Sport, Power, and Society

Sport, Power, and Society

INSTITUTIONS AND PRACTICES

A Reader

Robert E. Washington
and David Karen

Bryn Mawr College

WESTVIEW PRESS

A Member of the Perseus Books Group

Library of Congress Cataloging-in-Publication Data

    Sport, power, and society : institutions and practices : a reader / Robert E. Washington and David Karen.
        p. cm.
    Includes bibliographical references and index.
    ISBN 978-0-8133-4487-4 (alk. paper)
    1. Sports—Social aspects. I. Washington, Robert E., 1941– II. Karen, David.
GV706.5.S7358 2010
    306.4'83—dc22

                                    2009054050

10 9 8 7 6 5 4 3 2 1

CONTENTS

ACKNOWLEDGMENTS

During the course of putting this book together, we have accumulated a number of debts. The students who have taken our Sport and Society class have been instrumental in *teaching us* which readings were most analytically and pedagogically useful. Quite a few students worked with us as research assistants and organizational wizards in the course of collecting the many articles that we have included (and that we have not included!) here. Among them, we would like especially to mention: Steve Feder, Emily Schneider-Krzys, Sasha Toten, and Amy Scott. A number of scholars have helped us arrange free or reduced permissions fees: thanks to Michael Messner, Loïc Wacquant, and Rick Eckstein and Kevin Delaney. John Cheslock was very helpful in working with us on editing his Women's Sports Foundation piece. We would especially like to thank Randall Collins and Sherri Grasmuck for contributing original articles to this volume; we very much appreciate the extra care and time they took in producing these pieces. Andy Markovits and Jerry Karabel provided many, many kinds of support throughout this process and we are grateful. Karen Sulpizio once again helped in myriad ways, especially providing important secretarial and bibliographic support at key moments. We would like to thank Fred Courtright for his steady hand in guiding us through the permissions process. The Bryn Mawr College Provost's Office contributed in various ways to help defray the costs associated with this book. Alex Masulis at Westview Press has been a pleasure to work with and we thank him for his support throughout this process. Finally, each of us has accumulated some personal debts. Karen would like to thank his family for always letting him have the sports section first and for tolerating his long stints in front of the computer. Washington would like to thank Rose for her support and sense of humor throughout the summers and holiday breaks when his "free time" was consumed working on this book.

A NOTE TO THE READER

We developed the format for this book after teaching a Sport and Society course for many years. The general introduction sets out our vision of the uniqueness of sport as a social institution and discusses the ways that it articulates with many other social practices and institutions.

We divide the book into seven parts. Each part focuses on a given social institution or practice and presents several scholarly articles and one journalistic article to illustrate some of the key issues in that domain. Each part begins with a short introduction that details key analytical and/or theoretical issues regarding the given social institution (politics, media, political economy, fandom/community, and education) or social practice (violence, body culture). We demonstrate not only the ways that interactions with these social institutions or practices shape sport, but also how sport, in part through its enormous popularity, influences those social institutions or practices. We then discuss how each of the scholarly articles illuminates the issues we raise in the introductions. Finally, each part ends with a journalistic article that highlights a range of problems about the complex role of sport in modern society.

ROBERT E. WASHINGTON
DAVID KAREN

INTRODUCTION

Sport as a Model of Meritocracy

The year nears its end and the Gigantico Corporation, a major furniture manufacturer, will soon issue its annual report. In the first three quarters, profits showed significant improvements compared to those of last year. But what will the final two crucial weeks of the fourth quarter reveal? Will the company realize the highest profit margin of any furniture company this year? Or *ever*? How many people in the general public can (or will want to) observe the actual daily performances of this company coming down the stretch? Which employee is expected to be the "most valuable employee"? Who will rise heroically to the challenge and lead the company to a record-shattering year-end success? Will that employee be publicly acclaimed and adored like a Joe DiMaggio or a Michael Jordan? Will he or she become a national celebrity? Will magazines and newspapers clamor to interview her or him? Will s/he be able to go to a restaurant without being swarmed by autograph seekers? Needless to say, this would be ludicrous in the furniture industry—or, indeed, in the world of business more generally.

Yet it is business-as-usual in the world of professional sports—populated, it should be noted, by large corporations—which issues frequent, if not daily, reports to a curious public noting the relative value of employees (via rosters and depth charts on team websites) and providing long-term statistical summaries of individual and group performances. And if these data are insufficient, the public can gain further insight into the quality of the individual and group performances by taping and analyzing telecasts of the contests.

Many institutions claim to operate according to meritocratic norms. In fact, in open democratic societies, the entire social order is legitimated according to meritocratic precepts: the notion that rewards are allocated in proportion to *merit*, that is, the contributions that individuals make to society, how hard-working they are, the achievements they attain, and the like. The claim that society operates fairly is a major part of the ideological basis of contemporary democratic societies. For example, the capitalist economic system is based on the belief that individuals are rewarded relative to their contributions to profitability. Democratic polities are rooted in the notion that each citizen's voice is critical to their operation. In educational settings, students are rewarded in accordance with their performance on ostensibly objective tests. And the criminal justice system is supposed to operate on the premise that each citizen's rights are equally protected under the rule of law. Yet there is no visible, public demonstration that these institutions are actually adhering to meritocratic principles.

Much evidence suggests that democratic governments, criminal justice systems, schools, and corporate enterprises are widely believed to operate according to meritocratic principles, yet they in fact regularly depart from the principles they claim to follow. This does not obviate their ideological function of legitimating the democratic capitalist social order, however. As long as we *believe* they are operating according to rules we would all endorse, and that these rules are followed and enforced fairly and equally, the ideological function of the institutions remains intact. That is because their *actual* practices are usually *hidden*. Their daily operations are seldom open to observation.

Not so, in the case of sports. In sports, the competition is visible, public, and open to analysis and review. Any interested individual can observe the competition. Anyone who has played the game—and many who have not—feels perfectly comfortable scrutinizing a player's or a team's performance. Anyone familiar with the sport feels competent to question the coach's decisions. Moreover, even if they are upset about a referee's call, a team's fans (usually) accept that the contest was fair and that—on that particular day—the better team won.

The fact that "on any given day" an underdog can win gives sports contests their most compelling storylines. We have a host of unlikely outcomes that tell us that under the rules of fair competition, anything can—and *has*—happened. One does not have to be obsessed with sports trivia to know of the "miracle on ice" in hockey, Bobby Thomson's "shot heard 'round the world," Doug Flutie's "Hail Mary," Franco Harris's "immaculate reception," and on and on. We regularly witness the life stories of individual players, often including those who move up from a poor childhood in a rural hamlet or urban ghetto to become a wealthy celebrity in a global city.

But sport's central sociological significance does not derive from its popularity or from the passions that it generates. The fact that sports offers the possibility for team success and individual upward mobility, for those displaying talent and motivation in sports contests played in *public* on a *level playing field*, obliges sociologists and other analysts of society to take sports seriously as a meritocratic institution. This uniqueness of sport—its characteristic as the purest, most public model of meritocracy—is what compels us not only to understand its influence on the society as an embodiment of meritocratic practices but also, and equally important, to understand the societal influences on sport that may weaken or undermine those practices.

Our Framework

In this book, we present articles that explore the connections between sports and other social institutions. In examining the influence of sport on non-sports institutions and vice versa, we develop and employ a distinct analytical perspective. First, we argue that the world of sports is a unique social institution in which principles of fair competition and just reward for meritorious contributions find their clearest expression. The performances are transparent; they are open to public observation. They exist in a competitive environment where meritocratic principles are central and the major objective is to win. The singular goal of sports—winning—it should be noted, differs from that of most business enterprises. A Procter and Gamble, a CBS, or a Ford Motor Company may not aim to "win" but to reach a particular level of adequacy, to "satisfice," as the twentieth-century economist Herbert Simon might say. The goal might simply be to improve over last year's earnings, thereby pleasing stockholders. In sports, to quote the legendary Vince Lombardi: "Winning is not the most important thing, it's the only thing."

Achieving this objective in contests against opponents who have the same goal demands unwavering commitment to "instrumental rationality"—that is, to deployment of the most efficient means. Coaches and players, in other words, aim to translate meritocratic principles into specific practices, maximizing their likelihood of winning.

The outcomes of sports contests are, indeed, strongly correlated with the extent of use of meritocratic practices. In other words, meritocratic principles work in sports. Those who use them the most tend to win. Empirically, of course, teams vary in the degree to which they employ meritocratic practices. Although, as noted above, we believe that the sporting *contest* embodies the purest expression of meritocratic principles, the pure meritocratic organization should be viewed as an *ideal type*. We can think of teams employing meritocratic practices as an analytical construct of institutional perfection that—like pure democracy or pure justice—never exists in reality. The construct nevertheless provides a useful reference point for comparing the practices of actual sports entities to determine their levels of institutional development. Following the general theoretical orientations of Meyer and Scott (1983) and DiMaggio and Powell (1983, 1991), our idea of institutional development focuses on the degree to which organizations within a given organizational field* follow the underlying, taken-for-granted principles and practices of their institutional environment. To what extent do sports organizations *establish* cultural outlooks that define the objectives and strategies of action in the surrounding society? To what extent do they merely conform to these cultural outlooks? (See DiMaggio and Powell 1991, 28.)

To illustrate the idea of how "the 'most meritocratic' wins," let's take the example of the 1966 NCAA basketball championship game between the University of Kentucky and Texas Western University. Kentucky had an all-white team because legendary coach Adolph Rupp had a policy of recruiting only white players. Texas Western, in contrast, had a racially open recruitment policy and started five black players. Despite being the overwhelming favorite, Kentucky was defeated by Texas Western. Clearly, Texas Western's orientation to recruiting and playing the best players—following "proper" meritocratic practices—had led to the victory. The two schools had very different levels of meritocratic institutional development, and the outcome of the contest reflected that fact, as our argument would have predicted.

But how do we explain this disparity in the degree of institutionalization of meritocratic practices between Kentucky and Texas Western? Why were two teams that were similarly enmeshed in the institution of sport so different in terms of their adherence to meritocratic principles? How, in particular, can we explain Kentucky's weaker adherence to those principles? First, the school was located in the regional culture of the white American South where racial segregation was the norm. Second, Kentucky belonged to a southern white

---

* For an extended discussion of organizational fields, see DiMaggio and Powell (1983).

college basketball conference (the SouthEastern Conference—SEC), which followed the segregation norm of the region. So long as Kentucky was competing against other teams within its region, its racial recruitment policy entailed no disadvantage, since all teams were racially segregated. But when Kentucky moved beyond its regional organizational field and participated in the larger national organizational field (the NCAA), it paid a significant price. Simply put, when it was obliged to compete against teams with more open recruitment policies and higher levels of meritocratic development, it lost. Kentucky shortly afterward shifted to a more racially open recruitment policy.

Third, we argue that sport, more than any other institution, models the principles of meritocratic competition for the surrounding society. Though largely ignored, this is a critically important basis of sport's sociological significance. The world of sports teaches us principles of fair competition. The institutional logic of sport, in its most developed state, strives to produce objective and fair competitive outcomes. But, as indicated above, sports entities vary in the degree to which they actually embody meritocratic principles of fairness. The degree to which the sports contest models the meritocratic ideal for other institutions needs to be emphasized. Significantly, the meritocratic ideal of the sport contest has even seeped ideologically into our everyday discourse. When the Senate discusses the suitability of a potential Supreme Court justice, the focus is on the degree to which s/he will function like an "umpire." The metaphor is invoked to denote the ultimate cultural standard of fairness—the key criterion for a just society. Equally prevalent is the tendency of observers to assess the fairness of a situation, such as one involving competition for a job, in terms of whether it constitutes a "level playing field."

Our fourth point—also evident from the Kentucky–Texas Western example—is that other major institutions that interact with the world of sports may cause sports entities to deviate from meritocratic practices. Despite being perceived by most people simply as on-field contests, sport hardly exists in a vacuum. So much of what affects on-field sport performances occurs off-field, through the influences of the larger organizational fields within which those performances are embedded. Sports entities may be diverted into nonmeritocratic practices that undermine or supplant their putative objective of winning, even if, at times, the entities themselves do not recognize it. Many examples of these diverse influences can be cited. The commercialization and profit motive of sports, often driven by large media contracts, may supplant the objective of winning. Racial, ethnic, and religious prejudices among the owners, the fan base, or the alumni of a university may divert teams from meritocratic practices in the selection of players and coaches. The long history of blacks being excluded from the quarterback position would be an example of this. The fact that there are currently (in 2009) only seven black head coaches among the 119 Division I college football teams suggests that even education, the other ostensibly meritocratic field, still allows nonmeritocratic factors to influence its recruitment for sports teams.

Here's another example of how outside forces may influence how the game is played. Imagine two college football teams, one in the highly competitive, media-focused Division I, and the other in Division III, where games might not even be reported in the local newspapers. By NCAA rules, the Division I school has been able to provide scholarships for its players, while the Division III school has not. Simply by virtue of the fact that the two schools have very different locations in this organizational field, their orientations to "winning at all costs," as opposed to "developing the scholar-athlete," are radically different. Both schools certainly try hard to win every game. However, the D-I school might be focused on: ensuring that (especially) the star players remain academically eligible and not too bogged down with demanding courses; generating revenues by selling out its 100,000-seat stadium; increasing the number of national television appearances in a given season (as well as the number in prime time); garnering attractive bowl game opportunities; and recruiting successfully from among current high-school seniors (which may be related to television appearances). The D-III school is not overly concerned with revenues but does pay attention to the academic constraints and opportunities for their student-athletes. Indeed, the D-III school might even pressure star players to take a semester abroad during the *spring* in their junior year. Concerns about television are not even on the radar screen. The NCAA has not been as concerned with restricting the texting contacts between coaches and recruits in D-III as they have been in D-I. Needless to say, it would be very unlikely for a Division III school to receive the kind of alumni contribution—$165 million—that the Oklahoma State (Division I) Athletics Department (not the *university*, the *athletics department*) received from T. Boone Pickens in 2005.

These examples convey our idea that the relationships that obtain in given highly structured organizational fields (each of which must be understood in the given case) constitute, metaphorically, a power grid within which all the relevant actors operate. This power grid, and an organization's place within the field, affects the resources available as well as the organization's perceptions of the opportunity structure. A given organization's place within the field will determine its responses to the underlying pressures, constraints, incentives, and opportunities. It is important to recognize that the power that we're talking about includes regulatory and coercive power (usually exercised by the state but often by leagues or conferences); cultural/hegemonic power, which shapes perceptions; and economic power. As we move across organizational levels and integrate more elements of the organizational field, we can see the effects of these external factors—the "game outside the game"—more clearly. (For more about these influences, see Figure 1.)

Fifth, we believe that the long-term consequences of deviations from meritocratic practice will lead to failure and pressures to change. Failure matters: A sports organization that persistently manifests a lower level of on-field success than its competitors is likely to experience organizational strains that will oblige it either to change, by expanding its meritocratic practices, or to (at least implicitly) shift priorities from winning to satisficing. The latter may take many forms, the most common of which is to characterize the team's current state as in a "rebuilding phase." Whether a team chooses one or the other route depends on many specific situational factors (especially relating to the dynamics of its organizational field) that would have to be analyzed in each case.

Interestingly, despite Adolph Rupp's long-term practice of excluding blacks from his team, shortly after their defeat by Texas Western he recruited a number of black players for the University of Kentucky. Similarly, Major League Baseball's "gentlemen's agreement" that excluded blacks from participation broke down—though unevenly—after Jackie Robinson's successful debut with the Brooklyn Dodgers in 1947. And in perhaps the worst trade in sports history,

FIGURE 1   *Constraints on a University Football Team*

A university's resources and hopes and dreams for its football team (as well as its ability to realize those hopes and dreams) is subject to many constraints posed by different actors.

• Federal regulation:
    Discrimination
    Title IX
    Gambling
    Media

• University-related:
    Athletic department
    Administration
    Faculty
    Alumni
    Boosters

• Media:
    TV broadcasting
    Magazines, newspapers, radio
    Websites, bloggers, etc.

Football Program at Football State University

• Conference and NCAA:
    Rules and Regulations
    Competition

• Sales
    Tickets
    Apparel, etc.

• Fans

• Recruitment
    High-school talent
    Funding for recruitment

Note: The actors on the left are external forces, whereas those on the right are internal to the university. Those at the center at bottom are somewhere in between these two extremes. Another work that takes a look at a "multiorganizational field," though in a different context (the reform of college athletics), is Robert D. Benford, "The College Sports Reform Movement: Reframing the 'Edutainment' Industry," *Sociological Quarterly* 48 (2007): 1–28.

the St. Louis Hawks traded Bill Russell, the Olympic hero and leader of the two-time NCAA basketball champions, to the Boston Celtics because they did not want to offend their largely southern white fan base. This transaction led to eleven championship titles in thirteen years for the Celtics and, indirectly, to the Hawks' decline and subsequent move to Atlanta.

This Volume

This book examines the social context of sports from the perspective of five major societal institutions—with sections on the political economy of sports; sports and the media; sports and education; sports and politics; and fandom and community in sports, and two sets of institutional practices, those involving body culture and sports and those involving violence and injuries in sports. Our goal is to provide the reader with a clearer sense of the power grid within which sports operates. By selecting a set of readings that situates sports (contests, teams, leagues, and so on) in different institutional contexts, we aim to sensitize readers to the external factors that may tilt the level playing field and compromise the goal of winning. By exploring the dynamics of the organizational fields within which sports operates, we aim to present a broader conception of sports that takes into account the political, strategic, and cognitive elements of institutionalized action on the part of individuals and organizations within the field. In contrast to these sections on institutions, which highlight the ways in which sports affect and are affected by other major social institutions, the sections on violence and body culture show how routines and practices within sports can be transferred and become embedded in other spheres.

Each of the realms that we examine has its own taken-for-granted assumptions about how it operates in society. By looking at sport in the context of these other institutions, we hope to alert the reader to the importance of comprehending the structure and symbols of all of the institutions involved in order to understand the actions of the relevant individuals and organizations within sport. Our selections emphasize how the goals and cultural frames of external institutions differentially motivate and constrain the relevant individuals and organizations.

For example, consider a professional basketball game. The game itself seems to embody a meritocratic ideal of a contest played among equals on a level playing field. But once we begin to account for how the roster was assembled (why the team has precisely these players at this time), we would have to consider the history of the team, its management, the dynamics of its revenue streams over time, its current relative economic situation, its geographical location, and its potential fan base. We would have to consider the attractiveness of its arena, its relationship to the central league office (is it under any unique constraints?), and the like, and this would show us how quickly nonmeritocratic factors come to the fore. Its (team-wide and league-wide) contracts with media outlets, its collective bargaining agreements with players and referees, and the tax and regulatory arrangements that it is subject to (which vary by city, state, and country) may all affect the pressures and constraints the team faces. We could go even further and ask how professional basketball leagues compete with professional hockey, baseball, and football leagues for fan dollars, favorable tax situations, advantageous city locations, and beneficial media contracts. Thus we have moved very quickly from the referee throwing the ball up for the center jump to considerations of conflicts over, among other things, television rights among local, national, and international corporations.

The goal for the competitors in a sports contest is, of course, to win. From early on, athletes are told to "just win, baby," or that "nice guys finish last." Yet, Al Davis and Leo Durocher were not condoning cheating; they were pushing their players to do everything they could within the rules* to win the game. Such a mindset may lead to social practices

---

* By "within the rules," we mean that they wanted to make sure that the players who somehow bent the rules did not get caught. The rules, therefore, meant "what the official saw or called."

that are at odds with the dominant norms of the society. In this book, we examine two sets of social practices, one surrounding violence and one surrounding body culture, that not only have a central role in sports but also interact in significant ways with other sectors of society. Extending our notion that the institution of sport generates practices surrounding body culture and violence, these sections explore the dynamics of violence and conceptions of the body within sports contexts as well as their implications outside of sports—in the surrounding society. How does the taken-for-granted training of the boxer's body, or the basketball player's body, affect conceptions of body discipline in the larger society? How do athletes manage the differing expectations about the body and about violence from the larger society and even from sports insiders?

Overall, the selections that we have assembled were chosen because we believe they will help the reader understand the articulation between the normative demands of different institutions. In that sense they not only bring out insights specific to the world of sports and culture, but provide models for how one might analyze other types of institutions. Further, we hope that the selections demonstrate how central are principles and practices within sport for understanding other institutions in the larger society.

References

Benford, Robert D. 2007. "The College Sports Reform Movement: Reframing the 'Edutainment' Industry." *Sociological Quarterly* 48: 1–28.

DiMaggio, Paul J., and Walter W. Powell. 1983. "The Iron Cage Revisited: Institutional Isomorphism and Collective Rationality in Organizational Fields." *American Sociological Review* 48: 147–160.

DiMaggio, Paul J., and Walter W. Powell. 1991. "Introduction." Pp. 1–38 in Walter W. Powell and Paul J. DiMaggio, eds., *The New Institutionalism in Organizational Analysis*. Chicago: University of Chicago Press.

Meyer, John W., and W. Richard Scott. 1983. *Organizational Environments: Ritual and Rationality*. Beverly Hills, CA: Sage.

PART I

RAIDING THE PUBLIC TREASURY: THE POLITICAL ECONOMY OF PROFESSIONAL SPORTS

(Hustling Major-League Cities?)

Sports is big business. Fans and non-fans alike know this. It involves everything from the burgeoning sports equipment industry to international labor-migration issues, from the organization of professional sports leagues to the most sought-after times in television advertising. Indeed, one cannot think deeply about the structure and practice of the contemporary sports scene without considering its economic moorings. And we cannot understand the economics of sports without serious consideration of the political context in which it is embedded. As will be evident from Part II of this book on the media, many aspects of sports involve large corporations vying for advantage in a competitive economic environment of changing political regulation. Political and economic institutions intertwine to affect the social organization of sports.

Owners of professional sports teams operate within a very constrained set of parameters. The relationship between the owners and the government of the city in which the team resides is affected by, among other issues, tax and zoning laws, and the owners' negotiations with players are carried out in the context of league, state, and national labor laws. In the United States, for example, every National Football League (NFL) team has a "cap-ologist," a business and legal expert who can advise the team on its "salary cap"—that is, the spending constraints regulating its players' salaries—to ensure that the team maximizes its flexibility within the limits mandated by the league's collective-bargaining agreement with the NFL Players Association. There are no absolute rules about how such things should be governed, and other sports, as well as other countries, do it differently. Major League Baseball (MLB), with its much stronger players union, for example, does not operate with a salary cap and has a long-standing special relationship to the U.S. government. In Europe, a team's ability to sign a given foreign player is regulated by both league rules and national law. Teams must limit their number of foreign players, though some players can be claimed as citizens under a sports-specific law (for example, a foreign player may become a "football German" and thereby not count as a foreigner on a team).

A rather unique example of this interconnection between politics and economics is found in the United States, where Major League Baseball—alone among professional sports leagues—has a state-sponsored monopoly. Often referred to as the "special antitrust exemption," this exemption from laws concerning monopolies allows MLB to control where its teams are located, whether any new teams can come into the league, and various aspects of labor-management relations. This special treatment has been tested in court and has been reaffirmed in a number of different ways since it was established in 1922. (See Andrew Zimbalist's essay in this part, "May the Best Team Win: Making Baseball Competitive.") Currently, the Supreme Court has indicated that it is up to Congress to enact legislation to take away the exemption. Although it may seem rather ironic that the country that is most committed to a free-market ideology protects one of its most profitable industries by giving it monopoly status, the United States—with its relatively low-burden and unprogressive tax system—is also unique in that it protects big property to an extent greater than most other countries. Insofar as a consideration of professional sports leagues involves labor-employer issues, immigration issues, media control issues, and many others—all regulated by political institutions—one ignores the political-economic context only at one's peril.

A political-economy approach to sports examines how political forces affect the way that actors in the sports world vie for economic advantage. Perhaps the classic example of the way this happens in the United States is with stadium construction: A professional team seeks a new stadium to increase the team's value and revenues and asks the relevant government agencies to underwrite costs, which might include not only the actual construction costs for the stadium and the cost of the land on which it will be built but also the cost of providing the necessary parking lots or those involved in making improvements to the city's transportation infrastructure. As the selection by Kevin J. Delaney and Rick Eckstein, "Public Dollars, Private Stadiums, and Democracy," shows, privately owned professional sports teams regularly attempt to secure public dollars for private profit. In attempting to secure public funding for their arenas and stadiums, the private owners take advantage of notions of "civic pride" and of being a "major-league city." Allying with other powerful interests, the owners often succeed in wresting dollars and other concessions from the powers that be. The resulting increase in the team's value and its annual profits is privately appropriated.

Although politics is central to the business of sports, it is often owners' success in keeping politics (and politicians) *out* of their business that ensures economic success. In the article on NASCAR by Brian O'Keefe and Julie Schlosser, "America's Fastest Growing Sport," we see how a relatively unregulated sport can develop: In the context of a near-monopoly, there appear to be no limits to its commercialization. All sports, however, must try to get as much marketing exposure as possible through cable and free television. Media conglomerates, which sometimes own sports franchises, will gamble that they can attract sufficient advertising revenue to pay for televising given events. If the demographic numbers are "right" (that is, the people who are expected to watch the show have a lot of disposable income), the league can count on lucrative contracts from TV outlets. Of course, there are limits to the exposure that leagues and teams can receive—some TV channels reach many more homes than others, and there are, of course, better and worse times to be televised.

The examples of stadium construction and NASCAR represent two poles of the interpenetration of political and economic institutions in the realm of sports. The article in this section by David Morris and Daniel Kraker, "Rooting the Home Team: Why the Packers Won't Leave—and Why the Browns Did," on the unique situation of the Green Bay Packers is included to illustrate the variation that is possible in terms of ownership and in terms of the relationships between teams and their locales. The Packers are community owned, with ownership shares sold to the public. Community ownership, which U.S. professional leagues have largely banned (the Packers' situation is grandfathered), is more common in Canada than in the United States. But Morris and Kraker suggest that allowing such arrangements, along with other legal and economic variations from the current rules—especially revenue sharing among teams in a league—would change the dynamics of bargaining for professional teams and their locales.

The key point here is that, in understanding sports as a business, which it certainly is, we must always understand how the state—the political organizations that control the economic context—structures the economic playing field. Similarly, we must understand that the large private corporations and individuals who own sports teams make public policy by virtue of their decisions about their teams. Their decisions have huge implications for employment opportunities, mass-transit and a host of transportation issues, the media and advertising, and tax issues. In other words, these are major arenas of public policy that are subject to private control.

Chapter 1

PUBLIC DOLLARS, PRIVATE STADIUMS, AND DEMOCRACY

Kevin J. Delaney and Rick Eckstein

In this excerpt from the last chapter of their book *Public Dollars, Private Stadiums*, Kevin J. Delaney and Rick Eckstein review their argument about how democracy was subverted in the process of getting a recent spate of stadiums built. Their elucidation of how power operates in specific political-economic contexts highlights the extraordinary influence that sports and sports-team owners have in the contemporary United States. Using a comparative urban analysis, the authors demonstrate how "local growth coalitions" composed of many of the largest corporations in given metropolitan areas (it's key that the coalition be dominated by *non*-sports-related corporations) push forcefully for stadiums because of their supposed contributions to recruiting top executive talent and civic pride. . . . And politicians follow along.

Where's the Democracy?

Overall, the process of building private stadiums with public dollars in the United States is more akin to plutocracy and oligarchy than to democracy. Here, we include both a procedural definition of democracy (in which everyone affected by policy decisions has a meaningful say in making them) and a substantive definition (in which policy decisions reflect the real interests of affected parties without those interests being manipulated).[1] Sometimes the anti-demo-cratic processes are blatant and unmistakable, sometimes they are more subtle, and sometimes they are obfuscated by the workings of normal politics. Residents in and around Pittsburgh and Phoenix were crystal clear about not wanting to spend public dollars on private stadiums. But in both cases, powerful stadium advocates simply trampled on public sentiment and built the stadiums anyway.

Sometimes the threats to democracy are more subtle, although still obvious if you look in the right places. In Philadelphia, for instance, there was no need to blatantly trample on popular sentiment because the public was never given any say on the matter except indirectly through city council and state representatives. When a Pennsylvania state representative explained to us the inner workings of the legislature, it seemed to have little in common with democracy as we conventionally define it. He explained exactly how Pennsylvania decided to put up two-thirds of the money for the four new stadiums in Pittsburgh and Philadelphia:

Ninety-five percent of the calls we get on this issue are against it. . . . For dynamic issues like these that are wildly unpopular, the legislative leaders decide it will happen; and then they decide how many votes each side [Republican and Democratic] will give up and which representatives are least vulnerable—so they don't get taken out [for voting for something so unpopular].

This representative was clear that, even though Pennsylvania residents were overwhelmingly opposed to using public dollars for the four new stadiums, the legislative leadership did it anyway. The leaders selected which representatives would vote for the "wildly unpopular" issue by determining who was in a safe district and would thus be insulated from voter backlash. So, for example, a Democrat in a district that is 90 percent Democratic is cajoled into voting for the unpopular issue because she or he will be unlikely to lose reelection. Of course, that Democrat will not vote "correctly" without some serious horse trading. When we interviewed the representative just quoted a few months before the final vote, he predicted, "I would bet this [funding for new stadiums] will happen because

most members have their price" in terms of pet projects (such as, acquiring park land or resurfacing bridges), which others will vote for in exchange for supporting the stadium issue. It turns out he was correct.

In fact, we were told that one of the big inside fights on this issue concerned the fact that Republicans wanted to provide fewer than half of the total yes votes needed to pass the stadium bill. The Democratic leadership, however, argued that because Republican governor Tom Ridge wanted the bill so badly, the Republicans should give up more than half of the votes. The Republican leadership countered that because the stadiums would benefit the two largest cities in Pennsylvania, which are largely Democratic, the Democrats should give up more than half of the votes. All of this finagling may not surprise a cynical observer, but it is not exactly what you read about democracy in a high school civics text.

While such blatant and clandestine power plays pose clear threats to democratic institutions, we think there are even more sinister threats within the everyday political process. Here, the trappings of democratic procedure often mask very undemocratic social policies. The best ongoing examples are the referendums that seem to indicate community support for new publicly subsidized stadiums, apparently demonstrating that policies allocating public dollars for private stadiums reflect popular sentiment. But this belief assumes that the referendum process is balanced and fair—that all interested parties have an equal opportunity to influence public policy.

Referendum campaigns are anything but fair arenas for hashing out the advantages and disadvantages of using public dollars for new stadiums. Subsidy advocates have much more power in the referendum process than do stadium opponents. At the most basic level, advocates directly outspend opponents by at least ten to one and sometimes, as in San Diego, by much more. These powerful individuals and organizations also have far superior "unofficial access" to decision makers than do average citizens—access that often occurs in stadium luxury boxes! We heard a story in Pittsburgh about a city council member who spent Sundays at Three Rivers Stadium, not watching the Steelers but keeping track of who was meeting whom in the corporate boxes. In this way, the council member knew what was going on behind the scenes when certain people or companies tried to influence city policy.

In addition to these obvious advantages in the referendum process, stadium advocates also have a third-dimensional* advantage: citizens grant more legitimacy to powerful people (the so-called experts) than to average people such as themselves, especially when it comes to complex issues like stimulating economic growth. This advantage is paralleled by a political system that also grants much more legitimacy to the opinions of powerful individuals and organizations than to more ordinary ones. In a sense, then, stadium supporters rarely have to fight city hall to achieve their goals. With important exceptions, the default position among many political elites is to equate new stadiums with economic growth or heightened community self-esteem. Subsidy opponents have to convince politicians *not* to believe what they have already been conditioned to believe.

---

* The third dimension of power (Lukes 1974) is the deepest level of power. Though not entirely uncontested, it operates as a strong hegemonic ideology. [Eds.]

Why Growth Coalitions?

We have argued throughout the book that unraveling these stadium battles is best accomplished by examining the structure of each city's local growth coalition (or its proxy) and the strategies these coalitions use to build private stadiums with public dollars. As we have shown, the strength and unity of the growth coalition shapes the stadium battles in American cities. Both the structure of growth coalitions and the decisions they make are deeply embedded in the unique social characteristics of each city. Some combinations of structure, decisions, and social characteristics carve out relatively uncomplicated paths to publicly subsidized stadiums, while other combinations create many more challenges. Either way, no route is a shining testament to democracy in action.

We have built our analytical framework around growth coalition theory because it allows us to identify some of the covert threats to democratic institutions. We believe these threats are not just sporadic and temporary breakdowns of a fair, self-regulating system but are embedded in the workings of the system itself. Most academic and nonacademic studies of new sports stadiums, good as they usually are, miss an important part of the story because they focus only on the most obvious public-policy players: the politicians and the sports teams. But guided by our search for local growth coalitions, we have discovered a world of less discernible players; and they have tremendous power over the policies allocating public dollars for private stadiums. Like more public players, these individuals and organizations stand to gain from new stadiums, but in less noticeable ways. Because growth coalitions can be so powerful, because they are largely invisible, and because they are mostly unaccountable to other social actors, we think it is imperative to understand how they are involved in the battles over new stadiums and how this involvement poses an especially insidious threat to a democratic society.

This point has not been emphasized enough, even in critical discussions of sports-stadium funding. Instead, conversations on the issue generally take a corporate welfare approach, castigating wealthy team owners who ask for handouts and local governments that universally grant these requests. But team owners are acting in the way that team owners are *supposed* to act; so the brunt of criticism, from the corporate-welfare perspective, ends up being aimed at the spineless politicians who sell out the rest of the community for a private seat in the owner's luxury box or a future campaign contribution. In contrast, our growth coalition approach insists that we must also look at the large nonsports corporations in a community (with multibillion-dollar gross revenues) rather than just the teams themselves (with gross revenues close to $100 million) in assessing who might benefit from the public financing of new stadiums.

These corporations are far more powerful than any local sports team; and their influence over the policymaking process may be ideological (that is, third-dimensional), not just a matter of throwing their money around or threatening to take their huge companies elsewhere. Local politicians "naturally" turn to the leaders of corporations for advice on important matters. Executives are invited to sit on economic development task forces and be part of municipal stadium authorities. If these successful business leaders, who are also involved with local philan-

thropic organizations, think that publicly financed stadiums are good for the local community, then why should policymakers (or the general community) think otherwise? Thus, corporations' particular parochial vision of suitable growth strategies comes to rule the day. Too often, however, this vision is not portrayed as particular, parochial, or self-interested, but as civic-minded and altruistic. In this regard, nonsports corporations can more easily than sports teams conceal their organizational self-interest and maintain that community welfare is driving their interest in new publicly funded stadiums—if anyone even knows they are interested in the matter.

The Corporate Arm of the Growth Coalition

Why do the corporate members of a growth coalition want new stadiums? We found that business leaders (sometimes including team owners) were more likely than politicians to promise social rewards from new stadiums, such as increased civic pride or a closer-knit community. While politicians talked more of economic activity to justify opening the public coffers, business leaders knew very well that there were better ways to create jobs than by subsidizing a huge stadium that operates either eighty-one days per year (baseball) or ten days per year (football). Thus, when we interviewed growth coalition leaders about their advocacy of public dollars for private stadiums, they talked about "wearing their civic hat" rather than stimulating economic growth. But this attitude only begs the question, Why promote sports stadiums rather than any other type of civic good? What underlies corporate executives' interest in advocating public dollars for private stadiums?

We think a number of factors have led corporate elites to favor building new stadiums. First, corporations want to be able to use stadiums—especially their luxury boxes—and the aura surrounding professional sports to attract new executive talent. Many of the corporate executives we talked with spoke about the challenges they faced recruiting top talent to their city. This is a particularly strong sentiment in small cities with little allure for graduates from top law schools and business schools. Business leaders in Cleveland and Cincinnati told us that, when competing with firms in New York and San Francisco, the new stadiums gave them something to show off. We can't help but wonder whether a gender bias exists here. Of course, women can be interested in professional sports. But in all our conversations with executives about recruiting A-level talent, they always seemed to be talking about men. Although we aren't even sure whether A-level talent cares all that much about stadium luxury boxes, clearly the "real truth" doesn't matter. As long as current executives believe that future executives will care, they continue to treat new stadiums as part of their recruitment effort. And why not have the local government subsidize this particular recruitment tool?

We speculate that the growth coalitions in larger, more exciting cities have less success in emphasizing new sports stadiums as an executive recruitment tool. Places such as New York, San Francisco, Boston, Philadelphia, and Los Angeles have so many other amenities that they don't really need (or think they need) new sports stadiums to attract the A players. This is one reason why there has been little, or only very deliberate, progress toward new, pub-

licly financed stadiums in these cities. Simply put, in the minds of the local growth coalitions of midsized cities, the consequences are severe if they don't get a new ballpark. Therefore, getting a stadium is high on their agendas.

The recruitment effort put forth by local growth coalitions is also linked with the larger notion of community self-esteem. Many corporate executives desire an image of a city on the move. Cities such as Cleveland and Hartford, for example, seem to radiate negative impressions to the surrounding world. They are looked upon as decaying urban holes with declining and increasingly impoverished populations. Again, these images may be exaggerated far beyond empirical reality. But as long as the local growth coalition *believes* this is the projected image, corporate leaders will do tangible things to address it. Thus, members may see a flurry of new stadium construction as a visible and relatively fast way to counter the image of a city in decline. In hindsight, it seems to have been at least a moderately effective strategy. Outsiders are now more inclined to talk about turnarounds in places such as Cleveland and Baltimore, having absolutely no evidence except the presence of new stadiums and the growth coalition's constant reiteration that things have turned around.

It is also important to note that some corporate executives are simply big sports fans. They enjoy professional sports and want to be associated with building a new sports palace. Wearing their civic hats, executives will find it a lot harder to improve the test scores of inner-city schools (although a few do gallantly try) than to build a new stadium. Most want a visible monument to their efforts, and the stadium can serve that purpose. If you are a big-time sports fan, what better way to show your civic pride than to help give the team a new place to play and the community a new place to watch games? It would be grander still if you could manage to have the new stadium named after your company.

Today, many postindustrial cities in the United States are filled with hollow corporations: companies that split their administration from their production, the former staying in the home city and the latter moving elsewhere in the United States or even offshore. Thus, when we say that a firm's headquarters are located in a city, often this simply means that the company employs several hundred, or at most a few thousand, top managerial and administrative staff who work in the city. The production workers have left town—or perhaps more accurately, their jobs have left town—leaving only very low-wage workers who provide support services for executives. The result is a polarized social-class dynamic: cities have very well paid and very poorly paid workers on either end, with fewer people in the middle. The two polarized groups have very different stakes in the city itself. For the high-paid members of the local growth coalition, the city is a transient station for work and play before returning home to suburbia or moving on to their next outpost in another city. Their urban priorities include good roads or commuter rails, decent restaurants, and cultural diversions, which might include new sports stadiums with plenty of available parking. For minimum-wage workers, the city is usually a permanent place to work and live. Their urban priorities are more likely to include good schools, reliable buses, safe neighborhoods, clean streets and playgrounds, and decent grocery stores. Given

the recent wave of using public dollars for private stadiums, it seems clear that the needs of the growth coalition are winning out over the needs of poorer urban residents.

This disparity was illustrated for us by a Cleveland business leader, who said that, among many of the top corporations in the city, *no* employee had ever been directly exposed to the Cleveland public schools. This astounding statement would not have been made fifty years ago, when these companies still had relatively well paid production workers living in Cleveland. Gone are the Fisher Body Division workers from the Euclid plant (which closed for good in 1993) as well as members of the United Steel Workers, whose Cleveland-area membership dropped from 47,000 in 1980 to slightly more than 20,000 in 1990. Urban neighborhoods, which were built around such factories, increasingly face economic and social decay when the facility leaves town. This reduces the overall tax base and puts even more strain on the public sector to maintain services (such as schools) and deal with the fallout (such as crime) from deindustrialization. Unfortunately, in cities like Cleveland, the powerful local growth coalition and its political champions have been subsidizing new stadiums rather than decent housing, further exacerbating the metamorphosis of the city into a playground for suburbanites.

The frontier cities have very different development histories. Here, suburbanization was a major factor from the beginning rather than a threat to an older urban tradition. Thus, the frontier cities have a power structure with less entrenched political expertise and a wider field for stadium battles to play out. The population explosion in these cities sometimes mitigates the issue of fighting over a shrinking pie, which is so common in Rust Belt cities. At the same time, however, citizens in frontier cities opposed to the particular growth strategies of subsidized stadiums often find few political champions with either the will or the political acumen to take up their cause.

The Political Arm of the Growth Coalition

Clearly, the corporate arm of the local growth coalition has reasons to be interested in new publicly funded sports stadiums and has the power to help turn this interest into reality. Ultimately, however, local government is still responsible for the actual policies that will direct public dollars to private stadiums. As a result, local governments become important components of coalitions. In cities with weak or absent corporate communities, the local government often (but not always) takes the lead on new stadium projects. Why do some governors, mayors, and other political leaders want stadiums if they are increasingly unpopular? Why do they risk their political lives on this issue?

As we have suggested throughout the book, the coalition between local government and the corporate community can take different forms. One form, which we refer to as second-dimensional power, occurs when the corporations capture and control policymakers through campaign contributions, relocation threats, membership on key task forces or other overt types of influence. The other form, which we call third-dimensional power, occurs when policymakers "naturally" see a convergence between corporate interests and the overall community's interests without the application of any overt influence. These two types of relationships are by no means mutually

exclusive, and it is not particularly important which type of power prevails. We saw them overlap in Cleveland through the relationship between the mayor's office and Cleveland Tomorrow. The business group had produced an economic blueprint for the city, which the mayor completely supported. This alignment seemed predictable enough because the executive director of Cleveland Tomorrow at the time had previously been the mayor's chief assistant for economic development, illustrating what some have called a "circulation of elites." But the fact that the new mayoral assistant (who replaced the person now directing CT) also completely agreed with this blueprint suggests that the convergence of corporate and government interests is more than just a personal matter. Whatever the case, alternatives to the corporate vision of local economic growth are not seriously considered.

This more systemic bias is reflected by politicians who genuinely believe that, for their city to survive, they need to transform it into a tourist destination—and they are betting on stadiums to do the job. Particularly in cities that have experienced substantial decline, politicians may be understandably desperate to hold on to businesses and residents. Professional sports and, in particular, new stadiums are seen as a highly visible way to indicate that a city is still powerful and important. But when politicians make these choices and place huge monetary bets on them, they neglect other urban needs. Cleveland was once a well-known manufacturer of basic durable goods. In fact, its pattern of industry originally attracted many of the corporations that subsequently located their headquarters there. With this history in mind, Norman

Krumholz, a professor of urban studies at Cleveland State University and a former planning official in the city, is critical of the new civic tourism strategy:

> We haven't spent money on tool-and-die, metal bending, or steel, or certainly not comparable to the money we are spending reforming our image. It's at least worth a guess whether if we spent this kind of money on less spectacular but basic things, whether we'd put more of our industries back to work in jobs that people of this city could do.

You could, of course, argue that less visible factors are more important to the vibrancy of a city. For example, we were told by business leaders in several cities that the office sector would benefit most from improvements that were not stadium-related: enhancing Internet infrastructure, nurturing small business development through seed money, improving education beyond the most basic skills, and developing reliable and affordable mass transit. These kinds of improvements, however, are far less sexy, far less visible, and therefore far less attractive to politicians. You often see politicians holding a shovel during a stadium groundbreaking or throwing out the first pitch on opening day. But how many politicians are photographed sitting in the driver's seat and opening the doors on one of the city's brand-new low-pollution buses? Perhaps it is naïve to ask them to choose bread over circuses, but the question is still worth asking.

Some politicians fear threats (direct, implied, or imagined) that a sports team might leave town on their watch. Professional sports truly are different from any other kind of business because much more attention and emotion are attached to the home team. If a nonsports business that employed 150 people left town, hardly anyone would notice. But if that business were a professional sports team, thousands of hours of talk radio, hundreds of pages of print media, and millions of e-mail messages would be devoted to the news. Some politicians must also believe that they can contain the anger of citizens who are opposed to publicly financed stadiums, although many mentioned that they tried to schedule tax referendums as far away as possible from their own reelections. Some, too, believe that they just know better than the opponents of public funding, dismissing them, during several of our interviews, as "naïve," "naysayers," "CANEs" (Citizens Against Nearly Everything), or "crazed Naderite types," among even unkinder names.

In cities with a strong local growth coalition, elected leaders are better able to take a low profile in stadium initiatives, although they may choose not to. Politicians offer to serve as watchdogs over the political process, while the local growth coalition exercises its power behind the scenes. Conversely, in cities with weak or fractured growth coalitions, the teams or the politicians are forced to take the lead. This is much more problematic: if the teams are taking the lead, they are accused of holding the city hostage for a handout; if local government takes the lead, the entire process assumes the messy trappings of procedural democracy such as public hearings and rancorous city council meetings. These situations can sometimes derail a stadium initiative or at least slow it down, as in San Diego, Philadelphia, and Minneapolis. They usually also result in making the teams pay for a larger share of the new stadium. We aren't claiming that some cities are more democratic than others. But in cities with weaker growth coalitions, politicians often have trouble avoiding grass-roots input.

The Media Arm of the Growth Coalition

In every city we studied, the main local newspaper editorially favored using public dollars for private stadiums. Fortunately, this editorial bias rarely interfered with a relatively fair reporting of the stadium initiatives, and journalists and columnists often wrote scathing and embarrassing stories about the stadium-building process.

Publishers and high-level editors often seem to share the same ideologies and visions as the local growth coalition. This may be due in part to their sense that they know better than the masses. It may also be due to the fact that, as newspaper companies come to be part of larger media conglomerates, they are increasingly indistinguishable from the corporate arm of the growth coalition. High-level editors frequently rub elbows with growth coalition members and come to share a vision of what is needed for correct growth. Only in Pittsburgh did we find a maverick newspaper publisher with a strong set of libertarian beliefs who promoted significant media criticism from the top of the company. The opposition of the *Tribune* (and the Allegheny Institute for Public Policy) was a significant irritant to the growth coalition's plans to acquire public dollars for private stadiums. If more cities had competing mainstream media voices, their stadium initiatives might have taken much different paths.

What Is a Major League City Anyway?

During our interviews, we repeatedly encountered the socially constructed notion that professional sports teams are a necessary condition of being a major league city. The more teams you have (taking population into account), the more major league you are. In some ways, we understand that having sports teams gives a city the stamp of authenticity by providing publicity and media exposure. Stadium advocates have taken this idea, however, and manipulated it to extract maximum public financing. They argue that, without a new stadium like those popping up in other places, their city will quickly become second-rate. Its fall from grace will be even faster and more embarrassing if the sports team actually leaves town. Increasingly, however, there is no actual threat that a team will leave without a new stadium (although the threats are still occasionally verbalized). And often the team owners aren't even the ones making this argument; rather, the corporate and political arm of the local growth coalition is making the claim. Policymakers, it seems, have internalized the assumption that "a new stadium" equals "the team stays" (or "a new one comes") equals "our city is first-rate."

Ironically, those cities with other sources of community self-esteem are more immune to this kind of manipulation. Rarely do pro-subsidy advocates in New York, Los Angeles, Philadelphia, or San Francisco claim that the city will cease being major league without a new sports stadium. The reason is obvious: these cities do not need the imprimatur of a sports team to make them major league in their own eyes or the eyes of the world. They have a diverse economy, vibrant downtowns open after bankers' hours, and great restaurants. Can you imagine somebody saying, "Without new stadiums, New York will be just another Hoboken with tall buildings," or "San Francisco will only be Sacramento with a bay view"? Los Angeles lost its NFL team in the 1990s because the city refused to build a new publicly financed stadium. At last look, L.A. had not become second- or third-rate.[2]

San Francisco, in fact, is a great example of how the manipulation of community self-esteem is ineffective in cities that are already first-rate. The new Pacific Bell Ballpark opened in 2000* and has been touted as the only privately financed ballpark among the recent wave of new stadiums. While this claim is an exaggeration, as we will explain, it is true that the public share of the stadium is significantly below average.

Although some view the Giants as magnanimous in not asking for handouts, this perception misreads the history. The Giants got fewer public dollars to be sure, but not for lack of trying! The new stadium went to public votes four separate times and lost each referendum. The team wandered around the Bay Area looking for some municipality to pay for their new ballpark and failed each time. Finally, the team's most recent ownership group, headed by Peter Magowan, decided to build a stadium largely with private financing. The Giants raised about $65 million from the sale of personal seat licenses and another $121 million from naming rights and other corporate partnerships, with Chase Financing backing much of the remainder. The price of the stadium reached nearly $307 million, although, as in all of the cases in this book, ongoing debate continues about the true cost.

A certain amount of public money has gone into the project, despite proclamations to the contrary. San Francisco used a tax-increment financing plan to provide money for infrastructure and neighborhood improvements around the new ballpark. The Giants received some tax breaks; and the city agreed to fund the construction of all needed amenities outside the park, including a light-rail stop and street lighting, and provided all water, sewerage, and other public service connections. Nevertheless, the Giants are able to say that the park itself was built with 100 percent private financing and no public dollars.

Despite some linguistic maneuvers, the important point still holds: the Giants got fewer public dollars for their new stadium. The key to this difference is the chemistry between San Francisco's growth coalition and the potential efficacy of manipulating community self-esteem. San Francisco certainly has a corporate community far stronger and more cohesive than those in Hartford and Minneapolis and probably just as strong (or stronger) as those in Cincinnati, Cleveland, and Pittsburgh. But San Francisco's local growth coalition doesn't really need a stadium to attract executive talent or create the image of being first-rate. The rest of San Francisco can do that all by itself. Property values in the city are among the highest in the nation, and it would be laughable to argue that those values will decline if the Giants leave town.

Equally important, San Francisco has an affluent population and a large number of corporations willing to buy seat licenses (at least for now). Recognizing the unique features of the city, Jack Bair, the Giants' senior vice president and corporate counsel, said in an interview on Minnesota Public Radio (http://news.mpr.org/features/199911):

I can't speak for other communities. We faced our unique problem here in San Francisco and tried to fashion a solution that would work here. We also are blessed with

---

* Due to various corporate changes, the name was changed to SBC Park and is now AT&T Park. [Eds.]

having a community that has enjoyed great economic times and also is the home to many of the most successful companies: . . . the gateway to Silicon Valley. We have a very affluent population here. And so we have been successful where other communities might not be able to be successful.

Despite San Francisco's powerful local growth coalition, appeals to community self-esteem would have fallen on deaf ears. Many residents seemed perfectly willing to let the team walk away: after all, they voted down stadium deals over and over again. Eventually the Giants chose to stay and build their own park, but that decision may not work in cities without a strong demand for private seat licenses or enough money to buy them. Clearly, midsized cities and those fighting population decline are more vulnerable to being manipulated by arguments about major league status.

Stadium Battles and Competing Visions of Cities

Stadium battles are struggles over competing and contested views of cities in the United States. Are cities meant to be tourist attractions? Are they places to improve exchange value (that is, drive up real estate costs for speculators, sometimes at the expense of poor and middle class residents)? Should they be designed to attract high-priced corporate talent—the A players of the world? Are they places where people live and care about schools, parks, libraries, public safety, traffic congestion, and transportation systems?

The desire to become a tourist destination often informs the ideology of local growth coalitions as they press for new stadiums. In the postindustrial economy,

many cities, desperate for new revenues, have been chasing elusive tourist dollars, hoping to attract visitors to their city. There is often a certain faddishness to these attempts. For a while, many cities were trying to build festival markets in imitation of Faneuil Hall in Boston. Then cities began closing streets to create pedestrian shopping malls, mimicking malls in the suburbs. For the past ten years, building new sports stadiums has seemed to be the way to get tourists.[3] What we have learned from these experiences, however, is that the copy cats tend not to do as well as the originals because the novelty quickly wears off.

Being a tourist destination also depends in large part on uncontrollable things like weather and location. Only the most die-hard football fan will visit Cleveland in early January just to see a football game in the new lakefront stadium. Pittsburgh is also likely to have a difficult time attracting tourists, despite two new stadiums and the grand dreams of city politicians. Unlike Baltimore, Pittsburgh cannot count on a large population within easy driving distance that will come to the new stadium. For a time, Pittsburgh planners considered placing a major tourist attraction between the two new stadiums, but some joked that a steel industry museum might be too depressing. Others imagined a high-tech amusement park but had trouble articulating exactly what that might be. Perhaps they envisioned a very fast roller coaster, with cars shaped like ingots, careening through an abandoned steel plant.

There is also a clear downside to becoming a tourist city. Tourist economies are highly dependent on the health of the national economy; and in recessions, tourist spending lessens significantly. In addition, those economies provide a large number of low-wage service jobs, which can increase inequality in cities. For example, in Phoenix, several proposals are in the works for new single-room occupancy (SRO) housing in the downtown area near Bank One Ballpark. The demand for such housing is intimately related to the quality of jobs produced not just at ballparks but in the tourist economy as a whole. Hotel desk clerks, hot dog vendors, and ticket takers do not make high enough salaries to afford a place to live. Three developers have approached Phoenix Downtown Partnership with plans to build new, modern SROs. They are repackaged versions of the old flophouse hotel, only with amenities such as a security system and a fax machine for residents' use. Despite the high-tech wiring, however, the SRO illustrates a way to provide a very cheap, single room for someone who works in and around the ballpark, the hotel industry, or the restaurant industry and is simply not paid well enough to live anywhere else. A business leader who focuses his attention on downtown development described it this way:

This is a step above homelessness, obviously. . . . [SROs] are meant to house hospitality workers, students, and others on fixed incomes. They are very small units, your typical SRO, but they have security at the front door, cable TV, a little refrigerator. They have "business centers" in them, a whole bunch of amenities that obviously aren't flophouse amenities. . . . Because our economy is built so much on the hospitality industry, I think there is a pretty good market for it here.

To be fair, some political leaders really do not know how to make their cities more vi-

brant. They are not sure if investment in schools or basic work force training will pay off in the long run. Dependent on being reelected, politicians tend to favor a more visible project over a less visible investment in job training or public schools that might pay off only gradually over several decades. Sadly, though, sports stadiums may not be our urban saviors. As we showed in chapter 2, a growing body of anecdotal experiences and systematic research show they stimulate little economic growth. They probably provide notoriety and good publicity in the short run as well as temporarily shoring up a city's reputation. Nevertheless, this advantage is surely waning as the stadium boom peaks. These days, people seem much less excited about the next new stadium. Baltimore can only happen once. Recent data show that the increase in attendance at new stadiums is declining and that the honeymoon effect is lasting for a shorter period. Nine major league baseball teams have established new lows for single-game attendance in their stadiums, and all nine built new stadiums in the 1990s or 2000s (*Philadelphia Inquirer*, April 28, 2002, D18).

Stadiums don't seem to promote the kind of mixed residential, retail, and business development that actually builds vibrant neighborhoods in the long run. When urban governments finance new stadiums, they are really spending hundreds of millions of dollars to entertain suburbanites. Unfortunately, the political relationship between city and suburb is often so contentious that there is little regional cooperation between poorer and wealthier municipalities in funding stadiums. In Philadelphia, for example, the city decided to put a rental-car tax in place to help fund the stadium. City leaders approached suburban leaders about the possibility of instituting this tax in all of the counties surrounding Philadelphia. Not surprisingly, the suburbs politely declined. (Some local officials, we were told, actually laughed out loud.) As a result, the rental surcharge applies only to renting a car *in the city*. So city residents, who are generally poorer, must pay an extra tax for a rental car. Granted, this particular tax was designed as a visitor tax, but it will still have a detrimental effect on city residents who need a rental car.

Opposition and the Growth Coalition

It's tough being opposed to new sports stadiums, especially when you are up against a powerful local growth coalition that can obfuscate its vested interests in such social policies. Although we have described the role of opposition groups in the cities we have studied, we now want to place this opposition into the larger context that frames our conclusions. That is, what does the plight of new stadium opponents have to say about the state of democracy in the United States? We have seen several well meaning and occasionally well organized opposition groups rolled over by pro-subsidy forces. Supposedly democratic venues like referendums are almost inherently unfair because opposition groups cannot raise anywhere near the money generated by stadium advocates. Indeed, in cities such as San Diego, new stadium advocates wanted very much to have a public referendum because they thought it would be easier to manipulate the general public than to get prompt action from the local government without a public mandate. And what are opponents to think when apparent referendum victories such as those in Pittsburgh

and Phoenix are simply ignored by stadium advocates? Why even bother?

There is no monolithic pattern to these opposition groups. Like the growth coalitions they battle with, their existence, shape, and form are firmly tied to the social characteristics of a particular city. In Minneapolis, they coalesce around an anti-corporate welfare position that has roots in Minnesota's longstanding populist tradition. In Pittsburgh, one of the most effective opposition campaigns came from a wealthy newspaper owner with a libertarian streak, who just happened to live there. If Richard Scaife had lived in a different city, the opposition in Pittsburgh would have been far less effective. Arizona's relatively elderly population generated a fairly formidable opposition in Phoenix that was rooted almost totally in an anti-tax philosophy. They were simply ignored, however; and their single-minded anti-tax focus prevented them from forming more sustainable alliances with smaller bands of opponents with different philosophies. Members of Philadelphia's relatively middle class opposition were effective in preventing a downtown baseball stadium from being built in their neighborhood but were largely irrelevant to the more general issue of building the ballpark in the first place.

How can citizens build more effective opposition to subsidizing private stadiums with public dollars? One reform might be to create spending limits on referendums that concern stadium funding. This would at least even the playing field. Our research shows that proponents typically outspend opponents by at least a ten-to-one margin and sometimes much more. At the same time, we are aware that such a reform might not make a difference in the long run. Stadium proponents have ways to manipulate the community even without a funding disparity. Newspapers can still run an avalanche of editorials and print home team press releases documenting the economic pain that the franchise is enduring. Corporate elites can still pressure politicians or more subtly influence the political discussion over "correct" forms of economic growth and development. The teams can continue to threaten that they will leave the city, and politicians can wring their hands over the tragedy of becoming a minor league city. We are also wary of campaign finance reform because ultimately the referendums only seem to matter if ballpark proponents win, not if they lose. With that in mind, opposition groups might decide not even to bother trying to influence the outcomes via a popular referendum.

Stadium opponents often try to pressure the local sports teams who seem to benefit most from these policies, arguing that using public money for private stadiums is a form of corporate welfare for wealthy team owners. Opponents might publicize the finances of the team and its owners (in hopes of embarrassing them) or organize a boycott. But based on what we have learned in our research these tactics might not be very effective. For one thing, it is no surprise that teams are trying to use tax money to build their stadiums. They are forever trying to increase revenues through soaring ticket prices and six-dollar beers, so why not try to get the community as a whole to pay for a new stadium? Owners are lodged in an economic system (professional sports) that leads them to press for more than the other guy gets. So an obvious reform, suggested by other observers, involves pressing for reform of the economic structure of the leagues, which would benefit all teams and cities: for example, national legislation lim-

iting the amount (or percent) that a municipality can spend on a sports stadium or laws mandating that leagues pay a substantial share of new stadium costs. Other possibilities include placing limits on teams' mobility (particularly after receiving a large public subsidy in the stadium), thereby undercutting any future threat to leave town.[4]

More important, however, our identification of the growth coalition's leading role in building publicly financed stadiums suggests a different tactic for any opposition. Opponents need to target these nonsports organizations and try to raise awareness about their manipulation of policymakers and their influence over dominant ideologies. So instead of pressuring sports teams, opponents might pressure local businesses that advocate using public dollars for private stadiums. In Cincinnati, this could mean boycotting Chiquita bananas. In Pittsburgh, this might mean pulling accounts from PNC Bank or refusing to buy Heinz ketchup.

A successful opposition should also adapt to the shifting strategies of local growth coalitions and other stadium advocates. While some attention still must be paid to critiquing the alleged economic benefits of new stadiums, even more should be paid to countering arguments that link new stadiums with community self-esteem and community collective conscience. In other words, opponents must have a good response to "Keep Cincinnati a Major League City" and "Keep Cleveland from Becoming Akron." They must articulate ways in which public dollars can be better spent to keep their city vibrant and remind people that the public coffers are not bottomless. A stronger connection must be made for community development, stronger neighborhoods, lower crime, a vibrant downtown, and better schools instead of new ballparks. It might be easiest for opponents to highlight these community trade-offs in cities where advocates have mostly abandoned strategies that justify new stadiums in economic terms. By admitting that stadiums will not expand the public till, advocates can no longer make arguments that there will soon be enough money for new stadiums and new libraries and new public schools.

Thus, opponents must force a public realization that there are actual choices to be made about which of these amenities contributes most to enhancing community self-esteem and community collective conscience. At the moment, sports stadiums have been cornering the market on what makes a city first-class. But this perception is not inevitable, even though it will be hard to change. Perhaps political representatives and corporate leaders can be educated about the possible consequences of "wearing their civic hats" or "leaving their marks" through new stadiums rather than in less visible ways. For example, in 2001, racial unrest erupted in Cincinnati just as the city built two new sports stadiums that were supposed to enhance community collective conscience. We think that unfortunate situation in Cincinnati may foreshadow events in other cities where good stadiums have been defined as more socially important than good jobs, good libraries, and good schools.

So long as cities keep spending lots of public dollars on new sports stadiums rather than on public schools, affordable health care, and safe neighborhoods, social conditions will continue to deteriorate for a great number of urban residents. Perhaps we need an entirely new vision for what makes an American city a major league city.

Notes

1. The key to Lukes' (1974) third dimension of power is the distinction between perceived and real interests.

2. The population of Los Angeles increased by 6 percent between 1990 and 2000, despite losing the NFL Rams.

3. We thank Norman Krumholz for helping us think about stadiums in this way.

4. Several analysts have offered a host of suggestions for the reform of professional sports. See, for example, Costas (2000) and the final chapter of Weiner (2000).

References

Costas, Bob. 2000. *Fair Ball: A Fan's Case for Baseball.* New York: Broadway Books.

Lukes, Steven. 1974. *Power: A Radical View.* London: Macmillan.

Weiner, J. 2000. *Stadium Games: Fifty Years of Big League Greed and Bush League Boondoggles.* Minneapolis: University of Minnesota Press.

Chapter 2

MAY THE BEST TEAM WIN

Making Baseball Competitive

Andrew Zimbalist

In this short piece by Andrew Zimbalist, the economist explains clearly how legislative and judicial decisions and nondecisions can affect very fundamental aspects of a sport—in this case, baseball. The political context affects not only the structure of the league but managerial behavior as well. Though the article is slightly dated, Zimbalist's vision of a more competitive playing field has yet to be attempted.

The World Series of October 2001 between the Arizona Diamondbacks and the New York Yankees was more than just scintillating baseball. In that seven-game series, America's pastime became a healing ritual, and baseball helped bring the nation together after the shocking terror attacks of September 11. But the world of baseball was not what it may have seemed during that brief interval. Much was—and is still—amiss.

Just one month after the 2001 World Series ended, baseball commissioner Bud Selig went before Congress to plead poverty for his industry. To get its economic house in order, Major League Baseball proposed to eliminate two or more teams—at the same time that several potential host cities, including the nation's capital, were begging for a major league team. Meanwhile, various team owners were demanding public subsidies from their host cities for new stadiums—and threatening to move their teams if the subventions were not forthcoming. High-revenue teams such as the Yankees maintained their dominance over low-revenue teams, and threats of another player strike sapped fan interest. Ticket prices climbed ever higher, and attendance continued to fall, with 20 of the 30 major league teams dropping at the gate in 2002. Overall, attendance fell 6 percent in 2002 and, as of the All-Star break, attendance was down another 5 percent in 2003.

These recurrent problems are all related to baseball's special status as an unregulated legal monopoly. Alone among team sports, Major League Baseball enjoys a presumed exemption from the nation's antitrust laws. It is the only top-level professional baseball enterprise in the country, and each of its teams is assigned an exclusive territory (in a few megacities the territory is shared by two teams). Until 1992 the industry claimed that its "independent" commissioner would guard against abuses of baseball's market power and privilege. But the few commissioners who ever consistently behaved independently of the owners' wishes were usually dispensed with in short order by unappreciative owners. And even the illusion of independence was shattered in 1992 when Bud Selig, owner of the Milwaukee Brewers, was appointed acting commissioner—and then full commissioner in 1998.

The Antitrust Exemption

Baseball's antitrust exemption has been linked to its player reserve system, which for almost a century gave a team sole rights over a player and forbade players to solicit competitive bids for their services. In 1976, however, a collective-bargaining agreement between Major League Baseball and the Players Association ended that reserve system, lifting the reserve clause from players with six years of major league experience and instituting a system of limited "free agency." And in 1998 Congress passed legislation that lifted baseball's antitrust exemption as applied to labor relations. But even though the reserve system has been in history's dustbin for more than a quarter-century, the antitrust exemption itself remains—though its convoluted history is one for the books.

The exemption is founded in the 1922 *Federal Baseball* case. In *Federal Baseball* the Supreme Court affirmed a U.S. District of Columbia Court of Appeals ruling that baseball was a sport, not interstate commerce—and thus not subject to the Sherman Antitrust Act. In 1948 the Second Circuit Court of Appeals, calling the reserve clause "shockingly repugnant to moral principles . . . that have been basic in America . . . [since] the Thirteenth Amendment . . . condemning 'involuntary servitude,'" ruled that baseball was subject to antitrust law. But the Circuit Court suit was settled out of court before the Supreme Court could rule on appeal—and thus was born the ambiguity about whether baseball is subject to antitrust. That same ambiguity explains why the antitrust exemption is often referred to as baseball's "presumed" antitrust exemption.

In 1951, Major League Baseball requested Congress to affirm its exemption. The House Subcommittee on the Study of Monopoly Power held protracted hearings on the subject but passed no legislation. Many observers believe that the House committee thought that the 1948 ruling had superseded the 1922 ruling and that the failure to pass new legislation to grant MLB an exemption meant that the sport would be subject to the nation's antitrust laws.

Yet, in 1953, the Supreme Court reaffirmed the 1922 decision and handed the ball back to Congress, observing that "in *Federal Baseball* . . . this Court held that . . . professional baseball . . . was not within the scope of the federal antitrust laws. Congress had the ruling under consideration but has not seen fit to bring such business under these laws by legislation. . . . We think that if there are evils in this field which now warrant application to it of the antitrust laws it should be done by legislation."

Baseball's exemption became still more anomalous in 1957 when the Supreme Court ruled, in *Radovich v. NFL*, that the National Football League is subject to antitrust statutes. And in 1972 (in *Flood v. Kuhn et al.*) the Court once more affirmed the 1922 decision while calling it an "aberration" and an "anomaly"—prompting the *New York Times* to opine, "The Supreme Court made a mistake the first time it considered the subject 50 years ago and now feels obliged to keep on making the same mistake because Congress does not act to repeal the exemption it never ordered."

Since 1990 several judicial rulings on the status of baseball's exemption have resolved little. One state ruling and one federal ruling have held that the exemption applies narrowly to baseball's (now defunct) reserve clause and to no other aspects of the industry. One state and two federal rulings have held that it applies broadly to the entire business of baseball. Together the rulings cover only three of the eleven judicial circuits in the United States, leaving ample ambiguity in the status of the scope of the exemption in the remaining circuits.

Baseball's Ups and Downs

Despite the lingering presumed antitrust exemption, the fortunes of baseball (and its competitive balance) steadily improved between 1965 and the end of the 1980s, aided by the demise of the reserve system and by a reverse-order amateur draft in which teams with the worst records choose first. Before free agency, when players were stuck with a team for their whole careers unless they were traded or released, big-city owners bought good players from small-city owners. The extra revenue produced by these top players went to the owners, not the players, and

high-revenue teams disproportionately accumulated player talent. The free-agent market allowed weak teams to improve themselves rapidly and made it more difficult for winning teams to hold together. Competitive balance improved and the era of team dynasties seemed to be gone forever.

Then came the 1990s. Baseball's 1990–93 national television contract with CBS and ESPN awarded each team roughly $19 million a year—almost 40 percent of the average team revenue from baseball's central coffers to help equalize team strength and keep baseball competitive. But the value of the new 1994 TV contract fell more than 60 percent. With centrally distributed monies falling below $8 million per club, big-market teams like the Yankees and teams like the Baltimore Orioles with new, big-revenue-generating stadiums found their revenue edge growing rapidly.

The revenue disparity between the richest and poorest teams grew from around $30 million in 1989 to $208 million in 2001. As franchise values rapidly escalated, owners increasingly had to be extraordinarily wealthy individuals or corporations that frequently owned other businesses with ties to the baseball teams. In 2001 the Anaheim Angels, Atlanta Braves, Toronto Blue Jays, Chicago Cubs, Los Angeles Dodgers, Cleveland Indians, and Texas Rangers were owned by media companies or media moguls. And the Yankees, Boston Red Sox, and Philadelphia Phillies either owned media companies outright or had joint ventures with them. The baseball teams themselves were only small cogs in large enterprises, but teams like the Yankees and the Braves—inundated with revenue from many sources—grew into dynasties that smaller, low-revenue franchises could not hope to match.

Although baseball has seen and survived past dynasties, such as the storied Yankee teams of the 1950s and early 1960s, the game today is more vulnerable than it was half a century ago. Teams that perform poorly year after year and have few prospects for becoming competitive risk losing fans for good. The game's core base of fans is aging, and younger audiences are enticed by a growing list of professional sports and entertainment options.

Meanwhile, the problem of real and threatened franchise movement continues. Baseball's monopoly allows it to restrict artificially the number of franchises and to dally with cities that have no team to hold out to them the elusive promise of a franchise, pressuring existing host cities to build new stadiums or otherwise do MLB's bidding. As a consequence, cities and states compete against each other, leading to exorbitant stadium-financing packages and sweetheart leases. Cities have attempted on their own to include lease provisions that deter team relocation and provide a more equitable sharing of the facility returns. But usually only the largest cities have sufficient bargaining leverage to accomplish even part of these aims.

Moreover, baseball's insulation from competition has also contributed to a lax and inefficient management culture. Consider the World Series you are about to watch. Home field advantage this year for the first time was decided by the winner of this year's All-Star Game. Why? Not because it made any logical or competitive sense, but because baseball was desperately grasping for a way to boost its flagging ratings for the mid-season classic. (Despite this artificial inflation, the 2003 All-Star Game failed to improve its television ratings and even saw its ratings fall 9.7 percent in the

key 18–34 male demographic relative to its record-low ratings in 2002.) The pattern here is well established. Grab for the proximate dollar and never mind about the long-term consequences.

Or consider the revealing message in Michael Lewis's new book *Moneyball: The Art of Winning an Unfair Game*. For decades, baseball teams' front offices were run by "good old boys" who followed a dubious lore of player evaluation as if it were catechism. The enlightening statistical analyses of the game by innovators like Bill James went ignored until Sandy Alderson in Oakland decided that his team could benefit from James's insights in the mid-1990s. And benefit they did, creating a first-class competitive team on a shoestring budget. Now, after a 25-year delay, several teams are beginning to change their ways and introduce the teachings of Bill James and his followers.

Or take the absence of a Major League Baseball team in our nation's capital, the eighth-largest media market. The National Football League, the National Basketball Association, and the National Hockey League, all without antitrust exemptions, have teams in Washington, D.C., but not Major League Baseball.

Baseball may finally have mismanaged itself into a position where Congress may be willing to enact some meaningful public policy reforms to curtail MLB's monopoly powers. Congressional initiatives in this area, however, would have to rise above a history plagued by local chauvinism and myopia. In the past, sponsors of legislation have invariably reacted to a team movement problem in their state or district, opportunistically seizing the occasion to posture in defense of their constituents. While it is arguable that there could be a small gain in net global welfare when a team relocates from a smaller to a larger city, it is clear that proper public policy should be oriented toward increasing the supply of baseball franchises so that all economically viable cities have a team. In this as in other problem areas, the solution is to strip MLB of its antitrust exemption, exposing it to judicial review and additional competitive pressure.

Solving the Problem

In a 1972 decision involving the reserve clause, the chief justice of the Supreme Court stated, "It is time the Congress acted to solve the [antitrust exemption] problem." Nothing has transpired in the ensuing 30 years to lessen the urgency of that appeal.

But even if Congress were to resolve the ambiguity over the scope of baseball's presumed exemption in favor of judicial review and competition, lifting the exemption would not guarantee competition in the industry. It would merely potentially put a check on restrictive behavior—and encourage much-needed judicial discovery of facts and analytical challenge of baseball's assertions. To promote competition and resolve the problems noted above, Congress should contemplate a forced divestiture of MLB into two competing business entities. The entities would be allowed to collaborate on playing rules and on interleague and postseason play, but not to divide up metropolitan areas, establish common drafts or players' markets, or collude on broadcasting policy. Under these circumstances neither league would be inclined to vacate an economically viable city, and, if it did, the competing league would be likely to jump in, just as McDonald's and Burger King rush to beat the other to any viable strip mall. Other consumer-friendly consequences

would flow from such an arrangement, and lower local, state, and federal subsidies would scale down team revenues, owner profits, and player salaries. But competition would compel more efficient management practices and teams would remain solvent, albeit with reduced cost structures.

When he was still baseball commissioner, Fay Vincent referred to Washington, D.C., as an "asset" of baseball even though no team was playing in the nation's capital. Why? Because D.C. was and is a potential host of a team and could be used to leverage better deals from other cities. Baseball treated D.C., in a sense, as if it owned the town. This sense of ownership, in turn, derives from the artificial scarcity of franchises that baseball enforces as a monopolist. Were there two competing major leagues, Washington would have one franchise, or perhaps two, in a heartbeat.

With two competing baseball leagues, most, if not all, of MLB's competitive-balance issues would be resolved. Not only would cities now bereft of baseball find themselves hosting teams, but some host cities might find an additional team or two in their market. If sharing the New York City market with the two existing teams offered better prospects for a franchise than, say, having New Orleans to itself, New York City might once again have three (or more) baseball teams. If the Yankees and Mets had to share New York with additional teams, much of their competitive advantage over smaller markets would disappear. Indeed, with competition over time one would expect teams to allocate themselves across the country so as to equalize the expected incremental revenue from each venue.

One potential downside to divestiture is that competition between two leagues will tend over time to result in one league growing stronger and the other weaker. The weaker league may see some of its franchises fail and may eventually be absorbed by the stronger league. The result would first be instability, followed by the possible reassertion of monopoly. This possibility, however, seems both remediable (divestiture could be legislated again in the future) and a modest price to pay given the expected benefits of competition.

Play Ball!

The U.S. House of Representatives and Senate have been prompted to consider public policy remedies for baseball more than 60 times since 1950, 16 times since 1990. Congress has never acted either to regulate or to break up MLB. With one minor exception, it has also never acted to take away baseball's presumed antitrust exemption.

It is useful to remember that in the past, rational public policy toward baseball has been impeded by "rational politics"—that is, politics where politicians act in their own best interest. As sports franchises have sky-

rocketed in value, today's owners tend to be some of America's wealthiest and most powerful individuals and corporations. As such, baseball ownership has important and close ties to members of Congress and, needless to say, to the man in the Oval Office. Congressional reluctance to curtail MLB's monopoly powers is hardly surprising.

But while most baseball issues taken up by Congress over the years have been local in nature, baseball sometimes seems to do its best to agitate the whole country at once. The announced intention of the owners to eliminate at least two teams along with their minor league affiliates out of a dozen or so contraction candidates in 2001 (now postponed until 2006)* may arouse enough members of Congress to undo the historical record of inaction. There is no reason for public policymakers to sit back and hope that baseball's barons will finally get it right.

---

* As of this writing, contraction still does not appear likely. [Eds.]

Chapter 3

ROOTING THE HOME TEAM

Why the Packers Won't Leave—and Why the Browns Did

David Morris and Daniel Kraker

David Morris and Daniel Kraker, in an article that dovetails with the Zimbalist and Delaney-Eckstein pieces in this section, suggest that community ownership might be an important part of an answer to the question of how to fix sports leagues. Their argument, that Green Bay's arrangement with the Packers is a viable model for tying teams to locales *and* for raising adequate funds, presents an interesting contrast to Zimbalist's suggestion that we should allow more teams and leagues. Of course, there are many elements to consider and many combinations are possible, including the options of discarding the antitrust exemption; enabling community ownership; and adopting revenue-sharing in all leagues (something the NFL already does). There are many possibilities, but power relations among elites and between elites and the masses seriously constrain the outcomes.

In the last Sunday in January, an elated John Elway stood on the gridiron where his Denver Broncos had just beaten the Green Bay Packers 31–24, and announced to millions of worldwide television viewers that the best part about finally winning the Super Bowl was how much it meant to his longtime fans, the people of Denver. Mere months later, the owners of the newly crowned Super Bowl champions announced they might move the team to another city if Denver fails to come up with $250 million for a new stadium—even though the team itself is valued at only $182 million.

Denver's predicament is not uncommon. More than 50 million Americans in almost 30 urban areas stand to lose a professional sports team in the near future unless their local governments agree to subsidize new, amenity-laden stadiums. But why should a community pay millions more than a team is worth simply to keep it local for another 10 or 20 years—especially since tax revenue generated by a stadium is usually less than

David Morris and Daniel Kraker, "Rooting the Home Team: Why the Packers Won't Leave—and Why the Browns Did" from *The American Prospect* 9, no. 40 (September 1, 1998). Reprinted with the permission of *The American Prospect*, 1710 Rhode Island Avenue NW, 12th floor, Washington, DC 20036.

the cost of the subsidy? How can a city keep its home team without emptying the municipal coffers into the hands of a private owner?

The best answer to this last question may be provided by 1998's Super Bowl losers, the Green Bay Packers, the only community-owned team in America. Rather than paying a continuous stream of subsidies to fickle owners, communities ought to be able to emulate Green Bay and buy their teams outright. Community ownership, combined with effective revenue sharing within professional sports leagues, would prevent teams from leaving home and would save taxpayers huge amounts of money by protecting fans and taxpayers from owners who bid their team out to the city offering the best stadium and the biggest subsidy.

Faithful Fans

Professional sports is modernity's mass religion. The sight of Green Bay Packers fans baring their chests and wearing foam-rubber cheese on their heads leaves little doubt as to just how fanatic these modern zealots can be.

Yet support for a local professional team is more than frenzied enthusiasm. Stadiums bring together Americans from all walks of life—black and white, old and young, assembly-line worker and CEO—to share civic pride as they root for the home team. Detroit's population doesn't congregate in bars to watch Ford or Chrysler workers build cars; Seattle residents don't cluster around their televisions to watch Microsoft programmers design software. But the cities do root communally for the Tigers and the Seahawks. This intimate connection between fan and team is what makes it so unbearable for some people to see their favorite team shipped around the country like a packaged good.

But civic pride is not equivalent to job creation or tax revenue. The same year that Cleveland unsuccessfully offered $175 million to refurbish Memorial Stadium to prevent the Browns from leaving for Baltimore, the city closed 11 schools for lack of funding. Although team owners claim that the economic benefits created by building new stadiums justify sweetheart deals, new stadiums have little impact on residents. Andrew Zimbalist, a professor of economics at Smith College who has written extensively about sports, argues that professional sports teams are actually a "slight net drag on the local economy."

In the past six years, eight teams have changed addresses, uprooting themselves from Minneapolis, Quebec, Cleveland, Los Angeles (the Rams and the Raiders), Winnipeg, Houston, and Hartford. They moved either because their host cities wouldn't build them a new stadium or because competing cities made a relocation offer that owners couldn't resist. During the same period an additional 20 cities paid the extortion that team owners demanded, building a new facility or remodeling an existing one. And yet another 44 teams are planning a new stadium, or have expressed dissatisfaction with their current one, and are demanding new subsidies from their city governments. All told, $7 billion is expected to be spent on new sporting facilities by 2006, most of which will come from taxpayer pockets.

Failed Strategies

Communities have tried to use the law to stop wayward teams from leaving town. Oakland in 1982 and Baltimore in 1984 tried to invoke their legal authority to seize privately owned property to prevent their National Football League teams from moving, but the courts denied them that power. In the wake of the Cleveland Browns' move, Ohio Representative Louis Stokes and Senator John Glenn introduced the Fans Rights Act of 1995, which would have provided for a narrow antitrust exemption, shielding a league from a lawsuit if it blocks a relocation.

Most of the efforts at the national level have been focused on increasing the cost to cities that subsidize teams. New York Senator Daniel Patrick Moynihan introduced legislation two years ago to prohibit tax-exempt bonds from being used to build professional sports stadiums.

Yet no bill to curb the right of teams to move has ever made it out of a congressional committee, much less come up for a vote in either chamber. Cities are reluctant to support a limitation on tax-exempt borrowing for sports teams for fear that Congress would eventually limit their borrowing authority for other purposes. Also, for every two senators trying to keep a team in their home state, there are two more wrangling for a team for *their* state; for every city struggling to fund a stadium, there are two more cities claiming a willingness to pay whatever it takes.

When Baltimore built Camden Yards in 1992 and Cleveland opened Jacobs Field two years later, local residents were enthusiastic. Located downtown, these new baseball stadiums are smaller and more intimate than their predecessors and have great sight lines, modern amenities, and a traditional feel. Both were financed almost entirely by public money, and city leaders and urban experts alike touted them as sparks that would revive languishing city centers.

But the fiscal bottom line has been disappointing. Despite the Orioles' success on the field and at the ticket office, taxpayers haven't seen a return on their investment. Bruce Hamilton and Peter Kahn, economists at Johns Hopkins University, estimate that Camden Yards generates about $3 million annually in economic benefits but costs Maryland taxpayers $14 million a year. The new stadium for the Baltimore Ravens, built adjacent to Camden Yards, was much more difficult for politicians to approve, partly because its projected fiscal deficit is even higher than that of Camden Yards.

With the cost of sports arenas soaring, other cities are looking more closely at the promised economic benefits, and public opinion has taken a decidedly negative turn. Voters, when asked directly whether they would fund a sports facility, are increasingly refusing—as residents of Minneapolis, Pittsburgh, Columbus, and San Francisco have done. Last November the citizens of Minneapolis voted to amend the city charter to require any city contribution in excess of $10 million for a sports facility to be approved by voters in a special referendum. San Francisco Bay-area voters struck down *six* public financing initiatives for a new Giants ballpark in the last decade before the team owners finally agreed to finance a stadium themselves—the first 100 percent privately financed stadium in this country in 30 years.

In some cities, residents voted down proposals to finance a stadium with public funds only to watch helplessly as their legislators bypassed their votes with financing plans of their own. In 1995, by a margin of 64 percent to 36 percent, Milwaukee voters defeated a proposal to pay for a stadium with a sports lottery. A few months later, by a single vote, the state legislature passed a plan for $160 million in direct public funds, when Senator George Petak "changed his mind" at the eleventh hour. While the stadium circumvented the public will, Petak could not; he was immediately recalled by angry citizens and lost re-election, causing Republicans to lose their majority in the state senate.

Even the referenda that have succeeded have been extraordinarily close, and all were tainted by gross spending disparities. In Seattle in 1996, Paul Allen, cofounder of Microsoft and the third wealthiest human being on earth (with a fortune of some $17 billion), agreed to buy the NFL's Seahawks (who were close to moving to Los Angeles) on the condition that the state put up 75 percent of the $425 million cost of a new stadium. In an unprecedented step, Allen personally paid the $11 million for a referendum, then saturated the media with a $5 million pro-stadium advertising blitz and spent $1.7 million lobbying the Washington legislature. Stadium foes spent about $100,000 total. The result was a 51 to 49 percent victory for Allen.

Just a year earlier King County taxpayers had narrowly defeated a financing initiative for a Seattle Mariners ballpark despite facing the same spending disparities (the *Seattle Times* even donated free ad space to the pro-subsidy campaign). The next month, apparently stirred by the Mariners' playoff victory over the Yankees, Washington legislators appropriated $270 million in public funds for a new stadium. The stadium, still under construction, is way over budget, putting taxpayers on the hook for yet greater subsidies.

San Francisco voters passed a referendum on June 4, 1997, calling for $100 million in public funds to help finance a new stadium complex for the NFL's 49ers. It passed by the squeakiest of margins—1,500 votes out of more than 173,000 cast—and only after closing a 20 percent gap in the polls in the final two weeks. Stadium proponents outspent their foes by $2.5 million to $100,000 and enlisted the aid and rhetorical agility of Mayor Willie Brown, whose office allegedly went so far as to set up special polling places at selective public housing projects where support for the stadium referendum was especially high but voter turnout was historically low.

Community Ownership

For some years now, most communities with pro sports teams have been paying large subsidies to keep the teams around. But it is only recently that team owners have been demanding more public money than their teams are worth. Minnesota Twins owner Carl Pohlad tried to extract $250 million from the Minnesota state legislature for a state-of-the-art retractable roof stadium, but the team is only worth around $100 million [see Table 1, "Team Values vs. Stadium Subsidies," below].

The best way to reverse this trend and keep teams at home is to allow communities to own their teams. The Green Bay Packer organization is the poster child for community ownership of professional sports teams. Pre-NFL football champions in 1929, 1930, and 1931, and winners of Super Bowls I, II, and XXX, the Packers were incorporated in 1923 as a private, nonprofit, tax-exempt organization. Their bylaws state that the Packers are "a community project, intended to promote community welfare." The team can move only through dissolution, in which case the shareholders receive only the original value of their shares. A board of directors, elected by the stockholders, manages the team.

TABLE 1   *Team Values vs. Stadium Subsidies*

Team	Year Funding Was Approved	Amount of Public Subsidy (in millions)	Franchise Value (in millions) in Year Subsidy Was Approved
Baltimore Orioles	1992	$210	team sold for $70 in 1989
Cleveland Indians, Cleveland Cavaliers	1991	$295 (two stadiums)	$162 combined value
Cincinnati Bengals, Cincinnati Reds	1996	$540 (projected cost) (two stadiums)	$270 combined value
Milwaukee Brewers	1995	$160–310 (projected)	$96
St. Louis Rams	1993	$260	$148 (as L.A. Rams)
Seattle Mariners	1995	$340 (projected)	$80
Seattle Seahawks	1997	$300 (projected)	$171
Florida Panthers	1996	$171	$45
Tennessee Oilers	1996	$220–292 (projected)	$159 (as Houston Oilers)

This nonprofit status has been threatened only once, in 1949. The Packers needed to raise more than $100,000 to avoid insolvency, but instead of becoming a profit-making venture the board chose to authorize 10,000 shares of common stock at $25 a piece—4,628 of which were issued—and dissolve the stock that had been sold in 1923. To ensure that no one individual or company had too much control, each shareholder was limited to a maximum of 200 shares.

Green Bay's model works. While its surrounding metropolitan area is home to fewer than 200,000 people, the Packers rank in the top 20 percent of all professional teams in terms of franchise value. Extravagant player salaries have driven many cost-conscious franchises into competitive irrelevancy as they fail to bid for the best free agent players. Observing this trend,

Packer team shareholders decided in late 1997 that more revenue needed to be raised for the team to remain competitive. The 10,000 shares issued in 1950 were split into 10 million shares—400,000 of which were made available to the public at $200 a piece. A disclaimer on the opening page of the stock offering reads: "It is virtually impossible for anyone to realize a profit on a purchase of common stock or even to recoup the amount initially paid to acquire such common stock." Even so, by March the team had raised $24 million dollars, far short of its $80 million goal but enough to double its available cash, and ample capital to invest for the future construction of a new stadium 20 or 30 years from now.

Wisconsin residents support the team even through dismal seasons. Games at Lambeau Field have been sold out for more than 30 consecutive seasons, even through years of mediocrity in the 1970s and 1980s. Streets are deserted for three hours on autumn Sunday afternoons. The waiting list for season tickets is 36,000 names long for seats in a stadium that holds 60,000. It is common for season tickets to be willed from one generation to the next and to be hotly contested in divorce proceedings. For better or for worse, the Packers are like a community religion (even for the truly religious: nuns in northern Wisconsin proudly sport Packer T-shirts when doing social work in the community). Literal and figurative community investment in the team fuels such loyalty.

League Rules

If community ownership can make sports teams less transient, then why isn't it more widespread (though it should be noted that the Canadian Football League, the NFL's struggling junior sibling to the north, boasts four successful community-owned teams)? One simple reason, mainly: professional sports leagues have prohibited community ownership.

The NFL formally banned community ownership in 1961 at the same time that it adopted a radical revenue-sharing plan that distributes all revenue from merchandise, television, and gate receipts equally among all teams. It took NFL Commissioner Pete Rozelle two years to convince Congress to enact this essentially socialist redistributive mechanism. Revenue sharing made small-market teams viable. In fact, had the league not chosen to ban community ownership at the same time, we might now be rooting for NFL teams from Akron, Ohio, and Gary, Indiana. Major-league baseball has also managed to prohibit fan ownership, though without enacting a formal policy against it. In the 1980s when Joan Kroc, widow of McDonald's founder Ray Kroc, offered to donate the Padres to San Diego along with $100 million to cover operating expenses, the owners nixed the idea. Bud Selig, baseball's current acting commissioner—who as owner of the Milwaukee Brewers coerced Wisconsinites into building him a new stadium—has vowed to kill any community ownership proposal because it would be an "awkward" arrangement for the league.

Though clearly successful where implemented, community ownership remains illegal in most professional leagues. A bill introduced in the House of Representatives by Earl Blumenauer, a Democratic congressman from Oregon, would change that. The Give Fans a Chance Act of 1997 would override all league rules against public ownership. Under the bill, if a league refused to allow a community to purchase its team, the league would lose its sports broadcast antitrust exemption. The bill also would require leagues to take into account fan loyalty and whether an investor is willing to keep the franchise in its home community when considering whether to allow teams to relocate. If enacted, Blumenauer's bill would give fans the opportunity to give the home team genuine roots.

Community ownership is attracting increasing interest at the grassroots level. In 1995, Kansas City Royals owner Ewing Kauffman donated his team to charity with two conditions: the charitable foundation had to sell it to someone who would commit to keeping the team in Kansas City, and the proceeds from the sale had to go to local charities. The IRS approved the donation. While this arrangement does not call for community ownership, it does tie the team permanently to the city.

In Minnesota, Twins owner Carl Pohlad has offered to donate the club to a local foundation as part of a deal for a new publicly financed ballpark (as long as his accumulated losses of around $85 million are covered). Considering this an invitation to community ownership, several legislators have introduced a bill that would have the state buy the team and then sell a majority share to the fans within a year. If the fans failed to buy the shares, showing themselves unwilling to put their money where their cheers are, the team would go back on the market.

History indicates that fans are willing to pay top dollar for the home team. The

Boston Celtics went public in 1986 as a rare "pure play" limited partnership, meaning someone buying shares got part ownership in a company made up entirely of the basketball team and all its parent corporation's holdings. Shares in the Celtics were grossly overvalued at $18.50, did not grant voting rights, and lacked even the endorsement of star player Larry Bird, who deemed them "not a good investment." Still, 2.6 million shares, a 40 percent interest in the team, were sold in one day, raising $48 million dollars—more than triple the $15 million the team's owners had paid only three years earlier. Celtics shares are trading today for only around $20, but have paid out more than $16 per share in dividends since 1988. This comes to a healthy 10 percent annual return on investment.

Revenue Sharing

Yet community ownership, while necessary, is by itself an insufficient remedy for the disease currently afflicting professional sports. The Green Bay Packers, though the paragon of community ownership, would have died long ago if not for the NFL's revenue-sharing policy—which ensures that, for example, its recent $17.6 billion television contract will be divvied up among all the teams.

Baseball and—increasingly—basketball and hockey, on the other hand, are tied to the fortunes of their owners and the skybox-revenue-generating capacity of their stadiums. The four most victorious baseball teams in 1997 also had the largest payrolls; six of the eight top-spending teams have had stadiums built since 1989. As the same well-positioned teams continue to win while the small-market clubs flounder in division cellars, fan enthusiasm will erode,

taking with it the leagues' financial vitality. If baseball, basketball, and hockey are going to retain an interesting level of competitiveness, small-market vitality, and national fan support, these leagues must emulate the NFL's revenue-sharing system.

But revenue sharing alone will not make sports franchises less nomadic. In fact, the NFL's revenue-sharing policy has effectively encouraged team migration—the NFL has experienced more relocations than any other league over the last decade—because sharing revenue permits small cities to compete for teams. But since revenue from corporate suites, club seats, and other stadium sources are excluded from the revenue-sharing arrangement, owners feel compelled to demand new stadiums with more and bigger skyboxes. Despite average game attendance of more than 75,000, the highest TV ratings in the NFL, and Cleveland's 72 percent approval of a $175 million tax increase to redo Memorial Stadium, the Browns left for Baltimore in 1995 to enjoy a fancier, heavily subsidized stadium. Cleveland Mayor Michael White and Ohio federal legislators failed to keep the Browns from leaving, but they did reach a compromise that enabled Cleveland to retain the Browns name. The league also promised that Cleveland would receive an expansion team within three years. This kind of compromise should be the third element, with community ownership and revenue sharing, of a comprehensive solution to the professional sports problem.

Under such compromises, teams would remain free to move, but the league would be penalized when they do. If Los Angeles and Cleveland were granted expansion franchises when their teams left, each team's share of the league's total revenue would decrease because of the two additional teams that would join the league. In other words, by moving their teams to increase short-term revenue, the owners of the Rams and Browns would have decreased the average value of NFL teams in the long run. Owners would therefore have to weigh the short-term advantages of relocation against the long-term financial advantages of league stability.

Professional teams have become an integral part of our community fabric and our emotional and civic lives. This may justify stadium subsidies in certain communities, but common sense dictates that when an owner demands a subsidy two to three times the value of the team itself, fans would be much better off purchasing the team themselves.

Professional sports may be in decline. As taxpayers spend more on new stadiums, team values, player salaries, and ticket prices all increase. Many fans can no longer afford to attend games and will grow increasingly uninterested in sports. For fans and communities to reclaim their teams, they need to rewrite the rules of ownership to give priority to the civic value of teams; for leagues, new rules of ownership may be the smartest option even if it's not yet in their playbook.

Chapter 4

AMERICA'S FASTEST GROWING SPORT

TV ratings are soaring. Corporate money is flowing.
And the crowds just keep getting bigger.
How NASCAR is racing ahead.

Brian O'Keefe and Julie Schlosser

In this overview of the recent development of NASCAR, Brian O'Keefe and Julie Schlosser deal with a range of sociological issues: who competes; what the fan base is; how funding is generated; and the like. In terms of the political-economic context, we see in this article the opportunities and constraints that face growing sports industries. Relatively unregulated, the powerful owners have been able to integrate vertically (some own race-car teams, tracks, and the league itself), market creatively, and expand geographically in a relatively short time. At the same time, as the authors explain, their monopoly control has been challenged in court and their expansion has not been uncontested.

It's 10 minutes before race time at the Indianapolis Motor Speedway, and in the grandstand, a quarter of a million fans—some of them fresh from a two-day-long tailgate party—are settling onto their NASCAR seat cushions, sipping from their NASCAR cups, adjusting their NASCAR caps. All around the 2.5-mile track, 74 television cameras are poised to capture every angle of the 43-car, 400-mile race for millions at home. Out on the asphalt, amid the race officials and mechanics in fire-retardant jumpsuits, is the suntanned figure of Home Depot CEO Bob Nardelli. His mission: to introduce FedEx CEO Fred Smith, who's standing at his elbow looking slightly overwhelmed by the noise and fumes and August heat, to Tony Stewart, the roly-poly star driver of the bright-orange No. 20 Home Depot Chevrolet.

Nardelli strides over to Stewart, who beams at the Home Depot chief. The driver then turns the brights on for FedEx's Smith, as if he's welcoming a new member to the club—which in fact he is. FedEx is in its first year as the primary sponsor of a NASCAR team, meaning Smith is the latest FORTUNE 500 CEO to commit tens of millions of dollars to the pursuit of breakneck speed—and the best return on investment in professional sports. Stewart, for instance, isn't just Nardelli's ace driver. He's his top salesman. After winning the Pepsi 400, the 5-foot-8, 185-pound Stewart celebrated by climbing—awkwardly—the 20-foot fence at Daytona and seizing the checkered flag from amused race officials. Home Depot rushed out a print ad featuring a picture of Stewart's ascent with text that read, "Hey Tony, we have ladders," and offered a 10% discount to customers who brought it in. "Ladder sales," says Nardelli, "popped up double digits."

Commerce, of course, is all around the track. Leave aside that the cars are rolling billboards for corporate sponsors. And that the name of the race has been sold to an insurance company—it's now "the Allstate 400 at the Brickyard" (the latter a nickname for the Indy track). In the parking lots outside the speedway, where keg parties, pig roasts, and wet T-shirt contests evoke a Mardi Gras mood, a makeshift mall is also going gangbusters. Levi's is sizing up the waistlines and inseams of potential customers in its Fit Pit, while DeWalt is demonstrating jigsaws and drills from the side of an 18-wheeler known as Rolling Thunder. New sponsor Garnier Fructis, a division of L'Oreal, has dispatched a fluorescent-green-clad Fru Crew to sculpt the hair of fans in the style of its cute young driver Brian Vickers. Branded gear is hawked from foldout tractor-trailers, pickup beds, and bustling arena vending booths. All this on top of the $740 million Nextel has ponied up over ten years to headline NASCAR's

championship series—and the exclusive B-to-B summits NASCAR arranges for its sponsors to meet and greet each other.

This, race fans, is the new world of NASCAR, the fastest-growing, best-run sports business in America—with the emphasis on business. Once the province of moonshine runners and good ol' boys, the sport has courted corporate America for decades. But NASCAR's recent explosion in popularity—and the establishment of its racetracks as big-time commercial venues—is unprecedented. Stock-car racing is now a multibillion-dollar industry. The second-most-watched sport on television behind pro football, NASCAR has seen its ratings increase by more than 50% since it inked a six-year, $2.4 billion network deal five years ago. The sport is on pace this year for its highest TV viewership ever; the last time a major professional sport set a new high was the NFL in 1981. Licensed retail sales of NASCAR-branded products have increased 250% over the past decade, totaling $2.1 billion last year alone (up from $1.3 billion in 2000). Nascar.com is one of the most highly trafficked sports websites. The NASCAR name is so hot that market research firm PSB picked it as the country's No. 2 brand for 2005, ahead of both Google and iPod (BlackBerry was No. 1).

With NASCAR claiming one-third of all American adults as followers—including a growing swarm of blue-state and female fans—corporate America is stumbling all over itself to get in on the action. It doesn't hurt that while other major sports keep waking up to one PR nightmare after another—baseball's ongoing steroid scandal, last season's NHL lockout, fisticuffs between NBA players and fans—NASCAR drivers are media-savvy, fan-friendly marketing machines. (They never talk about their cars without mentioning their sponsors: "the Cingular Chevrolet," "the Viagra Ford," and so on.) According to the IEG Sponsorship Report, NASCAR had total corporate sponsorship revenue last year of $1.5 billion, compared with $445 million for the NFL and $340 million for Major League Baseball. "Talk to anybody in sports marketing right now," says Larry DeGaris, who runs the Center for Sports Sponsorship at James Madison University, "and NASCAR is the first thing out of their lips." There are 106 FORTUNE 500 companies involved as sponsors—more than in any other sport. "We had been talking about it for over a decade," says FedEx CFO Alan Graf Jr. of his company's decision to sponsor a team this year. "But the sport has gone to such a higher level, we decided we had to jump in."

At the center of it all is NASCAR itself, a private, family-controlled, for-profit company started 57 years ago in Daytona Beach, Fla., that now includes offices in midtown Manhattan, L.A., and the center of U.S. retail, Bentonville, Ark. Once focused on simply bringing order to the cheerful, low-down chaos of stock-car racing—where vehicle standards used to shift from track to track—the business today is run like a FORTUNE 500 company, dotcom, and media conglomerate rolled into one. In other big-money sports like football or baseball, local franchises own teams and stadiums and dominate league management. Stock-car racing is entirely different, with team owners—who spend millions outfitting cars and fronting drivers—and track owners reliant on an independent NASCAR (the National Association of Stock Car Auto Racing) to bring them together. There are no union troubles, and if a team fails to perform, it doesn't drag down

the league—it's simply replaced by the next new faster car and driver. If a track is getting shabby and failing to draw a capacity crowd, NASCAR can simply shift to another site. Meanwhile, beyond the high-profile, big-money events, NASCAR also oversees more than 1,000 races at tracks spread across 38 states.

The kingpin charged with executing this bare-knuckle business model is a 43-year-old college dropout named Brian France. The third generation in his family to run stock-car racing's governing body, France took over as NASCAR's CEO just a year and a half ago—and quickly made major changes, aggressively borrowing business tactics from other professional sports and recruiting some of their top next-generation talent. France sees the sport he grew up in not merely as a racing circuit, but as an entertainment empire that happens to move at 190 miles per hour.

The day that kicked off NASCAR's latest and greatest growth phase is also one of the saddest in its history. Legendary driver Dale Earnhardt—whose brinkmanship earned him the nickname "the Intimidator"—was rounding the final turn of the Daytona 500 in February 2001 when his car was bumped and then slammed into the wall. He was killed instantly. NASCAR nation erupted in grief, and the Intimidator became bigger than ever, his face on the covers of magazines and countless hats and T-shirts. His last race happened to be the first broadcast in NASCAR's huge TV deal with Fox, NBC, and TNT (Fox broadcasts the first half of the Nextel Cup season, NBC and TNT the second half). NASCAR's all-time leading money winner at the time of his death, Earnhardt had used his success and iconoclastic reputation to build a multimillion-dollar licensing business. His ability to monetize his fame became a template for other drivers, teams, and NASCAR itself.

It was a coming-of-age moment for a sport long considered a regional curiosity. When "Big Bill" France founded NASCAR in 1948, his goal was to bring a set of common rules to stock-car racing. Standing a sturdy 6-feet-5 with an outsized personality to match, Big Bill established what everyone inside the sport refers to today as NASCAR's "benevolent dictatorship." He didn't hesitate to disqualify drivers for unfairly souping up their vehicles or to banish them for trying to unionize. In 1972 his son Bill Jr. inherited the dictatorship—a fragmented web of independent track operators and drivers ignored by national marketers and TV execs. With limited financial options, NASCAR under Bill Jr. cultivated corporate sponsors with an ardor that other sports found unseemly. Logos were embroidered into the fabric of the sport.

The Brian France era has seen a new iteration of dictatorship. As television gradually discovered NASCAR during the '80s and '90s, individual tracks made their own deals with networks, usually getting a few million dollars for each race. The events were spread over multiple networks, giving each station less incentive to cross-promote or invest in extra cameras and graphics that would enhance broadcasts and ratings. Brian, then an executive vice president in charge of marketing, knew there was a better way. Working with Bill Jr. in the late '90s, he persuaded track owners to consolidate their TV rights and allow NASCAR to negotiate a package deal with the networks. The result was the $2.4 billion contract with Fox, NBC, and TNT. NASCAR is now negotiating a new package that is expected to be even richer.

Brian's business vision—and strong-arming—continued after his father turned over day-to-day operations to him in the fall of 2003. His first act: to rewrite the nearly 30-year-old formula for determining NASCAR's annual points championship. Rather than tally up points all season, the top ten drivers after 26 races would qualify to compete in a ten-race playoff called the Chase for the Nextel Cup. (The other drivers' motivation over the final two months would be to win races for their sponsors, or maybe muck up the works for their rivals.)

The outcry was immediate and vicious. "I compared it to Clinton starting right off the bat with health-care reform," says George Pyne, a former football player at Brown University who's now NASCAR's COO. "I said, 'Wouldn't it make sense to wait a year and get established first?'" But France was adamant that NASCAR, like baseball and basketball, would benefit greatly from a playoff run to keep it in the news, especially in the fall after the football season started. It turned out he was right. The race for the first championship in 2004 came down to the final lap, boosting viewership. This year, despite the fact that fan favorites Dale Earnhardt Jr. and Jeff Gordon are long shots to qualify, Cup series TV ratings are up 9%.

Sitting in an air-conditioned, Nextel-branded trailer near the garage area in Indianapolis, France explains that growing up, he didn't think he would make a career out of stock cars. "I thought I'd go into law or something," he says. "I always loved NASCAR, but I didn't view it as a business opportunity." After dropping out of the University of Central Florida, however, he went to work managing a small dirt track in Tucson and found he had an aptitude for the sales side of the business. Then, in 1994, NASCAR ran its first Brickyard race at Indy, drawing a sellout crowd and a sizable television audience. France began to see the potential. By then, his father had put him in charge of marketing, and he went at it with a vengeance. He took NASCAR to L.A., where he opened the first Hollywood office for a professional sports league. Now NASCAR's goal is one film a year with a stock-car-related plot (this summer it was Disney's *Herbie: Fully Loaded*; Will Ferrell has signed to play a driver in a comedy due next summer with the working title *Talladega Nights*), plus NASCAR placement inside the story lines of popular TV shows (as when driver Jamie McMurray appeared on *The West Wing* in January).

France has been equally aggressive elsewhere. NASCAR's New York office now includes marketing pros formerly employed by the NBA, the NFL, the NHL, and Major League Baseball. "It's not so much that we have a passion for the sport at first," says Justin Johnson, who recently came over from MLB. "We have a passion for the business of NASCAR." France feels strongly that stock-car racing doesn't get enough coverage in newspapers and on talk radio, so he's hired PR specialists in New York and Los Angeles; the publicity staff has grown from two full-timers in 2001 to 25 today. France has even talked about starting a news service to help increase coverage; NASCAR already has a password-protected website for journalists with suggested story ideas.

The night before the Allstate 400, just over 100 FedEx employees and clients sit down for dinner in the Murat Centre, a former Masonic Shrine Temple in downtown Indianapolis. The Centre's Egyptian room features hieroglyphics on the walls and art deco chandeliers; big-band stars such as Glenn Miller once entertained from its stage. On this night it holds a racecar. As the guests settle at tables decorated with FedEx-orange flowers in glass vases, the lights dim and up-tempo music begins to play. Behind the No. 11 FedEx Chevrolet Monte Carlo, the seven members of the car's pit crew, clad in their purple fire-retardant jumpsuits, take their positions. The stage lights flash on, the timpani swell, and the pit crew leaps into action. Fourteen highly choreographed seconds later, the car has four new tires and a virtual new tank of gas. The crowd, including CEO Fred Smith, erupts in applause at this display of post-modern automotive performance art.

In NASCAR parlance, this is called "activating" a sponsorship. A company like FedEx might pay as much as $20 million a year to be the lead sponsor for a top-notch race team. But the sponsor may also spend $20 million more on promotional campaigns, client entertaining, and other marketing to maximize the value of its NASCAR presence. In fact, NASCAR execs frown on sponsors who shirk their activation responsibilities. They like to see cardboard cutouts of drivers posted in retail stores and crowds of clients—potential new fans—flown to the racetrack on junkets. France's crew actually runs seminars to help sponsors make the most of their investments. Earlier this day, NASCAR hosted a lunch for representatives of about ten sponsors, including DuPont, UPS, and USG. A marketing manager from Sunoco (the official fuel of NASCAR since 2004) gave a PowerPoint presentation on his company's activation program, which features a joint contest with Nextel that gives away $250,000 and a full 9,000-gallon tanker of gasoline.

One of the guests at the FedEx gala is Norm Miller, the chairman of Interstate Batteries. Like FedEx and Home Depot, Interstate is a primary sponsor of a team owned by Joe Gibbs Racing, run by the

Redskins coach. When Miller first began sponsoring a team in 1992, the rate was just $2.5 million a year. But even as the cost of sponsorship has escalated, Miller insists his company has gotten its millions' worth. NASCAR, he says, has helped boost potential customers' "front-of-brain awareness" of his brand from 22% to 70%. There are other benefits too. A couple of years ago Miller asked Gibbs to make an introduction for him at Home Depot. Interstate now sells its lawn and garden batteries at the home-supply giant. "That's $4 million in business a year," says Miller.

Sponsors rave about the purchasing loyalty of NASCAR fans. According to a NASCAR licensing study, 72% of fans are more likely to buy a product if it has the sport's logo on it. (No wonder celebrity chef Mario Batali is writing a NASCAR cookbook.) Nextel says that it has found that NASCAR fans are several times more likely to try their service than the average person. Margie and Phil Chaney, both 45, who flew into Indianapolis from San Martin, Calif., to attend the Brickyard race, are living proof. "Absolutely," says Phil. "I don't care what it is—gasoline, auto parts, or whatever. If it has NASCAR on it, that's the one I'm going to buy."

The breadth and volume of licensed goods NASCAR sanctions—in more than 3,500 categories—is extraordinary. They range from standard T-shirts and baseball caps to vegetables. Yes, vegetables: Produce distributor Castellini Group now sells NASCAR-branded potatoes, lettuce, and tomatoes in supermarkets across the country. "It's been a big boost," says Jack Bertagna, Castellini's head of sales and marketing. "Apples to apples, our sales are up 20%."

A few chairs away from Senator Hillary Rodham Clinton on the stage of the St. George Theatre in Staten Island, N.Y., sits Lesa France Kennedy. A reserved, soft-spoken woman of 44, Kennedy is both Brian France's sister and the president of International Speedway Corp., a publicly traded company that owns or has interest in 12 racetracks around the country, all of which host Nextel Cup races. Her company is 62% controlled by the France family, making their Thanksgiving dinners akin to an industry conference. (NASCAR and ISC are headquartered in the same Daytona building.) She's here on a Thursday morning in early August speaking to a crowd of a couple of hundred women to garner support for putting a $600 million speedway nearby. To the France family, the New York City area is a crucial pushpin on NASCAR's national map, the gateway to full acceptance by blue-state America. Since the late 1990s, NASCAR has added Nextel Cup races in California, Chicago, and Kansas City. The goal: to make stock-car racing as popular in urban America as it is in the heartland.

Easy to say, hard to do. New York City politicos aren't exactly jumping up and down to bring NASCAR to town. Even NASCAR's tightly controlled universe has its skeptics. There are only 36 Nextel Cup events a year to be parceled out around the country, and 18 of them are run at ISC properties. Considering that an event like the Brickyard race might pump a couple of hundred million dollars into the local economy, those on the outside looking in tend to get jealous. In July the owners of the Kentucky Speedway in Sparta sued NASCAR and ISC in federal court, alleging that the companies are violating anti-trust laws by refusing to award them a Cup race. The track, built in 2000, hosts NASCAR-sanctioned Busch Series—the equivalent of Triple A for stock-car racing—and Craftsman Truck

NASCAR FOR NEOPHYTES

For the rest of America—beyond the 75 million adults that NASCAR claims as fans—here's a quick primer on the common misconceptions about the sport. *By Oliver Ryan*

MYTH: "All the fans are rednecks."
REALITY: NASCAR may have Southern roots, but that's no reason for pejoratives. One out of five fans has income above $75,000. Fans are also more likely to be professionals than the average American. Some 18% are black or Hispanic.

MYTH: "Women don't watch."
REALITY: NASCAR claims women make up 40% of its fan base. Of sports watched on TV, NASCAR boasts the second-highest percentage of women viewers, according to Nielsen. Families turn NASCAR weekends into outings that include kid-friendly face painting and teen-friendly concerts.

MYTH: "Crashes are the only entertainment."
REALITY: Racing involves strategy. Drafting can increase speed and save fuel, which makes for fewer pit stops. Good drivers can find the fastest line on a track. The timing of passing and pit stops is critical. At 190 mph, nothing is simple.

MYTH: "The fastest car always wins."
REALITY: Cars are tightly regulated to stay within certain mechanical norms. Teams do build engines from scratch, use computer models and wind tunnels to perfect body designs, and customize vehicles for different track conditions. But no amount of money will make up for poor driving, a lousy pit crew, or just plain bad luck.

MYTH: "Stock-car racing isn't really a sport, and drivers aren't athletes."
REALITY: Temperatures in a 3,400-pound, 850-horsepower stock car can reach 130 degrees, and drivers fight against three Gs of force while cornering. They make nonstop, split-second decisions for nearly four hours during a race—some lose as much as ten pounds of body weight. Unconvinced? Listen to Ernest Hemingway: "There are only three true sports: bullfighting, motor racing, and mountaineering; all the rest are merely games."

events and has become a favorite place for drivers to test racecars. But NASCAR has refused to give the speedway a chance at the big show. France settled a similar suit in 2004 by the proprietors of the Texas Motor Speedway outside Dallas, awarding that track a second Cup event. But France vows to fight the Kentucky suit—"We're going to be extraordinarily aggressive at defending our business practices," he says—and points to NASCAR's long history of making the sport work financially for an extensive network of interested parties. "There's no question that NASCAR has some vertical integration," says Tulane University's Gary Roberts, a sports-law expert. "On the other hand, you might say that there's nothing inherently anticompetitive about an entity vertically integrating, if it doesn't injure the consumer."

NASCAR is looking to expand demographically as well. On a race day, you're hard-pressed to find more than a handful of non-whites at a track, and the Confederate flags still wave from some tailgaters' RVs. There may be many people of color watching at home, but for now every single driver in the Nextel Cup races remains white and male. Last March, NASCAR traveled to Mexico City, filling 95,000 seats for a Busch Series race at the Autodromo Hermanos Rodriguez. "We want to be more relevant to the fastest-growing segment of the population—Hispanics," says France. He's launched a program to support minority drivers, and at NASCAR's Craftsman Truck Series race in Indianapolis, a young Hispanic named Aric Almirola was in the field against, among others, a 44-year-old African American named Bill Lester. Lester has a degree in electrical engineering from Berkeley and gave up a job with Hewlett-Packard to pursue his auto obsession. "I think there are a lot of closet African-American NASCAR fans out there," he says.

There is at least a chance that the first minority driver to make it big in stock-car racing will come via the NFL. Joe Gibbs is the most successful NFL alum in NASCAR, while former Dallas Cowboys quarterbacks Roger Staubach and Troy Aikman this summer received a commitment from Texas Instruments to sponsor a Nextel Cup team for 2006. But former Heisman Trophy winner Tim Brown created an even bigger stir

when, announcing his retirement from the NFL in July, he revealed plans to launch a NASCAR team with Jack Roush, one of the sport's top owners. At the Brickyard in Indy, the former Oakland Raider showed up to spark sponsor interest and talk up his intent to provide an opportunity for minority drivers. Such a team could tap into an urban market rich with potential, he says: "You know, it's not too cool to wear a Dale Earnhardt jacket in the neighborhood. We want to make it cool."

Brown admits he isn't much of an auto aficionado. The former business major at Notre Dame says that he first got interested in the late 1990s, when he started a lingerie company and "wanted to go after the NASCAR market." He approached Dale Earnhardt's people to discuss a deal, he says, and was told it would cost him $1 million to meet with the racer. "Just for a meeting," says Brown, who passed on the offer. "I never could get over that. But it's the kind of thing that sticks in your mind."

If stock-car racing has a spiritual home, it's a V-shaped slice of land between I-77 and I-85 near Charlotte, N.C. Often called NASCAR Valley, it's the home of nine out of every ten Nextel Cup teams. Many of the sport's drivers live in swanky houses on nearby Lake Norman. North Carolina has been a hotbed of racing since moonshiners first came down out of the Appalachians to race souped-up sedans on Saturday nights. The old Charlotte Speedway was the site of the first NASCAR-sanctioned "strictly stock" race, on June 19, 1949. When John Holman and Ralph Moody established their influential racing factory outside Charlotte in the late 1950s, it solidified the area as the place to build fast cars.

These days there's an arms race going on in the Valley—a high-tech effort by team owners to create the fastest stock car, fueled by the unprecedented flow of money into the sport over the past decade. Although the basic engine technology inside stock cars—a V-8 without fuel injection—is a relatively simple design dating from the 1950s (NASCAR regulates it to maintain competitive balance), virtually every part of the cars is handmade and heavily tested. Every major race team has its own office park with multiple buildings for the race shop, engine shop, and a research and development center—not to mention a museum of racing artifacts. And every new shop seems to be bigger and fancier than the last. Earlier this year Indy racing legend Roger Penske, who currently operates three NASCAR Nextel Cup teams, opened a new 424,000-square-foot facility on the site of a former Matsushita factory. In addition to a dazzling garage area, it has a 138-seat cafeteria, a one-mile nature trail, two baseball fields, and nine conference rooms on 105 acres of land—just in case he needs room to expand.

No one personifies the changes that NASCAR has gone through over the past few decades more than Richard Childress. Growing up outside Winston-Salem, Childress got his first taste of racing while selling peanuts at nearby Bowman Gray Stadium. Working nights at a filling station, he got to know some of the area's moonshine runners and often made local deliveries when he got off work. He was 18 when he got his first racecar, a 1947 Plymouth he bought for $20, and he started Richard Childress Racing six years later. He drove the Cup series for 12 years without a victory. Then, in the early 1980s, as an owner, he hooked up with Dale Earnhardt, and the two went on one of the most successful and profitable runs in the sport's history. Childress, 59, now owns three full-time Nextel Cup teams

and two Busch Series cars. His race shop and museum near Winston-Salem attract about 70,000 visitors a year. In the fall of 2004 he also opened Childress Vineyards a few miles away; the former moonshiner now loves his merlot.

"When I had one team, there was a lot of things I could go and do," Childress recalls. "Hell, I used to play golf. But with the commitments that everybody has today, that's impossible." He did more than 100 events with sponsors last year. The cost of running a team is enormous—as much as $1 million a year just for tires. Economies of scale help, which is why big players like Childress run multiple teams. But anyone on the margins is getting squeezed. "You're down to big owners that own a lot of race teams," says Childress. "And you have to operate more teams to survive. It's definitely swayed to the amount of teams and the amount of resources you can put together. Who would have ever dreamed a race team would have an in-house CFO and retainers with attorneys and human resource departments?" Childress worries that the rise of multiple-team operations could upset the balance of power that makes NASCAR's benevolent dictatorship work. "We don't need five owners with eight teams apiece running our show, even if I'm one of them," he says. "To make the sport healthy, you need 20 owners, and we're down to less."

One of the most powerful owners at the moment is Jack Roush. The veteran of drag and open-wheel racing now runs five Nextel Cup teams, and he's captured the last two championships with drivers Matt Kenseth and Kurt Busch. Roush Racing president Geoff Smith says the sponsorship market "is the hottest I've ever seen it." But that has a downside too. "One sponsor could come in, pull a Steinbrenner, and try to buy success," he says. Every new big spender ups the ante for the rest of the owners. Like Childress, he worries that the trend toward ultrapowerful, multiteam owners could throw up impenetrable barriers to entry and erode the competitive balance. Plus, he says, even for a big operation, the economics aren't getting any easier. The hotter the sport becomes, the more money drivers, crew chiefs, and even star tire changers demand. Not to mention the astronomical expense of building hundreds of engines a year.

Back in Daytona, at the NASCAR headquarters where Brian France keeps his office, they're well aware of the perils that confront the sport as it strives to challenge football and baseball. Most critical, perhaps: What happens to NASCAR's core fans as the sport continues to expand? Stock-car racing has long attracted a targeted audience—a way for sponsors to wrap themselves in the flag and have their brand displayed where PA announcers pray "in the name of Jesus Christ." In expanding its reach, NASCAR risks losing the distinctiveness of its audience and turning off its base. And that could dilute its fans' Pavlovian responsiveness to ads.

Other sports leagues would love to have those kinds of concerns. And so far, certainly, NASCAR's sponsors seem unworried. Home Depot's Nardelli, for one, has plenty of reasons to keep the faith. After more than three hours of racing at Indianapolis, his driver, Tony Stewart, took the checkered flag for the Allstate 400, his fourth victory in six races. This time not just Tony but his entire crew climbed the fence near the finish line. Home Depot was ready for the photo op with a dozen ladders out on the track. But an opportunistic sponsor's work is never done. In keeping with recent tradition at Indy, Stewart got down on pit road after the race and kissed the strip of red bricks that give the track its nickname. Sure enough, Home Depot quickly brought out an ad featuring his celebratory smooch. Bricks have been selling briskly ever since.

Chapter 5

BUILDING A MINI METROPOLIS KNOWN AS THE U.S. OPEN

Bill Pennington

When the United States Open begins this week at Oakmont Country Club outside Pittsburgh, a challenging, manicured golf course will be only part of the scene.

More striking will be the transformation of the grounds into a temporary metropolis of corporate tents, merchandise vendors, provisional roads, grandstands, concessions, hospitality centers, news media facilities, security outposts and every conceivable public service from baggage claim to bug-bite care. Supervised by a staff numbering in the thousands, the United States Open is far more than a golf tournament; it is an extravagant American sporting spectacle rising out of a lush field like a mirage.

Authentic as it may be, the once-a-year manifestation of the Open obscures an unseen, sophisticated operation that precedes the first golf shot in competition by seven to eight years.

About 300 miles east of Oakmont, in the Philadelphia suburbs, is Merion Golf Club, the host of the 2013 Open. At Merion, and

in the adjacent streets, towns and even at the local college, everyone already knows exactly how the tournament is going to transform a sleepy suburb into a small city for a week. Maps and overlays have been drawn, train and traffic schedules rethought, neighborhood schematics readied and many millions of dollars allocated from the budget of the United States Golf Association, sponsor of the Open.

A typical United States Open is estimated to net more than $25 million for the association, so cost is hardly an obstacle if it keeps the project moving along. For example, Merion, which was host to its first U.S.G.A. championship in 1904, is wedged into tight quarters and will have to rely on the benevolence of its closest neighbors, most significantly Haverford College.

Beginning in 2012, the college has agreed to give up the use of three of its athletic fields, including the varsity softball field, so the U.S.G.A. will have time to erect the platforms, roads, colossal tents and utility services for the cynosure of the event to many visitors: the five-acre corporate tent village.

The college will receive an undisclosed moderate fee from the U.S.G.A. for its co-operation, as well as some passes, a hospitality tent and a promise to restore the fields to their original condition. Still, that left the softball team without a field for one season.

No worries. The U.S.G.A. found a simple municipal field a short walk from the campus and agreed to pay for its renovation to meet the standards of Haverford's flourishing softball program.

"You learn quickly that the U.S.G.A. doesn't mess around; they are a well-oiled machine," said Ron Tola, Haverford College's director of facilities management. "I was awe-struck by the advance planning. Then again, when you go to an Open, and you walk into one of those giant buildings that they call corporate tents, you realize what you're dealing with.

"There's black walnut furniture in those tents and every other amenity. My wife would say, 'Give me this for my living room, and I'll be happy.' They call it a corporate village; it's really a city."

The core U.S.G.A. advance staff will usually visit a potential host site seven to eight years before play is to begin. At Merion in the past year, the U.S.G.A. has met with local public transportation officials to review how the nearby rail lines could deliver many of the 25,000 spectators expected daily.

Officials have begun devising a strategy for parking about 15,000 cars in outlying areas. (The Villanova University campus several miles away is one option.)

The U.S.G.A. has met with Haverford township officials and begun to rally a force of more than 5,000 volunteers. And it has asked about 20 families living in homes abutting the course to allow corporate tents to sprout in their yards. The homeowners could be paid enough to cover their mortgages for two or three months.

The Open is primarily about identifying a national champion, but it is also a perfect merger of powerful entities: golf culture and corporate America.

Because of that, and other reasons like golf's popularity in the Tiger Woods era, the Open has become a cash machine for the U.S.G.A. The association does not reveal its finances, but recent federal tax records show it reported about $40 million in annual profits from its 16 championships. (The U.S.G.A. also puts on men's, women's and junior amateur championships as well as the United States Women's Open.) The bulk of that profit, perhaps as much as 75 percent, comes from the United States Open.

A 2004 article in Golf Digest estimated that the 55 to 70 corporate tents at a typical Open rented for about $150,000 each. The massive merchandise tent, as big as a football field, brought in $7 million in revenue, according to the magazine. Television kicked in as much as another $20 million and ticket sales another $10.5 million. Those numbers have remained steady.

Mike Butz, the deputy executive director of the U.S.G.A., did not discuss the financial details of the Open but acknowledged that the revenue had to be high to cover the expenses.

"I think the only other sports event that compares in terms of advance planning is the Olympics," Butz said.

"The Olympics is obviously bigger, but each of their venues is like putting on a U.S. Open. And probably like a successful Olympics, it only works if the community hosting things buys into it completely."

In the late 1990s, the U.S.G.A. told Merion it would probably not be the site of another Open. The modern version of the event, some said, had grown too big for the old, traditional courses like Merion, which held its last Open in 1981.

"I think the club and the community around us took that as a challenge," said Rick Ill, the president of Merion Golf Club. "We lengthened some holes, and that solved one part of things, but the incredible community collaboration is truly what made this happen. It couldn't have happened, for sure, without Haverford College giving up its three fields."

Greg Kannerstein, the dean of the college, remembers being shocked that the availability of Haverford's grassy fields could be the deal-breaker.

"I had no idea they needed so much space," Kannerstein said. "But we all felt kind of badly that Merion wouldn't be part of the Open rotation, and we knew we wanted to help."

Haverford's incoming president, Dr. Stephen Emerson, had one complaint about the arrangement.

"I do wish they had included golf lessons targeted specifically for the college president," Emerson said. "Then again, had they seen what a project they would be taking on, the whole thing might have fallen through. Maybe it's best to leave things in the hands of the professionals."

A U.S.G.A. task force will descend on the campus and community in about five years, even living in campus housing while working. The temporary city will rise in the fields like a mirage. Then, after a boisterous week, it will begin to disappear.

Somewhere, the 2020 United States Open will have taken seed.

PART II

THE FAUSTIAN BARGAIN:
BIG-TIME SPORTS AND THE MEDIA

The marriage between sports and the media has transformed sports. From directly observed local events to virtually observed delocalized events that were transmitted—often over great distances—by media corporations, major sports morphed into media-sports. Beginning with a heavyweight boxing championship match that was broadcast in 1921, media-sports grew throughout the twentieth century, attaining its greatest impact with the development and expansion of television—and it soon became the dominant source of fans' sports experiences.

Despite its achievement in bringing sports contests into the living room of the ordinary fan, the sports/media marriage produced some unsettling effects. First, it increased greatly the financial wealth of major sports teams and organizations, which began to earn millions of dollars from selling broadcasting rights. Second, supported by advertising and commercialization, sports became linked with capitalist consumer culture, and soon afterward, almost every object associated with big-time sports—from T-shirts, jackets, and replicas of player jerseys to beer mugs and key chains embellished with team colors and logos—was being marketed for a profit. By the last several decades of the twentieth century, sports such as baseball, hockey, and football had evolved into major retail enterprises, promoting a vast and ever-expanding pool of consumer products, all with the objective of exploiting fan loyalties, to increase the team's financial wealth. This commercialization, in recent years, has extended even to the naming of sports stadiums.

Third, the sports/media marriage changed the patterns of sports-franchise ownership in the United States. Though less visible than some other effects of the linkage, this change had important implications for the way sports operated in society. As the enormous wealth generated from media contracts grew and sports became more commercialized, large corporations began to purchase family-owned sports franchises and sought to synergistically integrate them with their other corporate operations. Media conglomerates such as Rupert Murdoch's News Corporation, Comcast Cable Network, and Time Warner acquired sports franchises with the strategic objective of using sports revenue not just to increase their profits but also to expand the markets for their other corporate ventures.

Fourth, the marriage greatly increased the wealth and celebrity status of leading professional athletes. Generating multimillion-dollar sports contracts, often accompanied by additional millions from advertising endorsements, sports media made star professional athletes some of the world's most popular and highly paid professionals. The names of Michael Jordan, Tiger Woods, Roger Federer, or David Beckham are likely to be more familiar to ordinary people in Toronto, Paris, and Tokyo than are many of the names of the world's political leaders. Because of their high profiles, these star athletes often attract as much media attention for their off-field activities as they do for their athletic feats, feeding an insatiable and relentless public curiosity for athlete celebrity gossip.

Fifth, and finally, the media/sports marriage, and the resulting commercialization of sports, has played a large role in marginalizing many previously popular amateur sports. In fact, the very concept of "amateur sports" has lost much of its meaning. This can be seen perhaps most clearly in big-time college football and basketball, which continue to be formally defined as amateur sports while actually operating as quasi-professional enterprises. The "amateur" college leagues and teams compete for lucrative media contracts and postseason bowl invitations and manage, much like their professional counterparts, to generate lucrative financial returns. In fact, few people are surprised to learn that some college team coaches earn more money than many of their professional counterparts and that star athletes in big-time college sports programs sometimes receive secret payments, gifts, or other perks in violation of the rules of the amateur athletic associations. Given the stakes, this simply reflects the value of these star coaches and athletes in media-driven athletic programs.

Though some sports observers lament the commercialization of media-sports and the demise of the old amateur ethos of "playing for the love of the game," the sports/media marriage has produced such robust offspring—in the form of huge financial returns—that it would be unrealistic, if not delusional, to anticipate their future divorce. Capitalist media-sports are here to stay. Nevertheless, it is important to recall the positive side of media-sports, which its critics tend to gloss over or ignore—that is, its significance for the ordinary sports fan. As a consequence of the emergence of media-sports, many millions of fans can experience sports contests in real time, something that, in earlier years, was simply impossible. The sports experience for spectators has been transformed.

Another positive result of media-sports linkage is its role in normalizing images of racial and gender groups in society. In recent years, for example, the media has projected positive images of persons of color such as black sports superstars Michael Jordan and Tiger Woods. This was not always the case. The media has a long history of projecting images of black athletes as poster boys of social taboos and deviant behavior (Kellner 1996). An especially egregious example of such negative racial images appeared in a 1998 *Sports Illustrated* article on out-of-wedlock fathers that focused primarily on black NBA players. Because the article never bothered to note that these athletes were not representative of most blacks players in the NBA, it helped to nurture and reinforce pernicious racial stereotypes of black athletes (Wahl and Wertheim 1998). We see similar examples in the distorted images of women athletes in the media. Many studies have documented gender stereotypes of women athletes in media descriptions of women's sports and in media comments about the nonathletic aspects of the women's lives—including their clothing, physical appearance, and romantic relationships—personal information of the type that is rarely mentioned in articles about male athletes (Eitzen 1999). We need more studies of the portrayal of racial and gender groups in the sports media in order to expose patterns of distorted images as well as to expand our understanding of the complex social functions of the sports media in modern society.

Which brings us to a broader theoretical question: How have social scientists explained the functions of mediated sports? We will briefly describe three of the perspectives that have been used: critical theory, transactional theory, and circuit-of-capital theory. These are not the only perspectives that have been used to explain mediated sports, but they are common ones, and they are sufficient to indicate the variety and range of such perspectives. The critical theoretical perspective, which encompasses several different but related approaches, argues that media sports weakens the development and mobilization of progressive political consciousness in society. Because media sports divert people from concern about the social injustices of the surrounding political order, critical theorists maintain, media sports help to induce and sustain political false consciousness. Though provocative, these theorists unfortunately rely on a simplistic view of the functions of media sports, one that reduces those media to a conservative and one-dimensional political role.

The transactional theoretical perspective presents a more complex argument focusing on three areas: (1) audience experience (how it differs from stadium experience, its unique gratifications, and its socialization effect); (2) mediated sports content (the different languages presented—spoken, written, visual, the value motifs; and links to dominant societal values); and (3) the dynamics of the mediated sports production complex, which is made up of sports and media organizations that exert pressures on sports journalism around several issues: ownership, organization control, and internal decision making (Wenner 1989). This transactional perspective thus seeks to investigate a broad range of empirical questions rather than merely reducing media sports to a reactionary political function.

Finally, the circuit-of-capital perspective, which attempts to adapt Marxian theory to cultural analysis, views mediated sports as cultural discourse. It consists of four analytical components, which examine the following: (1) the production of cultural products; (2) the texts that are produced; (3) how these texts are read by ordinary people; and (4) "lived cultures" and social relations—the use that can be made of reading texts and their potential as materials for cultural production (Jhally 1989).

Though no dominant theoretical perspective has emerged in the study of media sports, it should be noted that the one characteristic that distinguishes the more complex and insightful analytical approaches is their view of sports media as part of a problematic process—a view that poses questions for empirical research. The readings in this chapter illustrate analytical approaches and issues that reflect these more complex empirical approaches to understanding the functions of mediated sports.

In his chapter "Football, Television, and the Supreme Court: How a Decision 20 Years Ago Brought Commercialization to the World of College Sports," Welch Suggs explains the legal context that underlies the huge expansion of U.S. college football on television. In the early 1980s, the National Collegiate Athletic Association (NCAA) controlled whether individual institutions could broadcast team sports on national television. Thanks to a U.S. Supreme Court decision in 1984 involving a lawsuit brought by two universities that challenged the NCAA's right to control access to television broadcasting of football games, the door was opened to full-fledged competition among universities for access to media economic benefits, a development that created huge potential conflicts with their explicit educational missions.

Looking at the other end of the spectrum, focusing on the power dynamics resulting from the media's expanding role in sports, David Rowe, in "Money, Myth and the Big Match: The Political Economy of the Sports Media," addresses the theme of corporate ownership and the issues pertaining to the political economy of sports media. He argues that television sports exist as battlefield sites of competition between media corporations seeking to generate revenue from various sources and that one result of these competitive battles was the increased power of capitalist media moguls such as Rupert Murdoch, who is among the most powerful people in the world of sports today. Rowe views this as a negative development.

Emphasizing a similar theme of corporate media power, Murray Phillips and Brett Hutchins, in "Losing Control of the Ball: The Political Economy of Football and the Media in Australia," show how both national and global media processes changed rugby in Australia. They examine the historical background of the league's commodification, the growth of the media-sport cultural complex, the role of pay television, and the control of the rugby league that is vested in Rupert Murdoch's transnational News Corporation; they also note the fan resistance to this corporate media control in sports.

The article by Alan Law, Jean Harvey, and Stuart Kemp—"The Global Sport Mass Media Oligopoly: The Three Usual Suspects and More"—broadens the discussion to look at the international dimensions of corporate media control by examining the corporate structure of major media entertainment conglomerates. The authors show how these "competitors" are involved in joint ventures that link them together into a dense web despite their rivalries. Expressing support for activist resistance, they conclude by arguing for democratic intervention to protect sports media consumers from the increasing power of the global media/entertainment oligopoly.

References

Eitzen, D. S. 1999. *Fair and Foul: Beyond the Myths and Paradoxes of Sport*. Lanham, MD.: Rowman and Littlefield.

Jhally, S. 1989. "Cultural Studies and Sports Media Complex in Media, Sports and Society." Pp. 70–93 in L. A. Wenner, ed., *Media, Sports, and Society*. Newbury Park, CA: Sage.

Kellner, D. 1996. "Sports, Media Culture, and Race—Some Reflections on Michael Jordan." *Sociology of Sport Journal* 13, no. 4: 458–467.

Wahl, G., and L. J. Wertheim. 1998. "Paternity Ward." *Sports Illustrated*, May 4, 64–71.

Wenner, L. A., ed. 1989. *Media, Sports, and Society*. Newbury Park, CA: Sage, 1989.

Chapter 6

MONEY, MYTH AND THE BIG MATCH

The Political Economy of the Sports Media

David Rowe

In this article David Rowe critically examines the increasing role of the corporate sports media, which view sports as a site for generating revenue. At the same time, one of Rowe's key insights is that we must consider the media in terms of their complex interpenetration of the sport, culture, and entertainment industries.

The influence of television is felt in the ever increasing number of on-site advertising banners and logos and sponsorship tie-ins. Some athletes have become walking billboards for their multiple sponsors and equipment suppliers. . . . The commercialization of sports, even at amateur level, continues apace, justified by the constant need to bring in more money, and limited only by initial resistance from the public, which inevitably overcomes its outrage and learns to accept yet more blatant salesmanship in sport as a necessary evil which subsidizes the undertaking. If in junk sports, it's tough to separate the junk from the sports, then in all sports it's equally tough to separate the business from the sport.

—Klatell and Marcus (1988, p.21)

Introduction: Valuing Sport

The discussion of sport and media economics leads into the second part of 'Unmaking the media sports text' for the slightly perverse reason that, just at the point where many other works in media and cultural studies tend to bracket off the rather unromantic 'business of business' and get down to the more freewheeling task of textual reading and interpretation, it is, I believe, all the more necessary to keep economic concerns to the fore. In this way, no artificial separation can be maintained between the 'light' sphere of culture and symbols and the 'heavy' world of economics and material objects. Instead . . . I will discuss below some of the latest twists and turns in media economics, but the chapter will inevitably reflect the extraordinary growth of media sport rather more than its current difficulties. As Toby Miller (1999: 115) has argued, expenditure on sport has heretofore seemed immune to 'conventional business cycles' and 'has grown through most recessions'. In recent memory, therefore, words like downswing and contraction have found little expression in the lexicon of the media sports cultural complex. It has been difficult, therefore, to question the 'article of faith for broadcasters that sports programming was a river of gold' (Maiden 2002: 33). But nothing undermines business faith more than the arrival of the receivers and the administrators, as has occurred in such high-profile media sport cases (discussed later in the chapter) as KirchMedia, XFL, C7 and ITV Digital.

The fortunes of individual sports and also of media companies can, in the ordinary course of things, shift rapidly in response to the involvement of sponsors, crowd attendance and TV ratings, broadcast rights, and so on. It is useful, then, to appraise the major forces in media sport, the ways in which they cooperate and conflict, and the consequences of this economic activity for sport and the wider society and culture. If no single party can be said to dominate the media sports cultural complex or to control its 'image bank', it can hardly be denied that the presence of major economic entities has resulted in far-reaching changes to the sport we see and read about, and to the culture in which it is located. To illustrate this point, we need only point to the cut-throat competition and multi-million dollar and pound investment involved in acquiring such mega media sports properties as the broadcast rights to the:

- Summer and Winter Olympics
- English Premier League soccer
- US National Football League

(Rowe and McKay 2003). That media sport involves serious money is obvious, but the cultural and economic consequences for media sports texts are less apparent. For this reason, we need to delve further into the place where economic and sporting muscles are flexed.

Sport, Media and Capital Accumulation

In chapter 1, I provided brief outlines of the intersecting development of sport and media, arguing that each institution had something that the other wanted—and with increasing urgency. The initial reluctance which both parties displayed in forming a deep alliance was, in part, due to the unprecedented nature of the economic and cultural relations that developed speedily from the late nineteenth century onwards (that is, consumer capitalism and national state-sanctioned media were 'feeling their way'), and partly because their initial economic base relied on direct exchange. So, when most of the revenue for sports enterprises stemmed from paying customers going through the turnstiles to watch sport in person in highly localized settings, not much in the way of mass marketing and promotion was needed. Word-of-mouth, wall posters and some rather staid newspaper advertisements were the major means of informing the paying public about forthcoming sports events, and the technological means did not exist (and when they did, were not initially welcomed) to record and transmit proceedings for those not present

(Stoddart 1986; Whannel 1992; Boyle and Haynes 2000). Similarly, for newspapers more dependent on revenue from cover sales than on advertising, and interested more in the great events of state (as in the establishment press) or in scandal-mongering (the province of the 'yellow press'), sport had only limited appeal. With the development of national and international sporting competitions, the maturation of media advertising and the emergence of broadcast media for which there was no or limited direct payment by the 'consumer', new revenue streams and uses of the sports media were created. In this way, the media sports text became increasingly valorized, a commodity that could be produced, sold, exchanged and distributed. To understand precisely how the media sports text becomes such a valuable economic and cultural object, it is necessary to view it in terms of large-scale social, economic and cultural transformations and also to appreciate the specific ways in which that object is desired or can be made to be or seem desirable.

Within the history of capitalist development, the sports media are not essential commodities: they are not vital for the maintenance of life like food, shelter and clothing, or 'consumer durables' that preserve food, wash clothes or transport whole families to work and school. Nobody has ever died as a direct result of media sport starvation, although passionate sports fans can do striking impressions of zombies during TV blackouts. Seen in this way, media sports texts are not very useful goods but they are, paradoxically, high prized. This is so because they exist in an economic environment where, as many goods have become easier to mass produce and standardize, only a relatively small proportion of their total

price is attributable to the cost of raw materials, labour and manufacture. Hence, the direct production cost of a compact disc or a dress or a child's toy can often be measured in pence and cents rather than in multiple pounds and dollars. Where, then, is the value added and capital accumulated? It is, increasingly, not in the material character of objects that can be reassuringly touched and used, but in the immaterial nature of symbolic goods (Hall 1989; Hesmondhalgh 2002). Value in this sense lies in design, appearance and in the capacity to connect different economic processes that exist in a complex interdependence (Hebdige 1989). An extensive and complex theoretical debate (that can only be addressed briefly and synoptically here) has been conducted since the late 1980s over the meaning of this development (see, for example, Harvey 1989; Hirst and Zeitlin 1989; Giddens 1991; Kellner 1995; Dunn 1998; Dandaneau 2001). This wide-ranging debate is over such far-reaching and difficult questions as:

- Are current circumstances an extension of the same 'logic' and process of modernity (which we might call 'advanced', 'late' or 'high') that brought industrialization, liberal democracy, humanism, and so on?
- Or have we moved on to a new 'condition' called postmodernity in which our social, economic, political and cultural life radically differs from its modernist predecessor?
- Has the mass production and consumption 'regime' pioneered by Henry Ford in the car industry (Fordism) changed a little (to neo-Fordism) or been replaced by a new, more targeted, smaller-scale and flexible way of producing and

consuming goods and services (post-Fordism)?

Posing such questions requires a command of a rather daunting language in which terms like 'flexible specialization' and 'reflexive accumulation' compete for theoretical and conceptual supremacy. It is necessary in the first instance only to be armed with the glossary of key terms provided and to follow the contours of the argument that media sport is at the leading edge of cultural and economic development. If cultural factors are emerging as central to economic process—and most contemporary analyses suggest that they are—then sport and the sports media, as cultural goods *par excellence*, are clearly a central element in a larger process (or set of processes) that is reshaping society and culture (Throsby 2001).

Of course, goods have always had a cultural character (Hesmondhalgh 2002)—the 'respectable' appeal of a type of family sedan, the 'reliable' qualities of a brand of vacuum cleaner, and so on—but more and more commodities have nothing else to declare but their status as cultural goods with appropriately high levels of 'sign value' (Baudrillard 1981), as opposed to the more conventional Marxist concepts of use value (what something can do) and exchange value (what something is worth in a direct transaction). As Lash and Urry argue:

[Yet] the objects in contemporary political economies are not just emptied out of symbolic content. They are also progressively emptied out of material content. What is increasingly being produced are not material objects, but signs. These signs are primarily of two types. Either they have a primarily cognitive content and thus are post-industrial or informational goods. Or they have primarily an aesthetic, in the broadest sense . . . , content and they are primarily postmodern goods (Eagleton 1989). This is occurring, not just in the proliferation of non-material objects which comprise a substantial aesthetic component (such as pop music, cinema, magazines, video, etc.), but also in the increasing component of sign value or image in *material* objects. This aestheticization of material objects can take place either in the production or in the circulation and consumption of such goods. (Lash and Urry 1994: 14–15)

If we consider this argument in relation to media sports texts, then they can be said to be particularly valuable not only because of their 'substantial aesthetic component' (the principal object of media sport is the aesthetics of bodies—their beauty, condition, size, effectiveness—in motion under specified conditions), but also because of their key role in the informational order (cognitive in only a limited sense in terms of 'patented' knowledge about training techniques and regimes, but certainly an informational sign given sport's major role in the news media). Media sports texts, with their almost unprecedented capacity to 'flow across and around these economies of signs and space' in both local and global contexts, their very high levels of 'sign-value', and with their intimate connection to all-pervasive *informational and communication structures*' (Lash and Urry 1994: 6), are almost perfect prototypes of signs in circulation, heavily loaded with symbolic value.

To develop this point a little further, Lash and Urry use the term 'reflexive accumulation' to describe a strengthening tendency in the processes of production and consumption of objects and images for the people involved to be in a position not just to be 'buried' in what they are doing, but to reflect on it, criticize it and adapt to it (Rowe and Lawrence 1998). In this way, human subjects can be partially disconnected from the social institutions, structures and identities (including class, gender, work, nation, locality and family) that they inhabit. Or, to put it another way, as the 'automatic' power of traditional social structures over individuals has weakened, new opportunities have emerged to behave, think and identify in less socially prescribed ways. This development, which is sometimes called 'postmodernity', may not be so very new and may still have much in common with 'modernity', but the existential and ideological fluidity of postmodern life is probably unprecedented. It has created, in one sense, a 'market' for collective identification, a vigorous competition between governments, business corporations and social movements for the 'soul'—and, not uncommonly, the discretionary income—of 'cultural citizens' (now described as 'postmodern subjects'; see Miller 1993, 1998a). In more obviously functionalist terms, perhaps a 'values vacuum' has been created whereby many people feel alienated, no longer believing deeply in anything, identifying with anyone, or feeling committed to any cause outside the immediate interests of themselves and their significant others. An opening exists, therefore, for enterprising parties to engage in the 'consciousness' trade (Enzensberger 1976), to help supply the meaning and commitment that rapid social change under late modernity or postmodernity have evacuated from many lives. But what phenomenon has the emotional force to bind symbolically the fragmenting constituents of society (evidenced, according to Enzensberger (1994) by proliferating civil wars from 'L.A. to Bosnia'), especially where there is abundant critical self-reflection, cynicism and a seeming 'exhaustion' of novelty? Not surprisingly, the answer in the context of this [article] is media sport.

There is a well known argument (e.g. Novak 1976) that sport is a secular religion, having taken over from the church as the primary place of collective and individual ritual, belief, ecstasy, and so on. When sports fans have their ashes spread on the 'hallowed turf' of their favourite sports stadium, the spiritual qualities of sport are very evident. When on occasion a sports team receives a blessing from a religious leader before a major sports event, it may appear that 'sacred sport' is supporting orthodox religion, rather than the other way round. If sport and religion have certain qualities in common, they also share an involvement with business, especially where the religion is, as Max Weber pointed out, the Calvinist form of Protestantism, which he argues supplied many of the values crucial to the formation of capitalism. Indeed, in one (unconsciously) prescient passage in *The Protestant Ethic and the Spirit of Capitalism*, Weber links all three institutions by stating that:

> In the field of its highest development, in the United States, the pursuit of wealth, stripped of its religious and ethical meaning, tends to become associated with purely mundane passions, which often actually give it the character of sport. (Weber 1930: 182)

If Weber's lifespan had stretched a few decades beyond the year of his death (1920), he would have seen not only 'the pursuit of wealth' in the USA and other capitalist nations given 'the character of sport', but also leisure pursuits like sport take on the character of the pursuit of wealth. He would also have seen sport appropriate many of the functions of established religion in increasingly secular societies dedicated to the worship of the god of conspicuous commodity consumption.

Irrespective of whether sport and its values are religions in the strict sense, in broad economic terms (concerned more with profits than prophets, to use a rather old pun) it is one of the key contemporary sites where the expression of strong emotions is translated into the generation of substantial capital. Or, more expansively, where (following Lash and Urry) aesthetic and informational signs meet popular emotion (which sometimes looks like mass hysteria) in a manner readily convertible into commodified pleasure. Media sport has, as we have seen, a proven capacity to bring potential consumers to the marketplace in numbers ranging from the respectable to the staggering. It is able at particular moments symbolically to reconstruct disparate human groups, to make them feel at one with each other (and perhaps, in the case of the Olympics and the World Cup of association football, the world). When contemporary advertising relies so heavily on making very similar items (such as sugared drinks, cars with shared components and 're-badged' computers) appear different, sport's capacity to stimulate emotional identification with people and things is priceless. Sport can connect the past, present and future, by turns trading on sepia-tinted nostalgia, the 'nowness' of 'live' action and the anticipation of things to come. Furthermore, even when our human sports 'subject' is being reflexively critical, rather than getting carried away by sporting affect, they can take an ironic, playfully postmodern approach to it, mocking the mangled language of sports commentators (like the satirical magazine *Private Eye's* 'Colemanballs' section and book series), watching self-consciously bad-taste sports TV programmes (like Australian rugby league's *The Footy Show*) and buying sports newspapers that are parodies of 'straight' tabloid reporting (like Britian's *Sunday Sport*). This chameleonic capacity of contemporary media sport makes it a key aspect of the commodity cycle, its flexibility of form and use fitting perfectly contemporary requirements for speedy change and customization.

Media sports texts are perhaps, then, at the leading edge of this culturalization of economics: they cannot be eaten or worn yet billions of people desire them in a bewildering variety of types, and media corporations are willing to expend billions of units of currency to supply them, often 'free of charge', to the user. In return, as we have seen, invaluable access is given to audiences, on a global scale, which can be cashed in for large sums of money exchanged between sporting associations, clubs, officials and players, TV and sports management companies, sponsors, advertisers and governments. Media sports texts are particularly valuable assets because of their flexibility and interconnectedness. A single sports 'live' TV broadcast can be shown in 'real time' and endlessly afterwards, and can be cut up and packaged in myriad ways, with its soundtrack separated from its visual images so that both can be continually manipulated and reproduced. The sports print media, both newspapers and magazines, can help stimulate interest before the event and 'keep it alive' for a lengthy period afterwards, aided and abetted by the celebrity status of elite sportspeople. In multi-media environments like the Internet, virtually any media sports text can be put to use in the virtual world. All manner of goods and services, from sports equipment and 'designer' leisurewear to beer, banking and tobacco, can invoke or be directly associated with media sports events, the associated messages adapted as necessary to the cultural sensitivities of different audience blocs around the globe (Rowe *et al.* 1994). It is for this reason that television broadcast rights to the major sports are often contested more fiercely than the sports events they are seeking to cover—even when those same media companies complain about how much money they lose by winning them. To understand this apparently economically irrational behavior (which perhaps has turned out to be irrational after all) means delving further into the media sports cultural complex.

How to Make Money While Losing It in Sports Television

Having set out the broad economic framework within which contemporary media sport operates, more precise explanations of why media corporations are prepared to expend huge sums on securing the rights to television sport are required. The Olympic Games constitutes a useful example of the economic appeal of broadcast sport and of the extent to which the rights pertaining to it are both protected and infringed. Detailing the statistics is not unlike recounting the latest world record time in the 100 metres sprint or the greatest number of points scored in the World Series, except that (at least until the early twenty-first century) more records have been broken more frequently in buying sports rights than in performing in sport. Taking the example of the USA's NBC television network, it transpires that in 1995 NBC won the US TV rights to the Sydney 2000 Olympics for US$715 million, as part of a deal in which it paid escalating fees of US$793 million and US$894 million for the 2004 and 2008 Olympics, respectively, to show the Games to American audiences in (then) unknown locations (which turned out to be, respectively, Athens and Beijing). Despite its capacity to sell subsidiary rights, charge vastly inflated advertising rates during key events, and make some other returns from various 'spin offs' (selling videos of Olympic highlights, for example), the cost of rights and of producing TV coverage ensured that NBC would lose large sums of money on the deal. But this does not mean that the NBC Board has suddenly become philanthropic, and is prepared to carry out a selfless task of public service by subsidizing the delivery of Olympics TV to the people of the United States of America and the rest of the world. It has a broader economic motive: the huge audiences for the Olympics raise the network's overall ratings, meaning that it is in a stronger position to negotiate advertising rights across its year-round, all-genre programming. The network also hopes for an Olympics 'spillover effect'—that viewers will be exposed to and stay with its other programmes or, even better, that it will 'get the habit' of switching on NBC first. Being the Olympics station brings with it a great deal of *kudos*, especially prima facie evidence (which might in practice be repudiated) that the network can handle with distinction one of the world's largest media events. In an image-saturated age where 'branded sign-value' is paramount, being known as the Olympic network—with all the brand recognition and prestige that the label entails—gives an important competitive advantage in the media industry. Securing the US broadcast rights to the Olympics also has a 'spoiler effect'—ambitious commercial rivals, such as Rupert Murdoch's Fox Network, can be thwarted (McKay and Rowe 1997) and induced to expend equally large sums of money on other broadcast rights on pain of being locked out of major TV sport altogether. They might also gain psychological ascendancy over other networks like CBS boasting a strong sporting culture who have lost out in the fight for key TV sport properties. All these justifications for paying out vast sums on broadcast rights for sport hold as long as it can be demonstrated that, by one means or another, over time benefits outweigh costs. As briefly noted above, and discussed in greater detail below, the orthodoxy that TV sport is more golden goose than dead duck has come under sharp challenge.

Historically, there is great symbolic and economic value to be gained from controlling the production and distribution of symbols and, in the case of Olympic sport, global images do not come any more desirable (Schaffer and Smith 2000). It is for this reason that there is so much antagonism between Olympic rights and non-rights holders, a struggle that also inevitably draws in sports organizations and even athletes. In Australia, for example, the zealous safeguarding of Seven Network's AUS$45 million television rights contract for the Sydney 2000 Olympics was the subject of considerable anxiety among its commercial and public rivals. At the earlier Atlanta Olympics, where Australian rights were also held by Seven, the Australian Olympic Committee (AOC) helped protect its 'investment' (that is, its opportunity to maxi-

mize rights revenue by guaranteeing exclusivity) by breaking up an interview between a non-rights holder (Network Ten) with two athletes, ejecting a Ten employee from an official function and, finally, by being instrumental in the withdrawal of the Network Ten staff's media accreditation (Moore 1997). For the Sydney 2000 Olympics, the AOC attempted to prevent the 'parasitical' behaviour of non-rights holders in making money out of athletes but not contributing to their upkeep by trading more liberal media access rules for a substantial subvention for its 2000 Olympic Medal Reward Scheme. In early colonial times bushrangers in Australia held up travelers on the open road, but in sport it is rights holders and official sponsors who are 'ambushed' in the various channels of the media. A diverting parallel game is thus played out, with non-rights holders trying to sneak as much sports coverage as possible, and unofficial sponsors seeking to associate their corporate logo as closely as legally permissible with major sports events. Their official counterparts, in true sporting style, do their best to stop them. If the sporting action is a little dull, especially in out-of-stadium events like cycling, the triathlon and marathon running, television viewers can search for 'ambush' corporate brand imagery strategically planted for the cameras.

By negotiating, honouring, helping police and strategically modifying broadcast rights, sports organizations and personnel become economic allies, even colleagues, of the media. Hence they need to be well versed in the arcane rules that govern rights, such as whether non-rights holders should be bound by the 'three by three by three' rule ('three minutes of Olympic footage three times a day in news programmes at least three hours apart') which has normally applied in countries like Australia, or by a stricter and more complicated variation of it which we could call the 'two by three minus eighteen minus two thirds rule' ('two minutes of coverage three times a day in established news programmes, but no events screened less than 18 hours after they took place', and no more than one-third of an event to be broadcast, even if it is the sub-ten seconds 100 metres final) as recommended by the IOC in Atlanta (Moore 1997: 4). Such deliberations also involve national broadcast policy priorities and the copyright laws with which any rights agreement must be in accord, and even whether the Olympics come under the rubric of 'news' (and, therefore, should be more fully reported on public interest grounds) or 'sport' (that is, more subject to broadcast restriction as just another form of entertainment). These issues continue to preoccupy the broadcast media and sports professionals because the entire economics of the media sports cultural complex turn on the careful rationing, packaging and sale of media sports texts in different markets. Hence, the idea of the global media sports spectacle is at its heart quite illusory: the images that appear to be so freely released have been subject to extraordinarily stringent pre-selection and control, and the sanctions taken against those who breach such arrangements (by, for example, implying official Olympic endorsement when it has not been negotiated and paid for) powerful indeed. High-end, especially 'live' broadcast sport appears to be in plentiful supply, but it is, in fact, subject to careful rationing and, as is discussed later in the chapter, would be controlled and harboured even more by highly concentrated commercial interests were it not for intervention by the state in the public interest.

The Summer and Winter Olympics, however, occur only over four-year cycles, which leaves large gaps between orgies of Olympic viewing, although after 1992 these were staggered at two-year intervals to ensure that the world did not have to wait so long for its Olympic television 'fix'. Other great media sports events—international tournaments like the soccer, rugby and cricket World Cups, world championships in sports such as athletics and swimming, and major annual competitions with international involvement like Wimbledon in tennis or the US Masters in golf—have important places on the sports calendar, but they are by their nature intermittent and out of the ordinary. Filling television schedules is a constant task that cannot wait for the next global media sports spectacular. The 'bread and butter' of sports television, then, is annual competition within nations.

NBC had become accustomed to its position as the main sports network and, not coincidentally, the top rating network overall, having the rights to such major US sports as American football, basketball and baseball to supplement its Olympic fare. Yet in 1998 it found itself 'frozen out of football for the first time in 33 years' (Attwood 1998: 39). Given that American football is the most important television sport in the USA, with broadcast rights valued in 1998 at US$2.25 billion a season, the scramble for broadcast rights to it is vigorous to say the least. This contest takes place over rights to a game that is barely played, understood or watched in other countries (although not for want of trying; see Maguire 1999), thereby revealing the pre-eminence of the USA as a media sport market in its own right. As noted above, their direct economic value is almost overshadowed by the image of being a 'winner' (analogous to that of breaking a world record while winning an Olympic gold medal). As Attwood states:

> Several morals can be drawn from this US price war. One is that, more than ever, sport is *the* most important commodity for TV. Another is that the desperation of grown men, most of whom have never played top-level sport themselves, to feel as if they are part of the game should never be underestimated. (Attwood 1998: 39)

The struggle for television sport can be seen to be more than a fight for profit: it reveals the cultural power of sport, particularly in the higher ranks of large corporate enterprises, where aggressive, competitive masculinity is as evident in the boardrooms as in the locker rooms (McKay and Rowe 1997). For example, the loss by the CBS network of its rights to Sunday football in 1993 to a Fox network prepared to pay over three times the amount for them (US$1.58 billion as opposed to US$500 million), had a demoralizing impact on the entire network that went beyond the concomitant fall in ratings. As Attwood (1998: 39) goes on to say, the four networks which paid unprecedented sums for the right to televise American football into the early part of the twenty-first century 'regard football as so crucial to their credibility and programming that they are prepared to pay almost any price', and that this phenomenon is not confined to the boundaries of the United States, but 'demonstrates how crucial major sporting events are to networks, worldwide, in an increasingly competitive TV market'. Thus, as Singer (1998: 36) notes, 'today's rule of thumb mandates that any viable network must have sports to help raise the profile of its other properties'; here he means

literally to 'have sports', listing the direct ownership of sports teams in the late 1990s by US media conglomerates, including Cablevision (the Knicks basketball and Rangers ice hockey franchises), Disney (the Angels in baseball and Mighty Ducks in hockey) and (the now AOL-merged) Time Warner (the Braves in baseball and Hawks in basketball). As Law *et al.* (2002) have demonstrated, media sport involves intricate 'supply chains' that go well beyond the 'usual suspects' (Disney, News Corp and AOL Time Warner) and the more obvious 'circuits of promotion' (Whitson 1998). While the cross-promotional possibilities of jointly owned media and sports enterprises are attractive, it is the cultural appeal of sport that ensures that old fears of club owners of 'oversaturation' and that '"giving away" the product on TV would kill the gate' are as 'misguided as Hollywood's fear of the VCR [video cassette recorder]' (Singer 1998: 36). Such popularity also allays the concerns of media proprietors in countries like the USA that sport is not worth the asking price:

> There's good reason why sports is a TV staple: It's human drama at a base level, it's cheap to produce and it's live. One can't minimize the power of immediacy in this time-shifting era when sports are the last remaining live coast-to-coast events—the Oscars, the Emmys, even 'Saturday Night Live' are tape delayed to the West Coast. Only sports has the nation, and sometimes the world, watching the same thing at the same time, and if you have a message, that's a potent messenger. (Singer 1998: 36)

Once again, the power of sports television to create and connect nations fragmented by space, time and social difference is shown to be its crowning economic advantage. With this power, though, comes contest and even chaos.

The "Strategic Chaos" of Media Sport

Network free-to-air television is, it should be noted, not the only player in the sports market. The fierce 'internal' competition between networks is replicated in the struggle between the network and pay television sectors. In some cases, as with Rupert Murdoch's News Corporation (which owns the Fox network and various pay satellite services like British-based BSkyB and the Hong Kong–based Star) or the Walt Disney Company (which owns both the ABC network and the leading sports cable channel ESPN), the enterprise is 'horizontally integrated' (that is, spread across different media and modes of delivery) and so is involved in both free-to-air and pay sports television. The continuing and accelerating realignment of organizations and convergence of technologies (as discussed in the Afterword) ensures that sports television will continue to be in a dynamic (which is often a euphemism for unstable) condition.

While it is premature to conclude that there is a single, integrated global sport or sports media market—for such a thing to exist much greater cultural homogeneity and economic rationalization would be necessary—there is a marked globalizing trend in media sport that makes it increasingly hard to insulate any aspect of sport and media in any particular country from external, disruptive forces (Maguire 1999; Roche 2000). Just how much power the media wield over sport can be seen through some brief case studies. In Australia, for example, a large country with a medium-sized population (now 19 million—as Turner (1990) has noted, a country with a land mass comparable to that of the USA and a population similar to that of Holland) some distance from the centres of power in media sport, there has been turmoil in sports television as the belated introduction of pay TV (in January 1995) precipitated a convulsion in the industry that is far from approaching a settled state. The intimidating presence in the free-to-air and pay TV market of Rupert Murdoch (who was born in Australia but gave up his citizenship to purchase key media assets in the USA) and his great commercial rival (and sometime strategic ally) Kerry Packer, owner of the top-rating Network Nine and (in)famous TV pioneer of one-day cricket, alongside a host of other 'players' like Telstra (the partially privatized national telecommunications company), Optus (whose major shareholder is the British-based communications company Cable & Wireless), the publicly funded ABC, Networks Seven (partially Murdoch-owned) and Ten (whose largest shareholder is the Canadian CanWest company) and many other interested organizations, has seen a story of almost medieval intrigue unfold. Notoriously, this epic narrative of communications and commerce involved, as is discussed below, unarmed combat over pay TV rights to the key Australian sport of rugby league that created a schism in the game from which it is yet to recover. Under circumstances in which a new conservative federal government was elected in 1996 on a platform that promised to reform the Australian system of media regulation (especially rules that restrict foreign ownership and prevent organizations having substantial holdings in both the print and the electronic media), sports television has been a cauldron of competing policy recipes and conflicting economic ingredients. Paul Sheehan, in surveying the global media sports scene, sees the Australia context as particularly chaotic and vulnerable to the domination of Rupert Murdoch:

> Strategic chaos is the one area where Australia is ahead of America. There has been a bloody insurrection against the old order financed by media money (Murdoch and Super League). There has been a horrendously expensive cable war (Murdoch/Foxtel v Optus) and there may be about to be a virtual merging of media and sport product if Seven and the AFL [Australian Football League] complete their mega deal [a free-to-air, cable, radio, Internet and foreign rights agreement until 2011].
>
> . . . In the biggest game of all, global TV sport, it is already game, set, match, Murdoch. Thank you, players, thank you, ball boys. (Sheehan 1998: 5)

In the ensuing shakedown of television ownership, control and regulation, Murdoch and Packer have both done well by cooperating rather than competing. Packer came to an accommodation with Murdoch over rugby league and took a stake in Foxtel. He (in cooperation with Ten) then successfully outbid Seven for the rights to Australian Rules Football. The failure of Seven's pay TV arm C7 (Eckersley and Benton 2002), the deep financial difficulties of the regional provider Austar and the capitulation in 2002 of Optus to Foxtel in the sharing of a common platform, ended significant pay TV competition in Australia. For all the political rhetoric concerning new players entering the media market, its two most powerful media barons retained and extended their influence. Sheehan's assessment of Murdoch's inevitable triumph in

TV sport is not, however, universally shared—*Los Angeles Times* in 1997, for example, described Murdoch's expensive attempt to control the sport of rugby league in Australia, Britain, France, New Zealand and the small number of other countries in which it is played as 'one of News Corp.'s bigger blunders' (quoted in Miller 1998b: 5). Expensive acquisition has, however, been a major part of News Corporation's global strategy (Andrews 2004). When a big financial player like Murdoch is sufficiently determined to make a major impact on a sport, the outcome is inevitably far-reaching, and the means by which that influence is exerted always involves media, especially television coverage. Thus, while Murdoch's strategy includes taking a stake not just in the sports media but in sport itself (hence his purchase of major stakes in rugby union and rugby league, and the ownership of individual sports outfits like the Los Angeles Dodgers baseball team), it is always the promise of wider TV coverage and cross-media exposure through his newspaper and magazine interests that forms part of the 'pitch'. Furthermore, when new forms of delivery involving subscription are involved, no media identity understands the importance of sport more than Rupert Murdoch. The turning around of his BSkyB satellite service in Britain (News Corporation is its 40 per cent majority shareholder) from a chronically loss-making to a highly profitable business entity can be traced directly to his securing of prime exclusive rights in 1992 to many of the most important games in Britain's nation sport—soccer. In this task, he was given substantial encouragement by the more neo-classical economic elements of the Conservative Government of Margaret Thatcher, who disliked the public/private free-to-air duopoly of the BBC and ITV in free market terms almost as much as they loathed the BBC's news and current affairs on political grounds (Goodwin 1998). Since 1992, BSkyB has made several multi-million pound deals in sports like golf (including the Ryder Cup), cricket, rugby union and boxing, sometimes in association with the BBC and Channel 4. Not only have these contracts, with their strong elements of exclusive 'live' rights, had the effect of raising subscription levels, but also they have in some cases (including boxing and soccer) included a pay-per-view element, with its opportunities for the kind of direct economic exchange between sports provider (now via an intermediary) and sports spectator that once existed only at the turnstiles of sports media.

By turning the television set-top decoding box into an electronic turnstile, pay-per-view and subscription sport are, paradoxically, via new media delivery technology, recreating an older cash nexus. But now sports themselves are ceding to the media, for a handsome price, responsibility for the presentation of great sporting occasions to the largest component of the audience. The political implications of this shift are serious (as is argued more fully below), in that the new services—and many of the old ones—are now available only to those citizens with the capacity to pay. As Combe (1997) notes, BSkyB's premium, live and exclusive sports coverage enabled it, by 1996, to gain 5.1 per cent of channel share of audiences in Britain for its two sports channels alone. Combe argues that with free-to-air public broadcasters like the BBC restricted by the political imperative of holding down the licence fee, and their commercial counterparts required to compete in a more aggressive 'audience sale'

market, BSkyB has been especially well placed to win broadcast rights auctions where the principal bargaining tool is the capacity to make an offer that is very hard to refuse, and which few if any competitors can match:

> BSkyB dominates the area of premium programmes with its stranglehold on Hollywood films and sporting events . . . In terms of consumer welfare, the multi-channel industry structure diminishes consumer protection and undermines the fundamental concept of pluralism in a democratic society. (Combe 1997: 19)

The deleterious consequences for media companies and, ultimately, for sport, of the hyperinflation of broadcast rights have been noted already, but the impact of this exercise of economic power in sports television on viewers is also regarded by Combe as less than liberating:

> The stranglehold on sports rights enjoyed by BSkyB has changed the economics of broadcasting such events and transformed the organization of the events themselves to fit in with the criteria set by television. The continuing domination of BSkyB is as unsatisfactory as was the old BBC/ITV duopoly. Now, large numbers of viewers are excluded from seeing major events on purely economic grounds. The imminent arrival of digital television will set off another round of negotiations between broadcasters and sporting bodies with the OFT [Office of Fair Trading] casting an enquiring eye over the outcomes. (Combe 1997: 21)

Murdoch's £623 million bid in 1998 for Manchester United, the world's best known and richest football club, highlighted the economic desirability of simultaneously owning both broadcast rights to sport and the sports teams that are being broadcast (Brown and Walsh 1999). Despite enthusiastic support by Murdoch newspapers like *The Times* and *The Sun*, the bid was opposed by the Blair Labour Government (despite its warm relationship with Murdoch) and blocked 'in the public interest' by the (then) UK Monopolies and Mergers Commission. The grounds were that it would reduce competition in the broadcasting industry (Murdoch would be on both sides of the negotiating table in buying and selling TV rights) and that it would damage the already weakened fabric of English football by exacerbating the inequalities between the clubs in the Premier League and the rest. The Commission was unpersuaded by precedents in other European countries, such as French broadcaster Canal Plus's ownership of Paris St German and Italian Prime Minister Silvio Berlusconi's control of A.C. Milan, or Murdoch's ownership of the LA Dodgers. While the *institutions* of sport and media may have substantially merged or interpenetrated, their constituent *organizations* have in most cases remained formally distinct. For systematic, comprehensive organizational integration to occur in sport will not only be determined by state and suprastate industry regulation. The synergies that appear so attractive on corporate business plans may not materialize in practice given the added complexity of the operation, with the media, entertainment and sports industries providing several instances of public floats, acquisitions and mergers (including AOL Time Warner, English Premier League and Italian Serie A club flotations, and European pay TV operations in Germany and

Italy) that have not performed as anticipated. Nonetheless, by 2002 Murdoch held stakes in English League clubs Manchester United, Leeds and Chelsea, and late in that year was expressing interest in the purchase of leading Serie A club Lazio from the Cirio food group (*The Australian* 2002: 29). The sport market, nevertheless, remains an uncertain one (Magee 2002; Wild 2002), as is graphically represented by the notorious 1995 incident (a photograph of which provides the cover image for Boyle and Haynes 2000) when Eric Cantona of Manchester United performed a flying kick on a spectator who was abusing him. The resultant bad publicity meant that 'more than £3m was wiped off Manchester United's share price', a 'minor fluctuation' that could be magnified many times by poor results on the field (Gardner 1998: 4).

The changing economics of broadcasting popular sports events—sometimes held in check as we have seen by public political values or by the desire of major sports organizations like the IOC to ensure maximum television exposure—nonetheless continually modify the conditions under which media sports texts are made. For example, the timing of 'live' sports broadcasts is now dictated by the need to stagger them over several days and nights, and/or to give a number of parties the opportunity to show whatever material to which they have gained access. Thus, while as recently as the 1970s most professional British soccer matches or Australian rugby league games started and ended on the same weekend day within 15 minutes of each other, the 'festival' of football now stretches over much of the week in the sports media equivalent of continuous process production. As seasons have extended and competitions proliferated in deference to the media hunger for sport—and to sport's appetite for media money—the prospect of creating a media sports cultural complex that defies the constraints of time and space—just as the first factory owners began to do in the eighteenth century—approaches closer. The difference, however, is that much of the population is now viewing the production process from the domestic sphere rather than participating within the factory walls. Watching, in this sense, is essential to complete the production cycle of relayed movement, meaning and imagery.

The constant availability of sport on television, though, is not necessarily coterminous with its popularity, even for some major sports events. This is because, despite occasional appearances to the contrary, even sports fans have to work, sleep, go to the supermarket, clean the toilet and offer emotional support to their families and friends. In other words, they have to make choices about when and what to view, in real time ('live') or otherwise. For this reason, the concept of prime time may have been stretched, but it has not been rendered meaningless. Grant Farred (2001: 3) makes this point about the Sydney 2000 Olympics, which he judges 'will be remembered as the Olympics that weren't' by East Coast American viewers at least. This comment would be something of a disappointment to the host broadcaster, the Sydney Olympic Broadcasting Organization (SOBO), which required some 3400 personnel, more people than were then (and since) 'employed by all the TV networks currently operating in Australia' (Gratton 1999: 122). Despite then IOC President Juan Antonio Samaranch declaring these to be 'the best games ever' at its Closing Ceremony, various factors made it for Farred and others 'turn-off television'. These included: 'the fact that 15-hour tape delay (if you're

on the East Coast) produces bad Nielsen ratings tells us not only that time-zone is everything, but that the old North-South economic paradigm is pivotal to culture' (Farred 2001: 3). It is suggested here that US TV sport viewers are accustomed to watching at convenient times and discomfited by too much distance from a land that, it should be recalled, describes its national domestic baseball competition as the World Series. Significantly, Farred argues that many viewers preferred the Internet's instantaneous provision of the 'pleasure of information' to the delayed 'pleasure of spectacle' (p. 4) offered by television. In such circumstances, television may attempt to be 'plausibly live', simulating events as if they are happening and shaping them into smoothly assimilated live narratives that are, in fact, recordings (Rivenburgh 2003). The Internet's developing capacity to marry informational and spectacular forms of pleasure threatens to reconfigure the economic structure of media sport, and is a strong motivation for the merging of media and Internet service providers, most spectacularly the (so far disastrous) 2000 merger of Time Warner and AOL (Hesmondhalgh 2002). The exciting prospect of radical vertical and horizontal integration of the Internet, media, sport and entertainment has faded somewhat, with AOL Time Warner reporting a US$98.7 billion loss for 2002, having a group debt in 2003 of US$26 billion (*Sydney Morning Herald* 2003: 33) and attempting to sell off various assets including its sports teams and events, which include:

The Atlanta Thrashers, the NHL's most recent expansion team . . . NBA [National Basketball Association] and MLB [Major League Baseball] teams in Atlanta, TNT Sports, the Goodwill Games, World

Championship Wrestling, the CNN/SI sports network, *Time*, and *Sports Illustrated*, and is the NBA's cable partner. (Miller *et al.* 2001: 66)

Irrespective of the state of the media, technology and information markets, however, computer users are yet to be allocated any more hours in the day and exemptions from work and family responsibilities than sports television viewers.

Irrespective of the logistical problems of bringing the viewer in front of the set, this economy of sports television is thoroughly representative of the newer 'economies of signs and space' discussed earlier, where power lies increasingly in the control of images and information by means of copyright and associated intellectual property rights, rather than by relying on the slower, more predictable processes of making goods or providing 'human' services. Of course, such exchanges do still go on and, somewhere and at some time, capital has to be exchanged. But following the 'money trail', as in contemporary tax and fraud investigations, is an ever more complex task. Television sport can, in strictly economic terms, be seen as a battlefield between media corporations seeking to generate revenue from all manner of sources—advertisers, sponsors, subscribing viewers and even from sports themselves (the more unfortunate ones who need TV exposure so much that they are prepared to pay for it). This state of affairs means that media mogul Rupert Murdoch frequently tops the *Sporting News*'s annual list of the most powerful people in sport rather than global sports celebrities like Michael Jordan, Tiger Woods, Serena Williams and David Beckham; powerful sports administrators like

current IOC President Jacques Rogge or FIFA President Sepp Blatter (Rowe and McKay 2003); or sport and leisurewear entrepreneurs like Nike founder Phil Knight. Why such a person is at the centre of power in sport can be explained succinctly by the following opening paragraphs from a newspaper feature article on Rupert Murdoch as the 'champion of world sports':

> Last month [January], American television networks spent [AUS]$26 billion on the broadcast rights for American football games for the next eight years. That is not a misprint. That's $26 *billion*. It works out to almost $1 billion for each of the 30 teams in the National Football League (NFL).
>
> This stratospheric number is a foretaste of the revolution that is about to engulf television, and Rupert Murdoch's global sporting empire is playing a central role in that revolution. The revolution will occur on several fronts, all at the same time. (Sheehan 1998: 4)

Given that, in 1980, NBC paid only US$72 million for the broadcast for the Summer Olympics, the coming revolution in television has clearly already arrived. Perhaps, in Trotsky's (1969) famous formulation, it is in a state of 'permanent revolution'. Sheehan referred explicitly to the imminent technological changes that are discussed here in greater detail in the Afterword, but even if we focus on the current 'Jurassic' period of television broadcasting (he refers to current TV networks as 'dinosaurs'), then the sports TV world has been in the grip of tumultuous 'climatic' change marked by a sharply rising temperature rather than a slow passage into a sportless ice age. What is confusing about these circumstances—and it is typical for the human sciences to have to confront a stubbornly reflexive complexity that is much less troubling for those in natural sciences like climatology—is that they often display counter-tendencies. Hence, for example, as Combe (1997) observes in his appraisal of statistics on channel share or audiences, in Britain between 1993 and 1996, when cable and satellite delivery really began to take hold (reaching over 15 percent of all television households), the total terrestrial share was at the same level (69.9 per cent) at the end of this period, and the hard-pressed, publicly funded BBC1 channel actually increased its audience share (from 23.8 per cent to 24.1 per cent). There may, then, be a significant role in an even more differentiated broadcasting market for 'mass' public organizations like the BBC with proved brand identity and loyalty after the digital 'revolution'. Perhaps, though, the resurgence of some parts of public broadcasting will come at the expense, as occurred in the period 1993–96 in Britain under the old regime, of niche broadcasters (like the BBC's own second channel and the innovative commercial Channel 4) and of 'commercial public service' broadcasters aiming to appeal to wider audiences (like ITV), who lost ground both to general public broadcasters and to pay TV (Goodwin 1998).

From this British instance it can be seen that the global sports television market is, despite attempts to portray it as a single entity following predictable trends, a series of smaller national, regional and local markets occasionally linked by spectacular mega media events or by the more routine circulation of content from core markets to secondary ones. In fact, as O'Regan (1992: 76) points out, there is a tendency to exaggerate the extent to which television programmes, especially from the United States, flow freely around the world. He notes that while the USA was in 1989 responsible for some '71 per cent of the *international* trade' valued at US$1.7 billion in an estimated world television export market of US$2.4 billion (one which, it should be acknowledged, has expanded considerably since), it was in the same year estimated that television 'product' twenty-nine times greater in value (US$70 billion) stayed in its 'nation of origin'. Of course, such raw figures do not take into account other forms of 'cultural exchange'—such as the 'uncompensated' imitation of American programme genres like soap operas and quiz shows in many different countries—but they do indicate that judgements of a smoothly competed 'project' of economic and cultural globalization are seriously premature. Culture has continued to be a major sticking point in attempts to create an open global market for good services with, as Ann Capling (2001: 165) has pointed out, the 'the audiovisual sector, especially films, videos and television programs' being an 'extremely contentious' area in multilateral trade negotiations. There are few more highly charged areas of audiovisual culture than sport, with many nations intervening in the TV marketplace to protect the broadcast of listed events of national significance—almost all of them sporting (Rowe 2002). Cunningham and Jacka (1996: 40), furthermore, observe that most sports programming does not travel well in the global mediascape, so that 'of the various genres of television . . . most are locally specific, and are not heavily traded', and genres like sport 'except for major international events like Grand Slam tennis, the Olympics, World

Cup soccer, or Formula One Grand Prix motor racing . . . are usually entirely local in character'. The aforementioned example of American football is just such a game that has had little success in its attempts to 'export itself' as popular sports television (Maguire 1990, 1999; McKay and Miller 1991). However, as Hollywood film and US network television discovered many years ago, a successful if expensive-to-produce item in a domestic market is doubly successful when it can be distributed and promoted 'fully formed' in other markets.

For this reason, there is an unending search for new ways to exploit the same or partially modified economic goods and, as Cunningham and Jacka (1996: 40–1) recognize, 'under the pressure of burgeoning channel capacity and commercialization, new tradeable international formats are emerging', including those 'prompted by new forms of delivery like pay television', leading to the 'growth of specialist sports channels [which] will lead to the televising of sports not previously considered television fare, in order to fill the demand'. Sports like boxing have been quick to appreciate the international economic potential of 'pay-per-view' bouts involving heavyweight (in more than one sense) stars like Mike Tyson and Lennox Lewis, where all the resources of the broadcast and print media can be used, through staged pre-fight confrontations between the combatants and other devices, to stimulate an urge to pay to see the event on screen as it happens. That it tends to happen on US soil or in East Coast time-zone friendly locations, or at times that are inconvenient for the boxers and ringside viewers but convenient for US TV viewers, reflects the aforementioned commercial clout of that country's television au-

dience. Avid sports fans have been lured over time in respectable numbers to subscribe to pay TV, especially when the siphoning of their favourite live sports from free-to-air television means that they have no other home viewing option (as has occurred with rugby union in New Zealand). What is intriguing about much of the content of satellite and other pay TV delivered sport, however, is that there is no discernibly strong demand for it. Multiple 24-hour pay TV sports channels are as subject to the scarcity of 'good' (in the sense of 'good enough to pay for') content as are those devoted to film, comedy or drama. Apart from blue chip and some emerging sports (with what in the industry is called a cult following), the content of pay TV sport outside its core markets is often simply 'channel filler'—an alternative to the test pattern. In such cases, pay sports TV resembles what Raymond Williams (1974) describes in *Television: Technology and Cultural Form* as the prevailing conditions existing during the invention of television (and radio) in the first place—a technology looking for a use.

Sport as Screen Filler

In addressing questions of the uses and abuses of television sport, it is worth quoting the following well-known passage from William's book, not least because of the central place it gives to sport:

Unlike all previous communications technologies, radio and television were *systems primarily devised for transmission and reception as abstract processes, with little or no definition of preceding content.* When the question of content was raised, it was resolved, in the main, parasitically. There were state occasions, public sporting events, theatres and so on, which would be communicatively distributed by these new technical means. *It is not only that the supply of broadcasting facilities preceded the demand: it is that the means of communication preceded their content.* (Williams 1974: 25, original emphasis)

When viewers, then, in one country switch on a 24-hour TV sports channel and encounter an obscure (to them) sport from another country (receiving the same broadcast, including commentary, as the citizens of that country), it is unlikely that they are receiving a service which they urgently demand. In such instances, it is not so much, as Cunningham and Jacka (1996) suggested earlier, a question of pay sports television growing to fill an emerging demand, but, somewhat curiously in economic terms, to supply the filler for what would otherwise be a newly created but empty space. Where sports are hoping to cultivate a new audience (and sometimes paying or subsidizing the broadcasters for the privilege), what is being offered for exchange is not TV sport for interested viewers but TV viewers for interested sports. The 'market' is constructed around the need to patch the holes created by technologically induced abundance; the opportunity to offer sports that cannot command huge broadcast rights revenue the chance to do so in the future by contacting some kind of television audience; and accommodation of those sports with more modest ambitions of receiving some valuable media coverage in the knowledge that some committed fans are willing to pay for it (Moore 1996). This form of sports TV delivery, unlike the networked free-to-air

television that is heavily reliant on 'blockbuster', ratings-based viewing figures, is in principle amenable to smaller-scale, targeted, niche-marketed, post-Fordist sport (Giulianotti 1999), as is indicated by the development of a cable channel for golf in the United States and a women's sport TV network in Canada. But, at least in Britain and Australia, the pattern to date in satellite and cable sport has mainly involved broadcasting well-established national and international sports, accompanied by entertainment-based packaged segments that show snippets of sporting moments (triumphant and disastrous), novelty sports, 'extreme' sports (Rinehart 1998) and material relayed from one country to another for no other apparent reason than it is sport and there is a space in the schedule for it.

The 'bonanza' for minority sports promised by multi-channel pay TV has not yet eventuated, with claims of increased broadcast sports diversity more closely resembling political and marketing rhetoric than the actual practice of expanding the range of sports on television. As Crosswhite (1996: 58) has pointed out in the Australian context, for example, women's sports have often been required to pay broadcasters (both free-to-air and subscription) to get on screen, have come under pressure to be more 'watchable', and so have been forced to confront such questions as 'Should athletes go into Lycra outfits, or the sport alter the size of the playing area, or speed up the flow of the game, or change the venue, increase the crowd, etc?' Appleton (1995: 32), however, is less concerned by television changing sport than the need for sports organizations to cater better for television. This means for her mobilizing to secure greater genuine broadcast sports

diversity rather than the 'resort to entertainment of the ilk of demolition derbies and
mud wrestling rather than "real" sport'. My
own research into questions of equity and
diversity in Australian sports TV has found
that, in a sample period of one month in
1999, only 5.8 percent of sports programming on free-to-air TV was devoted to
women's sport. One pay TV channel (Fox
Sports 2) carried no women's sport in the
sample period, but this was also the case
with all three commercial free-to-air channels, leaving the two public channels (ABC
and SBS) to carry almost 70 per cent of all
women's sport. Such arguments and evidence indicate that (as will be discussed
later in this chapter) the economics of
sports television are inextricably bound up
with questions of cultural politics. So, while
a more complex mix of coexistent market
forms of television sport does potentially
exist, and is characterized by very different
ways of creating and receiving media sports
texts, the (full or partial) realization of that
potential—or even its failure to materialize
significantly at all—is dependent on political as well as economic factors.

Free-to-air mega sports events like the
Olympics will continue to exist for the foreseeable future because, as the International
Olympic Committee has recognized, their
greatest economic (and cultural) asset is the
massive popularity that can give billions of
people the sense of simultaneously having
the same sporting experience (Wilson
1998). On the other hand, smaller sports
TV audiences can be catered for, targeted or
(even if notionally) created through various
forms of direct purchase. What Holger
Preuss (2000: 122) calls 'match TV: a combination of free TV and pay-per-view' he
believes to be 'the most probable variant for
future Olympic coverage' given the globalization of television infrastructure. The delicate balance between these forms of delivery of sports TV will, however, be
constantly under strain as commercial interests, governments and sports fans pursue
their various and often contradictory interests. Whatever the mode of delivery, and
even if national public broadcasters manage
to keep control over some 'hallmark' sports
events, economic processes of varying scale
and intensity are inevitably in play. This
mutability of the production of broadcast
media sports texts explains how they keep
emerging, 'hydra-headed', despite some
complaint that 'television has taken over
sport'. It should be remembered, of course,
that television is not the only means by
which sports culture is framed, dissemi-
nated, peddled and circulated. Radio and
print are also integral components of the
media sports cultural complex, their products just as pervasive in the everyday world.
Yet, while radio rights are contested for
popular international and national sports;
newspapers are committing greater resources to the sports pages, expanding print
and photographic coverage and headhunt-
ing their competitors' 'name' sports writers;
and new general and specialist sports magazines are launched (and closed) every year;
in sports television lies the most compelling
expression of naked economic power in the
media sports cultural complex. Accompanying this economic power to make media
sports texts for vast audiences comes, as
noted earlier, considerable political and cultural power. Because that arena is 'only
sport', the extent and potential of this
power is often underestimated, and it is important to draw out the political and cultural implications of the power to make
media sports texts for the national and
global citizenry.

Media Sports Policy, Politics and Myth

It is probable that many times a day, somewhere in the western world, a talk-back radio host or caller pronounces that 'sport and politics don't mix' or proclaims that 'politics should be kept out of sport'. Such comments are a little curious, given the many ways in which sport and politics interrelate. These include: deciding public spending priorities, such as allocations by national, state and regional governments to sporting organizations (Cashman and Hughes 1998) and by local governments for civic sports amenities (Mowbray 1993); anti-discrimination policies (such as Title IX section of the US Education Amendments Act of 1972, which denied 'federal financial assistance' to 'any education program or activity' that discriminated against any person 'on the basis of sex', and so had a substantial, positive impact on women's and girls' sport; see Guttmann 1991; Heywood 2000); and government restrictions on the advertising and sponsorship through sports such as Formula One motor racing and cricket of unhealthy products like tobacco and alcohol (Harris 1988). Sport and identity politics would also have to be for ever separated (Baker and Boyd 1997; Bloom 2000), and uncomfortable questions about, for example, the relationship between sport and violence against women suppressed (Benedict 1997). To be really vigilant about keeping sport and politics apart, it would be necessary to ban politicians from using sports metaphors like 'going the distance', 'levelling the playing field' and 'moving the goalpost after the game has started' in political speeches and interviews (Rowe 1995). The task of keeping sport and politics for ever separate is, then, not only difficult, but

inherently futile. While the sphere of sport—as, among others, John Hargreaves (1982) has noted—can never be reduced to 'pure' politics, neither can it be entirely insulated from it. As a result, the sports media, which it was argued in Chapter 1 are always already implicated in the politics of communication, are necessarily embroiled in the politics of sport—and the 'sport' of politics.

The media, in various ways, are called upon to:

- provide good, wholesome family entertainment through sport;
- offer sensationally dramatic coverage that will attract healthy audiences (but perhaps for 'unhealthy' reasons);
- describe and show what happened to those who were not present or who want to see it again and differently;
- subject sport to intense scrutiny as part of the media's Fourth Estate function;
- support local, regional and national sporting efforts; and
- further the Olympian ideals of sport by transcending petty, partisan politics in the name of international peace and good will.

No single organ of the media can fulfill all of these expectations (some of which are seen as unfortunate obligations), just as different types of media sports text are better suited to the performance of some tasks than others. To develop this logic to its fullest extent absolves the sports media of any general responsibility for their actions beyond the minimal observance ('actionable', in any case) of the laws of defamation, obscenity, and so on. The sports public, it is claimed, is provided with what it wants from the media on orthodox, market principles—if a demand exists for a type of sports coverage, then the market will provide it. No single sports programme or publication, from this perspective, need feel responsible for what its competitors currently or might do. The different elements of the sports media, it plausibly follows, do what they do until it is shown to be unprofitable or illegal to do otherwise. To take the sports media simply at their word and to accept this account of their motives, operations and effects would be as unwise as to confine analysis only to the surface properties of media sports texts. By pointing out the latent and sometimes manifest political significance of their practices, it is made more difficult for the sports media to evade the proposition that with cultural power comes political responsibility.

One major contention of this book is that, while the mythology of sport rests heavily on the belief that it is or should be free of the grubby workings of the political world, it cannot escape the less than glamorous struggle, both external and internal, for power and influence. In other words, sports culture—at least its official, 'legitimate' face—is highly romanticized. We have also seen that media have their own romantic myth—that of the fearless watchdog resisting the pressures of the state, capital and other powerful entities by exposing all and telling the truth. When isolated from each other, these two romantic dispositions pull in different directions; sporting mythology relies on the studied evasion of politics, while media mythology depends on a principled confrontation with it. The uneasy coming together of myths in making media sport helps explain the problems of professional practice and prestige for sports journalism analysed at some length in Chapter 2. An unsentimental take on how media sports texts are framed suggests that

both sports and media mythologies—and so, inevitably, sports media mythologies—are mythological in a rather unfashionable, unspecialized sense. The 'lay' meaning of myth is that it is untrue or a mistaken impression (such as, 'it's a myth that watching too much sport on television makes you go blind'), whereas in most recent social and cultural theory, the term does not so much denote a lack of correspondence between what is said and what is 'real', but demonstrates the power of particular symbols and narratives in expressing widely, unconsciously and deeply held beliefs as 'natural' in any given society, irrespective of any burden of 'proof' (like the myths of romantic love, the 'perfectibility of man', of national cultural identity, and so on). The tension between these two meanings of mythology can be traced in media and cultural studies back to the seminal work of Roland Barthes (1973). It is being discussed in this section on political economy, and not in the 'usual place' where textual analysis happens, to demonstrate the indissolubility of the making and unmaking of media sports texts.

In *Mythologies*, Barthes (1973) attempts to deal with these different kinds of 'truth'—what is believed and what can be established theoretically, empirically and so politically (in terms of a class struggle and other forms of political action) as true. While in later works (such as Barthes 1978) he was somewhat less definitive about the clear division between truth/reality and falsehood/myth (Rojek 1985), the analytical and political dilemma has not gone away (Sugden and Tomlinson 2002). In particular, the ways in which myths can function to obscure objective judgement and cloak it in mystifying ideology is still troubling if the rest of any 'truth claim' is reduced to a choice between available myths (Thwaites et al. 1994). In the light of the postmodern and post-structuralist assault on the enlightenment concept of 'truth' (see, for example, Norris 1993), how can we speak authoritatively about the way things 'really are' and so propose rational and progressive political values and actions? Rather than attempt to provide a simple answer to this question (which, if it existed, would mean that it need never be posed), it is preferable to develop and refine our understanding of the multiple phenomena and relationships that make the social world and its culture(s). Earlier in this chapter, for example, we saw the undeniable power of economic forces in the shaping of sport and of media sport, but it was also apparent that the mobilization of economic factors was dependent on cultural forces (including the popular appeal of sport in the first place). These symbolic and affective elements did not simply respond to economic imperatives but were critical in shaping economic possibilities (as shown, for example, by the stubborn lack of international 'transportability' of many sports no matter how slick the advertising and promotional campaign). An intellectually respectable political economy of the sports media, therefore, must seek to be aware of the many influences—strong and weak, constant and intermittent, predictable and unpredictable—on the making of media sports texts.

In illustrating this argument, it is useful to examine briefly some instances where the cultural politics of media sport are played out in contrasting ways. For example, in looking at the gender order in media sport above, it was clear that women have been subject to subordination and/or under-representation in two key organizational complexes—in media corporations as owners, senior executives and 'rank-and-file' professional personnel (Creedon 1994a,b) and in sporting organizations on governing bodies and as professional athletes (Jennifer Hargreaves 1994; McKay 1997). The intimate, longstanding linkage between sport and masculinity has helped secure the dominance of male sport in the media and of males employed to cover sport in the media. This is obviously not a simple question of capitalist logic in operation—male media proprietors and executives are drawn no less than other men to the expression of heroic, aggressive and competitive masculinity by associating themselves with the popular contact sports of which their fellows are so enamoured. In fact, there seems to be a strong streak of economic irrationalism in the desire for some businessmen to win at all costs in the boardroom as a form of compensation for not 'cutting it' at the highest level on the sporting field (McKay and Rowe 1997; Attwood 1998; Warren 2002). Yet, pressure to change this pattern of male predominance in media sport is coming from various sources. Sport is, somewhat belatedly, one of the important fronts on which battles for sexual equality are being waged, with both governments and feminist groups demanding an end to male exclusionism in sport (Jennifer Hargreaves 1994; Hall 1997). Women workers in the sports media have mobilized to improve their positions within media organizations (Cramer 1994), while women's sports organizations have demanded more air time and column inches, sponsorship and broadcast rights revenues (Crosswhite 1996). To a lesser extent, sport is also emerging as a site of contestation over gender and sexuality, with, for example, the Gay Games offering a challenge to the longstanding association of sport and 'hegemonic masculinity', Connell's (1987) conception of physically assertive, white male heterosexism that has historically dominated the institution of sport (Krane and Waldron 2000; Symons 2002).

These have not, however, all been external pressures: within the media sports cultural complex itself there has been a gradual realization that it is economically and otherwise senseless to alienate a large proportion of a market, which, if segregated too strictly on gender lines, would in the case of some sports (like the football codes) be close to saturation (Miller 2001). This is even without mentioning the key decision-making position of women in household consumption. Then there is the potential of new media technologies to provide more diverse sports fare, and the requirement for public and commercial broadcasters who have been outbid for sports broadcast rights by their rivals to make a virtue of necessity in 'signing up' some women's sports like basketball and netball. As a result, sports broadcast programmers and print editors have sought (with signal success in sports like soccer and rugby league) to attract substantial female audiences by adopting strategies such as overtly sexualizing sportsmen, explaining arcane rules to the uninitiated, giving greater and more sympathetic coverage of sportswomen, employing female sports commentators and writers, and so on (Miller 2001). In other words, commodity logic and cultural politics have interacted in new, intriguing ways—although not always with impeccably 'progressive' outcomes (as evidenced, for example, by the willingness of more women's sports and of individual sportswomen to emphasize sexual attractiveness as a marketing tool in pursuit of greater media, sponsor and advertiser attention). The issue of sex and gender equality in sport and media sport, and the ways in which it is confronted by governments and business enterprises, raises the wider question of the role of media sport in the whole domain of 'cultural citizenship'.

Fighting for the Right to Watch

The concept of cultural citizenship is a broadening of the traditional idea of the rights and responsibilities of states and citizens in recognition of the increased 'culturalization' of society. The outcome is a greater significance of culture and communication under 'postmodernity' in fostering the creation of informed, critically reflective persons capable of taking an active part both in their own lives and in those of the collectivities of various kinds—families, peers, pressure groups, political parties, and so on—in which they are involved. Just as, say, the idea of what constitutes a necessity and what a luxury has changed over many decades—possession of inside toilets, reticulated plumbing and domestic electrical power was, until well into the twentieth century, the exception rather than the norm for most of the population of the west (and still is in many non-western societies and in indigenous settlements in 'white settler' countries)—so what is considered to be an essential prerequisite for comprehensive participation in all of society's major institutions, debates and processes has been extended. In making informed choices, contemporary citizens need to have ready access to highly detailed information about the values, histories, performances and intentions of the various parties engaged in formal and informal political processes. Therefore, they must possess the means of ready communication in the public sphere (televisions, newspapers, radios, telephones, computers, and so on) and the appropriate educational means to decode, interpret, adjudicate on and respond to the messages that are circulating in that 'public sphere' (Murdock 1992, 1997; Golding and Murdock 2000).

As culture has become, across the past two centuries, industrially produced or provided and governed by the state (Bennett 1998), this entitlement to information for guidance in voting or family health, personal hygiene or even product choice (as applied both to commercial advertising and to state advice on safe and healthy consumer behaviour) has progressively expanded. It now involves the claimed right to certain kinds of cultural (including strictly entertainment) provision so that the citizen can take part fully in the cultural as well as the political life of the nation and even of humanity. Here a model of cultural heritage encompasses quite recent historical developments, like the twentieth-century practice of broadcasting major public events to the entire nation.

Because sports events have become the most important, regular manifestations of this national culture (Rowe *et al.* 1998), and despite the move towards their supply to the citizenry by commercial rather than by public broadcasters (Wilson 1998), media sport has become a major aspect of contemporary cultural heritage. Sport and television are, therefore, deeply implicated in debates about cultural citizenship in a way that would horrify cultural elitists (Tomlinson 1999).

Once, then, free-to-air television provided major national and international sports events at nominal direct expense to viewers, and these cultural items had been counted among the major rituals of national significance, they became incorporated into the citizen's cultural 'treasure house'. As a result, there would need to be compelling grounds indeed for the 'free list' of major television sport to be fully commodified, yet this is precisely what is threatened. The political value of (virtual) universal entitlement in the west has been challenged by market-based values, with the idea of abundant choice of television sports texts as the overriding imperative—a choice that involves a 'user pays' principle and one which positions sport as simply another commercialized entertainment option in an unforgiving and, ideally, unfettered cultural marketplace. The only rights that need to be safeguarded from this point of view, then, are those of sports media consumers from fraud, deception and other crimes of commercial practice, rather than in terms of any higher concept of the protection of significant cultural rights. The completed commodification of television sport would be consistent with its current direction, but would ultimately destroy the values associated with serving all citizens in favour of identifying, targeting and privileging affluent viewers. As Stan Correy puts it:

> Sporting tradition dictates that whatever the game, it was originally played for pure and honest motives. Money was the servant of the players not the master.
>
> In the 1990s, it's clear that sports tradition has lost out badly to commerce. The sports field is the battleground on which global TV corporations are fighting to test new television technology. The reward is not a gold-plated trophy but the traditional sports consumer. Profile: Male, 18–35, with enough disposable income to attract

the sponsors with the big dollars. (Correy 1995: 80)

Debates about the rights and responsibilities in sports television are played out differently according to national context. In most European countries and various former British colonies, for example, broadcast sport was first dominated by public broadcasters, their control gradually loosened first by commercial free-to-air broadcasters and then by pay TV companies. In the USA, with its much weaker commitment to non-commercial broadcasting, the sports media marker developed much earlier (Wenner 1989), although this did not destroy network free-to-air sports television, which has survived and prospered through a combination of anti-trust legislation, broadcast synergies and the economic power of the networks deriving from television audiences captured for mass advertising rather than targeted for subscription and pay-per-view. There is, then, a complex intrication (that is, perplexing entanglement) of the economic, the political and the cultural in the determination of how televised sport is to be delivered and to whom.

In Australia, for example, the belated introduction of pay TV in 1995 enabled the (then Labour) national government to avoid what was seen as the folly of Britain's Conservative Thatcher regime, which (as was noted above) had allowed political ally, Rupert Murdoch, to rescue his BSkyB satellite television venture by 'capturing' English Premier League soccer (Goodwin 1998). Australia embarked on what has been called 'the bravest effort at an effective anti-siphoning regime in the world' (Grainger 1996: 25) by amending in 1994 (just before the arrival of pay TV) Section 115 of its Broadcasting Services Act 1992. This law allowed the relevant minister (then for Communication and the Arts) to, in the words of the Act, 'by notice published in the *Gazette*, specify any event, or events of a kind, the televising of which, or the live televising of which, should, in the opinion of the minister, be available free to the general public'. Hence the Minister may list any event deemed to be of national importance or cultural significance that is usually broadcast on free-to-air television. The listed events exclusively involved sport, including horse and motor racing, soccer, tennis, basketball and golf, and covered events staged both in Australia and overseas. The provisions also allowed the minister to 'de-list' events if: 'satisfied that the national broadcasters and the commercial television broadcasting licensees have had a real opportunity to acquire, on a fair commercial basis, the right to televise the event live [and] that none of those persons has acquired that right within a reasonable time'.

This was a stronger regulatory regime than was devised in Britain, where the Blair government, elected in 1997, undertook to review and tighten up the weak anti-siphoning regulations of the Thatcher and Major regimes. The eventual framework of listed events created a hierarchy with full protection for 'A Level' sports events and diminished rights to watch sports events on the 'B' list 'live' and in full. In the European Union, a combination of general exemption and member state implementation has created a televisual patchwork of listed sports events (Roche 2000: 178–81; Rowe 2002). In all such cases there is direct intervention by the state in the workings of the sports television market, ostensibly in the interests of promoting the rights of cultural citizenship. As Law and Kemp (2002: 299–300) argue, without such 'national as well as international regulatory policy . . . sport spectacle consumers will remain . . . easy targets for those gradually filling in every moment of their attention'. In this case there is an assumed public right to watch major sports events free and 'live' as part of established national cultural heritage. This political determination, however, was not entirely immune from economic influences. The long-delayed introduction of pay TV in Australia has been attributed to the political influence of free-to-air broadcasters (Cunningham 1992), while the anti-siphoning regime may be seen as giving an unfair market advantage to the established free-to-air television sector over the fledgling pay sector. Indeed, criticisms of anticompetitive behaviour by government are not made only by pay TV broadcasters: netball, the only women's sport on the Australian list, quickly asked to be removed from the list because, as the National Executive Director of Australian Netball argued, 'it has not taken into account the fact that we have had to pay to get on free-to-air' (Smith 1996: 69), and pay TV held out the prospect, paradoxically, of being 'free' (even remunerable) for the sport and 'chargeable' for the viewer. As noted above, this has been a vain hope for most sports that were not already dominant. Furthermore, the Australian political apparatus did little more than watch from the sidelines while the sport of rugby league (as discussed above) disintegrated in the mid-1990s as Australia's two most powerful media barons, Rupert Murdoch and Kerry Packer, fought over free-to-air and pay TV rights to the sport.

Throughout the struggle (which ended in a truce in 1998 after two years of hugely expensive court action, a massively inflated and unsustainable rise in players', coaches' and referees' salaries, and a disastrous split

competition in 1997) each side tried to win the mythological war, with the Packer camp stressing class, loyalty, tradition, nationalism and 'blokeish' masculinity, and the Murdoch camp promoting values of upward mobility, flexibility, progressive change, globalism and a more sophisticated, even glamorous appeal (McKay and Rowe 1997). Broadcast and print journalists and presenters charged with the responsibility of reporting these events with objectivity and fairness tended, if employed by the contending parties, to report from behind their own battlelines (Packer TV versus the Murdoch press, with the rival Fairfax newspaper company revelling in the role of 'neutral' umpire and honest broker). The tragi-comedy (Rowe 1997b) dragged on for several more years, though, with the iconic South Sydney Club (the 'Rabbitohs') being first expelled in a blaze of anti-Murdoch publicity from the new National Rugby League competition on economic grounds, and then re-admitted after a court decision that their treatment had been unfair (Moller 2002). News Corporation was legally vindicated in 2003, but the 'Rabbitohs' club stayed in the league. The 'Super League' saga lost the various combattants a great deal of money—an estimated AUS$600 million for News Corporation alone (Eckersley and Benton 2002: 20). It presaged a development that many in media sport could barely imagine—the end of the TV rights party.

When Sports Television Fails

In recent decades, there has been a long boom in media sport. As noted above, sports desks and the pages that they create have greatly expanded (Tunstall 1996), and sports magazines have appeared and folded with signal frequency. Some inroads have been made by sports Internet services, with Rod Brookes (2002: 46) observing that 'whereas a number of household names on the Internet are only expected to be profitable in the long term, Internet companies producing sports content are already generating significant revenue'. For print and the Internet, technological innovations, convergence strategies, shifts in advertising revenue, changes in audience patterns, and the 'shakedown' from the 'dot.bomb' collapse of information technology stocks and investment, have all created a dynamic media sport environment. But, as we have seen, the major driving force of media sport has been television, which has injected funds in 'telephone book numbers' into sport in pursuit of broadcast rights. In parallel with the information technology boom (Shiller 2000), television sport has been deeply involved in a frenzied inflationary round of purchasing desirable business 'properties', in this case broadcast rights and, preferably, the entities that wholly or partially own those rights. Also in common with the bizarre billion-dollar venture capital purchase of startup Internet companies was the belief that the rise in the market would never end, that a 'new economy' had replaced the old one that was so chronically subject to a cycle of boom and bust, and that this investment could be used as a platform on which to increase revenue streams created by organizational synergies and emerging consumer needs.

The 'iron laws' of capital accumulation, however, are not so easily set aside, although the sports industry did for some time seem weightless (Miller 1999). At some point, investment, expenditure and revenue must be brought into the same ballpark (to use an appropriate sporting metaphor). In the early twenty-first century, it became apparent that television sport, for all its *fin de siècle* success, had in many cases over-reached itself. There has followed a retrenchment that is increasingly registering as a 'red needle' across the media sports cultural complex, with several instances of companies folding, advertising revenues shrinking, subscription numbers stagnating, broadcast rights deals contracting, sportspeople's incomes falling and TV screens fading to black. It is uncertain whether this is a temporary market correction or will have long-standing ramifications, but there is no doubt that television sport has experienced a sobering challenge to its belief in its own invincibility. As two commentators note:

It is widely acknowledged that the modern sports era began ten years ago [1992], when Foxtel Chairman, Sam Chisholm, then Chief Executive of Rupert Murdoch's satellite broadcaster BSkyB, was given approval by Murdoch to outbid BSkyB's rivals for the television rights to the new English Premier League.

BSkyB ended up paying what at the time seemed the enormous sum of £304 million for the four-year deal . . . Until this year [2002], television rights payments for major sports continued to be ratcheted up each time they came up for grabs. In 1993, Murdoch's US Fox Network virtually doubled what rival television networks had been paying for National Football League rights packages, and then went on to invest in ice hockey, college football and baseball. When the English Premier League's television rights next came up for negotiation, in 1996, BSkyB retained them in the face of spirited bidding, for £674 million, or £168.5 million a season, a rise of 121% and in June 2000, BSkyB won them for a further three years for £1.11 billion, another 120% jump. (Eckersley and Benton 2002: 20)

While some English soccer clubs claimed that the initial broadcast rights were originally undervalued, and that Murdoch quickly recouped his investment, there is no doubt that revenues to broadcasters would have to be spectacular indeed to match this escalating level of cost. They were not. Ironically, Murdoch, who famously told his shareholders in 1996 that he would 'use sports as a battering ram and a lead offering in all our pay television operations' (quoted in Millar 1998: 3), and was willing to acquire broadcast sports rights at almost any price, now complained that 'prices being paid to sport and sporting bodies have got beyond an economic level' (quoted in Eckersley and Benton 2002: 20). Sport, as noted above in the case of Super League, is crucial to the development of new broadcast services, and to converging telecommunications and computing services. As a result, it becomes (usually willingly) entangled with major corporate strategies, gambles and power plays. In this case, it was 'News's plans for a global pay TV network' that came unstuck 'when its bid to buy the DirecTV satellite pay TV operation from General Motors was rejected' (Maiden 2002: 33). The value of the broadcast rights fell, therefore, as the promise of fully globalized subscription services receded once more, leaving Murdoch's 'chief lieutenant, Peter Chernin, [to] put it even more bluntly, saying "clearly, you would have to say we've overpaid"' (Maiden 2002: 33). Compounding the problem was the post-recession and September 11th fall in advertising revenue, with Murdoch describing the advertising market as 'anaemic', but one finance journalist using more dramatic language in judging it to be the 'worst fall-off in overall ad spending since World War II' (McCarthy 2002: 2A). In discussing intense competition for advertising revenue between the 2002 Winter Olympics in Salt Lake City and Super Bowl XXXVI in New Orleans (the latter having been put back to just five days before the start of the former because of the assault on the Twin Towers), there is some surprise that there is seemingly not enough room in the huge American media sport market for two such prime events to flourish. Media sport seems now to be subject to orthodox laws of supply and demand, with Tony Ponturo, vice president of global media and sports marketing for the major brewer Anheuser-Busch, the biggest advertiser at the 2002 Super Bowl and Olympic sponsor, stating 'The U.S. media market is glutted with more sports and entertainment properties than there is ad money to go round' (McCarthy 2002: 2B). Ironically, on the same page, *USA Today* advertises its online coverage of the Winter Olympics, thereby illustrating the 'glutted' condition of the US media market.

The result has been a US$3 billion dollar write-down of US sports rights alone, about a third of which is accounted for by News Corporation (Chenoweth and O'Riordan 2002). This is not just an American problem, although the combination in the United States of over-production, cultural protectionism and sporting introversion has exacerbated and accelerated the decline of the media sports market (Miller *et al.* 2003). Competition in that market has also led to such desperate initiatives as the formation in 2001 of XFL, an American football tournament launched by the World Wrestling Federation and broadcast by the once dominant in sport, now eclipsed network NBC. The rationale was to offer a spiced up version of gridiron that borrowed from the hyped, parodic presentational techniques of the 'pseudo sport' of wrestling. XFL did not see another football or TV season, having 'delivered the lowest prime-time ratings of any of the four networks' and 'lost XFL and NBC [US]$35m each' (Brookes 2002: 14). NBC, locked out of broadcasting the major sports leagues by exorbitant rights, tried again in 2003 when it covered the Arena Football League, 'a hybrid sport that is much quicker and higher-scoring than the NFL' that has existed for 17 seasons (Rubino 2003), albeit promoting it in a more restrained manner than XFL (Sandomir 2003: 4). The establishment of such new sports competitions by media companies and sports is a sign not of the health of media sport, but of the unsustainable contractual arrangements that currently exist. Morgan Stanley has predicted that total major US TV network losses on sport in the period 2002–6 will be US$1.3 billion (Miller *et al.* 2003).

The shock to the sporting system that there can be such a thing as 'negative growth' (the expression used by economists when they can't bring themselves to say something straightforward like 'shriveling wealth') has now registered across the globe. The business pages of newspapers, by 2002, began to speak of media sport calamities and, for the first time, that sport had become the 'sick man' of the cultural industries in articles such as the following:

Suddenly, it seems, the business of sport is in serious trouble. The looming shake-out is likely to affect everyone from media to clubs, players and the fans. The warning flags have been flying for months, now the sirens are blaring. Sport is in real trouble around the world, and some large codes are

on life support. The drama that is unfolding this weekend in dressing rooms and club boardrooms is like nothing the sport industry has seen before. (Chenoweth and O'Riordan 2002: 21)

The cause of the crisis, given the co-dependent relationship of sport and television, lies with the failure of the media to match revenue to expenditure, a problem that they, in turn, pass on to the sports that they have enriched. The extent of the problem in television sport is revealed when it is recognized that the 'weekend' referred to immediately above occurred during probably its greatest global festival—the World Cup of association football, staged in Japan and Korea but reaching out to the four corners of the earth. It is extraordinary to talk of the crisis of media sport when, in the wake of the World Cup, FIFA issued the following press release containing information that trumpeted the global success of the tournament. Given that global audience figures for mega-media sports events have tended to be based on 'guesstimates' and marketing (de Moragas Spà *et al.* 1995), FIFA took a more cautious and rigorous approach to audience measurement, but still produced extraordinary figures:

Television coverage reached 213 countries, virtually every country in the world, with over 41,100 hours of dedicated programming. This represents a 38% increase in coverage over the 1998 event and sets a new record for a single sporting event. Contrary to some expectations, live audiences were not affected by the time zone differences for viewers in Europe and Central and South America. In fact, the cumulative live audience showed an overall increase on the 1998 figures.

Although the overall global audience was down on France 98, this decline was entirely due to the introduction of audited audience measurement in China for the first time, which allows for more accurate reporting . . .

The cumulative audience over the 25 match days of the 2002 event reached a total of 28.8 billion viewers. The corresponding audience for France 98, with unaudited viewing figures for China, reported 33.4 billion. However, if China is excluded from the statistics for both events, the totals show an increase of 431.7 million viewers (+2%) this year.

These impressive figures make the 2002 FIFA World Cup Korea/Japan™ the most extensively covered and viewed event in television history. Despite the time difference between Asia and the major football continents of Europe and South America, record audiences and market shares were reached in many countries . . .

Viewers the world over demonstrated their willingness to trade sleep for soccer and change their viewing habits and daily routine in order to watch the FIFA World Cup™. In terms of viewer hours, calculated as the total number of hours watched by all viewers, this year's tournament set a new record for a sports event of 49.2 billion worldwide . . .

Out-of-home viewing contributed to the 2002 Final being the most viewed match in FIFA World Cup™ history, with 1.1 billion individuals watching this game . . .

Soccer has long been seen as the perfect vehicle for sponsors to deliver messages to the dream male demographic, but statistics for the 2002 FIFA World Cup™ indicate that women's interest in the tournament is growing rapidly. For example in Japan, the audience split for the whole of the tournament was virtually even, at 51% men, 49% women. The FIFA World Cup™ attracts audiences outside the typically male-dominated arena of sports broadcasting . . .

Excluding China, the total global audience has increased by 431 million viewers over France 98. (FIFA 2002)

These statistics show vast numbers of men and women coming together before the television screens in their homes, commercial premises and public sites to watch football. Of the many figures produced, my personal favourite is the 94.2 per cent market share gained by Brazil's TV Globo when covering the England versus Brazil match (46 million viewers and a 30.2 per cent rating). The game took place at 3:30 am local time (FIFA 2002). It is important for international sporting bodies like FIFA to capture and promote these impressive numbers as they represent a massively lucrative lure for the purchase of broadcast and sponsorship rights and a powerful statement that they do, indeed, control 'the world game'. The IOC, as operators of rival mega-media sports spectacles, make similar claims to the global status of Summer and Winter Olympics. There is, consequently, a strong incentive to massage and inflate the 'guesstimate' figures that are spread around the world and become authoritative through repetition. Thus, for example, it has been claimed that 1 billion people watched the Opening Ceremony of the 1988 Seoul Olympics, then the 'largest television audience in history' (Rogers 1993: xiii) until exceeded by the Opening Ceremonies of the 1992 Barcelona and 1996 Atlanta Olympics, with their estimated global viewing audiences of 3.5 billion (Gordon and Sibson 1998: 209). When, for example, de Moragas Spà *et al.* (1995: 207) sceptically examined the claim of '3.5 billion people simultaneously watching the Barcelona Opening Ceremony' in 1992, they considered such factors as access to TV sets in developing countries, levels of interest in sport, viewing alternatives and time zone variations. The authors concluded that, even based on an optimistic estimate of a 'potential world television audience [of] 2.3 billion . . . the highest possible audience for a single event, such as the Opening Ceremony, must be estimated to be between 700 million and one billion' (p. 215). This is still a striking statistic, but one that at worst is only one-fifth of the original estimate. The International Olympic Committee (2002) estimated that the Sydney 2000 Olympic Games, broadcast in 220 countries, were 'the most watched sports event ever', with over '3.7 billion people tuned in to watch . . . representing a 20% increase over the 1996 Atlanta Olympic Games four years before'. Total viewer hours were estimated at 36.1 billion and 'Nine out of every 10 individuals on the planet with access to television watched some part of the Olympics'. Important for arguments above concerning access and cultural citizenship was the claim that '90% of coverage broadcast on channels available to the entire population of each country'. The economic significance of these audience ratings is clearly reflected in the statement on the revenue generated by the Sydney 2000 Olympic Games, with the value of broadcast rights recorded at US$1331 million, 45 per cent of total revenues of approximately US$3 billion. These far exceeded any other source of income with, for example, tickets to venues generating only US$551 million or 19 per cent of total revenue (IOC 2002).

Much of the attention that has been given to media sport, especially when dramatic simultaneous world viewing statistics are circulated by the very media who benefit from them, has involved analysing its relationship to the wider process of globalization, of which it can be seen as both significant expression and engine (Maguire 1999; Bairner 2001; Miller *et al.* 2001). While the globalization of sport has been judged to be, in various ways, uneven, inconsistent and subject to resistance and some market failure, it has been in the context of continuing expansion of the media sport industry. Only recently, therefore, has it been necessary to ponder the consequences of global recession. There are several disastrous post-millennial stories around the world in which the next great leap forward in media sport has resulted in a career-threatening hamstring injury. One of the most spectacular examples of these is Germany's KirchMedia, who seemed to hit paydirt in 1996 when FIFA sold them the broadcast rights to the 2002 and 2006 World Cups. The Kirch group bought the rights for a reported record 3.3 billion Swiss Francs (2.3 billion Euro; Bunn 1999: 5) as part of a consortium with Swiss sports marketing group ISL. But the cost of the investment and the delay in recouping it led to ISL's bankruptcy in May 2001, with Kirch acquiring the worldwide TV rights to the World Cup (Milmo 2001). KirchMedia had great difficulty in selling the rights at the inflated prices necessary to make its original investment profitable. Ambitions to sell high-priced fees to pay TV companies were in conflict with legislation in most European nations protecting free-to-air broadcast of listed events of national significance (as discussed above). European rights had previously been sold through the European Broadcasting Union (EBU), a group of mostly public service free-to-air broadcasters (some of whom, curiously, are in North Africa and the Middle East). National broadcasters, when required to negotiate individually, baulked at the higher broadcast rights fees. The BBC, for example, refused to pay for the 2002 World Cup a fee that it claimed was 70 times the figure for the 1998 World Cup (BBC Sport Online 2001). A game of 'brinkpersonship' ensued across various media markets, in which the unthinkable possibility emerged that the Korea/Japan World Cup would not be seen in countries where football was the dominant denomination in the secular religion of sport. This did not happen because Kirch was forced to accept much lower broadcast rights fees for the World Cup than it anticipated, precipitating its own collapse and the bizarre outcome of the German federal government having to underwrite the cost of broadcast infrastructure so that Germany, the host country for the 2006 World Cup, could watch the previous tournament. The disastrous collapse of Kirch was not, though, just the tragic tale of one company and one mega-media sports event (Rowe 2002). It also involved the collapse of Kirch's pay TV arm, Premiere, and resulted in a dispute over the buy-back of a £1 billion investment by News Corporation (Gibson 2002a). It caused problems for Formula One motor racing, for which Kirch also held broadcast rights and in which it had a significant financial stake. As income from Kirch was also of major importance to German football clubs, many of these now faced bankruptcy.

The TV sport picture was darkening. In the same year, the UK's ITV Digital went into administration with debts of £178 million, leaving several of the smaller clubs in the Nationwide League in dire financial straits. ITV also admitted that it had paid

too much—£183 million for a three-year deal—for Premier League highlights, with its in-season weekly Saturday night highlights programme estimated to be losing £750,000 per week in 2002 (Milmo 2002). In Italy, the two pay TV companies that had invested huge sums in the rights to football, the French Telepiu and News Corporation's Stream, were forced to merge (Chenoweth and O'Riordan 2002). Across the world, C7, the pay TV sport channel of Australia's Seven Network, lost Australian rules football coverage to a higher bid by a Foxtel-led consortium and folded. In summary, predictions of the emergence of a global, sports-led pay TV and interactive services industry have proven to be wildly optimistic, and many nation states (and some sports organizations like the IOC) remain stubbornly opposed to the exclusive capture of the prime sports content that would force a massive rise in subscription numbers. By 2003, the World Broadcasting Unions (WBU) organization and its constituent members like the EBU, the Asia-Pacific Broadcasting Union (ABU) and the Arab States Broadcasting Union (ASBU), mounted a strong counterattack in defence of open public broadcasting of sport. One Japanese broadcaster, for example, argued for a change to broadcasting arrangements that led to the sudden fading from Japanese consciousness of the World Cup that they had co-hosted. This state of affairs, its representative argued, was caused by the exclusive control of post–World Cup images by pay TV (Fujiwara 2003: 24). An Arab broadcaster, similarly, argued that sports federations should 'rehabilitate the roll of broadcasting unions to ensure that sport does not only become the privilege of those rich enough to afford it' (Harguem 2003: 23). There is, of course, a strong element of self-interest in such arguments, but they mark a detectable turning of the tide in the affairs of sports TV after several years of discursive dominance by neoclassical economic philosophy wedded to in-practice commercial oligopoly.

These developments might be the source of a little ironic pleasure in witnessing the puncturing of *hubris* and give comfort that television sport is still afforded some protection from complete commodification. But these positive feelings are mitigated by their disruptive impact on sport, which has become dependent on the television drip feed. Many sports organizations took the unsustainable amounts of media money and spent it on equally unsustainable player payments, which have often absorbed 75 per cent of total revenues. As clubs and teams concentrated their efforts on poaching each others' dim athletes, and caring little for smaller sports organizations or the long-term infrastructure of the game (such as 'bringing on' young sportspeople), many have accumulated huge debts. Having mortgaged their futures, sports reams bloated by force-fed TV funds now face severe cutbacks and even insolvency. In the case of UK soccer, for example, a boom has been proclaimed and validated by the signing of leading players from other countries (facilitated by international sports labour market de-regulation and lured by multimillion pound contracts; see Miller *et al.* 2001; Magee 2002; Magee and Sugden 2002; McGovern 2002). But there is now a strong sense of impending doom:

The British football industry is in financial crisis. Any other business might be pronounced dead and buried but this sector is different: when it comes to the people's game, the heart still very much rules the head.

Despite the financial turmoil—wiser heads might say reality—that has crashed down on the sport over the past 12 months, the hopes of fans, players and investors continue to require clubs to wield the cheque book even when the coffers are empty.

And it seems that all those who should know better—from banks to investors to the finance directors of the clubs themselves—appear happy for this suspension of credibility to continue . . .

As a result, most League clubs are in hock to two competing interests—their bank and Sky TV. As one football finance expert puts it: 'The sport has sold its soul to television'. (Wild 2002: 15)

Such analyses suggest that the full price of the sport's Mephistophelian compact with television is now being exacted. The dependency of clubs on television, with 'Only Murdoch's millions stand[ing] between many clubs and financial ruin' (Wild 2002: 15), is marked for the smaller clubs by both the trauma of the loss of ITV Digital funds and an almost pathetic gratitude for receiving very occasional appearance fees. For example, an FA Cup replay between non-league Dagenham and Redbridge and Second Division Plymouth Argyle was broadcast 'live' by BSkyB in early 2003. This game was reflective of the 'romance' of a competition that pits fulltime professionals against part-time players, and was therefore of some televisual interest. Although Plymouth had failed to beat their junior opponents in the first match, the additional income from BSkyB made this poor performance profitable, with the club's Chairman stating:

'If you'd asked before the game would I take a draw and get £265,000 in TV money for a replay, I would have said "yes"'.

'For a club like ourselves the FA Cup is all about maximizing your revenue'. (Errington 2003: 40)

The game was duly broadcast 'live' and Plymouth Argyle lost, with their manager describing the unaccustomed experience of appearing on national television (also broadcast, in fact, in other countries; see Afterword) and being humiliated: '"The whole of the nation has seen us having a poor performance and that hurts as much as anything else"' (Errington 2003: 43). The 'sport may have sold its soul to television', but the pain of loss on the field of play is still felt as keenly as on the balance sheet.

The evidence is clearly that the trade in sporting souls is a cross-border one. The 2002 football season was said to be 'getting off to a shaky start with the grim state of the television business resulting in growing doubts about the future of lucrative broadcasting deals and concerns over the finances of several major clubs' (McCathie 2002: 20). The commencement of the Italian season was, in fact, postponed because of disagreements over TV rights, with Italian public broadcaster RAI offering 'to pay the nation's football league only half the EUR88 million (AUS$157 million) it paid last year to show highlights of matches' (McCathie 2002: 20). The result has been stagnation in the player market as:

Worries about the balance sheets shredded by years of over-spending on players and fears the television-rights bubble is about to burst, mean club chairmen now tell their coaches a player's price matters as much as his quality. (Huggins 2003: 30)

Television executives like the Chief Executive of the Australian Nine Network, Ian Johnson, are now repeating minor variations on the mantra that:

'Sport is so expensive, the networks just cannot afford to be paying what we have in the past. Any sporting body that has been the recipient of huge sporting-rights fees should be putting it in the bank and thanking their lucky stars they signed those deals when they did, because it won't be happening again'. (Eckersley and Benton 2002: 20)

There is no doubt that the broadcast sports rights contracts being (re)negotiated in the wake of the recession in sports television will be, for the foreseeable future, rather less favourable for peak sports organizations and clubs, and that there will be a negative economic impact on coaches, elite athletes, and so on given the prime importance of media capital to sport. As noted earlier, many major sports have been 'loss leaders' for converged media corporations, but the principle of the 'loss leader' is that what is lost in the direct transaction is more than matched by the income from other sources that it stimulates. This balance has been, at least temporarily in many cases, lost. The recession in TV sport has also led to a round of collapses and mergers, creating a number of TV monopolies and quasi-monopolies. This has placed television in a stronger bargaining position with sport.

It is always dangerous to commit the sin of 'presentism', the belief that what currently holds will be for ever thus. Observers of the hi-tech Nasdaq stock market index will grasp this point well, and if they are investors will now have a visceral understanding of it. When the first edition of this book was written in the late 1990s, there was little sign of the wreckage in TV sport ahead. It might be that, in a further five years, circumstances will have again changed dramatically, and a new cohort of TV and sports executives, sportspeople and viewers will be afflicted with the amnesia that turns so much of contemporary life into a blur of buzzwords, beliefs and fantasies. In the English Premier League in 2003, for example, the Russian oil billioniaire Roman Abramovich has bought and paid millions of pounds into the ailing Chelsea—or 'Chelski' as the tabloids now describe the club. But whatever the economic trials and tribulations of media sport, its public visibility is undiminished and, if anything, enhanced. This is because although 'live' TV sport is the bedrock of the economy of sport, it is gossip and scandal that keep it in perpetual view both in and outside the formal framework of the sports media.

Sport as School for Scandal

It is worthwhile to look briefly at media sports scandals because they reveal how the political economy of media sport extends far beyond the production, distribution and consumption of sports reports and live television. We have noted how sport has notable popular appeal for large (especially male) sections of the population, and that media sports texts take many forms, from 'hard' objective reporting to the 'soft' news of gossip, background and 'colour' (Andrews and Jackson 2001; Whannel 2001a). However, sport's cultural prominence and the visibility of its celebrities make it a useful vehicle for carrying news stories 'outside' itself and its routine audiences. Some of these stories are positive in nature, drawing, for example, after success in major international competitions like the Olympics, on the nationalist impulse that can be activated in many citizens, irrespective of their usual involvement in sports spectatorship (Miller *et al.* 2001). But scandals are particularly

instructive because their inherently transgressive quality raises the possibility of 'contagion' or, as John B. Thompson (1997: 59) puts it, 'a corrosive impact on the forms of trust which underpin social relations and institutions'. As we have seen, sport for its adherents is the bearer of strong mythologies of nobility and fair competition, while even those who are not sports fans are of necessity aware of the material success and high standing of sports stars. Media sports scandals like those involving, for example, Ben Johnson's disqualification after winning the 100 metres at the 1988 Seoul Olympics for taking performance-enhancing drugs, or the trial of iceskater Tonya Harding for conspiring to injure her US teammate and rival Nancy Kerrigan, or Mike Tyson snacking on the ear of an opponent, directly transgress the 'fair play' values of sport. In other words, the contradictory mythological structure at the heart of sport—ennobling physical contest and benevolent universal values versus base competition and cynical exploitation—is ripe for the periodic production of scandals that explode through the media sports cultural complex with firestorm intensity. These may be exhausted or dowsed, but the embers of sports scandal glow perpetually, with the media providing the perfect accelerant.

A 'scandal' can be created even out of fairly routine occurrences in a sporting event of great significance, like the public pillorying of the English soccer 'golden boy', and then Spice Girl fiancé (now husband) David Beckham for being sent off for kicking an opponent (admittedly in a rather innocuous manner) in a 1998 World Cup match against Argentina (Miller 2001: 8; Whannel 2001b: 140). The case of Beckham is especially instructive in revealing the volatility of sport celebrity and scandal, with an ever-changing cast of heroes and villains in a constantly shifting pattern of deification, celebration, demonization, punishment, damnation, rehabilitation and redemption of Biblical proportions. The speed at which these shifts occur can be bewildering, with Beckham re-installed in enhanced form as English masculine exemplar in the space of a few years (Whannel 2001a,b) and is even potently if mutely manifest in the successful feature film *Bend it Like Beckham*. The most sublime moment of his restoration came during the 2002 Korea/Japan World Cup, when, as England captain, Beckham confronted his fate and scored a crucial penalty against his nemesis—Argentina. The press that had abused him in 1998, describing Beckham as 'One Stupid Boy' and 'an over-coiffed terp' (quoted in Brookes 2002: 98–9), now loved him to death. Beckham's 'moment' was now ecstatically shared and almost no inhabitant of the UK could have missed the banner headlines plastered across media space. Among these many texts the clichéd statement that 'When Beckham scored with that penalty it was better than sex' (Ridley 2002: 5) in a British tabloid paper captured the temper of the times that had seen Beckham transmute from whipping boy to Love God. The figure of Beckham could also be scrutinized by academics in sociology, media and cultural studies for signs that he embodies a positive shift towards a less ideologically constricted masculinity and sporting celebrity (Cashmore 2002). With Beckham constructed so improbably (perhaps impossibly), the potential for a fall from grace is ever-present. Thus, in the political economy of media sport, male celebrity figures like David Beckham, Michael Jordan and Tiger Woods (and, to a lesser extent, high-profile sportswomen like Serena Williams, Anna Kournikova and Marion Jones, who

nonetheless have to contend with sport's unequal gender order) function simultaneously as popular weather vanes for the exploration of social trends and ideologies, and as priming agents ensuring the cultural ubiquity of sport.

To qualify as media sports scandals, the transgressive behaviour does not, in fact, have to occur in the pursuit of sport. The Corinthian status of elite sportspeople means that, as in the case of the O.J. Simpson murder trial, a retired footballer turned sports commentator and film actor is still associated predominantly with his exploits on the field of play (McKay and Smith 1995), while the prosecution of boxer Mike Tyson for rape is directly connected in the media to his performance in the ring (not to mention his identity as an African American male; see Sloop 1997). In the case of high-profile HIV-positive athletes like Earvin 'Magic' Johnson and Greg Louganis, the stuff of scandal is provided by the positioning of sexuality within elite sports culture. The mere fact of being gay can be scandalous within this culture, as Justin Fashanu, the first soccer star to 'come out' and the first million-pound black footballer in Britain, discovered to his cost. He hanged himself in May 1998, largely ostracized by his footballing peers and facing allegations in the USA of the sexual molestation of a minor.

An especially striking case that illustrates how off-field behaviour can be massively newsworthy is that of Wayne Carey, the most famous Australian Rules footballer of his generation, who resigned from the North Melbourne club that he captained in 2002 after the public revelation of his affair with Kelli Stevens, the wife of his vice-captain, Anthony. This 'Downfall of a King' (*Who Weekly* 2002: 27) represented a double transgression, a 'betrayal' of both marital vows (Carey was also married) and of the compact between club-mates (the expression is used advisedly, given the strong male bonding in team contact sports). In a city where 'footy talk' dominates discourse in season (and not uncommonly outside it), this resulted in more 'morning after' stories in one Melbourne newspaper devoted to the Carey scandal than to the 11 September 2001 destruction of the World Trade Center (Robinson 2002). The Carey case also revealed something of the temporal rhythm of the sports scandal—in the space of a few weeks, coverage of Carey in Australian newspapers went from low-key (the scandal broke just before the start of the football season) to ubiquitous and then quickly subsided (Robinson 2002). This effervescence of scandal is obviously temporary, but all the 'data' generated by it is a cultural resource that can be quickly recalled and redeployed, as occurred in February 2003 when Carey, now reconciled with his wife Sally (as Stephens was to his) and playing for a new club in a new city (Adelaide), found himself embroiled in a scandal involving a 'luxury' hotel room, a party, various women to whom he was not related by marriage, and a spa. After a few days of intense media coverage of the incident, a young woman withdrew allegations made on radio that she had photographed Carey falling off a bed, drunk and naked except for a T-shirt, and that she had seen him kissing a blonde woman (McGuire 2003: 3). Her story and retraction were told to *New Idea* magazine, which had 'reportedly paid Sally Carey AUS$150,000 for an exclusive interview that appeared in the previous week's edition' (McClure 2003: 8). At this point the story petered out—until the next opportunity to reactivate the scandalous potential of the sports celebrity.

In general terms, scandal cannot be contained within the sports world even where it emanates directly from sporting activity, nor can the heroic mythology of sport be protected from scandal when the 'extra-curricular' behaviour of sportspeople brings it into disrepute by association. As Thompson (1997: 58) argues, scandals have wider social ramifications than is often acknowledged, being 'consequential not just for the lives and reputations of the individuals immediately affected by them'. In the case of sport, they do not merely damage the 'forms of trust' on which the institution relies, but also permit the use of a powerful and popular institution for the exploration and contestation of significant contemporary social issues. In the cases briefly cited above, these include: matters of resort to unethical means in the pursuit of approved goals; normative conceptions of the body and the use of drugs; private ambition versus the collective good; norms of conduct among women; the relationship between aggressive sporting masculinity and a propensity to violence; physical and other forms of abuse of women by men both inside and outside marriage; the racialized nature of the justice system; the stigmatization of homosexuality and celebration of male heterosexual promiscuity; gender inequality in sports fandom, and so on (Rowe 1997a).

In coming to an understanding of the political economy of the media sports scandal, it is, therefore, necessary to appreciate how the hunger for content, the power of celebrity, and the ready transportability of images and information within and across media, create the conditions for a full-blown media phenomenon, but that to prosper they must articulate with social questions that are of importance to media audiences and 'moral entrepreneurs' (Cohen 1980) alike. Media sport scandals, then, service the cultural economy by comprehensively connecting sport, economics and the wider socio-cultural order. They operate in the zone that the social anthropologist Victor Turner (1990) calls the 'liminoid', where social conventions become frayed at the edges, and the consequences of their transgression unpredictable, even subversive. Recurrent media sports scandals are, ultimately, no more than spectacular instances of the everyday product of the sports media. As grist for the media mill, keeping sport to the forefront of formal news coverage, celebrity gossip and everyday conversation, media sport scandals are structured into its systems of production rather than bizarre disruptions to them. Every fragment of sports report, snatch of commentary, still shot and flickering image, and all other elements of sports discourse, are couched in visual and verbal languages whose grammar and syntax, vocabulary and framing, carry within them a kind of politics. These need not be overt, clear or consistent, but they represent a politics of the popular that is pumped out unreflectively every day in the name of sport. As Barthes (1973) has famously noted, it is not when politics is close to the surface and easily recognizable that it is at its most popularly powerful, but when it is strongly present but apparently absent, allowing myths to do their work on the emotions, and ideologies to represent the interests of the privileged few as the natural order for the many. We underestimate the political economic weight of the media sports cultural complex at our peril.

Conclusion: Media Sport Lost and Found

In their programme for a revitalized and critical political economy of communications set out in the early 1990s, Golding and Murdock (1991: 17) are critical of the 'romantic celebration of subversive consumption' and the loss of interest in 'the way the mass media operate ideologically, to sustain and support prevailing relations of domination' that they see as marking the work of 'new populist' cultural studies theorists like Fiske (1989a,b). They go on to argue that even if it is conceded that there is value in focusing on 'the moment of exchange when the meanings carried by texts meet the meanings that readers bring to them', it leaves out far too much of the overall story:

> But even if this wider perspective is restored there is still the problem that cultural studies offers an analysis of the ways the cultural industries work that has little or nothing to say about how they actually operate as industries, and how their economic organization impinges on the production and circulation of meaning. Nor does it examine the ways in which people's consumption choices are structured by their position in the wider economic formation. (Golding and Murdock 1991: 17)

In this first part of the book, I have taken seriously the question of how the cultural industries work qua industries and their consequent impact on the meanings that we derive from media sport, in the process acknowledging (although not deeply analysing) their position in the wider economic and social formations (such as, respectively, the informational economy and the media sports gender order). This chapter has engaged with the political economy of the sports media, addressing and/or anticipating the 'three core tasks' of political economy 'in practice' proposed by Golding and Murdock (1991: 22), analysing the production cultural floods alongside the political economies of texts and of cultural consumption.

References

Andrews, D.L. and Jackson, S.J. (eds) (2001) *Sports Stars: The Cultural Politics of Sporting Celebrity.* London: Routledge.

Andrews, D.L. (2004) Speaking the 'universal language of entertainment.' News Corporation, culture and the global sport media economy, in D. Rowe (ed.) *Critical Readings: Sport, Culture and the Media.* Maidenhead: Open University Press.

Appleton, G. (1995) The politics of sport and pay TV, *Australian Quarterly,* 67(1): 31-7.

Attwood, A. (1998) Football crazy, *Sydney Morning Herald,* 17 January.

Bairner, A. (2001) *Sport, Nationalism, and Globalization: European and North American Perspectives.* Albany, NY: State University of New York Press.

Baker, A. and Boyd, T. (eds) (1997) *Out of Bounds: Sports, Media, and the Politics of Identity.* Bloomington, IN: Indiana University Press.

Barthes, R. (1973 [1957]) *Mythologies.* London: Paladin.

Barthes, R. (1978) *A Lover's Discourse.* New York: Hill & Wang.

Baudrillard, J. (1981) *For a Critique of the Political Economy of the Sign.* St. Louis, MO: Telos.

BBC (2001) *Annual Report and Accounts 2000/2001* (www.bbc.org.uk).

Benedict, J. (1997) *Public Heroes, Private Felons: Athletes and Crimes Against Women.* Boston, MA: Northeastern University Press.

Bennett, T. (1998) *Culture: A Reformer's Science.* Sydney, NSW: Allen & Unwin.

Bloom, J. (2000) *To Show What an Indian Can Do: Sports at Native American Boarding Schools.* Minneapolis, MN: University of Minnesota Press.

Boyle, R. and Haynes, R. (2000) *Power Play: Sport, the Media & Popular Culture.* Harlow: Pearson Education.

Brookes, R. (2002) *Representing Sport.* London: Arnold.

Brown, A. and Walsh, A. (1999) *Not for Sale: Manchester United, Murdoch and the Defeat of BSkyB.* London: Mainstream.

Bunn, R. (1999) 'The inflationary spiral in the cost of TV transmission rights', Interview in *Diffusion EBU,* Winter, pp. 4–7.

Capling, A. (2001) *Australia and the Global Trade System.* Melbourne, VIC: Melbourne University Press.

Cashman, R. and Hughes, A. (1998) Sydney 2000: Cargo cult of Australian sport?, in D. Rowe and G. Lawrence (eds) *Tourism, Leisure, Sport: Critical Perspectives.* Melbourne, VIC: Cambridge University Press.

Cashmore, E. (2002) *Beckham.* Cambridge: Polity.

Chenoweth, N. and O'Riordan, B. (2002) The sick business of sport, *Australian Financial Review,* 4 June.

Cohen, S. (1980 [1972]) *Folk Devils and Moral Panics.* Oxford: Martin Robertson.

Combe, C. (1997) Structural change in the UK broadcasting industry during the 1990's. Unpublished paper, University of Westminster, London.

Connell, R.W. (1987) *Gender and Power.* Sydney, NSW: Allen & Unwin.

Correy, S. (1995) Who plays on pay?, *Media Information Australia,* 75: 80–2.

Cramer, J.A. (1994) Conversations with women sports journalists, in P.J. Creedon (ed.) *Women, Media and Sport: Challenging Gender Values.* Thousand Oaks, CA: Sage.

Creedon, P.J. (1994a) Women in toyland: A look at women in American newspaper sports journalism, in P.J. Creedon (ed.) *Women, Media and Sport: Challenging Gender Values.* Thousand Oaks, CA: Sage.

Creedon, P.J. (1994b) From whalebone to spandex: Women and sports journalism in American magazines, photography and broadcasting, in P.J. Creedon (ed.) *Women, Media and Sport: Challenging Gender Values.* Thousand Oaks, CA: Sage.

Crosswhite, J. (1996) Pay TV and its impact on women's sport, in R. Lynch, I. McDonnell, S. Thompson and K. Toohey (eds) *Sport and Pay TV: Strategies for Success.* Sydney, NSW: School of Leisure and Tourism Studies, University of Technology.

Cunningham, S. (1992) *Framing Culture: Criticism and Policy in Australia.* Sydney, NSW: Allen & Unwin.

Cunningham, S. and Jacka, E. (1996) *Australian Television and International Mediascapes.* Cambridge: Cambridge University Press.

Dandaneau, S.P. (2001) *Taking It Big: Developing Sociological Consciousness in Postmodern Times.* Thousand Oaks, CA: Pine Forge.

De Moragas Spá, M., Rivenburgh, N.K., and Larson, J.F. (1995) *Television in the Olympics.* London: John Libbey.

Dunn, R. G. (1998) *Identity Crises: A Social Critique of Postmodernity.* Minneapolis, MN: University of Minnesota Press.

Eckersley, O. and Benton, N. (2002) The venue versus the lounge room, *Australasian Leisure Management,* 35: 20–3.

Enzensberger, H.M. (1976) *Raids and Reconstructions.* London: Pluto.

Enzensberger, H.M. (1994) *Civil Wars: From L.A. to Bosnia.* New York: The New Press.

Errington, C. (2003) Argyle cut by daggers, *Evening Herald,* 15 January.

Farred, G. (2001) TV's time's up: The forgotten Games, *Journal of Sport & Social Issues,* 25(1): 3–5.

FIFA (2002) 41,100 hours of 2002 FIFA World Cup TV coverage in 213 countries, *Press Release,* 21 November.

Fiske, J. (1989a) *Understanding Popular Culture.* Boston, MA: Unwin Hyman.

Fiske, J. (1989b) *Reading the Popular.* Boston, MA: Unwin Hyman.

Fujiwara, Y. (2003) World Cup: The lessons, *European Broadcasting Union Diffusion Sport Dossiers,* January, pp. 24–5.

Gardner, S. (1998) Football shares hit fever pitch, *The Sunday Times Money,* 13 September.

Giddens, A. (1991) *Modernity and Self Identity.* Cambridge Polity.

Gibson, O. (2002a) Kirch stalls on BSkyB buyback bid, *MediaGuardian,* 20 May.

Giulianotti, R. (1999) *Football: A Sociology of the Global Game.* Cambridge: Polity.

Golding, P. and Murdock, G. (1991, 2000) Culture, communications, and political economy, in J. Curran and M. Gurevitch (eds.) *Mass Media and Society* (first and third editions). London: Edward Arnold.

Goodwin, P. (1998) *Television under the Tories: Broadcasting Policy 1979–1997.* London: British Film Institute.

Gordon, S., and Sibson, R. (1998) Global television: The Atlanta Olympics opening ceremony, in D. Rowe and G. Lawrence (eds.) *Tourism, Leisure, Sports: Critical Perspectives.* Melbourne, VIC: Cambridge University Press.

Grainger, G. (1996) The Broadcasting Services Act 1992: Present and future implications, in R. Lynch, I. McDonnell, S. Thompson and K. Toohey (eds.) *Sport and Pay TV: Strategies for Success.* Sydney, NSW: School of Leisure and Tourism Studies, University of Technology.

Gratton, R. (1999) The media, in R. Cashman and A. Hughes (eds.) *Staging the Olympics: The Event and Its Impact.* Sydney, NSW: University of New South Wales Press.

Guttmann, A. (1991) *Women's Sport: A History.* New York: Columbia University Press.

Hall, M.A. (1997) Feminist activism in sport: a comparative study of women's sport advocacy organizations, in A. Tomlinson (ed.) *Gender, Sport and Leisure: Continuities and Challenges.* Aachen: Meyer & Meyer Verlag.

Hall, S. (1989) The meaning of new times, in S. Hall and M. Jacques (eds.) *New Times: The Changing Face of Politics in the 1990s.* London: Lawrence & Wishart.

Hargreaves, Jennifer (1994) *Sporting Females: Critical Issues in the History and Sociology of Women's Sports.* London: Routledge.

Hargreaves, John (1982) Sport, culture and ideology, in Jennifer Hargreaves (ed.) *Sport, Culture and Ideology.* London: Routledge & Kegan Paul.

Harguem, A. (2003) The Arab example, *European Broadcasting Union Diffusion Sport Dossier,* January, pp. 20–3.

Harris, K. (1988) What do we see when we watch the cricket?, *Social Alternatives,* 7(3): 65–70.

Harvey, D. (1989) *The Condition of Postmodernity: An Inquiry into the Conditions of Cultural Change.* Oxford: Basil Blackwell.

Hebdige, D. (1989) After the masses, in S. Hall and M. Jacques (eds.) *New Times: The Changing Face of Politics in the 1990s.* London: Lawrence & Wishart.

Hesmondhalgh, D. (2002) *The Cultural Industries.* London: Sage.

Heywood, L. (2000) The girls of summer: Social contexts for the 'Year of the Women' at the '96 Olympics, in K. Schaffer and S. Smith (eds.) *The Olympics at the Millennium: Power, Politics, and the Games.* New Brunswick, NJ: Rutgers University Press.

Hirst, P. and Zeitlin, J. (eds.) (1989) *Reversing Industrial Decline?* Oxford: Berg.

Huggins, T. (2003) Europe sees last of the big spenders, *Sydney Morning Herald,* 3 February.

International Olympic Committee (2002) *Marketing Fact File* (www.multimedia.olympic.org/pdf/en_report.344.pdf).

Kellner, D. (1995) *Media Culture: Cultural Studies, Identity and Politics between the Modern and the Postmodern.* London: Routledge.

Klatell, D. and Marcus, N. (1988) *Sports for Sale: Television, Money and the Fans.* New York: Oxford University Press.

Krane, V. and Waldron, J. (2000) The Gay Games: creating our own sports culture, in K. Schaffer and S. Smith (eds.) *The Olympics at the Millennium: Power, Politics, and the Games.* New Brunswick, NJ: Rutgers University Press.

Lash, S. and Urry, J. (1994) *Economies of Signs and Space.* London: Sage.

Law, A., Harvey, J. and Kemp, S. (2002) The global sport mass media oligopoly: The three usual suspects and more, *International Review for the Sociology of Sport,* 37(3/4): 279–302.

Magee, J. (2002) Shifting balances of power in the new football economy, in J. Sugden and A. Tomlinson (eds.) *Power Games: A Critical Sociology of Sport.* London: Routledge.

Magee, J. and Sugden, J. (2002) 'The world at their feet': professional football and international labour migration, *Journal of Sport & Social Issues,* 26(4): 421–37.

Maguire, J. (1990) More than a sporting touchdown: The making of American football in Britain 1982–1989, *Sociology of Sport Journal,* 7(3): 213–37.

Maguire, J. (1999) *Global Sport: Identities, Societies, Civilizations.* Cambridge: Polity.

Maiden, M. (2002) Odds blow out on TV sports gamble, *Sydney Morning Herald,* 25 February.

McCarthy, M. (2002) Bowl, Olympics compete for gold. *USA Today,* 31 January.

McCathie, A. (2002) Soccer stars see prices plummet, *Australian Financial Review,* 31 August.

McClure, G. (2003) The story that wasn't, *The Age Sporting Life,* 12 February.

McGovern, P. (2002) Globalization or internationalization? Foreign footballers in the English League, 1946–95, *Sociology,* 36(1): 23–42.

McGuire, M. (2003) Backflip puts pants back on Carey, *The Australian,* 11 February.

McKay, J. (1997) *Managing Gender: Affirmative Action and Organizational Power in Australian, Canadian, and New Zealand Sport.* Albany, NY: State University of New York Press.

McKay, J. and Miller, T. (1991) From old boys to men and women of the corporation: The Americanization and commodification of Australian sport, *Sociology of Sport Journal,* 8(1): 86–94.

McKay, J. and Rowe, D. (1997) Field of soaps: Rupert v. Kerry as masculine melodrama, *Social Text,* 50(1): 69–86.

McKay, J., and Smith, P. (1995) Exonerating the hero: Frames and narratives in media coverage of the O.J. Simpson story, *Media Information Australia,* 75: 57–66.

Millar, S. (1998) Courtship ends as soccer and TV are united, *The Guardian,* 7 September.

Miller, T. (1993) *The Well-Tempered Self: Citizenship, Culture, and the Postmodern Subject.* Baltimore, MD: Johns Hopkins University Press.

Miller, T. (1998a) *Technologies of Truth: Cultural Citizenship and the Popular Media.* Minneapolis, MN: University of Minnesota Press.

Miller, T. (1998b) Hopeful signs? Arthur Ashe/working class spectatorship (editorial), *Journal of Sport and Social Issues,* 22(1): 3-6.

Miller, T. (1999) Competing allegories, in R. Martin and T. Miller (eds.) *SportCult.* Minneapolis, MN: University of Minnesota Press.

Miller, T. (2001) *Sportsex.* Philadelphia, PA: Temple University Press.

Miller, T., Lawrence, G., McKay, J., and Rowe, D. (2001) *Globalization and Sport: Playing the World.* London: Sage.

Miller, T., Rowe, D., Lawrence, G. and McKay, J. (2003) Globalization, the overproduction of US sports, and the new international division of cultural labour, *International Review for the Sociology of Sport,* 38(4): 427–40.

Milmo, D. (2001) Kirch group scores with global World Cup TV rights, *MediaGuardian,* 16 July.

Milmo, D. (2002) Football cost too much, admits ITV, *MediaGuardian,* 27 November.

Moller, M. (2002) Reclaiming the game: Rugby league, globalisation and masculinity. Unpublished doctoral dissertation, University of Sydney, Sydney, NSW.

Moore, D. (1996) Pay TV: The Confederation of Australian Sport perspective, in R. Lynch, L. McDonnell, S. Thompson and K. Toohey (eds.) *Sport and Pay TV: Strategies for Success.* Sydney, NSW: School of Leisure and Tourism Studies, University of Technology, Sydney.

Moore, M. (1997) Seven's 2000 advantage, *Sydney Morning Herald—The Guide,* 9–15 June.

Mowbray, M. (1993) Sporting opportunity: Equity in urban infrastructure and planning, in A.J. Veal and B. Weiler (eds.) *First Steps: Leisure and Tourism Research in Australia and New Zealand.* Leisure Research Series No. 1. Sydney, NSW: ASZALS.

Murdock, G. (1992) Citizens, consumers, and public culture, in M. Skovmand and K.C. Schroder (eds.) *Media Cultures: Reappraising Transnational Media.* London: Routledge.

Murdock, G. (1997) Base notes: The conditions of cultural practice, in M. Ferguson and P. Golding (eds.) *Cultural Studies in Question.* London: Sage.

Norris, C. (1993) Old themes for new times: Postmodernism, theory and cultural politics, in J. Squires (ed.) *Principled Positions: Postmodernism and the Rediscovery of Value.* London: Lawrence & Wishart.

Novak, M. (1976) *The Joy of Sport.* New York: Basic Books.

O'Regan, T. (1992) The international, the regional and the local: Hollywood's new and declining audiences, in E. Jacka (ed.) *Continental Shift: Globalisation and Culture.* Sydney, NSW: Local Consumption Publications.

Preuss, H. (2000) *Economics of the Olympic Games: Hosting the Games 1972–2000.* Petersham, NSW: Walla Walla Press/Centre for Olympic Studies, University of New South Wales.

Ridley, J. (2002) When Beckham scored with that penalty it was better than sex, *Daily Mirror,* 21 June.

Rinehart, R.E. (1998) *Players All: Performances in Contemporary Sport.* Bloomington, IN: Indiana University Press.

Rivenburgh, N.K. (2003) The Olympic Games: twenty-first century challenges as a global media event, in A. Bernstein and N. Blain (eds.) *Sport, Media, Culture: Global and Local Dimensions.* London: Frank Cass.

Robinson, S. (2002) Salacious allegations: Culture, public relations and the sports scandal.

Unpublished honours thesis, University of Newcastle, Newcastle, NSW.

Roche, M. (2000) *Mega-Events and Modernity: Olympics and Expos in the Growth of Global Culture.* London: Routledge.

Rogers, E. (1993) Foreword, in J. Larson and H. Park, *Global Television and the Politics of the Seoul Olympics.* Boulder, CO: Westview Press.

Rojek, C. (1985) *Capitalism and Leisure Theory.* London: Tavistock.

Rowe, D. (1995) *Popular Cultures: Rock Music, Sport and the Politics of Pleasure.* London: Sage.

Rowe, D. (1997a) Apollo undone: The sports scandal, in J. Lull and S. Hinerman (eds.) *Media Scandals: Morality and Desire in the Popular Culture Marketplace.* New York: Columbia University Press.

Rowe, D. (1997b) Rugby League in Australia: The Super League saga. *Journal of Sport and Social Issues,* 21(2): 221-6.

Rowe, D. (2000a) Cathy Freeman: Live at Stadium Australia, 25 September 2000, *M/C Reviews Feature Issue on The Olympics,* 10(18): October (http://www.api-network.com/mc/).

Rowe, D. (2002) Public broadcasting: Populist multiplex or edifying ghetto?, paper to *The Changing Meanings of Popular Culture for Public Broadcasting,* European Science Foundation Workshop, Amsterdam, June.

Rowe, D. and Lawrence, G. (1998) Framing a critical sports sociology in the age of globalization, in D. Rose and G. Lawrence (eds.) *Tourism, Leisure, Sport: Critical Perspectives.* Melbourne, VIC: Cambridge University Press.

Rowe, D. and McKay, J. (2003) Sport: Still a man's game, in S. Tomsen and M. Donaldson (eds.) *Male Trouble: Looking at Australian Masculinities.* Melbourne: Pluto.

Rowe, D., Lawrence, G., Miller, T. and McKay, J. (1994) Global sport? Core concern and peripheral vision, *Media, Culture & Society,* 16(4): 661–75.

Rubino, R. (2003) Funky football risks niche for TV exposure, *The Press Democrat,* 9 February.

Sandomir, R. (2003) Good ratings for Arena League, *The New York Times,* 4 February.

Schaffer, K. and Smith, S. (eds.) (2000) *The Olympics at the Millennium: Power, Politics, and the Games.* New Brunswick, NJ: Rutgers University Press.

Sheehan, P. (1998) Game, set and match: Murdoch, the champion of world sports, *Sydney Morning Herald—The Guide,* 23 February–1 March.

Shiller, R.J. (2000) *Irrational Exuberance.* Princeton, NJ: Princeton University Press.

Singer, T. (1998) Not so-remote-control, *Sport,* March, p. 36.

Sloop, J.M. (1997) Mike Tyson and the perils of discursive constraints: Boxing, race, and the assumption of guilt, in A. Baker and T. Boyd (eds.) *Out of Bounds.* Bloomington, IN: Indiana University Press.

Smith, P. (1996) Pay TV: Perspective from a popular sport, in R. Lynch, L. McDonnell, S. Thompson and K. Toohey (eds.) *Sport and Pay TV: Strategies for Success.* Sydney, NSW: School of Leisure and Tourism Studies, University of Technology, Sydney.

Stoddart, B. (1986) *Saturday Afternoon Fever: Sport in the Australian Culture.* North Ryde, NSW: Angus & Robertson.

Sugden, J. and Tomlinson, A. (1998) *FIFA and the Contest for World Football: Who Rules the People's Game?* Cambridge: Polity.

Sugden, J., and Tomlinson, A. (2002) Theory and method for a critical sociology of sport, in J. Sugden and A. Tomlinson (eds.) *Power Games: A Critical Sociology of Sport.* London: Routledge.

Symons, C. (2002) The Gay Games and community, in D. Hemphill and C. Symons (eds.) *Gender, Sexuality and Sport: A Dangerous Mix.* Petersham, NSW: Walla Walla Press.

Sydney Morning Herald (2003) AOL Time ponders radical editing to reduce $44bn debt load, 3 February.

The Australian (2002) Murdoch in wings for Lazio, 2 December.

The Sun Newspaper Online (2003) 14 February.

Thompson, J.B. (1997) Scandal and social theory, in J. Lull and S. Hinerman (eds.) *Media Scandals: Morality and Desire in the Popular Culture Marketplace.* New York: Columbia University Press.

Throsby, D. (2001) *Economics and Culture.* Cambridge: Cambridge University Press.

Thwaites, T., Davis, L. and Mules, W. (1994) *Tools for Cultural Studies: An Introduction.* Melbourne, VIC: Macmillan Education.

Tomlinson, A. (1999) *The Game's Up: Essays in the Cultural Analysis of Sport, Leisure and Popular Culture.* Aldershot: Ashgate.

Trotsky, L. (1969) *The Permanent Revolution, and Results and Prospects.* New York: Merit.

Tunstall, J. (1996) *Newspaper Power.* Oxford: Oxford University Press.

Turner, V. (1990) Are there universals of performance in myth, ritual, and drama?, in R. Schechner and W. Appel (eds.) *By Means of Performance: Intercultural Studies of Theatre and Ritual.* Cambridge: Cambridge University Press.

Warren, I. (2002) Hyper-masculinity, Superleague and corporate governance, in D. Hemphill and C. Symons (eds.) *Gender, Sexuality and Sport: A Dangerous Mix.* Petersham, NSW: Walla Walla Press.

Weber, M. (1930 [1904/5]) *The Protestant Ethic and the Spirit of Capitalism.* London: Unwin University Books.

Wenner, L.A. (ed.) (1989) *Media, Sports, and Society.* Newbury Park, CA: Sage.

Whannel, G. (1992) *Fields in Vision: Television Sport and Cultural Transformation.* London: Routledge.

Whannel, G. (2001a) *Media Sport Stars: Masculinities and Moralities.* London: Routledge.

Whannel, G. (2001b) Punishment, redemption, and celebration in the popular press: The case of David Beckham, in D.L. Andrews and S.J. Jackson (eds.) *Sports Stars: The Cultural Politics of Sporting Celebrity.* London: Routledge.

Whitson, D. (1998) Circuits of promotion: media marketing and the globalization of sport, in L.A. Wenner (ed.), *MediaSport.* London: Routledge.

Who Weekly (2002) Downfall of a king, 1 April, p. 27.

Wiechula, F. (1997) 'I play in the big league, Gazza Disney!' says Les Ferdinand, *Mirror,* 27 March.

Wild, D. (2002) Networking—goal of the season, *Accountancy Age,* 29 August.

Wilson, H. (1998) Television's *tour de force*: The nation watches the Olympic Games, in D. Rowe and G. Lawrence (eds.) *Tourism, Leisure, Sports: Critical Perspectives.* Melbourne, VIC: Cambridge University Press.

Williams, R. (1974) *Television: Technology and Cultural Form.* London: Fontana/Collins.

Wilson, N. (1988) *The Sports Business: The Men and the Money.* London: Piatkus.

Chapter 7

LOSING CONTROL OF THE BALL

The Political Economy of Football and the Media in Australia

Murray Phillips and Brett Hutchins

In this article, Murray Phillips and Brett Hutchins use a Marxist-influenced political-economy approach to describe the historical changes in the relationship between Australia's Rugby League and the media, culminating in the current situation in which Rupert Murdoch's News Corporation controls "almost all commercial dimensions of sporting ownership, production, and delivery." The authors also describe rugby fans' resistance to these changes.

The control of spectator sport both in Australia and internationally has increasingly moved away from sports administrators and toward media executives. The global media hunger for sport is most obviously demonstrated by Rupert Murdoch's News Corporation (News Corp.) as its seeks to use sport as a major component in the development of its global digital television system (Herman & McChesney, 1997; Hutchins & Phillips, 1999; Rowe, 1999; Westfield, 2000). News Corp., whose sharemarket value runs at more than $A100 billion ("Bouncing off the Satellites," 2000), now owns television broadcasting rights, sporting leagues, and teams—or a combination of all three—in sports as diverse as baseball, basketball, ice hockey, Rugby League, Rugby Union, and soccer worldwide. The issue at hand is what happens to these sports as they are incorporated into the interests of transnational media corporations and their expansionist strategies.

In this article, we examine the changes that have occurred in Rugby League by adopting a Marxist-influenced political economy paradigm. We concur with David Rowe (1995) that value does not remain in a Marxist-influenced political economic approach that emphasizes the production and

Murray Phillips and Brett Hutchins, "Losing Control of the Ball: The political economy of football and the media in Australia" from *Journal of Sport and Social Issues* 27, no. 3 (August 2003): 215–232. Copyright © 2003 by Sage Publications, Inc. Reprinted with the permission of Sage Publications, Inc.

reproduction of power relations under capitalism, particularly given the continuing inroads into the realm of culture made by global corporate capital (p. 106). In our inquiry, the key issues are centered on how these inroads have been made and what they have given rise to.

Analysis of the political economy of Rugby League is framed around two interrelated concepts: MediaSport and the media sport cultural complex. As Wenner (1998) argued, MediaSport describes the intermeshing of corporate cultural capitalism with those who deliver and create sports media outputs. Sport and the media have come to adhere to the ideologies, structures, and practices of corporate capitalism as they have satisfied each other's commercial needs. This integration has reduced the economic and social autonomy of sport over the past half a century or more as the media, and in particular television, has come to dominate its transmission and exposure, thereby regulating both audience and sponsor appeal (Whannel, 1992). That the lines between sport and the media have blurred or even disappeared to become MediaSport appears to be the corollary of this media-dominated power relationship. The related concept is the media sports cultural complex (Rowe, 1999), which is an extension of previous work that has examined the relationship between sporting organizations, media and marketing organizations, and commercial/transnational companies (Maguire, 1993, 1999). Rowe (1999, p. 4) has reformulated Maguire's work by developing the media sports cultural complex that maintains the production element but further stresses the "two-way relationship between the sports media and the great cultural formation of which it is part":

That is, the extent to which the great engine of signs and myths itself symbolizes and helps create [our] current "being in the world." By gaining a better knowledge and understanding of how media sports texts are produced and what they might mean, it is possible to learn more about societies in which "grounded" and "mediated" experience intermesh in even more insidious and seemingly seamless ways. (p. 34)

This opens the way to examine the political economy of Rugby League through the interrelationships between key production processes and the cultural changes and patterns of resistance to these changes in the game.

Since the first decade of this century, Rugby League has been the major professional football code in two of the three states on the eastern coast of Australia. As a professional sport, it has always been associated with commodity value, but the acceleration of commercial involvement in the code over the past few decades has created significant change. Rugby League is now a commodity existing within a market framework structured by the carrier and deliverer of sports products—the media—particularly in its electronic forms.

The transnational media has literally overtaken many dimensions of the business of sport, and Australian Rugby League is a prime example of the takeover process. Although not discussed here, a similar phenomenon is also evident in English Rugby League that is now also managed by News Corp. (Arundel & Roche, 1998; Denham, 2000; Falcous, 1998; Kelner, 1996). A key argument of this article is that Rugby League represents a unique form of Media Sport, one in which almost all the major dimensions of the sport are subsumed within the objectives of a transnational media corporation. The term *transnational*, as opposed to *multinational*, is used deliberately throughout this article because this differentiation better expresses the "relative autonomy" of the media corporations and companies at a global level (Maguire, 1999, p. 22). We argue that the key transnational company in this case study, News Limited (News Corp.'s Australian arm), dictates the organization, the marketing strategies, media coverage, and sponsorship of Rugby League in Australia. A failure to understand and document such a power relationship can only lead to reductive social and cultural analysis of not only Rugby League but also any cultural forms influenced and/or controlled by the media.

To examine the power relationship between Rugby League and economic forces, the focus in this article is on the following four key issues: first, the historical development of professional Rugby League; second, the influence of television on the code; third, the advent and affect of pay television; and fourth, supporter resistance to growing corporate media control. These issues are also discussed in relation to wider trends in both Australia and North America. Initially, however, it is necessary to place the political economy of Rugby League within its historical context.

Commodity Value and Nonprofit Instrumental Rationality

The defining characteristic of Rugby League in its first 60 years is an underlying ethos of nonprofit instrumental rationality. Early administrators carefully calculated their actions to position their sport in an advantageous position compared to other sports, particularly Rugby Union. Profit was not the chief motive in this pursuit. When rebel administrators, players, and sympathizers decided to break away from the amateur Rugby Union competition in 1907, they could have simply played Rugby Union under professional rules. Instead, they chose to play Rugby League, which has fewer men on the field (13 as opposed to 15), no line-outs, and a more efficient way of clearing the ball from the ruck providing for a faster, less cluttered game of football. Rugby League was a superior spectacle, more likely to attract spectators and therefore raise the necessary finances to hire grounds, pay players, and compensate them for work time lost due to injury. These critical decisions were taken to give the new game the best chance of competing against its established and powerful Rugby Union rival. By securing high-quality players, providing an entertaining spectacle via rule modification, and attracting a strong working-class following, Rugby League won the battle for spectators and the single most important financial source for Australian sport at this time: gate receipts (Phillips, 1998). Like many professional sports in other countries during the early part of the 20th century (Gruneau & Whitson, 1993; Horne, Tomlinson, & Whannel, 1999), gate receipts dominated the economics of Rugby League. However, rather than going to private entrepreneurs or to companies as was usually the case with major North American sports, the money was recycled back into the development of the game.

A new dynamic introduced in the 1960s was licensed football social clubs that provided food, alcohol, and for the first time, poker (gambling) machines. Depending on the profitability of these social clubs, the effect was to significantly increase the budget for their associated football clubs. Even though the social clubs added to the financial resources of football clubs, and were directly responsible for doubling the wages for players, they did not challenge the underlying nonprofit ethos (Phillips, 1998). The president of the ruling body of Rugby League at the time, the New South Wales Rugby League (NSWRL), promoted the ethos in 1968: "the NSWRL is a truly socialist body because it has amassed very little in the way of profits over the past 60 years" (Heads, 1992, p. 335).

Although laced with ideological romanticism, his descriptions remained accurate: Rugby League was organized on membership-based clubs that were geographically stable and centered on suburban community identity. Also, the game was run by volunteer administrators who channeled surplus funds back into junior competitions, facilities, coaching, and interstate and international tours. In this sense, Rugby League was markedly different to spectator sport in the United States, which was characterized by private ownership and franchise relocation. As Ingham and Beamish (1993) argued, "Sport entrepreneurs [in the United States] were interested in profit ahead of any community service or responsibility" (p. 195). The profit-driven rationality of American professional sport contrasts markedly with the first 60 years of Rugby League.

Although no profits were accumulated, it is wrong to romanticize the governing practices of Rugby League. From its foundation, it was linked to Labor Party politics and working-class (mainly) Catholic communities. During times of social tension, such as World War I, Rugby League could not be separated from class conflict and sectarianism (Phillips, 1995). Volunteer administrators who ran both the NSWRL and the clubs could be self-serving, parochial, and patronizing to players. For instance, several clubs were refused entry into the competition for many years, and two clubs were excluded from the competition because of the threat they posed to the vested interests of existing clubs (Heads, 1992). There were also labor restraints, including the residential rule (1908 to 1959) and the transfer system (1960 to 1971), which severely restricted player mobility and limited their potential earnings (Phillips, 1996). Although the league's philosophy of nonprofit instrumental rationality may have been different from that of spectator sport in America, disputes, tensions, and problems existed that centered on different localized economic, political, and cultural issues.

Subordination: Capital Accumulation and the Media Sport Cultural Complex

From the 1970s, Rugby League underwent further structural changes and a philosophical shift by discarding nonprofit policies. The shift toward capital accumulation was closely related to the drawing realization that Rugby League, like many similar sports, had created a market for commercial companies who were willing to invest in the game to sell their goods and services (Sage, 1990). By the early 1980s, the realization resulted in administrative restructuring as, within a very short time frame, the NSWRL displayed many similar features to corporate and bureaucratic organizations. Professional administrators replaced volunteers, positions and roles were created that exhibited high degrees of specialization and formal-ization, and decisions were increasingly made via a centralized administrative body. The new administrative hierarchy was geared to expanding income and generating surplus funds. To this end, the NSWRL boasted an operating surplus of $2,067,509 in 1984 and an almost 300% increase to $5,996,007 by 1988 (New South Wales Rugby League, 1992). The ethos of the previous 70 years, epitomized by the comments of the president in the late 1960s already cited, proved anachronistic two decades later.

Closely linked to capital accumulation were strategies designed to expand the geographical base and market catchment of the competition. Within 13 years, the code expanded from city- to state-based, to interstate, to national, and then international. Growth began in 1982 when Canberra and Illawarra were admitted and, 6 years later, Brisbane, Gold Coast, and Newcastle entered the competition. The inclusion of the first privately owned franchise, the Brisbane club, epitomized the market-oriented direction of the game. In 1995, there was a total of 20 clubs including newcomers from Townsville, Perth, Auckland (New Zealand), and a second team from Brisbane. Distinguishing these club additions from previous growth are the motives for expansion. Whereas clubs had been added to accommodate major junior player nurseries, traditional Labor Party affiliations, Catholic connections, or changing working-class demographic patterns, the impetus for expansion in the 1980s and 1990s was a desire to increase the game's television audience and its associated commercial markets.

Administrative and organizational changes in Rugby League were closely aligned to changes in the wider political economy of Australian sport. As already mentioned, a key

dimension in the commercial trajectory of sport was the development of the media sport cultural complex. The complex took shape in Australia during the 1960s although, as McKay and Miller (1991) pointed out, it was the following decade that signaled the onset of major investment in sport by commercial and media companies. The Kerry Packer–inspired one-day cricket revolution (1977), victory by Australia II in the America's Cup yachting (1983), as well as government intervention in and regulation of sport from the early 1970s are seen as catalysts accelerating the commodification of Australian sport and leisure. In the case of Rugby League, those investing were initially local and national businesses, followed later by transnational companies and the media, particularly television.

Rugby League was first telecast on monochrome television screens in 1961. In a pattern similar to other sports such as Australian Rules football, the Rugby League administration embraced the medium after a period of skepticism centered on concerns about the possibility of reduced gate receipts (Linnell, 1995; Stewart, 1984). Following the introduction of color television in 1975, the commercial value of Rugby League ballooned with the NSWRL president enthusing:

> Colour television has been a big boost. Rugby League is a great sport for the medium, and rating figures show very clearly how popular our sport is with the viewer. (New South Wales Rugby League, 1975, p. 4)

From this moment, the market value of the code oscillated in relation to the state of the television industry. Overall audience ratings, however, have been consistent in most cases, and outstanding for some special events such as finals, interstate, and international fixtures (Phillips & Hutchins, 1998). In 1996, for example, the interstate competition between New South Wales and Queensland (promoted as "State of Origin") was not only the most watched sporting event in Australia but also the most popular program of any category on television (McKay, Hughson, Lawrence, & Rowe, 2000). The popularity of Rugby League with audiences ensured that administrators controlled a product desired by television networks, enabling them to exercise a degree of control over the form and content of the game and its television coverage. Nevertheless, it was television, the powerhouse of the sports media cultural complex (Rowe, 1999), that helped to initiate the shift toward capital accumulation away from nonprofit policies.

Color television was also a catalyst for corporate sponsorship. Sponsor involvement preceded color television, although it was irregular, insignificant in its visual branding of the game, and minor in terms of financial contribution. The new medium dramatically altered this relationship and spurred a proliferation of sponsorship of players, referees, clubs, and the competition. In 1982, for example, a transnational tobacco company invested $850,000 over 3 years for the commercial rights over intercity, interstate, and international games (Heads, 1992). With this financial commitment, the largest in any Australian sport to that time, the media sport cultural complex embedded its third, permanent, and powerful partner.

The commercial sponsorship of Rugby League highlights cultural variations within the media sport cultural complex. A striking feature of Rugby League, and much Australian sport, is the visual saturation of corporate sponsor logos and insignia—from changing rooms and training gear to players' uniforms, support staff apparel, and, most obviously, fields and stadiums. In this respect, Australian sport distinguishes itself from American professional sports, where television has traditionally required "clean screens" free from commercial clutter (Barnett, 1990). Rugby League's visual display of corporate capitalism and its relationship with television highlights that the media sport cultural complex, although a useful analytical tool, needs to be both culturally and historically contextualized.

Television helped to transform Rugby League from an activity with limited exposure, witnessed in person, broadcast on radio and reported in the press, into a commodified mediated spectacle with a national and international audience of millions by the late 1980s. There were many changes enabling this transition. Reduction of excessive violence helped the game appeal to a larger audience (Hutchins, 1997; Hutchins & Phillips, 1997), and the athleticism and (hetero-) sexual appeal of the male athletes was repackaged in high-profile promotional campaigns (Hutchins & Mikosza, 1998; Yeates, 1995). This repackaging culminated in the 1989 marketing campaign, the most successful in Australian sport history, featuring the Afro-American performer, Tina Turner (the Turner campaigns ran until 1995). Marketing manager of the NSWRL, Graeme Foster, summed up the 1989 campaign:

> The Tina Turner Campaign was the culmination of a three-year marketing plan to give Rugby League a more contemporary image. . . . It was a ballsy [sic] campaign that appealed to women and young men, broadened the game's appeal, and reached

into the white-collar audience without alienating [the] league's traditional blue-collar supporter base. (Shoebridge, 1989)

At this time, so-called show business formats featuring live entertainment, teams mascots, and cheerleaders were central elements in the code's presentation. Adoption of such marketing strategies could be interpreted as a form of cultural imperialism (Tomlinson, 1991), or, more specifically, as Americanization (Guttmann, 1994) that produces a homogenized global sporting culture. For example, the Rugby League Grand Final can be read as a copy of American football's Super Bowl. It is, however, more useful to view changes in Rugby League over the past few decades as part of the globalization of sport (Maguire, 1999). Globalization stresses that the forces operating in Rugby League cannot be seen as exclusively American influences but must be read as emerging from any number of cultural flows, including Asian and British influences (McKay & Miller, 1991). Theorizing global forces in this fashion allows for the possibility of cultural resistance by local cultures and acknowledges the multidimensional character of cultural power relations in sport (Donnelly, 1996; Rowe, Lawrence, Miller, & McKay, 1994). In the case of Rugby League, local issues of identity, geography, and consumer preferences still had to be negotiated by administrators in the game's production. For instance, it became necessary to move the American-inspired "Monday Night Football" league fixture to Friday nights, as the late week time slot proved more popular with Australian audiences (Phillips & Hutchins, 1998).

In summary, the establishment and subsequent development of the media sport cultural complex changed the culture of Rugby League. Commodification of the game accelerated and it gradually became inseparable from corporate capitalism (Phillips, 1998). Limited modifications to rules and scheduling were made to suit media interests, although it needs to be noted that Rugby League was positioned differently than other Australian sports—such as surf-lifesaving, cricket, and triathlon—that underwent major alterations to accommodate television demands (Goldlust, 1987). A reciprocal power relationship existed between Rugby League, the media, and sponsors up until the 1990s. League administrators maintained some autonomy in decision making as television networks and commercial companies competed for the rights to cover and sponsor Rugby League as they sought the game's large audience to promote their own products. In the process, Rugby League became slowly subordinated to commercial interests as it increasingly relied on the injection of media and corporate funding to run its operations. In effect, those running the game created the preconditions for its future domination by a transnational media company. As the next section illustrates, the power relationship between Rugby League and the media swung dramatically in favor of the latter with the introduction of pay television (also variously known as cable, pay per view, or satellite television) into Australia.

Domination: The Power of Pay Television

Part of the ARL's [the Australian Rugby League] dilemma is that it has unwittingly created the monster—a new game and spectator base beyond its wildest visions of the laborious '80s. (Crawley, 1995)

The dilemma referred to here centers on the introduction of pay television into Australia in 1995. Under a competitive system of tendering, the two most powerful players purchasing pay television licenses were Foxtel (at the time an alliance between Rupert Murdoch's News Limited and the national telecommunications carrier Telstra) and Optus Vision (at the time an alliance between Optus Communications, Continental Cable Communications, and Kerry Packer's Publishing and Broadcasting) (Westfield, 2000). Both commercial alliances wanted Rugby League for their pay television services, especially given its audience command in two of Australia's largest television markets, Sydney and Brisbane, and its residual appeal in the rest of the country (Rowe, 1997).

The rival pay operators built programming catalogues in predominantly two key areas—sport and movies—to lure subscribers. Sport has an established history of attracting viewers and subscribers (Bellamy, 1998), and Rugby League became caught in the battle between opposing media companies (Rowe, 1997). Optus Vision acquired the pay television rights to Rugby League, but to circumvent this acquisition, Foxtel audaciously created and set up an entirely new rival competition, Super League. Foxtel's controller, News Limited, invested $350 million in 1995 buying players and officials, purchasing and privatizing clubs (or franchises, as they became known), and selling the rebel competition to the press, sponsors, and the public (Colman, 1996). After protracted legal proceedings, two separate competitions—Super League and the ARL (that had superseded the NSWRL)—competed for all aspects of community and commercial support in 1997. Audiences fell away dramatically as playing talent was diluted between the two competitions, clubs no longer played traditional rivals competing in the opposing competition, and the acrimonious publicity battle for Rugby League waged in the media turned fans off the sport. A compromise was reached (if not forced by the code's plummeting popularity) the following year, providing joint broadcasting rights and a new organizing body, the National Rugby League (NRL), to run a reunited competition.

The clash over pay television in Australia highlights a relatively new dimension of the media's relationship. In the pre–pay television era, there was little organizational overlap between the commercial companies who sponsored the sport and the media interests that televised it. Companies investing in Rugby League sold a product, often cigarettes and alcohol, whereas television stations produced advertising income from audience ratings (Phillips & Hutchins, 1998). The common link between these discrete groups was Rugby League.

With the spread of transnational media power and influence, there are now new, more plentiful and intricate synergies at work between Rugby League and the media. The traditional interests of Murdoch's News Corp. are in electronic and print outlets, now located in North and South America, Australia, Asia, Europe, and the United Kingdom. Importantly, these holdings have diversified into ownership or partial ownership of airline, film, music, publishing, and technology interests also across several countries. On the establishment of Super League, some of these entities served as sponsors and, in tandem, the Super League competition was a vehicle to promote these businesses:

Murdoch owns the players that make up the Murdoch teams that make up the Murdoch-sponsored league that play the matches that feed the Murdoch TV networks that sell the Murdoch products that are endorsed by the Murdoch [news]papers. (*Inside Sport,* 1998, p. 104)

The indivisibility of these commercial interests highlights the intricate web of economic interdependencies that can constitute sport in the hands of a transnational media conglomerate.

The Super League imbroglio has been read in different ways: a masculine melodrama pitting media moguls Rupert Murdoch and Kerry Packer against one another in a battle over Rugby League and for corporate power, and/or corporate-driven globalism and economic rationalism conflicting with community, class, loyalty, and tradition (McKay & Rowe, 1997; Rowe, 1999, p. 90). Irrespective of how Super League is read, it is necessary to account for the dynamics of economic and political power over sport. Both Foxtel and Optus Vision well understood that Rugby League was inextricably linked to pay television, with the conflagration becoming the most costly ever in the Australian media industry and possibly any other industry (Ries, 1996). Pay television is strategically situated to take advantage of new technological advances involving the convergence of broadcasting, telecommunications, and other electronic technologies (Stoddart, 1997). For these reasons, Foxtel and Optus Vision needed Rugby League not only because it attracted customers to their current pay television and related services but also because it positioned these people as targets for future services as they come online. To

this end, more money was spent competing for Rugby League than the accumulated income of the game from gate receipts, sponsorship, merchandising, legal gambling, television, and radio broadcast fees since its establishment in 1907 (Phillips & Hutchins, 1998).

The culmination of the pay television battle was that a transnational media company took control over much of the structure, management, and organization of Rugby League. For example, in 1997, News Limited ran the board of Super League and established two new self-owned franchises to make their new competition viable. These franchises were News Limited versions of the traditional membership-based, community sporting club. Unlike these clubs, however, these franchises were based on principles involving the sale of a recognized product in a protected market that is positioned to maximize revenue (Gruneau & Whitson, 1993). The franchises could also be shut down or relocated with no consultation required with the communities that supported them. When the competition reunited in 1998, News Limited had attained a controlling interest in almost every facet of Rugby League. News Limited took ownership to a new level by surpassing the level of control of other media conglomerations—Cablevision, Disney, and Time Warner—that have purchased a range of sporting franchises including the Knicks and the Hawks in basketball, the Rangers and the Mighty Ducks in hockey, and the Braves and the Angels in baseball (Rowe, 1999). News Limited had gained 50% control of the NRL while retaining partial ownership in several clubs, secured broadcasting rights for 25 years for its pay television station—Foxtel—and through ownership and partial ownership of other commercial companies, and provided money and sponsorship for former Super League clubs and the reunited competition (Masters, 1999).

Although it is easy to overstate the supposedly monolithic power wielded by News Corp. in sport (Arundel & Roche, 1998, p. 70), in Rugby League's case, News Corp. had taken over. The previous decades show separate identities constituting the media and sport relationship. The introduction of pay television and associated global corporate forces created a new phenomenon in Rugby League. Through its partial ownership of Foxtel and other businesses, News Limited had consumed or partially consumed all parts of the sport: the administration of the sport, the media organization televising the sport, and the companies sponsoring the sport. As one non-Murdoch-owned newspaper argued, "We are told Rugby League is the people's game. It is not. It is Murdoch's game." (Masters, 1999b). Rugby League had become a specialized example of MediaSport in which a transnational media conglomerate had assumed control over almost all commercial dimensions of sporting ownership, production, and delivery.

Resistance: The Supporters Fight Back?

A key policy of the News Limited–dominated NRL was a program of club rationalization involving the reduction of the number of clubs from 20 to 14 by the year 2000. This represented a loss of more teams in 2 years than in the code's entire history as 6 teams were merged into 3, and 3 were removed altogether (1 has since been reinstated after protracted and expensive legal proceedings). This rationalization accelerated the process of "delocalization" that has pervaded North

American professional sport (Whitson, 1998). Teams or clubs or franchises are ruptured from meanings associated with place or community (Bale, 1994) and replaced with meanings associated with consumer choice (Gruneau & Whitson, 1993). The criteria used for assessing the inclusion of clubs in the NRL were crowd numbers, competition points, gate receipts, sponsorship (income), profitability, and annual revenue (see www.ozleague.com). The emphasis of the NRL's culling process was on the accumulation of profit at the expense of community sentiment, tradition, and history. At the level of public discourse, it is now realized that Rugby League is purely a commodity—purchased, partitioned, reconnected and rationalized by a transnational company for the sake of corporate strategy and profit.

Radical structural changes in Rugby League have resulted in significant community and supporter resistance. Politicized resistance groups have included Aussies for the ARL, who support the old administration, the Friends of Public Football Grounds, who object to the government funding of facilities used by Murdoch's pay television–driven competition, the registration of official political parties to run in local council elections, and many threatened club supporter groups. Other forms of resistance included clubs holding out against a merger with other clubs, supporter groups petitioning local and federal politicians, attempts to eject complaint administrative boards, the creation of cyber protest movements through Internet resistance sites, and one ejected foundation club (1908), South Sydney (eventually), successfully fighting its removal from the competition in court after refusing to merge with another team. Rugby League has become a key symbol in the battle between corporate controllers who wish to downsize sport and the communities fighting to save their team, identity, and history.

A growing body of research has examined supporter resistance in relation to the changes in professional sporting structures globally (Nauright & Phillips, 1996, 1997; Nauright & White, 1996; Schimmel, Ingham, & Howell, 1993; White, Donnelly, & Nauright, 1997). Some of this work has investigated resistance related to the attachments of fans to sporting teams and in terms of fans' nostalgic longing for an idealized past in an uncertain, rapidly changing present (Nauright & White, 1996; Phillips & Nauright, 1999). These issues are certainly relevant in Rugby League and underpin many supporter reactions as they express their view on the domination of community interests by business. What stands out in Rugby League is the clarity of public realization that they had lost their contribution to the administration and ownership of the competition. An indicator of this loss is that roughly half the competition's clubs are now privately controlled, as opposed to clubs' traditional public membership club base that operated unchallenged until the late 1980s.

News Limited is widely recognized as determining nearly all dimensions of Rugby League, and much of the protest is aimed squarely at them. The disgust of South Sydney President George Piggins was palpable when he declared,

> if you believe in truth and the rights of ordinary people not to be trampled upon by multinational media corporations, then I ask you all to cancel that other journal [the Murdoch-owned *Daily Telegraph* newspaper] and stick with the *Sydney Morning Herald*. (Elliott, 1999)

Supporters also circulated via e-mail a list of News Limited–owned companies and products such as newspapers, pay television services, film companies, and airlines and encouraged a boycott "because we the punters are what business like News Limited rely on for profits. If we get angry enough and united enough, we can hurt the 'big end of town' and win" (personal communication, Anonymous, September 16, 1999). Although this approach fails to fully recognize the power, wealth, and control of companies such as News Corp., whose assets, like other transnationals, outstrip the economies of many nations (Coakley, 1998), it does acknowledge that it is the corporate ownership of Rugby League fueling supporter resistance.

Supporter resistance is notable as it comes at a time when it is sometimes difficult to acknowledge, assess, and reflect on the commodification of culture (Jameson, 1991). Rugby League disrupts what Whitson (1998, pp. 71–72) has referred to as the "natural" ways corporate capital has penetrated all aspects of sport from playing surfaces to equipment to stadia and that often escapes the sustained attention of fans. The pay television battle and the rationalization of Rugby League has created, at a popular level, a critical distance that allows supporters to question and challenge the corporatization of sport. Unfortunately, for many of Rugby League's fans, their resistance has failed to bring about a tide change in the control of the game.

Conclusion

As it stands, Rugby League is a specialized version of the MediaSport phenomenon in that News Corp.'s takeover has extended well outside media coverage. News Corp.'s variety of holdings, encompassing media, airline, film, music, publishing, and technology companies, has seen the game used to benefit not only its media arms but also these other commercial operations. Many of these commercial enterprises, in turn, have then been used to boost News Corp.'s investment in Rugby League. The business of sport is now a transnational's business and vice versa. Ownership of Rugby League, its media coverage, and its sponsors—once three relatively distinct identities with a mutual interest—are now largely in the hands of one corporation, News Corp. The question now is how this transnational chooses to exercise its power over Rugby League, as well as its other sporting investments, in relation to their value for its global media and corporate strategies.

Finally, Australian Rugby League provides another dimension to the conceptualization of contemporary global spectator sport. Wenner (1998), through his concept of MediaSport, made the case that our cultural sensibilities about sport have shifted to create an almost indivisible and naturalized interrelationship between sport and the media. An issue that needs addressing, then, is whether any sustained future challenge will (or can) be made to the corporate power bloc controlling sport as the wider commodification of culture comes into question. Is there any expectation or possibility that sport will escape from being used as a major site of anticorporate and globalization sentiment, as manifest in movements such as S11 and the continuing worldwide publishing phenomenon of Naomi Klein's *No Logo* (2001)? The MediaSport concept is yet to be sufficiently developed to account for socially and culturally situated countermovements away

from the naturalized acceptance of corporate sport. This is why Rowe's theorization of a media sports cultural complex is particularly useful as it emphasizes the signs, myths, and codes that mediate and ground consumer culture and, therefore, allows for an understanding of the discourses and meanings of supporter resistance. Taken together, MediaSport and the media sports production complex provide complementary parts of a useful analytical framework that can account for both the historical and social production of sports industries and their cultural consumption.

References

Arundel, J., & Roche, M. (1998). Media sport and local identity: British Rugby League and Sky TV. In M. Roche (Ed.), *Sport, popular culture and identity* (pp. 57–91). Aachen, Germany: Meyer and Meyer Verlag.

Bale, J. (1994). *Landscapes of modern sport*. Leicester, UK: Leicester University Press.

Barnett, S. (1990). *Games and sets: The changing face of sport on television*. London: FBI.

Bellamy, R. V. (1998). The evolving television sports marketplace. In L. A. Wenner (Ed.), *Mediasport* (pp. 73–87). London: Routledge.

"Bouncing off the Satellites." (2000, February 3). *The Sydney Morning Herald*, p. 210.

Coakley, J. J. (1998). *Sport and society: Issues and controversies* (8th ed.). Boston: Irwin McGraw-Hill.

Colman. M. (1996). *Super League: The inside story*. Sydney, Australia: Pan Macmillan.

Crawley, C. (1995, March 13). Fine kick-off but reality will soon bite. *Australian*, p. 25.

Denham, D. (2000). Modernism and postmodernism in professional Rugby League in England. *Sociology of Sport Journal, 17*(3), 275–294.

Donnelly, P. (1996). The local and the global: Globalisation and the sociology of sport. *Journal of Sport and Social Issues, 20*(3), 239–257.

Elliott, G. (1999, November 11–17). Advantage rule in dispute. *Australian Media Magazine*, p. 9.

Falcous, M. (1998). TV made it all a new game: Not again!—Rugby League and the case of Super League in England. *Occasional Papers in Football Studies, 1*(1), 4–21.

Goldlust, J. (1987). *Playing for keeps: Sport, the media and society*. Melbourne, Australia: Longman Cheshire.

Goodwill soars as rabbitohs chase foxes. (2000, June 16). *The Sydney Morning Herald*, p. 5.

Gruneau, R., & Whitson, D. (1993). *Hockey night in Canada: Sport, identities and cultural politics*. Toronto, Canada: Garamond.

Guttmann. A. (1994). *Games and empires: Modern sports and cultural imperialism*. New York: Columbia University Press.

Heads, I. (1992). *True blue: The story of the NSW Rugby League*. Sydney, Australia: Ironbark.

Herman, E. S., & McChesney, R. W. (1997). *The global media: The new missionaries of corporate capitalism*. London: Cassell.

Horne, J., Tomlinson, A., & Whannel, G. (1999). *Understanding sport: An introduction to the sociological and cultural analysis of sport*. London: E & FN Spon.

Hutchins, B. (1997). Mediated violence: The case of state of origin Rugby League. *Sporting Traditions, 13*(2), 19–39.

Hutchins, B., & Mikosza, J. (1998). Australian Rugby League and violence, 1970 to 1995: A case study in the maintenance of masculine hegemony. *Journal of Sociology, 34*(3), 246–263.

Hutchins, B., & Phillips, M. G. (1997). Selling permissible violence: The commodification of Australian Rugby League, 1970 to 1995. *International Review for the Sociology of Sport, 32*(2), 161–176.

Hutchins, B., & Phillips, M. G. (1999). The global union: Globalization and the Rugby World Cup. In T. J. L. Chandler & J. Nauright (Eds.), *Making the rugby world: Race, gender, commerce* (pp. 149–164). London: Cass.

Ingham, A., & Beamish, R. (1993). The industrialisation of the United States and the "bourgeoisification" of American Sport. In E. G.

Dunning, J. A. Maguire, & R. E. Pearton (Eds.), *The sports process: A comparative and developmental approach* (pp. 169–206). Champaign, IL: Human Kinetics.

Inside Sport. (1998). Sydney: Gemkitt Publishers (p. 10).

Jameson, F. (1991). *Postmodernism, or, the cultural logic of late capitalism*. London: Verso.

Kelner, S. (1996). *To Jerusalem and back*. London: Macmillan.

Klein, N. (2001). *No logo*. London: Flamingo.

Linnell, G. (1995). *Football Ltd.: The inside story of the AFL*. Sydney, Australia: Pan Macmillan.

Maguire, J. A. (1993). Globalization, sport development, and the media/sport production complex. *Sport Science Review, 2*(1), 29–47.

Maguire, J. A. (1999). *Global sport: Identities, societies, civilizations*. Cambridge, UK: Polity.

Masters, R., (1999a, July 31). Murdoch finally gets his way. *The Sydney Morning Herald*, p. 37.

Masters, R. (1999b, September 29). Piggins builds barricades as rebellious rabbitohs refuse to go quietly. *The Sydney Morning Herald*, p. 40.

McKay, J., Hughson, J., Lawrence, G. & Rowe, D. (2000). Sport and Australian society. In J. M. Najman & J. S. Western (Eds.), *A sociology of Australian society* (pp. 275–300). South Yarra, Australia: Macmillan.

McKay, J., & Miller, T. (1991). From old boys to men and women of the corporation: The Americanisation and commodification of Australian sport. *Sociology of Sport Journal, 8*(1), 86–94.

McKay, J., & Rowe, D. (1997). Fields of soaps: Rupert v. Kerry as masculine melodrama. *Social Text, 50*(1), 69–86.

Nauright, J., & Phillips, M. G. (1996). A fair go for the fans? Super Leagues, sport ownership and fans in Australia. *Social Alternatives, 15*(4), 43–45.

Nauright, J., & Phillips, M. G. (1997). Us and them: Australian professional sport and resistance to North American ownership and marketing models. *Sport Marketing Quarterly, 6*(1), 33–39.

Nauright, J., & White, P. (1996). "Save our jets": Nostalgia, community, professional sport and nation in contemporary Canada. *AVANTE,* *2*(4), 24–41.

New South Wales Rugby League. (1975). *Annual Report* (p. 4). Sydney Australian Rugby League Archives.

New South Wales Rugby League. (1992). *Annual Report* (pp. 10–11). Sydney Australian Rugby League Archives.

Phillips, M. G. (1995). Football, class and war: The rugby codes in New South Wales, 1907–15. In J. Nauright & T. J. L. Chandler (Eds.), *Making men: Rugby and masculine identity* (pp. 158–180). Essex, UK: Cass.

Phillips, M. G. (1996). Rugby League and club loyalty. In D. Headon & L. Marinos (Eds.), *League of a nation* (pp. 106–111). Sydney: Australian Broadcasting Commission.

Phillips, M. G. (1998). From suburban football to international spectacle: The commodification of Rugby League in Australia, 1907–1995. *Australian Historical Studies, 29*(110), 27–48.

Phillips, M. G., & Hutchins, B. (1998). From independence to reconstituted hegemony: Rugby League and television in Australia. *Journal of Australian Studies, 58,* 134–147.

Phillips, M. G., & Nauright, J. (1999). Sports fan movements to save suburban-based football teams threatened with amalgamation in different football codes in Australia. *International Sport Studies, 21*(1), 23–38.

Ries, I. (1996, September 27). A 796 black hole in Pay TV. *Australian Financial Review,* pp. 47 & 76.

Rowe, D. (1995). *Popular cultures: Rock music, sport and the politics of pleasure.* London: Sage.

Rowe, D. (1997). Rugby League in Australia: The Super League saga. *Journal of Sport and Social Issues, 21*(2), 221–226.

Rowe, D. (1999). *Sport, culture and the media.* Buckingham, UK: Open University Press.

Rowe, D., Lawrence, G., Miller, T., & McKay, J. (1994). Global sport? Core concern and peripheral vision. *Media, Culture & Society, 16*(4), 661–675.

Sage, G. H. (1990). *Power and ideology in American sport: A critical perspective.* Champaign, IL: Human Kinetics.

Schimmel, K., Ingham, A., & Howell, J. (1993). Professional team sport and the American city: Urban politics and franchise relocation. In A. Ingham & J. Loy (Eds.), *Sport and social development* (pp. 211–244). Champaign, IL: Human Kinetics.

Shoebridge, N. (1989, October 13). League's new tack wins converts. *Business Review Weekly,* p. 164.

Stewart, B. (1984). The economic development of the Victorian Football League, 1960–1984. *Sporting Traditions, 2*(1), 2–26.

Stoddart, B. (1997). Convergence: Sport on the information superhighway. *Journal of Sport and Social Issues, 21*(1), 93–102.

Tomlinson, J. (1991). *Cultural imperialism: A critical introduction,* Baltimore, MD: Johns Hopkins University Press.

Wenner, L. A. (1998). Playing the mediasport game. In L. A. Wenner (Ed.), *Mediasport* (pp. 3–13). London: Routledge.

Westfield, M. (2000). *The gatekeepers: The global media battle to control Australia's pay TV.* Annandale, Sydney, Australia: Pluto.

Whannel, G. (1992). *Fields in vision: Television sport and cultural transformation.* London: Routledge.

White, P., Donnelly, P., & Nauright, J. (1997). Citizens, cities and sports teams. *Policy Options, 18*(3), 9–12.

Whitson, D. (1998). Circuits of promotion: Media, marketing and the globalization of sport. In L. A. Wenner (Ed.), *Mediasport* (pp. 57–72). London: Routledge.

Yeates, H. (1995). The league of men: Masculinity, the media and Rugby League Football. *Media Information Australia, 75,* 35–95.

Chapter 8

THE GLOBAL SPORT MASS MEDIA OLIGOPOLY

The Three Usual Suspects and More

Alan Law, Jean Harvey, and Stuart Kemp

In this article, Alan Law, Jean Harvey, and Stuart Kemp discuss the international dimension of global media control by examining the structure of major media conglomerates. Going beyond a consideration of just the "three usual suspects"—Disney, News Corporation, and AOL–TimeWarner—the authors alert us to the breadth and depth of big media's control of sport. They raise serious concerns about the effects of such massive corporate concentration and collaboration on sports and on global culture production and distribution more generally.

Around the World, Around the Clock . . . Virtually every minute of the day, in every time zone on the planet, people are watching, reading and interacting with our products. We're reaching people from the moment they wake up until they fall asleep. We give them their morning weather and traffic reports through our television outlets around the world. We enlighten and entertain them with such newspapers as The New York Post *and* The Times *as they have breakfast, or take the train to work. We update their stock prices and give them the world's biggest news stories every day through such news channels as FOX or Sky News.*

When they shop for groceries after work, they use our SmartSource coupons to cut their family's food bill. And when they get home in the evening, we're there to entertain them with compelling first-run entertainment on FOX or the day's biggest game on our broadcast, satellite and cable networks. Or the best movies from Twentieth Century Fox Film if they want to see a first-run movie. Before going to bed, we give them the latest news, and then they can crawl into bed with one of our best-selling novels from HarperCollins.

—News Corp (1999)

Alan Law, Jean Harvey, and Stuart Kemp, "The Global Sport Mass Media Oligopoly" from *International Review for the Sociology of Sport* 37 (2002): 279–302. Copyright © 2002 by International Sociology of Sport Association and Sage Publications. Reprinted with the permission of Sage Publications, Inc.

Introduction

Contemporary literature on media and globalization of sport argues that professional as well as amateur sport are increasingly integrated into an emerging global 'sports/media complex' (Andrews, 2001; Gruneau and Whitson, 2001; Maguire, 1999; Wenner, 1998; Whitson, 1998). However, empirical evidence in support of this claim has been primarily limited to three major corporations, which have traditionally occupied prime positions in the media oligopoly: News Corp, Disney and AOL–Time Warner. Further, commentary has also stopped short of elucidating the contours of corporate structures which house sport and other interests within conglomerates. These gaps in the literature lead us to further explore two issues. First, we wish to examine the extent of heterogeneity across a sample which goes beyond the three usual suspects. Second, we wish to examine the role of corporate structure in the commerce of signs traditionally conceived in the sport sociology literature as a battle between titans—somewhat akin to battles between 'old rival' sports teams.

Based on the construction of detailed corporate holdings maps, this article traces interlinkages between entities in the sports/media complex. There are two main arguments pursued here. First, while the three 'usual suspects' indeed occupy extensive 'territory', the global sports/media complex is more diverse than the current sociology of sport literature suggests. That is in terms of the number of actors involved, the shape of their corporate structures, as well as the corporate links between them. Second, and drawing on Whitson (1998), corporate structure has itself become a

method of capital accumulation for media/entertainment conglomerates by accelerating the profitability of sports and other symbols through 'synergies' achieved in relatively closed 'circuits of promotion'. While this argument illuminates some dynamics of competitive practice, we also tentatively suggest the emergence of a somewhat different model of intercorporate profitability based on positioning in dense and expanding inter-related supply chains of symbols. In summary, the combined processes of proliferating agencies, markets, 'synergies' and joint ventures are simultaneously expanding the modes of consumption of sport in the world marketplace, as well as the power of the sportsmedia complex to determine what becomes available to people (and how) for consumption. As a result, these trends potentially reduce the range of choices among distinct sport spectacle products available, as well as the space for public information and deliberation on these same products.

The next section briefly reviews the most recent literature on sport and media infrastructure in relation to the issues we wish to address. Then, the discussion turns to the corporate structure of what we argue are the major players of the sport/media oligopoly, to make the point that expansion of media delivery systems also means fragmentation of the oligopoly. We then offer a characterization of the emerging oligopoly that departs somewhat from traditional concepts. That is, the proliferation of multidimensional profit zones enabled by new technologies, commercial practices and internationally mobile capital has shifted the terms of competition from between relatively independent dominant players to between consumption supply chains, while reducing the diversity of sport spectacle available for consumption.

Review of Literature

The growth of media control of sports, accelerating during the 1990s, has received attention from a number of authors in the sport sociology literature. At the level of political economy, most agree that the sports media complex is controlled by a small number of corporations, which own or lease the visual product from source to point of consumption by a globally expanding audience, and then rent out 'their viewers' and listeners' attention' (Sage, 1998: 123). If audience reach is broad and deep enough, generated advertising revenues allegedly extend well beyond the billions of dollars paid out.

Market presence for media interests is obtained in a number of ways, each adding to the diversity of inter-relationships making up the global complex. The types of relationships, in Maguire's words, vary 'over time and within and between continents . . . (and) from one sport to the next'. This being said, sport relationships with media are predominantly cemented by exclusive media coverage rights and equity ownership, both of which exert high levels of control. The important point to make here, however, is that equity ownership brings revenue streams in the form of savings on coverage rights, revenues from multi-platforms distribution and cross-promotion of within-conglomerate product (Andrews, 2001; Gruneau and Whitson, 2001; Harvey et al., 2001).

Whitson (1998) notes a globalization of business practices that contain growth functions dependent on 'synergies' derived through cross-promotion of commodities and achievable through corporate integration. Corporate integration enables 'product lines' to promote each other through mutual association (Alger, 1998; Andrews, 2001; Whitson, 1998). In this context, sports teams (in some cases entire leagues) supply content that is used to promote other contents such as television shows or other commodities, which also act to promote sports. Whitson refers to these 'circuits of promotion' (Whitson, 1998), a function of conglomerate structure, as one of the more compelling reasons pushing the rise of media corporation ownership of sports teams. Bellamy (1998: 46–7) argues that the predominance of integrated corporate structure is a feature of a 'new oligopoly' within the United States, emerging from the conglomerate business practices identified by Whitson as an increasingly standard practice in global competition.

Some authors argue that those engaged in sport, either as athletes, teams, leagues and even nations, have lost control of their own product, now known in media circles as mere 'software', in the process of its commodification, increasing in intensity along with the vertical integration of sports product media distribution conglomerates. Carrington et al. (1999: 1) refer to this dynamic as 'high-jacking' of sovereignty. Maguire (1999: 150) argues that the interdependencies between the key groups making up the global sports media complex (sports teams, marketing companies and transnational corporations) have placed sports teams in dependent positions, where they no longer have control over the nature and form in which their sport is televised, reported and covered. To this we might add observations of slippage of control over how, when, where and what sports are played (e.g. Fox's purchase of British Rugby League and consequent shifting of seasonal play as well as names of teams; or Kerry Packer's night cricket).

Further, the global circulation of sport through its electronic delivery disconnects audiences from traditional forms of cultural affiliation based on locality and dynamic that drives the entire complex. Several writers have commented on the disconnection of sport from space attendant on the rise of global media and the consequent expansion of commodity markets (e.g. Miller et al., 1999; Rowe et al., 1994). Rupert Murdoch claims with glee that sports are his 'battering ram' (quoted in Andrews, 2001) for entry into new markets because of the audience share they demand. This does not automatically imply cultural homogenization but is arguably a disruptive dynamic causing cultural hybridization (Pieterse, 1994), giving rise to new forms of cultural space (Morley and Robins, 1995; Richardson and Meinhof, 1999).

Alger (1998) identifies five dimensions through which we can characterize and compare conglomerate structures important for oligopolistic competition in the media sector: (1) horizontal integration (concentration with one media, e.g. multiple newspapers held by the same corporation); (2) vertical integration (ownership of the entire supply chain from product to consumer delivery); (3) product and service extension into other media realms (e.g. extension from newspapers to broadcast to cable, etc.); (4) geographic market extension (e.g. from one locality to another, between nations, across nations, etc.); (5) Industrial-media conglomerate structure (financial links with previously unaligned businesses

for the purpose of asset acquisition), including industry inter-relationships. The following section sets out and discusses the corporate maps of six conglomerates presented here as case studies. These are News Corporation, Disney, AOL–Time Warner, Viacom, Bertelsmann, and Vivendi-Universal. Each case is presented in a visual map and verbally presented according to Alger's dimensions. Following the presentation of the six cases, discussion focuses on structural similarities, dis-similarities and, most importantly, inter-conglomerate relationships.

Case Studies

News Corp

As of 30 June 2001 News Corp had total assets of US$42.9 billion and had achieved annual revenues of roughly US$13.8 billion (News Corp, 2001), making it the largest and among the most diversified of global media entertainment corporations. As can be readily seen in Figure 1, News Corp exhibits high degrees of *horizontal integration* in delivery platforms including print media, television broadcasting, cable television and Internet.

Product and service extension is located primarily in media properties with sports-oriented 'product' for distribution. What we now know as Rupert Murdoch's News Corp was initially capitalized from print media inherited from his father in 1952 and aggressively expanded on a global scale in the mid-1980s. Following the massive expansion of the print empire, Murdoch acquired delivery platforms, primarily through takeovers, to progressively expand his share of the attention of 'consumers'— translatable to advertising revenue. According to Murdoch, sport, with a particular

FIGURE 1   *News Corp corporate holdings (simplified)*

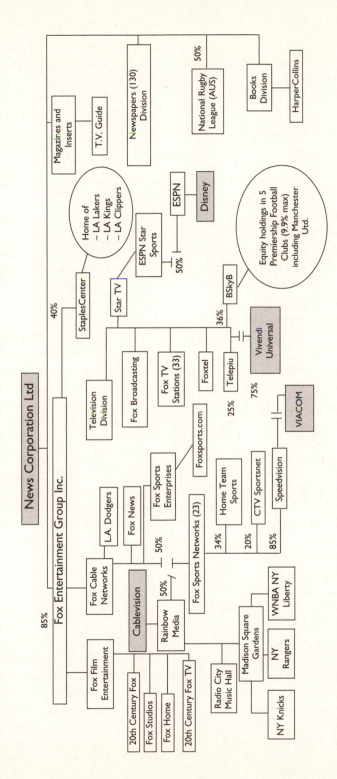

Note: Unless otherwise shown, holdings represents 100% ownership.

Sources: Corporate website, Business Wire, Hoovers Online and Annual reports.

Updated from: Harvey et al., 2001: 444.

emphasis on football, has been his 'battering ram' to establish the competitive success of his media properties.

Vertical integration for News Corp is dominated by sport product—controlled through global and local broadcasting rights as well as equity interest. News Corp assumed control of the Los Angeles Dodgers in March 1998 and has an interest in the New York Rangers and Knicks under its alliance with Rainbow Media and Madison Square Gardens (News Corp, 1999). News Corp also has full ownership of Los Angeles' Dodger Stadium, and a 40 percent interest in the US$300 million Staples Center, home to the Los Angeles Kings, Lakers and Clippers. Further equity holdings include 9.9 percent (the most allowable) of Chelsea, Manchester United and Manchester City football clubs, 5 percent of Sunderland and 9.1 percent of Leeds (*Guardian,* 2000). News Corp also owns the British Rugby League as well as 50 percent of the Australian National Rugby League formed through merger with Super League and Australian Rugby League in 1997.

These equity interests certainly enhance access to content material for expanding delivery mechanisms. However, broadcast rights continue to play the dominant role in acquiring sport products. The importance for the right to broadcast American football (NFL) is underscored by the $395 million increase over the previous contract (Landreth, 2000) and that the league now has the right to renegotiate its eight-year contract after only five years. Further, 71 of the 76 teams in the American big four leagues have agreements with Fox Sports Regional Networks (Andrews, 2001) for local broadcast. Exclusive broadcasting rights are held for the Super Bowl, NHL games, the MLB World Series, as well as the World Cup of Cricket and English Premiership Football. News Corp's acquisition of Twentieth Century Fox in the 1980s has enabled the company to employ its own film and television content onto its worldwide platforms.

In terms of *geographic market extension,* News Corp is both an international (across national borders) and intra-national (within national borders) corporation. Holdings that distribute across borders include virtually all media, while those contained within borders include mostly national papers and domestic radio and television news programming. In addition to presence in Europe, North America and the Antipodes, the last decade has seen expansion into India, Latin America and China. One important characteristic of News Corp expansion has been its willingness to ignore popular opposition and circumvent national regulation. For example, News Corp was able to skirt British regulations that no newspaper proprietor should own more than 20 percent of a TV company (in this case BSkyB) by claiming that its broadcast actually emanated from Luxembourg where the satellite network was based. Initial market failure, no matter how colossal, is little deterrent. The $1.2 billion BSkyB lost between 1989 and 1992 was absorbed as a short-term cost of market expansion (APTN, 2000: 6). Football was leveraged as a cultural product that would inevitably attract domestic and international paying customers to News Corp's satellite services. Here we can see News Corp using vertical integration for its geographic market extension strategy.

News Corp *industry inter-relationships* are numerous. News Corp has extensive and critical linkages with major global competitors including AOL–Time Warner, Disney, and Vivendi-Universal through joint venture investments, namely Rainbow Media (American), ESPN Star Sports (American and Asian networks) and BSkyB (British). ESPN Star Sports is a 50–50 owned Asian-based network that expands each conglomerate's series of global networks and subsequent consumer audiences. In 2001 News Corp entered into yet another joint venture with Vivendi through the merging of its Stream subsidiary, its 50 percent owned Italian pay TV operator, with Telepiu, then owned at the 75 percent level by Vivendi-Universal (News Corp, 2001). In 2002, News Corp purchased all Vivendi assets in Telepiu. Such strategic alliances and venture of a profoundly global magnitude enable News Corp to reach approximately three-quarters of the wired world. (Baker, 1998).

Disney

Disney entertainment products are rooted in American values and tradition. Examination of Disney's corporate structure reveals dynamics at play that are different but related to those of News Corp. News Corp's vertical structure was rooted in the use of content product to boost the profitability of distribution networks. In contrast, Disney began with content product and simultaneously expanded both product and distribution networks.

Horizontal integration is substantial for Disney across entertainment product and distribution divisions, readily discernible from its corporate map. Founded on film and television production, Disney has ventured into the Internet and the world of sport substantially in the last 10 years. Of particular interest is the density of retail involvement at both the product and distribution channel ends of the supply chain. This feature in particular adds a cross-promotional dimension not included in News Corp's empire.

As mentioned above, Disney's roots in image production have meant the emergence of multiple lines of *verticle integration* connecting product with audience. Sport is only one among several quite dense product lines. We are able to observe an array of sport rights, properties and related distribution channels, similar in structure to News Corp. Disney's two major North American franchise teams include 100 percent of the Mighty Ducks for $50m from the NHL in 1992 (Landreth, 2000) and 25 percent of the Anaheim Angels (then the California Angels) from Gene Autry in 1996 (Johnson, 1998). Disney's broadcasting portfolio flows through ESPN and ABC networks. ABC holds rights to over $6 billion worth of sports coverage in college football, PGA Golf, the NHL, NFL and Major League Soccer over eight years. ESPN extends this trend with no less than four major broadcast agreements. Two of these (Major League Soccer and the PGA) are shared with the sister ABC network, but the NFL and MLB contracts stand alone at $4.8 billion for eight years and $440 million for four years respectively (Landreth, 2000).

Disney's Internet activities use sport to distribute Disney symbols. ESPN formed an agreement with the NFL in 1996 to co-produce the league's site in return for shared revenue and the opportunity to use the site for promoting other Disney interests, namely ESPN and its various media properties. A similar arrangement is in place with both the NBA and NASCAR. Infoseek and the other Disney web ventures all cross-promote the league sites of the NBA, NHL and NASCAR. Thus an alliance has been formed between these groups along with ABC.com, ABCNEWS.com and the Disney and ESPN site.

The cross-promotional capabilities of Disney's empire that characterize its product and *service extension strategy* are substantial to say the least. Disney distributes, promotes and buys its own products. As much as possible, the conglomerate keeps manufacturing and production 'in house', enabling the 23 internal divisions to work together and for one another (Ricker, 1996). Organized under three main umbrellas, Theme Parks and Resorts, Filmed Entertainment, and Consumer Products, Disney's assets are categorized most distinctly compared to other conglomerate exemplars. Interestingly, coherence of business lines does not result in corporate 'silos', rather, it enables clear and easy distribution of overarching Disney symbols. Branded products were responsible for $67 million in worldwide character merchandise licensing in 1996 alone (Ricker, 1996).

Figure 2 shows substantial *inter-industry relationships*, even with traditional competitors. Perhaps the most important of these is the 50–50 joint ownership of ESPN with News Corp, created in November of 1996, extending Disney's reach to over 45 million homes throughout India, Taiwan, the Philippines, China, Thailand, Malaysia and a number of other Asian and Pacific nations.

AOL–Time Warner

AOL–Time Warner is a conglomerate with three distinct components, representing the merged interests of four corporations, making for highly dense *horizontal integration* in media production and distribution interests. Figure 3 shows the reasonably coherent clustering of: sport content production within the Turner group; magazine, book and movie production and distribution within the Time Warner Holding group; and most interestingly, the suite of 'blue chip' components of the electronic distribution system within the AOL family.

With the exception of *Time, vertical integration* has been a growth strategy of each independent corporation and substantially amplified through *the product and service extension* strategy achieved by merger. There is not enough room here to retrace the growth strategies of each corporation in detail, however, each will be briefly canvassed to illustrate the core point.

Time magazine was founded in 1923 as the world's first news weekly and later expanded sideways with *Life, Fortune* and then *Sports Illustrated.* Warner Brothers Motion Picture Co. was also incorporated in 1923. However, over the course of the 20th century, Warner Brothers expanded both horizontally and vertically into television and film production and distribution along with music labels in over 70 countries. Turner Broadcasting Systems joined the conglomerate in 1996. It should be noted that the purchase of the Turner properties was directly aimed at adding branded material to the existing holdings of Time Warner so that content could be distributed across a greater number of platforms and cross-promotional strategy could be extended (*The Economist,* 2000: 22). Turner brought to the table the Home Box Office network (HBO), CNN (arguably the world's first global news gathering and disseminating broadcaster) and other cable and entertainment properties including the Atlanta Braves, Atlanta Thrashers, Atlanta Hawks, the Phillips Arena, the Goodwill Games, World Championship Wrestling. The latter two properties represent Turner's attempts to create his own

FIGURE 2 *Disney Corp corporate holdings (simplified)*

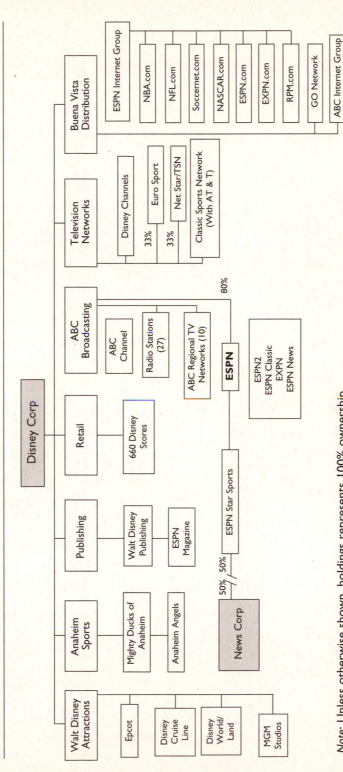

Note: Unless otherwise shown, holdings represents 100% ownership.

Sources: Corporate websites, Hoovers Online and Annual Reports.

FIGURE 3 *AOL–Time Warner corporate holdings (simplified)*

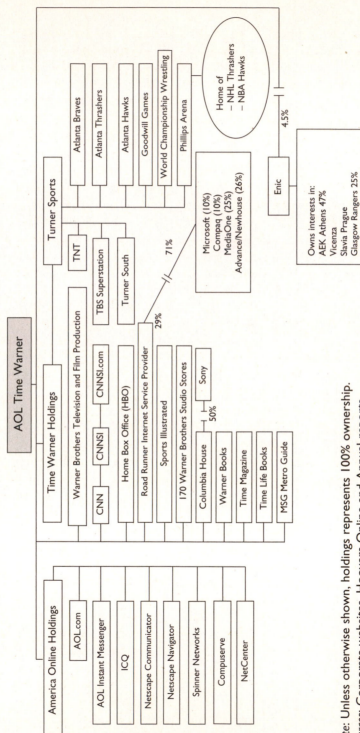

Note: Unless otherwise shown, holdings represents 100% ownership.
Sources: Corporate websites, Hoovers Online and Annual reports.

sport content, avoiding expensive broadcast rights and scheduling issues.

In January 2000, AOL joined the group. AOL began in 1985 with 500,000 subscribers. In 2000, it had over 17,000,000. Acquisition of Instant Messenger added 35,000,000 users (Krigel, 1999). The addition of Netscape Communicator and Navigator enabled AOL to capture a substantial proportion of the Internet access market. In addition to its primary service, providing consumers with access to the Internet, AOL went to great pains to keep the user within its 'walled garden' of content in order to attract the consumer to its line of e-products and services. Nearly 40 percent of AOL users' time is spent in this area (*The Economist*, 2000).

Inter-corporate links are extensive to say the least. AOL–Time Warner collaborates with Microsoft, Compaq, MediaOne and Advance/Newhouse in a combined venture to provide high-speed Internet access to its collective group of customers. This service, Road Runner ISP, was launched in 1998 and for Time Warner's Chairman and CEO Gerald Levin was envisioned as a means to 'develop a powerful, branded package of content that will become the high-speed online service of choice for our customers'. Other links of note include News Corp's content agreement with AOL–Time Warner's Road Runner. This agreement sees News Corp's online branch, News America Digital Publishing (formed in November 1997) provide news and sports programming for the Road Runner service and its 180,000 customers (Business Wire, 1999). The last links worthy of consideration are Philip's investment in the Hawks and Thrashers arena ($180 million over 20 years) (Landreth, 2000) and Sony's 50 percent interest in Columbia House.

The merger between Time Warner and AOL attempts to combine brand name media, entertainment, news and broadband delivery systems with the extensive array of AOL Internet franchises and the infrastructure itself that reaches such a large online consumer audience. The cross-promotional strategy that the conglomerate will be able to achieve is vastly superior to other members of the oligopoly as no other company has access to such a large Internet infrastructure.

Consolidation of 'branding' is perhaps best illustrated in reference to sport with the joining of the CNN news reputation and the success of *Sports Illustrated* magazine. Here, the two have been merged for a sports news cable network (CNNSI was launched in December 1996) and a website devoted to sports news (CNNSI.com launched in July 1997) (CCNSI.com 1997). Such cross-promotional activity is a key ingredient in the synergy of such new and old media.

In terms of *geographic and market extension*, although AOL–Time Warner's properties are mainly North American based and aimed at North American markets (especially their sport-based properties), some of their most high-profile holdings are very much global in scope. The emergence of CNN as an international news gathering and disseminating source epitomizes their eagerness to be a transnational company. International AOL alliances with other members of the oligopoly exist. AOL received a $75 million payment from Bertelsmann as part of an agreement to expand the two companies' online service in Europe via the CompuServe platform. This agreement dictates Bertelsmann's online presence in Europe (CompuServe Europe), but also extends AOL–Time Warner's consumer reach.

Viacom

The new Viacom will be the 21st Century media company, with strong brands that will lead the industry in all aspects of our operations, a wealth of world-class content in film, television, radio, publishing and the Internet and the best distribution system in the business in both the established and new media. (Milner, 1999: B9)

Specializing in TV and film, Viacom produces movies via Paramount Pictures and television via Spelling Entertainment. It also owns half of the United Paramount Network (UPN) and is a major player in the cable television industry with cable networks like MTV, VH1 and Nickelodeon, as well as pay-per-view channel Showtime, all of which have large subscriber bases. Viacom also extends its grasp on entertainment into the home with its 82 percent ownership of the Blockbuster video rental chain that was acquired (US$8.2 billion later) in an effort to raise capital for the 1994 purchase of Paramount. Viacom's global strategy and ability to cross-promote are ideal. Youth-oriented Paramount films are promoted heavily on MTV, with other rental tie-ins following at Blockbuster once the film is out of the theatre.

The history of Viacom itself is long and complex as it is the result of a series of mergers and acquisitions dating back 90 years. The original conglomerate was CBS, but after the US Federal Communications Commission (FCC) ruled in 1970 that networks could not own cable systems and TV stations in the same market, CBS formed Viacom to take care of its programme syndication division. One of the most recent moves by Viacom was to reclaim CBS for US$34.5 billion and this again marries a large media entertainment company with a well-recognized media platform.

CBS has long been a television powerhouse in North America and its recent sport-related gain was its acquisition of NFL rights from the previous holder, NBC. The US$4 billion deal accompanies the network's new venture, 1999's US$6 billion deal with the NCAA for exclusive rights across all media platforms to the college basketball championship tournament.

Viacom's access to sport content was the CBS Sports acquisition. CBS sports gained exclusive rights (broadcast, cable, radio, satellite) to the NCAA college basketball championship tournament for 11 years, confirming its spot among the sport-media elite. CBS also owns the rights to the AFC games of the NFL. Viacom also owns 18 percent of the Internet sports information site, Sportsline.com. Through these moves Viacom has positioned itself with sports programming for its film, television and Internet platforms.

Just as previous mergers have extended media platforms into cyberspace, Viacom continues to expand its presence on the Internet in many cases by utilizing similar news and sport content for online properties such as CBS.Sportsline.com and MVP.com. In terms of *geographic market extension*, a number of Viacom products are available to a global audience. Paramount pictures, CBS news and sports Internet services, Famous Players Theatres and music programming are the strengths of Viacom's international presence. This content is primarily American-based and rooted in American culture but proliferated worldwide as American cultural goods. There is little evidence to suggest that Viacom alters or reconfigures its products to suit the tastes and needs of its consumers worldwide.

FIGURE 4 *Viacom corporate holdings*

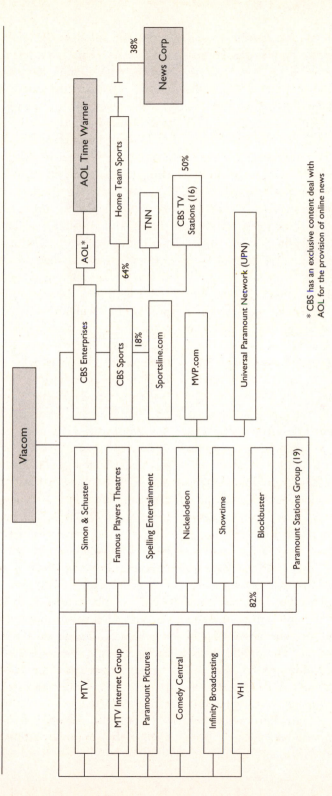

Note: Unless otherwise shown, holdings represents 100% ownership.
Sources: Corporate websites, Hoovers Online and Annual reports.

In order to foster its *industry inter-rela-tionships*, Viacom has completed a deal that would see it provide music content to America Online, which links it with competitor, AOL–Time Warner. The deal sees AOL develop content for its sites based on Viacom's VH1 music network. AOL users will have exclusive multimedia and cross-promotions with Viacom music properties. Terms of the agreement for both companies are unclear but appear to benefit each in the form of additional content for AOL and exposure for Viacom (Seminario, 1997).

Bertelsmann AG

German company Bertelsmann began to publish hymnals in 1835 and has evolved into one of the largest media companies in the world, in a virtual tie with News Corp. In terms of *horizontal integration*, Bertelsmann, with the acquisition of Random House Publishing, is now the largest publisher of English-language books in the world. Bertelsmann's properties can be categorized under five headings: books/publishing, magazines, music, broadcast and multimedia. Since its inception, Bertelsmann has acquired numerous publishing houses whose most famous names include Bantam Doubleday and Random House. The conglomerate purchased Random House in 1998, 51 percent of Bantam Books in 1977 (and the rest in 1981). Bertelsmann's publishing holdings have been integrated into their multimedia division through their 41 percent acquisition of barnesandnoble.com, the online bookseller. Magazine holdings amount to 28 publications in North America and Germany (*Columbia Journalism Review*, 2000). Bertelsmann owns over 200 music labels through BMG Entertainment.

Bertelsmann has tried diligently to make the Internet central to its media properties, and their 50–50 joint venture with AOL in creating CompuServe Europe was one such move. However, the stability of this move is now in doubt as the AOL–Time Warner merger may take exception to being of such assistance to one of its biggest publishing competitors. Thus, the AOL–Time Warner merger may spoil an important part of Bertelsmann's global strategy (*The Economist*, 2000: 24).

In terms of vertical integration, UFA Sports' parent company, UFA, was purchased by Bertelsmann in 1964 and has become a leading European TV and film producer. Through its extensive network of marketing agreements and exclusive broadcast rights, UFA provides content to Bertelsmann's numerous RTL networks in England, France, Germany, the Netherlands and Hungary. UFA Sport is the marketing partner of close to 300 football clubs in Europe and 45 football associations in Europe and Asia, as well as 12 clubs in the German Bundesliga. The company has retained the European broadcast rights to sporting events such as qualifying matches for Euro 2000, the Asian Cup, The World Cup, and the UEFA cup. UFA Sports also covers tennis as the European rights holder of Wimbledon, the US Open and the Davis Cup (UFA, 2000). With reference to multimedia, Bertelsmann's joint venture with America Online was initiated in 1995 and this helped bring about AOL CompuServe Europe and AOL Australia. This venture is the company's most important new media move and aims to incorporate content from other holdings.

In terms of *geographic and market extension*, Bertelsmann's venture with AOL,

FIGURE 5   *Bertelsmann AG corporate holdings*

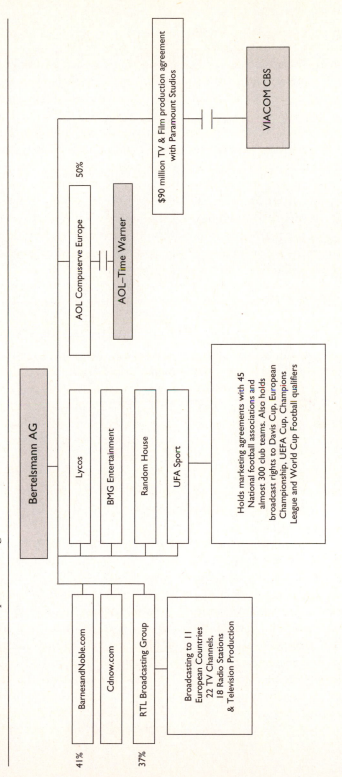

Note: Unless otherwise shown, holdings represent 100% ownership.
Sources: Corporate websites, Hoovers Online and Annual reports.

BMG, Lycos and others has added North American content to a complex European company. This synthesis can also be seen as having added a European flavour to the mix of mostly American corporations that have penetrated the sport mass media complex. The Internet is a crucial element of Bertelsmann's global expansion strategy. Of note here is that, in the search for content, it is not expected that Bertelsmann will seek a major merger, as has been the trend. As Bertelsmann is not a publicly traded company (and consequently less susceptible to a hostile or shareholder-forced take-over) it is more likely to continue its series of joint ventures and alliances to expand its content and platform growth.

In terms of *industry inter-relationships*, a further co-operative venture with the competition is Bertelsmann's agreement with Paramount (a division of Viacom). This $90 million venture (UFA, 2000) has UFA working with Paramount Studios for the production of made-for-television films. In producing content for European and American audiences in Hollywood, the venture is an example of production and consumption patterns that are not dependent on states, but rather global agreements. Alliances with AOL and others have provided assets to Bertelsmann not otherwise available within the existing conglomerate and at the same time met the needs of the mostly 'new media' companies by expanding their consumer base worldwide. However, viewing the AOL-Bertelsmann agreement as sleeping with the enemy (in reference to AOL's merger with news giant Time Warner) would be premature as Time Warner may have other plans once their merger has been consolidated.

Vivendi-Universal

As of May 2002, the latest merger in the global media/entertainment complex being put in place is the acquisition of Seagram/Universal by Vivendi. The new conglomerate brings together a number of elements spanning the range of entertainment-based and distribution platforms for the expressed purpose to create a European based AOL–Time Warner. Like other new conglomerates, this strategy represents a way to gain leverage from already dense horizontal integration by growth in product and service extension.

Seagram's empire began during the Depression as a distillery and grew to become one of the world's largest liquor companies. In 1995, Seagram purchased 80 percent of Universal, which added an entirely new dimension to Seagram's 'family' of entertainment product and image distribution capabilities, resulting in four global business units known as: Music, Filmed Entertainment, Recreation, and Spirits and Wine (Seagram, 2000).

Universal Music is the world's largest recorded music distributor and operates globally. Universal Studio's Networks division established in 1997 oversees 13th Street, which is broadcast to France, Germany and Spain where it has 1.3 million, 900,000 and 700,000 viewers respectively. It also operates the Studio Universal Movie Network in Italy and Germany, the Sci Fi network in the UK to an audience of 5.4 million, and the USA Network in Brazil and Latin America to 11 million homes (Universal, 2000). In the US Universal has distribution control over a library of 24,000 TV episodes and 4000 motion pictures. Apart from the proliferation of its main TV

FIGURE 6   *Vivendi–Universal corporate holdings (simplified)*

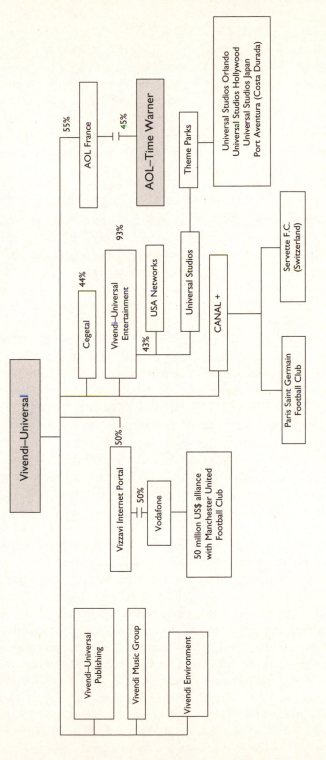

Note: Unless otherwise shown, holdings represents 100% ownership.
Sources: Corporate websites, Hoovers Online and Annual reports.

shows and movies, Universal produces programming for its international audiences with local tastes in mind. Universal's website describes this strategy in the following manner: 'Universal Studios Networks is building global television brands, created and managed locally for distinct consumer audiences' (Universal, 2000). Universal is also responsible for the licensing of merchandising rights to their film and television properties.

Beginning in 1853, Compagnie Generale des Eaux supplied water to Paris, Lyons, Venice, Nantes and Constantinople. Expansion of the company came in the waste management, energy, transport, construction and property sectors. By 1976, water distribution comprised 46 percent of revenues, civil engineering and construction 28 percent, and energy 12 percent (Vivendi, 2000). Expansion into the communications industry first came in 1983 when Generale des Eaux teamed up with the Havas media group to create Canal+ that also extended vertical integration through ownership of the Paris Saint-Germain football club. In 1997 this alliance was taken to the next level when Generale des Eaux purchased a 30 percent stake in Havas publications. With the company's properties now extremely diversified, Generale des Eaux formed Vivendi to control its holdings other than those based on water management. Vivendi's formation in 1998 created a global company that operates utilities (Water, Energy, Waste management and Transport) and Communications (Telecommunications, Publishing and Multimedia). This move also included the incorporation of Havas into the Vivendi conglomerate (Vivendi, 2000). With a large European consumer base (14 million subscribers to Canal+ and 8 million to SFR),

Vivendi's next moves were aimed at penetrating the North American market and acquiring content and more distribution platforms. A first step in this direction was made with the acquisition of 43 percent of USA Networks (Reuters, 2001). In 2002, Havas was regrouped under Vivendi-Universal Publishing along with other publishing assets.

Product and service expansion: the June 2000 take-over of Seagram/Universal by Vivendi SA valued Seagram at US$33 billion and illustrated the strength of the existing oligopoly in that the company had to merge in order to compete with other media-entertainment powerhouses of similar or greater magnitude. Further it was necessary for Vivendi to acquire substantial content (in this case the music and movies of Universal and Polygram) for its already considerable communications platforms.

In terms of *geographic market extension*, existing Vivendi companies Vizzavi and Canal Plus enable the new French conglomerate to tap into 80 million European mobile and TV subscribers who currently consume sports products on mobile, satellite and pay-per-view bases. The acquisition of 43 percent of USA Networks firmly set Vivendi-Universal's foot in the US TV market. Vivendi-Universal rivals the three main American-based media conglomerates and, as a European-based company, the merger illustrates the internationalization of the mass media oligopoly. Rather than the majority of media power emanating from the west, it is now apparent that there is a global dynamic at work with production and capital flowing between states like the US and France in this case. The addition of Universal content and networks will add to this audience base substantially. Like Bertelsmann, Vivendi-Universal is now a truly global media conglomerate with an assortment of products and holdings that are not produced in one setting only, and both accommodate local tastes and transcend state boundaries as well.

In terms of *industry inter-relationships,* Canal Plus's coverage of sport and Vivendi-Universal's joint venture with Vodafone that sees Vodafone interacting with Manchester United Football Club properties for $50 million are worthy of note. Vivendi-Universal's sports programming is primarily European-based and includes football, rugby, hockey, basketball and boxing. In terms of indirect sports content, it is vital to recognize Vivendi's 25 percent stake in BSkyB, Murdoch's leviathan of British sport and Vivendi-Universal competitor. While Vivendi-Universal may not own as many sports rights and properties as their competitors, their merger is facilitating new platforms and technologies for access to sports information and related content beyond direct ownership.

Conclusion

For the sport spectacle consumers, horizontal and vertical integration within conglomerates, as well as their interconnectedness, may amount to bad news. The following trends, some of which are already in place, may indeed unfold in the upcoming years. (1) If the number of producers collapses as the dense web of relationships expands, there may be a diminution of the diversity of available sport spectacle, jeopardizing the extent of the world's sport-cultural heritage. (2) The integration of sport entities into media/entertainment conglomerates may reduce the availability of sport spectacle to its commodified forms, the remaining being increasingly indistinguishable from it (as we

already witness with the broadcasting of the Olympic Games). (3) Further integration of these cultural supply chains may lead to a relative disappearance of critical accounts of the sport spectacle, thus eliminating what is left from the already limited freedom of the sport press and therefore jeopardizing the structured rights of the sport consumers to 'independent' sport information.

Moreover, for countries like Canada, France, Germany, Britain and more so for Third World countries, even for emerging new forces in the world's economy like China, media conglomerates are pushing national cultural policies and to an even greater extent national mass media policies to their last retrenchments. Indeed, with satellite television and Internet technologies, media/entertainment are no longer concerned by these policies since borders, national territories, do not exist for them. For example, LaFeber underlines that CNN does not divide its market between domestic US and foreign, but into regions of the world. Ted Turner even banned the word 'foreign' from being used in CNN coverage (LaFeber, 1999).

In the face of such flows of symbols, catalysed by corporate structure as profit technology, there seems little room for national cultural sovereignty and hence access to a state-centred politics of critique. Perhaps the only alternative left for countries as coherent entities is to make sure that they are represented in the new mass media by encouraging if not subsidizing national/local production of films and television broadcasts nationally produced—thus entering these circuits of promotion at strategic points. However, as suggested by New and LeGrand (1999), the acquisition and control of exclusive broadcasting rights of premium sports events by these conglomerates creates 'natural monopolies' in specific markets, therefore holding consumers hostage. Perhaps national as well as international media regulatory policy is called for, such as Britain's 'crown jewel' list reserving certain sports events for free-to-air distribution. However, in the current deregulated world economy, sport spectacle consumers will remain, for a long time, easy targets for those gradually filling in every moment of their attention.

This article has illuminated several facets of the sport/media complex that advocate caution when over-characterizing the operation of circuits of promotion and certainly emphasizes the need to look beyond the three usual suspects in order to grasp important features of the global sports/media complex. However, the article was only able to scratch the surface of how this web operates. We are yet to explore exactly how symbol combination operates differently in closed and open circuits of promotion. We are yet to explore in detail how patterns of corporate shape-shifting affect the stability of branding. We are yet to explore the extent to which corporate interlinkages enable or distort circuits of promotion across profit zones dominated by multiple interests. We have also presented a very limited number of cases begging questions of penetration of these practices elsewhere, particularly Asia. Further, the role of sports teams, leagues and stadiums in corporate profit models certainly invites us to question the efficacy of purchasing our last shred of control through expensive private and public subsidies taken at the gate or from the tax return. Finally, structured investigation into the impact of such concentration of media properties on the content of the sport spectacle is greatly needed.

Note

1. Corporate maps represent condensed versions of empires that, if presented in their full detail, would obscure the overall structures.

References

Alger, D. (1998) *Megamedia*. Lanham, MD: Rowman & Littlefield.

Andrews, D.L. (2001) 'Sport', in R. Maxwell (ed.) *Culture Works: Essays on the Political Economy of Culture*. Minneapolis: University of Minnesota Press.

AOL.com (2000) *History*. Retrieved 28 Sept. 2002 from http://www.aol.com/nethelp/misc/history.html

Asia Pacific Technology Network (2000) *A Multimedia Global Empire: Changing Technology, Politics and Commercial Strategy in the Globalization of Murdoch's Newscorporation*. Retrieved 29 Sept. from http://www.aptn.org/ibis/newscorps.htm

Baker, R. (1998) 'Murdoch's Mean Machine', *Columbia Journalism Review*. Retrieved 5 Jan 2000 from http://www.cjr.org/98/3/murdoch

Bellamy, R. (1998) 'The Evolving Television Sports Marketplace', in L. Wenner (ed.) *Media Sport*. New York: Routledge.

Business Wire (1999) *News Corporation's News America Digital Publishing and Road Runner Announce Content and Distribution Partnership*. Retrieved 10 Feb. 2000 from http://www.businesswire.com/webbox/bw.021799/1103022.htm

Carrington, B., Sugden, J. and Tomlinson, A. (1999) 'Network Football: Trans-national Capital and the Incorporation of World Football', paper presented at the annual conference of the NASSS, Cleveland, OH, 3–6 Nov.

CNNSI.com (1997) 'CNN and Sports Illustrated Deliver Sports News with Immediacy and Depth', *CNN Sports Illustrated*. Retrieved 21 Feb. 2000 from http://www.cnnsi.com/about_us/index.html

Columbia Journalism Review (2000) 'Media Owners, Bertelsmann'. Retrieved 29 Sept. 2000 from http://www.cjr.org/owners/bertelsmann.asp#magazines

The Economist (2000) 'The Net Gets Real' (5 Jan.) 354 (8153): 22–4.

Gruneau, R. and Whitson, D. (2001) 'Upmarket Continentalism: Major League Sport, Promotional Culture, and Corporate Integration', in V. Mosco and D. Schiller (eds.) *Continental Order? Integrating North America for Cybercapitalism.* Lanham, MD: Rowman & Littlefield.

Guardian (2000) 'BSkyB's Grip on Premiership Tightens' (3 March). Retrieved 29 Sept 2000 from http://www.guardian.co.uk

Harvey, J., Law, A. and Cantelon, M. (2001) 'North American Professional Sport Franchises Ownership Patterns and Global Entertainment Conglomerates', *Sociology of Sport Journal* 18(4): 435–57.

Johnson, T. (1998) 'Autry is Rememberd as a Man Who helped Shape OC'. Retrieved 2000 from http://www.angelsbaseball.com/history/autry/tribute.html

Krigel, B.L. (1999) 'Microsoft Plays Catch-up with Instant Messenger' (19 July). Retrieved 28 Sept. 2000 from http://www.canada.cnet.com/news/0–1005–200–345065.html

LaFeber, W. (1999) *Michael Jordan and the New Global Capitalism.* London: Norton.

Landreth, N. (2000) 'Broadcast Rights'. Retrieved 28 Jan. 2000 from http://www.foxsports.com/business/resources/broadcast

Maguire, J. (1999). *Global Sport: Identities, Societies, Civilizations.* Cambridge: Polity Press.

Miller, T., Lawrence, G, McKay, J. and Rowe, D. (1999) 'Modifying the Sign: Sport and Globalization', *Social Text* 17(3): 15–32.

Milner, B. (1999) 'CBS Merges with Viacom in Blockbuster Deal Worth $34.5 Billion', *Globe and Mail* (Toronto, 9 Aug.): B9.

Morley, D. and Robins, K. (1995) *Spaces of Identity: Global Media, Electronic Landscapes, and Cultural Boundaries.* London: Routledge.

New, B. and Le Grand, J. (1999) 'Monopoly in Sports Broadcasting', *Policy Studies* 20(1): 23–6.

News Corporation (1999) *Around the World Annual Report 1999.*

News Corporation (2001) *Annual Report 2001.*

Pieterse, J.N. (1994) 'Globalisation as Hybridisation', *International Sociology* 9(2): 161–84.

Reuters (2001) 'Vivendi renforce sa position aux Etats-Unis' (Vivendi solidifies its position in the USA), *Le Devoir* (18 Dec.): B3.

Richardson, K. and Meinhof, U.H. (1999) *Worlds in Common: Television Discourse in a Changing Europe.* London: Routledge.

Ricker, A. (1996) *Critical Arts* 10(1). Retrieved 27 Sept. 2000 from http://www.und.ac.za/und/ccms/articles/ricker.htm

Rowe, D., Lawrence, G., Miller, T. and McKay, J. (1994) 'Global Sport? Core Concern and Peripheral Vision', *Media Culture and Society* 16: 661–75.

Sage, G. (1998) *Power and Ideology in American Sport.* Champaign, IL: Human Kinetics.

Seagram (2000) *Overview.* Retrieved 20 September 2000 from http://www.seagram.cm/overview/overview.asp

Seminario, M. (1997) 'Yet More Web TV Convergence: AOL, Viacom Inc Deal' (29 Sept.). Retrieved 29 Sept. 2000 from http://www.zdnet.com/zdnn/content/zdnn/0929/zdnn0014.html

UFA (2000) 'The UFA: A Growing International Success'. Retrieved 29 Sept. from http://www.ufa/de/ufa_firmen/info/profile_engl.html

Universal (2000) 'TV and Film'. Retrieved 29 Sept. 2000 from http://www.universalstudios.com/tv

Vivendi (2000) 'Vivendi-Universal Merger Press Release'. Retrieved 21 June from http://www.vivendi.com

Wenner, L. (ed.) (1998) *Media Sport.* New York: Routledge.

Whitson, D. (1998) 'Circuits of Promotion: Media, Marketing and the Globalization of Sport', in L. Wenner (ed.) *Media Sport.* New York: Routledge.

Chapter 9

FOOTBALL, TELEVISION, AND THE SUPREME COURT

How a Decision 20 Years Ago Brought Commercialization to the World of College Sports

Welch Suggs

In this selection, Welch Suggs discusses the increasing commercialization of college sports. He explains the historical, legal, and financial contexts that underlie the huge expansion of U.S. college football on television. He suggests that some university athletics departments have become so profit-oriented—especially in their pursuit of television revenues—that they threaten the nonprofit tax status of the universities of which they are a part.

Twenty years ago last week, the U.S. Supreme Court rewrote the rulebook for college sports.

Siding with the boards of regents for the Universities of Georgia and Oklahoma in 1984, the court declared that college football games, particularly ones played on television, were an ordinary business practice—not an idealistic venue for universities to promote amateur sports and academic ideals. Because of that, the court ruled, the National Collegiate Athletic Association had no right to force its members to abide by a central plan to broadcast games.

The decision freed colleges to pursue their own broadcast contracts, enabling them to make millions of dollars. In doing so, it brought economic competition to college sports, making money at least as important as the games on the field. The "haves" of college sports signed their own television deals, setting one athletic conference against another in the race for network dollars.

The ultimate result was today's athletic landscape, in which a few universities control the most-lucrative bowl games, conferences are raiding each other for members, and the NCAA has little control over any of it.

"When one looks back, the tipping point for the commercialization of collegiate sports began with the victory by Georgia and Oklahoma against the NCAA," says Sheldon E. Steinbach, then and now the general counsel of the American Council on Education.

Challenging the NCAA

From the earliest days of the medium, the NCAA exercised complete control over which football teams got to play on television. Its purpose, according to the association's officers, was to protect colleges from losing fans who would stay home and watch television instead of paying to see games in person.

The NCAA was more aggressive about television than it ever was about scandals or rules violations. The only college ever to lose its membership in the association was the University of Pennsylvania, which tried to defy the NCAA and schedule its own broadcasts in 1951. (Penn relented quickly and was restored to full membership.)

The NCAA also used the television agreement to structure its membership. In the late 1970s, the association's executive director, Walter F. Byers, tried to persuade lower-tier colleges to move from Division I-A to Division I-AA by promising them television time if they made the move.

By the 1970s, universities like Oklahoma and Georgia with big-time football teams had become fed up with the system. Their squads were the ones the networks wanted, but the NCAA insisted on limiting each institution to one or maybe two television appearances per year. In addition, the entire membership voted on the terms of the NCAA's contracts with CBS and ABC, so the powerhouse colleges were effectively outnumbered.

"The NCAA kept watering down the scotch," says Charles M. Neinas, then the Big Eight commissioner. "The NCAA started having more requirements for the networks to carry certain games, and at the same time did not increase the number of appearances for those that actually drove the TV engine."

In 1977 the Atlantic Coast, Big Eight, Southeastern, Southwest, and Western Athletic conferences formed the College Football Association, along with major unaffiliated institutions like Pennsylvania State University and the University of Notre Dame, to lobby for their interests within the NCAA. They hired Mr. Neinas as director.

Four years later, the group struck its own television deal with NBC. At the time it was the second-largest sports television contract ever signed, according to the association's lawyer, Philip R. Hochberg. Even though its bylaws said nothing about television rights, the association threatened to ban from championship events every team in every sport, not just football, from any college that participated in the CFA deal.

Oklahoma and Georgia then sued in federal court, arguing that the NCAA was acting as a monopoly in violation of the Sherman Antitrust Act. "It evolved into Oklahoma and Georgia suing to protect their property rights," recalls Mr. Hochberg. "They had not ceded to the NCAA all of their property rights, and that was a fundamental aspect of why the lawsuit was brought."

Despite the NCAA's argument that it was protecting its members' gate receipts and preserving competitive parity among football teams, Judge Juan G. Barciaga ruled that the association was behaving like a "classic cartel," inflating prices and restricting output to make more money.

Moreover, he and a majority of judges on the U.S. Court of Appeals for the 10th Circuit and the Supreme Court said that "live college football television" was a unique product that consumers desired, just like professional football on television or even Coca-Cola. The NCAA could pass and enforce some kinds of rules, like scholarship limits and requirements that athletes were amateurs, but it had no right to restrict its members' opportunities to make money from televising football games.

"The NCAA plays a critical role in the maintenance of a revered tradition of amateurism in college sports," wrote Justice John Paul Stevens in the Supreme Court's majority decision. "The preservation of the student-athlete in higher education adds richness and diversity to intercollegiate athletics and is entirely consistent with the goals of the Sherman Act. But consistent with the Sherman Act, the role of the NCAA must be to preserve a tradition that might otherwise die; rules that restrict output are hardly consistent with this role."

The court's decision could not have come at a better time for the television industry. Cable was just gaining a foothold in American households, and ESPN and other channels desperately needed programming.

"The immediate reaction is that since more games were available, the price of each game went down, and the number of games went up," says James E. Delany, then the commissioner of the Ohio Valley Conference and now of the Big Ten Conference. "As you might expect, those unable to fend for themselves in the marketplace were losers, whether they were in Division I-AA or II or III, and the winners were

those schools that were strongest in the marketplace—the CFA, the Big Ten, and the Pac-10."

Athletics departments were hungry for new sources of income, Mr. Neinas says. The passage of Title IX of the Education Amendments of 1972 and the NCAA's 1981 decision to begin holding women's championships had forced colleges to add an assortment of teams for women, and those teams needed money to operate.

The College Football Association took over the NCAA's role in orchestrating television appearances for football teams at most of the country's elite sports conferences. However, even that kind of organization was too restrictive for the most-popular members, leading Notre Dame to defect in 1991 and the Southeastern Conference to do the same in 1994. That put the CFA out of business.

High Stakes

The NCAA, for its part, was essentially shut out of the business side of football. The association received a legal opinion two years after the Supreme Court's decision saying that it could not exercise any control over postseason bowl games either, leaving conferences free to make deals with bowls and television networks for their teams.

The financial stakes quickly became enormous. The Southeastern Conference divided $16 million in revenue among its members in 1990; this year, the league will distribute almost $109 million. Nearly all of Division I-A has been rearranged over the past 14 years as colleges have tried to make the best television deals: The SEC grew from 10 to 12 teams; the Big Eight acquired four members of the Southwest Conference to form the Big 12; and most recently, the

ACC reached far beyond its Tobacco Road roots to create a league stretching from Boston to Miami.

Salaries for top football coaches have shot past $1 million, and the best-paid, Nick Saban of Louisiana State University, will make roughly $2.5 million this year, following the Bayou Bengals' national championship in January. And costs for all colleges playing Division I-A football have skyrocketed: The average program budget in 2002–3 was $6.6 million, up 63 percent from a decade earlier.

Along the way, the NCAA's arguments about the need to protect attendance at football games and to preserve amateurism have been disproved. Attendance at college football games has soared, and most Division I-A institutions have expanded their stadiums dramatically to keep up with demand. Ohio State University, Penn State, the University of Michigan, and the University of Tennessee will all draw more than 100,000 fans per game this year, even though almost all of their games will be televised.

College football is as amateur as it ever was. Over the past two years, the NCAA has introduced sweeping reforms to relax standards for incoming players and to increase requirements for athletes already in college. Players get scholarships, but none are paid overtly.

An Important Dissent

The Supreme Court ruled 7 to 2 in favor of Oklahoma and Georgia in 1984, with Justices William H. Rehnquist and Byron R. White dissenting. Justice White, who had been an All-American football player at the University of Colorado at Boulder, argued that his colleagues had misconstrued college sports.

"The Court errs in treating intercollegiate athletics under the NCAA's control as a purely commercial venture in which colleges and universities participate solely, or even primarily, in the pursuit of profits," he wrote.

Rather, the NCAA's purpose is to regulate amateur sports that enhance higher education, he wrote, and such a system could not exist in a purely commercial marketplace.

The NCAA's limitations on television appearances would not be countenanced as an ordinary business practice, but neither would its rules preventing athletes from being paid, limiting the number of coaches a team could have, or limiting the scholarships teams may award, he wrote.

And permitting a small number of colleges, even popular ones, to have unlimited television appearances "would inevitably give them an insuperable advantage over all others and in the end defeat any efforts to maintain a system of athletic competition among amateurs who measure up to college scholastic requirements," Justice White predicted.

The second part is debatable, but the first part has certainly come true. The colleges in the six current elite conferences—the ACC, Big East, Big Ten, Big 12, SEC, and Pacific-10—have much more money, much better facilities, and for the most part, much better teams than the rest of the NCAA. That worries William C. Friday, president emeritus of the University of North Carolina and chairman of the Knight Foundation Commission on Intercollegiate Athletics.

"I am one who thought Judge White was correct in his dissent," Mr. Friday says. "What he predicted is going on now, and . . . academic institutions are not as free to act as they ought to be." Colleges must ratchet up spending on sports, especially football, continue paying coaches exorbitant amounts, and take on more and more capital debt to maintain their visibility, Mr. Friday says.

For that reason, the Knight Commission voted 9 to 2 (with Mr. Friday abstaining) in May to call on the NCAA to take control of football's bowl games as an initial step toward controlling the commercialism of college sports. The games are now managed by television networks and conference commissioners. They tend to be more overtly commercialized than the NCAA's own championships. The NCAA does not sell naming rights for its events, for example, and stadiums and arenas are precluded from having most sponsors' signs visible to spectators or cameras, unlike at bowl games.

The court's decision defined the NCAA's right to maintain certain kinds of rules. But if colleges continue to ratchet up their pursuit of money through sports, Mr. Friday warns, the Internal Revenue Service could determine that athletics departments are business entities and not part of the nonprofit mission of a university. "It's a huge business, and we can't go on giving it a tax exemption when it goes on building what it builds," Mr. Friday says. "No other part of an institution has such a situation."

Mr. Hochberg, the NCAA lawyer, says that's possible, but there are other reasons to control the bowls and other commercial aspects of college sports. "I'm not sure it would necessarily play out the way President Friday would say, but I see an even more imminent impact," says the lawyer. "With so many bowl games, you're going to have half the schools in Division I-A needed to fill out the bowl schedule, and you're going to start having teams with losing records. I think that weakens the entire bowl structure."

In 1951 Congress voted to give the National Football League an exemption from antitrust laws so it could negotiate collective television deals for its teams. The NCAA, Mr. Hochberg says, passed up the opportunity to apply for an exemption of its own, believing that it didn't need one because of its ties to higher education.

The rising cost of college sports, along with continuing questions about scandals and rules violations, are causing more people to question how strong those ties really are, and the Knight Commission and even Congress have begun talking again about the question of an antitrust exemption and other solutions. Something, Mr. Friday says, has to be done. "The issue without a doubt is the pursuit of money, and what money does in excessive coaches' salaries and greater bonding debt," he says. "Intercollegiate sports has got to stop this arms race."

Chapter 10

MARKETERS ARE JOINING THE VARSITY

Stuart Elliott

Athletes, if they are talented, train hard and get a break or two, can climb the sports ladder from high school to college to the pros. Madison Avenue, sensing a lucrative opportunity, is heading the other way.

Decades after marketers began selling products by capitalizing on consumer interest in professional teams, then college teams, they are becoming big boosters of high school sports.

Big media companies are getting into the market as well, in part by offering high school competitors a taste of the exposure that is typically lavished on college and pro athletes. In March, the CSTV Networks division of the CBS Corporation—the "CS" stands for college sports—acquired Max-Preps, which operates a Web site (max-preps.com) and has more than a million high school athletes in its database. Last month, CSTV began creating video-on-demand television channels under the Max-Preps brand carrying high school sports programming.

Another media giant, the Time Inc. division of Time Warner, formed an alliance in December with Takkle, which operates a social-networking Web site for high school athletes (takkle.com). Visitors to the site can nominate students for the familiar "Face in the Crowd" feature in Sports Illustrated magazine.

"High school kids are more sophisticated than a generation ago," said Mark Ford, president and publisher of Sports Illustrated in New York, "and brands like Nike and Gatorade are on this, reaching athletes at a much earlier stage than they previously have."

The goal is to gain favor with student athletes and also their coaches, teachers and principals—not to mention their fans, friends and families.

"Energy for student athletes, and the moms who keep up with them" is, for instance, the theme of advertisements for EAS AdvantEDGE nutritional bars and shakes, sold by Abbott Laboratories.

High school athletes buy all the obvious products—sneakers, gear, sports beverages—along with general items like grooming aids, magazines and video games. Many high schoolers shop for the family while their parents work, so they may be buying groceries along with items for themselves.

Students can also influence the purchasing choices of their parents in important categories like cars, cellphones and computers.

For example, in 2005 Allstate Insurance started coordinating a program for local agents "to demonstrate their support of high school athletes," said Lisa Cochrane, vice president for integrated marketing communications at Allstate in Northbrook, Ill. Today, the brand is present in more than 700 high schools where agents sponsor teams and make donations to athletic departments.

"In many, many communities, high school athletics is one of the premier events," Ms. Cochrane said, adding: "Teenagers themselves are not big customers for insurance, but their parents are. And they will be, in the future."

The trend is also visible in the popular culture, as two TV series—"Friday Night Lights" on NBC and "One Tree Hill" on CW—are centered on high school teams that play football and basketball, respectively. Both have attracted sponsors willing to pay to weave their brands into plot lines; among them are Applebee's restaurants, Cingular Wireless and Secret deodorant.

"We've spent more than 30 years building our relationships with customers," said Jeff Webb, chief executive at Varsity Brands in Memphis, which specializes in goods and services for high school cheerleading and dance teams. "In the last 10 years, our programs with consumer marketers have expanded dramatically."

Companies like Bic, S. C. Johnson & Son, Nike, PepsiCo and Playtex Products work with Varsity Brands, which sends 300 field representatives to high schools across the country to give away product samples and coupons and operates cheerleader camps that draw about 280,000 high school students each year.

"They're trying to find unique ways to reach the teen audience," Mr. Webb said of marketers, adding that cheerleaders and other student athletes are especially attractive because "they're visible, they're leaders and they're influential."

The ardor among advertisers to go back to high school coincides with the rising national attention to junior sports. Examples include the basketball star LeBron James appearing on the cover of Sports Illustrated when he was still in high school, coverage of high school sports tournaments and all-star games in mainstream media, and programming on CSTV devoted to "Generation Next" high school football and basketball players (and which colleges might recruit them).

One reason that high school is getting its own chapter in the sports-marketing playbook is the large number of athletically inclined students in grades 9 through 12.

Call them Millennials, Generation Y or baby boom babies, the 7.2 million children who played sports in high school during the 2005–6 school year, as estimated by the National Federation of State High School Associations, represent a target market that has grown 80 percent since the 1971–72 school year.

"We're seeing sports becoming increasingly important for young girls as more and more of them are being empowered through athletics," said Lela Coffey, associate North American marketing director for the Tampax brand of feminine hygiene products owned by Procter & Gamble in Cincinnati.

Another reason that advertisers are crowding high school gymnasiums is their newfound ability to use the Internet, in the form of social-networking Web sites, to unite what had been diffused audiences.

"Technology allows you for the first time to aggregate small, fragmented communities in one place and try to reach the athletes themselves," said Brian Bedol, president and chief executive of CSTV Networks. "It's a very different approach from fan-based college and pro sports."

The eagerness among marketers to clamber down the sports ladder worries those who are concerned with the intensifying presence of marketing in the American culture.

"Youths are overwhelmed with commercial messages," said Robert Weissman, managing director at Commercial Alert in Washington, a nonprofit advocacy organization that decries what it considers to be creeping commercialization.

"To the extent possible, schools should be a haven from those pressures," he added.

Most marketers turning their attention to athletes in high schools already "are linked up with sponsorships at the professional level and the college level," Mr. Weissman said, "so they get to exploit the kids on the cheap."

And by sponsoring local teams, advertisers "get the benefit of seeming to be part of the community," he added, even when they are not.

Needless to say, the companies involved with high school sports describe themselves as sensitive to the potential pitfalls.

"We don't want to be too intrusive," said David Birnbaum, chief executive at Takkle in New York, which is owned by investors that include Greycroft Partners and the Wasserman Media Group.

For instance, no ads appear on the takkle.com home page, Mr. Birnbaum said, because "it's not just about the dollars."

And although "I'm not going to say we wouldn't" ever accept sponsors that peddle products like candy or soft drinks, he added, the intent is to run "the ads that the athletes want to see, that speak to their passion and engage them the way they want to be engaged."

(When Varsity Brands works for PepsiCo, employees distribute Propel Fitness Water to high school cheerleaders rather than soda.)

As Under Armour, the maker of athletic apparel, completes plans for a campaign to begin on July 15, carrying the theme "Team Girl," the inclusion of high school athletes with their college counterparts is being handled carefully, said Steve Battista, vice president for brand marketing in Baltimore.

Female high school athletes were assembled in focus groups to gather opinions, he added, which led to changes in marketing approaches.

For example, "we've had a women's campaign featuring Heather Mitts, a women's soccer star, on her own, not with the rest of her team," Mr. Battista said, "but the girls said they want to see her with her team."

As CSTV adds MaxPreps to its operations, Mr. Bedol of CSTV said, "often it comes down to judgment calls" when determining how to speak to students younger than the college students.

"We need to be vigilant," he added, "and make sure we're responding to the needs of our audience, not just to the needs of our marketers."

What about going even younger? "I don't think we're looking to go into middle school or younger," Mr. Bedol said.

At the cheerleader camps that Varsity Brands operates, however, Mr. Webb said, about 25,000 students who attend each year are from junior high and middle schools.

PART III

TRUE LOVE, OR A MARRIAGE OF CONVENIENCE? SPORTS AND EDUCATION

In the contemporary world, elementary schools focus on teaching basic literacy and numeracy. Recognizing, however, that "all work and no play makes Johnny and Mary dull children," schools also provide opportunities for recreation. From elementary school onward, students take courses in physical education and participate in sports, though these opportunities vary tremendously in terms of the types of organizations involved (private vs. public, school-related or not, and so on), the children's ages, and the country they are in. In the United States, scholarships to private high schools are regularly given to highly skilled fourteen-year-old basketball or football players. College coaches may spend time watching players who are even younger. One cannot imagine increasing one's likelihood of admission to Oxford or to a *grande école* in France because of one's superiority on the pitch, yet one's probability of being accepted to Harvard increases tremendously if one is a recruited athlete (Karen 1991).

In university communities in the United States, there are often concerns that once a talented athlete is enrolled in college, he or she may receive special treatment, or that athletes may contribute to an anti-intellectual atmosphere on campus. Big-time college sports is a business that conjoins media conglomerates, universities, and consumer-products companies (think beer and sports drinks) in a set of mutually reinforcing and profitable relationships (Sperber 2001), but the interests of faculty, researchers, and even many alumni, parents, and students do not always coincide with the interests of the athletic department.

To understand the main issues in the sports-education equation, it is critical to take the relationships among all the relevant organizations into account. If we wanted to examine a Division I college football team in the United States, for example, we would have to situate it within its athletic conference (for example, the SEC, the Big Ten, and so on) and within the National Collegiate Athletic Association. We would need to look at its relationship within the Athletic Department of the university, and we would need to explore whether and how much the presence of a booster club affected its daily operations. Funding from a university is affected not only by the university's competitive status but also by various federal and state regulations (such as Title IX). The other major relevant actor is the mass media: What kind of contract does the school (and/or conference) have with ESPN or another corporation for televising games? How does this contract affect university policy vis-à-vis the football team? Such a neo-institutional perspective—a perspective that takes account of all the organizations that regulate, compete with, or otherwise affect daily operations—is critical for a clear understanding of stability and change in the sports-education relationship. (See DiMaggio and Powell 1983 as well as our introduction to this book.)

Sport plays different roles in the educational systems of different societies. Sociologists ask a variety of questions about the sports-education relationship. For example, What are the effects on education and on larger patterns of social mobility of the integration of organized, interscholastic sports competitions into the educational system? What is the relationship between sports participation and academic achievement? Do athletes do better or worse in school than students with similar social and academic characteristics? Are they more likely to go to college, and if so, are they more likely to graduate than their peers who do not participate in sports? Are scholastic and collegiate athletes who sign lucrative professional contracts (a *very* small proportion of athletes) as successful as other students socioeconomically in later life? Are they more successful? When colleges and universities participate in big-time athletics, what effect does the intense competition have on the quality of education offered to students? What effects do the institution's inevitable relationships with corporate sponsors and wealthy boosters have?

Sociologists use a number of different theoretical perspectives to address such questions. Pierre Bourdieu's social reproduction framework addresses the broad issue of the relationships among individuals' social origins (defined by their location in the distribution of economic, cultural, and social capital), the educational and other strategies that they direct toward their social mobility project, and their final social destination (Bourdieu 1977). In their article included in this section, "Race, Cultural Capital, and the Educational Effects of Participation in Sports," Tamela McNulty Eitle and David Eitle explore how sports participation articulates with social background and academic achievement among males in U.S. high schools. Their findings are somewhat unexpected insofar as they suggest that participation in football and basketball may detract from one's grades but may also increase one's attachment to school. Their comprehensive examination suggests that different sports have different effects for different groups of students.

The article by Douglas Foley, "High School Football: Deep in the Heart of South Tejas," shows how school and sports articulate with one another in a Texas town. As Foley portrays it, the local high school, ostensibly only an educational institution, is a site of status competition among race-, gender-, and class-based groups. Though one might think of the competition of the football season as a key field of struggle for high-school status, Foley suggests instead that the football team itself and associated events and relationships play a central role in conferring status within the high school. Activities connected to football—powder-puff football, cheerleading, and pep rallies—also confer status, reinforcing and reaffirming the status structure of the surrounding community.

The report from the Women's Sports Foundation by John Cheslock, "Who's Playing College Sports? Trends in Participation," reviews what has happened to women's sports participation in institutions of higher education in the thirty-five years since Title IX was passed in 1972. Overall, women's participation in college sports has skyrocketed, though it remains far behind men's. Further, the increases that were evident during the 1990s have fallen off considerably. The most recent data lead one to question whether athletic participation means something different for the more recent women college students than it did for previous generations of graduates, and if so, what form that meaning takes. How are these students—students who, perhaps, would not have gone to college in previous decades—different from previous cohorts? Are they more likely to come from working-class backgrounds, for example, or to have more careerist orientations? What are the implications—for colleges and for sports—if this is, indeed, the case?

In the selection "The Game of Life: Taking Stock," James L. Schulman and William G. Bowen raise questions about how athletics and academics articulate with one another in the context of selective institutions of higher education. Although their book *The Game of Life: College Sports and Educational Values*, where this piece was originally published, deals primarily with the conflict between academic values and culture and the increasingly commercialized world of college sports, this selection summarizes some of the key findings of a study that highlights the *changes* that have occurred in the nature of college athletes and the nature of college athletics. Their work addresses important questions about how athletics affects central aspects of higher education as well as how athletics should function within the context of institutions of higher education. Although Schulman and Bowen make many specific contributions, their most important one is to highlight the ways that college athletics brings many sets of actors together who, consciously and unconsciously, strongly affect the decisions—and tradeoffs—that are made by institutions of higher education.

References

Bourdieu, Pierre. 1977. "Cultural Reproduction and Social Reproduction." Pp. 487–511 in Jerome Karabel and A. H. Halsey, eds., *Power and Ideology in Education*. New York: Oxford University Press.

DiMaggio, Paul J., and Walter W. Powell. 1983. "The Iron Cage Revisited: Institutional Isomorphism and Collective Rationality in Organizational Fields." *American Sociological Review* 48: 147–160.

Karen, David. 1991. "'Achievement' and 'Ascription' in Admission to an Elite College: A Political-Organizational Analysis." *Sociological Forum* 6, no. 2 (June 1991): 349–380.

Schulman, James L., and William G. Bowen. 2001. *The Game of Life: College Sports and Educational Values*. Princeton, NJ: Princeton University Press.

Sperber, Murray. 2001. *Beer and Circus: How Big-Time College Sports Is Crippling Undergraduate Education*. New York: Holt.

Chapter 11

WHO'S PLAYING COLLEGE SPORTS?

Trends in Participation

John Cheslock

In this report from the Women's Sports Foundation, John Cheslock reviews the thirty-fifth anniversary of Title IX's effect on athletics in higher education. Title IX, passed by the U.S. Congress in 1972, stipulates that educational institutions that receive federal funding cannot discriminate against women. Its major effect has been to provide more opportunities for women to participate in athletics. This report focuses on the types of changes that occurred in women's and men's athletics during the decade from 1995 to 2005. As you read this selection, consider the types of policies that might lead to a gender-equitable athletic environment at U.S. colleges and universities.

Introduction

The year 2007 marks the 35th anniversary of the passage of Title IX, which prohibits discrimination by gender in any federally funded educational institution. Although Title IX applies broadly to all aspects of education, the focus of this report is its application to intercollegiate athletic participation. Since the passage of Title IX in 1972, athletic opportunities for female undergraduates have expanded considerably.

To what extent has women's athletic participation continued to increase over the last 10 years? Have recent gains addressed the historical gender inequities within intercollegiate athletics? Such questions are important but sometimes missing within the Title IX debate. In contrast, much attention focuses on whether male athletes continue to enjoy their high participation levels. Some assert that men's athletics have been severely reduced, but these claims are rarely based on definitive statistical evidence. When sound data and analyses are utilized, how have men's participation levels changed over time?

In the past, these questions were difficult to answer due to a scarcity of data on intercollegiate athletics participation levels, which has prevented researchers from conducting

Table 1 Women's Participation by Sport, 10-Year/738 NCAA Institutions Sample			
Sport	**1995-96**	**2001-02**	**2004-05**	**Change: 95-04**
Soccer	10,752	14,902	15,632	4,880
Rowing	3,184	5,759	5,963	2,779
Softball	9,706	11,553	11,909	2,203
Swimming	7,088	8,436	8,718	1,630
Lacrosse	3,038	4,432	4,588	1,550
Golf	1,795	2,749	2,956	1,161
Ice Hockey	377	1,222	1,348	971
Water Polo	221	850	950	729
Equestrian	331	848	1,041	710
Volleyball	9,191	9,669	9,896	705
Field Hockey	3,953	4,307	4,356	403
Basketball	10,316	10,721	10,626	310
Other Sports*	279	590	573	294
Bowling	29	224	289	260
Fencing	506	590	622	116
Gymnastics	1,208	1,285	1,310	102
Sailing	361	428	461	100
Rifle	110	123	135	25
Skiing	373	368	389	16
Tennis	6,244	6,355	6,256	12
Squash	324	327	311	-13
Subtotal	**69,386**	**85,738**	**88,329**	**18,943**
Cross Country	(Estimated increase of 1,426 participants)			
Indoor Track & Field	(Estimated increase of 3,478 participants)			
Outdoor Track & Field	(Estimated increase of 1,998 participants)			
Total	**(Estimated increase of 25,845 participants)**			

* Other Sports include archery, badminton, ice skating, judo, lightweight rowing, pistol, polo, rodeo, rugby, synchronized swimming, track & skeet shooting, water skiing, and wrestling. None of these sports have more than 10 teams in any year.

substantial longitudinal analyses. As a result, estimates of participation trends can only be drawn from a limited number of reports, which contain contradictory findings in terms of men's participation levels and often possess serious shortcomings. A previous Women's Sports Foundation report (Sabo, 1997) and a 2001 Government Accounting Office (GAO) report found that men's sports have increased over time, yet a recent College Sports Council (CSC) study and a 1999 GAO report produced contradictory results.

The passage of the Equity in Athletics Disclosure Act (EADA) in 1994 created the opportunity for greater clarity and unanimity. This act requires colleges and universities to report detailed data on their athletic program to the general public. While some of the reported data are flawed, most notably the fi-

nancial data, the participation data contain relatively few errors, and researchers can identify and adjust for these errors.

This report utilizes available EADA data to provide the most accurate and comprehensive analysis of how intercollegiate athletic participation levels have changed over time.

Due to changes in the reporting requirements of the EADA over time, we use two samples of higher education institutions throughout this study. Our "10-year/738 NCAA institution sample" includes the 738 NCAA institutions that reported data for the 1995–96, 2001–02, and 2004–05 academic years. Our "complete four-year/1,895 institutions sample" contains the 1,895 higher education institutions that reported data for 2001–02 and 2004–05, a nearly complete roster of all postsecondary institutions that offer athletic departments. We use a smaller sample for the 10-year period, because the EADA did not require institutions to report participation data to the Office of Postsecondary Education (OPE) until 2000–01. As a result, a more limited amount of data is available for 1995–96.

Findings

Women's Participation

As demonstrated by Table 1, female participation in intercollegiate athletics increased by approximately 25,000 athletes over the 1995–96 to 2004–05 period for the 10-year/738 NCAA institutions sample. These gains were concentrated in the early years of the period as progress towards gender equity slowed considerably during the last three years of the period. Almost 85% of the increases in women's participation occurred between 1995–96 and 2001–02.

Participation trends varied significantly across sports. Soccer grew by more than 4,000 participants, while rowing (+2,779), softball (+2,203), swimming (+1,630) and lacrosse (+1,550) also experienced substantial gains. Our estimates also demonstrate similarly sized increases for cross country, indoor track and field, and outdoor track and field. In contrast, a number of sports (squash, tennis, skiing, rifle, sailing, gymnastics and fencing) experienced relatively little or no growth for women.

The results in Table 2 demonstrate that participation levels for women increased by more than 11,000 athletes between 2001–02 and 2004–05 for the complete four-year/1,895 institutions sample. The trends across sports did not differ from those reported for the 2001–02 to 2004–05 period in Table 1. The number of participants in squash, gymnastics and tennis fell, while the largest increases occurred in soccer, track and field, cross country, softball, swimming, volleyball and golf.

The number of women's teams also grew substantially in the late 1990s, but this growth slowed in the early 2000s. (See Table 3.) For the 10-year/738 NCAA institutions sample, 876 teams were added between 1995–96 and 2004–05, an increase of more than one team per school. For the complete four-year/1,895 institutions sample, the increase was 394 between 2001–02 and 2004–05, suggesting that only a minority of institutions added women's teams during this period. The differences by sports were similar to those reported for participation levels, except that one sport, golf, became more noticeable as a growth sport. An additional golf team does not create as many extra participants as other sports do because the average roster size for golf is relatively small (7.2).

Table 2 Women's Participation by Sport, Complete Four-Year/1,895 Institutions Sample

Sport	2001–02	2004–05	Change
Soccer	26,312	28,576	2,264
Softball	25,118	25,897	779
Swimming	10,731	11,371	640
Volleyball	20,781	21,409	628
Golf	4,237	4,783	546
Lacrosse	5,385	5,791	406
Equestrian	1,467	1,751	284
Rodeo	337	554	217
Ice Hockey	1,427	1,638	211
Rowing	6,580	6,780	200
Basketball	24,219	24,381	162
Bowling	428	589	161
Water Polo	1,618	1,768	150
Field Hockey	5,176	5,308	132
Sailing	510	595	85
Fencing	616	661	45
Rifle	173	198	25
Skiing	503	523	20
Badminton	144	153	9
Squash	338	322	-16
Gymnastics	1,483	1,424	-59
Other Sports*	1,142	1,021	-121
Tennis	10,212	10,023	-189
Subtotal	**148,937**	**155,516**	**6,579**
Cross Country		(Estimated increase of 837 participants)	
Indoor Track & Field		(Estimated increase of 1,815 participants)	
Outdoor Track & Field		(Estimated increase of 1,813 participants)	
Total		**(Estimated increase of 11,043 participants)**	

* Other Sports include archery, ice skating, judo, lightweight rowing, pistol, polo, rugby, synchronized swimming, table tennis, team handball, water skiing, weight lifting, and wrestling. None of these sports have more than 10 teams in any year.

Table 3 Changes in Team Offerings, Women		
Sport	1995–2004*	2001–2004*
Soccer	162	86
Golf	141	68
Softball	92	33
Track and Field, Indoor	71	48
Lacrosse	72	22
Track and Field, Outdoor	46	18
Swimming	40	15
Cross Country	34	18
Bowling	30	17
Water Polo	37	7
Ice Hockey	38	6
Rowing	43	2
Volleyball	18	18
Basketball	10	25
Field Hockey	20	7
Equestrian	17	8
Rodeo	1	19
Other Sports	7	11
Sailing	2	4
Rifle	1	-1
Squash	0	-1
Fencing	-1	-1
Skiing	-2	1
Gymnastics	-5	-6
Tennis	2	-30
Total	**876**	**394**

* The first column of results contains the number of teams added, on net, between the 1995-96 to 2004-05 period for the 10-year/738 NCAA institutions sample. The second column contains the same information for the complete four-year/1,895 institutions sample for the 2001-02 to 2004-05 period.

Men's Participation

Male participation in intercollegiate athletics increased by approximately 7,000 athletes over the 1995–96 to 2004–05 period for the 10-year/1,895 NCAA sample. (See Table 4.) This increase was steady over the period, occurring during good economic times for colleges and universities (the late 1990s) as well as relatively bad economic times (the early 2000s). The gain in men's overall participation masked differences across individual sports; increases in the growing sports were substantially larger than the declines in the remaining sports. Four sports accounted for almost all of the increase in men's participants: football grew by more than 4,000 participants, while

baseball (+1,561), lacrosse (+1,091) and soccer (+758) also rose sharply. Meanwhile, only two sports declined by more than 80 athletes, and these declines were relatively small at -680 (for tennis) and -488 (for wrestling). In general, the trends by sport were similar for men and women in that the sports experiencing no growth for women were those that had declines for men.

Although small in terms of total athletes, the reductions in some of the individual men's sports were relatively large in percentage terms. For example, rifle fell by only 41 athletes, but that was a 20% decline from 1995–96 levels. To demonstrate how important scale is, consider the following: in 2004–05, the combined number of participants for men's water polo, volleyball, skiing, rifle, fencing, squash, sailing and gymnastics was 3,693. In contrast, the number of football participants grew by 4,063 between 1995–96 and 2004–05. In other words, if the 4,063 increase in participants occurred in these eight sports rather than football, each of these sports would be more than twice as large in 2004–05.

As indicated by Table 5, the growth in men's sports between 2001–02 and 2004–05 was even larger when one considers all higher education institutions (i.e. the complete four-year/1,895 institutions sample). During this period, men's participation levels increased by close to 10,000 for the 1,895 institutions reporting data for both years. This increase is very similar to the 11,000 participant increase reported for women in Table 2 for the same set of

Table 4 Men's Participation by Sport, 10-Year/738 NCAA Institutions Sample				
Sport	1995-96	2001-02	2004-05	Change: 95-04
Football	43,814	46,716	47,870	4056
Baseball	19,482	20,506	21,043	1561
Lacrosse	4,482	5,148	5,573	1091
Soccer	13,492	13,847	14,250	758
Swimming	6,146	6,136	6,274	128
Other Sports*	536	454	626	90
Water Polo	602	651	684	82
Volleyball	719	845	768	49
Rowing	2,388	2,396	2,436	48
Basketball	11,828	11,842	11,868	40
Skiing	417	402	405	-12
Ice Hockey	3,027	3,057	3,003	-24
Rifle	210	210	169	-41
Fencing	628	542	586	-42
Squash	418	374	368	-50
Sailing	509	403	436	-73
Golf	6,008	6,001	5,932	-76
Gymnastics	354	280	277	-77
Wrestling	5,089	4,787	4,601	-488
Tennis	6,252	5,780	5,572	-680
Subtotal	**126,401**	**130,377**	**132,741**	**6,340**
Cross Country	(Estimated increase of 48 participants)			
Indoor Track & Field	(Estimated increase of 915 participants)			
Outdoor Track & Field	(Estimated increase of 202 participants)			
Total	**(Estimated increase of 7,101 participants)**			

* Other Sports include archery, bowling, cricket, equestrian, judo, sprint football, lightweight rowing, pistol, polo, rodeo, rugby, track & skeet shooting, and water skiing. None of these sports have more than 10 teams in any year.

institutions. Almost two-thirds (16 of 25) of men's sports experienced gains between 2001–02 and 2004–05. Table 5 shows that the declines in individual men's sports were very slight in relation to the gains in other sports. Only two men's sports experienced declines of more than 60 athletes, while 12 men's sports had increases of at least that amount. As in Table 4, the men's sports that experienced the largest gains were football, baseball, soccer and lacrosse, whose gains dwarfed the losses experienced by volleyball and tennis, the two sports with the largest declines.

This overall growth in participation, however, did not translate into growth in the number of men's teams. As indicated in Table 6, the overall number of men's teams experienced almost no change over time. The number of teams for some individual sports, however, did increase or decrease over the period of study. There are two reasons why the overall number of men's participants increased but the overall number of men's teams did not. First, the average roster size increased between 1995–96 and 2004–05 for several men's sports, most notably football (+7.0), baseball (+2.3), lacrosse (+3.4) and soccer (+1.2). Second, the sport experiencing the largest decline was tennis, which had teams with an average roster size of 9.4 in 2004–05. Meanwhile, the average roster sizes in 2004–05 were quite large for growing sports such as lacrosse (32.9), baseball (30.0) and soccer (24.6).

Female Share of Athletes

While women's participation increased more than men's participation, females still comprise a minority of athletes. For the complete four-year sample of 1,895 institutions,

Table 5 Men's Participation by Sport, Complete Four-Year/1,895 Institutions Sample			
Sport	*2001–02*	*2004–05*	*Change: 95-04*
Football	73,714	76,639	2,925
Baseball	44,367	46,511	2,144
Soccer	28,542	29,903	1,361
Lacrosse	6,964	7,730	766
Swimming	7,917	8,349	432
Basketball	28,235	28,589	354
Other Sports*	786	1,064	278
Golf	11,129	11,374	245
Sailing	498	581	83
Water Polo	1,384	1,461	77
Bowling	232	302	70
Rodeo	1,058	1,125	67
Fencing	568	6,202	52
Squash	385	380	-5
Wrestling	7,483	7,478	-5
Skiing	578	562	-16
Ice Hockey	4,043	4,026	-17
Rowing	2,899	2,876	-23
Rifle	263	232	-31
Gymnastics	353	295	-58
Volleyball	1,752	1,624	-128
Tennis	9,391	9,052	-339
Subtotal	**232,541**	**240,773**	**8,232**
Cross Country	(Estimated increase of 84 participants)		
Indoor Track & Field	(Estimated increase of 759 participants)		
Outdoor Track & Field	(Estimated increase of 890 participants)		
Total	**(Estimated increase of 9,965 participants)**		

* Other Sports include archery, cricket, judo, sprint football, lightweight rowing, pistol, polo, rugby, table tennis, team handball, and water skiing. None of these sports have more than 10 teams in any year.

ing the late 1990s. Between 1995–96 and 2001–02, the female share of athletes increased from 38.2% to 42.2%. The female share only increased four-tenths of a percentage point between 2001–02 and 2004–05 (from 42.2% to 42.6%).

The much higher participation levels for men do not imply that a larger number of men's teams were offered. Among our complete four-year/1,895 institutions sample, the average institution offered 6.3 men's teams and 6.7 women's teams in 2004–05. The contrast between the participation and team numbers mainly reflects the large average roster size for football, which was 93 for the 823 institutions offering the sport in 2004–05.

the reported number of men's participants in 2004–05 was 291,797 while the corresponding number for women was 205,492. In combination, these figures demonstrate that as of 2004–05, only 41% of athletic participants were women, and 151,149 female athletes would need to have been added (assuming no reduction in male participants) to reach a share of 55%, the female share of full-time undergraduates in the fall of 2004 (NCES, 2005).

As demonstrated in Figure 1, the female participation share changed little (from 41.1% to 41.3%) between 2001–02 and 2004–05 for our complete four-year/1,895 institutions sample. Figure 2 shows similar findings over this period for the 10-year/738 NCAA institutions sample, but it also depicts substantial improvement dur-

Compliance with Title IX

To demonstrate compliance with Title IX, higher education institutions must meet requirements in three areas: participation, athletic financial assistance and other program areas. To determine whether colleges and universities are providing equitable participation opportunities to female athletes, the Office for Civil Rights (OCR) has developed the following three-prong test.

Prong One: Substantial Proportionality. This part of the test is satisfied when participation opportunities for men and women are "substantially proportionate" to their respective undergraduate enrollments.

Prong Two: History and Continuing Practice. This part of the test is satisfied when

an institution has a history and continuing practice of program expansion that is responsive to the developing interests and abilities of the underrepresented sex (typically female).

Prong Three: Effectively Accommodating Interests and Abilities. This part of the test is satisfied when an institution is meeting the interests and abilities of its female students even where there are disproportionately fewer females than males participating in sports. (U.S. Department of Education, 1997)

An institution fulfills the participation requirement if it adheres to any or just one of the three tests listed above. The Equity in Athletics Disclosure Act (EADA) data allow one to make several broad-brush inferences with regard to compliance with the first two prongs of the Title IX athletic participation standards.

Table 7 contains detailed information on the extent to which participation opportunities were "substantially proportionate" to undergraduate enrollments. For the complete four-year/1,895 institutions sample in 2004–05, the female share of undergraduate enrollments was 55.8%, while the female share of athletes was 41.7%. In combination, these figures mean that the average institution had a proportionality gap of 14.1 percentage points and was far from compliance with the first prong of the test. The figures were only slightly better for the 10-year/738 NCAA institutions sample, which had an average female share of athletes of 42.7% and an average proportionality gap of 12.5 percentage points.

Table 6 Changes in Team Offerings, Men		
Sport	*1995-2004**	*2001-2004**
Track & Field, Indoor	34	37
Lacrosse	20	9
Baseball	3	15
Soccer	2	15
Other Sports	4	12
Cross Country	10	5
Track and Field, Outdoor	7	8
Golf	8	3
Rodeo	1	10
Basketball	2	8
Football	3	1
Sailing	2	2
Ice Hockey	2	0
Water Polo	5	-3
Skiing	0	-3
Squash	-2	-1
Rifle	-1	-3
Rowing	0	-7
Fencing	-5	-2
Swimming	-7	-3
Volleyball	0	-19
Gymnastics	-10	-5
Wrestling	-32	-8
Tennis	-44	-48
Total	**2**	**23**

* The first column of results contains the number of teams added, on net, between the 1995–96 to 2004–05 period for the 10-year/738 NCAA institutions sample. The second column contains the same information for the complete four-year/1,895 institutions sample for the 2001–02 to 2004–05 period.

In a 1996 policy clarification, the Office for Civil Rights (OCR) stated that they would:

consider opportunities to be substantially proportionate when the number of opportunities that would be required to achieve proportionality would not be sufficient to sustain a viable team, i.e., a team for which there is a sufficient number of interested and able students and enough available competition to sustain an intercollegiate team. (Office for Civil Rights, 1996)

Depending on the size of the institution's athletic department, an institution would need a proportionality gap between one and three percentage points to meet this

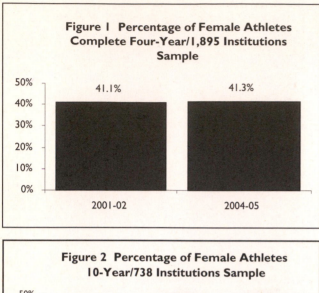

Figure 1 Percentage of Female Athletes Complete Four-Year/1,895 Institutions Sample

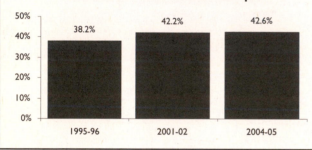

Figure 2 Percentage of Female Athletes 10-Year/738 Institutions Sample

teams they offer. Some of these institutions, however, may not be in compliance with Prong Two (a history and continuing practice of program expansion), because the 1996 OCR Policy Clarification suggests that a more thorough examination is required. The results in Table 7 indicate that a much larger share of institutions (66%) added a female sport on net between 1995–96 and 2001–02. However, no OCR guidelines suggest that increases in such an historical time frame without additional expansion would demonstrate a history and continuing practice of program expansion.

In combination, the figures in Table 7 clearly indicate that the majority of institutions would not meet either of the first two prongs of the three-prong test. More than 86 percent of institutions would not meet the substantial proportionality standard, and 75 percent did not increase their number of women's teams in the early 2000s. A reliable estimate of Prong Three compliance cannot be conducted using EADA data and is therefore beyond the scope of this report.

standard. As Table 7 indicates, the large majority of institutions (somewhere above 86.9% or 1,620 institutions) did not achieve substantial proportionality in 2004–05 because their female share of athletes was below their female share of undergraduates. Furthermore, many institutions were far from compliance with the first prong; for example, 46% of the complete four-year/1,895 institutions sample had a proportionality gap greater than 15 percentage points.

Table 7 also demonstrates that approximately a quarter of institutions added a female sport on net between 2001–02 and 2004–05; that is, around 25 percent of institutions increased the number of women's

Distribution of Institutions Across Athletic Organization Affiliations and Divisions

To this point, we have discussed colleges and universities in the aggregate. The following two sections examine how participation trends and compliance levels vary by an institution's organizational affiliation and the division within the organization in which it competes. It is helpful to first provide some perspective regarding the location of most

Variable	10-Yr NCAA Sample	Complete 4-Yr Sample
Table 7 2004-05 Substantial Proportionality and Program Expansion Estimates		
% Undergraduates, Female	55.3%	55.8%
% Athletes, Female	42.7%	41.7%
Average Proportionality Gap (Prop Gap)	12.5	14.1
Percent of Institutions:		
with Prop Gap > 3	85.2%	86.9%
with Prop Gap > 5	76.8%	80.7%
with Prop Gap > 10	58.3%	65.8%
with Prop Gap > 15	39.3%	46.3%
with Prop Gap > 20	23.3%	28.6%
with Prop Gap > 25	10.2%	14.4%
with Prop Gap > 30	2.6%	6.3%
Percent of Institutions Adding Women's Teams on Net:		
Between 2001-02 and 2004-05	24.4%	26.0%
Between 1995-96 and 2001-02	65.9%	n/a

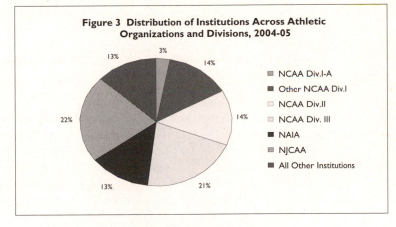

Figure 3 Distribution of Institutions Across Athletic Organizations and Divisions, 2004-05

- NCAA Div.I-A
- Other NCAA Div.I
- NCAA Div.II
- NCAA Div. III
- NAIA
- NJCAA
- All Other Institutions

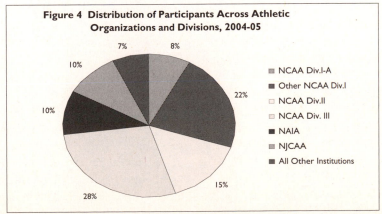

Figure 4 Distribution of Participants Across Athletic Organizations and Divisions, 2004-05

- NCAA Div.I-A
- Other NCAA Div.I
- NCAA Div.II
- NCAA Div. III
- NAIA
- NJCAA
- All Other Institutions

Table 8 Participants by NCAA Division, 10-Year/738 NCAA Institutions Sample

	# Inst.*	Total Participants			Participants per Institution		
		1995-96	2004-05	Change	1995-96	2004-05	Change
Women							
All NCAA Institutions	738	101,570	127,415	25,845	137.6	172.6	35.0
Division I	269	46,346	58,739	12,393	172.3	218.4	46.1
Div. I-A (BCS)	60	13,636	17,335	3,699	227.3	288.9	61.7
Div. I-A (Non-BCS)	39	6,278	8,471	2,193	161.0	217.2	56.2
Div. I-AA	88	15,823	19,718	3,895	179.8	224.1	44.3
Div. I-AAA	60	7,334	9,008	1,674	122.2	150.1	27.9
Division II	180	16,574	21,571	4,997	92.1	119.8	27.8
Division III	264	35,866	43,449	7,583	135.9	164.6	28.7
Men							
All NCAA Institutions	738	163,998	171,099	7,101	222.2	231.8	9.6
Division I	269	74,513	72,736	-1,777	277.0	270.4	-6.6
Div. I-A (BCS)	60	22,395	21,918	-477	373.3	365.3	-7.9
Div. I-A (Non-BCS)	39	11,685	10,766	-919	299.6	276.1	-23.6
Div. I-AA	88	26,363	26,312	-51	299.6	299.0	-0.6
Div. I-AAA	60	8,933	8,953	20	148.9	149.2	0.3
Division II	180	28,769	31,886	3,117	159.8	177.1	17.3
Division III	264	55,988	61,210	5,222	212.1	231.9	19.8

* An institution is only reported in a division and subdivision if it is in that classification for 1995-96, 2001-02, and 2004-05.

intercollegiate athletes, because the vast majority of these athletes compete outside the limelight of the national media. The casual observer may believe that intercollegiate athletics primarily takes place within large athletic departments that offer football and compete in Bowl Championship Series (BCS) athletic conferences (Big-10, Pac-10, Big 12, SEC, ACC, Big East). But as Figures 3 and 4 demonstrate, BCS institutions comprise only 3% of the higher education institutions that offer athletics and account for only 8% of intercollegiate athletes.

Nearly half of the colleges and universities that offer athletics are not in the NCAA (around 48%), although the smaller size of athletic programs at non-NCAA institutions cause them to contain only 27% of the total athletes. These schools mostly reside in the National Association of Intercollegiate Athletics (NAIA) and the National

Junior College Athletic Association (NJCAA). The other 49% of athletic departments reside at institutions that are in the NCAA but in other conferences within Division I or in Divisions II or III. Unlike Divisions I and II, Division III institutions do not offer athletic scholarships; also, schools in Division II face limits on the number of athletic scholarships allowed that are different from those in Division I.

Participation Levels by Affiliation and Division

Table 8 describes changes in participation levels by NCAA division and subdivision between 1995–96 and 2004–05 for the 10-year/738 NCAA institutions sample. The results indicate that the average institution in the 10-year NCAA sample added 35 female athletes, with steady growth throughout the NCAA, as each division increased its number of female participants by at least

Table 9 2004-05 Substantial Proportionality and Program Expansion Estimates, 10-Year/738 NCAA Institutions Sample							
	All NCAA	*Div I*	*Div II*	*Div III*	*Div I-A (BCS)*	*Div I-A (non-BCS)*	*Div I-AA*	*Div I-AAA*
Average								
Proportionality Gap	12.5	9.2	16.5	13.3	6.2	8.6	12.5	8.3
Percent Undergraduates, Female	55.3%	54.3%	57.4%	55.0%	50.1%	53.2%	54.3%	58.5%
Percent Athletes, Female	42.7%	45.0%	40.9%	41.7%	44.0%	44.6%	41.8%	50.2%
% with Proportionality Gap > 3	85.2%	78.1%	92.2%	89.0%	73.3%	69.2%	85.2%	78.3%
% with Proportionality Gap > 5	76.8%	62.1%	87.2%	85.2%	51.7%	59.0%	73.9%	56.7%
% with Proportionality Gap > 10	58.3%	40.9%	72.2%	67.0%	26.7%	38.5%	56.8%	35.0%
% adding women's teams: 01-04	24.4%	18.6%	31.7%	25.4%	13.3%	25.6%	15.9%	23.3%
% adding women's teams: 95-04	65.9%	72.1%	61.1%	61.4%	75.0%	74.4%	79.5%	53.3%
# of Institutions*	738	269	180	264	60	39	88	60

* An institution is only reported in a division and subdivision if it is in that classification for 1995-96, 2001-02, and 2004-05.

20 percent. The largest gains, in terms of number of participants, occurred in Divisions I-A and I-AA. The results presented earlier in Table 1 demonstrate that most of the gains (about 85%) took place during the first six years of the period.

Table 8 also reports information on how changes in men's athletic participation varied across organizations and divisions. The figures in Table 8 demonstrate that the overall gains for men reported in Table 4 were driven by substantial gains for male athletes in Divisions II and III. The average institution in these divisions increased the number of male participants by about 17–20 over this period. In contrast, NCAA Division I institutions reported declines in men's participation levels. Furthermore, these declines were concentrated within the upper levels of Division I. Division I-AAA schools (which don't offer football) and Division I-AA schools (which have a lower football scholarship limit of 63) saw little change in men's participation levels over time. The declines solely occurred for Division I-A institutions (which can offer up to 85 football scholarships). Within Division I-A, the largest reductions occurred for schools lo-

cated outside of the BCS conferences; they saw a drop of 24 participants per institution, much higher than the eight-participant drop for BCS schools.

Title IX Compliance by Affiliation and Division

As indicated in Table 9, some variation existed across the 10-year/738 NCAA institutions sample in terms of our very rough estimates of compliance with Prongs One and Two of the participation requirement of Title IX. In 2004–05, institutions in Division I-A BCS conferences had the smallest average proportionality gap, but that was not because they had the highest share of women among their athletes. Although these institutions had a relatively high share of female athletes (44%), the primary reason why they had the lowest average proportionality gap was their relatively low female share of undergraduates (50%). In contrast, Division I-AAA schools had a substantially higher female share of athletes (50%) but an even higher female share of undergraduates (58.5%). Similarly, Division I-A schools that were not in BCS conferences had a similar female share of

Table 10 2004-05 Substantial Proportionality and Program Expansion Estimates, Complete Four-Year/1,895 NCAA Institutions Sample

	All	NCAA	NAIA	NCCAA	NJCAA	COA	NWAAC
Average							
Proportionality Gap	14.1	13.0	15.9	6.9	16.3	19.4	9.5
Percent Undergraduates, Female	55.8%	55.8%	57.6%	49.3%	56.1%	55.4%	54.8%
Percent Athletes, Female	41.7%	42.8%	41.6%	42.4%	39.8%	36.0%	45.3%
% with Proportionality Gap > 3	86.9%	86.2%	89.1%	75.6%	90.7%	94.7%	84.4%
% with Proportionality Gap > 5	80.7%	78.8%	84.9%	63.4%	86.1%	88.4%	78.1%
% with Proportionality Gap > 10	65.8%	61.2%	78.7%	31.7%	71.2%	85.3%	43.8%
% adding women's teams: 01-04	26.0%	25.9%	36.0%	34.1%	19.7%	17.9%	12.5%
# of Institutions*	1895	964	239	41	431	95	32

* An institution is only reported in a division and subdivision if it is in that classification for 1995-96, 2001-02, and 2004-05.

** NCAA refers to the National Collegiate Athletics Association; NAIA refers to the National Association of Intercollegiate Athletics; NCCAA refers to the National Christian College Athletic Association; NJCAA refers to the National Junior College Athletics Association; COA refers to the California Community College Commission on Athletics; NWAAC refers to the Northwest Athletic Association of Community Colleges.

athletes (45%) as their BCS counterparts, but had a higher average proportionality gap because 53% of their undergraduates were female. Divisions II, III and I-AA had the lowest female share of athletes and the highest proportionality gaps among all NCAA classifications.

In terms of program expansion for females, Division II boasted the largest share of institutions that added women's teams between 2001–02 and 2004–05, while Divisions I-A (BCS) and I-AA had the lowest shares. In contrast, Divisions I-A and I-AA had the highest share of institutions that added women's teams over the 1995–96 to 2001–02 period, while Division I-AAA had the lowest share.

As indicated by Table 10, athletic organizations in the complete four-year/1,895 sample differed substantially in meeting Prongs One or Two of Title IX's three-prong test. Among the largest organizations, NAIA and NJCAA schools had slightly higher average proportionality gaps than those in the NCAA. Note that relative to the NCAA, the female share of under-graduates was higher at NAIA institutions, while the female share of athletes was lower at NJCAA schools. Among the smaller organizations, the NWAAC and the National Christian College Athletic Association (NCCAA) had relatively low average proportionality gaps, while the California Community College Commission on Athletics (COA) had a very high gap. These figures resulted from a relatively low female share of undergraduates at NCCAA institutions (49.3%), a relatively high female share of athletes at NWAAC colleges (45.3%), and a low female share of athletes at COA colleges (36%).

In terms of expanding women's athletics, the three organizations representing four-year institutions did considerably better than the three representing community colleges. Slightly more than one-third of institutions within the NAIA and NCCAA, and about one-quarter of NCAA schools, added at least one female team on net between 2001–02 and 2004–05. The analogous figures for NJCAA, COA and NWAAC ranged between 13% and 20%.

What Explains These Participation Trends?

This report provides the most accurate and comprehensive description to date of how men's and women's participation in intercollegiate athletics have changed over time.

After substantial growth during the second half of the 1990s, gains in female participation nearly leveled off between 2001–02 and 2004–05. While the fiscal challenges experienced by colleges and universities during the early 2000s may account for some of the slow growth in overall female participation, they do not explain why male and female participation levels increased by similar amounts even though female athletes still only comprise 41% of athletes. Given that the rapid gain in women's participation levels coincided with the Clinton administration, while the much slower growth occurred during the Bush administration, any changes in support of Title IX across these two different administrations could provide an additional explanation.

The steady gains for male participation certainly counter claims that Title IX has led to widespread reductions in men's sports. In fact, men's participation grew between 1995–96 and 2001–02, a period containing the *Cohen v. Brown* decision, which pushed colleges and universities to take Title IX more seriously. In addition, between 2001–02 and 2004–05, many colleges and universities faced extremely difficult financial situations as a result of the general slowdown in the national economy. In such a budgetary environment, institutions would welcome any opportunity to cut costs. Yet, overall participation in men's athletics continued to grow. Thus, the evidence does not support the argument that

pressures to comply with Title IX led to overall reductions in men's sports over the 10 years spanning 1995–96 and 2004–05.

We do find reductions in men's participation levels for Division I-A institutions, especially those in non-BCS conferences. Division I-A institutions may face the greatest pressure to comply with Title IX because many female athletes desire the opportunity to participate at the highest level of competition. Such considerations may explain the high growth in women's participation at these institutions over the period of study. But Division I-A schools face another concern that is much more severe: the pressure to increase spending levels by an amount similar to their competitors, especially in high-profile men's sports.

These pressures have contributed to extremely high expenditures among Division I-A institutions. According to a recent NCAA study (Fulks, 2005), the average Division I-A athletic program has expenditures of $27.2 million, far above the $7.5 million spent by Division I-AA programs or the $2.7 million spent by Division II programs with football. Furthermore, Division I-A institutions devote a much greater share of their dollars to men's football. Among those expenditures allocated to specific sports, 41.6% of Division I-A expenditures go to football, while the corresponding shares are only 26.6% and 29.0% for Division I-AA and Division II (with football), respectively.

The results of this study also demonstrate that participation trends differed across individual men's sports. For example, we find that men's lacrosse and soccer have grown steadily while men's tennis and wrestling have declined. What is the cause of these trends? Neither Title IX nor spending on men's football seems like a good explanation.

A variety of sport-specific factors is more likely the culprit.

Policy Implications

For too long, policymakers have been forced to rely upon a set of confusing and contradictory estimates of how intercollegiate athletics participation has changed over time. This report addresses this problem. It produces clear evidence regarding participation trends and, furthermore, it demonstrates that two recent reports on Title IX have yielded erroneous findings due to shortcomings in their data analysis and methodology. The participation trends revealed by this report have several important implications for the ways that policymakers think about Title IX and shifting patterns of female and male athletic participation.

Implication #1: Further weakening of Title IX, as represented by the March 2005 policy clarification, is unjustified.

Women continue to be significantly underrepresented in college athletics and the growth in their participation slowed considerably in the early 2000s. These findings provide no support for weakening Title IX, but the March 2005 policy clarification did exactly that. By allowing institutions to use an online survey to demonstrate compliance with Prong Three of Title IX's participation standard, this clarification substantially reduced the pressure on institutions to ensure gender equity by expanding opportunities for women. Past research and basic methodological principles demonstrate that exclusive reliance on such a survey will not fairly reveal the interests and abilities of female athletes (Sabo & Grant, 2005).

Implication #2: Title IX does not need to be reformed to stop large overall decreases in men's athletic participation because such decreases have not occurred.

Debates over Title IX have focused more on maintaining the numerous athletic opportunities that men have historically enjoyed rather than ensuring that women gain access to the opportunities they have been historically denied. Within these debates, some claim that institutions rely heavily on cuts in men's athletic participation to achieve gender equity. The results of this study clearly refute this claim. Recent improvements in gender equity were driven by increases in female participation rather than decreases in men's participation levels. In fact, overall men's participation has increased. For the 10-year/738 NCAA institutions sample, male participation levels grew by around 7,000 athletes between 1995–96 and 2004–05, an average of almost 10 athletes per institution. For the complete four-year/1,895 institutions, male participation levels grew by almost 10,000 athletes between 2001–02 and 2004–05, an average of slightly over five athletes per institution.

Implication #3: The debate over Title IX should not be based on the experience of a few individual sports.

Figures for a few specific sports, such as wrestling or tennis, are often used to support claims that men's sports are in serious decline. But such claims would make little sense if participation trends for growing men's sports, such as lacrosse or soccer, are used instead. The policy debate over Title IX must consider the broader experiences of all men's and women's sports and should never be based on data for a few individual sports.

Implication #4: Efforts to analyze and stem reductions in men's sports should focus on Division I-A institutions, the only set of institutions that experienced declines. Future attempts to explain the declines of men's athletic participation at Division I-A institutions should consider institutional policies and practices associated with the "arms race" in athletic spending.

This report demonstrates that a reduction in men's sports occurred solely at Division I-A institutions. Given the scale of expenditures within these athletic programs, sufficient funds exist for additional participation opportunities if costs are controlled. Furthermore, the competitive pressures driving the "arms race" in expenditures is most severe at the highest level of competition, as represented by Division I-A of the NCAA, and will likely absorb any additional dollars generated by alternative reforms.

References

Anderson, D.J. & Cheslock, J.J. (2004). Institutional strategies to achieve gender equity in intercollegiate athletics: Does Title IX harm male athletes? *American Economic Review*, 94(2), 307–311.

Anderson, D.J, Cheslock, J.J., & Ehrenberg, R.G. (2006). Gender equity in intercollegiate athletics: Determinants of Title IX compliance. *Journal of Higher Education*, 77(2), 225–250.

College Sports Council. (2007). *Longitudinal study of NCAA participation study.* Available at http://savingsports.org/presentation/; last accessed April 23, 2007.

Fulks, D.L. (2005). *Revenues and expenses of Divisions I and II intercollegiate athletics programs re-port.* Indianapolis, IN: National Collegiate Athletic Association.

General Accounting Office. (1999). *Intercollegiate athletics: Comparison of selected characteristics of men's and women's programs.* Available at http://archive.gao.gov/paprpdf2/162342.pdf; last accessed April 23, 2007.

General Accounting Office. (2001). *Intercollegiate athletics: Four-year colleges' experiences adding and discontinuing teams.* Available at http://eric.ed.gov/ERICDocs/data/ericdocs2/content_storage_01/0000000b/80/25/a7/6c.pdf/; last accessed April 23, 2007.

National Center for Education Statistics. (2006). *Digest of education statistics, 2005.* Available at: http://nces.ed.gov/programs/digest/; last accessed May 8, 2007.

Office for Civil Rights. (1996). *Clarification of intercollegiate athletics policy guidance: The three-part test.* Available at: http://www.ed.gov/print/about/offices/list/ocr/docs/clarific.html; last accessed April 23, 2007.

Sabo, D. (1997). *The gender equity report card.* East Meadow, NY: Women's Sports Foundation.

Sabo, D. & Grant, C. (2005). *Limitations of the Department of Education's online survey method for measuring athletic interest and ability on U.S.A. campuses.* Available at http://www.dyc.edu/crpash/limits_of_online_survey.pdf; last accessed April 23, 2007.

U.S. Department of Education. (1997). *Title IX: 25 years of progress.* Available at: http://www.ed.gov/pubs/TitleIX/index.html; last accessed April 23, 2007.

U.S. Department of Education, Secretary's Commission for Opportunity in Athletics. (2002). *San Diego town hall meeting transcript, November 20, 2002.* Available at: http://www.ed.gov/about/bdscomm/list/athletics/transcripts.html; accessed April 23, 2007.

Vincente, R. (2006). *1981–82—2004–05 NCAA sports sponsorship and participation report.* Indianapolis, IN: National Collegiate Athletic Association.

Chapter 12

THE GAME OF LIFE

Taking Stock

James L. Shulman and William G. Bowen

In this excerpt from *The Game of Life: College Sports and Educational Values*, James L. Shulman and William G. Bowen examine the relationship between collegiate and athletic culture in the United States. Using survey data from 90,000 undergraduate students who entered thirty different colleges in 1951, 1976, and 1989, the authors were able to assess the changing relationship between sports and academics on various types of college campuses (especially the differences between Division IA and other NCAA divisions and between large public universities and small liberal arts colleges). Their work is notable for its use of a neo-institutional perspective, which examines as fully as possible all the major actors (students, alumni, boosters, corporate media, high schools, and the like) that impinge on the educational and athletics organizations as they make decisions.

A major unifying theme of this study is that an ever larger divide has opened up between two worlds. One is an ever more intense athletics enterprise—with an emphasis on specialized athletic talent, more commercialization, and a set of norms and values that can be seen as constituting a culture of sports. The other is the core teaching-research function of selective colleges and universities, with its own increasing specialization, a charge to promote educational values such as learning for its own sake, and a strong sense of obligation to provide educational opportunity to those who will make the most of it—all in a time when the good of the society is increasingly dependent on the effective development and deployment of intellectual capital. This widening athletic-academic divide—its pervasiveness and subtlety—is the core of this book's message.

The Changing Face of College Sports

Rationing Educational Opportunity

Today, . . . many of those who play college sports enjoy the experience and benefit from it. But supporting the extensive intercollegiate programs that exist today also entails substantial costs, and the most important may not be the readily apparent dollar outlays required to field teams, build facilities, and (in the case of the Division IA schools) provide athletic scholarships. One of the most valuable resources that the leading colleges and universities must ration is the limited number of places in each entering class. For the most academically selective schools, admissions is a zero-sum game: the more athletes who are recruited, the less room there is for other students.

Recruiting athletes for up to 40 intercollegiate teams at colleges and universities that are vastly oversubscribed by talented applicants has major opportunity costs—especially at the smaller Ivy League universities and the coed liberal arts colleges. In this crucial respect, the consequences of athletic recruitment are far more serious for these schools than for large universities with big-time programs. In the words of a former president of a distinguished public university, "Yes, it was embarrassing when there was a scandal of one kind or another, but the number of athletes was so small relative to the size of the student body that whatever they did or didn't do in the classroom or on the campus didn't really affect the place as a whole." *Athletics is a much more serious business, in terms of its direct impact on admissions and the composition and ethos of the student body, at an Ivy League school or a coed liberal arts college than it is at a Division IA university.* This basic point is often overlooked. Highly publicized incidents at big-time schools get all the press—and they are very important for what they say to both campus communities and a broad public about the values of the institution—but the issues of direct educational consequence

flowing from the recruitment of large numbers of athletes are much more serious at the schools where athletes constitute anywhere from 15 to 35 percent of the student body.

Unlike some situations in big-time sports, in which coaches and players are literally at each other's throats, highly visible athletes are arrested for beating up their girlfriends, or self-important boosters contribute to the exploitation of athletes without any thought for their well-being, there are no villains associated with this part of the story. In writing about the implications of athletic recruitment for the rationing of educational opportunity, we most emphatically do not mean to suggest that the athletes who are admitted are bad people, that they will not benefit from attending these schools, or that attending one of these institutions will fail to help them achieve their personal goals. The more difficult, and more relevant, question is whether admitting other students in their place might not have done even more to fulfill the educational mission of the school.

The greatly increased competition for places in the leading schools makes this question far more important today than it used to be. . . . One factor in the increasingly competitive college admissions process is that, over the past fifty years, new players have been allowed into the game—as women, minority students, and individuals from all socioeconomic classes have been encouraged to seek places where previously they may not have been welcome. Moreover, as our society has moved increasingly toward a knowledge-driven economy, the pressure to obtain the best possible education and to obtain credentials that will open the right doors has become ever more intense. Many students could further their individual goals by attending great universities like the

University of North Carolina at Chapel Hill and Columbia, or colleges like Wellesley and Williams, but only so many can attend each year. These schools provide a flexible pool of opportunity that can be utilized in many ways. In addition to the educational advantages that they offer are reputational advantages and the connections that one makes by attending these schools. Having a degree from a leading college or university is helpful in getting a job on Wall Street, getting into graduate school, or making connections in the art world. Deciding who should have such opportunities is extremely challenging, and the outcomes of the admissions process reveal a great deal about how a college or university truly sees—and pursues—its mission.

Taking Full Advantage of Academic Opportunities

Faculty often remark that the most discouraging aspect of teaching is encountering a student who just does not seem to care, who has to be cajoled into thinking about the reading, who is obviously bored in class, or who resists rewriting a paper that is passable but not very good. Such students are failing to take full advantage of the educational opportunities that these colleges and universities are there to provide.

Uninspired students come in all sizes and shapes, and no one would suggest that athletes are uniformly different from other students in this regard. But the evidence presented in this book does demonstrate a consistent tendency for athletes to do less well academically than their classmates—and, even more troubling, a consistent tendency for athletes to underperform academically not just relative to other students, but relative to how they themselves might have been expected to perform.[1] *These tendencies have become more pronounced over time and all-pervasive: academic underperformance is now found among women athletes as well as men, among those who play the Lower Profile sports, as well as those on football and basketball teams, and among athletes playing at the Division III level of competition as well as those playing in bowl games and competing for national championships.*

If we take seriously the notion that students should take full advantage of what are very scarce educational opportunities, evidence of high graduation rates should not end the conversation. It is not good enough, we believe, just to get by. Respect for core academic values and the educational mission of these schools requires more than that. Otherwise, colleges and universities are failing to put their most valuable resources—their faculty and their academic offerings—to their highest and best use. . . . They are not focused on fulfilling their educational missions.

Rationing Athletic Opportunity

Everyone agrees that opportunities to play on teams can be beneficial (and fun!) for the participants, and in earlier days many college students played several sports, sometimes even learned to play sports they had not played before, and were able to enjoy the satisfaction of dramatically improving their skills. One of the many ironies of the ever increasing intensification of college sports, even at the Division III level, is that many of those who might arguably have benefited the most from college athletics now have little or no chance of being on a team. Standards of performance have risen so dramatically, specialization has become so important, and youngsters hone their skills at such a young age that there is less and less opportunity for the true "walk-on" or late-developing athlete to participate. As recruiting intensifies and incoming athletes become more and more proficient, the benefits of playing on college teams are bestowed increasingly on those who are already "trained up."

Concurrently, intercollegiate programs demand more and more of those who, as a result of extensive pre-college preparation, can qualify for the team. Swimmers are often in the pool up to four hours per day Monday through Friday, and year-round training, in one form or another, is common in most sports; the notion of a clearly demarcated "season" is becoming an anomaly. One obvious consequence is the decreasing number of students who play two or more intercollegiate sports. Another direct consequence is that the more broadly interested student who wants to play sports but also to do many other things is conflicted and may just opt out. We learned a great deal about these conflicts through talking with an Ivy League graduate who had been a star soccer player in high school. He spoke with great regret about his decision to limit his goal-scoring talent to intramural contests. "I just didn't think that I could spend the time that I would have had to in order to play at that [varsity] level, and still be able to cut it academically." What was fascinating was that this student saw his decision not to go out for the team to be *his* failing rather than that of a program that placed such heavy demands on students who wanted to do more than just play soccer. In another scenario, this talented soccer player might have been able to enjoy the thrill of playing for his college, gotten the education that he wanted, and not blamed himself for failing to be able to do both at what the sports marketing brochures speak of as "the highest level of excellence."

The Athlete Culture: Campus Ethos

In part because of the increased degree of high-intensity "professionalization" that discourages ordinary students from competing, intercollegiate athletes have become a less and less central part of the main campus scene. This reality is of course attributable not only to changes in intercollegiate athletics. The broader changes in faculty cultures . . . (perhaps especially the greater emphasis on academic disciplines and specialized research accomplishments) have almost certainly made it harder for the highly focused athlete to feel truly welcome on many campuses. As we pointed out in the introduction to this chapter, it is the *combination* of greater intensity athletics and greater academic intensity that has led to the growing divide between athletes and much of the rest of the campus community at many of the schools in this study.

The separateness of many athletes is most evident in the case of those playing High Profile sports at universities with big-time programs. Such students may be housed in athletic dorms, have their own tutors, and in large measure exist in their own world. But our research and the work of others suggests that an athlete culture has spread quite widely and can now be found in small coed liberal arts colleges and Ivy League universities as well as in Division IA universities offering athletic scholarships and other amenities. Social psychologists have documented these self-isolating tendencies in the norms and values of Ivy League athletes as well as in the ways that they spend their time, and we have tracked how male and female athletes are increasingly "banding together" in certain fields of study. The declining tendency for athletes and especially High Profile athletes, to demonstrate their general interest in the school through financial contributions may be another harbinger of where current trends in athletics are leading us.

We have little direct evidence as to the effects of this culture on the rest of the campus community, and it would be a mistake to exaggerate them. At the same time, it would also be a mistake to be too sanguine, especially since differences in values and interests between athletes and other students continue to widen, women's athletic programs look more and more like those of the men, and athletes are increasingly being recruited on the basis of talent that differentiates them from other students.

Campus interest in attending sports events still serves as one way of bringing students, faculty, alumni/ae, and townspeople together under the school's banner. The long-term decline in student attendance at college sporting events reminds us, however, that this contribution of intercollegiate competition to the campus ethos has become less and less important. There is no denying the appeal of other activities, from playing recreational sports to spending time online, at the same time that aggressively marketed professional sports events are now available on too many television channels to count. Looking ahead, it would be a serious error to expect any resurgence of campus-based attendance at college sports events.

The Athletic Culture: Life after College

Including in the class a large number of highly recruited athletes has a number of other, less direct, effects on the rationing

of opportunity since, as a colleague once put it, "people come in packages." In the case of men, in particular, we have seen that there is a strong correlation between being an athlete, having a strong interest in achieving financial success, seeing college as a means to this end, and pursuing careers in fields such as finance. The strong tendency for athletes to concentrate in the social sciences and to opt for business and communications majors (where they are offered) is clearly related to these goals, as is their subsequent tendency to enroll in MBA programs. More generally, the "athlete culture" has a set of norms, values, and goals that are coherent, largely independent of socioeconomic status, and different from those of other groups of students attending the same institutions. This culture has natural affinities with what University of Chicago economist Frank Knight has called the "business game." Games with clear goals and rules, where competitive instincts, team play, and discipline are rewarded, provide a link between the culture of sports and marketplace pursuits.

There is certainly nothing wrong with this confluence of the values of sports and those of the business world. Colleges and universities are surely right to take pride in the accomplishments of their graduates who succeed in the "business game." There are, however, two questions that give us pause and deserve consideration.

First, is there a risk that the focused career interests of many athletes will cause them to neglect the broader educational opportunities offered by schools that describe themselves as liberal arts colleges and universities? These schools want to educate business leaders, but they want to educate business leaders who will understand the complexities of the world in which they are working and the importance of participating effectively in shaping that world in positive ways. The utility of the strong competitive drives associated with athletics depends on the values and the ends to which these drives are directed. As Knight put it, "If . . . one adopts the view that the end of life is to get things done, the case for competition becomes much stronger; but even here misgivings arise. It is hard to avoid asking, *what things.* If it is thought to be important which things are done, competition may be entirely indifferent and unselective, equally effective as a drive toward worthy and unworthy ends."[2]

One of the great advantages of attending colleges that emphasize the liberal arts, as their catalogues properly proclaim, is that the breadth of the educational experience, and the emphasis on values and first principles, *can* help students harness their learning and their energies in ways that serve the broader goals of the society. This is, in fact, a core educational mission of these schools. It is not, however, a "treatment" that "takes" without the willing participation of those given the opportunity of learning in such an environment; in this regard, the decidedly weaker interest in gaining a broad liberal education expressed by the athletes is problematic. . . .

The second question focuses on the effects of athletic recruitment on the mix of students in the school. When recruited athletes make up such a substantial fraction of the entering class in at least some colleges and universities, is there a risk that there will be too few places for others who want to become poets, scientists, and leaders of civic causes? Is there a possibility that, without realizing what is leading to what, the schools themselves will become unbalanced in various ways? For example, will they feel

a need to devote more and more of their teaching resources to fields such as business and economics that are disproportionately elected by athletes, in lieu of investing more heavily in less "practical" fields such as classics, physics, and language study? Similarly, as one commentator put the question, what are the effects on those students interested in fields like philosophy? Could they feel at risk of being devalued?

In an ideal world, we would suppose, schools would like to see a diversity of majors, values, and career choices among all subgroups of students. In our view, society is best served when the financial services sector "inherits" some students who have a deep commitment to understanding history and culture (rather than mainly those with a more narrow focus on earning a great deal of money as an end in and of itself). In the same way, academia benefits when some of those who pursue Ph.D.s also have learned some of the lessons about life that one gains on the playing fields (rather than just those with a more narrow focus on an arcane, if not obscure, realm of academic research). In short, the heavy concentration of male athletes, in particular, in certain fields of study raises real questions of institutional priorities and balance.

Allocating Financial Resources

If intercollegiate sports was self-financing and raised no resource allocation questions for colleges and universities, the issues discussed thus far would still be consequential. Unmeasured "costs," including especially the opportunity costs associated with admitting Smith but not Jones, matter enormously at academically selective institutions. But it is also true that intercollegiate athletics programs involve the expenditure of a great deal of money. We were surprised to learn how high the net costs are (after taking account of revenue offsets) at the vast majority of the schools in our study. An obvious question is whether so much money really needs to be spent to achieve the benefits of well-conceived athletic programs. This is an issue for colleges and universities of all kinds, not just for those that are academically selective.

Here we note only that students who might be interested in other extracurricular pursuits—putting out the school paper or acting on stage, for example—have no comparable, equally expensive, infrastructure supporting them. Each assistant football coach takes the place of the nonexistent journalism coach who would indubitably make the campus paper even better than it is absent such coaching. Disproportionate funding follows disproportionate athletic recruiting and succeeds in enabling a level of professionalism—but only in one particular area. It is useful to remember that per-student expenditures on *all* student services combined (including core functions such as the admissions office) are in the range of $2,000 to $3,000 at these institutions, as compared with athletic outlays of $8,000 per individual athlete in the Ivies, to take that one point of comparison.

As he altered the university's funding structure to provide more resources for the athletic program at Vanderbilt, Chancellor Joe Wyatt acknowledged the reality of competing claims on scarce funds. As long as unrestricted university funds are being used to subsidize athletics, he noted, "the long-term effect may be to seriously impair Vanderbilt's ability to invest in some critical educational and research programs. And there is little doubt that such an outcome could jeopardize Vanderbilt's standing among the best universities in the nation."

Wyatt also drew attention to the findings of a survey of parents of current students that found that they placed the highest priority on the quality of teaching, the quality of the faculty, the emphasis on undergraduate education, and preparation for future employment. Parents were pleased with Vanderbilt's performance on these scales, but they were split on the question of whether Vanderbilt was doing a good enough job controlling costs. Although they were willing to pay more to improve educational quality, Wyatt observed, "It seems safe to conclude that real or perceived increases in cost that do not contribute directly to the priorities related to educational quality would not be well received by Vanderbilt parents."[3]

Commercialization

One way of limiting the expenditure of general funds on athletics is to attract revenues from commercial sponsors, and this is an approach that has proved increasingly attractive to schools. At the schools with big-time athletic programs, winning consistently in the High Profile sports has very large financial consequences. There is no denying the attendant incentives and pressures: on coaches, the admissions process, academic programs followed by athletes who must stay eligible, scheduling of games, housing and training athletes, and on and on. Controlling these pressures is not easy, and there is an obvious danger that the academic integrity of the institution will be corrupted.

These risks are greatest at private and public universities that both compete at the Division IA level and have demanding academic programs. As President Emeritus Arnold Weber of Northwestern has stressed, such issues are qualitatively different in Division IA than elsewhere. But these temptations and pressures are by no means confined to the Division IA level of play or to athletic programs that generate large amounts of revenue. . . . "Self-funded" teams, in the language used by the NCAA, can all too easily move outside the control of the institution. To whom will the coach paid by the "friends" group feel the most loyalty?

No revenues come without costs, some of which are less a threat to the budget than to the institution's mission. Selling students' uniforms as billboards to sneaker companies becomes tricky when an athlete decides that he or she objects to the labor practices of the company and refuses to wear the symbol. Letting boosters have an important say in the admissions process (sometimes subtly, through their relationships with coaches) represents another kind of infringement of material interests on the practices of the schools. These dangers are akin to similar dilemmas elsewhere on campus; one common example can be seen in how universities manage medical, scientific, or technological research with major commercial potential that is funded by external sponsors. It would be naïve to believe that financial inducements affect only the conduct of the athletic department; commercialization of athletics does, however, serve as a prism through which broader issues of institutional mission can be seen in clear relief.

In need of funds to carry out their mission, schools (and museums and zoos and orchestras) go into the marketplace. Sometimes, the revenue found there becomes habit forming, leading orchestras to perform Beethoven's Ninth night after night, magazines to resist commissioning investigative stories about companies that advertise in their pages, and colleges to offer just one more accounting class in place of one more course in philosophy. It is unrealistic to deny . . . a place in the museum for museum shops or to ignore entirely what prospective students want to study when designing a curriculum. Nevertheless, maintaining an appropriate balance between the pulls of the marketplace and the core educational values of colleges and universities produces a very real predicament: the more that colleges tell students and their parents that their $120,000 "investment" is the best one they will ever make, the greater the temptation to define the purposes of education in the currency of the marketplace.

It is abundantly clear that colleges and universities today face an array of market realities that are only partly—and in some schools, only in relatively small measure—the result of the increasing commercialization of athletics. In pursuing a wider and wider range of opportunities to earn income (the burgeoning interest in making lectures available over the Internet is a recent example), schools and other not-for-profits may be required to act like businesses: examples range from the fancy marketing brochures that schools distribute in their search for applicants to the highly professionalized fundraising machinery that now exists at almost all private and public institutions. More complex, and ultimately as important, are the financing and marketing of patented inventions and other forms of intellectual property. Done correctly, all of these activities can benefit the educational purposes of the host institution. But there is also the risk of what has been called "mission drift."

As always, the hard question is how to garner the resources needed to mount a scholarly exhibition or provide a good liberal education without subverting the mission of the institution in the process. An unavoidable question is whether the norms and values associated with an athlete culture end up having an overly commercialized impact on the campus ethos, and eventually, on how an institution interprets its mission.

Sending Signals

High school students, their parents, and their schools watch attentively for the signals that colleges and universities send. The more that leading colleges and universities signal *through their actions* how much they value athletic prowess, the greater the emphasis that potential applicants will place on these activities. The issuing of rewards based on sports accomplishments supports (and in fact makes real) the message that sports is the road to opportunity.[4] Young people in schools of all kinds—from prep schools to inner-city schools—are less likely to get a

message that the way upward is to learn to write computer code or take chemistry seriously when it is not only the pros and the big-time schools, but also the Ivies and the most selective liberal arts colleges, that place a large premium on athletic prowess, focus, and specialization. Athletic scholarships and tickets of admission to non-scholarship schools provide a more powerful incentive than the promises contained in high-minded proclamations.

Some of the clearest signals are those sent to secondary schools that rate themselves by their success in getting their students admitted to the most selective colleges and universities. The admission of talented athletes to these highly selective and academically oriented colleges and universities sends signals to many parties, as Peter Philip, former dean of admission and financial aid at the Hotchkiss School and now headmaster of the Tower School, explained in an interview:

Henry Louis Gates, W.E.B. DuBois Professor at Harvard University, on just how clearly the signals are read among young African Americans:

The blind pursuit of attainment in sports is having a devastating effect on our people. Imbued with a belief that our principal avenue to fame and profit is through sports and seduced by a win-at-any-cost system that corrupts even elementary school students, far too many black kids treat basketball courts and football fields as if they were classrooms in an alternative school system. "O.K., I flunked English," a young athlete will say. "But I got an A plus in slam-dunking."[5]

Look first at the message sent to the athlete. She or he may well be confused as to the true reason for the offer of admission. Even if she had an excellent academic record, she might rightly conclude that she was admitted because she is an outstanding athlete. This cheapens her academic accomplishments and suggests that her athletic achievements in college will be more highly regarded than anything she accomplishes academically.

Look next at the message sent to a school community when a disproportionate number of admissions to the most selective colleges go to prominent athletes. Again, whatever the academic accomplishments of the admitted athlete, the community will read a mixed message. Needless to say, there are occasions when the admitted athlete is not a particularly successful student. This admission sends a very clear message. As students who have assembled virtually perfect academic records are denied by the most selective colleges while their peers whose athletic accomplishments have earned recognition are accepted, the perceived value of the academic program is diluted.

Finally, look at the message sent to the [secondary] school's administration. Especially if it is an independent school, it will naturally be concerned with its "college list." Like it or not, the fancier the college list, the more attractive the school will be to many families. When the school sees that many of its "most successful" college applicants are recruited athletes, it will . . . begin its own recruitment of athletes.

Taken together, this signaling process has a powerful impact. We were told of one specific situation in which almost *half* the students from a leading prep school admitted to an Ivy League university were either outstanding hockey or lacrosse players—and not particularly noteworthy students. When asked at a recruiting session in a large city about the success of his prep school in placing its students in the most prestigious colleges, the school's representative gave the absolute number of students admitted to this Ivy League school, hoped that no one would ask him how many of the admittees has been athletes, and went home with mixed feelings about his presentation. The real issue, however, is not about how forthcoming the prep school representative was in explaining his school's success in placing students than the nature of the reality that underlies that "success."

Forces at Work Shaping the Face of Athletics

The present-day face of intercollegiate athletics at academically selective colleges and universities is seen most clearly when it is juxtaposed with a corresponding snapshot taken in the 1950s. Much has changed, and it is important that those who grew up in those days understand how profound the changes have been. In 1955, the offensive linemen at Denison University averaged 196 pounds; in 1999, they averaged 251 pounds. In 1955, the 50-yard freestyle swimming record at Denison was 22.8 seconds; by 1999, it had dropped to 19.9 seconds. Much has changed, throughout the system. How has this happened?

Specialization, Athletic Recruitment, and Admissions

One of the most powerful forces driving these changes has been the increasing proficiency of high school athletes and the attendant increase in sports specialization by athletes at younger and younger ages. Outstanding goalies, lacrosse players, field hockey stars, squash and tennis players, golfers, swimmers, and runners (never mind punters and point guards) are identified much earlier than used to be the case. Stories abound about parents pushing children to excel in soccer or softball in the hope they will thereby gain admission to a good college and maybe even earn an athletic scholarship. The extent of the problem is illustrated vividly by a recent account of an effort by one thoughtful community leader to discourage a zealous basketball coach from starting a *second-grade* traveling team.[6]

This world of highly proficient and highly specialized young athletes calls out for a different kind of athletic recruiting than what sufficed before. Coaches must be sure that they enroll the right position players, that the prospective athletes they are recruiting can fit within the system they use, and that the right mix of talents is assembled. Lists of desired recruits drawn up by coaches are much more closely tailored to specific needs than they used to be. It is easier than in earlier years to know who is *the* most talented point guard or high school tennis player (thanks to camps, regional tournaments, and other structured ways of ranking individuals), and since the team's success now depends much more than before on the athletic skills that recruited athletes bring with them to campus, the pressure to admit the top-ranked athletes is strong indeed.

The most obvious consequence of this evolution in standards of performance and specialization of skills is that the coaches play a far more important role in determining *which* athletically talented applicants gain admission. It will not do to rely on the admissions office to look at a longish list of athletically talented candidates and then choose, say, half of them on the basis of criteria related marginally, if at all, to the very specific needs of the basketball or softball team. Assuming that the candidates on a coach's list are above the required academic threshold (defined by SAT scores, Academic Index requirements in the Ivy League, NCAA standards in the Division IA programs, and so on), admissions staff are understandably reluctant to override ("usurp") the coach's judgment as to which individual candidates will be the most valuable additions to the team.[7]

We infer that this changing model of athletic recruitment and admissions goes a long way toward explaining the changes that

have occurred in the characteristics and performance of athletes over the time period covered by our study. Consider the women athletes in the '76 cohort. The mid- to late 1970s were still relatively early days for women's intercollegiate sports, and it is noteworthy that only a tiny number of women athletes in this cohort said that they had been recruited. We also know, however, that these women athletes enjoyed a considerable admissions advantage. Presumably the admissions offices identified fine athletes who were also attractive candidates for the school on other grounds, and it was the *combination* of qualifications that gave such candidates an edge in the admissions competition. We do not think it is coincidental that the women athletes in the '76 cohort ranked well in their class academically, did not underperform academically, and went on to earn advanced degrees in above-average numbers. In sharp contrast, large numbers of the women athletes in the '89 cohort reported having been recruited (especially in the Division IA programs and in the Ivies), and we surmise that coaches were playing more of a role, relative to the admissions staff, in deciding who made the final cut. This cohort of women athletes did not do as well in class, underperformed academically, and no longer enjoyed an edge in advanced degree attainment.

This same point can be made by comparing the male athletes in the '51 cohort with the male athletes in the '76 and '89 cohorts. The men in the '51 cohort were not nearly as actively recruited as their counterparts in the '76 and '89 cohorts, and their highly credible records in school and after college mirror those of the women athletes in the '76 cohort. Athletic recruitment for men intensified further between the '76 and '89 cohorts, and the differences in outcomes achieved by athletes in these three cohorts are consistent with what one would have expected to find, given the line of argument being developed here. However the data are analyzed (by gender, by sport, by level of competition, by cohort), there is at least a crude correlation between the degree to which athletes report having been recruited and the degree of academic underperformance. All of these effects are magnified in the Ivy League and the coed liberal arts colleges by an inescapable need to over-recruit. Because there are no athletic scholarships that bind recruited athletes to playing, a considerable number of first-year students may not continue with their teams. In order to allow for this attrition, larger numbers of athletes must be recruited initially.

The Well-Rounded Individual versus the Well-Rounded Class

We believe that the changes in the face of athletics between the 1950s and today can be related to a still broader shift in admissions philosophies. In the 1950s, much was said about the desirability of enrolling "well-rounded students." One consequence (among many others) was that athletes needed to have other attributes—to be ready to take advantage of the broad range of the school's academic offerings, to be interested in being part of the larger campus community (many of them were class officers, not just team captains), and so on. We suspect that the subsequent success of a number of the athletes of this era in gaining leadership positions, including positions as CEOs, owes something to their having had a strong combination of attributes.

Without being able to date the change precisely, we believe that, sometime in the late 1960s or the 1970s, this admissions philosophy was altered in major ways. At some of the schools with which we are familiar, the attack on the philosophy of the well-rounded individual came from faculty. For example, one group of mathematicians objected vehemently to the rejection of candidates who had extremely high math aptitude scores but were not impressive in other respects.[8] A new admissions mantra was coined: the search was on to enroll the "well-rounded class," rather than the well-rounded individual. The idea was that the super-mathematician should definitely be admitted, along with the super-musician and maybe even the super-gymnast. It was argued that, taken together, this array of talented individuals would create an attractively diverse community of learners. For some years now, most admissions officers at academically selective schools have talked in terms of the well-rounded class.

The former dean of admissions and financial aid at Hotchkiss, whom we quoted earlier, provides a sharp insight into how this new way of thinking about admissions has evolved:

> For years now, parents have heard college admission officers espousing the virtues of a well-rounded class over well-rounded students. Colleges believe that they can build a well-rounded class by assembling a group of students with particular talents in specific areas. These talents are often referred to as "hooks" and the students who possess them are called "spiky." The most visible evidence of this for many families is the admission of talented athletes to highly selective academically oriented colleges and universities. . . .
>
> Altogether the impact of the college admission office's search for "spiky" kids has become enormously significant. From the beginning of a child's high school career

(and often much earlier) an increasing number of parents and children are concerned with building a "hook" rather than with getting the most out of the totality of the high school experience. As a result, there are more and more students concentrating their efforts in a particular field rather than experimenting with the broader range of available options. More and more students play only one sport in a given year, for example, instead of three. And more and more students concentrate immediately and precisely on theater or music instead of experiencing the full range of artistic disciplines. Of course, this early concentration is completely antithetical to the notion of a liberal arts education. The fact that liberal arts colleges are those most likely to be sending these messages to high schools, therefore, is particularly unfortunate.

In our view, the mathematicians who lobbied for the admission of high school students with off-the-scale mathematical potential were absolutely right. "Spiky" students of that kind belong in a great university that has a great mathematics department. We are much more skeptical that "spikiness" can be used to justify the admission of a bone-crushing full-back whose high school grades were over the academic threshold but who otherwise does not seem a particularly good fit for the academic values that colleges and universities espouse. There are many types of spikiness, and the objective, we believe, should be to assemble a well-rounded class *with a range of attributes that resonate with the academic and service missions of the college or university.* Looked at from this perspective, the arguments for spiky mathematicians and spiky golfers seem quite different. We also wonder how well some of the increasingly spiky ath-

letes of the '89 (and later) cohorts will do in the long run. Not as well, we suspect, as their male predecessors in the '51 cohort and the women athletes from the '76 cohort, who appear to have had, as the saying goes, "more arrows in their quivers."

Competitiveness, Emulation, and "Fairness"

The forces described thus far operate primarily at the level of the individual athletics program within the individual school. But the broad changes in the intercollegiate landscape that have occurred at academically selective colleges and universities over the past 40 to 50 years (and especially over the past 20 years) have also been driven by system-wide forces. First among them is competitiveness. Although colleges and universities compete for faculty, for grants, and for talented (and tuition-paying) students, athletics can come to represent an arms race without end. Even winning is never enough, since there are always more levels to aspire to, more ways to excel, and, if all else fails, future seasons to think about. Part of the reason that sports is so alluring as a field for competition is that it is so results-driven and so quantifiable. Everyone knows (or can find out) who won the Rose Bowl, which women's basketball team is the national champion, and which Division III college was the swimming champion at its level. It is much harder to avoid endless arguments as to whether this program of study is superior to that one (although in recent years magazines such as *U.S. News and World Report* have sought to resolve those debates, too). There is also something about competition in sports that reminds people of courage and even victory in war. (It is not coincidental that the image of the arms race keeps reappearing in stories about intercollegiate sports.) Seeking anything but the top of the sports rankings may seem like surrender.

Resisting these pressures is made even more difficult by the frequent failure to distinguish between *levels of play* (which depend on how talented the athletes are, how much time and how many resources are devoted to preparing for a contest, and so on) and *vigorous competition* (which can occur, or fail to occur, at any level of play). A competitive cluster of like-minded schools "gets the competitive juices flowing" and contributes to the community spirit of a campus whatever the level of play—from Hamilton College field hockey to Penn State football. Heroes in uniforms help to build identity, and they help campus and alumni constituencies to coalesce under a common banner. That is clear. What is more difficult to understand is why it is so hard to convince people that, within the closed ecosystem of the conference, healthy competition and the concomitant benefits for school spirit do not depend on how expert the play is. A Denison-Kenyon swim meet from 1955 presumably inspired passion even though the times were seconds (or even dozens of seconds) slower than they are today.

Healthy competition requires a rough parity that makes the game worth playing, and sustaining such competition is anything but easy. Even among seemingly like institutions, differences that from a distance would be difficult to detect provide profound competitive advantages (or disadvantages). For example, within the Ivy League, student bodies of different sizes mean that it is much easier to absorb a few more athletes with lower qualifications in a relatively large school than in a smaller peer group. Professional teams recognize that such persistent advantages are detrimental to all and employ revenue sharing, salary caps, and draft pick systems to redress imbalances systemically.

Since the college equivalents of these measures (NCAA regulations and conference rules) never really end the race, an individual school will inevitably continue to act in ways that may make it 5 percent better off, although the whole system may end up 10 percent worse off. Building a new artificial turf field may help your team recruit, but only until the other schools in your league catch up. Then everyone has paid for a new field and its subsequent maintenance, but no one is any better off competitively. The classic example of this sort of behavior occurs when someone viewing a parade stands on his tiptoes and no one will see any better. No one wants to miss the parade, and the competitive dynamic in sports has unquestionably fueled the increases in expenditures on coaching and facilities at all levels of play. It has also put tremendous pressure on the admissions process. With the unimpeded flow of more and more information about the pre-college achievements of athletes, and the mobility of coaches between institutions, there seems to be no limit to the contagion of athletic expectations.

As important a driver as competition is in shaping the face of athletics, there is an equally (or almost equally) powerful force. It can be referred to simply as envy or emulation. It is not news that people tend to want what others have. And it is not surprising, therefore, that within the Division IA scholarship schools the so-called "minor sports" of another day have sought to share as fully as they can in the attributes of the ambitious, well-funded High Profile programs. Many more specialized coaches have been hired, facilities have been improved, and scholarships have been provided. Such moves in the direction of equality are often urged in the name of "fairness." Because men who play football "get something," men playing other sports are said to "deserve," in the name of fairness, equal treatment. This same way of thinking is found within the Ivy League and the Division III coed liberal arts colleges. There is, for example, the recurring complaint among the football players in the Ivies or in the New England Small College Athletic Conference that, because members of all other teams have the chance to go to a national championship, "fairness" mandates that they be given this opportunity too. Part of the ethos of sport is to "refuse to lose"—to refuse to accept anything less than what anyone else has.[9]

The most widely publicized—and most consequential—arena for the application of the fairness doctrine is of course women's sports. At the present time, Title IX seems to be exporting to the domain of women's athletics all the salient characteristics of men's sports. An entirely understandable desire on the part of women to have the same opportunities that men enjoy is basic to this transfer of attitudes, policies, resources, and even values.

The women athletes of the late 1970s resemble the male athletes of the 1950s in their in-school and post-college success. It is only in the '89 cohort that we see the patterns for the women athletes that resemble those displayed by the male athletes in the '76 cohort and, even more strongly, by male athletes in the '89 cohort. The women swimmers on today's teams demonstrate the same dramatic gains in performance in the pool that are so evident in the case of the men. There are now many more coaches assigned to women's teams, and expenditures on women's athletics, although they still lag behind expenditures on men's teams, have grown dramatically.

In other words, with determined effort and considerable investment, it has been possible to increase the number of women playing intercollegiate sports and to improve the talent level of women athletes. But whether these developments provide access and opportunity to those women who are best able to take advantage of the resources of a selective college or university remains an entirely separate question. This too should be considered an issue of "fairness." To follow the men's approach to athletics is to follow historical precedent; but to do so unhesitatingly is to assume that history optimizes. We do not believe that this is necessarily true.

Directional Signposts

Comparisons over time, across institutional types, and between men's and women's athletic programs all lead to a single conclusion: intercollegiate programs in these academically selective institutions are moving steadily in the direction of greater intensification, increased tension with core educational values, and more substantial calls on the tangible and intangible resources of their host institutions. We cannot think of a single set of data that contradicts this proposition. Furthermore, the most recent cohort for which we have full data entered college in the fall of 1989. The limited data available for a much more recent cohort (the one that entered in the fall of 1999) suggest that the trends favoring the recruitment of highly specialized athletes have all continued—and, if anything, gained speed.

We are unable to identify any forces inside the systems that—without considerable help—can be expected to alter these directions. On the contrary, there is an intergenerational dynamic that seems likely to accelerate the pace of the changes we see occurring. The more intensively recruited athletes of today, men and women, will become the next generation of alumni/ae, and in the fashion of their predecessors they can be expected to press for increased emphasis on supporting winning sports programs as they become trustees and assume other leadership positions. Two pieces of evidence that support this conclusion are the data on the priorities of former athletes who have become alumni/ae leaders and the data showing the effects of winning teams on the giving behavior of former athletes from the Division III coed liberal arts colleges. These may be no more than straws in the wind, but we believe that they should be taken seriously.

Institutionalization of Athletics in the Academy

Looking back at the history of college sports over the course of the 20th century, one of the most important changes can be seen clearly only with the help of a long-distance lens: intercollegiate sports have become institutionalized in institutions of higher education. Whereas athletics programs were once a wild stepchild held at arm's length from the schools, run mainly by the players themselves and their devotees, they have by now been thoroughly enfolded into the fabric of these institutions. In an effort to control excess and police the games, schools took charge. In doing so, it was assumed, the strength of the institution's discipline and sense of purpose would moderate the passions inspired by athletics. There was, however, always the risk that, having gained a solid foothold inside the walls, the troubling aspects of the athletics enterprise would affect the academy at the very time

that the academy was working to control them. Sports once seen as merely an outlet for passions and energy or as a community-building ritual are now justified as a training ground for leaders, a school for character, or "the sweatiest of the liberal arts." While there are positive sides to taking sports so seriously, doing so also legitimizes a possible confusion between the dictates of the playing field and the lessons of the classroom.[10]

For years, people have understood that one can view life as a game. "Play the cards that Fate deals you," we are often told. But the country's leading colleges and universities have a special role to play in shaping the game of life, in setting the values (as opposed to the rules) of the game. The role of these institutions is not simply to be a facilitator of what each individual who "wins" the preliminary heats of the competition (the admissions game) sees the game to be. Colleges and universities are tax-favored, not-for-profit institutions because society agrees that they have a broader role to play in a far more consequential societal game. These institutions are charged to resist the narrow impulses of the marketplace, as well as ideological and political strictures of every kind: they are meant to live, as E. M. Forster once described the poet Cavafy, "at a slight angle to the universe." Pursuing their academic mission will produce better filmmakers, journalists, medical researchers, and yes, better bankers and lawyers too. But this will be accomplished by accepting those whom the schools believe will make best use of their educational resources and by insisting on the validity of their own missions.

In embracing intercollegiate athletics, colleges and universities gambled on their ability to "control the beast"—to harness the energies and many good qualities of sports to their own purposes, rather than to be subverted by them. The open question is whether this gamble was a good one: whether colleges and universities can rise to the challenge of rebalancing objectives and strengthening what we regard as the purer values of athletic competition. Leaders of these venerable academic institutions have difficult choices to make.

Notes

1. There is also evidence of academic underperformance among minority students (see William G. Bowen and Derek Bok. 1998. *The Shape of the River: Long-Term Consequences of Considering Race in College and University Admissions*. Princeton, NJ: Princeton University Press), and—while some, but by no means all, of the causes are similar to those that apply to athletes—the issues involved in assessing underperformance are quite different.

2. Frank Knight, *The Ethics of Competition* (New Brunswick, N.J.: Transaction, 1997), p. 60.

3. Joe B. Wyatt, "Chancellor Responds to Athletics Committee Report," *Vanderbilt Register* 15(30) (1996): 8–9.

4. The controversy over the suspension of St. John's point guard Erik Barkley for violating NCAA rules on accepting money from "athletic interests" to help cover prep school tuition provoked a number of revealing comments. *New York Times* columnist Harvey Araton has written about how discouraging it is for innercity students with reasonable grades at schools like Kennedy High School in Paterson, New Jersey, to have to struggle constantly to figure out how they can possibly pay for college when athletes with much lower grades "will go to some college, somehow, some way, and free of charge." At this school, there was not a lot of sympathy for Barkley by college coaches like Mike Krzyzewski at Duke, who preach about society's obligation to educate students like Barkley—provided, as Araton puts it, that "they can rebound and spot up for 3," Araton concludes: "Coach's sanctimony does not add up, or compute." "An Education Isn't a Game to Squander," *New York Times*, March 2, 2000, p. D1.

Similarly, in controversies over the initial eligibility standards that have been imposed by the NCAA, critics have complained that minority students will lose out on an education. Tulane University School of Law Professor Gary R. Roberts responds with outrage, "The notion that poor black kids are being denied opportunities . . . is nonsense. . . . I only wish that those who are so driven to allow schools to take academically unprepared black athletes would be more concerned about creating educational opportunities for minority students, whether or not they play basketball." David Goldfield, "Weaker NCAA Standards Won't Help Black Athletes," *Chronicle of Higher Education*, April 9, 1999, online edition.

5. "Delusions of Grandeur: Young Blacks Must Be Taught that Sports Are Not the Only Avenue of Opportunity," *Sports Illustrated*, August 19, 1991, p. 78.

6. Just as this book was going to press, an article appeared reporting an effort by parents in Wayzata, Minnesota, to resist the trend toward overscheduling of children's activities. Examples illustrate what is bothering the parents: "At Kristin Bender's house, where commotion of the 'I can't find my cleats' variety reigns as her three children rush to participate in three different sports simultaneously, she shoehorns in family time by having everyone meet near the sports fields for half an hour. Margaret Roddy's son, Drew, 17, a basketball player, has been benched for taking a family vacation."

The reporter also points out that "Coaches and program directors are judged on their programs' success, creating pressure to schedule more practices and year-round playing seasons, and discourage talented children from cutting back." The tensions parents feel are all too real. "'In theory I support it [the cutback] 100 percent,' said Greg Rye, who said that because his 9-year-old son Michael's soccer takes up four days a week, the boy often eats 'on the fly.' But Mr. Rye worries that if Michael misses a season or does not play on the more competitive traveling teams, he may be denied opportunities later."

As always, competitive pressures are a concern. What if other towns do not follow the Wayzata example? "If the quality is going to go down [because of fewer practices, for example], you are going to have difficulty retaining [coaches] who want to excel." And less competitive programs, one person observed, "can hurt your chance for a college scholarship." Pam Belluck, "Parents Try to Reclaim Their Children's Time," *New York Times,* June 13, 2000, p. A18.

7. Coaches are very well aware of the academic thresholds that they must meet. Although, as one admissions director noted, coaches push things as far as they can, they have no interest in wasting their own time pursuing candidates who will not be admissible under any circumstances. In this person's words, "They're very clear people. If you tell them, 'this is what you can have,' they accept it and do it. But I learned that it's impossible to let them have any gray area, because that's when they just can't stop testing to see how much they can get—how iffy a candidate, how many players. I made the mistake at one point of telling them that if they came up with a way to do well with the admissions process, I'd, in effect, reward them. But it was too gray, too jury-rigged. Each came up with some plan and then was angry when they didn't 'get' what Coach X had gotten. It only works when there are black and white boundaries. Gray they just push too hard." But within the boundaries, coaches are likely to feel that they "own" the admissions slots set aside for their teams.

8. In some instances, there were also issues of race, religion, and ethnicity involved. For instance, a disproportionate number of extremely smart students from schools like the Bronx High School of Science were Jewish. The shift from the notion of a well-rounded student to the notion of the well-rounded class also incorporated a greatly increased interest in enrolling diverse student bodies.

9. Another doctrine that has played a role in building the case for higher levels of athletic achievement and more generous funding is the idea that excellence for an educational institution carries with it the responsibility to seek excellence in *all* endeavors. This notion—which we discuss in some detail in the next chapter—leaves endless space for improvement in athletic programs at any one institution, and the forces of competition and emulation then tend to spread such improvements system-wide.

10. This same tension is described vividly in a recent account of a high school basketball program. The head of the Montrose Christian School, Ray Hope, is quoted as expecting the big-time high school basketball program directed by Stu Vetter to increase the school's name recognition, enrollment, and revenue. To some degree, it has achieved these objectives. "Just as important to Hope," the author writes, "is the basketball team's role in helping the church [which operates the school] spread the word of God. As a Southern Baptist, Hope is unapologetic about his desire to convert people to Christianity, and the arrival of big-time basketball has given him the opportunity to preach the Gospel to a whole new group of potential converts. . . . According to some Montrose students, however, it's the basketball players who appear to be converting the school. 'Montrose used to be really spiritually oriented,' says Rob Gallalee, a senior who has been at Montrose for four years. 'But when you bring in all of these basketball players who aren't Christian, of course that changes the atmosphere of the school. Things are now ignored that didn't used to be ignored. Like cussing in the hallway. I know that wouldn't be a big deal at other schools, but it used to be a big deal at Montrose. Now, if a teacher overhears you cussing in the hallway, they'll look the other way.'" Jason Zengerle, "The Portable High-School Hoops Factory," *New York Times Magazine,* February 6, 2000, p. 56.

Chapter 13

RACE, CULTURAL CAPITAL, AND THE EDUCATIONAL EFFECTS OF PARTICIPATION IN SPORTS

Tamela McNulty Eitle and David Eitle

This article by Tamela McNulty Eitle and David Eitle uses a large, longitudinal, quantitative dataset to examine how high-school boys' backgrounds, sports participation, and academic achievement are related. The authors ask what aspects of one's background lead to participation in what sports and how both background and specific sports participation affect different aspects of academic achievement. Further, they examine whether the same relationships exist for different races. Eitle and Eitle's serious consideration of measurement issues and their carefully presented statistical results demonstrate how sociologists often construct and test multivariate analytical models.

Understanding the effect of extracurricular activities on students' achievement has been a focus of sociological inquiry for the past three decades. The inspiration for this research was Coleman's (1961) seminal work, *The Adolescent Society,* in which Coleman argued that adolescent society emphasizes acceptance by peers, with academic achievement one possible avenue toward acceptance. Interpretations of Coleman's work have indicated that extracurricular activities, including participation in sports, pose additional paths to peers' acceptance that may divert energies away from academics (Marsh 1993). The popularity of sports among high school students is not debated and is demonstrative of the fundamental role that sports participation plays as a vehicle to achieve status that Coleman wrote about. Ironically, according to Coleman, schools play a fundamental role in structuring and promoting sports among adolescents that ultimately undermines the objective of maximizing learning (see also Heckman and Neal 1996).

Other scholars, however, have challenged the notion that participation in sports detracts from the educational mission. For instance, Snyder and Spreitzer (1990) suggested several reasons that sports may promote academic achievement, including increased interest in school, the need to maintain good grades to stay eligible, boosts to one's self-concept, increased attention from adults like teachers and coaches, membership with others who are academically oriented, and expectations to play college sports. Hanks and Eckland (1976) observed that students' participation in extracurricular programs like sports serves two important functions for schools: (1) the generation and reinforcement of educational goals via exposure to a network of social relations, serving to attach the student to the school and its norms, and (2) the facilitation of achieving such goals by empowering students with personal resources, such as interpersonal skills and self-confidence. Hence, a polemic exists regarding the association between participation in high school sports and academic outcomes: whether sports participation serves to increase or decrease students' academic achievement.

Unfortunately, research to date has not been able to resolve this question satisfactorily. For example, a third possibility, that participation in high school sports has *no* significant effect on students' achievement, is frequently raised ad hoc but rarely tested empirically. . . .

Furthermore, many of the prior studies of the educational consequences of sports participation failed to consider the possibility that the purported association between sports and academics may differ for different social groups—that participation in sports may have positive educational conse-

quences for some and adverse (or no) effects for others. . . .

It is not surprising that different explanations have emerged to explain such variation. On the one hand, Edwards (1986) contended that the overemphasis on sports among blacks, coupled with obstacles for social mobility for blacks, leads many young black men on a "treadmill to oblivion" that offers faint hopes of high-paying professional jobs for a select few. This drive toward professional athletics comes at a cost, according to Edwards—participation in sports diverts energies away from efforts to excel academically. On the other hand, social reproduction theory, the notion that institutions, such as schools, serve to reproduce social relationships and attitudes that characterize stratified societies like the United States (Bowles and Gintis 1976) has also been extended to explain the association between participation in high school sports and race-based differences in educational outcomes (Sage 1990). Sabo et al. (1993) suggested that sports participation promotes such stratification in two ways: (1) the institutional matrix of high school sports helps those who are already advantaged more than it helps the disadvantaged (the reinforcement hypothesis) and/or (2) the advantages afforded by sports participation are more effectively taken advantage of by those who are already advantaged (the cumulative advantage hypothesis).

If the social reproduction argument has validity, one would expect that such family factors as cultural capital and household educational resources would be associated with both participation in sports and the subsequent advantages sports would offer the participant. While the notion of the "treadmill to oblivion" produces no definitive hypothesis, findings that differences in cultural capital and household educational resources are predictive of both sports participation and subsequent academic achievement is reconcilable with its basic sentiment. That is, even among disadvantaged black youths, those who have (relatively) few household resources to support educational pursuits may be more likely to perceive of sports as a primary vehicle for social mobility, creating a vicious cycle of sorts, in which the resource deficient place more emphasis on sports, leading to a deemphasis on academics. This thesis is particularly poignant in light of established racial differences in educational performance and achievement.

Finally, virtually all the prior studies that have examined the association between sports participation and educational outcomes have treated such participation as a monolithic entity—all sports produce (or fail to produce) the same effect on academic outcomes. There are valid reasons to question this assumption. Foremost, if participation in sports is (partially, at least) a product of self-selection, it is plausible that students from different backgrounds will be more inclined or less inclined to play particular types of sports. There is some evidence to support such group-based differences in the orientation toward particular sports. For example, Phillips (1993) argued that there is a sports opportunity structure that funnels blacks into those sports in which facilities, coaching, and competition are available to them. The two sports that stand out in this regard are basketball and football. Consistent with the "treadmill to oblivion" thesis, blacks represent a much higher percentage of professional football players (65 percent) and basketball players (77 percent) than does the other of the "big three" American sports, baseball (18 percent) (Eitzen and Sage 1997: 264). Thus, it is plausible that the race-specific effects of playing basketball and/or football on educational outcomes is distinct from the effects of playing other sports in high school because of the perceived importance of such sports as an opportunity for social mobility. Fully understanding the relationship between participation in sports and academic achievement means examining both the factors that predict participation in different sports and the influence (if any) that participation in specific sports has on students' subsequent achievement.

The purpose of this article is to examine the family factors and resources that predict participation in high school sports for select sports and their consequent influence on academic achievement. Specifically, we seek to determine if (1) there is a connection between a male adolescent's cultural capital and household educational resources and the likelihood that he will participate in specific sports; (2) whether participation in specific sports is positively or negatively associated with academic achievement, independent of such resources; and (3) whether the influence of such capital on sports participation and subsequent academic achievement differ by race. By examining whether family educational resources are associated with participation in high school sports in addition to examining the consequences of participation, we hope to illuminate further the relationship between sports and student outcomes.

Background

Most of the studies of the effects of extracurricular activities on student outcomes have examined the role of sports on such outcomes as dropout decisions, educational aspirations, grades, achievement scores, teachers' and parents' aspirations for the student, performance in college, earnings in adulthood, self-esteem, and delinquency (e.g., Hanks 1981; Hanks and Eckland 1976; Landers and Landers 1978; McNeal 1995; Otto and Alwin 1977; Spady 1970). The results of these investigations have not been unequivocal. While earlier studies of the effects of sports participation on students' achievement largely found that athletics served as a positive force, rather than an energy drain, on achievement, Marsh (1993) aptly reported that these examinations suffered from several methodological limitations, including the failure to consider the relationship between sports and achievement for any group other than white males and the use of small convenience samples and cross-sectional data.

More recent research, which has used larger, nationally representative samples and longitudinal research designs, has not found a clear and consistent positive relationship between participation in sports and students' achievement, especially when racial and class differences have been considered. For instance, some studies have found that the effects of sports participation on selected student outcomes generalize across racial and ethnic lines (Fejgin 1994; Marsh 1993; McNeal 1995), while others have discovered that the effects of sports participation on students' achievement vary, depending on the racial and class characteristics of the participant (Melnick et al. 1992; Melnick, Vanfossen, and Sabo 1988; Messner 1990; Sabo et al. 1993). These latter studies suggest that sports participation may positively contribute to the achievement of some groups (e.g., whites and middle-class males) but may not have any significant influence on the educational outcomes of other groups (e.g., lower-socioeconomic strata youths and minorities).

Some previous inquiries (e.g., Otto 1982) into the link between sports participation and students' achievement have questioned whether findings that involvement in sports predict students' academic success are simply due to self-selection. Unfortunately, little research, using longitudinal designs and representative samples, has been conducted on how family factors predict involvement in sports, which could serve to illuminate this issue. Research that has explored the question of why youths participate in sports has found that the family is the primary agent responsible for stimulating a young person's interest (Loy, McPherson, and Kenyon 1978; Messner 1990). Research has also indicated that black families place more emphasis on sports than do white families and that they reward participation in sports more than other activities (Carrington 1986; Edwards 1986; Oliver 1980). However, additional research has suggested that other agents in a student's environment, like teachers and coaches, may be more consequential to participation and the intensity of commitment to sports than are parents (Carrington 1986; Harris 1994; Oliver 1980). More recently, McNeal (1999) found that school contextual factors, such as school size, pupil-teacher ratio, and mean SES of the student body, affect participation in athletics. But there has been no research on the influence of family educational resources on participation in sports.

There is, however, no shortage of research on how family factors influence academic performance. Such studies have already demonstrated that family characteristics, such as SES and family structure, influence students' achievement in myriad ways, including the characteristics and quality of the school that the child attends (Bowles and Levin 1968; Coleman et al. 1966; Roscigno 1998), academic track placement (Dauber, Alexander, and Entwisle 1996; Oakes 1985) and teachers' expectations (Alexander, Entwisle, and Thompson 1987). Even within socioeconomic strata, however, there is important variation in the family's contribution to the child's academic achievement. Central among these influential factors is cultural capital.

The concept of cultural capital, introduced by Bourdieu (1977) and extended by DiMaggio (1982), has been used to explain how social inequality is reproduced through such institutions as schools. According to Lamont and Lareau (1988), cultural capital can be defined as high-status cultural signals, such as attitudes, behaviors, preferences, and credentials, that are commonly used for social and cultural inclusion and exclusion. Hence, cultural capital comprises those aspects of the middle-class lifestyle that serve to separate their members from working- and lower-class individuals. Bourdieu argued that children who display these cultural attributes are more likely to fare well in middle-class institutions (including school) because these institutions value and reward these attributes. Lower- and working-class children are more likely to lack these cultural attributes and therefore are at an academic disadvantage in school. Lareau and Horvat (1999) extended this argument by illustrating that although possession of cultural capital is important, groups may differ in their ability or opportunity to activate these resources in different settings.

Sociologists have typically measured cultural capital by examining elite cultural practices like cultural trips (trips to museums and art galleries) and taking extracurricular classes in "high" culture areas (dance, art, and music) (DeGraaf 1986; DiMaggio 1982; Roscigno and Ainsworth-Darnell 1999). While the practice of these "high" cultural activities is associated with family SES (DiMaggio and Ostrower 1990), there is still variation in the practice of these activities within any given SES stratum.

Another way of measuring capital advantage has been to examine the level of household educational resources available to the student. It has been argued that household educational resources (books, computers, magazines, encyclopedias) shape the academic orientation of a child (Lareau 1989; Mercy and Steelman 1982; Teachman 1987), although the impact of these resources has been found to vary according to the number of siblings who share the resources in the household (the resource-dilution effect) (Downey 1995; Steelman and Powell 1989, 1991; Roscigno and Ainsworth-Darnell 1999).

Consistent with prior research on the effects of cultural capital and household educational resources on academic orientation and achievement, we assume that black and lower-SES teenagers have relatively fewer educational resources and less cultural capital overall than do their white and middle-class counterparts. In addition, Lareau and Horvat (1999) suggested that race has an independent effect on social interactions within schools and between parents and schools. They contended that although the presence of cultural capital is important, the activation and acceptance of that capital in educational settings may differ by race. In other words, the return to cultural capital and other educational resources (perhaps even participation in sports) may be different for white students than it is for black students.

Why would there be a relationship between family educational resources and involvement in sports? At least two possible explanations exist. First and specifically for blacks, children with low family educational resources may be more vulnerable to social forces that encourage an overemphasis on sports, regardless of the source of that message: parents, overzealous coaches or teachers, or the generic reinforcements of the media and its glorification of professional athletes (Lederman 1990; Messner 1990; Siegel 1994). Second, all children who lack academic resources may be attracted to sports because of the benefits that one can acquire by participation, either short term (such as popularity, attention from adults, and enhanced self-esteem) or long term (a future in professional sports). These overlapping explanations point to the importance of examining how differences in family academic support influence participation in sports and subsequent academic achievement.

The association between family educational resources and involvement in sports may differ by the type of sport being examined. While the aforementioned explanations may account for lower-SES students' interest in playing popular sports, such as football or basketball, students from advantaged backgrounds may find other sports more appealing, partially because they are reflective of their advantaged backgrounds. Sports like swimming or golf may not even be available to students who attend schools in poor communities. To the extent that more advantaged students may be more attracted to elite sports, however, their experiences in such sports can contribute to a social reproduction of status differences, in that they are likely to be playing with other advantaged students. Although the question of peer "effects" on educational achievement has been thoroughly debated in the literature (see Heckman and Neal 1996), the failure to consider educational resources in the family may serve to produce illusory findings that may be due to such sorting.

Because of the issues surrounding the possible associations between family educational resources, race, participation in sports, and academic achievement, we believe an examination of these relationships is warranted. The following questions guided our research:

1. Are young black males more likely to participate in basketball and football than are young white males, after opportunity to participate in the sport in high school (there are opportunity differences, such as the number of potential competitors for limited spots on sports teams) is controlled? Edwards (1986) and others suggested that there are important racial differences in the types of sports that black males are attracted to; hence, we partitioned those sports from others to evaluate the linkages between the variables of interest more closely.

2. Are male students with few cultural capital resources more likely to participate in football and basketball than are those with more cultural capital resources?

3. Do the effects of cultural capital on participation in the various sports differ by race?

4. Are there any academic benefits and/or costs of sports participation for students once cultural capital resources are considered?

Given previous scholarship, we make the following predictions:

1. Black male students are more likely to play basketball or football than are white male students.
2. Students with fewer cultural capital resources are more likely to participate in football or basketball (regardless of race).
3. The benefits of sports participation are positive for white males once cultural capital resources are considered (Melnick et al. 1992).
4. For black males, playing football or basketball has little influence on academic achievement, after cultural capital resources are considered.

Our predictions are guided by the extension of social reproduction theory. In summary, we believe that race, cultural capital, and educational resources are critical factors that need to be incorporated into analyses of the linkages between participation in sports and academic achievement.

Data and Methods

Sample

We used data from the first two waves of the National Education Longitudinal Survey (NELS), conducted by the National Center for Education Statistics (NCES), a nationally representative study that collected information from students, parents, teachers, and administrators. The first wave of the survey was conducted in 1988 and drew random samples of approximately 25 eighth graders in each of approximately 1,000 randomly selected middle schools. The students were then administered further surveys and tests in 1990 during the second wave of the longitudinal study (see NCES 1992).

The longitudinal design of NELS allowed us to minimize questions of causal ordering in the analyses by using variables measured at the first wave (1988), when students were in the eighth grade, to predict sports participation in 1990 and academic achievement at the end of that academic year (NCES 1992). We limited our analyses to male black and white public school students who are still in school in 1990. We explored potential differences between black and white male students in the effects of family factors on their participation in football, basketball, and other sports and of participation on academic outcomes.[1] . . .*

Table 1 presents the description and summary statistics of the major variables used in our analyses.

Analytic Strategy

The analyses proceed in sequential steps. First, we examine the differences between black and white students on selected factors. Next, we explore the extent to which interscholastic participation in football, basketball, and other sports is a function of family SES and structure, cultural capital and educational resources, and prior achievement (controlling for other factors), and whether there are racial differences in the effects of these factors on participation in sports. Two logistic regression analyses are conducted for each of the sports. The first model introduces the factors to be explored and focuses on the direct effects of these factors on sports participation. The second model introduces race interactions

---

* For information about sample weights and the specific indicators used to measure the conceptual variables, see the original article. [Eds.]

Table 1   Variables, Descriptions, and Standard Errors for Weighted Mean Estimates: 1990 Black and White Male 8th Graders in 1988 (Unweighted N = 5,018)

Variable	Description	Metric	Mean or proportion (SE)
1990 Sports Participation			
Basketball	Student's report of whether or not he participated in varsity or junior varsity basketball in 1990.	0 = did not participate 1 = did participate	.16 (.01)
Football	Student's report of whether or not he participated in varsity or junior varsity football in 1990.	0 = did not participate 1 = did participate	.24 (.01)
Other sports	Student's report of whether or not he participated in any varsity or junior varsity sport other than football or basketball in 1990.	0 = did not participate 1 = did participate	.39 (.01)
1990 Academic Achievement			
Mathematics-reading test composite	Standardized composite of math and reading test scores (1990).	30.68 = lowest score 71.82 = highest score	50.45[a] (.25)
Grades composite	Student's reported grade composite using English, mathematics, science, and social studies grades (1990).	.5 = mostly less than Ds 4.0 = all As	2.73[b] (.02)
8th-Grade Sports Participation			
Interscholastic sports	Student's report of whether or not he participated in interscholastic sports in the 8th grade (1988).	0 = did not participate 1 = did participate	.52 (.01)
Intramural sports	Student's report of whether or not he participated in intramural sports in the 8th grade (1988).	0 = did not participate 1 = did participate	.45 (.01)
Family Characteristics/ Structure			
Family SES	Standardized composite of father's educational level, mother's educational level, father's occupation, mother's occupation, and family income (1988).	-2.23 = lowest score 2.56 = highest score	-.03 (.02)
Single-parent household	Student lives in a single-parent household (1988).	0 = not in a single-parent household, 1 = in a single-parent household	.20 (.01)
Stepparent household	Student lives in a stepparent household (1988).	0 = not in a stepparent household 1 = in a stepparent household	.17 (.01)
Family Cultural Capital and Resources			
Cultural trips	Student goes to (1) art museums, (2) science museums, (3) history museums (1988).	0 = none of these museums 3 = all these museums	1.45 (.03)

(continues)

Table 1 *(continued)*

Variable	Description	Metric	Mean or proportion (SE)
Cultural classes	Student attends classes outside his or her regular school to study: (1) art, (2) music, (3) dance (1988).	0 = none of these classes 3 = all these classes	.34 (.01)
Household educational resources	Which of the following does the student have in his home? (1) daily newspaper, (2) regularly received magazine, (3) an encyclopedia, (4) an atlas, (5) a dictionary, (6) a computer, (7) more than 50 books, (8) a pocket calculator in the 8th grade (1988).	0 = none of these items 8 = all of these items	6.30 (.04)
Racial Group Identification			
Race	Student's racial identification	0 = white non-Hispanic 1 = black	.14 (.01)
Prior Achievement			
Student math-reading composite	Standardized composite of math and reading test scores (1988).	31.81 = lowest score 75.81 = highest score	50.74 (.24)
Student grade composite	Student's reported grade composite using English, mathematics, science, and social studies grades (1988).	.5 = mostly less than Ds 4.0 = all As	2.85 (.02)

[a] $N = 4,930$.
[b] $N = 4,951$.

to explore if racial differences exist in the effects of family characteristics, cultural capital, educational resources, and prior achievement on participation in sports. The significance of interaction terms for basketball, but not for football or other sports, suggests that racial differences do exist but not for all sports. Next we explore the consequences of sports participation for academic achievement. We estimate the direct effects of participation in football, basketball, and other sports on mathematics-reading achievement and self-reported grades using ordinary least squares (OLS) regression. This analytic strategy allows us to explore whether the return on participation differs by sport. We follow it by introducing race-sport interactions into the analyses to see whether the effects of participation in football, basketball, and other sports differ by race. We control for prior achievement to assess the contemporary importance of sports participation.

Results

Family Resources, Race, and Sports Participation

Table 2 presents summary statistics by race for selected variables and includes difference of means or proportions tests for black versus white students. The Wald statistic in-

Table 2 Weighted Mean Estimates and Standard Errors: Differences In 1990 Black and White Male 8th Graders In 1988 (Unweighted N = 611 for black students and N = 4,407 for white students)

Variable	Black Students: Mean or Proportion (SE)	Wald Statistic (F-test)	White Students: Mean or Proportion (SE)
1990 Sports Participation			
Interscholastic football	.36 (.04)	10.58**	.22 (.01)
Interscholastic basketball	.33 (.04)	20.72***	.13 (.01)
Interscholastic sport			
(other than football or basketball)	.31 (.04)	5.38*	.41 (.01)
1990 Academic Achievement			
Math-reading test composite[a]	43.92 (.57)	154.03***	51.54 (.25)
Grades composite[b]	2.64 (.05)	2.90	2.74 (.02)
Prior Sports Participation			
8th-grade interscholastic sports	.50 (.04)	.20	.52 (.01)
8th-grade intramural sports	.42 (.04)	.72	.45 (.01)
Family Characteristics/Structure			
Family SES	-.45 (.04)	141.43***	.04 (.02)
Single-parent household	.20 (.01)	.86	.16 (.01)
Stepparent household	.40 (.04)	38.52***	.16 (.01)
Two-parent household	.40 (.03)	61.43***	.68 (.01)
Family Cultural Capital and Resources			
Cultural trips	1.20 (.10)	7.30**	1.49 (.03)
Cultural classes	.24 (.03)	11.34***	.35 (.01)
Household educational resources	5.26 (.18)	45.60***	6.47 (.03)
Educational Achievement			
8th-grade math-reading test composite	44.25 (.45)	225.80***	51.83 (.24)
8th-grade grade composite	2.68 (.05)	13.80***	2.88 (.02)

[a] N = 595 black students and N = 4,335 white students.
[b] N = 595 black students and N = 4,356 white students.
* $p < .05$, ** $p < .01$, *** $p < .001$.

cluded in Table 2 indicates whether the statistical estimates for black male students are significantly different from the estimates for white male students.

There are racial differences in participation in football, basketball, and other sports. Black males are 1.6 times as likely as white males to participate in interscholastic football in high school and 2.5 times as likely to participate in interscholastic basketball. On the other hand, white males are 1.3 times more likely than black males to participate in other interscholastic sports (baseball, soccer, swimming, track, and so forth). These differences exist in spite of no meaningful racial differences in 8th-grade

sports participation. The failure to find meaningful racial differences in 8th-grade sports participation is likely due to the use of a global measure of playing sports instead of measures of participation in specific sports (as was the case in assessing sports participation in the 10th grade).

As expected, black male students come from families with significantly lower SES; have fewer household resources; take fewer trips to museums; and are less likely to attend art, music, or dance classes than white male students. In addition, 68 percent of the white male 8th graders were living in two-parent families; in contrast, only 40 percent of the black male 8th graders were living in two-parent families, and another 40 percent were living in households with stepparents.

The results of the logistic regression analyses examining the effects of family characteristics and cultural capital, prior educational achievement, and race on participation in football, basketball, and other sports are presented in Table 3. Previous studies suggested that family SES is positively associated with overall participation in high school sports. Our models indicate that SES does not have a consistent effect on participation in particular sports. The relationship between family SES and participation in basketball and other sports is positive, but SES has no effect on participation in football. Likewise, unlike studies of the influence of family characteristics on measures of academic outcomes, household structure in this study, measured as a two-parent, single-parent, or stepparent family, was not found to be a direct predictor of sports participation.[2]

The central independent variables, cultural capital measures and household educational resources, provide consistent support for the notion that culturally disadvantaged males are more likely to turn to football and basketball than are other high school students. As predicted, participation in other sports is not significantly related to the measures of cultural capital and household educational resources. Taking cultural trips has a small but significant effect on participation in basketball, but not in football. Students who have participated in cultural trips are less likely to participate in basketball (.88). For example, this finding means that each additional type of cultural trip increases the odds of *not playing* high school basketball by a factor of 1.1.[3] The effect of participation in cultural classes was also

found to be a significant predictor of participation in football and basketball. Each additional cultural class makes the odds of *not playing* high school football or basketball 1.3 times greater. Clearly, some measures of cultural capital are predictive of whether a male participates in basketball or football at the interscholastic level. On the other hand, the effect of the measure of household educational resources was only significant in the football participation model, and even there, it was negligible in terms of substantive importance.

Prior academic achievement, as measured by test scores, has the predicted association with participation in football and basketball. A 10-percentage point decrease in the mathematics-reading composite increases the odds of participating in football by a factor of 1.11 and in basketball by a factor of 1.35.[4] This finding supports the notion that males with fewer academic resources are more likely to participate in some sports. On the other hand, the measure of prior grades is positively associated with participation in basketball and other sports. A one-letter increase in a student's grade composite increases the odds of participating in basketball by 1.59 times and the odds of participating in other sports by 1.45 times. Although seemingly inconsistent, the effects of these two measures of prior achievement are not surprising, given the earlier insights about grade inflation, curriculum selection, and teacher selection that can mask true associations between academic learning and sports participation (Snyder and Spreitzer 1990). Furthermore, because students often must maintain some minimal grade point average to try out for or participate in interscholastic athletics in junior high school and high school, there may be some threshold that selects out some

Table 3   Logistic Coefficient Estimates for Regression of Football, Basketball, and Other Sports Participation on Race and Background Characteristics: 1990 Black and White Male 8th Graders in 1990[a] (Unweighted N = 5,018)

Variable	Football Participation Model 1		Basketball Participation Model 1		Other Sports Participation Model 1	
	b	Exp (b)	b	Exp (b)	b	Exp (b)
Family Characteristics/Structure						
Family SES	.11	1.12	.33**	1.39	.43***	1.53
	(.10)		(.12)		(.12)	
Single-parent household	-.03	.97	.004	1.00	.12	1.13
	(.17)		(.20)		(.17)	
Stepparent household	.02	1.02	-.23	.79	-.13	.88
	(.15)		(.19)		(.15)	
Family Cultural Capital and Resources						
Cultural trips	-.05	.95	-.13*	.88	-.03	.97
	(.05)		(.07)		(.04)	
Cultural classes	-.25**	.78	-.22*	.80	-.08	.92
	(.09)		(.10)		(.09)	
Household educational resources	-.10*	.91	-.09	.91	.05	1.06
	(.05)		(.06)		(.04)	
Race (black = 1)	.93***	2.54	1.74***	5.68	-.11	.90
	(.21)		(.24)		(.19)	
Educational Achievement						
Centered math-reading composite	-.01*	.99	-.03***	.97	.001	1.00
	(.01)		(.01)		(.01)	
Centered grade composite	-.01	.99	.46***	1.59	.37***	1.45
	(.09)		(.10)		(.09)	
Controls						
8th-grade interscholastic sports	.95***	2.59	.99***	2.69	.58***	1.79
	(.12)		(.15)		(.10)	
8th-grade intramural sports	.24**	1.27	.41***	1.51	.36***	1.43
	(.10)		(.12)		(.10)	
Student in the 10th grade (versus in school but not in the 10th grade)	.54*	1.72	.76*	2.15	.90***	2.47
	(.25)		(.35)		(.25)	
10 to 49 percent minority enrollment in the 10th grade	-.07	.93	-.39**	.68	.09	1.09
	(.12)		(.15)		(.11)	
50 to 100 percent minority enrollment in the 10th grade	-.56**	.57	-.63**	.53	.18	1.20
	(.22)		(.26)		(.18)	
800-1,599 students enrolled in the 10th grade	-.25*	.78	-.66***	.52	-.13	.88
	(.13)		(.15)		(.12)	
1,600 or more students enrolled in the 10th grade	-.40**	.67	-1.26***	.28	-.49***	.62
	(.17)		(.19)		(.15)	
Intercept	-1.41		-2.00		-1.94	
F-test, Model 1	11.51		19.17		16.94	

[a]Metric coefficients (standard errors).
* $p < .05$, **$p < .01$, ***$p < .001$ (one-tailed test).

athletically oriented students and excludes them from participation.

Perhaps the most important and compelling finding is the effect of race on sports participation. Controlling for the other factors, the odds that a black male will participate in interscholastic football or basketball are 2.54 times greater and 5.68 times greater, respectively, than the odds of participation for a white male. However, no such relationship exists between race and participation in other sports. This finding is supportive of the importance of participation in football and basketball, rather than other sports, for black males relative to whites.

There are also some interesting effects associated with the control for school minority enrollment.[5] Enrollment at a school that has a 50 percent to 100 percent minority enrollment vis-à-vis a school that has less than a 10 percent minority enrollment substantially decreases the odds of participating in football and basketball. Similarly attending a school that has a 10 percent to 49 percent minority enrollment vis-à-vis a school that has less than a 10 percent minority enrollment decreases the odds of participating in basketball. This effect provides some support for the notion that participation in football and basketball is important in the black community—the more minorities in a school, the more competition for limited opportunities to play football and basketball.

Although these models provide basic support for the idea that cultural disadvantage increases the likelihood of participating in the popular sports of football and basketball, the models do not investigate differences in the relationships between the independent variables of interest and sports participation for black versus white males. Table 4 presents the results of the logistic re-

gression analyses using interaction terms to examine whether the effects of the measures of family characteristics and structure, cultural capital and resources, or prior educational achievement on sports participation differ by race.

The most important finding illustrated in Table 4 is that race interactions are significant only in the basketball participation model.[6] We found support for the idea that there are racial differences in the effects of some of the measures of family characteristics, family cultural capital and educational resources, and prior academic achievement on participation in basketball but not in football or other sports. A significant difference was found between black and white males regarding the influence of living in a stepparent household on basketball participation. For white males, living in a stepparent versus a two-parent (non-stepparent) family increases the odds of *not playing basketball* by a factor of 1.79. For black students, there is no significant relationship between family structure and participation.

With regard to family cultural capital, the effect that differs by race is the influence of taking cultural classes on basketball participation. For white males, participating in cultural classes has no significant effect on the odds of participating in high school basketball. For black males, it decreases the odds of participating in high school basketball by a factor of .47. In other words, for each additional cultural class that a black student takes part in, the odds of *not participating* in basketball increase by a factor of 2.13. The effect of household educational resources on basketball participation is similar. Each additional household resource increases the odds of *not participating* in basketball by a factor of 1.22 for black

Table 4 Logistic Coefficient Estimates for Regression of Football, Basketball, and Other Sports Participation on Race and Background Characteristics with Race Interactions: 1990 Black and White Male 8th Graders in 1988[a] (Unweighted N = 5,018)

Variable	Football Participation Model 2		Basketball Participation Model 2		Other Sports Participation Model 2	
	b	Exp (b)	b	Exp (b)	b	Exp (b)
Family Characteristics/Structure						
Family SES	.09	1.09	.22**	1.25	.41***	1.51
	(.09)		(.09)		(.13)	
Single-parent household	-.12	.89	-.03	.97	.06	1.06
	(.16)		(.18)		(.19)	
Stepparent household	-.09	.92	-.58**	.56	-.18	.83
	(.15)		(.19)		(.17)	
Family Cultural Capital and Resources						
Cultural trips	-.08*	.92	-.18***	.83	-.01	.99
	(.04)		(.05)		(.04)	
Cultural classes	-.21*	.81	-.14	.87	-.07	.93
	(.10)		(.10)		(.09)	
Household educational resources	-.07*	.94	.02	1.02	.06	1.06
	(.04)		(.05)		(.04)	
Race (black = 1)	1.64*	2.27	2.11**	8.26	-.30	.74
	(.95)		(.92)		(.78)	
Educational Achievement						
Centered grade composite	.03	1.03	.53***	1.71	.41***	1.51
	(.09)		(.10)		(.09)	
Centered math-reading composite	-.01	.99	-.02***	.98	.00	1.00
	(.01)		(.01)		(.01)	
Controls						
8th-grade interscholastic sports	.96***	2.60	1.03***	2.81	.58***	1.79
	(.11)		(.13)		(.10)	
8th-grade intramural sports	.25**	1.29	.45***	1.57	.37***	1.44
	(.10)		(.12)		(.10)	
Student in the 10th grade	.61	1.83	.94**	2.56	.97***	2.63
(versus in school but not in the	(.27)		(.39)		(.25)	
10th grade)						
10 to 49 percent minority	-.05	.95	-.35	.70	.09	1.10
enrollment in the 10th grade	(.12)		(.14)		(.11)	
50 to 100 percent minority	-.54**	.59	-.59**	.56	.17	1.18
enrollment in the 10th grade	(.19)		(.21)		(.18)	
800 to 1,599 students enrolled in the	-.23*	.79	-.62**	.54	-.13	.88
10th grade	(.12)		(.13)		(.12)	
1,600 or more students						
enrolled in the 10th grade	-.39**	.68	-1.25***	.29	-.48	.62
	(.16)		(.18)		(.15)	
Race Interactions						
Family SES	.07	1.08	.32	1.37	.08	1.09
	(.31)		(.33)		(.31)	
Single-parent household	.54	1.71	.45	1.57	.41	1.51
	(.43)		(.46)		(.43)	
Stepparent household	.59	1.80	1.13**	3.08	.49	1.63
	(.38)		(.41)		(.41)	
Cultural trips	.13	1.14	.13	1.14	-.16	.85
	(.17)		(.16)		(.15)	
Cultural classes	-.36	.70	-.62*	.54	-.17	.84
	(.33)		(.36)		(.29)	
Household educational resources	-.08	.92	-.22*	.81	.01	1.01
	(.12)		(.12)		(.11)	
Centered grade composite	-.28	.75	-.36	.70	-.38	.68
	(.26)		(.27)		(.25)	
Centered math-reading composite	-.02	.98	-.08**	.93	-.02	.98
	(.03)		(.03)		(.03)	
Intercept	-1.65		-2.86		-2.07	
F-test, Model 2	8.14		15.06		12.02	
F-test for race interactions	1.29		3.69***		1.58	

[a]Metric coefficients (standard errors).
* $p < .05$, ** $p < .01$, ***$p < .001$ (one-tailed test).

males. Household resources have no significant impact on basketball participation for white males.

One measure of prior academic achievement also varies by race. Prior mathematics-reading composite scores are negatively associated with participation in basketball for both black and white males. For white males, a 10-percentage point (approximately one standard deviation) increase in the mathematics-reading composite score increases the odds of *not participating* in basketball by a factor of 1.26. For black males, a 10-percentage point increase increases the odds of *not participating* in basketball by a factor of 2.78. This finding supports the general idea that males who are not doing well academically are more likely to turn to sports and, more specifically, that black males in this situation are much more likely than white males to turn to sports.

To clarify the effects of the independent variables on the likelihood of participating in sports, we present the predicted probabilities that black and white males with selected characteristics will play basketball or football in high school. The predicted probabilities illustrate the striking effects of the factors being manipulated in Table 5 when other factors are at their mean or modal values. In particular, they highlight the impact that having cultural capital has on the probability that a male will participate in interscholastic basketball.

However, it is important to remember that the opportunity structures for basketball and football participation vary considerably, with the chance of playing football generally greater than the chance of playing basketball. Hence, it is somewhat difficult to make cross-sports comparisons. With that caveat in mind, black males are much less likely to participate in basketball and

football, but particularly basketball, if they are involved in cultural classes and trips. Given the characteristics of other factors noted in the table, black males who have high or even the mean level of cultural capital versus low cultural capital will be less likely to play these sports. For example, a black male who lives in a two-parent family has a 26 percent likelihood of playing basketball and a 52 percent likelihood of playing football if he has low cultural capital. But if a similarly situated black male has high exposure to cultural activities, the likelihood that he will play interscholastic basketball or football drops to 3 percent and 30 percent, respectively. Although the effect of cultural capital on football participation is of the same magnitude for black and white male students, this is not the case for basketball participation. A decrease in the level of cultural capital results in a greater change in the probability of playing basketball for black males than for white males.

The effect of changes in the measure of household educational resources on the likelihood that black and white males will participate in basketball or football are similar to the effect of changes in the measures of cultural capital. The exception is that household educational resources have no impact on basketball participation for white males. On the other hand, a black male who lives in a two-parent family and attends no cultural classes has a 31 percent likelihood of participating in basketball if his level of household educational resources is one standard deviation below the mean. If the same student has the mean level or one standard deviation above the mean level of household educational resources, his likelihood of participating in basketball drops to 25 percent and 20 percent, respectively.

Table 5 Predicted Probabilities of Participating in Interscholastic Basketball and Football for Male Students with Selected Characteristics[a]

Characteristics of Students	Basketball: White Students	Basketball: Black Students	Football: White Students	Football: Black Students
Two-parent family	.111	N.A.	N.A.	N.A.
Stepfamily	.065	N.A.	N.A.	N.A.
Two-parent Family				
Low cultural capital (0 cultural classes, 0 cultural trips)	.146	.261	.295	.515
Mean cultural capital (mean level of cultural classes and trips)	.111	.203	.263	.476
High cultural capital (3 cultural classes, 3 cultural trips)	.061	.030	.144	.300
Two-parent Family, No Cultural Classes				
1 standard deviation below the mean score on the math-reading composite	.142	.467	.303	.525
Mean score on the math-reading composite	.116	.247	.280	.497
1 standard deviation above the mean score on the math-reading composite	.094	.110	.257	.468
1 standard deviation below the mean level of household educational resources	N.A.	.306	.310	.533
Mean level of household educational resources	N.A.	.247	.280	.497
1 standard deviation above the mean level of household educational resources	N.A.	.197	.251	.460

[a] All the students reported here were in the 10th grade; participated in interscholastic but not intramural sports in the 8th grade; were in a school with 10–49 percent minority enrollment and 800–1,599 students; and were at the mean for SES, household educational resources, cultural classes, cultural trips, prior grades, and prior math-reading composite score unless otherwise noted.

The probabilities associated with changes in prior achievement, as measured by mathematics-reading composite scores, also illustrate the racial differences in the impact of prior mathematics-reading composite scores on participation in basketball. A black male from a two-parent family who attends no cultural classes has a 47 percent likelihood of participating in basketball if his prior test scores were one standard deviation below the mean score, while a similarly situated white male has a 14 percent likelihood of participation. The likelihood of participation decreases to 11 percent for the black male and to 10 percent for the white male if his prior test scores were one standard deviation above the mean score. This finding is particularly compelling, since it demonstrates that among the academically gifted, race has no bearing on the likelihood of playing basketball—it is relatively low for both high-performing whites and blacks.

These findings of racial differences in the impact of cultural capital, household educational resources, and prior achievement on participation in basketball (but not in football or other sports) are consistent with a number of observations about the relative importance of basketball among many in the black community. Basketball at the professional level is the sport in which the highest percentage of blacks participate. Hobermann (1997:6), who argued that a sports fixation in the black community has exacted a toll on black intellectual development, called basketball "the black sport par excellence." Thus, the finding that black males who lack cultural capital (relative to those who have cultural capital) are much more likely to play basketball supports the idea that black males participate in basketball if they do not have the cultural advantages that will help them succeed scholastically.

Involvement in cultural classes, access to more household educational resources, and higher mathematics-reading composite scores are all related to lower participation in football; that these relationships do not differ for black and white males is also compelling, especially since the relationships between these factors and participation in basketball differ by race. One explanation may simply be differences in the aforementioned opportunity structure for the respective sports. Another explanation is that for working-class white males, playing football has a somewhat loftier status (akin to basketball for black males) than do other sports, particularly given the level of physical violence in football relative to basketball. Although the opportunity for social advancement (a professional career) may not be the driving force for white males with low cultural capital, football may be seductive for satisfying more immediate needs, such as self-esteem, masculinity, a sense of belonging, or a legitimate social outlet for expressing frustration (Coakley 1990; Messner 1990).

So while we are unable to determine if sports are used as a means for social and economic mobility or merely as a way of fulfilling more immediate status needs and wants, it is clear that culturally disadvantaged black males are much more likely than both similarly situated whites and culturally advantaged black males to participate in football and basketball. Furthermore, this relationship is specific only to football and basketball, since participation in other sports was unrelated to cultural capital, household educational resources, or prior standardized test scores.

Race, Sports Participation, and Achievement

The models presented in Table 6 are OLS regressions of two measures of academic achievement (mathematics-reading achievement and grades composite) on students' race, family SES and structure, family cultural and educational resources, prior achievement, and sports participation. These models show results consistent with prior research on the effects of family SES, cultural capital, and household educational resources on mathematics-reading achievement, but the models offer new evidence to support the idea that the relationship between sports participation and mathematics-reading achievement depends on the sport and the race of the participant.

Models 1 and 2 predict change in the dependent variable (mathematics and reading achievement, relative to others) from 1988 to 1990. They illustrate that the effect of participation in sports on mathematics-reading achievement varies by sport even after controlling for two measures of prior achievement. This inclusion of prior grades and achievement scores should help disentangle earlier effects of sports from current effects. In Model 1, both football and basketball participation are negatively associated with mathematics-reading achievement, while participation in other sports is not associated with achievement. In Model 2, we find no racial differences in the impact of participation in football, basketball, or other sports on changes in achievement. Therefore, and somewhat contrary to our expectations, participation in football and basketball appears to cost students in their subsequent academic achievement, regardless of whether they are black or white. Although participation in other sports appears to enhance students' subsequent performance on these tests, playing football or basketball seems to drain resources away from academic achievement.

Models 3 and 4 include similar OLS regressions of self-reported grades (10th grade) on students' race, family SES and structure, family cultural and educational resources, and sports participation. It is not surprising that both prior test scores and prior grades are significant predictors of self-reported grades (Models 3 and 4). Many of the associations between family measures (family SES, cultural trips, and cultural classes) and self-reported grades appear to be mediated by prior measures of academic performance (test scores and prior self-reported grades). However, the effect of being raised in a single-parent household still exerts a direct influence on such grades, with those living with one parent reporting relatively lower grades, all things being equal. The indicator of race is still a significant predictor of grades, controlling for prior test scores and grades.

The patterns of association between participation in sports and self-reported grades, while somewhat distinct, are generally supportive of the overall findings that participation in different sports has differential consequences for academic achievement. First, the associations between playing football and basketball and grades fail to reach significance when prior grades and test scores are included in the analyses. However, participation in other sports appears to have benefits for grades, but only for whites. Indeed, the interaction coefficient between race and participation in other sports reveals that for black students, playing such sports actually has a significant negative effect on self-reported grades (see Model 4). This

Table 6 OLS Coefficient Estimates for Regression of Student's Mathematics-Reading Test Composite Score and Grades Composite on Race, Background Characteristics, Sports Participation, and Prior Achievement: 1990 Black and White Male 8th Graders in 1988[a]

Variable	Mathematics-Reading Test Composite Model 1	Mathematics-Reading Test Composite Model 2	Grades Composite Model 3	Grades Composite Model 4
Sports Participation				
10th-grade interscholastic football	-.53*	-.41	-.02	-.05
	(.22)	(.23)	(.03)	(.03)
10th-grade interscholastic basketball	-.80**	-.72**	.08	.08**
	(.25)	(.26)	(.04)	(.03)
10th-grade interscholastic sport (not football or basketball)	.19	.11	.14***	.18***
	(.20)	(.21)	(.03)	(.03)
Family Characteristics/Structure				
Family SES	.54**	.54**	.02	.02
	(.17)	(.17)	(.02)	(.02)
Single-parent household	.07	.06	-.08**	-.08*
	(.24)	(.24)	(.06)	(.04)
Stepparent household	-.48	-.46	-.03	-.03
	(.29)	(.29)	(.05)	(.05)
Family Cultural Capital and Resources				
Cultural trips	.24**	.25**	.02	.02
	(.09)	(.08)	(.02)	(.01)
Cultural classes	-.18	-.18	.02	.02
	(.18)	(.18)	(.02)	(.02)
Household educational resources	.15*	.14*	-.02	-.02
	(.07)	(.07)	(.02)	(.01)
Race (black = 1)	-.21	-.10	.17**	.21**
	(.36)	(.46)	(.06)	(.07)
Controls				
Student in the 10th grade (versus in school but not in the 10th grade)	1.20***	1.24***	.19**	.18**
	(.35)	(.35)	(.06)	(.06)
10 to 49 percent minority enrollment (10th grade)	-.23	-.22	.02	.02
	(.23)	(.23)	(.03)	(.03)
50 to 100 percent minority enrollment (10th grade)	-.29	-.32	-.06	-.05
	(.33)	(.32)	(.06)	(.05)
8th-Grade Achievement				
Math-reading test composite	.80***	.80***	.02***	.02***
	(.01)	(.01)	(.00)	(.00)
Grades composite	1.39***	1.38***	.46***	.46***
	(.15)	(.15)	(.02)	(.02)
Race Interactions				
10th-grade interscholastic football		-.81		.17
		(.66)		(.12)
10th-grade interscholastic basketball		-.30		.03
		(.62)		(.13)
10th-grade interscholastic sport (not football or basketball)		.81		-.36*
		(.58)		(.14)
Intercept	4.12	4.14	.46	.45
R^2	.765	.765	.40	.40
Unweighted *N*	4,930	4,930	4,951	4,951

[a]Metric coefficients (standard errors).
* $p < .05$, ** $p < .01$, *** $p < .001$ (two-tailed test).

finding may help to account for the mixed results of prior research that sometimes supported a positive relationship (Braddock 1981; Otto 1982) and sometimes supported a negative relationship (Coleman 1961) between sports participation and achievement—participation in some sports may enhance academic achievement for some students, but participation may serve as a drain on academics for others. Again, while grades may be a less-than-perfect measure of actual learning, the findings reveal that what sport one plays and who is playing the sport are important considerations for understanding the link between sports and academic outcomes.

Discussion

Our findings suggest that the relationship between participation in sports and academics may be more complex than previous studies have acknowledged and that future studies that explore this relationship should incorporate an understanding of factors that contribute to participation in sports. Coupled with previous research that indicated that cultural capital influences academic outcomes, our findings suggest that the link between sports and academics may differ, depending on the cultural resources that the student brings to school, as well as the particular sport or sports that the student plays. Considering Roscigno and Ainsworth-Darnell's (1999) finding that black and low-SES students receive less educational return for their level of cultural capital than do white and higher-SES students, we argue that it is vital to understand how the nexus between cultural resources, participation in sports, and educational outcomes may differ substantially according to a student's racial and class background.

Among our central findings were the following: (1) black males were more likely to be involved in sports generally than were whites, *ceteris paribus*; (2) differences in cultural capital (participation in cultural classes) were strong predictors of participation in basketball and football, but not in other sports; (3) the cultural capital measures did not make nearly as dramatic a difference in predicting the participation of white males as they did in predicting the participation of black males in basketball; (4) participation in basketball and football has a negative relationship with standardized achievement scores for its participants; (5) participation in basketball and football has neither benefits nor costs with regard to grades; and (6) playing other sports is associated with higher grades for whites but lower grades for blacks.

It was somewhat surprising that participation in football and basketball was found to be a drain on academic achievement (as measured by test performance), regardless of the race of the student. Although it is not clear if all these students are drawn to sports because of the hope of a professional career, as Edwards (1986) suggested is the case for black athletes, and/or because their participation satisfies more immediate social or personal needs, the implication of our research is that cultural disadvantage may contribute to an increased interest in and dependence on particular sports and that this dependence on sports may have additional adverse consequences for its participants in terms of academic achievement. Indeed, the temporal ordering of the relationship between involvement in sports and academic achievement may be more complicated than some have previously assumed. Rather than sports serving simply as a drain on energies that could be spent in maximizing academic achievements, males may end up pursuing some sports because they lack the resources necessary to perform well academically, which only serves to disadvantage them further in achieving academic excellence.

Clearly, our models omit important factors that lead to participation in sports. We have no measures of parents' level of involvement in their sons' sports activities, parents' participation in sports, whether the parents play sports with their sons (or teach or coach their sons in sports), or even the extent of parents' interest in sports (e.g., parents' attendance at games). Furthermore, we have no measures of interpersonal support for involvement in sports from such key actors as friends, coaches, or other influential members in the community. However, our primary interest was to investigate whether differences in educational resources and cultural capital in black males would be related to involvement in particular sports and whether such involvement would have different academic implications for different participants, and we found support for these notions. Whether or not families intentionally push their sons toward participating in sports (at the expense of educational objectives), our analyses suggest that participation in cultural trips and classes may protect socioeconomically disadvantaged black and perhaps white males and provide benefits in terms of academic achievement.

Our analyses of academic outcomes were also limited by a lack of data on sport-specific sports participation in Wave 3 of NELS.[7] Future research should explore longer-term effects of sports participation, such as graduation, 12th-grade achievement, and even college attendance. While

our analyses included 8th-grade general participation in sports, measures of sport-specific participation in the 12th grade might have helped disentangle issues related to the effects of a short versus long-term commitment to different sports. Finally, female and other racial and ethnic groups should also be studied.

In his analysis of the effects of school factors on participating in high school extracurricular activities (including sports), McNeal (1999) contended that involvement in extracurricular activities serves to increase levels of human (defined as one's level of skills, knowledge, and educational attainment), social (one's network of relationships established with other persons, such as peers, parents, and teachers, and the intrinsic value of such bonds), and cultural capital. Our analysis could not directly address whether McNeal's assumptions are true for people across racial and SES categories and for every extracurricular activity. However, we offer the following conjecture based on our analysis. McNeal and others may be right that participation in such activities increases capital. If that is the case, it likely explains why people who lack such capital may be more drawn to participation in sports than are those who have significant levels of educational and cultural capital. Playing a sport may be a rational choice for a teenager with few resources to increase his or her level of overall capital. But the fact that participating in sports may increase one's social and human capital does not necessarily mean that it is a maximizing pathway for acquiring valuable capital in the future. As our analysis revealed, it may be particularly true only for the effects of certain sports (e.g., football and basketball) on academic achievement. Our analysis suggests that Edwards (1986) and others, on the one hand, and McNeal (1995, 1999) and others, on the other hand, can both be right—generally, participation in sports is positively associated with (or has little negative consequences for) desired student outcomes, but especially when the sport being played is football or basketball, it detracts from meaningful acquisitions of educationally related capital for blacks as well as for others who play such sports.

Notes

1. We included other sports as a comparison to examine whether the effects of factors that precipitate participation in sports when there are high-profile professional opportunities (especially for black males) will be different from factors that precipitate participation in other sports. We explored similar models for females, and these models suggest that the relationships differ by sport and by gender.

2. Family size was included in original models not reported here, but was found to have no direct effect on sports participation.

3. To calculate the effect of the independent variables on the odds of the student not participating in the sport, we calculated the inverse of the effect on the odds of the student participating in the sport.

4. While some collinearity exists between the two measures of prior achievement (the mathematics-reading composite and the grades composite), it does not substantially alter the results. When entered individually, each measure has a similar coefficient estimate and significance with the exception of the effect of math-reading achievement on participation in other sports. The effect of mathematics-reading achievement on participation in other sports is positive and significant when the measure of prior grades is excluded from the analysis.

5. We recognize that the inclusion of organization-level measures of school characteristics violates the assumption of independent errors, since many of the students in the sample attended schools with other students in the sample. In response to this concern, we reanalyzed all our models using a hierarchical linear model for continuous outcomes and a hierarchical generalized linear model for binary outcomes. We found little difference in the results of the logistic or OLS models versus the hierarchical models (i.e., significance did not change and coefficients differed little in magnitude). In addition, reliability issues surfaced in the hierarchical models when we used only a subset of the students originally included in the NELS 88–92 panel (we included only black and white males), which resulted in a low number of students per school (see Carbonaro 1999). In fact, the modal number of students per high school in our sample was one student, with greater than 20 percent of the students in our sample in this situation. Hence, we report the results of our logistic and OLS regression analyses.

6. The *F*-test for the race interactions is reported in Table 4. This test indicates the significance of the inclusion of the race interactions as a group.

7. The third wave (second follow-up) NELS survey asked students a global question regarding sports participation, but did not ask which sports they played.

References

Alexander, Karl L., Doris R. Entwisle, and Maxine S. Thompson. 1987. "School Performance, Status Relations, and the Structure of Sentiment: Bringing the Teacher Back In." *American Sociological Review* 52:665–82.

Bourdieu, Pierre. 1977. "Cultural Reproduction and Social Reproduction." Pp. 487–511 in *Power and Ideology in Education,* edited by Jerome Karabel and A. H. Halsey. New York: Oxford University Press.

Bowles, Samuel, and Herbert Gintis. 1976. *Schooling in Capitalist America: Educational Reform and the Contradictions of Economic Life.* New York: Basic Books.

Bowles, Samuel, and Henry M. Levin. 1968. "The Determinants of Academic Achievement:

An Appraisal of Some Recent Evidence." *Journal of Human Resources* 3:3–24.

Braddock, Jomills H. 1981. "Race, Athletes, and Educational Attainment." *Youth and Society* 12:335–50.

Carbonaro, William J. 1999. "Opening the Debate on Closure and Schooling Outcomes: Comment on Morgan and Sørensen." *American Sociological Review* 64:682–86.

Carrington, B. 1986. "Social Mobility, Ethnicity and Sport." *British Journal of Sociology of Education* 7(1):3–18.

Coakley, Jay. 1990. *Sport in Society: Issues and Controversies* (4th ed.). St. Louis: Times Mirror/Mosby.

Coleman, James S. 1961. *The Adolescent Society.* New York: Free Press of Glencoe.

Coleman, James S., Ernest Q. Campbell, Carol F. Hobson, James M. McPartland, Alexander M. Mood, Frederic D. Weinfeld, and Robert L. York. 1966. *Equality of Educational Opportunity.* Washington, DC: U.S. Government Printing Office.

Dauber, Susan L., Karl L. Alexander, and Doris R. Entwisle. 1996. "Tracking and Transitions Through the Middle Grades: Channeling Educational Trajectories." *Sociology of Education* 69:290–307.

DeGraaf, Paul M. 1986. "The Impact of Financial and Cultural Resources on Educational Attainment in the Netherlands." *Sociology of Education* 59:237–46.

DiMaggio, Paul J. 1982. "Cultural Capital and School Success: The Impact of Status Culture Participation on the Grades of U.S. High School Students." *American Sociological Review* 47:189–201.

DiMaggio, Paul J., and Francie Ostrower. 1990. "Participation in the Arts by Black and White Americans." *Social Forces* 68:753–78.

Downey, Douglas. 1995. "When Bigger Is Not Better: Family Size, Parental Resources, and Children's Educational Performance." *American Sociological Review* 60:746–61.

Edwards, Harry. 1986. "The Collegiate Athletics Arms Race." Pp. 21–43 in *Fractured Focus,* edited by Richard A. Lapchick. Lexington, MA: Lexington Books.

Eitzen, D. Stanley, and George H. Sage. 1997. *Sociology of North American Sport.* Madison, WI: Brown & Benchmark.

Fejgin, Naomi. 1994. "Participation in High School Competitive Sports: A Subversion of School Mission or Contribution to Academic Goals?" *Sociology of Sport Journal* 11:211–30.

Hanks, Michael P. 1981. "Youth, Voluntary Associations, and Political Socialization." *Social Forces* 60:211–23.

Hanks, Michael P., and Bruce K. Eckland. 1976. "Athletics and Social Participation in the Educational Attainment Process." *Sociology of Education* 49:271–94.

Harris, Othello. 1994. "Race, Sport, and Social Support." *Sociology of Sport Journal* 11:40–50.

Heckman, James J., and Derek Neal. 1996. "Coleman's Contributions to Education: Theory, Research Styles and Empirical Research." Pp. 81–102 in *James S. Coleman,* edited by Jon Clark. London: Falmer Press.

Hoberman, John. 1997. *Darwin's Athletes: How Sport Has Damaged Black America and Preserved the Myth of Race.* Boston: Mariner Books.

Lamont, Michele, and Annette Lareau. 1988. "Cultural Capital: Allusions, Gaps, and Glissandos in Recent Theoretical Developments." *Sociological Theory* 6:153–68.

Landers, Daniel, and Donna Landers. 1978. "Socialization via Interscholastic Athletics: Its Effects on Delinquency." *Sociology of Education* 51:299–303.

Lareau, Annette. 1989. *Home Advantage: Social Class and Parental Intervention in Elementary Education.* New York: Falmer Press.

Lareau, Annette, and Erin McNamara Horvat. 1999. "Moments of Social Inclusion and Exclusion: Race, Class, and Cultural Capital in Family-School Relationships." *Sociology of Education* 72:37–53.

Lederman, Douglas. 1990, April 25. "Panel Examining Blacks and Sports Discusses Possibility of Boycotting Colleges that Fail to Educate Black Athletes." *Chronicle of Higher Education*:A36.

Loy, John W., Barry D. McPherson, and Gerald Kenyon. 1978. *Sports and Social Systems: A*

Guide to the Analysis, Problems, and Literature. Reading, MA: Addison-Wesley.

Marsh, Herbert W. 1993. "The Effects of Participation in Sport During the Last Two Years of High School." *Sociology of Sport Journal* 10:18–43.

McNeal, Ralph B. 1995. "Extracurricular Activities and High School Dropouts." *Sociology of Education* 68:62–81.

———. 1999. "Participation in High School Extracurricular Activities: Investigating School Effects." *Social Science Quarterly* 80:291–309.

Melnick, Merrill J., Donald F. Sabo, and Beth Vanfossen. 1992. "Educational Effects of Interscholastic Athletic Participation on African-American and Hispanic Youth." *Adolescence* 27:295–308.

Melnick, Merrill J., Beth Vanfossen, and Donald F. Sabo. 1988. "Developmental Effects of Athletic Participation Among High School Girls." *Sociology of Sport Journal* 5:22–36.

Mercy, James A., and Lala Carr Steelman. 1982. "Familial Influence on the Intellectual Attainment of Children." *American Sociological Review* 47:532–42.

Messner, Michael A. 1990. "Boyhood, Organized Sports, and the Construction of Masculinities." *Journal of Contemporary Ethnography* 18:416–44.

National Center for Education Statistics. 1992. *First Follow-Up: Student Component Data File User's Manual.* Washington DC: U.S. Department of Education.

Oakes, Jeannie. 1985. *Keeping Track: How Schools Structure Inequality.* New Haven, CT: Yale University Press.

Oliver, M. 1980. "Race, Class and Family's Orientation to Mobility Through Sport." *Sociological Symposium* 30:62–86.

Otto, Luther. 1982. "Extracurricular Activities." Pp. 217–33 in *Improving Educational Standards and Productivity,* edited by H. J. Walberg. Berkeley, CA: McCuthan.

Otto, Luther, and Duane Alwin. 1977. "Athletics, Aspirations, and Attainments. *Sociology of Education* 50:102–13.

Phillips, John C. 1993. *Sociology of Sport.* Boston: Allyn & Bacon.

Roscigno, Vincent J. 1998. "Race and the Reproduction of Educational Disadvantage." *Social Forces* 76:1033–60.

Roscigno, Vincent J., and James W. Ainsworth-Darnell. 1999. "Race, Cultural Capital, and Educational Resources: Persistent Inequalities and Achievement Returns." *Sociology of Education* 72:158–78.

Sabo, Donald, Merrill J. Melnick, and Beth E. Vanfossen. 1993. "High School Athletic Participation and Postsecondary Educational and Occupational Mobility: A Focus on Race and Gender." *Sociology of Sport Journal* 10:44–56.

Sage, George H. 1990. *Power and Ideology in American Sport: A Critical Perspective.* Champaign, IL: Human Kinetics.

Siegel, Donald. 1994. "Higher Education and the Plight of the Black Male Athlete." *Journal of Sport & Social Issues* 18:207–23.

Snyder, Eldon E., and Elmer Spreitzer. 1990. "High School Athletic Participation as Related to College Attendance Among Black, Hispanic, and White Males: A Research Note." *Youth & Society* 21:390–98.

Spady, William. 1970. "Lament for the Letterman: Effects of Peer Status and Extracurricular Activities on Goals and Achievement." *American Journal of Sociology* 75:680–701.

Steelman, Lala Carr, and Brian Powell. 1989. "Acquiring Capital for College: The Constraints of Family Configuration." *American Sociological Review* 52:844–55.

———. 1991. "Sponsoring the New Generation: Parental Willingness to Pay for Higher Education." *American Journal of Sociology* 96:105–29.

Teachman, Jay D. 1987. "Family Background, Educational Resources, and Educational Attainment." *American Sociological Review* 52:548–57.

Chapter 14

HIGH SCHOOL FOOTBALL

Deep in the Heart of South Tejas

Douglas Foley

In this piece by Douglas Foley, we are given an insider's view of how football fits into a small South Texas high school and how the town, the school, and football together tend to reinforce the central divisions of the community. Even as "homecoming" was an annual expression of school and community unity, gender and race divisions were embedded in the rituals surrounding football games. Foley's examination of North Town High and its football team illustrates how the status hierarchy of the town and of the school articulate with one another.

The Study: North Town

The setting of my study was "North Town," a small (8,000 population) South Texas farming and ranching community with limited industry, considerable local poverty, and a population that was 80 percent Mexican-American. North Town High had an enrollment of 600 students. Its sports teams played at the Triple-A level in a five-level state ranking system. North Town High usually made a habit of winning their conference and occasionally the bi-district. As in many other Texas towns, people took their football very seriously.

Shortly after arriving in North Town I attended my first pep rally. Students, whether they liked football or not, looked forward to the Friday afternoon pep rally. Perhaps nothing is more uniquely "American" than these events that are supposed to whip the student body into a frenzy to support the team. The exchange student from Norway found its blaring brass band and bouncy cheerleaders strange and exciting, "very different from our high school sports." Meanwhile, the coaches and players were upfront on the stage stammering through cliché-filled speeches about beating the "Tigers." The crowd seemed to accept

Douglas Foley, "High School Football: Deep in the Heart of South Tejas" from *Inside Sports*, edited by Jay Coakley and Peter Donnelly. Copyright © 1999. Reprinted with the permission of Routledge.

their inarticulateness as a virtue. They were strong and silent types. Men of action, not words.

Meanwhile, the cheerleaders were on the gym floor doing dance and jumping routines in unison for the crowd. They were acknowledged as some of the prettiest young women in the school, and they aroused the envy of students who had reputations as "nobodies" and "nerds." Male students incessantly gossiped and fantasized about these young women and their reputations. Particularly the less attractive, "uncool" males plotted the seduction of these young women. They reveled in the idea of having them as girlfriends, but they often accused the cheerleaders of being "stuck up" or "sluts." Most of their talk about cheerleaders was sheer fantasy and laced with considerable envy. Only those males with very high social status could actually risk relating to and being rejected by these dangerous, status-confirming young women.

Many young women who were not athletic or attractive enough to be elected also fantasized about becoming a cheerleader. Such young women joined the pep squad as an alternative. The North Town pep squad comprised a group of fifty young women in costume who came to the games and helped the cheerleaders arouse crowd enthusiasm. The pep squad also helped publicize and decorate the school and town with catchy team-spirit slogans such as "Smash the Seahawks" and "Spear the Javelinos." In addition, they helped organize after-game school dances. Their uniforms expressed loyalty to the team, and pep squad members were given a number of small status privileges in the school, such as being released from classes early for pep rallies and away games.

The other crucial part of any pep rally is the marching band. Indeed, some community members scrutinized the quality of the marching band as carefully as they did the football team. Although the band director, Dante Aguila, disliked turning music into a team-like competition, he did it to conform to community wishes. Like sport teams, marching bands competed in local, district, and statewide contests, attempting to garner high rankings. Individual band members could also achieve top rankings in various instruments, but the emphasis was on attaining a high group ranking. A certain segment of the student body began training for the high school marching band during their grade-school years. Band members were generally in the advanced academic tracks and perceived by the more marginal, deviant students as "goodie goodies," "richies," and "brains." Not all band members were top students or rich, but they were generally loyal, school-oriented students. Many female band members were "cool" and socially prominent, but others were studious homebodies and uncool.

On the other hand, "real men" supposedly did not sign up for the North Town band. According to the football players, only the physically weaker, more effeminate males were in the band. Consequently, males in the band were often derisively labeled "band fags." The only exceptions were a few "cool guys" who did drugs and had their own rock and roll band. Regrettably, males who emulated jocks and hoped to hang with them picked on band fags. However, the players themselves rarely picked on band members. They were too powerful and prestigious to use this as a status-boosting strategy. Consequently, they showed physical restraint towards obviously weaker males. Such a show of restraint enhanced the players' social status among peers.

In anthropological jargon, the pep rally, with its inarticulate heroic male warriors, adoring cheerleaders and pep squad, maligned yet irrepressible "band fags" and audience of loyal "nobodies," is a major American cultural ritual. Among other things, this ritual reproduces what feminists call the patriarchal order of male privilege. One can see this pattern especially well in a curious event called the "powder-puff football game." Exactly how widespread powder-puff football games are, I cannot say, but students from all over Texas and various states report similar practices in their high schools. In North Town, a powder-puff football game is staged by the junior and senior classes on the Friday before the seniors' final game. A number of the senior girls dress up as football players and form a touch football team to play the junior girls. The male football players serve as coaches and referees. Some also dress up as girls and act as cheerleaders. Perhaps a quarter of the student body, mainly the active, popular, successful students, drifted in and out to have a laugh over this game.

This event struck me as a priceless example of what anthropologists call "rituals of reversals." During such events people break or humorously play with their everyday cultural rules and roles. Such reversals are so clearly marked as being out of the ordinary that everyone knows the participants are "just playing." No male who is acting like a female will be accused of being a girl or homosexual, nor will the women be accused of wanting to be men. In this instance, however, it is crucial to note that the males used this moment of symbolic inversion to parody females in a burlesque and ridiculous manner. Males used this event to act in silly

and outrageous ways. They pranced around in high heels, smeared their faces with lipstick, and flaunted their padded breasts and posteriors in a sexually provocative manner. This was their way of expressing their social and physical dominance. Conversely, the females took few liberties with the male role being played. They donned the football jersey and helmets and huffed and puffed soberly under the watchful eyes of the boys. They blocked and shoved with considerable gusto. They tried to play a serious game of football. They wanted to prove that they were equal. Their lack of playfulness was a poignant testimony to their subordinate status in this small town.

Another part of any football season is the annual homecoming celebration. It also reproduces male privilege but has a much broader community function as well. Ideally, North Town graduates return to the homecoming bonfire and dance to reaffirm their support and commitment to the school, team, and town. Typically, the local paper plays up the homecoming game, and it draws a bigger crowd. On this particular homecoming day, three groups of boys with pickup trucks created a huge pile of scrap wood and burnable objects in the school parking lot. Unlike the school pep rally, a number of adults and ex-students joined the band, cheerleaders, pep squad, and players and coaches. The mood was even more festive and informal than the after-school pep rallies. The adults attending laughed about the "borrowed" packing crates and were pleased that others "donated" things from their stores and houses to feed the fire.

During the homecoming game, a king and queen and their attendants were presented and crowned during half-time. The royal court, typically the most popular and attractive students, was elected by the student body. The queen and her court, dressed in formal gowns, were ceremoniously transported to the crowning in convertibles. The king and his attendants, who were often football players, escorted the young women from the convertibles to their crowning in their dirty, sweaty uniforms. After the game, the king and queen and their respective courts were presented at the homecoming dance. The dance was primarily for high school students, but ex-students, especially those in college, were noticeably present at the informal beer parties after the dance. The homecoming pep rally, crowning, dance, and informal beer parties struck me as a particularly heightened expression of tradition and community solidarity.

Another major aspect of any football season is how the community, beyond being spectators and fans, actively involves itself in the football ritual. North Town was the type of community in which male teachers who had athletic or coaching backgrounds were more respected than other teachers. North Town school board members, many rugged farmers and ranchers, generally preferred that their school leaders be ex-coaches. In addition, the North Town Booster Club—composed mainly of local merchants, farmers, and ranchers—had the all-important function of raising supplementary funds for improving the sports program and for the post-season awards banquet. The Booster Club was the most direct and formal link that coaches had with North Town civic leaders. According to many ex-coaches, players, and fans, North Town had a long history of Booster Club and school board interference. North Town students and adults often expressed fears and suspicions that the school board and Booster Club imposed their racial and class

preferences on the coaches and team. In this case, the role of the Booster Club illustrates nicely that the football ritual reproduces class and racial inequalities as well as gender inequalities.

Early in the season, the North Town Booster Club became outspoken against coach Trujillo, their "weak Mexican coach." He was generally perceived as too "nice" and not enough of a "disciplinarian." Prominent Anglos frequently compared him unfavorably to an earlier, highly successful Anglo coach who had a much more military style. Early in the season, conflict surfaced over the selection of the varsity quarterback. Coach Trujillo chose the son of an Anglo businessman, and underclassman, over a senior, the son of a less prominent Anglo. The less educated Anglo faction lambasted the coach for giving preference to the children of socially and politically prominent families. Several other controversial player decisions also occurred, but selecting the varsity quarterback, the symbolic leader of the team, was especially sensitive.

Later in the season, the Booster Club also became critical of how coach Trujillo handled the selection of the freshman quarterback. The local restaurants staged many coffee-drinking debates over which of the two freshman quarterbacks should start, the "strong-armed Mexican boy" or the "all-around, smart Anglo boy." The Anglo boy was the son of a prominent car dealer and Booster Club activist. The Mexican boy was the son of a migrant worker and small grocery store manager. Eventually, the Anglo boy became the starter, which aroused several prominent Mexican political leaders to blast coach Trujillo as a *vendido* (sell-out) for succumbing to the Booster Club and "their freshman coach," whom they considered a racist "redneck." These incidents generally illustrate how prominent citizens from all races can and do put considerable pressure on coaches. The Booster Club was a particularly powerful voice, and its racial and class prejudices clearly enter into some decisions about players.

Having briefly portrayed the racial and class politics that surrounded player decisions, I must add that on a day-to-day basis, there was considerable racial harmony among players. North Town Mexicans and Anglos played side by side with few incidents during the regular season. Although the team never quite lived up to pre-season predictions, they did win six of their ten games. More importantly, these young players displayed a great deal of team unity in the face of much racial squabbling among the adults.

But what about the players? What did they think about their sport and being athletes? Only a very small percentage of players were skilled enough to play college or professional football. As already suggested, the social rewards from playing football are mainly local and cultural. Small town football is a way "to meet cute chicks" or to get preferential treatment from teachers to retake a test or get out of class early. Some players parroted a chamber of commerce view that football builds the character and discipline needed to succeed in life. Others evoked patriotic and civic ideals about beating rival towns and "showing that South Texas plays as good a football as anybody."

On a more personal level, however, playing was a way of proving that you were a virile man. Players talked incessantly about being "hitters" and "studs." They were always trying to prove that they could inflict pain and play with pain. But not all young men found an honored place in society through sports. A few simply ignored foot-

ball and excelled in other forms of self-expression and achievement from art to science. Most non-playing males fitted into the football ritual as spectators, academic advisors to the players, hangers on, band members, and sports fans.

One group of non-players stood out, however, because of their marginal racial and class position. The most conspicuous anti-footballers were working-class Mexicans called "vatos" (cool dudes) who were into a hip, drug-oriented lifestyle. They considered sports straight and "kid-stuff for suckers and suck-asses." They went to games to establish "reps" as tough guys who beat up kids from other towns and "hit on their chicks." After each game, the vatos regaled me with tales of their foray into enemy territory—the fights they won, the women they conquered. They saw themselves as warriors who were not under the thumb of "dumb coaches" and restrictive training rules. They were tough, unconventional North Town patriots who helped establish the town's reputation as a cool, hip place.

In actual fact, many "straight" North Town football players actually shared some aspects of the vatos' rebellious lifestyle. They often broke their strict training rules by drinking and smoking pot at private teen parties. Publicly, however, most jocks acted like all-American boys. Unlike the rebellious vatos who flaunted their drinking and drugs publicly, jocks hid their pleasures and represented themselves as "clean cut" and "straight." If jocks got caught breaking training, prominent men in the community tended to explain away these infractions as natural male temptations. Most fathers believed that "boys will be boys." Players were rarely criticized publicly the way rebellious vatos, non-playing males, and young women were. As long as they were not out-rageously indiscreet through public drunk-enness or getting a "trashy girl" pregnant, their training infractions were forgiven. They often seemed to revel in their privi-leged role and were not above telling "I-got-drunk/stoned-before-the-game stories" to the school "nobodies."

To sum up, North Town football is a powerful metaphor of American capitalist culture (Foley 1990a). Football is an enjoy-able, seemingly innocent popular cultural practice, but it is deeply implicated in the reproduction of the local ruling class of white males, hence class, patriarchal, and racial forms of dominance. All too often, coaches and players become ensnared in the local politics of the Booster Club. Local sports, especially football, socialize every new generation of youth into the local sta-tus hierarchy, both inside and outside the school. Each new generation of males learns to be individualistic, aggressive, and com-petitive within a group structure, thus bet-ter prepared for military and corporate life.

References

Foley, Douglas. (1990a) *Learning Capitalist Cul-ture: Deep in the Heart of Tejas,* Philadelphia: University of Pennsylvania Press.

Chapter 15

ODD JOBS HELP COLLEGE TEAMS STAY AFLOAT

Teddy Kider

One Sunday morning every fall, members of the Penn State fencing team spend hours scraping nacho cheese, chewing tobacco, peanut shells and cigarette butts off the floor of the university's 107,000-seat football stadium.

Cleaning after a home game is an annual fund-raising ritual for the team, a coed varsity program that is one of the most successful in national competition. Unfortunately for Division I athletes in sports like fencing, winning championships does not guarantee financial stability.

The cash cow of college athletics returns next week, when multimillion-dollar television programming begins with college football and continues through the end of the N.C.A.A. men's college basketball tournament in April. But for many athletes who compete in sports that do not produce revenue—the sports other than football and basketball—the arrival of the college football season means the return to working for the programs they see on television in order to support their own teams.

At N.C.A.A. Division I universities, football and basketball generate most of the revenue that comes from teams, and even some of those programs cannot make ends meet. For other sports, universities often leave it up to players and coaches to find other sources of funding.

For Butler softball players, that has meant working the gates at football games and cleaning the basketball arena. At Utah, that has led to having swimmers serve as hospitality workers in the suites at football games. And in the case of Penn State's fencing program, that has involved cleaning the trash left behind by the crowds that attend home football games at Beaver Stadium.

"It's one of the grossest things I'll ever have to do—hopefully—in my life," said the Penn State senior Megan Luteran, a captain of the fencing team, which last season won its 10th national title in 18 years.

Joe Paterno, Penn State's football coach, only underscored the uncomfortable nature of the fencers' job when he said his team would help clean Beaver Stadium on Sundays this season without compensation. The decision was a punishment for several football players' suspected connection to an off-campus fight.

Some coaches and administrators insist that it is unreasonable to ask Division I athletes to participate in small moneymaking projects, especially those that involve working for more profitable programs.

Billy Martin, the coach of U.C.L.A.'s men's tennis team, a perennial national championship contender, acknowledged that his program could not make any money for the athletic department, but he called some of the small projects "high schoolish."

Bob Reasso, the men's soccer coach at Rutgers, said: "You're not going to ask a major Division I football or basketball athlete to do a car wash. We have the same caliber athletes."

At Butler, a university that recently cut its men's lacrosse and men's swimming programs, the softball coach Jeanne Rayman raises about 15 percent of her program's annual budget through fund-raisers. Her team has sold cookie sheets and held a beanbag-tossing tournament.

"I'm always looking to find something unique, where people don't just say, Oh, this is just another fund-raiser," said Rayman, who says she discloses her team's efforts when recruiting players.

Butler softball teams have also worked the gates at football games, sold concessions at men's basketball games, cleaned the basketball arena and helped direct cars at Indiana Pacers and Indianapolis Colts games.

"The reality of where we are today is that we need to find a way to supplement bud-

gets," said Barry Collier, Butler's athletic director. "This is part of it."

Andrew Brown, a senior on the men's swimming team at Utah, said that male and female swimmers at his university have had to stock suite refrigerators before football games, then hand out marketing materials at the stadium gates and make sure guests in the suites and the press box have enough food and drinks.

"I'm just happy we still have a swimming team, because a lot of Division I teams are being cut," said Brown, who has an athletic scholarship that pays for his tuition and books.

Other programs choose to avoid small-scale, time-consuming fund-raising work in favor of relying entirely on other sources of funding, like donations. Doug Smith, the associate athletic director for development at Baylor, said he did not believe in "project-oriented programs," which he said involve too much work and time and produce an inadequate financial return. Penn State's fencing team sells university merchandise at football games, and the money they gather from stadium cleaning—several thousand dollars a year—enables them to take an overseas trip once every four years.

Jimmy Moody, a junior on the fencing team, said he found the stadium cleaning experience humbling and understood that Penn State's football team brought in money that benefited his team. But he was also interested in finding out how the football players would react to the dirty work.

"I'm glad for once that they'll have to do it," Moody said. "They'll get a taste of it. They get to see what we do every year."

N.C.A.A. bylaws limit the number of hours student-athletes can spend on "athletically related activities." But those activities do not include fund-raising, said Stacey Osburn, a spokeswoman for the N.C.A.A. Osburn said most rules about fund-raising were left up to individual universities.

At Butler, Rayman said, the continual projects can seem like a burden for some of her players.

"They have so much going on in their college lives, trying to be the best athletes they can be and trying to have somewhat of a social life," Rayman said. "It just becomes a daily grind. It's more of a drain on them than a morale booster."

For many student-athletes, including Brown, the Utah swimmer, the choice between working for high-profile teams and abandoning the sports they love is easy to make.

"It's unfair that we have to put in extra work because our sport might not be as much fun to watch," Brown said. "But it is fair that the school is giving us a chance to work to keep the program around."

Emmanuil Kaidanov, Penn State's fencing coach, said he thought cleaning the stadium, however unpleasant it might be, was a good team-building effort. He emphasized his 10 national titles and asked how anybody could question him.

"We bond through our misery," Moody said.

PART IV

THE POWER OF ATHLETICS: SPORTS AND POLITICS

There is an expectation that politics and sports do not and *should not* mix. No matter that the celebrity status provided by a career in professional sports has catapulted untold numbers of athletes into national legislatures—and even into the California governor's mansion. Yet, somehow, sport is seen as an arena of *play* and is therefore excluded from "the real world." After all, "it's just a game." We expect that, because of his or her lifelong socialization into the discipline of the game, the individual athlete will be largely unconcerned with, if not disconnected from, the realm of politics. Although we do not necessarily have this same expectation for other highly trained professionals (for example, physicists, doctors, architects, and the like), we somehow expect our athletes to keep their noses out of politics—and, if they do show interest, to keep it to themselves.

Why, when there are so many examples of athletes in politics, when the quadrennial Olympics and World Cups are festivals of nationalist politics, and when so many countries have some kind of national sports ministry, do we have this notion that politics and sports do not mix? In *Playing by the Rules* (1994), John Wilson usefully divides society into three domains organized by different principles and types of associations: (1) the state, organized by coercion and regulation and comprising all who officially make, influence, and enforce policy; (2) the market, focused on profitability and dominated by large corporations; and (3) the voluntary sector, focused on mutuality and friendly association, the primary locus of sports. As we suggested in Part I on the political economy of sports, once sports becomes institutionalized, these domains intersect deeply; it becomes impossible to understand the meaning of sports for society without considering the political and economic moorings of sports as well as the constraints and opportunities offered by sports.

Yet, the desire by fans to see the game as "pure" is strong. They do not want to think about whether Michael Jordan is a Republican or a Democrat (indeed, Jordan self-consciously decided that he wished to be perceived as apolitical, and famously quipped, in response to why he wasn't supporting black progressive Democrat Harvey Gantt in his election race

209

against white Republican Jesse Helms, who was widely considered to be racist, "Republicans buy sneakers, too") or what Peyton Manning's position is on universal health care. They *do* want to know about who Tom Brady is dating and about the latest shopping exploits of David and Victoria Beckham. Sports are fun; politics is serious; never the twain shall meet.

It is certainly helpful for the stability of sports (and the stability of given political regimes) to keep these domains as seemingly separate as possible. The reigning powers-that-be in the world of sports would like everyone involved to think that all the decisions within games and about the composition of teams are about winning. Does a basketball fan really want to hear that the coach doesn't want to call a timeout because there's a TV timeout coming up? Does that fan ever want to consider that a player who was free for a layup didn't get the ball because his teammates are freezing him out because of his views on race or neoliberal trade policy? Fans want to believe that the game is pure—that the decisions of coaches and players are based on strategic issues within the game. Such a belief leads fans to have a narrow, insulated, and—literally—conservative (in the sense of conserving the status quo) view of sports. The idea is that the game should be, in some sense, unspoiled by outside factors and that each athlete or coach should focus solely on playing or coaching to the best of his or her ability—*and* on winning.

Perhaps this conception of sports and of the relationship between sports and society would explain the disproportionate share of ex-athletes who, for example, take up the Republican mantle in the United States. Trading on their stardom, ex-jocks such as Steve Largent, J. C. Watts, Arnold Schwarzenegger, and Jim Bunning present themselves as Horatio Alger–like success stories who, relying on individual determination, were able to use athletics to realize the American Dream. Indeed, in many cases their experiences reflect that dream. Although these success stories are very rare events, they legitimate the rags-to-riches myth.

In general, professional athletes are pressured to stay out of politics, which is, of course, ironic, given that athletes are presented as symbols of patriotism as they stand solemnly when the national anthem is played or when they attend a White House ceremony to celebrate their championship. When an athlete does take some kind of critical political stand, the response by the team or league is usually swift and harsh (though tempered by the athlete's perceived contribution to team and league success). Witness how quickly Craig Hodges was out of the National Basketball Association (NBA) after he criticized the way the United States was dealing with poverty. Steve Nash's criticism of the Iraq War, though, led only to columnists suggesting that he keep his nose out of U.S. politics (Nash is Canadian). Witness as well the silence of the Red Sox and Major League Baseball in general in response to Curt Schilling's continual expressions—on radio and on his website—of support for the Iraq War.

At the same time, there is no doubt that sports and politics are strongly linked. Not only, as just implied, are sports used by regimes to underscore their legitimating myths; in addition, sports have been used by subordinate groups to bring attention to injustice. In the context of the U.S. civil rights movement, Tommie Smith and John Carlos brought attention to issues of race and sports on the biggest stage of all, the 1968 Olympics. Similarly, the Gay Games represent an attempt by lesbian, gay, bisexual, and transgender athletes to claim public space for their principles of "participation, inclusion, and personal best" in the context of "fellowship and friendly competition" (www.gaygames.com; see also Helen Jefferson Lenskyj's article, "Gay Games or Gay Olympics? Implications for Lesbian Inclusion"). According to Alan Klein (1995), baseball in the Dominican Republic, insofar as it reflects relations of domination and resistance along various dimensions, may not only provide avenues of social mobility for fortunate and talented baseball players but may also be a source of resistance in struggles against dictatorial regimes. Finally, it is worthwhile to remember the devotion of African Americans and political progressives to the Brooklyn Dodgers after the team broke the "color line" with the signing of Jackie Robinson in 1947.

Questions abound concerning why and how athletes become connected to particular political positions. Does the discipline of sports, including respect for the coaches' authority and subordination of self to team goals—which is central to the athletes' experience—predispose athletes toward conservative political positions? Do such predispositions vary by type of sport? Is the predisposition more likely in team sports than in individual sports? Are positions on teams that allow for greater creativity—say point guards—less likely to produce these conservative tendencies? How, if at all, are viewers of sports affected by watching them? Does such viewing affect their political preferences? And, of course, in a key question that motivates the selection of readings below, how do these tendencies vary by country?

In their article "Where Are the Jocks for Justice?" Kelly Candaele and Peter Dreier raise questions about the social conditions that produce an orientation to political engagement in the United States. They suggest that the fact that pro-athletes typically do not speak out on key issues may have much to do with the large paychecks they receive. The situation in Argentina is very different, according to Leslie Ray in "Argentina's Left-Wingers." There, football (soccer) has had specific connections to national political movements. Moreover, class and regional attachments to football teams have often had strong political orientations. Even in Argentina, however, there were hesitations about linking sports and politics. Similarly, Helen Jefferson Lenskyj, in "Gay Games or Gay Olympics? Implications for Lesbian Inclusion," presents a case where athletes embraced sports in order to engage a political issue (gay rights), but found that pressures from within sports attempted to minimize the politics. In Ben Carrington's piece, "Sport, Masculinity, and Black Cultural Resistance," we see, through an examination of a specific cricket club in England, how politics is engaged at multiple levels: The club is a place where race and gender identities are contested, where community is reinforced, and where white racism is resisted.

So, despite the necessary yet conflicted nature of the relationship, sports and politics are each strongly imbued with the symbols and metaphors of the other. Politicians often claim that they will use a "full-court press" to get their legislation passed, and coaches and players talk about games as "battles" and "wars." In his article "Televised Sport, Masculinist Moral Capital, and Support for the Invasion of Iraq," Carl Stempel goes even further, arguing that fan attachment to certain kinds of televised sports helps to explain the fans' commitment to certain political positions. Stempel's evidence is very suggestive, and it is well worth considering how our sports television viewing articulates with other orientations to the world.

References

Klein, Alan. 1995. "Culture, Politics, and Baseball in the Dominican Republic." *Latin American Perspectives* 22, no. 3 (Summer): 111–130.

Wilson, John. 1994. *Playing by the Rules: Sport, Society, and the State*. Detroit, MI: Wayne State University Press.

Chapter 16

WHERE ARE THE JOCKS FOR JUSTICE?

Kelly Candaele and Peter Dreier

In this selection, Kelly Candaele and Peter Dreier document the pressures on U.S. athletes to avoid any semblance of political dissent. Using many examples of athletes who have been silenced after an initial engagement with politics, the authors argue that athletes' wealth, potential future income, and social connections all conspire to keep them quiet. Candaele and Dreier suggest that the position of athletes in the larger political economy also provides them with many opportunities to intervene politically in progressive directions.

Adonal Foyle, 29, is a 6-foot, 10-inch center for the NBA's Golden State Warriors.* Like most pro athletes, he spent his youth perfecting his game, hoping for a shot at big-time sports. But off the court he's an outspoken critic of America's political system. "This mother of all democracies," Foyle insists, "is one of the most corrupt systems, where a small minority make the decisions for everybody else."

Three years ago Foyle started a grassroots group called Democracy Matters (www.democracymatters.org). Its goal is to educate young people about politics, mobilize them to vote and bring pressure on elected officials to reform the nation's campaign finance laws. When he's not playing basketball, Foyle is frequently speaking at high schools, colleges and conferences about the corrupting role of big money in politics. "I have lots of support [from fellow players] and I explain to them a lot what I'm doing," says Foyle. "The players understand that I want people to be excited about the political system."

Foyle's activism is rare in the world of professional sports. Many athletes visit kids in hospitals, start foundations that fix inner-city playgrounds, create scholarship funds to help poor students attend college and make commercials urging kids to stay in school and say no to drugs. But when it comes to political dissent, few speak out on big issues like war, sweatshop labor, environmental concerns or the increasing gap between rich and poor. While Hollywood celebrities frequently lend their fame and

Kelly Candaele and Peter Dreier, "Where Are the Jocks for Justice?" from *The Nation* (June 28, 2004). For subscription information, call 1-800-333-8536. Portions of each week's *Nation* magazine can be accessed at http://www.thenation.com.

* As of 2008, Foyle plays for the Orlando Magic. [Eds.]

fortune to candidates and causes, athletes are expected to perform, not pontificate. On the few occasions when they do express themselves, they are often met with derision and contempt.

Last year, for example, just before the United States invaded Iraq, Dallas Mavericks guard Steve Nash wore a T-shirt to media day during the NBA's All-Star weekend that said No War. Shoot for Peace. Numerous sports columnists criticized Nash for speaking his mind. (One wrote that he should "just shut up and play.") David Robinson, an Annapolis graduate and former naval officer, and then center for the San Antonio Spurs, said that Nash's attire was inappropriate. Flip Saunders, coach of the NBA's Minnesota Timberwolves, told the Minneapolis *Star-Tribune*: "What opinions you have, it's important to keep them to yourselves." Since then, no other major pro athlete has publicly expressed antiwar sentiments.

Although political activism has never been widespread among pro athletes, Foyle is following in the footsteps of some courageous jocks. After breaking baseball's color line in 1947, Jackie Robinson was outspoken against racial segregation during and after his playing career, despite being considered too angry and vocal by many sportswriters, owners and fellow players. During the 1960s and '70s some prominent athletes used their celebrity status to speak out on key issues, particularly civil rights and Vietnam. The most well-known example, boxing champion Muhammad Ali, publicly opposed the war and refused induction into the Army in 1967, for which he was stripped of his heavyweight title and sentenced to five years in prison (he eventually won an appeal in the Supreme Court and didn't serve any time). Today he is among

the world's most admired people, but at the time sportswriters and politicians relentlessly attacked him.

Many others were also unafraid to wear their values on their uniforms—and sometimes paid the price. Coaches and team executives told Dave Meggyesy, an All-Pro linebacker for the St. Louis Cardinals in the late 1960s, that his antiwar views were detrimental to his team and his career. As he recounts in his memoir *Out of Their League*, Meggyesy refused to back down, was consequently benched, and retired at age 28 while still in his athletic prime. Tennis great Arthur Ashe campaigned against apartheid well before the movement gained widespread support. Bill Russell led his teammates on boycotts of segregated facilities while starring for the Boston Celtics. Olympic track medalists John Carlos and Tommie Smith created an international furor with their Black Power salute at the 1968 Olympics in Mexico City, which hurt their subsequent professional careers. When St. Louis Cardinals catcher Ted Simmons came to the majors from the University of Michigan in 1967, some teammates were taken aback by his shaggy hair and the peace symbols on his bat, but they couldn't argue with his All-Star play. In 1972, almost a year before the Supreme Court's landmark *Roe v. Wade* ruling, tennis star Billie Jean King was one of fifty-three women to sign an ad in the first issue of *Ms.* magazine boldly proclaiming, "We Have Had Abortions." Washington Redskins lineman Ray Schoenke organized 400 athletes to support George McGovern's 1972 antiwar presidential campaign despite the fact that his coach, George Allen, was a close friend of McGovern's opponent, Richard Nixon.

Contemporary activism hasn't infiltrated the locker rooms as it did in the past, in large measure because of dramatic improvements in athletes' economic situation. A half-century ago, big-time sports—boxing and baseball in particular—was a melting pot of urban working-class ethnics and rural farm boys. Back then, many professional athletes earned little more than ordinary workers. Many lived in the same neighborhoods as their fans and had to work in the off-season to supplement their salaries.

Today's athletes are a more diverse group. A growing number come from suburban upbringings and attended college. At the same time, the number of pro athletes from impoverished inner-city backgrounds in the United States and Latin America has increased. Regardless of their backgrounds, however, all pro athletes have much greater earning power than their predecessors. Since the 1970s, television contracts have brought new revenues that have dramatically increased salaries. The growing influence of players' unions—particularly in baseball, since the end of the reserve clause in 1976—has also raised the salaries of stars and journeyman jocks alike. For example, the minimum salary among major league baseball players increased from $16,000 in 1975 to $100,000 in 1990 to $300,000 last year, while the average salary during those years grew from $44,676 to $578,930 to $2.3 million. Even ordinary players are now able to supplement their incomes with commercial endorsements. At the upper echelons of every sport, revenue from product endorsements far exceeds the salaries paid by the teams superstars play for or the prize money for the tournaments they win.

Thanks to their unions, pro athletes now have more protection than ever before to speak out without jeopardizing their careers. But, at the same time, they have much more at stake economically. "Athletes now have too much to lose in endorsement potential," explains Marc Pollick, founder and president of the Giving Back Fund, which works with pro athletes to set up charitable foundations. "That has neutralized their views on controversial issues. Companies don't want to be associated with controversy."

A few years ago labor activists tried and failed to enlist basketball superstar Michael Jordan in their crusade to improve conditions in Nike's factories. But with a multi-million-dollar Nike contract, he was unwilling to speak out against sweatshop conditions in overseas plants. In 1990 Jordan had refused to endorse his fellow black North Carolinian Harvey Gantt, then running for the US Senate against right-winger Jesse Helms, on the grounds, Jordan explained at the time, that "Republicans buy sneakers, too." (The criticism must have stung. Six years later he contributed $2,000 to Gantt's second unsuccessful effort to unseat Helms. And in 2000, like many NBA players, he publicly supported former New York Knicks star Bill Bradley's campaign for President. In March he contributed $10,000 to Illinois State Senator Barack Obama, who recently won the Democratic Party's nomination for an open US Senate seat.)

Early in his professional career, golfer Tiger Woods stirred some political controversy with one of his first commercials for Nike after signing a $40 million endorsement contract. It displayed images of Woods golfing as these words scrolled down the screen: "There are still courses in the United States I am not allowed to play because of the color of my skin. I've heard I'm not ready for you. Are you ready for me?" At the time Woods told *Sports Illustrated* that it was "important . . . for this country to talk about this subject [racism]. . . . You can't say something like that in a polite way. Golf has shied away from this for too long. Some clubs have brought in tokens, but nothing has really changed. I hope what I'm doing can change that."

According to Richard Lapchick, executive director of the National Consortium for Academics and Sports at the University of Central Florida, and a longtime activist against racism in sports, Woods was "crucified" by some sportswriters for the commercial and his comments. Nike quickly realized that confrontational politics wasn't the best way to sell shoes. "Tiger seemed to learn a lesson," Lapchick says. "It is one that I wish he and other athletes had not learned: no more political issues. He has been silent since then because of what happened early in his career." Woods remained on the sidelines during the 2002 controversy over the intransigence of the Augusta National Golf Club, host of the annual Masters tournament, on permitting women to join.

Like Lapchick, former New York Yankees pitching ace Jim Bouton, whose 1970 tell-all book *Ball Four* scandalized the baseball establishment, bemoans the cautiousness of today's highly paid athletes. "I'm always disappointed when I see a guy like Michael Jordan, who is set up for life, not speaking out on controversial issues," said Bouton. Today's athletes, he observed, "seem to have an entourage around them that they have to consult before making a statement or getting involved in something. Ali was willing to go to jail and relinquish his boxing title for what he believed in. He was a hero. It's a scared generation today." And it may be no coincidence that some of today's more outspoken athletes grew up outside the United States. Foyle, now a US citizen, is from the Grenadines, and the Mavericks' Nash is a Canadian.

American sports—from the Olympics to pro boxing to baseball—have long been linked, by politicians, business leaders and sports entrepreneurs, to conservative versions of nationalism and patriotism. At all professional sports events, fans and players are expected to stand while the national anthem is played before the game can begin. No similar expressions of patriotism are required, for example, at symphony concerts or Broadway shows.

Over the past century presidents have routinely invited championship teams to the White House for photo ops. A few weeks after 9/11 President Bush attended a World Series game at Yankee Stadium. His press secretary explained that Bush (who once owned the Texas Rangers) was there "because of baseball's important role in our culture." In January, just before the Super Bowl, Bush invited New England Patriots quarterback Tom Brady to sit in the gallery during his State of the Union address. Of the more than 900 Americans who have died in Afghanistan and Iraq, none were singled out for as much attention—by the media or politicians—as Arizona Cardinals safety Pat Tillman, who was killed in Afghanistan in April. Sometimes politicians' efforts to align themselves with sports figures can backfire. In 1991, for example, when President George H.W. Bush invited the Chicago Bulls to the White House to celebrate their NBA championship, Bulls guard Craig Hodges handed Bush a letter expressing outrage about the condition of urban America.

While most pro athletes are silent on political issues, many team owners regard political involvement as essential to doing business. Owners like Jerry Colangelo of the Phoenix Suns and Arizona Diamondbacks, Art Modell of the Baltimore Ravens,

Charles Monfort of the Colorado Rockies and George Steinbrenner of the New York Yankees make large campaign contributions to both Republicans and Democrats; invite elected officials to sit next to them at games; and lobby city, state and federal officeholders on legislation and tax breaks for new stadiums.

The emergence of professional players' unions should have been a voice for athletes on political and social issues. According to Ed Garvey, who ran the NFL Players Association from 1971 until 1983, racial turmoil was critical to the union's early development. The union "was driven by the African-American players, who knew there was an unwritten quota on most teams where there would not be more than a third blacks on any one team," says Garvey, who now practices law in Wisconsin. "And they knew they wouldn't have a job with the team when their playing days were over." The players also understood that team owners were "the most powerful monopoly in the country," he says.

Garvey brought the association into the AFL-CIO—the only professional sports union to do so—to give the players a sense that they were part of the broader labor movement. In the early 1970s several NFL players walked the picket lines with striking Farah clothing workers, joined bank employees in Seattle to boost their organizing drive and took other public stands. But "now they're making enough money, so they want to keep their heads down," he says. When Marvin Miller, a former Steelworkers Union staffer, became the first executive director of the Major League Baseball Players Association (MLBPA) in 1966, he sought to raise players' political awareness. "We didn't just explain the labor laws," he recalls. "We had to get players to understand that they were a union. We did a lot of internal education to talk to players about broader issues."

But those days are long gone. Bouton believes that athletes' unions now consider themselves partners in the sports business. They are "part of the same club," Bouton says, negotiating mainly to give players a greater share of proceeds from ticket sales, television contracts and the marketing of player names and team logos. Donald Fehr, the MLBPA's executive director, argues that players' unions should stick to the issues that directly affect them. "It is not our role to go around taking positions on things for the sake of taking positions," he insists. "Only if it's a matter involving baseball or the players do we look at an issue and determine what to do."

Like its counterparts in other sports, the MLBPA occasionally goes beyond the narrow confines of business unionism. For example, Fehr sent letters asking ballplayers to honor the recent United Food and Commercial Workers picket lines in Southern California and gave verbal support to the striking workers of the New Era Cap Company, who make major league baseball's caps in a Derby, New York, facility.

The players associations could usefully go beyond such symbolic gestures. After the 234-day 1994–95 strike ended, catcher Mike Piazza, then with the Los Angeles Dodgers, donated $100 for every home run he hit to the union that represented the concessionaires, who lost considerable pay while 921 games were canceled. It was an individual gesture of empathy with Dodger Stadium's working class—ushers, ticket takers, parking-lot attendants and food vendors—that generated tremendous good will among the Dodgers' fan base. As an organization, the MLBPA could have followed Piazza's example and set aside a small part of its large strike fund to help stadium employees who were temporarily out of work.

A glaring example of the MLBPA's short-sightedness is its reaction to a recent exposé by the National Labor Committee (NLC, www.nlcnet.org/campaigns), reported in the *New York Times*, revealing that Costa Rican workers who stitch Rawlings base-balls for the major leagues are paid 30 cents for each ball, which is then sold for $15 in US sporting-goods stores. According to a local doctor who worked at the Rawlings plant in the 1990s, a third of the workers developed carpal-tunnel syndrome, an often-debilitating pain and numbness of the hands and wrists. When the *Times* asked Fehr about the situation, he said he didn't know about it, despite the fact that the Rawlings plant had been the subject of news stories for several years. (Another recent NLC report documented that NBA sweat-shirts are made in Burmese sweatshops.)

Echoing growing concern about corporate responsibility and runaway jobs, professional players associations could demand that teams purchase their uniforms, bats, helmets and balls solely from companies—in the United States and abroad—that provide workers with decent wages, working conditions and benefits. The associations could send fact-finding delegations of athletes to inspect the working conditions at factories where their uniforms and equipment are made. The associations could demand that teams provide a living wage for all stadium employees, encourage politically conscious athletes to express their views and endorse candidates for office, support organizations like Adonal Foyle's Democracy Matters and even walk picket lines and do commercials for labor causes. As Foyle understands, taking stands on such issues could help the players forge better relations with the community whose support is critical to their continued economic success.

Foyle has refused to be intimidated by those sportswriters and fans who object to his beliefs. "How can we say we are creating a society in Iraq based on democracy and freedom and tell people here who have the audacity to speak out to keep quiet?" he says. "If people shut down because they are afraid the media is going to spank them or fans are going to boo them, then the terrorists have won." A history major at Colgate University, Foyle says, "The 1960s generation was against the war, people coming home in body bags, dogs gnawing at black people's feet. Today issues are more complicated, and you have to read between the lines. When you talk about campaign finance reform, you are talking about all of the issues—war, civil rights, environment, gender, globalization—because they are all connected." He adds: "If people want us to be role models, it's not just saying what people want you to say. It's pushing the boundaries a bit, saying things that you may not want to think about. That's good for a society. Morality is much bigger than athletics."

Chapter 17

SPORT, MASCULINITY, AND BLACK CULTURAL RESISTANCE

Ben Carrington

In this selection, Ben Carrington reports on his field research about a cricket club in England whose members were predominantly West Indian. Carrington deftly shows that the sport and the club played a major role in the construction of the men's black masculine identities as well as in the construction of a larger sense of community. In addition, the club and the practices associated with it were important resources in black resistance to white racism.

On sport's level playing field, it is possible to challenge and overturn the dominant hierarchies of nation, race, and class. The reversal may be limited and transient, but it is nonetheless real. It is, therefore, wrong to see black sporting achievement merely as an index of oppression; it is equally an index of creativity and resistance, collective and individual.

—Marqusee (1995, p. 5)

This article traces the meanings associated with cricket in relation to Black masculinity by examining the role of sport as a form of cultural resistance to the ideologies and practices of White racism. The article then shows the absences within contemporary sociology of sport theorizing around race, which has led to incomplete understandings of the complex ways in which gender operates in and through discourses of race. It is argued that it is necessary to produce more critical theorizations of the intersections of race with gender, nation, and class if we are to fully appreciate how social identities are constructed. A theoretical account follows of the historical and contemporary significance of sport within racialized societies (the racial signification of sport).

The theoretical arguments are then explored in more detail by an extensive empirical analysis. Drawing on participant observation and in-depth semistructured interviews, an account is given of how a

Ben Carrington, "Sport, Masculinity, and Black Cultural Resistance" from *Journal of Sport and Social Issues* 22.3 (August 1998): 275–298. Copyright © 1998 by Sage Publications, Inc. Reprinted with the permission of Sage Publications, Inc.

Black cricket club in the north of England is used by Black men as both a form of resistance to White racism and as a symbolic marker of the local Black community. Three themes are traced in this regard, namely (a) the construction of Black sports institutions as Black spaces, (b) the use of Black sports clubs as symbolic markers of community identity, and (c) the role of cricket as an arena of both symbolic and real racial and masculine contestation. The theoretical framework developed and the empirical analysis presented begin to provide a more critical understanding of the complexities of racial identity construction and resistance in sport than has so far been developed within the sociology of sport. . . .

Black Masculinity and the Limits to Sports Sociology Theorizing

In analyzing the historical development and social significance of sports during the 19th and early 20th centuries, it is now commonplace within the sociology of sport to assert that sport functioned as a key male homosocial institution whereby "manly virtues and competencies" could be both learned and displayed as a way of avoiding wider social, political, and economic processes of "feminization." Sport, in effect, symbolized and reinforced a patriarchal structure of domination over women. However, such accounts have consistently failed to acknowledge that this view can only be sustained if the inherently racialized nature of social relationships and the position of Blacks, and in particular Black males, within Western societies, generally, and within sport, in particular, is ignored. Historically, the entry of Black males into the social institutions of sport was conditional with formal segregation, particularly in the

United States, often imposed. When Black males did compete directly and publicly with Whites, such competition was organized on the premise that the "White man" would eventually win, thereby maintaining the racial order, and where this could not be guaranteed the prohibition of Blacks was quickly instated.

Thus, the claim that is repeatedly made concerning sport's early development as the preservation of male authority needs to be critically reexamined as it more accurately relates to the preservation of certain notions of White male identity and authority. To acknowledge this challenges many of the Eurocentric accounts that have themselves been guilty of reproducing racist discourses that have denied both the importance, and the very presence, of Black peoples throughout the modern history of the West.[1]

One notable exception to such accounts can be found in the work of Michael Messner (1992), who has argued that men's historical and contemporary experiences in sport clearly demonstrate that it is overly simplistic to view sport as a patriarchal institution that reinforces men's domination and power over women. Rather, "the rise of sport as a social institution in the late nineteenth and early twentieth centuries had at least as much to do with men's class and *racial relationships* [italics added] with other men as it did with men's relations with women" (Messner, 1992, p. 17). Messner continues,

We can see that the turn-of-the-century "crisis of masculinity" was, in actuality, a crisis of legitimation for hegemonic masculinity. In other words, upper- and middle-class, white, urban heterosexual men were the most threatened by modernization, by changes in the social organization of work, by the New Woman's movement into public life, by feminism, and by the working-class, ethnic minority, immigrant, and gay men. (p. 18)

Such a radical reconceptualization of the meaning of sport's historical development would help us to better understand the heightened significance of sport within colonial and contemporary societies and, specifically in relation to this article, the critical role that sport continues to play in narrating relations between Black men and White men. . . . Kobena Mercer (1994) has drawn attention to these questions in criticizing the Eurocentrism of many of the theoretical approaches to masculinity that have stubbornly refused "to recognize that not all men in the world are white or even that white masculinities are informed by the ethnicity of whiteness" (Mercer, 1994, p. 153).[2] The historically constructed social position of Black males, which raises profound questions for contemporary sports sociology theorizing, is accurately described by Mercer when he writes,

Whereas prevailing definitions of masculinity imply power, control and authority, these attributes have been historically denied to Black men since slavery. The centrally dominant role of the white male slave master in eighteenth- and nineteenth-century plantation societies debarred black males from patriarchal privileges ascribed to the masculine role. . . . In racial terms, black men and women alike were subordinated to the power of the white master in hierarchical social relations of slavery, and for black men, as objects of oppression, this also cancelled out their access to positions of power and prestige which in gender terms are regarded as the essence of mas-

culinity in patriarchy. Shaped by this history, black masculinity is a highly contradictory formation of identity, as it is a subordinated masculinity. (pp. 142–143)

It is clear then that we need to move toward more sophisticated and nonreductionist models of analysis that do not treat the significance of race as being epiphenomenal to the development of modern sports and that take seriously the "intersectionality" (Brah, 1996) of race, gender, nation, class, and the other multiple relational identities individuals have.

The Racial Signification of Sport

When you talk about race in basketball, the whole thing is simple: a black player knows he can go out on the court and kick a white player's ass. He can beat him, and he knows it. It's that simple, and it shouldn't surprise anyone. The black player feels it every time. He knows it from the inside. (Rodman, 1996, p. 129)

Given that sport is one of the few arenas where public displays of competition, domination, and control are openly played out (Birrell, 1989), it is not surprising, as bell hooks (1994) suggests, that, historically, "competition between black and white males has been highlighted in the sports arena" (p. 31).
Messner (1992) highlights the way in which sport provides opportunities for subordinated groups to challenge the established order. Messner argues that subaltern groups are able to "use sport as a means to resist (at least symbolically) the domination imposed upon them. Sport must thus be viewed as an institution through which domination is not only imposed, but also

contested; an institution within which power is constantly at play" (p. 13). Therefore, within racially inscribed societies we can see how the sociocultural, psychological, and political meanings of public displays of sporting contestation come to take on specifically racial significance. . . .

A further, pertinent, question would be to ask what happens when sporting contests between Black men and White men actually take place? What is the significance for those involved, both Black and White, and how do wider racialized discourses affect the game itself?

Michael Messner's (1992) arguments pertaining to the role of sport in allowing for the realization of a masculine identity for subaltern groups is relevant here. Messner suggests that "subordinated groups of men often used sport to resist racist, colonial, and class domination, and their resistance most often took the form of a claim to 'manhood'" (p. 19). It is precisely this attempt to reconstruct Black masculinity, which colonialism had configured "as feminised and emasculated" (Verges, 1996, p. 61), that is central to Frantz Fanon's (1986) analysis of colonial racism, and further shows why it is impossible to separate, in any simple way, questions of masculinity from race. . . .

It is not surprising then that it is the traditionally highly masculinized arena of sports through which Black men often attempt to (re)assert their Black identity, that is, gender acts as the modality through which a racialized identity is realized (Gilroy, 1993, p. 85). As the quote from the enigmatic basketball player Dennis Rodman suggests, sports can therefore be seen at one level as a transgressive liminal space where Black men can attempt, quite legitimately, to (re)impose their subordinated masculine identity through the symbolic, and sometimes literal, "beating" of the other, that is, White men.[3] Therefore, what we might term the "racial signification of sport" means that sports contests are more than just significant events, in and of themselves important, but rather that they act as a key signifier for wider questions about identity within racially demarcated societies in which racial narratives about the self and society are read both into and from sporting contests that are imbued with racial meanings.

Cricket, Colonialism, and Cultural Resistance

The whole issue [of racism] is quite central for me, coming as I do from the West Indies at the very end of colonialism. I believe very strongly in the black man asserting himself in this world and over the years I have leaned towards many movements that follow this basic cause. (Richards, 1991, p. 188)

It is within this context that we can begin to more fully understand the centrality of sports to Black resistance. As Douglas Hartman (1996), correctly in my view, points out, sport has "long constituted an important, if under-appreciated, set of activities and institutions in the black community providing many of its leaders and one of its most established spaces for collective action (second only perhaps to the Church itself)" (p. 560).[4] In the Caribbean, complex class, gendered, and racial antagonisms within the Caribbean itself, and of course between the West Indians and the British, were most often played out in the arena of cricket. C.L.R. James's (1963/1994) seminal work *Beyond A Boundary* is testament to what he saw as the inherent relationship between culture, and in particular cricket, politics, and Black resistance in the anticolonial struggles of the time. James argued that cricket was central in helping to shape a political sense of West Indian identity during the period of colonial rule by the British. In a way, cricket could be seen as being more than a metaphor for Caribbean politics; in many ways, it was Caribbean politics.[5]

Cricket, in particular, due to its position both as perhaps the cultural embodiment of the values and mores of Englishness and its "missionary" role within British imperialism and colonialism, occupied a central site in many of the anticolonial struggles both within the Caribbean and elsewhere within the Empire. Thus, the game itself assumed political importance in narrating unequal power relations between the British and the West Indians: "beating them at their own game" taking on deeper and more profound meanings. In discussing this, Grant Farred (1996) has argued that it "is precisely because the colonised were immersed in and observant of the codes of the native British game that they were able to transform the sport into a vehicle for Caribbean resistance" (pp. 170–171).

Viv Richards (1995), captain of one the most successful West Indian teams in cricket history, extends this connection between sport and Black resistance to the Black diaspora, when he reflects: "In my own way, I would like to think that I carried my bat for the liberation of African and other oppressed people everywhere" (p. vii).[6] Cricket, especially for certain generations of West Indian men, came to occupy a central position in their social identities, whether they were living in the Caribbean or elsewhere within the Black diaspora. As Ossie Stuart (1996) notes, for many Black men cricket itself occupied a symbolic posi-

tion in articulating an empowered sense of self within White supremacist societies; "cricket represented social status, social mobility, it meant modernisation and it meant West Indian success" (p. 125). It is to ground these theoretical issues, relating to the importance of cricket and notions of cultural resistance in the lived experiences of Black men, that I now turn.

The Setting: The Racialization of Chapeltown

This study focuses on the Caribbean Cricket Club (CCC), which is situated near an area of Leeds, a large city in the north of England, where the majority of the city's Asian and Black residents live.[7] The 1991 census data for Leeds showed that those classified as Black-Caribbean numbered just under 7,000, of whom nearly 60% lived within the two wards known as Chapeltown (Policy Research Institute [PRI], 1996). Because of the relatively large concentration of Black people, Chapeltown has come to be known in the city as a Black area, and as such, has been subject to a racialized discourse, fueled by local and national media representations (Farrar, 1997) that have labeled the area (and by default the Black residents of Chapeltown) as a deviant, dangerous, and sexually promiscuous place.

In keeping with many of Britain's multiracial, inner-city areas, Chapeltown is a largely working-class area with few public amenities and considerable economic problems, such as higher-than-average levels of unemployment and poor housing conditions (Farrar, 1997; PRI, 1996). Partly as a result of these socioeconomic conditions, the area has twice seen major disturbances, which attracted both regional and national attention in 1975 (see Farrar, 1981; Gilroy,

1987; Sivanandan, 1982) and during the summer of 1981, when many areas of Britain were gripped with violent Black and working-class political revolts (see Farrar, 1981). Despite, and probably because of, these economic conditions and the difficulties faced by the city's Asian and Black populations, the large number of political and cultural organizations in the area, of which the cricket club is a central part, have maintained, and even increased, their importance to social life.

The Club: Caribbean Cricket Club

The CCC is one of the oldest Black sports clubs in Britain. It was originally formed in the late 1940s as a social and sporting club by a group of West Indian soldiers who had fought in the Second World War and had settled in the city (Wheatley, 1992; Zulfiqar, 1993). Over the years, the club became more successful, culminating in the late 1970s when it won the league three years running and won the treble on a number of occasions. In the late 1980s, the CCC moved on to play in one of the strongest leagues in Yorkshire County, the Leeds League, where it has played for the past 10 years. It currently has three senior men's teams and three junior boy's teams. Nearly all of the senior players are Black except for three Asian players and three White players.

The club's current ground, called The Oval, is a relatively new acquisition. With money from the local council, wasteland just outside of Chapeltown was transformed, over many years, into a cricket pitch and a few years later the club's current pavilion was built—the plaque inside proudly confirming the opening as "The Realisation of a Dream." The surrounding area is largely overgrown grassland, over-looked by a working-class council estate and tower blocks on one side, with a panoramic view of the city's skyline on the other.

The clubhouse has been the constant subject of vandalism and break-ins over the years—another break-in occurred during the research, in which the television, phone, drinks, and money from the till and pool table were stolen. The most serious setback to the club has been an arson attack that unfortunately destroyed nearly all of the club's memorabilia. This has left the clubhouse looking somewhat empty without all the team photos that usually adorn cricket clubhouses. There is often talk within the club that such attacks are racially motivated, with the prime suspects being the youths from the nearby, predominantly White, council estate, although on each occasion the police have been unable to prosecute anyone. Earl, the third team wicket-keeper, suggested,

I think it's down to, "Oh, it's a Black club, we don't want them to get far." I think it's a racial thing again because I've seen words daubed up, "Niggers Out," and things like that. Because once you've been done over once, and it happens again, you know there is a pattern to it.

The spacious wasteland of the surrounding area tends to attract youngsters riding motorbikes and sometimes cars. Presumably due to this activity, a police car or two, and sometimes even a police helicopter, will circle the ground (as occurred on my very first visit to a game at the club). The well-documented history of police and state regulation, surveillance, and harassment of Black community spaces within Britain (Gilroy, 1987; Hesse, 1997b; Keith, 1993; Sivanandan, 1982), a key factor in the disturbances in Chapeltown in 1975 and

1981, gives this constant police activity (that symbolically infringes on the bounded space of the club) heightened significance. This inevitably leads to the feeling among many that the police are keeping an eye on the club as much as looking out for the joyriders. The location of the club and its somewhat troubled history seems to give the club and its members an embattled feel and adds to the widely held notion of the club's struggle both on and off the pitch.

Black Space as Cultural Resistance

I wish now to explore briefly how members of the club use the CCC as a discursively constructed Black social space.[8] In relation to the racialization of space, Farrar (1997) remarks,

> In everyday speech, many residents of an urban area of black settlement would readily comprehend a phrase such as "black space" . . . in terms of their effort to forge discourses and practical activities in a particular part of town which are, to some extent, "free" from the discourses and practices which they associate with a coercive white power structure. Establishing nearly autonomous territory is the conscious aim of all sorts of actors in the black inner city—in churches, mosques, temples, community centers, clubs, pubs, and in certain "open" spaces. (p. 108)

Such movements to create nearly autonomous spaces are an attempt to resist what might be described as the "terrorizing white gaze" (hooks, 1992) within public spaces. Here, Black people, and Black bodies, become subject to a panoptic form of "white governmentality" (Hesse, 1997b) that seeks to oversee, control, and regulate

the behavior of Black people and is underpinned by the constant threat of racial harassment and violence. In this sense, we can see how the club's significance goes beyond merely being a cricket club and assumes a heightened social role as a Black institution within a wider White environment, providing many of the Black men with a sense of ontological security. This can operate on a number of related levels, from being a space removed, albeit not entirely, from the overt practices of White racism, as a social and cultural resource for Black people, and as an arena that allows for Black expressive behavior. These elements can be traced in the various ways in which the importance of the CCC was discussed by its members. The club was often labeled by the players and members in the interviews and discussions as a *Black space*, by which was often meant a place where Black people could be themselves (for example, in being able to tell certain jokes and speak in Caribbean patois), free from the strictures imposed by the White gaze. Thus, the club's importance transcended its sporting function.

The current chair and manager of the CCC, Ron, came to Leeds in the late 1950s and joined the CCC in the 1970s, when in his early 20s. For Ron, it was important to acknowledge the historical social role of the club within the area. When asked whether he saw the club as being more than just a sporting club, he replied,

> Oh yeah, because when it started in '47 it wasn't just a sports club, it was a focal point for those people who were black and in a vast minority, because in 1947 I don't think there were the amount of black people in Leeds that there are now. It was a focal point, it was a survival point for the people that were here. So it was more than a club

then and it's still more than a club now, so it will always be that.

The use of the language of survival is interesting. It highlights the historical significance of the club in providing a safe space within a wider (hostile) environment for the earlier Caribbean migrants, which is then mapped onto the present, showing the continuities of the club and its role in the light of the persistence of racism: "It was more than a club then and it's still more than a club now, so it will always be that."

Nicholas, a 17-year-old who played for both the senior and junior sides, referred to the CCC as an important social space for Black people. As he played for another junior cricket team in another part of Yorkshire, he was able to contrast his experiences of playing for White and Black teams. Nicholas had experienced racial abuse from an opposing player while playing junior cricket for his other team, Scholes, which had increased his feelings of isolation at his predominantly White club.

Nicholas: Some teams, if you're batting against them, and you start hitting them all over the place they always have to come out with their racist remarks to try and put you off. . . . It even happened to me this season when we played a team from Garforth, and I was hitting the opening bowler who has played for Yorkshire [Juniors]. I was hitting him for quite a lot of fours, and then he started to go on and call me names on the pitch . . . and then he got me out, and then, he was all "mouthy mouthy."

BC: But how did that make you feel?

Nicholas: Well, it's the first time it's happened, it made me feel kind of funny. I didn't know whether to answer him back or to walk away from him.

BC: If you were playing for Caribbean do you think he would have said it?

Nicholas: If I were playing for Caribbean he wouldn't have dared say it because if he was saying it to one person he's really saying it to the whole team . . . but at Scholes there is only two of us there, and all the rest are White, so it was more easier for him to say it there.

Such incidents compounded his feeling of isolation and otherness in a White setting, and he thus felt more relaxed and secure when at the CCC. In this sense, the CCC can be seen as providing Nicholas with an environment where his Blackness takes on a lesser significance and offers, in both a symbolic and very real sense, protection from the more overt practices of White racism.

The achievement of creating and sustaining a cricketing Black space within a White environment was often reflected on, somewhat nostalgically, by the club's members, particularly the older ones. There was a sense of pride among many of the players and members that despite all the problems the club had faced, including increasing financial pressures, the CCC was still going and now had its own ground and pavilion. Pete, one of the older players, who had come to England from Barbados in the late 1960s, echoed these views, while being interviewed in his car at The Oval. He said,

I tend to think there are people out there who don't want us to have this. . . . But I hope we can carry on. I mean look at this [he gazes at the panoramic view across the ground overlooking the city], this is great as far as I'm concerned!

Community, Resistance, and Cricket

It is important to remember the wider context of the CCC's recent development. Its current ground and clubhouse materialized in the 1980s and can be seen as emerging from a wider Black political struggle that was taking place during this period. Following the violent disturbances of the early 1980s, there was a shift in government spending toward social expenses as a means of trying to placate inner-city tensions. The provision of leisure facilities was a key part of this process, even while government expenditures were generally being squeezed as the welfare state was restructured (Henry, 1993). Although state funding of such leisure provisions has been criticized as a form of "soft policing" (Hargreaves, 1986) that increased state control of Black and working-class communities and simultaneously diverted attention away from the underlying economic causes of the social deprivation these areas were facing, the outcomes of these policies were more ambiguous. Although it was clear that the primary motive behind such funding was designed to (re)impose social integration, many Black organizations were willing to take the money available and to use it to their own advantage. Thus, the negotiations with the local state to achieve the aims of the CCC were contradictory. To a degree, this allowed the state to use sport, as John Hargreaves (1986) suggests, to further its own ends, while the Black community fought for space to negotiate a different set of cultural possibilities (cf., Hall, 1996).

Ron, who worked for the local council and was instrumental in securing local government funding for the development of the ground and the subsequent building of the clubhouse, was well aware of the underlying political motives of such provision.

It was after 1981, the uprisings, or the disturbances, whatever you want to call them. The authorities decided that they had to keep the "natives" happy, and they looked at something that the natives liked, and obviously cricket was what the natives liked.

Ron's deliberately ironic self-description of the "natives" is instructive. It highlights how the colonial discourse of British imperialism still resonates as a point of reference within the popular contemporary White imaginary in relation to Black people living in Leeds. Indeed, as late as the 1970s Chapeltown was actually referred to in the local press as "the colony within" (Farrar, 1996), reinforcing popular local misconceptions of Chapeltown and its residents as alien and potentially violent, a place to be overseen and policed as a colonial settlement.

The "natives," then, had, after almost 40 years, secured their own ground and pavilion—a physical marker of the club's (and in some ways, Chapeltown's Black communities') presence and progress in the area. However, it is argued here that although the CCC now has a physical presence, that is, a clubhouse and a pitch, the sense in which the club comes to represent the community for some of its members is largely as a symbol, that is to say, it is imagined. As Cohen (1985, p. 19) notes, "Symbols are mental constructs: they provide people with the means to make meaning. In so doing, they also provide them with the means to express the particular meanings which the community has for them."

The polyvocal nature of signs can be seen in the way in which the CCC is itself used interchangeably with the Black community in discussions at the club, standing as a symbolic marker of the community (which depending on the context can take on both local, that is, Chapeltown, or wider, that is, diasporic, dimensions), and assumes a specifically racial, that is, Black, association. We can see then that the language of community, especially for Blacks living in Britain, connotes both political (as a form of resistance) and moral (as a place of transcendence) associations. What we might term "Black community discourse" (Back, 1996) is used strategically as a way of articulating wider Black struggles within a specific locality by labeling it as a Black area. The Black community discourse can be understood as a narrative that locates a particular area "as the site of Black struggles and institutions, a place where Black people have fought to make something their own. This construct is also invested with a notion of political agency and locates Black resistance to racism and self-affirmation in this particular area" (Back, 1996, p. 113). Such attempts at establishing (partially) autonomous institutions and spaces, such as the CCC, as part of wider community projects are mechanisms in the development of "communities of resistance" (Sivanandan, 1990), which are inherently political maneuvers. As Gilroy (1987) notes, the invocation of community refers to more than just the concentration of Black people within a particular bounded area.

It has a moral dimension and its use evokes a rich complex of symbols surrounded by a wider cluster of meanings. The historical memory of progress from slave to citizen actively cultivated in the present from resources provided by the past endows it with an aura of tradition. Community, there-fore, signifies not just a distinctive political ideology but a particular set of values and norms in everyday life: mutuality, co-operation, identification and symbiosis. For black Britain, all these are centrally defined by the need to escape and transform the forms of subordination which bring "races" into being. (Gilroy, 1987, p.234)

Thus, given the symbolic significance attached to the club and its central position within the local Black community discourse, the success of the club on the field came to be seen as reflecting on the standing of the Black community of Chapeltown too. For example, during team meetings, management and other senior players would often stress the need for the players to be aware that they were not just playing for themselves, or even the team, but also for the community as a whole: "for everyone down at Chapeltown" as Ron once put it. Despite the CCC's achievements over the years, the club had not won the Leeds League since its acceptance, after a number of unsuccessful applications, in 1988, and this was a constant source of frustration for many at the club. Both Ron and Earl felt the need for the club to win the league title.

Ron: Because we need to be champions one day.
Earl: For the community as well as the club.
Ron: And it would lift the community like Earl says. . . .

For Pete, the CCC was important to Chapeltown because "it's the only sporting club, cricket club, that black people have got in the area, and when I say black I mean West Indian." Pete was aware that the CCC was perceived by White people as a Black club and symbolically represented Chapeltown and Black people in general to them, therefore, it was vitally important that the club was not only successful but run well: "I've had my hands down the loo! 'Wash this, wash that.' Because I'm buggered if I want anyone to come up here and believe, 'Ah, is this the way Black people live?'" He therefore spoke disparagingly and with a sense of bewilderment and incomprehension about those members who did not realize the wider social significance of the club: "Most members come up here and all they want to do is play cricket!"

Cricket and Racial Contestation

C.L.R. James (1963/1994, p. 66) noted long ago the wider social significance of cricket contests: "The cricket field was a stage on which selected individuals played representative roles which were charged with social significance." Given that the CCC has a predominantly Black membership (and its name, and location, as suggested earlier, signify the club as Black) and given too that it plays its cricket in a league in the heart of Yorkshire (a regional identity historically constructed through a notion of Whiteness), the racial meanings invested in the actual matches are heightened even further.[9] Many of the players felt sure that the opposing teams were well aware of the wider racial significance of the contests and that the cricket matches were more than "just a game"; the war metaphor was often used to describe the contests.

Overlaid on this of course, as outlined earlier, is the specificity of cricket itself as a cultural practice and its central, almost metaphoric, position as a site of hegemonic struggle between the British and the West Indians. The competition between Black and White men within this context be-

comes a symbolic and real contestation of masculine and racial pride, and specifically for the Black participants a way of attempting to reassert a unified sense of self, and of rejecting, even if temporarily, the notion that their Black identity is a subordinated, and inferior, identity. As Westwood (1990, p. 68) notes in her brief analysis of a Black men's football team, the victory of Black teams over White teams "is, in effect, an injury to White masculine pride and a source of power and celebration to Black masculine pride when White teams are beaten."

These themes emerged constantly during the discussions at the club and the interviews conducted. For instance, referring to opposing White sides, Nigel said, "I think they see us purely as colour first, end of story, and then the cricket club comes [second]." Nigel was therefore dismissive of the notion that the cricket arena was somehow free of racial contestation and significance and that it could bring people together. When I suggested this to him, he replied,

Oh come on, come on! We are talking about cricket here aren't we Ben? We're talking about the one county that we're based in being the one that always said, [puts on a strong mock Yorkshire accent] "You can't play for Yorkshire unless you're born in bloody Yorkshire lad!" That's still got to come through and that's been so strong within Yorkshire, the country on its own inside of another country, that's almost how strong they feel, and particularly around cricket.

This passage is important as it pulls together a number of key issues. It shows how a regional identity can become conflated with notions of nation and indeed race. The view that Yorkshire is a "country on its own inside of another country" is a powerful one that gives the county a particularly strong regional identity. That sport, and in particular cricket, is central to this, and that until recently only those born in Yorkshire could play for Yorkshire, excluding Asian and Black immigrants from being "true Yorkshiremen" and thus giving the identity a racial connotation, means that the players come to assume representative roles that are charged with social significance; the games themselves become, in effect, Black (West Indian)/White (Yorkshire) contests.

For example, Pete was clear, as he saw it, on the wider significance of the CCC and the matches within a context of a racist society. The relationship of the players to the actual national West Indian Test team went beyond a rhetorical identification and extended to the view that they actually were in some sense part of the West Indies side:

Pete: As far as I'm concerned we're just an extension of the West Indies national team.
BC: Is it more than just a cricket game to you?
Pete: Yes it is. You see I've heard the opposing teams talk you see. I've been at a game when we've lost and I've heard the words coming out of the dressing room, "We've beaten the fucking Black bastards dem, again!" [thumps steering wheel] So then it takes the game away from being a game, it's war then.

Such views were reflected in a number of the interviews undertaken in this study. Errol, who was in his 30s and had played for the club for a number of years and who had also played with a predominantly Asian cricket team, similarly noted the racial, and hence national, significance that was at-tached to the games: "They [White teams] don't want a West Indian team to beat them or they don't want an Asian team to beat them. For them it's like, England versus the West Indies, or England versus India." Errol suggested that White teams would consciously raise their game to ensure they were not beaten by a Black side:

Errol: At the end of the day we are living in England. Nobody want us to do better. It's like if there were an English [i.e., White] team in the West Indies, there's no way that the West Indies players or teams are gonna want them to win.
BC: How do you think other teams see Caribbean?
Errol: It's like, to me, they don't want a Black team to beat them. We've played against teams who never win a game but yet when they're playing Caribbeans you'd think that they were unbeatable! . . . It's because they don't want a Black man to beat them.

We can begin to see here how the wider discourses of the racial signification of sport become constituted in the actual contests themselves. The view that other teams played differently against the CCC because they were seen as a Black club was widely held among the players and supporters. . . .

Given the racial signification of the contests, the immense emotional and personal investment made in the games for the Black men was significant. At both a symbolic and very real level, winning became a way of challenging the logic and efficacy of the racism they faced in their day-to-day lives, even if the victories were always, ultimately, transitory. As Bob, an older player in his 40s, acknowledged, racial and masculine pride was at stake in contests between the

CCC and other White sides, thus it became paramount for the CCC, and the players themselves, not to lose.

> At the end of the day you don't want to be beaten. You think "Let's show these lads who's the boss here." You try your best because you don't want to be beaten because it's like they go away all cocky and that, "We showed them, they can't play cricket, English game's the best!" all that business. You want to go out there and hopefully shut them up.

Conclusion

Westwood (1990) has argued that as "a counter to racism black masculinity is called up as part of the cultures of resistance developed by black men in Britain" (p. 61). This article has shown how for a number of Black men, sport, and in particular cricket, can provide a modality through which Black cultural resistance to racism can be achieved. Sports provide an arena whereby Black men can lay claim to a masculine identity as a means of restoring a unified sense of racial identity, freed, if only momentarily, from the emasculating discourses imposed by the ideologies and practices of White racism.

However, we should be cautious not to overstate unproblematically the benefits of such sites of resistance. For one, Black women often occupy marginal positions within sports clubs such as the CCC (especially those that do not have women's teams), which are perhaps more accurately described, as I have tried to make clear throughout, as Black men's cricket clubs. Without acknowledging such limitations, the complex positioning of Black women, in particular, within "white supremacist

capitalist patriarchal societies" (hooks, 1994) gets overlooked. Thus, any claims for such cultural practices as being in some way emancipatory must be qualified. Otherwise, as Black feminists have consistently pointed out, the requirements for Black resistance become equated with the need for Black male emancipation. The overcoming of the crisis of Black masculinity is frequently misrecognized as the panacea for the Black community as a whole, thereby silencing the voices and needs of Black women; the politics manifest within certain (conservative) Black nationalisms being the most obvious example of this.

There is also, of course, the further problem with the zero-sum notion of resistance and power, most evidenced in the competitive sports arena, which inevitably leads to a conceptualization of resistance that can only be understood via notions of domination and physical conflict. Richard Burton (1991, 1997), for instance, has provided an interesting analysis in arguing for cricket to be situated within carnivalesque aspects of Caribbean street culture. Burton suggests that the carnival's symbolic subversion is central to how cricket is watched and played, as a more diffuse and stylized site of popular cultural resistance in challenging dominant social hierarchies.[10] This should alert us to the point that such modes of resistance as have been analyzed here should not be thought of as the only positionings possible. They ultimately need to be embedded within wider struggles.

It is perhaps necessary therefore to understand and explore both the benefits that such forms can have for a number of Black men while simultaneously acknowledging the limitations of sport as a modality of resistance to racism. Only when we have more ethnographically informed analyses in a greater variety of different communities across differing locations will we be able to more fully understand the complexities of Black cultural resistance through sport and its emancipatory possibilities.

Notes

1. Eurocentrism is used conceptually to refer to those discourses and relations of power that privilege culturally hegemonic European notions of Western universality and that therefore elide, within its frame of reference, the voices of others, both within and outside the West. In another sense, Eurocentrism can be understood as an attempt to recenter the West in conditions when its universality can no longer be guaranteed due to the multifaceted interrogations of the West by various postcolonial movements and critical multiculturalisms (cf., Hesse, 1997a; Sayyid, 1997; Shohat & Stam, 1994).

2. It is worth mentioning here that if the literature within the sociology of sport and leisure studies (and indeed elsewhere), on race, racism, and sport is inadequate, then the acknowledgment within these fields of study of White ethnicity is even worse. There are too few studies that have seriously considered how sport is central to the construction of White racial identities or even demonstrated an awareness of the fact that Whiteness is a racial category. As researchers, "we" are in the habit of equating race with the Black (and/or Asian) experience (just as in an earlier period gender equaled female experience), which as a number of scholars have demonstrated, only serves to reinforce current racist discourses and obscures the normalizing power of Whiteness (see Bonnett, 1996; Dyer, 1988, 1997; Feagin & Vera, 1995; Frankenburg, 1993; hooks, 1992; Ware, 1992).

3. Interestingly, Rodman's comments were echoed by a Black professional rugby league player when interviewed as part of a survey looking at racism within rugby league (Long, Tongue, Spracklen, & Carrington, 1995). He said, "I think a lot of Black players play rugby league, in my opinion . . . as they see it as a way to get their own back, or to take their aggression out on people, white people. . . . You couldn't do it on the street, but you can

do it on the pitch" (as cited in Long, Carrington, & Spracklen, 1996, p. 13; see also Long, Carrington, & Spracklen, 1997). It is also within this context that we can understand the comments made by the cricketer Brian Lara, currently captain of the West Indies, after his side's inexplicable loss to Kenya in the cricket World Cup in 1996. In private remarks to the Kenyan side after the game, which were eventually reported by the media and for which he later apologized, he said, "It wasn't that bad losing to you guys. You are Black. Know what I mean. Now a team like South America is a different matter altogether. You know, this White thing comes into the picture. We can't stand losing to them" (as cited in Marqusee, 1996, p. 136). St. Pierre (1995) similarly suggests, in relation to cricket, that West Indian Test players "will tell you, privately, that a victory against England carries with it a special savour" (p. 77). Clearly, as I explore further in the rest of the article, the significance of these last two examples has as much to do with historical colonial and political relationships as it has with race.

4. There is a complex history, which is yet to be fully theorized, or indeed written, concerning the connections, crossovers, and interplay between the roles and lives of Black athletes and Black political radicals within the Black diaspora. I have begun to tentatively map this out elsewhere via the concept of the "sporting Black Atlantic" (see Andrews, Carrington, Jackson, & Mazur, 1996). I am thinking here, for example, of the relationships between figures such as C.L.R. James and Learie Constantine (see Note 6) and Muhammad Ali and Malcolm X, and in a somewhat different context, the quite literal connections made by Jean-Michel Basquiat in his painting *All Colored Cast (Part II)* (1982), between the boxer "Jersey" Joe Walcott and Toussaint L'Ouverture.

5. The continuing relevance of, and insights from, James can still be seen in contemporary writings on cricket and the Caribbean that demonstrate the inherent relationship between Black political struggle and cricket. Consider the titles of recent books on cricket and the Caribbean, all of which are heavily influenced by a Jamesian analysis; for example, see Beckles's (1994) *An Area of Conquest: Popular Democracy and West Indies Cricket Supremacy*, Beckles and Stoddard's (1995) *Liberation*

Cricket: West Indies Cricket Culture; and Birbals- ingh's (1996) *The Rise of West Indian Cricket: From Colony to Nation*. See also the essays by St. Pierre (1995), "West Indian Cricket as Cultural Resis- tance," and Yelvington's (1995) "Cricket, Colonial- ism, and the Culture of Caribbean Politics."

6. Richards can be seen to be operating within a longer lineage of great West Indian cricketers who were aware of the wider significance of cricket. This can be traced back to Learie Con- stantine. The grandson of a slave, Constantine was a vocal advocate of West Indian indepen- dence and spoke out against racial injustice, both within cricket and more generally, eventually serving in Dr. Eric Williams's government in Trinidad and Tobago from 1957 to 1961 (Birbal- singh, 1996). Indeed, C.L.R. James credits Con- stantine as being a central figure in James's political development in relation to his racial awareness, anticolonial sensibility, and views on West Indian nationalism. As James (1963/1994) remarks, "Constantine had always been political, far more than I had ever been. My sentiments were in the right place, but I was still enclosed within the mould of nineteenth-century intellec- tualism. Unbeknown to me, however, the shell had been cracked. Constantine's conversations were always pecking at it" (p. 113).

7. The research is based on my doctoral study. In-depth semistructured interviews conducted between 1995 and 1997, and participant observa- tion during the summer cricket seasons of 1995, 1996, and 1997, have been used to collect the data. Pseudonyms for the players and club mem- bers are used throughout. I am using the nomen- clatures Black and Asian to refer to those groups who, due to the process of racialization, are visibly marked as belonging to different races. Within this context, those referred to as Black are those people of sub-Saharan African descent and those referred to as Asian are of South Asian descent.

8. The concept of space invoked here is not used simply as reference to a geographically bounded area, although clearly this is a dimension of any use of the term, but rather refers to the so- cial production of space, that is, the ways in which socioeconomic, cultural, and political discourses construct spatial relations and the ways in which individuals themselves negotiate and reconstruct these discourses. As Lefebvre (1976) argues, space should be seen as having been "shaped and moulded from historical and natural elements . . . this has been a political process. Space is political and ideological. It is a product literally filled with ideologies" (as cited in Farrar, 1996, p. 295).

9. Due to a number of high-profile incidents of racist abuse from supporters at Yorkshire cricket grounds and statements, widely seen as racist, by prominent members of the Yorkshire County Cricket Club over the years, the county has a rep- utation as an "unwelcoming territory for Black cricketers" (Searle, 1990, p. 43; see also Searle, 1996). As Marqusee (1994) accurately notes, "The roots of racism in Yorkshire cricket are set deep in the county's peculiar regional chauvinism, a chau- vinism warped by years of cricket failure. . . . The powers that be at Yorkshire have for many decades preferred the spurious roots of racial and cultural identity to the living roots of the game as it is ac- tually played in the locality. It stands proudly not for the mixed culture of contemporary York- shire—industrial and urban, black and white, im- migrant and native—but for a reified, hollow culture of boastfulness and bigotry. It is, at its core, profoundly exclusive" (pp. 143–144).

Despite over a century of Asian and Black in- volvement in cricket throughout England at both the county and national levels, Yorkshire disgrace- fully remains the only County Cricket Club never to have fielded a British-born Asian or Black cricketer in its first team. Although Yorkshire County Cricket Club now officially promotes an open policy in its selection, evidence suggests that racial discrimination is still prevalent in Yorkshire cricket, despite the work of a number of commit- ted individuals at the club to change this situation (see Long, Nesti, Carrington, & Gilson, 1997). The county's emblem, a white rose, has therefore become a rose, has therefore become a powerful signifier for racist sentiments in the county in wanting to keep the "white rose white."

10. In fact, following Michel de Certeau, Bur- ton (1997) makes the distinction between resis- tance, that is, those forms of contestation from outside a particular discursive regime, and opposi- tion, that is, those forms of contestation from

within a system. Discerning readers will have noticed that I have used the term resistance rather more generally and descriptively in this article when perhaps opposition would have been more analytically precise. Such distinctions have not been central to my arguments in this article.

References

Andrews, D., Carrington, B., Jackson, S., & Mazur, Z. (1996). Jordanscapes: A preliminary analysis of the global popular. *Sociology of Sport Journal, 13,* 428–457.

Back, L. (1996). *New ethnicities and urban culture: Racisms and multiculture in young lives.* London: University College London Press.

Beckles, H. (Ed.). (1994). *An area of conquest: Popular democracy and West Indies cricket supremacy.* Kingston, Jamaica: Ian Randle.

Beckles, H., & Stoddard, B. (Eds.). (1995). *Liberation cricket: West Indies cricket culture.* Manchester, UK: Manchester University Press.

Birbalsingh, F. (1996). *The rise of West Indian cricket: From colony to nation.* Antigua, Jamaica: Hansib.

Birrell, S. (1989). Racial relations theories and sport: Suggestions for a more critical analysis. *Sociology of Sport Journal, 6,* 212–227.

Bonnett, A. (1996). Anti-racism and the critique of "White" identities. *New Community, 22,* 97–110.

Brah, A. (1996). *Cartographies of diaspora: Contesting identities.* London: Routledge.

Burton, R. (1991). Cricket, carnival and street culture in the Caribbean. In G. Jarvie (Ed.), *Sport, racism and ethnicity.* London: Falmer Press.

Burton, R. (1997). *Afro-Creole: Power, opposition and play in the Caribbean.* London: Cornell University Press.

Cohen, A. (1985). *The symbolic construction of community.* London: Routledge.

Dyer, R. (1988). White. *Screen, 29,* 44–64.

Dyer, R. (1997). *White.* London: Routledge.

Fanon, F. (1986). *Black skin, White masks.* London: Pluto.

Farrar, M. (1981). Riot and revolution: The politics of an inner city. *Revolutionary Socialism, 2,* 6–10.

Farrar, M. (1996). Black communities and processes of exclusion. In G. Haughton & C. Williams (Eds.), *Corporate city? Partnership, participation and partition in urban development in Leeds.* Aldershot, UK: Avebury.

Farrar, M. (1997). Migrant spaces and settlers' time: Forming and de-forming an inner city. In S. Westwood & J. Williams (Eds.), *Imaging cities: Scripts, signs, memory.* London: Routledge.

Farred, G. (Ed.). (1996). *Rethinking C.L.R. James.* London: Basil Blackwell.

Feagin, J., & Vera, H. (1995). *White racism: The basics.* London: Routledge.

Frankenburg, R. (1993). *White women, race matters: The social construction of Whiteness.* London: Routledge.

Gilroy, P. (1987). *There ain't no Black in the Union Jack: The cultural politics of race and nation.* London: Hutchinson.

Gilroy, P. (1993). *The Black Atlantic: Modernity and double consciousness.* London: Verso.

Hall, S. (1996). Politics of identity. In T. Ranger, Y. Samad, & O. Stuart (Eds.), *Culture, identity and politics: Ethnic minorities in Britain.* Aldershot, UK: Avebury.

Hall, S., & Jefferson, T. (Eds.). (1976). *Resistance through rituals: Youth subcultures in post-war Britain.* London: Hutchinson.

Hargreaves, J. (1986). *Sport, power and culture.* Cambridge, UK: Polity.

Hartman, D. (1996). The politics of race and sport: Resistance and domination in the 1968 African American Olympic protest movement. *Ethnic and Racial Studies, 19,* 548–566.

Henry, I. (1993). *The politics of leisure policy.* London: Macmillan.

Hesse, B. (1997a). It's your world: Discrepant M/Multiculturalisms. *Social Identities, 3,* 375–394.

Hesse, B. (1997b). White governmentality: Urbanism, nationalism, racism. In S. Westwood & J. Williams (Eds.), *Imaging cities: Scripts, signs, memory.* London: Routledge.

hooks, b. (1992). Representing Whiteness in the Black imagination. In L. Grossberg, C. Nelson, & P. Treichler (Eds.), *Cultural studies.* London: Routledge.

hooks, b. (1994). *Outlaw culture: Resisting representations*, London: Routledge.

James, C.L.R. (1994). *Beyond a boundary*. London: Serpent's Tail. (Original work published 1963).

Keith, M. (1993). *Race, riots and policing: Lore and disorder in a multi-racist society*. London: University College London Press.

Lefebvre, H. (1976). Reflections on the politics of space. *Antipode,* 8, 2. Trans. by Michael Enders from the French journal *Espaces et Sociétiés*, No.1, 1970.

Long, J., Carrington, B., & Spracklen, K. (1996, April). *The cultural production and reproduction of racial stereotypes in sport: A case study of rugby league*. Paper presented to the British Sociological Association annual conference, Reading, UK, April.

Long, J., Carrington, B., & Spracklen, K. (1997). "Asians cannot wear turbans in the scrum": Explorations of racist discourse within professional rugby league. *Leisure Studies,* 16, 249–260.

Long, J., Nesti, M., Carrington, B., & Gilson, N. (1997). *Crossing the boundary: A study of the nature and extent of racism in local league cricket*. Leeds, UK: Leeds Metropolitan University Working Papers.

Long, J., Tongue, N., Spracklen, K., & Carrington, B. (1995). *What's the difference? A study of the nature and extent of racism in rugby league*. Leeds, UK: The Rugby Football League/Leeds City Council/The Commission for Racial Equality/Leeds Metropolitan University.

Marqusee, M. (1994). *Anyone but England: Cricket and the national malaise*. London: Verso.

Marqusee, M. (1995). Sport and stereotype: From role model to Muhammad Ali. *Race and Class,* 36, 1–29.

Marqusee, M. (1996). *War minus the shooting: A journey through South Asia during cricket's World Cup*. London: Heinemann.

Mercer, K. (1994). *Welcome to the jungle: New positions in Black cultural studies*. London: Routledge.

Messner, M. (1992). *Power at play: Sports and the problem of masculinity*. Boston: Beacon.

Morley, D., & Chen, K-H. (Eds.). (1996). *Stuart Hall: Critical dialogues in cultural studies*. London: Routledge.

Policy Research Institute. (1996). *Community profile of Chapeltown Leeds*. Leeds, UK: Leeds Metropolitan University.

Richards, V. (1991). *Hitting across the line: An autobiography*. London: Headline.

Richards, V. (1995). Foreword. In H. Beckles & B. Stoddard (Eds.), *Liberation cricket: West Indies cricket culture*. Manchester, UK: Manchester University Press.

Robson, C. (1994). *Real world research: A resource for social scientists and practitioner-researchers*. Oxford, UK: Basil Blackwell.

Rodman, D. (1996). *Bad as I wanna be*. New York: Delacorte.

Sayyid, B. (1997). *A fundamental fear: Eurocentrism and the emergence of Islamism*. London: Zed Books.

Searle, C. (1990). Race before wicket: Cricket, empire and the white rose. *Race and Class,* 31, 31–48.

Searle, C. (1996, August 18). Running a gauntlet of hate at Headingley. *The Observer,* p.12.

Shohat, E., & Stam, R. (1994). *Unthinking Eurocentrism: Multiculturalism and the media*. London: Routledge.

Sivanandan, A. (1982). *A different hunger: Writings on Black resistance*. London: Pluto.

Sivanandan, A. (1990). *Communities of resistance: Writings on Black struggles for socialism*. London: Verso.

St. Pierre, M. (1995). West Indian cricket as cultural resistance. In M. Malec (Ed.), *The social roles of sport in Caribbean societies*. Luxembourg: Gordan & Breach.

Stuart, O. (1996). Back in the pavilion: Cricket and the image of African Caribbeans in Oxford. In T. Ranger, Y. Samad, & O. Stuart (Eds.), *Culture, identity and politics: Ethnic minorities in Britain*. Aldershot, UK: Avebury.

Sugden, J. (1996). *Boxing and society: An international analysis*. Manchester, UK: Manchester University Press.

Verges, F. (1996). Chains of madness, chains of colonialism: Fanon and freedom. In A. Read (Ed.), *The fact of Blackness: Frantz Fanon and visual representation.* London: Institute of Contemporary Arts.

Ware, V. (1992). *Beyond the pale: White women, racism and history.* London: Verso.

Westwood, S. (1990). Racism, Black masculinity and the politics of space. In J. Hearn & D. Morgan (Eds.), *Men, masculinities and social theory.* London: Unwin Hyman.

Wheatley, R. (1992). *100 Years of Leeds League cricket.* Leeds, UK: White Line Publishing.

Williams, J. (1994). "Rangers is a Black club": "Race," identity and local football in England. In R. Giulianotti & J. Williams (Eds.), *Game without frontiers: Football, modernity and identity.* Aldershot, UK: Arena.

Yelvington, K. (1995). Cricket, colonialism, and the culture of Caribbean politics. In M. Malec (Ed.), *The social roles of sport in Caribbean societies.* Luxembourg: Gordan & Breach.

Zulfiqar, M. (1993). *Land of hope and glory? The presence of African, Asian and Caribbean communities in Leeds.* Leeds, UK: Roots Project.

Chapter 18

TELEVISED SPORT, MASCULINIST MORAL CAPITAL, AND SUPPORT FOR THE INVASION OF IRAQ

Carl Stempel

In this suggestive piece, Carl Stempel, using U.S. survey data, finds a strong link among three factors in people's lives: watching certain kinds of sports on television, feelings of patriotism, and support for the Iraq War. This study is an excellent example of how sociologists use data to test theories about how the world works. Stempel finds interesting variations in support for the war by race and by type of sport watched, leading him to propose a new theory about the kind of morality that underlies both support for the Iraq War and the sports that we watch.

If we broaden the traditional parameters of sports violence to include violent acts related to sport (and I think there are good sociological reasons to do so), it becomes clear that our subject may be far more heterogeneous than simply acts of violence perpetrated by athletes or members of sports crowds.

—K. M. Young (2002, p. 208)

The Bush Doctrine of Preemptive Attacks

America's power position in the world system is in decline, and for the foreseeable future, there will be a strong structural inclination for the United States to use its superior military power to maintain or improve its waning economic and political power position (Wallerstein, 1999, 2003). After Al-Qaeda's attacks on the World Trade Center and the Pentagon on September 11, 2001 (hereinafter, 9/11), neoconservatives in the Bush administration used the fears of terrorism to implement their long-standing plans to overthrow Saddam Hussein (Kessler, 2003; Woodward, 2004). In building support for their plans, they argued that the Iraqi government was stockpiling and

Carl Stempel, "Televised Sport, Masculinist Moral Capital, and Support for the Invasion of Iraq" from *Journal of Sport and Social Issues* 30.1 (February 2006): 79–106. Copyright © 2006 by Sage Publications, Inc. Reprinted with the permission of Sage Publications, Inc.

hiding chemical and biological weapons and was close to securing nuclear weapons that could be used on the United States. Furthermore, they claimed that the Hussein regime had strong links to the Al-Qaeda terrorist organization and was thus at the core of the terrorist threat to the United States.

The invasion of Iraq went hand in hand with a major change in American foreign policy in the direction of asserting unilateral military hegemony for the United States in the name of protecting American security and freedom and preventing the proliferation of weapons of mass destruction among terrorist groups and nations that support them. In his 2002 State of the Union address, President Bush publicly identified Iran, Iraq, and North Korea as an "axis of evil" that "by seeking weapons of mass destruction . . . pose a grave and growing danger." Moments later, he added, "I will not wait on events while dangers gather. I will not stand by as peril draws closer and closer" (Bush, 2002a). In his speech to West Point graduates in early June 2002, Bush directly discounted the value of the strategies of containment and diplomacy in the post-9/11 era and articulated a policy of preventive attacks by declaring, "If we wait for threats to fully materialize, we will have waited too long" (Bush, 2002b). This marked a new imperial doctrine that asserted the right of the United States to attack nation-states that have not attacked, threatened to attack, or even secretly planned to attack the United States or its allies.

The events of 9/11 strengthened Americans' support for militaristic imperialism, but there is reason to believe that most Americans will not go along with this strategy for long. The failure to discover weapons of mass destruction and the breadth of the armed resistance to the occupation contradict Bush administration depictions of Americans as hero-liberators. Likewise, there is a growing disconnect between the hero-liberator metaphors and evidence that most Iraqis, however glad they are to be rid of Saddam, view the United States as an occupying force motivated by imperial, political, and economic interests ("How Iraqis View the U.S.-Led Coalition," 2004). It is also becoming increasingly clear that an invasion that intended to create a shining example of Arab democracy is increasing the militarization and masculinization of antimodernist and anti-imperialist resistance to American and Northern hegemony (Burns & Eckholm, 2004).

Compared to the trajectory of Americans' reactions to the Vietnam War, the opposition to the Iraqi occupation in the United States has grown faster, despite Hussein's record of genocide and brutality and greater efforts by the U.S. military to control the images of war in Iraq. In early January 2003, before the invasion of Iraq, a Gallup poll found only 53% of Americans supporting the war, with 42% against it. Support for the war was greatest during the invasion, peaking on April 9, 2003, when Gallup found 76% of Americans polled agreeing that the war was a good idea and only 19% disagreeing. As Iraqi resistance to the occupation grew and weapons of mass destruction were not found, support for the war declined sharply. Since the middle of January 2004, less than 10 months after the invasion, support for the war has never risen above 52% (Gallup Organization, 2004). This is consistent with the view that many Americans learned (or were easily reminded of) important lessons about the universality of national self-determination from the Vietnam War and from other anticolonial movements after World War II.

Alan Wolfe's (1998) study of middle-class Americans prior to 9/11 supports this view. Using inductive, semistructured interviews, Wolfe found a strong streak of "mature patriotism" in the United States, a nationalism that rejects the "America, right or wrong" mentality though still believing that America is a special land of freedom and opportunity. Most of those he interviewed were skeptics about wars to bring "freedom" to the less "civilized" regions of the world or to protect our national security against threats that are less than imminent. It is hard to know how deeply habituated these views are and how much the events of 9/11 have changed things, but clearly 9/11 strengthened the hand of militaristic imperialists. In this climate of fear and distrust, neoconservatives successfully portrayed diplomacy, working through international organizations, and containment as evidence of "softness," "weak character," and "moral relativism," keywords that I will show metaphorically link support for the war to sports.

To Wolfe's (1998) mature patriotism we must add a somewhat less sanguine perspective on Americans' national habitus that captures important elements missed by Wolfe, perhaps because his research was structured to uncover high moral status signals (Lamont, 2000)—the part of our national habitus that idealizes our democratic nature. Another aspect of our national habitus emphasizes special qualities that make us stand out among other nations. Wallerstein (2003) clearly summarizes many Americans' sense of distinction, so I will quote him at length:

I think that Americans tend to believe that others have *less* of many things than we have, and the fact that we have more is a sign of grace. . . . Other countries are less modern, the meaning of modern being the level of technological development . . . and that therefore we are certain to win the wars into which others may drag us. Americans also consider their society to be more efficient. Things run more smoothly—at the workplace, in the public arena, in social relations, in our dealings with bureaucracies. . . . Others do not seem to have American get-up-and-go. They are less inventive about finding solutions to problems major and minor. They are too mired in traditional or formal ways. And this holds the others back, while America forges ahead. . . .

. . . Is there any other country where social mobility, for those with merit, is so rapid? And which country can match us in the degree to which we are democratic? Democratic not merely in the continuing openness of our political structures, the centrality of a two-party system, but also in our quotidian mores? . . .

We can put this all together in a phrase that Americans have not used much, at least until September 11, but which we largely think in our hearts: We are more civilized than the rest of the world, the Old World, as we used to say with a token of disdain. We represent the highest aspirations of everyone, not merely Americans. We are the leader of the free world, because we are the freest country in the world, and others look to us for leadership, for holding high the banner of freedom, of civilization. (pp. 195–198)

As Wallerstein (2003) notes, openly stating this viewpoint would embarrass many Americans, though somewhat less so after 9/11. Democratizing developments and movements have entailed suppressing or even repressing such feelings of superiority (Wouters, 1998). Borrowing from Hochschild (1989), we might describe the American habitus as democratic on top and aristocratic on the bottom, a bottom that some have more openly embraced after 9/11. Many Americans are committed to living up to their democratic ideals, but their feelings of superiority, outlined by Wallerstein, are an important, less acknowledged part of their national habitus, as well. Furthermore, it appears, ironically, that Americans' feelings of superiority are closely tied to their sense that they are beacons of democracy. I believe that Americans' willingness to support the invasion of Iraq demonstrates that as their power position continues to decline, it will take a great deal of work to redefine, sustain, and build on their democratic ideals.

Masculinist Sports and Militaristic Imperialism

Sports are our most explicit and mythologized public spectacles of competition, power, and domination. Consequently, they are important sites where Americans are registering, managing, and shaping the complex feelings about their power position in the post-9/11 world. As the costs of the military intervention in Iraq become clearer to more and more Americans, there will be opportunities to engage in reflection on the morality and rationality of resolving differences through war and on the realities of trying to sustain dominance in an interdependent world system (Schell, 2003). A part of this national self-reflection ought to include asking why so many of us went along with the invasion of Iraq with very little questioning. And if we are serious about understanding the causes of the invasion, we need to consider the ways our cultural institutions contributed to and reinforced the discourses, fears, and beliefs that made the war appear righteous, justified, and necessary to so many. I posit that popular masculinist sports are among the cultural institutions that functioned to buttress support for the Iraqi war and for the broader Bush doctrine that asserts the authority and obligation of America to attack countries and enemies prior to direct threats to the United States. This study is the first to present systematic data demonstrating the existence of a "televised masculinist sport–militaristic nationalism complex" (MS-MN complex) that contributes to support for imperialistic wars by the United States. The MS-MN complex includes a variety of televised sports that represent, iconize, and naturalize a combination of masculinist and nationalistic ideals and morals and a field of politics where imperialist military projects are imagined and popular support and acquiescence is garnered.

Using data from a nationally representative survey of 1,048 Americans, conducted for the Scripps Howard News Service, I will show that in the summer of 2003, level of involvement in televised masculinist sports was correlated with support for the Iraqi war and for the unilateralist doctrine of preventive attacks and with strong patriotic feelings for the United States. Because nationalism is a hegemonic process of defining the values, meanings, and goals of large, impersonal "survival units," support for imperialist wars can be found across genders, races, social classes, religions, and political and regional groups. However, there is a social structuring of support for and resistance to imperialist wars. Support for the invasion of Iraq was and is strongest among men, Whites, and those who identify as born-again in terms of their religion, but other than party identification, involvement in televised masculinist sports has the strongest, most robust correlations with the measures of imperialistic nationalism.

The Structural Linkage Between Masculinist Sports and Imperialistic Nationalism

If masculinist sports and imperialistic nationalism are interrelated, then a crucial question is, what is the structure of this relationship? One possibility is that youthful sports involvement in masculinist sports operates as an explicit or de facto training and proving ground for future soldiers and military leaders. If masculinist sports functioned in this way, then we would expect masculinist sports and soldiering to form overlapping social networks. This is clearly not the case among highly visible professional athletes, who so rarely sign up for military service that the exceptions are often highly publicized, perhaps in a strained effort to assert a linkage that does not exist in social network terms. High school athletes may be somewhat more likely to enter the military than nonathletes, but even this is doubtful. To my knowledge, this question has not been systematically tested, but we do know that high school athletes disproportionately come from the middle and upper-middle classes, and military personnel are disproportionately those who are not going on to college, so it is unlikely that the correlation is very strong.

Another possible structural linkage is that sports and war have similar social structures and are structured around or embedded with similar ideals, belief systems, worldviews, or habitus. I will be arguing that their isomorphism is based on being structured around a common system of "masculinist moral capital." This structural family resemblance between sports and war leads to a cognitive-emotional affinity between a masculinist interpretation of sports and a readiness to go to war to defend one's national interests and to a predisposition to view imperialist wars as opportunities for heroism and as part of our duty as world leaders.

If we conceptualize masculinity as a habitus or worldview that is embodied and institutionalized in practices across various social fields, then it may be an important mediating structure that links support for war and involvement in masculinist sports. Despite increasing opportunities for girls and women to participate in sports, masculinist sports and war are both, to a considerable degree, still male preserves where fighting strength, competitiveness, and controlled aggression are valued. Both construct and channel camaraderie, sacrifice, and risking one's body for the team as high moral values, and both require disciplined training and submission to clear authority. Risking one's body, intense physical training, submission to authority, sacrifice, and so on are conceived of as "character building" tests. Both masculinist sport and military training are perceived by many as exemplary means of building manhood. From this view, the similarities between masculinist sport and militarism appear to be substantial. The overlap between the version of manhood idealized in many sports and in militaristic nationalism is so great that Nagel (1998) concludes,

Terms like honor, patriotism, cowardice, bravery, and duty are hard to distinguish as either nationalistic or masculinist, since they seem so thoroughly tied both to the nation and to manliness. . . . The "microculture" of masculinity in everyday life articulates very well with the demands of nationalism, particularly its militaristic side. (pp. 251–252)

A great deal of work has been done on sports and violence, but surprisingly little systematic analysis has been done on the relationship between popular sports and war. For example, Young's (2000) excellent summary essay in the *Handbook of Sport Studies* on the research on sport and violence touches on a wide range of issues but does not mention war. In the same volume, Allison (2000), on sport and nationalism, and Houlihan (2000), on sport and politics, also reflecting the state of their subfields, make only passing mention of war. There is, nevertheless, a thread of research and analysis that supports the view that a hard or macho type of masculine habitus mediates the relationship between support for nationalistic wars and involvement in masculinist sports (Burstyn, 1999; Faure, 1996; Hoch, 1972; Jansen and Sabo, 1994; Jeffords, 1989, 1994; McBride, 1995; Sabo, 1994; Sabo and Jansen, 1998; Wakefield, 1997).

I will begin by presenting two theories that develop an analysis of the relationship between mass-mediated sports, gender, and militaristic nationalism: critical feminism and the figurational sociology most associated with Norbert Elias. Both perspectives have done important work to uncover the linkages between sports and masculine domination. I also find both of these theories wanting in their relative silence about what I label masculinist moral capital. I believe that this silence stems from their primary interest in countering the structures of masculine domination in sports. This has placed them in a position of demythologizing powerful ideologies such as the belief that sports build "character" and promote clean, manhood-making aggression and violence. The masculinist myths are challenged by focusing on the underbelly of masculinist sports: destructive violence, physical abuse, homophobia, misogyny, sexual coercion, high levels of injuries and disabilities, and pressure to play with debilitating injuries (Dworkin & Wachs, 2000; Hoch, 1972; Messner, 1992, 1994; Messner & Sabo, 1990; Nelson, 1994; Nixon, 1994; Sabo, 1994; Sabo, Gray, & Moore, 2000; White, Young, & McTeer, 1995; Young, 1993, 2000, 2002; Young, McTeer, & White, 1994).

Breaking with the myths of character and heroism is an important function of sport sociology, but as Bourdieu showed for the reproduction of social class, critical sociology is also advanced when one breaks from that initial break to view these myths as well-founded myths. By *well-founded myth*, I do not mean that the myths are true or partially accurate but that they are exemplars of the moral schemes of evaluation or system of metaphors that are instituted as an "illusio" that makes a social game possible and structures the purpose, meaning, and socially valued identities for those involved (Bourdieu, 1990a, 1990b; Bourdieu & Wacquant, 1992). I will argue that George Lakoff's (2002) work on the conservative worldview uncovers a system of metaphors that constitutes the schemes of masculinist moral capital that centrally underpin the association between televised masculinist sport and support for imperialist wars.

Critical Feminist Perspectives on Televised Sport, Masculinity, and Militaristic Nationalism

Although it is difficult to generalize about feminist perspectives of the relationship between sport, masculinity, and war, there is a clear tendency to draw strong linkages between war and sports, such as football, that emphasize physical domination and an extreme form of masculinity that associates manhood with physical domination and with heroically risking and sacrificing one's body. I will label this perspective *critical feminism* and illustrate it with a few of the best critical feminist analyses, focusing on how they conceptualize the form of masculinity that mediates between sports and war, developing a critique of this conceptualization as I go.

Jansen and Sabo's (1994) analysis of the use of sport (primarily football) metaphors by military leaders and media commentators to heroicize and mythologize the 1991 Persian Gulf War exemplifies a critical feminist view that an aggressive macho masculinity was legitimated and reproduced through war-as-football metaphors. Raising vital issues on the racial, national, and class gendering of sport and, through sport, support for the war, they summarize the prowar masculinity as a hypermasculine one that emphasizes "aggression, competition, dominance, territoriality, and instrumental violence" (Jansen & Sabo, 1994, p. 10).

Burstyn (1999) provides a sociohistorical explanation for the emergence of hypermasculinity in sports, arguing that the erosion of and challenges to the systems of masculine domination have led to hypermasculine responses in the popular culture, particularly in televised sports. The hypermasculine popular culture is then drawn on to build support for war (Burstyn, 1999; see also Jeffords, 1989).

Hypermasculinity is typically viewed as an exaggerated masculinity found among those who are compelled to constantly defend their masculine honor against continuous assaults and challenges or against feelings of shame for failing to meet the standards of masculinity. For Burstyn (1999), hypermasculinity in mass-mediated sports and in male popular culture more generally is a lowest-common-denominator masculinity that reduces and essentializes masculinity to a primal or pure form of violent physical domination stripped of withering Victorian associations with character, sacrifice, and fairplay. Drawing from and expanding on Jeffords (1989), she argues that a central cause of the rise of hypermasculinity has been the ways "the sport-media complex both draws on and supports a militarist response to men's feelings of frustration, alienation, isolation and rage" (Burstyn, 1999, p. 179).

Men's feelings of alienation have roots in a variety of social developments, including the increased social power and independence of women and gays, the neoliberal political economy that has increased the economic insecurity of many working-class and middle-class families, the absence or remoteness of fathers in many American families today, and especially feelings of national embarrassment and disgust about losing the Vietnam War. On the supply side, competitive pressures within the segmenting entertainment industry contribute to the production of hypermasculinist heroics and idols.

Burstyn's (1999) and Jansen and Sabo's (1994) analyses are supported by Messner, Dunbar, and Hunt's (2000) content analysis of televised sports, sports news, and the surrounding ads. They uncovered a "master discourse" that they labeled the "televised sports manhood formula," which identifies real men as aggressive, violent, tough "winners" who are such "true warriors" and possess so much competitive drive that they heroically play through pain and injuries and risk their bodies for victory. Echoing Jansen and Sabo's finding of the discursive integration of football and war, they found that play-by-play coverage and reporting of masculine televised sports closely associates sports with war and weaponry by describing sport using military terms and metaphors, sometimes quite directly framing the contest as a war. The National Football League (NFL) and National Basketball Association (NBA) used the language of war much more than Major League Baseball and extreme sports did, a finding that should be kept in mind when we turn to the survey findings.

I agree with Burstyn (1999) that there has been a broad remasculinization of American popular culture since the 1980s, that something like a lowest-common-denominator hypermasculinity has grown in televised sports during the same period, and that it plays a role in the MS-MN complex (Whannel, 2002). However, I do not believe that it is the lowest-common-denominator forms of masculinity that primarily underpin the MS-MN complex. Rather, the qualities or forms of masculinity that Burstyn claims are being eroded in mass-mediated sports, things such as moral order and character, centrally underlie and stitch together the MS-MN complex in the United States. The critical feminists' conception of hypermasculinity is more congruent with a Social Darwinist or Machiavellian view that the world is a war of all against all. I believe that by itself, this worldview is an extreme version of a conservative worldview that is not hegemonic. I argue that the hegemonic masculinist worldview combines Machiavellianism with moral metaphors such as moral strength, character, and moral order, which provide a vision of how one should bring and sustain moral order to the war of all against all.

From the perspective developed here, critical feminist analyses of masculinity leave out central aspects of the televised sports manhood formula by not adequately capturing the linkages between televised sports discourse and conservative metaphors of moral character, family, and nation, which are at the heart of the moral capital of masculine sports. I believe this is not because they do not recognize the metaphors of masculinist moral capital but because their demythologizing analysis is working to frame these metaphors as ideological to develop a critical analysis of sports that brings the negative aspects of masculinist sports into view. Although indispensable, this strategy may prevent us from more clearly understanding important aspects of how masculine domination operates by limiting us too much to the analytical tool of ideology (distorted images, narratives, and beliefs that naturalize hierarchies and distinctions and secure consent). To this valuable analytical tool I want to add (not replace with) an analysis of habitus or worldview that attempts to empathetically uncover the masculinist schemes of moral and cultural evaluation.

Figurational Sociology, Masculinist Sport, and Violence

The other major approach to studying the relationship between sports, masculinity, and violence is the figurational sociology pioneered by Norbert Elias and Eric Dunning. Figurational sociology is particularly well suited for this task because it provides empirically developed theories and concepts that have at their center issues related to state processes, nationalism, violence control, emotional controls, masculinity, democratization, and long-term social figurations or structuring processes (Dunning, 1999; Dunning & Sheard, 1979; Elias, 1994, 1996; Elias & Dunning, 1986; Maguire, 1999; Stempel, 1992). Given the primacy of Elias's claim that "modern" sport emerges as it gains autonomy from mock battles and the preparation for war, it is somewhat surprising that the figurationalists have done little work on contemporary linkages between sport and war. Nevertheless, Dunning, Sheard, and Elias have analyzed a number of "civilizing spurts" that involved improving the power positions of women, reducing the level of violence in sport contests, and increasing the autonomy of sports from war (see Dunning, 1999, and Maguire, 1999, for summaries).

During civilizing spurts, greater constraints are placed on men from using physical domination and the threat of physical domination as a power resource. Under these conditions, men whose power chances are in decline may turn to male preserves such as masculinist sports, male-exclusive clubs, sports and sex bars, and so on to bond around the ethos and practices of masculine domination and nostalgic feelings about the past, when "men were men." Male preserves are important power resources for militarists during decivilizing spurts such as wars or violent revolutions (Elias, 1996). Wars, aftermaths of lost wars, violent revolts, or other decivilizing spurts dissolve controls on violence and increase the level of fear and insecurity and, often, the masculinist solutions to fear and insecurity. The "taste" for masculinist solutions to fear and insecurity is expressed in recreational and leisure activities, such as participation in violent or macho sports. In this regard, Dunning (1999) cites as support for the figurational approach Sipes's (1973) classic study that found that hunting and football

grew in popularity during World War II, whereas the popularity of baseball declined.

Thus, figurational sociology is in substantial agreement with critical feminism that masculinist sports, resistance to gender equality, and a warrior ethos form a historically shifting but relatively obdurate complex. Like critical feminists, figurationalists expect that those who are most involved in the most male exclusive and most battle-like sports will, other things being equal, be most likely to support wars in response to threats to national security.

Televised Sports as Forms of Mimetic Leisure

On the other hand, Elias and Dunning (1986; Dunning, 1999) also initiated a line of analysis into spectator sports as mimetic forms of leisure that diverges from critical feminism and may help in understanding how televised sports are interpreted by viewers. Earlier, we saw Burstyn (1999) argue that the hypermasculinization of sports stemmed in part from the transformation of sports into commercialized spectacles aimed at wide audiences. The concept of mimetic leisure points to a different side of sport as spectacle by illuminating how viewing violent masculinist sports on television is congruent with a more advanced level of revulsion toward violence than actually playing violent sports. For spectators, mimetic sports, such as televised sports, operate on a different plane or register than direct physical involvement in the contest, action, or drama. Through mimetic sports, one can emotionally experience violent, dangerous, and intensely competitive games and drama without being overwhelmed by them or having to live the real-life consequences of direct participation. Thus, for example, people who enjoy the danger and physical domination of watching boxing or American football on television might be disgusted or overwhelmed by participation that drew them closer to the physical violence.

Violent mimetic sports fit societies where violence and masculine aggression has been hedged in to some degree and where some steps have been taken in the direction of gender equality. Conversely, they fit societies of "late barbarism," where violent masculine domination is still celebrated, admired, and found to be thrilling, at least at a distance.[1]

This view of mimetic sport is strongly supported by sport and theater historians (Gorn, 1986; Guttmann, 1986; Kasson, 1990; Levine, 1988), and professional wrestling is an illuminating present-day case because it hyperbolizes macho masculinity and violence much more than legitimate sports (Messner et al., 2000). Pro wrestling can only stay on the acceptable side of its audience's level of revulsion against violence by making it clear that the blows and falls are not real and that no one really gets hurt (even if many do suffer serious injuries; Atkinson, 2002). The level of revulsion against violence may be one reason efforts to transfer the professional wrestling formula to legitimate sport as a form of "smashmouth" football failed so quickly and resoundingly.

The producers of other televised sports that are working at the boundary between legitimate and illegitimate mimetic violence and domination understand the threshold of repugnance in legitimate sports and carefully manage spectators' impressions of levels of violence, injuries, and domination. Pointing out that athletes are stoically playing hurt, for the team and because they are "competitors," is a common theme in sports coverage that reinforces the masculinist account of games and polices those athletes who might be tempted to put their health ahead of the team. However, routinely reporting the pervasiveness or cumulative effects of injuries is a politically and economically incorrect move that, in our late barbaric society, upsets the impression of the level of violence that makes spectating pleasurable (Sabo & Jansen, 1998).

Analyzing televised sports as mimetic leisure raises the possibility that many viewers of mimetic combat sports view them within more of a "quest for excitement" frame that disembeds hypermasculinism from the masculinist morality that I maintain holds the MS-MN complex together. When combined with an analysis of masculinist moral capital, this thread of figurational sociology leads us to somewhat different conclusions than its primary analysis, which supported the critical feminist analysis.

Masculinist Moral Capital

To describe masculinist moral capital, I will turn to a reading of Lakoff's description of the conservative worldview through the lenses of Bourdieu's work on masculine domination (Bourdieu, 1990b, 2001). According to Lakoff, the conservative worldview, which he considered labeling a patriarchal worldview, pulls together a variety of metaphors to form a "strict father" model of the family—a "cognitively real idealized model" (Lakoff, 2002, p. 67). I am interpreting Lakoff's account of the conservative worldview as the system of deep metaphoric schemes that constitute internalized masculinist moral capital. This moral-cultural system is reproduced in social figurations such as sports that produce, recognize, and circulate masculinist moral capital.

The strict-father model views the world as a cold, dangerous place where survival and success are difficult to achieve. In this perspective, evil is alive in the world and within ourselves, and morality is the courage and self-discipline to stand up to and resist evil. The family is headed by the father, whose primary parenting function is, through clear rewards and punishments, to instill self-discipline and self-reliance—the moral habits needed to succeed and prevail against children's natural tendency to sloth and ease. The greatest danger in this process is that a child will end up "weak," "spoiled," and easy prey to the many temptations of evil. The phrase *tough love,* which became popular in the Reagan era, captures important elements of this ethos, updating and downplaying the violence of the somewhat quaint "spare the rod and spoil the child" and, through a "nation as family" metaphor (see below), linking parenting to a model of how government leaders (ruling fathers) should govern their citizens (children).

Central metaphors in the strict-father morality include the complex and flexible metaphors of moral strength, moral order, and moral authority. At the level of embodied symbolism (Bourdieu's body habitus), moral strength is conceived of as standing upright and being upstanding, straight, and on the up and up. Moral strength is the backbone and fortitude to stand up to or resist evil. Evil can take the form of external threat to one's family or nation or the internal weakness of the body that gives in to desire, escapes from duty, and chooses the easy life. Like physical strength, moral strength is cultivated through self-denial and strict self-control, which is why physi-

cal training or displays of the physically well-trained body can be readily articulated with the strict-father morality (cf. Hoberman, 1984).

A moral father must have the moral strength to set and expect clear standards and take strong corrective action when necessary, including using physical punishment. A moral father also needs to instill respect for authority in general, whether it is his law, the law of the state, or the rules of organizations such as schools and businesses. In this way, the strict father contributes to his children's success and strengthens the moral fabric of the community.

The strict-father morality also sets a vision of the structure of a moral society and of the moral individual. A moral individual is one who is competitive and "self-disciplined enough to make his own plans, undertake his own commitments and carry them out" (Lakoff, 2002, p. 69). A moral society is a competitively structured society that rewards self-disciplined and competitive individuals with wealth, status, and power. Thus, a just society has a hierarchical social structure that reflects a moral hierarchy (remember "*up*right" and "*up*standing").

The conservative moral system, familiar to us because it is a central part of our symbolic order, is actually a system of flexible, embodied metaphors that operate as interpretive schemes, which can be applied to various situations and excluded from application to others. For example, one might apply this worldview only to public, impersonalized, bureaucratic life and use another more "feminine" cognitive-emotional system of metaphors while operating in one's private life. Similarly, a wide variety of moral-political positions is created by focusing more on particular metaphors and focusing less on others, by adhering to the moral system to varying degrees, or by approaching the moral system either more idealistically or more as a pragmatic means of personal advancement. Thus, Lakoff purports to explain a wide range of actual perspectives and position takings in terms of variations on this relatively obdurate system of cognitive-moral schemes.

Masculinist Moral Capital and the Televised Sport

More encompassing systematic content analyses are needed, and there are no doubt multiple readings of televised sports, but from my less systematic observations, the conservative worldview appears to mediate televised sport and support for the war in Iraq.

Televised sport discourse is to varying degrees structured by several metaphors that are closely connected to the conservative worldview:

1. Self-discipline, self-reliance, self-control and competitiveness are virtues that are highly rewarded and extolled (moral order).
2. The televised sports world richly mythologizes character (competitive, self-denial, moral strength). It reinforces the view that character underlies success in sports and in the world. Winners are viewed as possessing the most moral strength or character, keeping in mind that moral strength is equated with competitiveness and the "will to win" (moral strength, moral authority, moral order).
3. Character is defined in masculinist and essentialist terms of being the "go-to" guy under intense competitive pressure and being a true warrior who sacrifices his body and is resolute in the pursuit

of victory (the will to win) in the face of great obstacles. Those possessing character or moral strength are the ones who stand up to adversaries when the going gets tough. Sports are a test of and crucible for constructing masculine honor or character (moral strength).

4. The "us-versus-them" structure of most sporting contests can easily operate as a metaphor for good versus evil, which is prominent in the conservative worldview. Sports provide clear guidelines and boundaries that closely match the conservative metaphor of the moral order having clear boundaries between right and wrong and between good and evil. The rules of conduct are clearly demarcated, and order is maintained through strict enforcement of the rules. The presumption is that the playing field is a dog-eat-dog world and that chaos would prevail without clear absolute authorities imposing strict control (moral order).
5. The popular discourse on the history and traditions of many sports closely matches the conservative vision of decaying and eroding values and of declining respect for authority. The purity of the game for testing and forging character is believed to be corrupted by money and by eroding respect for the legitimate authority of coaches and referees. Conversely, nostalgia is cultivated, and timeless sport traditions and memories are actively constructed and highly honored, especially in the media buildup to the most sacred events, championship tournaments (tradition, moral character resisting corruption).

6. Less often stated but highly sacralized when it comes up is the assertion that the virtues of televised sports heroes are the same virtues of defending our country. Reactions to the death of Pat Tillman, NFL defensive back turned Army Ranger, in Afghanistan were illustrative. On ESPN, a leader and innovator of masculinist sport discourse, the tone of the coverage of his death was deferential, with a mixture of pride that Tillman was one of us and mild shame that sports are, after all, just games that only "play" at this courage and heroism stuff. Tillman was the "real hero." In somber tones somewhat at odds with their norms, they quoted NFL Commissioner Paul Tagliabue: "Pat Tillman personified all the best values of his country and the NFL" (Anderson & Shapiro, 2004).

I present this provisional analysis of the conservative metaphors in televised sports as a crucial part of the *illusio* (Bourdieu, 1990a, 1990b; Bourdieu & Wacquant, 1992; Wacquant, 2003) that underlies the value of televised sports and the worldview or habitus that recognizes and identifies with the value of masculine moral capital in both sports and war. But to understand how closely this habitus connects with militaristic nationalism, we must add the metaphor *nation as family*. The schemes of nation as family are used to project the strict-father metaphors into politics. Thus, without thinking, we speak of forefathers, Uncle Sam, and when we conceive of government as intrusive, Big Brother. Lakoff (2002) argues that there are no "higher generally accepted moral principles" (p. 326) and that it is thus not possible to have political values that are separate from fam-

ily values, a fact that conservatives make use of much more than liberals (Lakoff, 2002, chaps 8, 19).

Masculinist Moral Capital and Support for the Iraqi War

Although Lakoff focuses on liberal-conservative differences internal to the United States, I believe that Americans operating within the conservative worldview conceive of their relations with other nation-states and international relations using the same metaphors. That is, those who rely heavily on the strict-father morality to think about local and national politics tend to interpret foreign policy issues within the same framework. Within this conservative worldview, I believe that with regard to the war in Iraq, the United States is conceived of as a strict-father country that was "born again" in the Reagan years after failing for a period of time to rule or lead the world because it fell victim to sloth, hedonism, and a loss of courage (Jeffords, 1989, 1994). At the same time, our greater economic and military power is seen as a sign of the moral virtues of self-discipline, independence, competitiveness, and self-reliance that make the United States special. Finally, the conservative metaphors of moral strength and so on, applied to international relations, closely link with the metaphor of America as courageous hero rescuing the Iraqis and the Middle East from evil and bringing our special way of life to them. The conservative worldview, projected to the sphere of global politics, appears to be the worldview that President Bush is speaking to and from when he addresses the American people on the war.

To illustrate this, I will briefly analyze a speech Bush made before his news conference on April 13, 2004. This speech was symbolically structured to demonstrate resolve and a clear sense of the enemy as desperate, marginal evildoers in the face of growing doubts in the United States about the war and to displace a growing awareness that many "ordinary" Iraqis saw the U.S.-led coalition as an illegitimate occupying power.

In the speech, Bush made subtle but metaphorically clear reference to our "exit strategies" from the Vietnam War and first Gulf War, in which the United States showed signs of moral weakness.

As I have said to those who have lost loved ones, we will finish the work of the fallen [moral strength, character].

We're carrying out a decision that has already been made and will not change [resolute, unwavering; moral strength, moral authority].

A free Iraq will confirm to a watching world that America's word, once given, can be relied upon, even in the toughest times [stand*up* nation, moral strength]. (Bush, 2004)

The American people are now more resolute and are willing to pay the costs of freedom. This is because we now understand that there is great evil in the world and we are strong in our resolve to stand up to it:

And the enemy has seen that we will no longer live in denial or seek to appease them. For the first time, the civilized world has provided a concerted response to the ideology of terror—a series of powerful, effective blows [moral strength].

Now is the time, and Iraq is the place, in which the enemies of the civilized world are testing the will of the civilized world [moral strength, character, moral order]. (Bush, 2004)

Notice how "testing the will" metaphorically evokes conservative views on parent-child relationships. The contemporary conservative heirs to the belief that children are born with the devil in them are the beliefs that children are always testing the boundaries or testing parents' authority. Conservative parenting experts, such as the popular James Dobson (1996), are constantly advising parents to have the courage or will to discipline in this permissive era.

The internal evils, which we have previously succumbed to (prior to being reborn in the Reagan era), loom in the background as the imagined derision of the enemy, should we lose our nerve.

Yet in this conflict, there is no safe alternative to resolute action. The consequences of failure would be unthinkable. . . . Every enemy of America in the world would celebrate, proclaiming our weakness and decadence, and using that victory to recruit a new generation of killers [moral order, moral strength]. (Bush, 2004)

By now, the differences between critical feminism and figurational sociology and the analysis that I am developing here should be much clearer. Through the lenses of Lakoff's analysis of the conservative worldview, Burstyn's (1999) hypermasculinity is an element of the conservative worldview (masculinist moral capital), but on its own, it is an extreme and marginalized form of masculine domination that is disembedded from the dominant moral framework. That is, Burstyn and other critical feminists may be presenting an extreme form of masculinity as the dominant form in an effort to highlight its negative aspects. This is a common rhetorical strategy that we should avoid because it leads to misunderstandings about the nature and uses of hegemonic masculinity. Burstyn might counter that there has been both a long-term and a recent spurt in the coarsening of popular American sports in the direction of representing a Darwinian war of all against all, where raw power rules and aggressive, violent domination is legitimate. I believe she is right about the recent coarsening or decivilizing spurt but not her analysis of the dominance of hypermasculinity and its linkage to support for the war. If she is right about hypermasculinity, then we should find that the fans of the most hypermasculinist of televised sports are the most supportive of the war in Iraq.

Survey Analysis

To compare the claims of the different theories, I analyzed the results of a nationally representative telephone survey of 1,048 adults conducted for the Scripps Howard News Service between July 30 and August 12, 2003. The survey is one of three or four that Scripps Howard conducts each year to generate political and human interest stories. Questions were asked about how often respondents watched 14 different sports or sporting events on television or read about them in the newspaper or on the Internet. Respondents were selected using a random-digit-dialing technique, and the analyses presented here utilize sample weights that brought the sample in line with valid national estimates on key demographic variables. None of these analyses varied substantially from the same tests done using unweighted data.

Three survey questions make up the measures of support for the Iraqi war and militaristic nationalism: support for the Iraqi war, support for U.S. military policy of pre-ventive attacks, and the respondents' feelings of patriotism toward the United States. The fixed choice questions measuring these variables along with the univariate percentages are presented in Table 1. Support for the war and support for preventive attacks were strongly correlated (Spearman's r = .514), but patriotic self-identity was only moderately correlated with the other two variables. This is not surprising, because many of those who are antiwar and antimilitarist identify as being patriotic, sometimes pointedly in an effort to articulate protesting the war as a patriotic position. Conversely, many who are most in favor of the Iraqi war acknowledge that the antiwar protesters are patriotic, perhaps in deference to Americans' identity as beacons of democracy.

Table 2 looks at bivariate relationships between support for the war and several important social structural variables. We see that Whites, men, and those who identify as being born-again were the most likely to support the war. African Americans were the most antiwar, and race had the strongest impact on support for the war. On the other hand, there were not statistically significant differences in support for the war by level of education, although those with 4-year college degrees were slightly more supportive than either the high school graduates or those with postgraduate degrees. Not shown were data on income and region attendance, which had no statistically significant differences, or on city type, age, and church attendance, which found weak positive but significant relationships ($p < .05$) between living in small cities and attending church last week and support for sending troops to Iraq. Being age 65 and older had a weak negative relationship with support for the war.

Table 1
Dependent Variables: Question Wording and Response Percentages

	%	n
Support for the Iraqi war: As you know, the United States sent troops into Iraq to force it to disarm its weapons of mass destruction. Are you absolutely certain, pretty certain, or not certain that this was the correct thing to do?		
Not certain	41.1	431
Pretty certain	20.5	215
Absolutely certain	31.9	334
Don't know or refused	6.5	68
Support for preventive attacks: Thinking about America's foreign policy, how do you feel about our policy of preventive military attacks on countries that we feel threaten our national security?		
Strongly disagree	7.0	73
Somewhat disagree	16.6	174
Neutral	19.4	203
Somewhat agree	30.6	321
Strongly agree	18.6	195
Don't know or refused	7.7	81
Patriotism toward the United States: Generally speaking, how would you describe your own feelings of patriotism toward the United States?		
Very unpatriotic	1.9	20
Somewhat unpatriotic	2.3	24
Neutral	5.1	54
Somewhat patriotic	27.5	288
Very patriotic	59.8	626
Don't know or refused	3.4	36

Table 2
Support for War in Iraq by Gender, Education, Race, and
Born-Again Religious Identity (July 30, 2003, to August 12, 2003)

	Male	Female	High School	College	Postgraduate	Black	Hispanic	White	Born-Again	Not Born-Again
N	473	507	240	225	144	120	108	690	334	572
How certain that troops to Iraq was a good idea (in percentages)										
Absolutely certain	41.0	27.6	35.0	37.8	31.3	20.0	29.6	38.7	41.6	31.3
Pretty certain	22.6	21.3	18.3	24.0	19.4	14.2	13.0	24.6	22.8	19.8
Not certain	36.4	51.1	46.7	38.2	49.3	65.8	57.4	36.7	35.6	49.0
Pearson correlation	$-.160^{**}$		$-.063_a$		$-.098_b$	$-.194_c{}^{**}$	$-.116_d{}^{*}$		$.129^{**}$	

a. Test for relationship between college degree and high school degree.
b. Test for relationship between college degree and postgraduate degree.
c. Test for relationship between Blacks and Whites.
d. Test for relationship between Hispanics and Whites.
$^{*}p \leq .05.$ $^{**}p \leq .001.$

The Televised Masculinist Sport–Militaristic Nationalism Complex

If the critical feminist and figurational perspectives are right, viewers of the most macho or hypermasculinist and male-exclusive sports should have the strongest association with support for the war. As an initial test, I conducted a separate ordinary least squares (OLS) regression for each of the 14 sports, with support for the war as the dependent variable. Each regression model included gender, education, region of the country, racial identity, church attendance, born-again religious identity, married-with-children status, and age as control variables. With these controls, often watching baseball was associated with support for the war at a .001 level of significance; NFL, college football, National Association for Stock Car Auto Racing (NASCAR), and tennis were associated at .01; golf, extreme sports, and boxing were associated at a .05 level of significance; and NBA basketball ($p = .057$) and Indy car racing ($p = .058$) approached significance (results available on request). It is striking that baseball, tennis, and NASCAR had the largest standardized regression coefficients and that the sports that most dramatize direct physical domination and/or are most narrated with the discourse of war (Messner et al., 2000) were not the sports whose viewers were most likely to support the war.

A similar pattern emerged when I conducted a regression that entered all of the televised sports simultaneously along with the control variables. This is a quite different model because for each sport, it controls for the effects of watching the other 13. In this model, only watching baseball and tennis were associated with support for the war, using a .05 significance level as the cutoff.

Watching the Olympics was negatively associated with support for the war. Both college football ($p = .092$) and NASCAR ($p = .101$) had positive associations, and figure skating ($p = .086$) had a negative association with support for the war that approached significance. NFL football ($p = .590$), NBA basketball ($p = .417$), and boxing ($p = .219$), all sports that critical feminists and/or figurationalists would expect to have strong associations with support for the war, had weak nonsignificant positive relationships with support for the war. Thus, the hypothesis drawn from critical feminism and the figurationalists, that sports which are most combat-like or display the most violent domination, would be most associated with support for the war was not supported by these initial tests.

There is a clear racial dimension to the connection between support for the Iraqi war and involvement in televised masculinist sport. The sports most strongly associated with support for the war are, within the American racial formation, coded as White. Virtually all of the NASCAR drivers and most professional tennis players are White, and Major League Baseball has by far the highest proportion of White players (and lowest proportion of African American players) of the big three American sports. Conversely, many of the sports that most emphasize violence and/or direct physical domination (NFL football, NBA basketball, boxing, and college basketball) have the highest proportions of African American and Latino players and are not associated with support for the war. Even college football, the apparent exception to this pattern, stands out as the most White-coded of the sports emphasizing direct physical domination: A considerably higher proportion of Division I college football players and coaches are White than their counterparts in the NFL, basketball, or boxing (Lapchick, 2003).

A brief side note on encoding is in order here. It is now widely recognized that encoding occurs on both the production and reception sides, but less recognized is the importance of field or relational encoding. That is, the encoding of any particular sport is formed in relation to the other televised sports. So, for example, it may be that hypermasculine sports are coded as brash, youthful, unrestrained, and Black, whereas baseball, tennis, golf, and NASCAR are coded in relation to the hypermasculine sports as disciplined, mature, courageous, and White.

The preliminary analyses were the impetus for developing three indexes of televised sport viewing:

1. The number of White-coded masculinist sports on television (baseball, tennis, NASCAR, golf, Indy car racing, and extreme sports) often watched
2. The number of non-White-coded hypermasculinist sports (NFL, boxing, college football) often watched
3. The number of non-White-coded masculinist sports (soccer, NBA, and college basketball) often watched

In constructing these indexes, I created the groupings based on two overlapping but somewhat separate dimensions: (a) the degree of direct physical violence and domination sanctioned in the sports and (b) the racial coding of the sports, which is closely related to the racial makeup of its players and coaches. Two sports or events, the Olympics and figure skating, were left out of this analysis. The Olympics was left out because it is an event with many sports (and

is thus hard to categorize) and because it is produced and received through strong internationalist frames that run against militaristic nationalism, as evidenced by its viewers' antiwar tendencies. Figure skating was left out because it is the one sport whose fans are primarily women, as are its most famous athletes, and because it is structured around traditionally feminine frames.

I conducted OLS multiple regression analyses that compared the explanatory power of each of the televised sport indexes on support for the war, using the same social structural control variables used in the previous regressions. The results shown in Table 3 add strong support to the preliminary finding that the White-coded masculinist sports, not the hypermasculinist sports, are the sports most associated with support for the war.

I first conducted separate regressions for each index, the results of which are shown in Models 1 to 3. The non-White hypermasculinist and the White masculinist sport indexes are positively related with support for the war at .001 levels of significance, and the non-White masculinist sports are not associated with support for the war at a .05 level of significance. However, the White masculinist sport index had a larger standardized regression coefficient, and when all three indexes are entered into the same regression (Model 4), neither the non-White hypermasculinist sports nor the non-White masculinist sports were associated with support for the war at $p = .05$, whereas the White masculinist sports are associated with support for the war at a high level of confidence ($p = .001$).[2] Thus, for this nationally representative sample, White-coded masculinist sports, which I contend are, for many Americans, the sports that are en-

Table 3

Ordinary Least Squares Regression Coefficients for Social Structural Variables and Indexes of Masculinist Televised Sports Viewing on Support for the Iraqi War

	Model 1			Model 2			Model 3			Model 4		
Male[a]	-.267	.059***	-.150	-.309	.060***	-.174	-.253	.061***	-.143	-.242	.061***	-.136
Black[b]	-.492	.091***	-.184	-.525	.095***	-.196	-.524	.092***	-.195	-.520	.094***	-.194
Hispanic[b]	-.264	.095**	-.094	-.297	.097**	-.106	-.289	.096**	-.103	-.278	.096**	-.100
Asian or Other[b]	-.532	.148***	-.116	-.563	.150***	-.123	-.531	.150***	-.116	-.527	.148***	-.115
Married with children[c]	.197	.062***	.111	.206	.063***	.116	.191	.063**	.108	.186	.063**	.105
Some college[d]	-.018	.073	-.009	-.022	.074	-.011	-.035	.074	-.018	-.017	.074	-.008
College graduate[d]	.041	.080	.020	.013	.081	.006	.000	.081	.000	.028	.080	.013
Postgraduate[d]	-.118	.093	-.048	-.159	.094	-.065	-.167	.093	-.068	-.127	.093	-.052
Northeast[e]	.048	.091	.021	.053	.092	.023	.041	.091	.018	.056	.091	.024
South[e]	-.091	.077	-.049	-.100	.078	-.054	-.107	.078	-.058	-.094	.077	-.051
Midwest[e]	-.002	.085	.001	-.010	.086	-.005	-.026	.086	-.012	-.003	.085	-.002
Born-again	.260	.064***	.141	.260	.066***	.141	.271	.065	.147	.256	.065***	.139
Church attend	.124	.061*	.069	.121	.062	.068	.118	.062	.066	.120	.061	.067
Age 18 to 24[f]	.271	.112*	.105	.228	.116*	.088	.203	.114	.079	.250	.115*	.097
Age 25 to 34[f]	.381	.104***	.165	.362	.105**	.157	.367	.104	.158	.374	.104***	.162
Age 35 to 44[f]	.133	.096	.064	.107	.097	.052	.115	.097	.056	.132	.096	.064
Age 45 to 54[f]	.134	.102	.057	.110	.104	.047	.123	.103	.052	.127	.102	.054
Age 55 to 64[f]	.240	.110*	.090	.218	.111	.082	.227	.110	.085	.242	.110*	.091
Small city[g]	.166	.074*	.083	.195	.075*	.097	.185	.075	.092	.173	.074*	.086
Suburb[g]	-.067	.082	-.029	-.054	.084	-.023	-.043	.083	-.019	-.060	.083	-.026
Rural[g]	.029	.083	.013	.030	.084	.014	.020	.084	.009	.024	.083	.011
White-coded masculinist sports	.164	.031***	.173							.138	.034***	.146
Non-White-coded masculinist sports				.084	.050	.059				.017	.052	.012
Non-White-coded hypermasculinist sports							.140	.036***	.133	.064	.042	.061

a. Reference category is female.
b. Reference category is White.
c. Reference category is unmarried and/or no children.
d. Reference category is high school or less.
e. Reference category is West.
f. Reference category is 65 and older.
g. Reference category is large city.

$*p \leq .05$. $**p \leq .01$. $***p \leq .001$.

coded as exemplars of masculinist moral capital, are most strongly associated with support for the war.

It should be noted that because respondents' race was controlled for in all of the regressions reported here, the lack of association in the full model between the non-White-coded sports (masculinist and hypermasculinist) and support for the war is not because those sports have higher rates of non-White viewers, who, as we saw earlier, were less supportive of the war. However, further analysis uncovered an interaction effect involving race that may be an important piece to the puzzle of why the White-coded masculinist sports that emphasize physical domination less are most strongly related to support for the war.

To test interaction effects by race and the different types of masculinist sports, I conducted separate regressions for each of the three sport indexes among Whites and then among non-Whites (available on request). For both Whites and non-Whites, the White masculinist and the non-White hypermasculinist sports were associated with support for the Iraqi war. However, the non-White masculinist index was associated with support for the war only among non-Whites.[3]

Taken together, the evidence closely fits a model that the racial coding of different televised sports goes hand in hand with different racial-moral readings of those sports. My hypothesis, which closely fits the evidence presented here, is that the White-coded sports are more often "read" within the hegemonic schemes of masculinist moral capital (the strict-father morality), which I contend is a central mediating framework between televised sports and support for the Iraqi war, and thus these are the sports that are more strongly associated

with support for the war. Conversely, the non-White-coded sports are more often read within a "quest for excitement" or "hypermasculine as spice" framework that is less connected to masculinist morality. This is why the non-White-coded hypermasculinist sports are more weakly associated with support for the war and why White fans of non-White-coded masculinist sports, such as NBA basketball, do not support the war in Iraq: They are not relating to basketball within the framework of masculinist moral capital.

If we view the field of televised sport as a racialized social space where hegemonic masculinity is contested and constructed, the patterns uncovered here are consistent with Lamont's (2000) finding that White, lower-middle-class males view themselves as superior to African Americans on moral grounds, identifying strongly with what she calls the "disciplined self" that they believe many African Americans lack. It is also consistent with a racial order where Whiteness and Whites are conceived of as the mature race that is neither too effeminate nor overly masculinist, both of which are perceived as childlike qualities. And at the level of the field of nations, this interpretation fits a theory that the habitus schemes of many Americans, the middle-class nation par excellence, entail a national identity of being neither too civilized (European) nor too uncivilized (Third World or Muslim), a perspective whose general contours go back at least to postrevolutionary republicanism.[4]

Intensity of Involvement in Masculinist Sports and Imperialist Nationalism

We have seen that the televised sports central to the MS-MN complex are somewhat different than expected by the prevalent theories in the field, and we have found strong indirect support for the alternative explanation put forward here. With these findings as a foundation, I turned to gauging the strength of the relationship between masculinist televised sports and militaristic nationalist beliefs. To be able to present measures of strength that are intuitively and statistically accurate, I conducted three binary logistic regressions, using strong support for war, preventive attacks, and feelings of patriotism as dependent variables. For the measure of involvement in televised masculinist sports, I added the scores on the White-coded masculinist sports index with the scores on the non-White-coded hyper-masculinist sports to form a single index. The non-White-coded masculinist sports index (college and NBA basketball and soccer) was left off because its effects were virtually eliminated when the other two indexes were included in the earlier regression model. Thus, the index used consisted of nine sports: baseball, tennis, golf, NASCAR, Indy car racing, extreme sports, NFL, college football, and boxing.

Logistic regression generates estimated odds ratios for each category of the independent variables, so to ensure that there were enough cases in the high category of the index, anyone who often watched four or more of the nine sports was coded 4. Table 4 shows the estimated odds ratios for the variables in each of the three logistic regressions. Several structural variables have some explanatory power on one or more of the dependent measures of militaristic nationalism, but the dummy variable for African Americans and the masculinist sport index are consistently the two most powerful explanatory variables. This is strong support for the existence of the MS-MN complex. Note also that with the marginal exception of *feels very patriotic*, the masculinist sport index is linearly related to measures of militaristic nationalism. That is, increased involvement in televised masculinist sports increased the estimated odds of feeling strong patriotism and of supporting the war and the policy of preventive attacks. For example, often watching one masculinist sport increased the odds of strongly agreeing with preventive attacks to 1.471 (relative to not watching any masculinist sports often), and the odds ratios increased markedly with greater involvement, up to 5.21 for those who often watch four or more masculinist sports.

Conclusion

Previous studies have analyzed the historical roots, structural relationships, and discursive similarities between masculinist sports and war. They have developed a compelling case that televised masculinist sports are cultural and social supports for militaristic nationalism and imperialist wars. The findings from a nationally representative survey presented here provide strong evidence that level of involvement in masculinist sports on television is robustly associated with strong feelings of patriotism and with support for the American invasion of Iraq in 2003 and the Bush doctrine of preventive attacks. Following others, I have interpreted these findings as evidence that televised masculinist sports constitute a central institution in producing and reproducing militaristic nationalism, surpassing social class, religion, age, gender, family structure, and region in explanatory power. This finding suggests that political sociologists can no longer afford to ignore the importance of televised sports and the sports culture more generally in their efforts to explain support for militaristic nationalism.

Table 4
Estimated Odds Ratios From Logistic Regressions of
Structural Variables and Index of Masculinist Sports Viewing
on Militaristic Nationalism Variables

	Is Absolutely Certain About Troops to Iraq	Strongly Agrees With Preventive Attacks	Feels Very Patriotic
Male[a]	1.835***	1.301	.854
Black[b]	.347***	.376**	.305***
Hispanic[b]	.690	.627	.334***
Asian or Other[b]	.317***	.178*	.517
Married with children[c]	1.547*	1.048	1.208
Some college[d]	.841	.624	1.402
College graduate[d]	.940	.623	1.353
Postgraduate[d]	.657	.584	1.631
Northeast[e]	1.013	.619	.736
South[e]	.662	.828	.958
Midwest[e]	.788	.456**	.731
Born-again	1.685**	1.354	1.579**
Church attend	1.327	1.201	1.093
Age 18 to 24[f]	1.091	1.012	.199***
Age 25 to 34[f]	1.929*	.760	.320***
Age 35 to 44[f]	1.130	1.243	.330***
Age 45 to 54[f]	1.180	.746	.845
Age 55 to 64[f]	1.753*	1.948*	1.114
Small city[g]	1.481*	1.003	1.107
Suburb[g]	.801	.896	.996
Rural[g]	1.037	.753	1.429
Number of masculinist sports viewed			
One[h]	1.493*	1.464	1.537*
Two[h]	2.149***	2.325**	3.478***
Three[h]	2.165**	3.463***	2.878***
Four or more[h]	3.329***	5.177***	3.814***

a. Reference category is female.
b. Reference category is White.
c. Reference category is unmarried and/or no children.
d. Reference category is high school or less.
e. Reference category is West.
f. Reference category is 65 and older.
g. Reference category is large city.
h. Reference category is watches zero masculinist sports.
$*p < .05.$ $** p < .01.$ $*** p < .001.$

However, the analysis presented here differs from previous studies that have pointed to institutionalized representations of violent, aggressive, macho hypermasculinity as the social form that links masculinist sports to militaristic nationalism. At the core of this perspective is the view that both masculinist sports and war are best characterized as testing and forging masculinity through violent domination while risking life and limb. The evidence presented here suggests that a hypermasculine-prowar connection exists for some sports fans but that for more, the cognitive-emotional linkage consists of a system of masculinist moral metaphors that Lakoff labels a strict-father morality.

At the core of the strict-father morality are metaphors of moral character, moral strength, and moral order. I found strong and consistent support for this interpretation throughout a variety of empirical tests, which found that hypermasculinist sports, such as boxing and NFL football, were less strongly associated with support for the invasion of Iraq than several other masculinist sports that do not emphasize violence and direct physical domination, such as baseball and tennis.

I believe that including a greater focus on masculinities built around the strict-father morality could have practical political and analytical benefits in the field of sports and sport studies. If we are interested in working against hegemonic masculinity in ways that will have the greatest chance of getting people to rethink their practices and perspectives, recognizing the symbolic power of the strict-father morality should help us avoid stereotyping hegemonic masculinity as a violence-based masculinity that those we would like to reach do not see themselves in. At the same time, it may help us clarify the nature of the task before us, which includes recognizing and articulating moral and ethical alternatives to the strict-father morality in the field of sports along with challenging hypermasculinist tendencies.

This study also uncovered important racial patterns that should be followed up in more detail in future studies. The division between hypermasculinist and masculinist sports is, to a great extent, a racial divide. Viewing White-coded masculinist sports is more strongly associated with support for the Iraqi war than non-White-coded hypermasculinist or masculinist sports are. Also, White viewers of non-White-coded masculinist sports, such as NBA basketball, were not more likely to support the Iraqi war, whereas the non-White viewers were. Although not anticipated, these patterns closely fit my emphasis on masculinist moral capital when we conceive of the televised sports market as a racialized field of contested masculinities. A provisional interpretation is that in the field of televised sports, Whiteness is more strongly associated with the capital of moral character and moral strength, and this association goes hand in hand with limits on direct physical violence and domination in the White-coded sports. Conversely, Blackness is more associated with brute strength, physical above mental prowess, passion, and uncontrolled violence, and these qualities, however exciting and thrilling to watch, poorly mediate support for military aggression framed as liberation and spreading civility and democracy.

Notes

1. Note that this is neither a "catharsis" theory nor a theory that fits very easily with other abstracted empirical questions, such as whether watching violent sports causes one to act violently. Rather, it links the development and popularity of mimetic forms of combat sports to the emergence of highly routinized and somewhat pacified societies and hypothesizes that a taste for mimetic forms of violent masculine domination fall on a scale of violence control somewhere between being repulsed by such forms and participating directly in those activities.

2. To make sure that the strong association for the White index was not simply the result of baseball, which has a much larger following than the other sports, I did the same test using the White index minus baseball and baseball entered as a separate dummy variable. The White index minus baseball and baseball had almost identical standardized regression coefficients, and both were significant at $p < .01$. The non-White indexes continued to be nonsignificant at $p < .05$.

3. Non-Whites included African Americans, Hispanics, Asian Americans, and Other. Non-Whites' views on the war and televised sport viewing habits are fairly similar across races.

4. Here it is noteworthy that baseball, the sport most strongly associated with support for the war, has long been dubbed the national pastime, is the subject of the most intense nostalgia, and has strong middle-class origins (Adelman, 1986).

References

Adelman, M. (1986). *A sporting time: New York City and the rise of modern athletics.* Urbana, IL: University of Illinois Press.

Allison, L. (2000). Sport and nationalism. In J. Coakley & E. Dunning (Eds.), *Handbook of sport studies* (pp. 344–355). Thousand Oaks, CA: Sage.

Anderson, S., & Shapiro, M. (Executive Producers). (2004, April 23). *Sportscenter* [Television broadcast]. Bristol, CT: ESPN TV.

Atkinson, M. (2002). Fifty million viewers can't be wrong: Professional wrestling, sports entertainment and mimesis. *Sociology of Sport Journal, 19*(1), 47–66.

Bourdieu, P. (1990a). *In other words: Essays towards a reflexive sociology.* Stanford, CA: Stanford University Press.

Bourdieu, P. (1990b). *The logic of practice.* Stanford, CA: Stanford University Press.

Bourdieu, P. (2001). *Masculine domination.* Stanford, CA: Stanford University Press.

Bourdieu, P., & Wacquant, L. (1992). *An invitation to reflexive sociology.* Chicago: University of Chicago Press.

Burns, J., & Eckholm, E. (2004, August 29). In western Iraq, fundamentalists hold U.S. at bay. *The New York Times.* Retrieved September 9, 2004, from LexisNexis database.

Burstyn, V. (1999). *The rites of men: Manhood, politics, and the culture of sport.* Toronto, Canada: University of Toronto Press.

Bush, G. (2002a, January 29). *State of the union address.* Retrieved May 1, 2004, from http://www.cnn.com/2002/ALLPOLITICS/01/29/bush.speech.txt/

Bush, G. (2002b, June 1). *President Bush delivers graduation speech at West Point: Remarks by the President at 2002 graduation exercise of the United States Military Academy, West Point, New York.* Retrieved May 1, 2004, from http://www.whitehouse.gov/news/releases/2002/06/20020601–3.html

Bush, G. (2004, April 13). *Tough weeks in Iraq* [Transcript of president's news conference statement]. Retrieved April 30, 2004, from http://abcnews.go.com/sections/US/World/bush_transcript_040413.html

Dobson, J. (1996). *The new dare to discipline.* Wheaton, IL: Tyndale House.

Dunning, E. (1999). *Sport matters: Sociological studies of sport, violence, and civilization.* London: Routledge.

Dunning, E., & Sheard, K. (1979). *Barbarians, gentlemen, and players: A sociological study of the development of rugby football.* New York: New York University Press.

Dworkin, S. L., & Wachs, F. L. (2000). The morality/manhood paradox: masculinity, sport and the media. In J. McKay et al. (Eds.), *Masculinities, gender relations, and sport* (pp. 47–66). Thousand Oaks, CA: Sage.

Elias, N. (1994). *The civilizing process.* Oxford, UK: Basil Blackwell.

Elias, N. (1996). *The Germans: Power struggles and the development of habitus in the 19th and 20th centuries.* New York: Columbia University Press.

Elias, N., & Dunning, E. (1986). *The quest for excitement: Sport and leisure in the civilizing process.* Oxford, UK: Basil Blackwell.

Faure, J.-M. (1996). Forging a French fighting spirit: The nation, sport, violence and war. In J. A. Mangan (Ed.), *Tribal identities: Nationalism, Europe and sport* (pp. 75–93). London: Frank Cass.

Gallup Organization. (2004). *Iraq.* Retrieved September 9, 2004, from http://www.gallup.com/poll/content/default.aspx?ci=1633&pg=1

Gorn, E. (1986). *The manly art: Bare-knuckle prize fighting in America.* Ithaca, NY: Cornell University Press.

Guttmann, A. (1986). *Sports spectators.* New York: Columbia University Press.

Hoberman, J. M. (1984). *Sport and political ideology.* Austin: University of Texas Press.

Hoch, P. (1972). *Rip off the big game: The exploitation of sports by the power elite.* Garden City, NJ: Doubleday.

Hochschild, A. (1989). *The second shift: Working parents and the revolution at home.* New York: Viking.

Houlihan, B. (2000). Politics and sport. In J. Coakley & E. Dunning (Eds.) *Handbook of sport studies.* (pp. 213–227). Thousand Oaks, CA: Sage.

How Iraqis view the U.S.-led coalition and post-Iraq invasion. (2004, April 30). *USA Today.* Retrieved May 1, 2004, from http://www.usatoday.com/news/world/iraq/2004–04–29-gallup-poll-post-invasion-full.htm

Jansen, S. C., & Sabo, D. (1994). The sport/war metaphor: Hegemonic masculinity, the Persian

Gulf War, and the new world order. *Sociology of Sport Journal, 11,* 1–17.

Jeffords, S. (1989). *The remasculinization of America: Gender and the Vietnam War.* Bloomington: Indiana University Press.

Jeffords, S. (1994). *Hard bodies: Hollywood masculinity in the Reagan era.* New Brunswick, NJ: Rutgers University Press.

Kasson, J. (1990). *Rudeness and civility: Manners in nineteenth-century urban America.* New York: Hill and Wang.

Kessler, G. (2003, January 12). U.S. decision on Iraq has puzzling past: Opponents of war wonder when, how policy was set [Electronic version]. *The Washington Post.* Retrieved May 1, 2004, from http://www.washingtonpost.com/ac2/wp-dyn/A43909–2003Jan11

Lakoff, G. (2002). *Moral politics: How liberals and conservatives think.* Chicago: University of Chicago Press.

Lamont, M. (2000). *The dignity of working men.* Cambridge, MA: Harvard University Press.

Lapchick, R. (2003). *2003 racial and gender report card.* Orlando, FL: Institute for Diversity and Ethics in Sport. Retrieved December 15, 2004, from http://www.bus.ucf.edu/sport/public/downloads/media/ides/release_05.pdf

Levine, L. (1988). *Highbrow/lowbrow: The emergence of cultural hierarchy in America.* Cambridge, MA: Harvard University Press.

Maguire, J. (1999). *Global sport: Identities, societies, civilizations.* Cambridge, UK: Polity.

McBride, J. (1995). *War, battering and other sports: The gulf between American men and women.* Atlantic Highlands, NJ: Humanities Press.

Messner, M. A. (1992). *Power at play: Sports and the problem of masculinity.* Boston: Beacon.

Messner, M. A. (1994). When bodies are weapons. In M. A. Messner & D. F. Sabo (Eds.), *Sex, violence, and power in sports* (pp. 89–100). Freedom, CA: Crossing.

Messner, M. A., Dunbar, M., & Hunt, D. (2000). The televised sports manhood formula. *Journal of Sport and Social Issues, 24,* 380–394.

Messner, M. A., & Sabo, D. F. (Eds.). (1990). *Sport, men, and the gender order: Critical feminist perspectives.* Champaign, IL: Human Kinetics.

Nagel, J. (1998). Masculinity and nationalism: Gender and sexuality in the making of nations. *Ethnic and Racial Studies, 21,* 242–269.

Nelson, M. B. (1994). *The stronger women get, the more men love football: Sexism and the American culture of sports.* New York: Harcourt Brace.

Nixon, H. L. (1994). Coaches' views of risk, pain, and injury in sport, with special reference to gender differences. *Sociology of Sport Journal, 11,* 79–87.

Sabo, D. (1994). Pigskin, patriarchy and pain. In M. A. Messner & D. F. Sabo (Eds.), *Sex, violence, and power in sports* (pp. 82–88). Freedom, CA: Crossing.

Sabo, D., Gray, P. M., & Moore, L. A. (2000). Domestic violence and televised athletic events. In J. McKay et al. (Eds.), *Masculinities, gender relations, and sport* (pp. 127–146). Thousand Oaks, CA: Sage.

Sabo, D., & Jansen, S. C. (1998). Prometheus unbound: Constructions of masculinity in sports media. In L. A. Wenner (Ed.), *Mediasport* (pp. 202–220). New York: Routledge.

Schell, J. (2003). *The unconquerable world: Power, nonviolence, and the will of the people.* New York: Henry Holt.

Sipes, R. G. (1973). War, sports, and aggression: An empirical test of two rival theories. *American Anthropologist, 75,* 64–86.

Stempel, C. (1992). Towards a Historical Sociology of Sport in the United States: 1825–1875 (Doctoral dissertation, University of Oregon, 1992). *Dissertation Abstracts Online, 53*(09A), 3374.

Wacquant, L. (2003). *Body and soul: Notebooks of an apprentice boxer.* New York: Oxford University Press.

Wakefield, W. E. (1997). *Playing to win: Sports and the American military, 1898–1945.* Albany: State University of New York Press.

Wallerstein, I. (1999). *The end of the world as we know it: Social science for the twenty-first century.* Minneapolis: University of Minnesota Press.

Wallerstein, I. (2003). *The decline of American power.* New York: New Press.

Whannel, G. (2002). *Media sport stars: Masculinities and moralities.* New York: Routledge.

White, P., Young, K., & McTeer, W. (1995). In D. Sabo & D. F. Gordon (Eds.), *Men's health and illness: Gender, power and the body* (pp. 158–182). Thousand Oaks, CA: Sage.

Wolfe, A. (1998). *One nation, after all: What middle-class Americans really think about God, country, family, racism, welfare, immigration, homosexuality, work, the right, the left, and each other.* New York: Viking.

Woodward, B. (2004). *Plan of attack.* New York: Simon & Schuster.

Wouters, C. (1998). How strange to ourselves are our feelings of superiority and inferiority? *Theory, Culture and Society, 15,* 131–150.

Young, K. M. (1993). Violence, risk, and liability in male sports culture. *Sociology of Sport Journal, 10,* 373–396.

Young, K. M. (2000). Sport and violence. In J. Coakley & E. Dunning (Eds.), *Handbook of sport studies* (pp. 382–407). Thousand Oaks, CA: Sage.

Young, K. M. (2002). From "sports violence" to "sports crime": Aspects of violence, law, and gender in the sports process. In M. Gatz et al. (Eds.), *Paradoxes of youth and sport* (pp. 207–224). Albany: State University of New York Press.

Young, K. M., McTeer, W., & White, P. (1994). Body talk: Male athletes reflect on sport, injury, and pain. *Sociology of Sport Journal, 11,* 175–194.

Chapter 19

GAY GAMES OR GAY OLYMPICS?

Implications for Lesbian Inclusion

Helen Jefferson Lenskyj

This selection addresses one of the few arenas of sport that was organized on a specifically political basis. Attempting to overcome the homophobia of the traditional world of sports, gay and lesbian athletes organized the Gay Olympic Games in 1982. Helen Jefferson Lenskyj's account of the history of the Gay Games highlights both how sport can be used to highlight progressive, inclusive politics *and* how, even within such a context, struggles may ensue about whether and how politics and sport should mix.

The Purpose of the Gay Games is "to foster and augment the self-respect of lesbians and gay men . . . and to engender respect and understanding from the non-gay world."

—**Federation of Gay Games (1997)**

When the first Gay Games, at that time called the "Gay Olympic Games," were held in San Francisco in 1982, they were hailed as an empowering sporting and cultural celebration organized by and for lesbians, gays and their allies on the principles of inclusion and participation. (The Gay Games are open to participants who are gay, lesbian, bisexual, transgendered, queer, and heterosexual, but the terms most often used

in reference to the Gay Games–related communities are *lesbian and gay*. Since most of the discussion here concerns events of the 1980s and 1990s, the terms lesbian and gay are historically appropriate.)

From their inception, discrimination based on "sexual orientation, gender, race, religion, nationality, ethnic origin, political belief(s), athletic/artistic ability, physical challenge, or HIV status" was prohibited. Since their modest beginnings in a San Francisco football stadium, the Gay Games have grown into an international sporting spectacle and business enterprise, with more than 20 core sporting events, a high level of competition between bidding cities, budgets exceeding US$7 million, corporate sponsors and more participants than most Olympic Games have attracted.

Organizing for Social Change

For many Canadian and American lesbian and gay activists in the early 1980s, an enterprise such as the Gay Games represented a radical departure from their usual political work, in that it was primarily a proactive initiative—a sport and cultural festival designed to celebrate lesbian and gay existence. Unlike activists lobbying for legislative or policy change, Gay Games founders were less interested in reforming the mainstream than in creating an alternative, inclusive model of sporting competition. Although, for many, the Games represented a reaction to homophobia in mainstream sport, significant numbers of participants with little prior sporting involvement were attracted by the principle of inclusion and the promise of community that the Games offered.

Gay Games Organizing and Activism

The first two Gay Games were organized by San Francisco Arts and Athletics, a group founded by former Olympic decathlete Tom Waddell in 1981. By 1989, this organization had become the Federation of Gay Games (hereafter the Federation) and included board members from a number of participating countries outside North America. Gender parity in committee structures was a key principle from the outset. The year 1990 marked the first Gay Games held outside the U.S., with the Metropolitan Vancouver Athletic/Arts Association (MVAAA), Canada, hosting the event with 29 sports and more than 7,000 athletes. It is

noteworthy that the words lesbian and gay were not part of the names of these first organizing groups, an omission that at least one critic viewed as an attempt to blend into the mainstream (Syms, 1990).

The 1994 Gay Games in New York, with 11,000 athletes from 45 countries, marked the first time that there had been competition between two bid cities; for the 1998 Games, there were three bids, and for 2002, five. The total cost of all five bids for the 2002 Gay Games exceeded the budgets for the first two Gay Games themselves (Boson, 1998), an indication of the growing trend towards emulating the Olympic model.

In the early 1980s when Waddell and others first began organizing the Gay Games, the principle of inclusion had different connotations—different for Waddell, a closeted gay man for much of his athletic career, and for most lesbian and gay athletes. Billie Jean King's experience of homophobic backlash and her loss of commercial endorsements amply illustrated the safety of the closet for competitive athletes. Similarly, jobs in coaching, sport administration and physical education were in jeopardy if sport leaders' lesbian or gay identities became public knowledge, while athletes at every level risked harassment and ostracism if they came out. Twenty years later, with sport still representing the last bastion of sexism and homophobia, legislative and policy changes are addressing some—but certainly not all—of the problems of discrimination facing lesbian and gay athletes.

Gay Games founders sought to provide an opportunity to participate in an openly lesbian and gay sport festival. As Waddell explained, "[T]he message of these games goes beyond validating our culture. They were conceived as a new idea in the meaning of sport based on inclusion rather than exclusion" (cited in Coe, 1986: 7). He envisioned the Gay Games as a way of raising consciousness and enlightening people both outside and inside lesbian and gay communities (Messner, 1984). Participation in the Games would challenge homophobia in the heterosexual world, and sexism, ageism, racism and nationalism among lesbian and gay people. He hoped that his dream of an "exemplary community" would be achieved through inclusive policies and practices: age-group competition, recruitment and outreach to ethnic minority athletes and those from the developing countries, and social and cultural events to break down the barriers of gender, class, ethnicity and dis/ability among gays and lesbians. Two decades later, there are continuing debates about the realization of these goals.

Media Representations of the Gay Games

In most written accounts of the Gay Games, lesbian and gay commentators seemed just as eager as their non-gay allies to *normalize* this sporting spectacle and its participants. There was a consistent emphasis on similarity rather than difference: "We" (lesbian and gay athletes) can break "their" (heterosexual) records; we can organize events that are officially approved by their international federations; and we can produce one of the biggest international sporting spectacles in the world.

In the extensive lesbian and gay media coverage, there is a clear emphasis on using conventional sporting practices to counter homophobic stereotypes and to achieve lesbian and gay visibility and empowerment.

In *The Story of Gay Games II*, Roy Coe described them as "an important demonstration of our love for each other and our presence in the world community. Our statement as a minority group was clearly made through the wonderful spirit of camaraderie and friendly competition" (Coe, 1986: 7). And, in the 1990 photo-journal of Gay Games III, the editors stated that the Games

symbolized for thousands of gay men and women one more step along the road of self-discovery. And for one astounding week in time it was a road they could travel without ever having to apologize for their existence, or even having to suffer the strain of maintaining an appearance alien to their very nature. (Forzley and Hughes, 1990: 110)

Although the emphasis on empowerment is valid, to reduce the idea to simply "being oneself" and publicly showing "love for each other" is to overlook the sociocultural diversity of lesbian and gay communities. The choice whether to "be oneself" or to "pass" as a member of the dominant group is not available, for example, to lesbians and gays who are Black, or to those who have disabilities. Liberal individualistic notions of self-discovery and self-expression are insufficient for authentic, universal empowerment because they overlook the double or triple oppressions suffered by minority members of lesbian and gay communities. Furthermore, simply bringing together diverse groups of lesbians and gay men in sport does not in itself guarantee "love for each other," and it is naive to hope that sexism, racism, ableism and other entrenched forms of discrimination that divide communities will simply evaporate during Gay Games. On a more grandiose scale, Olympic industry rhetoric calls for peace and harmony, and presents Olympic competition as a transcendent human experience, at the same time ignoring the labour practices and human rights abuses of its multinational sponsors, its impact on low-income and homeless people in host cities, and countless other negative social and environmental impacts (Lenskyj, 2000, 2002a).

Although lesbian and gay community newspapers are an obvious forum for Gay Games debate, they face competing pressures. On one hand, they are expected to generate support for upcoming bids and games, to congratulate organizers and participants, and to celebrate the event as a success story in a homophobic world. On the other hand, since they are the most accessible source of analysis and critique of the Gay Games movement, they will fail in that role if they avoid controversy and self-criticism.

A brief review of selected newspaper coverage of Gay Games III in Vancouver shows few differences between mainstream and lesbian/gay media. *Kinesis*, a Vancouver feminist newspaper, published a supportive information article in July and a five-page, mainly favourable report in September; in Toronto, the coverage in *Xtra*, the major lesbian and gay paper, was mostly positive. In both papers, the only serious criticism was reserved for the homophobic Christian fundamentalists who picketed sporting and cultural events, and threw bottles at Gay Games participants. The American lesbian and gay magazine *The Advocate* was similarly uncritical. Mainstream Canadian newspapers, such as the *Toronto Star*, the *Globe and Mail* and the University of Toronto student paper, *The Varsity*, were largely supportive of the Games and critical

of right-wing backlash (Brunt, 1990; MP, 1990; UBC, 1990; Vancouver, 1990).

One of the most obvious attempts to support MVAAA at all costs was Esther Shannon's commentary published in *Kinesis*. Discussing some anecdotal accounts of the Games, she wrote the following:

> A friend of mine told me about . . . getting a politically correct earful from two British lesbians . . . according to them, the Games were nothing more than an appalling white, middle-class North American spectacle. My friend . . . knew these earnest criticisms were valid but she kept thinking, "they're missing the point." [Vancouver] Gay Games organizers are at pains to keep "politics" out of the Games . . . [They] kept public debate on the Games' shortcomings to a minimum. (Shannon, 1990: 13)

One might argue that, in the face of the right-wing backlash, a public united front was crucial to the success of the Games. However, the naive aim of keeping "politics" out of sport—also a popular notion among Olympic boosters—is especially inappropriate in relation to a sporting event that is by its very nature political.

Rites, a Toronto lesbian and gay newspaper, published some of the few critical commentaries. Anne Vespry, a *Rites* collective member, and Shawn Syms, an athlete, identified a number of organizational problems that threatened the Games' commitment to inclusion and visibility. Syms was critical of the composition of the MVAAA board: seven white, university-educated members, four men and three women (Syms, 1990). Vespry focused on the shortcomings of the cultural events, including access problems for people with disabilities, failure to subsidize tickets for low-income participants, and underrepresentation of people of colour (Vespry, 1990).

Both Syms and Vespry targeted the MVAAA's assimilationist approach to advertising. Its "straight looking, straight acting" board members, they claimed, opted for a "puritan image," and rendered lesbian and gay people invisible by omitting the words *gay* or *queer* from advertising in mainstream media. Although MVAAA might have argued that their low-key advertising and sanitized public image were justified in light of virulent right-wing opposition, Vespry and Syms are persuasive in their argument that the Games' principle of inclusion requires, at the very least, unequivocal solidarity with openly lesbian and gay members of the community, including the large numbers who reject assimilationist strategies (Syms, 1990; Vespry, 1990).

Given the increased levels of competition among bid cities, pressure on community media to limit negative commentary will be especially strong during the Gay Games bidding process. There was evidence of this trend in Sydney's major lesbian and gay newspaper, the *Sydney Star Observer*, which published mostly positive articles and encountered criticism from Team Sydney (the Sydney Gay Games bid committee) whenever it didn't, or when the timing of a particular article (e.g., Boson, 1997b) did not "suit" Team Sydney's purposes. This did not prevent the *Star's* sport reporter, Mary Boson, from writing, among other critical articles, an insightful piece titled "Are we cheap dates?" in which she identified the danger that lesbian and gay organizations like Team Sydney would abandon their social justice agendas in the rush to get government and corporate funding, and in their efforts to demonstrate the power of the (gay male) "pink dollar" to the non-gay world (Boson, 1997a, 1997c). Given the double economic disadvantage experienced by lesbians—as women and as members of a stigmatized sexual minority—Boson's analysis was particularly cogent.

Gay Games or Gay Olympics?

Since their inception, Gay Games have involved a number of sport celebrities and former Olympic athletes, including Tom Waddell, Betty Baxter, Bruce Hayes, Martina Navratilova and Greg Louganis, and the biographies of Federation representatives and bid committee members usually include their athletic credentials (except for those organizing the cultural festival). The liberal notion of lesbian and gay celebrities serving as "role models" appears to hold sway in the Gay Games movement, and undoubtedly their positive examples and personal courage are inspirational to many. At the same time, however, this emphasis serves to entrench the mainstream competitive sporting ethos modelled on the Olympics, rather than to promote genuinely alternative and inclusive visions of sporting participation, where winning is less important than participating.

Research studies on lesbian and gay community sport demonstrate that it is difficult for those who have been socialized into the ethos of mainstream sport to abandon their often unexamined acceptance of competition and the "no pain, no gain" mantra for an alternative model that values fun, friendship and the pure pleasure of bodily movement. Socialized gender differences make it somewhat easier for women than men to embrace a new ethos of cooperation rather than competition in sport contexts (Lenskyj, 1994a). Greater involvement of feminist women in leadership roles would no doubt help the Gay Games movement to achieve its original radical goals. One troubling trend remains: Only 25 percent of Gay Games III and about 36 percent of Gay Games IV participants were women (Verry, 1998). This increased to 45 percent for Gay Games V in Amsterdam, largely as a result of the Women's Outreach Committee and direct marketing efforts.

From 1982 to 1986, Gay Games organizers were engaged in a lengthy and unsuccessful court battle against the United States Olympic Committee (USOC) to keep their original name, the Gay Olympic Games. Ambivalence over the key political question, "Gay Games or Gay Olympics?" was evident when Sara Lewinstein (Waddell's partner) told the press, "The perception has been created that somehow gays hate the Olympics . . . we love the Olympics. We just don't like the dumb bureaucrats who run the USOC" (Waddell and Schaap, 1996: 234). She went on to cite the improved sport facilities that would result from a successful Olympic bid.

In light of these early events, it is somewhat ironic that Sydney hosted the Summer Olympic Games in 2000, two years before Gay Games VI. In fact, according to Sydney's Gay Games bid book, most events would be using facilities constructed in the 1990s for Sydney 2000. Equally important, widespread popular support for Sydney 2000, achieved in large part by the Olympic Bid Committee's pressure on the mass media to suppress any negative reports (Booth and Tatz, 1994; Lenskyj, 2000, 2002a) helped pave the way for lesbian and gay community efforts to win Gay Games VI. The Gay Games bid book stressed the excellence of the Olympic facilities, and stated that the New South Wales government would provide these venues either free

of charge or with major subsidies (Sydney 2002, 1997: 57). One section, however, presented an unexpected critique of the Olympic Games: "The [Gay] Games' ideals and prominent sporting participants will be used to contrast the elitism of the modern Olympics and to gain [media] coverage in the run up to Sydney's Olympic Games in 2000" (15).

The Gay Games represent an alternative to the Olympic Games, but they are modelled in large part on an international sporting competition with over 100 years of checkered political history (and, in the late 1990s, a seriously tarnished image; see Lenskyj, 2000). From the outset, Gay Games' winners were named and recognized, medals were awarded, records were kept, and some events were "sanctioned" (conducted according to international federation standards); highly trained and talented athletes whose careers had been impeded by homophobia now had their own "Olympics." Only a minority of commentators problematized these trends.

Conclusion

The issues examined here confirm that tension remains between the radical view of the Gay Games as an alternative, inclusive and empowering lesbian and gay community event, and the liberal goal of mounting an income-generating, international sporting spectacle modelled on the Olympic Games. The key principle of inclusion, particularly in relation to lesbians, low-income people, participants from developing countries, and people with disabilities, is unlikely to be realized if organizers allow the Olympic model to dominate. However, if leaders can maintain an uncompromising political stance on the issues of inclusion, participation and accessibility, the Gay Games movement has transformative potential.

References

Booth, D. and Tatz, C. (1994). Sydney 2000: The games people play. *Current Affairs Bulletin* 70 (7), 4–11.

Boson, M. (1997a). We won! Government goes for gold. *Sydney Star Observer* (November 20) [www.sso.rainbow.net.au]

_____. (1997b). Gay Games License: Sydney hit with $1.4 million fee. *Sydney Star Observer* (December 11).

_____. (1997c). Are we cheap dates? *Sydney Star Observer* (December 18).

_____. 1998. Games bids "too costly." *Sydney Star Observer* (May 1).

Brunt, S. (1990). Inside the gay 90s: The name of the Games is pride. *Globe and Mail* (August 4), A24.

Coe, R. (1986). *A sense of pride: The story of Gay Games II*. San Francisco: Pride Publications.

Federation of Gay Games. (1997). The Purpose [www.gaygames.org].

Forzley, R. and Hughes, D. (Eds.). (1990). *The spirit captured: The official photojournal of Celebration '90—Gay Games III*. Vancouver: For Eyes Press.

Lenskyj, H. (1994a). Girl-friendly sport and female values. *Women in Sport and Physical Activity Journal* 3 (1), 35–46.

_____. (2000). *Inside the Olympic industry: Power, politics, and activism*. Albany, NY: SUNY Press.

_____. (2002a). *The best Olympics ever? Social impacts of Sydney 2000*. Albany, NY: SUNY Press.

Messner, M. (1984). Gay athletes and the Gay Games: An interview with Tom Waddell. *M: Gentle Men for Gender Justice* 13 (Fall), 22–23.

MP Praises Gay Games as "rainbow" of diversity. (1990). *Toronto Star* (August 6), A2.

Shannon, E. (1990). Can you believe the roar of the crowd? *Kinesis* (September), 12–14.

Syms, S. (1990). Celebration '90: Physique and critique. *Rites* (September), 13.

Vancouver holds the third and largest Gay Games. (1990). *Globe and Mail* (August 6), A7.

Vespry, A. (1990). Reflections on the Gay Games. *Rites* (September), 11–13.

Chapter 20

ARGENTINA'S LEFT-WINGERS

Leslie Ray

In this short selection about the relationship between politics and soccer in Argentina, we learn about the personal politics of specific players, the historical connections between particular teams and specific political orientations, and the ways that the government uses sports for political purposes. At the end of the article, author Leslie Ray suggests that traditional divisions among workers can be overcome through sports and through the creation of new forms of association that sports can foster.

On April 18th, 2004, Diego Maradona was admitted to the Swiss Clinic in Buenos Aires in an extreme condition. A crowd immediately began to form outside and soon developed into a mass vigil of a quasi-religious kind—devotees clutched candles, Virgin Mary statuettes, rosary beads and flowers, and held banners declaring 'Jesus in Heaven and Diego on earth'; 'Diego of the soul, after so many joys, give us one more'; 'God forgive the journalists, they know not what they do.' For British observers, there was an obvious parallel to be made with the collective grief following the death of Princess Diana.

That 'San Diego' (St Diego) is much loved is no surprise in a country so crazy about football, but why such reverency? For huge swathes of Argentina's working class,

despite his dalliance with drugs, Maradona encapsulates their own religiosity, nationalism and political identity to an extent that would be inconceivable with a player in Britain. But while millions adore him, Argentina's elite and its beleaguered middle classes loathe him with an equal intensity for declaring himself a Peronist, as the presence of the populist demagogue whose presence still looms large over Argentine politics, decades after he was in power.

In Argentina, football is divided along political lines: if you are a Boca Juniors fan, you are likely to be a working-class Peronist; if you follow River Plate, you tend to be a middle-class radical, Argentina's other main political grouping. The origins of this division are probably rooted in early twentieth-century differences of geography, wealth and na-

Leslie Ray, "Argentina's Left-Wingers" from *History Today* 54.12 (December 2004): 36–38. Reprinted with the permission of History Today Limited.

tionality. Boca is the port area where the poor immigrant Italians first settled, while River Plate is in more affluent Liniers, in northern Buenos Aires, where the middle-class Spanish and Jewish tended to live. Radical River fans cannot forgive Maradona for his very public association with communism—he has a tattoo of Che Guevara displayed prominently on his forearm—and with Castro's Cuba. Yet this support for Cuba has a nationalist, rather than an internationalist, slant; after a meeting with Fidel, Diego said of him: 'He defends his flag, in Argentina we gave ours away to the United States.'

The twin tracks of nationalism and socialism have been constants in Argentina's footballing history. The nationalism is easily recognized by England or Scotland supporters, as it mirrors their own. As historian Eric Hobsbawm has said, 'the imagined community of millions seems more real as a team of eleven named people.' England and Argentina have a World Cup history of great pitch battles: Michael Owen's winning goal in 2002, David Beckham's leg wave at Simeone, his subsequent disgrace and rehabilitating penalty, in 1998; England's victory over Rattin's hackers in 1966, when Sir Alf Ramsey called the Argentine team 'animals', and of course Maradona's unforgivable crafty 'hand of God' in Mexico in 1986. Argentine fans are often keener to bring up this particular bone of contention with England than the Falklands/Malvinas War. For them, the stadium is not just a battlefield; it is also the terrain of class struggle, nationalistic fervour and ecstatic religious experience. This is not unique to Argentina, of course, but the intermingling of these elements on the football pitch seem all the more obvious here.

Curiously, the founding of Argentina's football clubs around the turn of the twentieth century would seem to be due in equal measure to the empire-building efforts of the British bourgeois elite and to the organising forces of socialism. The English names of major clubs are many: Racing Club, Boca Juniors and River Plate are Argentina's three leading clubs. However, it is Newell's Old Boys, from the Primera Division A, which has the strongest connection with England. It was founded in 1903 in honour of Isaac Newell, originally from Kent, who was the headmaster of the Anglo-Argentine College in the city of Rosario from 1883 to 1900, where he taught the boys the skills and values of this character-forming sport. In 1903 his son Claudio and other alumni of the school founded Newell's Old Boys in Isaac's honour. The club's red and black shield have prompted many Argentine anarchists to believe that its founders had anarchist sympathies, though the club's official history stresses that in fact black was supposed to represent eloquence and red wisdom.

In Argentina Rosario is renowned for developing two great traditions: attacking football and radical politics. Gabriel Batistuta, Argentina's star striker of the 1990s, learnt his football on the streets of Rosario, and his first club was Newell's. An even more famous local boy was Maradona's hero, a certain Ernesto 'Che' Guevara. Che was in fact a keen rugby player, but chronic asthma forced him to abandon the oval ball in favour of the round one. His chosen position was in goal, so he could be close to his inhaler. In the 1940s—as today—most Argentine youngsters supported River or Boca, but Che, ever on the side of the underdog, decided to follow his local team, lowly Rosario Central.

Football was looked upon rather ambivalently by the theorists of the left. In 1917 the anarchist newspaper *La Protesta* condemned it as the 'pernicious reducing to idiocy through the repeated kicking of a round ball'. But socialists and anarchists were in the forefront of Argentina's new football enthusiasts. Founded in 1904, the Club 'Mártires de Chicago' (Martyrs of Chicago), later to become Argentinos Juniors and now in Primera B Nacional, was named in homage to the Chicago Haymarket Martyrs, hanged in 1886 for demanding an eight-hour working day. The Club El Porvenir (The Future), from predominantly working-class southern Buenos Aires, also in the Primera B Nacional, was founded by utopians; Chacarita Juniors, in the Primera División A, by the members of a libertarian library, appropriately enough on May 1st, International Workers' Day. Independiente, also in the Primera, was another socialist club, so named because it considered itself independent of the factory in Avellenada where its players worked.

As the twentieth century developed, football gradually divested itself of its British identity (though British referees were still invited to preside over matches to ensure that they were played in a proper, ethical fashion) and became increasingly associated with the urban working class of Italian and Spanish origin. The powerful forces of 'fanaticism' that football unleashed began to be exploited by politicians pursuing a nationalist agenda. Juan Domingo Perón loved football, but he also recognized the part it could play in building the nation. Perón wanted Argentina to occupy a more prominent role on the world stage, and he saw it as essential to modify the elitist profile of many of the country's institutions, including sports, and open them up to the popular sectors. In a 1998 article for *Entrepasados* magazine, Eugenia Scarzanella describes how the Peronist government con-

tributed to the expansion of sport: 'Racing drivers, marathon runners, boxers and footballers received decorations and favours. New football stadiums and sports facilities were built. Children were given free entry to matches and special tournaments were organized under the aegis of Evita.' Such forceful promotions of football, along with other sports, might have led to success at the 1950 World Cup, had the event not been held in Brazil, with whom Argentina's relations were—not for the first or last time—rather strained at the time.

Perón had seen that soccer could play an important role in forging a modern national identity for Argentina, but it was later generals who were the most determined to tap its immense power. So it was that when Argentina hosted the World Cup in 1978 during the military junta of Jorge Rafael Videla, the so-called 'Dirty War'—perhaps the greatest battle between ideologies in Argentine history—was waged inside and outside the stadiums. The Junta had spent an estimated $700 million on the World Cup project, seriously increasing Argentina's already large national debt. Although 60,000 foreign tourists were expected, only 7,000 actually turned up, most of whom were journalists. So the panicking government commissioned the American PR firm Burson & Marsteller to improve the country's image. Theirs was the slogan that was seen all over Argentina during the 'Mundial': *los argentinos somos derechos y humanos* ('we Argentines are upright and humane')—a pun that subverted and downplayed the accusation that grave abuses of human rights (*derechos humanos*) were taking place in the country at the time.

The national side progressed all the way through the competition—not without controversy, as when they beat a suspiciously supine Peru team 6–0—eventually making it to the final against Holland, which was played at the River Plate Stadium. It was somehow fitting that the great showpiece event pitted against the Generals' team a side from a liberal democracy whose 'total football' was more than just a tactical system, it was the egalitarian principle in practice, as every player was capable of playing in every position, with commitment, empathy and without hierarchy. Mixed among the sea of blue and white banners, and the occasional orange one, were others drawing attention to Argentina's thousands of 'disappeared'. The cameras strained to avoid them, but by this stage it was too late, the cat was out of the bag. Every day during the World Cup, despite attempts to silence them, the Mothers and Grandmothers of the Disappeared had walked silently and courageously around Plaza de Mayo in Buenos Aires, their white headscarves embroidered with the names of their missing loved ones. Amid the fuss surrounding the final—with thousands demonstrating their passion for the game, others their outrage at the Junta's repression—the great but irremediably elitist writer Jorge Luis Borges showed his utter disdain for the whole event by intentionally calling a conference on the theme of immortality on the very day, at the very time, that the Argentine team was playing. Few attended.

Argentina won 3–1, and the head of the Junta, Videla, gleefully handed the trophy to captain Daniel Passarella. Glory then, but anger or indifference now. Last year, to mark the twenty-fifth anniversary of the victory, a paltry crowd of just over 6,000 watched a match between a current Argentine side and a team including three members of the 1978 World Cup winning side. Once again many held banners inside and

outside the stadium denouncing human rights' abuses. One banner read, 'Inside they played a World Cup. Outside, a country was being lost.'

One irony of Argentina's victory was that the team's manager was Cesar Luis Menotti, who has never made a secret of his left-wing views. Menotti has always been understandably defensive about his work in 1978. He has said 'Revolution is not made by footballers, musicians or actors.' He was on tour in the USSR when the coup that brought Videla to power took place in 1976, and he has since confessed that he hesitated over whether to return to his country or go into exile. Return he did, his high profile and match-winning importance to the regime keeping him safe, despite his views.

Angel Cappa is a former midfielder and coach, and was Menotti's right-hand man when he managed Boca Juniors in 1987 and later Atlético Madrid. What makes Cappa unusual for a footballer is that he is truly a soccer intellectual, a professor of philosophy and sociology, who has written a number of books on the sociological aspects of the beautiful game. He is also the living demonstration of the fact that socialist ideas are still alive and well in football. Cappa believes with former Liverpool manager Bill Shankly that 'football isn't a matter of life and death: it's much more serious'. In an interview earlier this year he criticized the way that European soccer drains Argentina of two hundred players a year:

Eduardo Galeano once said that the South sells not only arms to the North, but also legs. The centre of world footballing power has a permanent 'factory' of players in South America and other marginalized regions, some of whom are already in Europe without ever having played in our own premier leagues. At best, in their countries of origin they are only ever seen on TV. This is nothing but total dependency on the centres of economic power.

In December 2001, at the peak of the social upheaval in Argentina, when thirty people were killed and hundreds injured as the government struggled to maintain the rule of law, the decision was made to allow the final day's matches on the fixture list to be played—thus ensuring that Racing won the championship for the first time in three decades. Three years later, this still arouses Cappa's bitter condemnation:

It was disgusting. A cruel way of accepting that money is what counts most for those in power, perhaps it is the only thing that counts. Undoubtedly it was television, and the other sectors profiting from Racing winning the championship after so long, that needed the matches to be played. It's one thing to sell products taking advantage of fresh euphoria and quite another to allow too much time to pass. Money has no patience. The same happened with the bombs in Madrid on March 11th [2004], when some Spanish teams didn't want to play in the European tournaments, and were forced to, with the whole country in shock. If anything were needed to show that all they care about is money, that is the proof.

Today Argentina's stability is precarious, but at the time of the millennium it was a country in ferment. Many factory owners,

unable to meet their debts, abandoned their businesses. Faced with no jobs, the workers at a number of factories decided to run them themselves. One of these was Zanon, in Neuquén, Patagonia. In the late 1990s Zanon had a trades union leadership that was corrupt and complicit with the bosses. Surprisingly, it was football that enabled a group of activists to wrest the control of the unions from the bureaucrats and plan the factory occupation. Syndicalist Raul Godoy tells the story:

We decided to hold a soccer tournament, with every sector of the factory taking part, as there was much rivalry between them. There was a team for each sector, and each team had its own delegate, so there we took advantage to talk to everyone. We talked about organizing the tournament, but we also began to chat about other things, the problems in the factory. So a network formed within the factory with comrades from different places, and we were able to find out their views, when we went to play, because you were not allowed to talk openly inside the factory. That's how it came about. First it was matches, nothing more, every Sunday spent barbecuing sausages, selling beer and playing football. It was tough, but it was worth it, because it meant we were eventually able to organize.

Even though a hundred years have passed since some of Argentina's first football clubs were founded by left-wingers, the country's soccer-socialists are still organizing.

Chapter 21

CARLOS DELGADO STANDS UP TO WAR

Dave Zirin

Toronto Blue Jays first baseman Carlos Delgado is known throughout the baseball world as one of the most feared sluggers in the game. In 2003, the thirty-two-year-old All-Star hit forty-two homers and drove in 145 runs. He has averaged almost forty home runs a year over the last six seasons. With his imposing physical frame, bald scalp, and gold earring, Delgado is one of the most recognizable figures in the game. And he has put the baseball world on notice that he will use his fame to fight the U.S.'s war on the world.

In a very sympathetic story on the pages of the *Toronto Star,* Delgado went public with his decision not to stand on the dugout steps for the seventh-inning-stretch singing of "God Bless America" that was added to the MLB program after 9/11. "I never stay outside for 'God Bless America,'" Delgado said. "I actually don't think people have noticed it. I don't (stand) because I don't believe it's right, I don't believe in the war."

Delgado also made clear that he couldn't abide the priorities of the U.S. military machine. "It's a very terrible thing that happened on September 11," he said.

It's (also) a terrible thing that happened in Afghanistan and Iraq. I just feel so sad for the families that lost relatives and loved ones in the war. But I think it's the stupidest war ever. Who are you fighting against? You're just getting ambushed now. We have more people dead now, after the war, than during the war. You've been looking for weapons of mass destruction. Where are they at? You've been looking for over a year. Can't find them. I don't support that. I don't support what they do. I think it's just stupid.

Historically, athletes have paid a steep price for standing up to the way sports is used to package patriotism and war. As we have seen, Muhammad Ali was stripped of his heavyweight title for refusing to go to Vietnam in the 1960s. In 1991, Bulls guard Craig Hodges found himself blackballed from the NBA after protesting the Gulf War during a visit to George Bush's White House with the champion Chicago Bulls. A similar fate befell shooting guard Mahmoud Abdul-Rauf in 1998 when he refused to stand for the national anthem. Delgado doesn't care.

"Sometimes, you've just got to break the mold. You've got to push it a little bit or else you can't get anything done," he told the *Toronto Star*. Delgado, fortunately, is aided by both his superstar status and the fact that he plays in Canada where the media is less likely to take orders from the Pentagon and slam the slugger. But his resolve comes from a deeply personal place. You might say that, for Delgado, the human toll of the U.S. military hits home.

Delgado is from Puerto Rico and has campaigned for years to end the U.S. Navy's presence in Vieques, an island that had been a weapons testing ground for sixty years. The Navy recently left Vieques, but it has also left behind an area with abnormally high cancer rates, 50 percent unemployment, and deep poverty. Delgado is now part of a movement to get the U.S. government to clean up their mess. He sees the people of Vieques as casualties—collateral damage—from the war on Iraq because they served as guinea pigs for the weapons that have wreaked havoc throughout the Persian Gulf. "You're dealing with health, with poverty, with the roots of an entire community, both economically and environmentally," Delgado has said. "This is way bigger than just a political or military issue. Because the military left last year and they haven't cleaned the place up yet."

The catalytic event for his activism was the killing of a Vieques man, David Sanes,

by an errant bomb on April 19, 1999. Delgado wanted to act, so his father hooked him up with "an old Socialist Party pal" named Ismael Guadalupe. The high school teacher, "a leading figure in the island's protest movement," had spent six months in prison in 1979 for protesting on "Navy property" in Vieques. "He wanted to help out with more than just the situation with the Navy," Guadalupe, fifty-nine, said of Delgado. "He wanted to help the people there. He wanted to help the children." Delgado has done more than talk a good game. Together with singer Ricky Martin and boxer Félix "Tito" Trinidad, he took out full-page advertisements about Vieques in the *New York Times* and the *Washington Post*. The ads included the names of fellow Major League All-Stars Roberto Alomar, Juan González, and Iván "Pudge" Rodriguez. Boxer John Ruiz and golfer Chichi Rodríguez also signed on. Delgado didn't fear reprisals for these ads, which were very critical of the Navy and ran in April of 2001. "What are they going to do, kick me out of the game? Take away my endorsements?"

Delgado has put his money where his mouth is for other causes as well, donating $100,000 to youth sports, schools, and activism on the island. He also travels to Vieques every January to run clinics for and give gifts to the children. "You'll need millions and millions of dollars to clean Vieques up. So, we try to make [the money] as effective as we can. We make it work for kids. I can't clean up Vieques by myself. It's going to take a lot of people." You get the feeling Carlos Delgado wants to see a cleanup far beyond the borders of Puerto Rico.

PART V

MORE THAN A GAME: FANDOM AND COMMUNITY IN SPORTS

On a typical Sunday morning before a Philadelphia Eagles football game, the city pulsates with activity as tens of thousands of loyal Eagles fans congregate in various places throughout the metropolitan area for social gatherings—from stadium parking lots for tailgate cookouts—to restaurants, sports bars, and people's homes. A festive mood warms the chilly fall air. Two sports talk radio stations buzz with arguments about the team's performance and speculations about the outcome of the contest and its meaning for the team's ultimate goal—the Superbowl title. Like citizens in most NFL cities, Philadelphians, on fall Sunday mornings, are transformed into a single-minded civic association in eager anticipation of football games. Arguably the most sociologically freighted events of the year, these Sunday-morning gatherings reveal the city's spirit of civic solidarity. In fact, without its professional sports teams—the Eagles, the Phillies (baseball), the Flyers (hockey), and the Sixers (basketball)—Philadelphia would be little more than a cluster of neighborhoods segmented by class and racial boundaries, surrounded by similarly segmented suburban towns.

Though typically viewed as simply an array of hyper-energized boosters, sports team fans constitute a special type of social community in modern urban society. Transcending the boundaries of class, racial, ethnic, religious, and political divisions, sports fandom—in its most expansive form—galvanizes people from diverse backgrounds and lifestyles into a civic fraternity. Whether the fans are congregating on the smaller scale of Little League baseball and high-school basketball, or on the larger scale of professional soccer and professional football, sports fandom constitutes a form of what sociologists term *social capital*. In one definition, "social capital refers to features of social organization, such as networks, norms, and trust that facilitate coordination and cooperation for mutual benefit" and "stocks of social capital . . . tend to be self-reinforcing and cumulative" (Putnam 1993). But most important, the ties, norms, and trust that social capital builds are "transferable from one social setting to another." In short, social capital is a civic resource that facilitates collective action. Through the social capital it creates, sports stimulates and sustains civic engagement and civic morale in modern urban life. The influence of social capital created by sports can be seen in the following examples:

- West Germany's World Cup soccer victory in 1954 helped to solidify a new German collective identity nine years after the defeat of the Nazi regime and thereby was a major influence in legitimating the new democratic German Federal Republic (Heinrich 2003).
- The Iraqi soccer team's success in the Asia Cup in July 2007 brought a rare moment of unity among Iraqis despite the sectarian violence that divided the nation at that time (Reuters 2007).
- The success of an Australian community's rugby team created a positive symbolic image for the city that submerged the perceptions of its divisions and inequalities (Rowe and McGuirk 1999).

Sports fandom not only strengthens social structures but also enriches the emotional quality of fans' personal lives. In the words of psychiatrist Daniel Wann, "Sports fandom is really a tribal thing. . . . We've known for decades that social support—our tribal networks—is largely responsible for keeping people mentally sound, whether it's our religious organizations, our business or vocation affiliations, our communities, or our families. We have a psychological need to belong" (Wann, cited in Kirchheimer 2004). It is this type of emotional gratification that attracts people to sports teams. Sports competitions create feelings of community that counteract the social fragmentation, distrust, and anomie of modern urban life. "These days," said Wann, "people don't live within walking distance to 20 members of their family like they did 50 or 100 years ago. People don't go to church as often. . . . So one option . . . is sports fandom. By going to a game, or even watching it, you get that sense of tribalness, of community, of a common bond you can embrace" (ibid.).

The importance of this sense of belonging is perhaps felt most dramatically when it is lost, destroyed by administrative or political decisions beyond the control of the fans. One of the most famous examples of this kind of loss occurred in Brooklyn, New York, in 1957, when the owner of the highly celebrated and beloved Brooklyn Dodgers decided to move the team to Los Angeles, California. That move did more than devastate Dodger fandom; it crushed Brooklyn's civic spirit, a loss from which the borough never recovered. Similar traumatic losses have been experienced by fans of the Boston Braves, the St. Louis Browns, the Syracuse Nationals, the St. Louis Hawks, the Cleveland Browns, and the Baltimore Colts, to name only a few examples of sports teams that abandoned cities for greener financial pastures elsewhere. Though some of the cities were able to replace the teams, many could not do so and hence failed to reconsolidate their dissipated social capital and restore civic morale.

Though we tend to think of the fandom created by sports as leading to positive, expansive developments of community, this is not always the case—negative effects of sports-generated social capital should also be noted. These can be observed in places where sports contests have become settings for mobilizing racial, ethnic, and religious expressions of bigotry and intolerance. We see examples of this in the acts of football (soccer) hooligans in

Europe who physically attack opposition fans (Dunning 1986); and soccer fans in places such as Spain and the Ukraine who shout racial taunts and insults at African players. We also see these negative effects of sports social capital in the white American South, prior to the civil rights reforms, where sports often functioned as bases for mobilizing and reinforcing feelings of white racial pride and unity in opposition to racial integration.

Many questions need to be researched on the impact of sports on social community. Social scientists have barely begun to explore this broad and complex landscape, which remains a fertile terrain for new theoretical ideas. Among the analytical questions that need further exploration are the following:

1. What have been the major historical changes in the communal functions of sports in industrial capitalist societies? Is the role of sports more or less prevalent in urban life now than it was a hundred years ago?
2. To what extent has sports fandom functioned as an effective social force that counteracted urban fragmentation and anomie? What are some of the most successful examples?
3. How do sports differ in their capacity to generate social capital? What are the characteristics of the sports with high capacity for social capital? What are the characteristics of those with low capacity for social capital? Are team sports more likely to generate high levels of social capital than individual sports?
4. Under what social conditions are sports likely to operate as integrative or divisive social forces?
5. Comparing societies cross-culturally, how do they differ in the amount and types of sports social capital they generate?
6. What is the effect of ownership, obligations, and stakeholding on the formation of sports social capital? Is voluntary nonprofit ownership more conducive to generating sports social capital than private corporate ownership?

The articles in this section focus on the effects of sports on social identity and social community. In "Joe Louis Uncovers Dynamite," Richard Wright describes how the outcome of a heavyweight boxing match sparked feelings of pride and solidarity in a politically oppressed black American community. Wright concludes by suggesting that Joe Louis's victory over a white opponent sparked a spirit of resistance—potential social capital—that could be harnessed and directed into political action. Sports have had an enormously positive role in solidifying the black American community. The achievements of great black athletes (such as Jessie Owens, Jackie Robinson, Wilt Chamberlain, Willie Mays, and Muhammad Ali) have stood in sharp contrast to the mostly negative images of blacks projected by American popular culture and have affirmed positive images of black identity, enhancing feelings of community and cultural solidarity.

This sports-generated black social capital no doubt contributed to successful black political mobilization during the civil rights movement. Viewing the effects of sports on identity from a different angle, Nick Trujillo and Bob Krizek, in "Emotionality in the Stands and in the Field: Expressing Self Through Baseball," use ethnographic methodology to illustrate fans' expressions of their emotions and identities in reaction to the closings of two major league baseball parks. The article demonstrates the depth of feelings fans attach to the artifacts and symbols of their sports memories.

In contrast to the first two articles, which illustrate the impact of sports on fans' identities, the next article addresses an aspect of fan identity that has been largely ignored, namely, the ways in which the patterns of identity have changed. In "Supporters, Followers, Fans, and *Flâneurs*: A Taxonomy of Spectator Identities in Football," Richard Giulianotti examines the effects of economic changes—specifically, the impact of the hyper-commodification of soccer—on fan identification with the sport. Differentiating fan identities by means of a well-designed typology, he argues that the trend is shifting away from the more emotionally intense local fan to the more detached, cool, and consumer-savvy fan. This pattern of change implies a lower level of social capital; however, further research is needed to determine the extent of these changes across different sports.

Finally, in "Something About Baseball: Gentrification, "Race Sponsorship," and Competing Class Cultures in Neighborhood Boys' Baseball," Sherri Grasmuck highlights the broader theme of sports-generated social capital as a dynamic social force. Grasmuck presents an insightful, ethnographically based account of how Little League baseball became a key social force (aided by gentrification) that led to the integration of a previously racially segregated urban neighborhood. In addition to discussing the features of neighborhood baseball that helped to bring about that outcome, she explains how the competing class cultures of diverse parents created different attitudes about public space and voluntary organizations. This study is an excellent example of the way sports sometimes bridges social divisions, facilitating the formation of social capital. It should serve as a model for future research on the potential impact of neighborhood sports in strengthening urban communities.

References

Dunning, E. 1986. *The Roots of Football Hooliganism*. London: Routledge.

Heinrich, A. 2003. "The 1954 Soccer World Cup and the Federal Republic of Germany's Self-Discovery." *American Behavioral Scientist* 146, no. 11: 1491–1505.

Kirchheimer, Sid. 2004. Reviewed by Michael Smith, MD. "Why the Super Bowl Matters," http://www.medicinenet.com/script/main/art.asp?articlekey=41850.

Putnam, R. 1993. *Making Democracy Work: Civic Tradition in Modern Italy*. Princeton, NJ: Princeton University Press.

Reuters. 2007. "Iraqis Ready to Defy Bombs to Back Soccer Team," http://www.reuters.com/article/latest Crisis/idUSL26780468.

Rowe, D., and P. McGuirk. 1999. "Drunk for Three Weeks: Sporting Success and City Image." *International Review for the Sociology of Sport* 34, no. 2: 125–141.

Chapter 22

EMOTIONALITY IN THE STANDS AND IN THE FIELD

Expressing Self Through Baseball

Nick Trujillo and Bob Krizek

In this engaging article on how fans relate to baseball and its shrine-like stadiums, Nick Trujillo and Bob Krizek present observational and interview data from the period immediately before the closing of the Chicago White Sox home, Comiskey Park, and the Texas Ranger home, Arlington Stadium, outside of Dallas. Their evidence suggests that the connections among baseball teams, stadiums, and fans (and stadium employees) are broad and deep, reflecting key aspects of identities and often articulating with the strongest human emotions of loss and love.

This ballpark means a lot more to me than just baseball. There's a lot of personal things tied up in it, and that's why I feel so strongly that she shouldn't have been torn down. Instead of spending 100 million on that monstrosity across the street, they could have sunk it in here and we would have had the ballpark for another hundred years and our ties to the past would have been preserved. I can't just cut the ties with her so easily.

> Fan, male, 20–25 years old,
> Comiskey Park, 1990

I started cryin' when we parked the car. We came out here a week ago, but I said we got to come back [for the last game]. I've got a lot of memories here, all good, with friends, and a friend at the time who became my husband. I have mixed feeling about losing this stadium. I know I'll like the new one. But there are lots of good memories here.

> Fan, female, 30–35 years old,
> Arlington Stadium, 1993

This article is about the emotionality experienced in the field. It is about the emotions

Nick Trujillo and Bob Krizek, "Emotionality in the Stands and in the Field: Expressing self through baseball" from *Journal of Sport and Social Issues* 18.4 (November 1994): 303–325. Copyright © 1994 by Sage Publications, Inc. Reprinted with the permission of Sage Publications, Inc.

expressed by members of the cultures we studied. It is about the emotions that we as researchers experienced as we studied members of these cultures. It is about how doing ethnographic research is extremely personal. *It is about baseball.*

Specifically, this article discusses two field studies that examined how people enacted their emotions and expressed their identities at the closing of "their" major league ballparks. In each case, a new stadium was being built for the team very close to the old ballpark. The first ballpark studied was Old Comiskey Park, the former home of the Chicago White Sox, on the occasion of the final series played there during September 27–30, 1990. Old Comiskey was a ballpark with an 80-year baseball tradition developed in World Series games (including the Black Sox scandal of 1919), the first All-Star game in 1933 (and its 50th reenactment in 1983), and infamous occurrences such as the introduction of uniform shorts in 1976 and the 1979 "Disco Demolition Night" fiasco inspired by the late owner, Bill Veck.[1] One of the authors conducted an ethnographic study of Comiskey's closing, focusing on how *fans* at the event experienced the final series.

The second ballpark studied was the lesser known (and far more dilapidated) Arlington Stadium, the former home of retired baseball legend Nolan Ryan and the Texas Rangers, on the occasion of the final series played there during October 1–3, 1993. Arlington Stadium was a reconstituted minor league ballpark, first called "Turnpike Stadium," with very little tradition, and it was one of the few in history that never hosted an All-Star game or a playoff game. Both authors conducted an ethnographic study of Arlington's closing.

However, one author focused on how *fans* experienced the closing whereas another author focused on how *ballpark employees* experienced the closing.[2]

During both studies, we conducted observations of those in attendance acting and interacting with each other (i.e., fans with fans, fans with employees, and, in the case of Arlington Stadium, employees with employees) before, during, and after each game in the final series. At each event, we arrived at least 3 hours prior to the first pitch and departed at least 2 hours after the final out. Our pregame strategy was to walk and talk with people as they participated in their natural pregame activities as fans or employees. We traveled along with fans as they walked from the parking lot to the ballpark entrances. We stood in lines with fans as they purchased programs, caps, and other souvenirs and as they purchased hot dogs and beer. Following a brief introduction and an abbreviated explanation of our purpose, we would engage them in guided conversations or more extensive informal interviews, asking a variety of questions to stimulate their memories and feelings of the ballparks, such as the following: Why are you here today? Do you remember the first time you came to this ballpark? Can you share some of your other memories of this ballpark? What, if anything, will you lose when they tear this place down?

Once inside the ballparks, our techniques remained much the same. We positioned ourselves in runways, empty seats, and near concession booths to find opportunities for informal interviews, being careful not to interrupt the flow of the day for fans or employees. During the game, we struck up conversations with fans whenever there was a lull in the action on the field. When interacting with employees, we moved with them so as not to interfere with their job performances. After the games, we roamed the stands and inner caverns of the parks, talking to fans who lingered and to employees who had postgame duties. And our questions continued. Why was it important for you to be here today? How do you feel now that it is over? We used both tape recorders and field notes to record their answers.

Despite the differences in the ballparks, the cities, and the types of individuals observed and interviewed (i.e., fans vs. employees), the people we studied enacted and expressed similar feelings and emotions about the importance of baseball in their lives and of the places where it is played. Perhaps more importantly, as we studied and interpreted the closing of these two ballparks, we experienced similar feelings and emotions about the importance of baseball in our own lives as researchers. Thus this article reveals as much about the meanings of ballpark culture for fans and workers as it does about the meaning of ballpark culture for ourselves as sons and ex-ballplayers.

In this article, we present several quotations from the two ethnographies that reveal various aspects of emotionality in the (baseball) field. Each of these statements displays a different dimension of ballpark culture and shows how the people we studied define themselves through baseball.

The Investment of Identity in Our National Pastime

I've been coming here since the Rangers came here back in '72. This place has been a big part of me for 22 years. It's like losing an old friend. It's hard to tell an old friend goodbye.

Fan, female, 60 years old, Arlington Stadium

I drove all night from Philly to get here. I paid 50 bucks to get in and I'm gonna drive all night to get back home. I want somethin' to show for my time. I grew up over by the stockyards and used to come here a lot with my dad. I want somethin' to remember this day by and to remember my dad. I'm gonna take this damn brick home to help me remember my father, that's why.

Fan, male, 30–35 years old, Comiskey Park

For fans and ballpark employees, major league baseball is not merely an industry; it is revered symbolically as our "national pastime." The local franchise is not just another bank, department store, or amusement park; rather, it is experienced as a public trust that engenders a powerful sense of identification and identity for fans and franchise employees alike. Fans and franchise employees consider the team to the "their" team, even though it usually is owned by a small elite group of wealthy capitalists who often exercise unpopular control. As Margaret Duncan (1983) concluded, "Team loyalties developed over the course of many years provide spectators with a sense of roots, of stability often missing in industrial America" (p. 32).

Fans and franchise employees invest much of their individual identities in baseball and in their favorite teams and ballparks. For many of these fans and employees—especially for those who grew up playing organized baseball—this investment of identity begins in childhood when they fantasize about being major league players. Although working at the front office is not experientially equivalent to playing on the field, franchise employees express a special feeling about their jobs and about their work environment. As the Rangers' director of stadium administration put it, "I can show you a paper I wrote when I was in the second grade that said I was going to make my living in baseball. I feel like I'm the luckiest guy in the world."

Baseball also provides special meaning to the lives of fans who do not work for a franchise. The ballpark is the place where these fans locate many of their childhood, adolescent, and adult memories, and so reminiscing about those memories was a natural occurrence at the closing of their ballparks. The nun quoted earlier had never been to a baseball game in her life until she went to a game in 1972; with the help of local merchants who purchased season tickets for the nun and her colleague from 1972 until 1993, she ultimately defined part of her adulthood through baseball as a devoted (and devout) Ranger fan. The White Sox fan who drove all night from Philadelphia to be in Chicago at Comiskey Park's last game also provides powerful testimony to the importance of ballpark memories; in fact, he was willing to risk being arrested to remove a brick from that ballpark that would help him to remember his youth and his father.

Another fan at the closing even identified his own male rites of passage in terms of Comiskey. As he revealed:

I've had so many experiences here at Comiskey, I mean major things a guy never forgets. I took my first real date, unchaperoned, . . . to a game in 1965. I was 16 and had just gotten my license. I drank my first beer at Comiskey. Bought it from a vendor. . . . I felt a girl up for the first time at Comiskey and I got laid for the first time in my life after a Friday night game here. Comiskey was a part of all these things.

For this fan, his identity as a male is forever tied to the ballpark.

Experiencing Home (Plate) in the Ballpark Community

I feel like I've been their [the employees'] mother. There's one kid I've had here with mental and physical disabilities. He's 35 years old now, and this was the first job he ever had. Every year his mother would call to see how he was doing. He now works at American Airlines during the day. He's a cashier at an ice cream stand, and he was an employee of the month last year. He's dependable, reliable. He now lives in his own apartment and has his own car. He came in the other day and his biggest concern was to make sure the new company [that will run concessions at the new ballpark] understands my problem. [She pauses.] Now that wrenches me. I've got a lot of employees like that who I've worked with over the years.

Personnel director of concessions, female, 45 years old, Arlington Stadium

I got married here July 16, 1977. I carried my wife over the turnstiles. . . . I was just thinking about it. I made a lot of friends down here. I met them here.

Fan, male, 30–35 years old, Comiskey Park

In some ways, a baseball stadium is a *community* in a literal sense. Each ballpark is a self-contained environment that accommodates thousands of regular residents (season ticket holders) and one-time visitors. Each has food and drink to keep citizens nourished, medical facilities to treat the injured, security forces to keep the peace, retail stores to provide clothing (with the home team logo), media facilities to inform people about community events, and entertainment for residents and guests.

The ballpark is experienced as community in a richer sense as a place where friends and families come together to work, to play, and to share in community celebrations. "Sports stadiums, arenas, and even parking lots," wrote Anderson and Stone (1981), "frequently become meeting places for social interactions which provide involvement in a community event" (p. 169). For fans, the ballpark is a meeting place for families and friends who play together on dates and picnics in the park. For employees, the ballpark is a place where members work together and play together—and, as they are fond of saying, "live" together—from April to October.

Through their social interactions at the ballpark, fans and workers develop important, and often lasting, relationships. Many of them come to see the ballpark symbolically as a *home* and themselves as *family* members. For example, the personnel director quoted earlier considers herself a "mother" of her employees, and she went on to comment on how the new ballpark will be very different for everyone:

> It's a joke around here that we live here during the baseball season. It's like a house that you've lived in for most of your life or that you grew up in. And you move away and your parents sell the house. And then they get another house, but when you visit them, it's not home.

The financial controller of the franchise used a similar metaphor of the ballpark, though one that may reflect a more traditionally masculine (and less nostalgic) view of Arlington Stadium: "This ballpark is like your first car. You had great times in it and loved it, and you have a whole lot of memories. But you never want to drive it again."

Yet the ballpark is not only a symbolic home for families. In some cases, it is the place where actual families—or at least marriages—have begun. Several couples met at Arlington Stadium as employees and took their vows during the off-season *at home plate,* turning the ballpark into a church. The White Sox fan quoted earlier carried his wife over the ballpark turnstiles, turning the ballpark into a ceremonial honeymoon home. In their best-selling book, *In Search of Excellence,* Peters and Waterman (1982) reported that people in many companies use the "family" metaphor to characterize their organizations; but how many people at IBM or Hewlett-Packard really *get married in their offices* or *carry their spouses over their desks* (or onto their laptop computers)?

Clearly, the way relationships are developed and/or celebrated in our ballparks is different from that in other organizational contexts, and those differences were vividly articulated when these symbolic and actual family members spent the last moments in their symbolic homes. Even those non-regulars who came to the last games at the two ballparks expressed unusual feelings of closeness with fellow attendees. Anthropologist Victor Turner (1974) developed the notion of "communitas" to describe the "homogeneous, unstructured, and free community" (p. 169) experienced by people who transcend ethnic, gender, and class lines at religious pilgrimages. We believe that as they shared their stories and expressed their feelings at Comiskey Park and

Arlington Stadium, these fans experienced at least a momentary sense of "communitas" during their own ballpark pilgrimages.

The Generational Continuity of Ballpark Fans

Seventy years ago, I was 8 years old. I came with my dad. He was a White Sox fan from way back when they came into the league in 1900. I've been coming through those 70 years, off and on, and it's been great, I've enjoyed it. This is my grandson, that is Adam, and this is my younger son, Paul, that's Adam's father. And this young man is, this is Marty, he's from St. Louis, my oldest son. They came with me for the first time to this park. [Paul now speaking.] That's why I thought it would be kind of sentimental to have three different generations of the family. My dad's been coming here for 70 years, I've been coming here for 35 years, he's [Marty] about the same, just a little bit longer, and Adam now for 3 years. What better of a way to celebrate our relationships?

> Fan, male, 78 years old, accompanied by two
> sons and a grandson, Comiskey Park

If the ballpark symbolizes a sense of community for fans and workers, it also establishes a *continuity* in the lives of these fans and workers. For the people just quoted, the old ballpark was a concrete symbol that connected generations of family members together and that linked their pasts with their own futures.

When they removed these two ballparks, they removed this powerful sense of generational continuity for these family members.[3] As another Comiskey fan, a 35-year-old male, put it:

My grandfather came from the old country, Eastern Europe. He was only about 18 years old when they built this park, and sentimentally I guess that makes a connection, maybe with dates or with ages or times. But it's just not possible to understand how they're gonna tear it down. History is just gonna disappear.

As the ballpark brings together these generations of families and friends, it also becomes a place where older people experience their own youth vicariously as they interact with and observe the children and grandchildren of their own family and of other families. In Arlington Stadium, for example, middle-aged ushers and gray-haired (and some blue-haired) ticket sellers reenacted their own glory days as they worked with teenagers who directed cars in parking lots and who sold programs in the stands. The middle-aged supervisor of the parking lot kids told of one of his recurring dreams: "I have this dream where I'm dressed in a baseball uniform and I'm batting at home plate. Only the plate is in the parking lot and I'm 16 again, just like the other kids out there." As the Rangers' spring training director, who turned 75 during the 1989 season, put it: "How can I retire from the ballpark? Working with all these kids keeps me young."

It is the *ballpark* that unites generations of fans and workers together and keeps them forever young.

The Narrativity of Ballpark Culture

In 1990, I got hit by a drunk driver. [He gestures to his missing left arm.] I finally got out of the hospital . . . and my brother loaded me up and brought me here to see Nolan Ryan try to win his 300th game. He didn't win it, but it was a real special deal. [He pauses.] I'll never forget that day. [He pauses again.] My brother passed away 6 weeks ago. One of the last things he did before he died was to buy 28 tickets to this game, for all his friends. He did that, and then a couple weeks later his heart stopped workin'. He was 31 years old. So there are 28 of us here, all together here this weekend. He's not—well, he's here too. [He pauses again.] That's why we're here. He wanted all of his friends to be here for the final weekend.

Fan, male, 35–40 years old, Arlington Stadium

We came here, seven of us, right before I left for 'Nam. I remember I was home on leave and seven of us came down here and we joked that this could be for some of us our last ballgame, so we came to see the Sox. Three of those guys eventually were killed over there, and I guess I'm saying goodbye to them. This park was my bond with them, and now I'm gonna lose that tie. So I know that it's weird that I kiss this wall, but I'm just saying goodbye to some buddies I saw in here for the last time back then.

Fan, male, 40–45 years old, Comiskey Park

People who attend baseball games as fans and workers are fond of telling stories. Some of these stories are about events that occurred on the field, such as when Nolan Ryan finally achieved his 5,000th strikeout at Arlington Stadium or when fans went wild on Disco Demolition Night at Comiskey Park. These stories are triggered by virtually anything: a greeting or question from another fan or worker (or field researcher), a moment of action on the field, a walk by a familiar section. These stories reveal the rich *narrativity* of ballpark culture and inform fans and workers about the unique *oral history* of the franchise itself.

Other stories, however, are very personal ones; consider the powerful ones told by the two fans who came to the closings not only to say goodbye to the ballparks but to say goodbye to dead friends and family members. These stories reveal the unique identities and emotions of people who define themselves as fans and the unique status of ballparks as symbolic places where their stories are retold. *And as they retell these stories,* these people relive their own memories and redefine their own lives through the ballparks they loved. "A tale or anecdote," as Erving Goffman (1974, p. 504) told us, "is not merely any reporting of a past event. In the fullest sense, it is . . . something that listeners can empathetically insert themselves into, vicariously reexperiencing what took place" (see also Bauman, 1986; Chatman, 1978; White, 1981).

When stories are passed on, they become part of the narrative folklore of the franchise that unites people together as members of ballpark culture with the same history and tradition. Such stories unite players, coaches, fans, and workers together as they share the episodic tales of each game, in the serial dramas of each season, in the oral history of the franchise, and in the ontology of baseball as our national pastime.

Baseball as Therapy

I'm not rich or anything. I've never done anything really great. I'm just a nobody, you know, just a nobody. And I come out here, and this place makes me feel like, man, I am somebody. . . . When the sweat starts running down my forehead in the late innings and I can barely walk back to the car after the game, I know that I have given it all I've got. And I know something good will happen if I keep trying. . . . I do these things for the Rangers, the children everywhere, God, Texas, and to show everybody that we can make a difference if we try.

Fan, male, 25 years old, Arlington Stadium

Every major and minor league ballpark attracts certain fans who act in ways that distinguish them from average spectators.[4] Two of the most distinctive fans at Arlington Stadium were a working-class couple named Jimmy and Bobbie Jo Fowler. The Fowlers attended almost every Ranger game and usually sat in the uppermost 400 section of the park, or at the top of the center field bleachers several rows above the nearest fan. Throughout the game, this blue-collar couple waved white towels—or confederate flags when "them Yankees" were in town—and Jimmy yelled "Ranger Fever" after every Ranger hit and after every opponent out.

Jimmy explained that he and Bobbie Jo waved their towels for years. "The hotel where we stayed on our honeymoon 6 years ago," Bobbie Jo revealed, "was nice enough to give us these towels." Jimmy clutched his towel against his chest. "To other people, this is just a towel," he said, "but to me, this is like a flag. I don't even want it to touch the ground."

Jimmy also volunteered proudly that Tom Grieve, the Ranger general manager, had come up to the 400 section to thank him for his support and that Grieve had sent him a letter as well—a letter that Jimmy "framed and put in the living room." The letter was signed by Grieve and Mike Stone, who was then team president. But this was no ordinary letter of thanks for fan support. The letter was sent to Jimmy Fowler, care of a local hospital, and it read as follows:

Dear Jimmy:

We want you to know that you have our admiration and respect for your courageous struggle. Just as the Rangers must take it "one game at a time," your personal commitment to "one day at a time" makes absolute sense.

We miss your unfailing support and towel waving enthusiasm, but we are glad to hear of your commitment to improve the quality of your own life. Just as we must eliminate self-defeating behavior/choices in order to be the best, so must you.

Again, you have our support in your efforts to win control of your life. We look forward to seeing you back at the ballpark.

Jimmy disclosed that, in 1988, he had suffered a serious injury to his knee that required hospital care, and then he suffered a serious depression while in the hospital. "I was having some tremendous problems," he confided, "and I was really sad that I couldn't make it to the games. So my counselor at the hospital said I should write Tom Grieve a letter. I told him 'no,' but he said that I might be surprised." Jimmy stood up and yelled "Ranger Fever" as the Rangers took the field to start the second inning. "That letter was the turning point in my life. And as long as I can breathe, I'll come out to Ranger games."

In a personal letter that accompanied the copy of the letter from the Rangers, Jimmy wrote:

Some people who know me tell me that since I'm always so broke, I shouldn't go to games because the money I spend there should be used for things like bills, clothes, and food. But we get to the ballpark any way we can because we want to show the people around here how we can make a difference.

We have mixed feelings about the fanaticism experienced by fans like Jimmy Fowler. Part of us believes that Jimmy has invested too much of his psychological, financial, and spiritual identity in baseball and that he should continue his counseling sessions. As Jimmy himself recognized jokingly in a postscript to his letter, "Do you think I'm ready for the madhouse?" From this viewpoint, baseball may be a kind of drug therapy, the "opiate" that early Marxist critics of sport suggested (see Coakley, 1982, for a review).

However, another part of us believes that baseball serves a healthy therapeutic function in Jimmy's life by providing meaning that he may not be able to find in other institutions in society. Although psychiatrist Arnold Beisser (1976) offered a general critique of the "madness" in sports, he did suggest that sport has the potential to help some disturbed individuals to overcome their neuroses, as in the case of a man named "Benny" whose fan support for the Brooklyn Dodgers helped him change from a fearful, estranged young man into a healthy, integrated individual who could relate better to members of his family (pp. 126–127). Lawrence Wenner (1990, p. 227) agreed: "In the short run, the therapeutic value of [sports] may be limited. . . . However, because of the centrality of sports to American life . . . [a fan] is integrated more fully into the larger community over the long haul." In his honest belief that his actions really make a difference, Jimmy Fowler expresses a childlike faith that most of us had when we were "immature" children but that we have outgrown as "rational" adults. Jimmy still believes, and his ballpark rituals of flag waving and yelling "Ranger Fever" revealed a therapeutic engagement with the game; it also served as a testament to the spirituality of the game. But he did wonder at the closing: "We love the new stadium, but I don't know if I'm gonna fit in over there. We fit here."

The Ballpark as a House of Worship

I come here in part, really more than just part, to visit with my husband. He was a Sox fan and sort of half joking, half serious, he once said to me quite a while back that when he died he would rest easiest if he could be buried under home plate at Comiskey Park. . . . After he died, that was on November 17, I had him cremated and kept his ashes at the house in one of those funeral urns and kept it in a closet. . . . When the baseball season rolled around the next year, I remembered what Frank said to me about being buried at the park. . . .

I remembered seeing planes sometime flying over the park when I'd go with Frank to the Sunday doubleheaders. . . . So I just called around and got a guy who agreed to fly me over the park. At first I didn't tell him why. But anyway, he agreed to fly me over the park on a day the Sox weren't in town. When I got to Megg's Field, I told him what I wanted to do and the guy said, "Okay, lady, if that's what you want to do." That's what we did, circled the park once and then he told me to pour the ashes out and I did.

So Frank's a part of this park. It don't matter if his ashes made it into the park or blew away years ago, I know Frank's here. He has been for over 10 years now. What's gonna happen now? Where's he gonna go? I always knew his spirit was happy here and I could come here and feel close to him. I don't know what I'm gonna do. Nothing I guess. There ain't much I can do except come here for the last couple of times. It's like he's dying all over again. When I heard they were tearing the park down, I thought, "What will happen to Frank? Where will he go?"

Fan, female, 60 years old, Comiskey Park

Some students of the game suggest that the ballpark can be interpreted as a place of worship (see Hoffman, 1992; Sage, 1981). Even in a cynical age, we can find genuine *hero worship* at the ballpark. Children still flock to the railing before the game during batting practice and wait at the clubhouse gates after the game to catch a glimpse of (and hopefully an autograph from) their favorite players. In addition, ballpark culture involves *magic and superstition,* beliefs that have flourished in a sport in which the best teams lose more than one third of their games and the best hitters fail almost 7 out of 10 times (Gmelch, 1971). "It requires no giant leap of logic or intuition," wrote George Grella (1985, p. 268), "to recognize that the magical qualities of primitive religion also exist in baseball." Expressions such as "ran out of luck," "being at the right place at the right time," and "miracle win" are familiar to fans and players alike as acceptable accounts for ballpark events that cannot be explained in rational terms. Just ask any Cub fan.

Yet hero worship and superstition cannot explain the sense of religion invoked by the woman who scattered her husband's ashes over Comiskey Park. For this woman, there is genuine *spirituality* to the ballpark, and attending the closing of that ballpark was very much a religious ceremony. As she talked about the details of her husband's "burial," she kept touching, almost caressing, the chairs around her as she "wrote" her text. She spoke affectionately of her husband and his spirit's soon-to-be demolished

home. As his spirit had rested contentedly in the park for more than a decade, so also had she rested. With the impending destruction of Old Comiskey close at hand, she now was faced with a new reality couched in fear. She was about to lose the inner tranquility that had permeated her life following the extraordinary measures she had taken to honor his request to remain in Comiskey forever.

Old Comiskey was a sacred place, infused with the spirit of her late husband. It was a place where she experienced and expressed a powerful emotional investment. As we studied the emotionality of this woman and of the many others we met in the field, we came to understand better our own emotionality as human beings who have experienced baseball in very personal ways and our own positionality as human researchers who study ballpark culture. For example, one of the authors empathized fully with the anxiety of the widow at Comiskey, as he came to grips with the loss of the "place" where the presence of his late father had always been the strongest for him. He would once again, and perhaps really for the first time, confront the death of his father, just as the widow faced the death of her husband for a second, and perhaps more difficult, time.

Concluding Remarks

Critics focus on the negative aspects of sport in society, especially on how sport engenders alienation, promotes commercialism and militarism, encourages sexism and racism, and is used by business and the state as a tool for control (see Coakley, 1982; Hargreaves, 1982; Lipsky, 1981; Trujillo, 1991). From a critical perspective, it is clear that those in positions of power in sports (such as franchise owners and media organizations) commodify and exploit fan identity, community, and emotionality in an effort to sell baseball (and baseball merchandise) to consumers and to reaffirm the ideology of American capitalism through baseball to members of society. As media critic Sut Jhally (1989) concluded, sports "ritually celebrate the most alienating features of the capitalist labor process" by transforming "structures that are hierarchical and exploitative into ones that become identified by the personal and human" (p. 86).

Despite these problems with sport, true fans seem to have an emotional attachment to baseball that is resilient to ticket prices, labor disputes, and media spectacles. As we documented in this article, basball fans and ballpark employees express genuine affection for baseball and for how baseball affects their lives. Indeed, as they expressed their feelings and emotions, these fans revealed (knowingly or unknowingly) powerful senses of identity, community, continuity, narrativity, therapy, spirituality, and self-discovery.

We believe that all researchers—even so-called "quantoids" who espouse the most radical detachment from their data—should pay closer attention to the emotions of the people we study as well as to the emotions we experience as researchers.

We believe that field research, by its very nature, encourages a constant interaction between the personal and emotional on the one hand and the intellectual and scientific on the other hand. By paying closer attention to the emotionality of others, we may better understand the cultures of the people we study and, in the process, we may better understand ourselves.

Notes

1. On Disco Demolition Night, a Chicago disc jockey was hired to blow up thousands of disco records during the break between games of a twilight doubleheader. When the disc jockey hit the detonator, hundreds of the mostly youthful fans who came to the promotion stormed the field and stayed there for several hours. The White Sox were forced to forfeit the second game.

2. One author had already conducted a 2-year ethnographic study of the ballpark culture of Arlington Stadium a couple years before the closing.

3. For these two ethnographies, we interviewed men and women as well as boys and girls. Although both males and females assign special meaning to our national pastime, we found that males generally attributed more personal significance to baseball and to the ballpark than did females. Perhaps this finding is due to the fact that more men and boys have played baseball than have women and girls, although more girls now are playing Little League baseball than ever before. Perhaps this finding was a function of the fact that many of our closest contacts at the ballpark were males whose beliefs about the importance of baseball in society corresponded to our own male views of baseball. In short, we recognize that much of ballpark culture is male dominated; some might even say that the ballpark is a bastion of male bonding.

As we analyzed the communicative actions of the male fans and workers we observed, however, we discovered that some of the qualities associated with this seemingly male-dominated ballpark are stereotypically *feminine* in nature. For example, many of the male fans and workers we interviewed and observed were openly sentimental about baseball and about the ballpark. Many of them talked lovingly about their fathers and about "celebrating" their relationships with them at the park. Many of them wept at the Comiskey closing; one did so while kissing a brick from the park's structure. Interestingly, many of them described Old Comiskey itself as a "she," as "The Grand Old Lady," who was about to "give birth" to the new park.

In the final analysis, we believe that some of the "male bonding" that occurs at the ballpark does so through a structure that is identified with feminine labels and through processes that are guided by traditionally feminine values such as warmth, openness, supportiveness, and sentimentality. For some men, the ballpark, as a "womb," is a place where they can act and interact in ways that are not tied to a traditional sense of masculinity. In sum, the ballpark is a place where men experience and express *emotionality.* We encourage other students of the game to examine these and other dimensions of the gender ideology of ballpark culture.

4. Historian David Voigt (1983) reported that baseball lore is filled with fanatics such as San Diego's "tuba man," Shea Stadium's "sign man," Philadelphia's "umpire-baiter," Atlanta's "rabble-rouser," and others. At Comiskey Park, some of these characters included "The Lone Ranger," "The drummer boy," and "Andy the clown."

References

Anderson, D. F., & Stone, G. P. (1981). Sport: A search for community. In S. L. Greendorfer & A. Yiannakis (Eds.), *Sociology of sport: Diverse perspectives* (pp. 160–175). West Point, NY: Leisure.

Bauman, R. (1986). *Story, performance, event: Contextual studies of oral narrative.* Cambridge: Cambridge University Press.

Beisser, A. (1976). *The madness in sports.* New York: Appleton-Century-Crofts.

Chatman, S. (1978). *Story and discourse: Narrative structure in fiction and film.* Ithaca, NY: Cornell University Press.

Clifford, J., & Marcus, G. E. (Eds.). (1986). *Writing culture: The poetics and politics of ethnography.* Berkeley: University of California Press.

Coakley, J. (1982). *Sport in society: Issues and controversies* (2nd ed.). St. Louis, MO: Mosby.

Duncan, M. C. (1983). The symbolic dimensions of spectator sport. *Quest, 35,* 29–36.

Geertz, C. (1988). *Works and lives: The anthropologist as author.* Stanford, CA: Stanford University Press.

Gmelch, G. (1971, June). Baseball magic. *Transaction,* pp. 39–41, 54.

Goffman, E. (1974). *Frame analysis.* New York: Harper & Row.

Goodall, H. L. (1989). *Casing a promised land: The autobiography of an organizational detective as cultural ethnographer.* Carbondale, IL: Southern Illinois University Press.

Grella, G. (1985). Baseball and the American dream. In D. L. Vanderwerken & S. K. Wertz (Eds.), *Sport: Inside out* (pp. 267–279). Fort Worth: Texas Christian University Press.

Hall, D. (1985). *Fathers playing catch with sons.* New York: Laurel.

Hargreaves, J. (1982). Sport and hegemony: Some theoretical problems. In H. Cantelon & R. Gruneau (Eds.), *Sport, culture, and the modern state* (pp. 103–135). Toronto: University of Toronto Press.

Hoffman, S. J. (1992). *Sport and religion.* Champaign, IL: Human Kinetics.

Jhally, S. (1989). Cultural studies and the sports/media complex. In L. A. Wenner (Ed.), *Media, sports, and society* (pp. 70–93). Newbury Park, CA: Sage.,

Lipsky, R. (1981). *How we play the game: Why sports dominate American life.* Boston: Beacon.

Peters, T. J., & Waterman, R. H. (1982). *In search of excellence.* New York: Harper & Row.

Sage, G. S. (1981). Sport and religion. In G.R.F. Luschen & G. S. Sage (Eds.), *Handbook of social science of sport* (pp. 136–156). Champaign, IL: Stipes.

Trujillo, N. (1991). Hegemonic masculinity on the mound: Media representation of Nolan Ryan and American sports culture. *Critical Studies in Mass Communication, 8,* 290–308.

Turner, V. (1974). *Dramas, fields, and metaphors: Symbolic action in human society.* Ithaca, NY: Cornell University Press.

Van Maanen, J. (1988). *Tales of the field: On writing ethnography.* Chicago: University of Chicago Press.

Voigt, D. Q. (1983). *America through baseball, Vol. 3: From postwar expansion to the electronic age.* University Park: Pennsylvania State University Press.

Wenner, L. A. (1990). Therapeutic engagement in mediated sports. In G. Gumpert & S. L. Fish (Eds.), *Talking to strangers* (pp. 223–224). Norwood, NJ: Ablex.

White, H. (1981). The value of narrativity in the representation of reality. In W.T.J. Mitchell (Ed.), *On narrative* (pp. 1–23). Chicago: University of Chicago Press.

Whyte, W. F. (1984). *Learning from the field.* Beverly Hills, CA: Sage.

Chapter 23

JOE LOUIS UNCOVERS DYNAMITE

Richard Wright

In this article Richard Wright describes the scene in the streets of Chicago after Joe Louis defeated Max Baer in a key heavyweight boxing match in 1935. Wright draws our attention to the impact of Louis's victory in generating feelings of pride and solidarity in the black American community.

Wun—tuh—three—fooo—fiiive—seex—seven—eight—nine—thuun!"

"Joe Louis—the winnah!"

On Chicago's South Side five minutes after these words were yelled and Joe Louis's hand was hoisted as victor in his four-round go with Max Baer, Negroes poured out of beer taverns, pool rooms, barber shops, rooming houses and dingy flats and flooded the streets.

"Louis! Louis! Louis!" they yelled and threw their hats away. They snatched newspapers from the stands of astonished Greeks and tore them up, flinging the bits into the air. They wagged their heads. Lawd, they'd never seen or heard the like of it before. They shook the hands of strangers. They clapped one another on the back. It was like a revival. Really, there was a religious feeling in the air. Well, it wasn't exactly a religious feeling, but it was *something,* and you could feel it. It was a feeling of unity, of oneness.

Two hours after the fight the area between South Parkway and Prairie Avenue on 47th Street was jammed with no less than twenty-five thousand Negroes, joy-mad and moving to they didn't know where. Clasping hands, they formed long writhing snake-lines and wove in and out of traffic. They seeped out of doorways, oozed from alleys, trickled out of tenements, and flowed down the street; a fluid mass of joy. White storekeepers hastily closed their doors against the tidal wave and stood peeping through the plate glass with blanched faces.

Something had happened, all right. And it had happened so confoundingly sudden that the whites in the neighborhood were dumb with fear. They felt—you could see it in their faces—that *something* had ripped loose, exploded. Something which they had long feared and thought was dead. Or if not dead, at least so safely buried under the pretence of good-will that they no longer had need to fear it. Where in the world did it come from? And what was worst of all, how far would it go? Say, what's got into these Negroes?

And the whites and the blacks began to feel themselves. The blacks began to remember all the little slights, and discriminations and insults they had suffered; and their hunger too and their misery. And the whites began to search their souls to see if they had been guilty of something, sometime, somewhere, against which this wave of feeling was rising.

As the celebration wore on, the younger Negroes began to grow bold. They jumped on the running boards of automobiles going east or west on 47th Street and demanded of the occupants:

"Who yuh fer—Baer or Louis?"

In the stress of the moment it seemed that the answer to the question marked out friend and foe.

A hesitating reply brought waves of scornful laughter. Baer, huh? That was funny. Now, hadn't Joe Louis just whipped Max Baer? Didn't think we had it in us, did you? Thought Joe Louis was scared, didn't you? Scared because Max talked loud and made boasts. We ain't scared either. We'll fight too when the time comes. We'll win, too.

A taxicab driver had his cab wrecked when he tried to put up a show of bravado.

Then they began stopping streetcars. Like a cyclone sweeping through a forest, they went through them, shouting, stamping. Conductors gave up and backed away like children. Everybody had to join in this celebration. Some of the people ran out of the cars and stood, pale and trembling, in the crowd. They felt it, too.

In the crush a pocketbook snapped open and money spilled on the street for eager black fingers.

"They stole it from us, anyhow," they said as they picked it up.

When an elderly Negro admonished them, a fist was shaken in his face. Uncle Tomming, huh?

"Whut in hell yuh gotta do wid it" they wanted to know.

Something had popped loose, all right. And it had come from deep down. Out of the darkness it had leaped from its coil. And nobody wanted to say. Blacks and whites were afraid. But it was a sweet fear, at least for the blacks. It was a mingling of fear and fulfillment. Something dreaded and yet wanted. A something had popped out of a dark hole, something with a hydra-like head, and it was daring forth its tongue.

You stand on the borderline, wondering what's beyond. Then you take one step and you feel a strange, sweet tingling. You take two steps and the feeling becomes keener. You want to feel some more. You break into a run. You know it's dangerous, but you're impelled in spite of yourself.

Four centuries of oppression, of frustrated hopes, of black bitterness, felt even in the bones of the bewildered young, were rising to the surface. Yes, unconsciously they had imputed to the brawny image of Joe Louis all the balked dreams of revenge, all the secretly visualized moments of retaliation, AND HE HAD WON! Good Gawd Almighty! Yes, by Jesus, it could be done! Didn't Joe do it? You see, Joe was the consciously-felt symbol. Joe was the concentrated essence of black triumph over white. And it comes so seldom, so seldom. And what could be sweeter than long-nourished hate vicariously gratified? From the symbol of Joe's strength they took strength, and in that moment all fear, all obstacles were wiped out, drowned. They stepped out of the mire of hesitation and irresolution and were free! Invincible! A merciless victor over a fallen foe! Yes, they had felt all that—for a moment . . .

And then the cops came.

Not the carefully picked white cops who were used to batter the skulls of white workers and intellectuals who came to the South Side to march with the black workers to show their solidarity in the struggle against Mussolini's impending invasion of Ethiopia; oh, no, black cops, but trusted black cops and plenty tough. Cops who knew their business, how to handle delicate situations. They piled out of patrols, swinging clubs.

"Git back! Gawddammit, git back!"

But they were very careful, very careful. They didn't hit anybody. They, too, sensed *something*. And they didn't want to trifle with it. And there's no doubt but that they had been instructed not to. Better go easy here. No telling what might happen. They swung clubs, but pushed the crowd back with their hands.

Finally, the streetcars moved again. The taxis and automobiles could go through. The whites breathed easier. The blood came back to their cheeks.

The Negroes stood on the sidewalks, talking, wondering, looking, breathing hard. They had felt something, and it had been sweet—that feeling. They wanted some more of it, but they were afraid now. The spell was broken.

And about midnight down the street that feeling ebbed, seeping home—flowing back to the beer tavern, the pool room, the café, the barber shop, the dingy flat. Like a sullen river it ran back to its muddy channel, carrying a confused and sentimental memory on its surface, like water-soaked driftwood.

Say, Comrade, here's the wild river that's got to be harnessed and directed. Here's that *something*, that pent-up folk consciousness. Here's a fleeting glimpse of the heart of the Negro, the heart that beats and suffers and hopes—for freedom. Here's that fluid something that's like iron. Here's the real dynamite that Joe Louis uncovered!

Chapter 24

SUPPORTERS, FOLLOWERS, FANS, AND *FLÂNEURS*

A Taxonomy of Spectator Identities in Football

Richard Giulianotti

This article presents an interesting typology of sports spectators. Richard Giulianotti argues that, with the enormous changes in the political economy and globalization of sport, the structure of opportunities for spectator identities has changed. Using two dimensions of attachment—hot vs. cool and traditional vs. consumer—Giulianotti's scheme yields four types: supporters, followers, fans, and *flâneurs*. The typology not only illuminates how people watch and enjoy sports but reveals some of the underlying dynamics that produce these spectator identities.

No one would deny that world football (or soccer, as it is sometimes known) has undergone a fundamental structural transformation. At the elite level, football's finances have grown exponentially, while there have been major changes in the cultural organization of the game as experienced by players, spectators, and media commentators. The United Kingdom (particularly England) has perhaps witnessed the most dramatic change in football's social and economic standing, because in the mid-1980s the English game was synonymous in the global public imagination with spectator violence and an entrenched infrastructural decline.

One area of substantial discussion over the past decade has concerned the impact of football's new political economy on its grassroots custodians, the football spectators. In the United Kingdom, there have been persistent criticisms of this boom on the basis that established (but relatively poorer) football spectators are being squeezed out of any stakeholder position within their clubs, most notably the biggest ones, in exchange for wealthier new spectators.[1] The *Guardian* newspaper described these disenfranchised spectators as "football's new refuseniks."[2] Football's burgeoning popularity, its increasingly serpentine ties with corporations and other business institutions, the reduction of stadium capacities to create high-priced seating, and the advent of pay-per-view television are four key ingredients identified in this process of commodification. A government-appointed football task force, with a mandate to identify and recommend on spectator interests, produced two rival, concluding reports and has had a negligible effect beyond promoting antiracist work within the game. Nevertheless, concern with the impact of this commodification remains strong in the public sphere, notably in the United Kingdom and also in Spain, Germany, Italy, and France.

In this article, I seek to examine the impact of football's commodification on spectator identities relative to their association with professional football clubs. I set out a model of four ideal-type spectator identities that may be found in the contemporary football world. In doing so, I seek to redefine more precisely and sociologically four particular spectator identities, and these are supporters, followers, fans, and *flâneurs*.

The analysis mapped out here applies principally to professional football clubs, particularly those whose corporate structures are owned or controlled on market principles by individuals or institutions. These privately owned clubs are most apparent across Western Europe (with the partial but declining exception of some clubs in France, Germany, Scandinavia, Spain, and Portugal) and increasingly in Eastern Europe. Similar processes of commodification look set to affect other football societies and other sporting codes. In Latin America (as in Iberia), clubs have traditionally existed as

private associations, under the ownership and political control of their many members (socios). However, there are signs, notably in Brazil, that future legislation will enable single investors or institutions to buy a controlling interest in football clubs. In North America, elite baseball, basketball, American football, and, to a lesser extent, ice hockey have all undergone extensive commodification and remarketing, resulting in different and new kinds of spectator relationships to clubs.[3] In Australia, there have been intensive attempts in recent years to construct national leagues for elite level clubs in Australian Rules Football (AFL), rugby league, and soccer (A-League). The AFL appears to have been most successful in constructing a popular, lucrative national profile for its sport and in the process generating new kinds of spectator identification, which have experienced resistance from more traditional supporters (Hess & Stewart, 1998). This apparent trend toward a homogenization of the corporate structures of professional sports suggests that the arguments presented here do not just pertain to football but, instead, have a cross-code and cross-cultural purchase.

The article develops critical sociological and normative arguments presented elsewhere on the nature of football's commodification (Giulianotti, 1999; Giulianotti & Gerrard, 2001a; Walsh & Giulianotti, 2001). Following earlier work, I take commodification to mean that process by which an object or social practice acquires an exchange value or market-centered meaning. Commodification is not a single process but an ongoing one, often involving the gradual entry of market logic to the various elements that constitute the object or social practice under consideration. As I argue below, the marked intensification of this process in recent years is of a different order to that which was experienced up until the late 1980s, and so might now be described as a period of hypercommodification.

Football's contemporary commodification—its hypercommodification—has been driven by extraordinary and different volumes of capital that have entered the game from entirely new sources: satellite and pay-per-view television networks, Internet and telecommunications corporations, transnational sports equipment manufacturers, public relations companies, and the major stock markets through the sale of club equity.

Concomitantly, a new set of social and cultural relations have arisen since the late 1980s, notably featuring the greater migration of elite labor, a gradual proliferation of continental and global competitions, astronomical rises in elite player salaries, new media outlets for football (for example, satellite television, club television stations, the Internet, and in future, mobile telephones), and new forms of cultural encoding of football through these media.

These transformations have been symptomatic of the contemporary condition of "disorganized capitalism" identified by Lash and Urry (1987, 1994). It is characterized by the genesis of intensified flows between individuals, social groups, objects, and institutions across an increasingly globalized terrain, rather than through a more organized chain of relations within national boundaries (cf. Lash & Urry, 1994, p. 10). Part of this transformation involves the increased social and sociological relevance of communication flows, not merely in the electronic media, but also in terms of the aestheticization of consumer culture and the semiotic expression of social identity within an information age (cf. Castells,

1996). The old institutions and organizations that had regulated economic and cultural relations throughout the 20th century entered what may be a terminal decline toward the new millennium (Lash, 1994, pp. 213–214). Within football, that transformation may well be illustrated through the rising power and influence of transnational corporations (TNCs) and the political and economic decline of some national or continental associations. Among the rising TNCs, we might certainly list major media corporations and sports merchandise corporations, but increasingly top football clubs such as Manchester United, Real Madrid, and Juventus possess transnational characteristics in consumer profile, flexible labor recruitment practices, and the global diffusion of corporate symbolism. The most powerful of these "superclubs" have formed an organization called (with some statelike irony) the "G14." Following warnings of an impending breakaway from established football structures, Union des Associations Européennes de Football (UEFA—European football's governing body) agreed in 1999 to amend Europe's top club tournament (the Champions League) to suit G14 demands for more lucrative fixtures. Reflecting the disorganized political structure within European football, continuing speculation has surrounded the future format of top club tournaments, as a range of institutional actors (old and new) jockey for positions that are most advantageous economically to their respective owners, shareholders, and officials. Finally here, as I have indicated, these transformations are all constituent of the broader, immensely complex process that is the contemporary globalization of football.

In what follows, I concentrate on one critical social relationship that has undergone transformation throughout football's modern and postmodern eras of hypercommodification. I refer to the identities of spectators and their relationships to football clubs.

Contemporary Spectator Identities: The Principles Behind the Taxonomies

I argue that there are four ideal-type categories, into which we may classify spectators. The main criterion for classifying spectators relates to the particular kind of identification that spectators have toward specific clubs.

As Figure 1 demonstrates, the four spectator categories are underpinned by two basic binary oppositions: hot-cool and traditional-consumer. Thus, there are four quadrants into which spectators may be classified: traditional/hot, traditional/cool,

consumer/hot, consumer/cool. The four quadrants represent ideal-type categories, through which we may map the historical changes and cultural differences experienced by specific spectator communities in their relationships with identified clubs. The traditional/consumer horizontal axis measures the basis of the individual's investment in a specific club: Traditional spectators will have a longer, more local and popular cultural identification with the club, whereas consumer fans will have a more market-centered relationship to the club as reflected in the centrality of consuming club products.

The hot-cool vertical axis reflects the different degrees to which the club is central to the individual's project of self-formation. Hot forms of loyalty emphasize intense kinds of identification and solidarity with the club; cool forms denote the reverse. The hot-cool opposition is indebted to at least

Figure 1

	HOT		
THICK SOLIDARITY	Topophilic Spaces	Product-mediated Distances	THICK/THIN SOLIDARITY
Supporter		**Fan**	
Grounded Identity	Subcultural relations	Non-reciprocal Relations	Market Identity
TRADITIONAL			CONSUMER
Nested Identity	Symbolic exchange relations	Virtual Relations	Cosmopolitan Identity
Follower		**Flâneur**	
THICK/THIN SOLIDARITY	Instrumental spaces	Simulation spaces Non-places	THIN SOLIDARITY
	COOL		

two sources. First, theorists of the mass media, such as Marshall McLuhan (1964) and Jean Baudrillard (1990), have employed this opposition to explain the cool social relations that structure the communicative processes involving the electronic media. Second, the hot-cool distinction is also derived from an essay by Bryan Turner (1999) on the changing historical and cultural meanings of body marks.

Turner argued that in more traditional societies, body marks were relatively obligatory and employed to designate hot forms of loyalty to the collective. Conversely, in postmodern societies, identification with the collective is voluntary and transient, reflecting cooler, postemotional forms of personal identity. Thus, tattoos in Western societies have traditionally demarcated the individual's hot and permanent masculine loyalty toward a specific social entity (such as the nation, family, female partner, military unit, football club, etc.). Latterly, postmodern tattoos have emerged that are impermanent, are unisex in bearer, are heavily aesthetic (often borrowed from Eastern cultures in design), and reflect a cool or nonexistent association with a specific social group. Turner also employed the binary distinction between thick and thin forms of solidarity. These latter categories tend to be congruent with his earlier binary, so that hot loyalties reflect "thick" forms of social solidarity, whereas cool identification produces "thin" forms of social solidarity.

By way of redeveloping Turner's model, it is important to return to the cultural form and to the social relations surrounding the game itself to map out the spectator identities. Each of the four spectator categories shows a distinctive synthesis of hot, cool, traditional, and consumer qualities. Each category displays distinctive kinds of

identification with a specific club and a particular motivation for such a personal association. Each category evidences a particular form of spatial relationship to the club. As ideal types, these categories do allow for degrees of empirical variation and difference among their constituents, for example in their relative manifestations of thick or thin solidarity.

Traditional/Hot Spectators: Supporters

The traditional/hot spectator is defined here as a supporter of the football club. The classic supporter has a long-term personal and emotional investment in the club. This may be supplemented (but never supplanted) by a market-centered investment, such as buying shares in the club or expensive club merchandise, but the rationale for that outlay is still underpinned by a conscious commitment to show thick personal solidarity and offer monetary support toward the club. Showing support for the club in its multifarious forms (including market ones) is considered to be obligatory, because the individual has a relationship with the club that resembles those with close family and friends. In South America, supporters talk of their respective clubs as "mothers," whereas they are its "sons" or "children." More routinely, whereas the players at the club may change, the ground is always "home." Renouncing support or switching allegiances to a rival club is impossible; traditional supporters are culturally contracted to their clubs.

Traditionally, the club is an emblem of its surrounding community, from whence it draws its core supporters. To establish themselves, clubs may have "raised the banner of town chauvinism, and prospered under it" (Hopcraft, 1968, p. 186), but the social and cultural impact of a club is always more relevant to local supporters than its unstable economic impact. Localist solidarity is strong, although some clubs with ethnic traditions might retain the deep affections of diasporic supporters. To continue the Durkheimian metaphor, the club might be seen as a totemic representation of the surrounding community. Thus, the various supporter rituals surrounding match day (not least the chanting of the club's name and the oldest supporter songs) coalesce to become a ceremony, through which the supporters worship themselves. The body becomes a key vehicle for communicating these hot and permanent forms of solidarity with club/community: Club crests are tattooed onto arms and torsos; club colors are worn perennially; during matches, the supporter corpus comprises hands, arms, and bodies that move in unison as part of the various supporter chants.

Supporters attend regularly, coming to know the ground's nooks and crannies in a very familiar, personal manner. The ground enhances their thick solidarity with fellow supporters, crowds of whom generate an atmosphere on match days that is considered to be special or unique. Supporting the club is a key preoccupation of the individual's self, so that attending home fixtures is a routine that otherwise structures the supporter's free time.[4] Supporting the club is a lived experience, rooted in a grounded identity that is reflected in an affectionate relationship to the ground that is regularly revisited. Moreover, the supporter's emotional investment in the club is reciprocated in several ways. The club might be seen to repay that faith by winning some matches or even some trophies, but less instrumental elements of reciprocated affection are at least as crucial. The club's players might play in a style that is favored by the sup-

porters and the club's traditions (whether this is flamboyant, fluent, tough, or efficient), perhaps even reflecting some distinctive local values. Outwith match day, supporters may enjoy some community benefits through use of club facilities or social engagements with officials and players.[5]

Supporters themselves husband these strong senses of hot, traditional identification in a subcultural manner. New generations of supporters are socialized into the core subcultural values by their parent groups or by older peers. Key forums for the debating of local club questions and the reproduction of subcultural values emerged through the creation of specific supporter associations, or latterly through the production of "fanzines" that are sold on the streets outside the ground. Yet within the support, there are inevitably various status gradations. To borrow from Thornton's (1995, pp. 8–14) development of Bourdieu (1984), some supporters seek to display greater volumes of "subcultural capital" to authenticate their support to the extent of claiming greater status over their fellow supporters. In the United Kingdom, subcultural capital is really reserved for those supporters who continued to attend and to live through those periods when their clubs were unsuccessful rather than become part-time supporters; distinction is also acquired by those football spectators who did not emerge during the post-1990 boom in the sport's fashionability.[6] The embodiment of key values is also accorded status, such as dedication to the club or vocal appreciation of the aesthetics behind the team's playing style. Moreover, the supporters' commitment to the team's cause does not preclude a deep interest and understanding of the various qualities and subcultural values of other clubs and their players. Supporters are both custodians of football qua game and hot participants in active rivalries with other clubs, notably those from neighboring communities (Armstrong & Giulianotti, 2001). For traditional/hot supporters, one cannot acquire subcultural capital in a purely market manner simply by purchasing the latest club commodities.

Traditional/Cool Spectators: Followers

The traditional/cool spectators are followers of clubs, but they are also followers of players, managers, and other football people. The follower is so defined not by an itinerant journey alongside the club but, instead, by keeping abreast of developments among clubs and football people in which he or she has a favorable interest. The follower has implicit awareness of, or an explicit preconcern with, the particular senses of identity and community that relate to specific clubs, to specific nations, and to their associated supporter groups. But the follower arrives at such identification through a vicarious form of communion, most obviously via the cool medium of the electronic media.

Traditional/cool followers may evince either thin or thick forms of solidarity toward their favored football institutions. In its thin solidarity form, the follower might be drawn to a particular club because of its historical links to his or her favored club, such as in one club hiring the other's players or manager. The distant club might have ideological attractions for specific individual followers, such as the anarcho-leftist St. Pauli club in Hamburg, the ethno-national culture of Barcelona, or the fascistic subcultures at clubs such as Lazio, Verona, Real Madrid, or some clubs from the former East Germany. In its thick form of solidarity, groups of followers might establish friendship relationships with the traditional/hot

supporters at these clubs. In Italy, for example, there are complex, subcultural lineages of friendship and strong rivalry that exist across club supporter groups, which might, for example, encourage Sampdoria supporters to be Parma followers.[7] In the United Kingdom, there are friendships that link club supporter groups through religious-ethnic sentiments.[8] Among some hooligan groups in particular, there are signs of informal transnational friendship networks, such as those between English firms and hooligans in the Benelux countries, or Scottish groups with ties to some English club hooligans and some ultras in southern Europe.

Informal communities are ritually cemented through the symbolic exchanges of football paraphernalia and the generous hosting of visiting friends. In its fullest sense, very thick senses of social solidarity might be reproduced through the club in a nationalist sense, enabling the "imagined community" to be socially realized—such as when Turkish clubs visit Germany and find that the local "guest workers" are in massive attendance, magically recreating their national identity whereas their actual identification with the specific club is typically a cool, instrumental one.

In both thick and thin versions of solidarity, we have a set of noneconomic, symbolic exchange relationships involving the follower and the favored club. The latter is accorded the interest or backing of the follower, but the favored club does offer something in return that accords with the follower's habitus or established football interests, such as in terms of employing a favored player or in the club's cultural politics. The follower may seek to authenticate in normative terms this association with the club by appealing beyond principles of mere football success to more abstract social and cultural values. Typically, these values harmonize with those associated with the follower's other, more established focus for support. Followers may define themselves against consumer values to authenticate their traditionalist motives, such as through a stylized denial of the role of team success or "fashionability" in inspiring their club allegiance (as one finds among Scandinavian followers of such unlikely football teams as Cowdenbeath or Stenhousemuir in Scotland).

To borrow from Cohen (1978), the notion of a set of "nested identities" might help to explain how the self seeks to integrate these different objects of allegiance.[9] There may be no simply ranked pyramid set of affiliations that the follower has for organizing his or her allegiances. Instead, these affiliations may be composed in a rather complex manner, with no obvious way of determining which identification is favored when different favored entities rub up against one another (such as when a favored manager comes up against a favored team). Nested identities instead function to provide the follower with a range of favored clubs and football people in different circumstances, ensuring that the follower's football interest is sustained when his or her supported true team is no longer competing. The proliferation of televised football now means that, to sustain the traditional spectating habit of favoring a particular team, the viewer must become a follower of some clubs. But, the follower is suitably inured with the cultural politics of football to know that certain elements cannot combine to construct a viable nest: Only flâneurs (see below), for example, would declare a penchant for both Liverpool and Manchester United, or Fiorentina and Juventus.

Moreover, the follower lacks the spatial embedding of the supporter within the club and its surrounding communities. For followers, football places may be mere practical resources with few symbolic meanings: a stage upon which favored players and officials might pitch up to perform before moving on. In circumstances of thicker solidarity, the public geography surrounding the favored club may be respected by followers, but from a distance, typically with no deep personal knowledge or engagement within this particular lifeworld.

The Hot/Consumer Spectators: Fans

The hot/consumer spectator is a modern fan of a football club or its specific players, particularly its celebrities. The fan develops a form of intimacy or love for the club or its specific players, but this kind of relationship is inordinately unidirectional in its affections. The fan is hot in terms of identification; the sense of intimacy is strong and is a key element of the individual's self. But, it is a relationship that is rather more distant than that enjoyed by supporters. Football's modern move into the market and its more recent hypercommodification have served to dislocate players and club officials from supporters, particularly in the higher professional divisions. The individual fan experiences the club, its traditions, its star players, and fellow supporters through a market-centered set of relationships. The fans' strength of identification with the club and its players is thus authenticated most readily through the consumption of related products. Such consumption might take the direct form of purchasing merchandise, buying shares, or contributing to fundraising initiatives. More significantly in future, more indirect forms of consumption come into play, particularly purchasing football magazines and pay-per-view or other subscription rights to the club's televised fixtures. The consumer relationship to the club is thus at its strongest among the wealthiest of football clubs.

The hot/consumer spectator can incline toward relatively thicker or thinner versions of social solidarity. In its thicker manifestation, bordering on the supporter identity, the fans' consumption practices are orientated toward enhancing the collective consciousness, intensifying the rituals of support. If large groups of fans attend matches in club shirts or other trademarked colors, then this striking display of visual solidarity may energize the players during matches. Thinner forms of solidarity are evinced from a greater distance. In its more extreme manifestation, buying into club regalia or shares becomes one of the few means by which fans scattered across the world may continue to signify their deep allegiance to a local team.

The fan recognizes that in contemporary professional sport, the amoral free market dominates, consequently the club's survival and successes are dependent upon greater financial contributions from all kinds of backers relative to the wealth of other clubs. Purchasing shares in clubs may be investments in football's boom time, but fans are reluctant to sell in the interests of personal profit. The brand loyalty and inelastic demand of fans for club shares and merchandise are consciously intended to provide the club with financial stability, typically to enable the purchase of better players (Conn, 1997, p. 155). But in promoting the transformation of its spectators into rather consumer-centered fan identities, the club tends to generate a set of utilitarian conditions for its consumers to continue attending. If the club fails to deliver on its market promises (such as "brand improvement" of the team), then the fans may drift into other markets (other leisure activities, other football leagues, though probably not supporting rival teams) in the deculturalized pursuit of "value for money." If solidarity is rather thicker, then fans may collectivize and agitate to unseat the incumbent controllers, such as by sacking the board or forming independent shareholder associations. Most typically, the club's fans are politically passive, strong in their affections for club and players, probably geographically removed from the club's home, and especially separated from the entertainment "star system" in which the players circulate.

Consequently, football fans resemble the fans of leading musicians, actors, and media personalities, through their largely unidirectional relationship toward these household names. Thompson (1997) described this social framework in terms of "non-reciprocal relations of intimacy with distant others" (pp. 220–222). Fans refer to stars by first name, discuss their private lives and traits, collect biographical snippets, surround the family home or workplace with their images, and perhaps even fantasize about a loving, sexual relationship with their objects of affection. Star footballers, like other celebrities, are rarely in a position to reciprocate. Football matches before live audiences only afford a temporary break in the distance between stars and fans, but in any case, the divisions are symbolically retained. Football players at matches, or even when signing autographs or visiting sick children in hospital, continue to play the star role. Their "work with the public" is a form of emotional labor, necessitating a form of professional "deep acting," which Hochschild (1983) has previously documented. Thompson viewed fan identity as a strategy of the self, a deliberate entry into a relationship that is fundamentally different from those founded on face-to-face interaction. Consequently, we may add that such a relationship is dependent on specific media that allow for a continuous and multifarious flow of star-related signs toward the fan. In the West particularly, this must mean capital-governed signifiers, through product endorsement, television interviews, and even forays into other realms of popular culture, such as pop music. Again, for such public relations, football players and club officials are trained to draw upon an ever-expanding reservoir of clichés and dead metaphors to confirm typified public constructions of their personality. These more shallow, mediated forms of acting help to preserve the highly profitable, parallel football universe that has been constructed to supply the fan market.

The commodity-centered mediation of football qua entertainment intensifies, so the fan identity comes under pressure to enter the realm of the flâneur, the unreconstructed cool consumer. This process is most apparent as market representations of football are increasingly telescoped onto playing stars and their celebrity lifestyles (rather than what they do on the field of play). The process first appeared in the United Kingdom with the public identity of George Best, but it has reached a new category of representation with Beckham, whereas in global terms, Ronaldo is the tragic exemplar.[10] As commodity logic comes to prevail, we encounter a redoubled fetishizing of the star's exchange value, beyond merely transfer worth and club wages, but into the highly unstable environment of general marketability, fashion, and exposure in popular media. Thus, football stars are quickly nudged out of the limelight by new performers and are liable to experience a decline in their "rating" among distant fans to a degree that far outstrips their continuing regard among supporters or those within the game. The hot identification that fans once attached to stars embarks upon a categorical decline, as fans generally learn to cool their affections, in expectation that the next player qua commodity sign will arrive sooner than ever.

Cool/Consumer Spectators: Flâneurs

The cool consumer spectator is a football flâneur. The flâneur acquires a postmodern spectator identity through a depersonalized set of market dominated virtual relationships, particularly interactions with the cool media of television and the Internet.

The flâneur constitutes a distinctive urban social type first chronicled and characterized by Baudelaire in the mid-19th century, remolded sociologically by Simmel, expounded upon more critically by Walter Benjamin (1973, 1999) during the 1930s, and latterly the flâneur has been the subject of substantial debate among cultural theorists.[11] In its original sense, the flâneur was a modern urban stroller: Male and bourgeois, typically in full adulthood, he would promenade through boulevards and markets. For the true flâneur, "kaleidoscopic images and fragments whose novelty, immediacy and vividness, coupled with their fleeting nature and often strange juxtaposition, provided a range of aesthetic sensations and experiences" (Featherstone, 1995, p. 150). Benjamin's (1999) flâneur is understood in part as an idler and traveler, a student of physiognomy and character among the passing throng, essentially semidetached in his engagement with the crowds and commodities of the labyrinthine metropolis.

In its contemporary manifestation, I would suggest the flâneur is less gender specific. Class differences must remain, because the flâneur has the economic, cultural, and educational capital to inspire a cosmopolitan interest in the collection of experiences. Accordingly, the flâneur's social practices are increasingly oriented toward consumption.

The football flâneur may tend to be more male than female, but not by definition. The flâneur is more likely to be bourgeois and thus in pursuit of a multiplicity of football experiences. The flâneur adopts a detached relationship to football clubs, even favored ones. A true football flâneur, the cool consumer belongs only to a virtual community of strollers who window-shop around clubs. In the most extreme manifestation, national allegiances may also be exchanged on the grounds of competitive successes or mediated identification with superstar celebrities. The adornment of a team's attire is in tune with a couture aesthetic, drawn to the signifier (the shirt color, the shirt design, its crest, even its sponsor logo) rather than to what is signified conceptually (the specific, grounded identity of the club or the nation). The flâneur thereby avoids any personal consumption by the appended signs but instead consumes these signifiers in a disposable and cliché-like fashion, as if adopting a temporary tattoo. Moreover, the football flâneur's natural habitat is increasingly the virtual arena, seeking the sensations of football as represented through television, Internet, or perhaps in the future, the audiovisual bodysuit. Thus, television presentation of football is tailored toward a flâneur-type experience. Television compresses time-space differences, distilling entire matches or tournaments into 100-second transmissions of blinding, aestheticized action, to an accompanying backbeat that drifts between techno and opera.

The cool/consumer seeks relatively thin forms of social solidarity with other fellow fans. Within the context of a postemotional panoply of social relations, the flâneur is definitively low in genuine collective affect. Nevertheless, there are occasions when flâneurs congregate and thus come to simulate in a playful manner the football passion that they have witnessed in prior media representations of those who appear to be true supporters.[12] The cool consumer is a cosmopolitan, but not in the classical sense whereby constant perambulations produce a worldly merchant in ideas. Rather, this cosmopolitan has relatively little biographical or strategic interest in discerning an underlying meta-narrative from the medley of football signifiers around which the flâneur dances, save for the instrumental identification with an avant-garde, winning brand. Flâneurs evidence the "transferable loyalties of the postmodern passenger" (Turner, 1999, p. 48); accordingly, they are liable not only to switch a connection with teams or players, but also to forsake football for other forms of entertainment. And the true cosmopolis, the cultural setting, for the community of strollers is the non-place, such as the airport departure lounge or the most contemporary shopping mall (Augé, 1995).

Some of the largest world clubs have provided the flâneur with an increasingly welcoming shop window in which to gaze, thereby creating a quasi-community of cosmopolitans. And thus, relatively more committed, regular forms of engagement with these clubs (so long as they continue to win or to be chic) encourages the germination of a proxy form of narcissistic self-identity for the cool consumers. Invariably, association with winning is particularly favored, but so too are cosmopolitan signifiers of conspicuous wealth, European sophistication (French, Italian), or an avant-garde setting (high-tech stadium). Clubs thus become appendages, selected for what they may say about the flâneur's personality.

Flâneurs may seek to authenticate their cosmopolitan identity through direct and unfavorable representation of spectators that possess traditional or hot characteristics. Traditionalists are constructed as regressive figures from the past—chauvinists, romanticists, xenophobes—in sum, truculent locals who refuse to reconcile themselves to the ineluctable hegemony of neoliberal principles within football. Flâneurs might try to depict hot spectators as emotionally driven and thus intellectually incapable of appreciating the fineries of the game. Yet as we have noted, the real identity of the flâneur is rooted in persistent motion, classically in material terms but increasingly in virtual terms, through switching affiliations like television channels. Thus, the flâneur who endeavors to authenticate a stable football identity relative to other spectators is something of a contradiction in terms.

Motives, Landscapes, and the Paradoxes of Cross-Category Relationships

The four spectator categories examined above have been distinguished according to their different football identities and the distinctive, underlying relationships that they have toward the game. I shall avoid treating the reader as a flâneur and providing a highlighted recapitulation of arguments, but it is useful to elucidate briefly these categorical differences by reference to two analytical heuristics—the specific motivations and the spatial relationships of these spectator identities.

In terms of motive, supporters give their support to clubs because they are obligated to do so. The club provides the supporter not simply with an element of personal identity but a complex and living representation of the supporter's public identity. Followers forward various allegiances to clubs because it helps to sustain and spread their personal senses of participation in football. This diffusion of allegiances is structurally facilitated by an increasingly complex, mediated networking of football information and images. Fans are motivated to produce non-reciprocal relationships with distant others, which are qualitatively different to face-to-face relationships and which promote a consumption-oriented identity to bridge symbolically the socio-spatial divide. Finally, flâneurs are motivated to seek sensation, excitement, and thus to switch their gaze across clubs, players, and nations. The greater commodification of football, and emphasis on association with success, structures the flâneur's peripatetic pursuit of winning or chic teams.

In terms of their relationship to the material environment, supporters have inextricable biographical and emotional ties to the club's ground, which is a key cultural emblem of the surrounding community. Similarly, followers are cognizant of the symbolic significance of the ground to the club, but their dependency on mediated representations of favored clubs reflects their circumscribed ties to this other community. Fans experience a distant socio-spatial relationship to favored clubs and their stars. Consumption of star-focused products might affirm and demonstrate fan loyalties, but the communicative divisions remain even in face-to-face interludes as stars consciously reaffirm their celebrity identity. Finally, the flâneur's preferred habitat is replete with audiovisual stimulation, such that high-tech electronic media are particularly favored. As a mobile cosmopolitan, the flâneur lives in a cosmopolis of consumption and thus has no capacity to secure personal alignment with a club qua locally defined institution. Instead, club signifiers are adorned in a cool, market-oriented style, such that the most congruous landscapes for these displays must be the character-free non-places of what Augé would prefer to term "supermodernity."

The model forwarded here suggests a structural relationship between the various spectator categories. Fans and followers share some primary, paradoxical qualities in their basic constitution. As hot/consumers and traditional/cool spectators, their dichotomous identities border on oxymoron. Followers have a traditional position in regard to the game's culture, but that is tempered by a cool relationship toward the clubs followed. Fans possess a hot sense of loyalty to players and to clubs, but that is tempered by a market-centered approach toward surmounting symbolic distances. Consequently, this synthesis of apparently conflicting qualities ensures that followers and fans can display relatively thick and thin forms of social solidarity. Historically, we may also view these spectator categories as intermediary retreats, as part of a strategy of negotiation and accommodation, whereby gradually the traditional/hot properties of the supporter are dissolved into the cool/consumer practices of the flâneur, although this does point toward a deeper social paradox.

As presented here, supporters and flâneurs are literally in diametrical opposition to one another, but they do appear to be dependent on each other for different reasons. In an increasingly neoliberal financial environment, local supporters practicing realpolitik come to recognize that the club must attract the custom of cosmopolitan flâneurs to preserve its status and perhaps push on for more successes. But can the same be said of the wealthy cosmopolitan who flits over the locals? After all, the contemporary structures of football are geared toward global consumption. Football is dominated by transnational corporations, particularly the merchandise companies (Nike, Reebok, Adidas), the world's governing bodies (notably the Fédération Internationale de Football Association and UEFA), and the largest football clubs. Unquestionably, the football flâneur is the cultural consumer that these transnational corporations are committed to seduce; their overtures are motivated by the rather hazardous aim of securing the flâneur's attention and thus securing his or her conversion into a warmer (more regular) consumer. Such a fundamental transformation in football, as in other sports or other realms of popular culture, threatens a Pyrrhic victory for the neoliberal agenda. As the political philosopher Michael Walzer has argued in a broader context, "There is a sense in which the cosmopolitan is parasitic on people who are not cosmopolitans . . . you could not exist if there were not people who sat still and created the places that you visit and enjoy" (as cited in Carleheden and Gabriëls, 1997, p. 120).

Otherwise stated here, if supporters become flâneurs, then the spectacle that is created by the spectators themselves will be threatened. There will be no more curious displays of football tribalism past which to stroll or on which to gaze.[13]

Notes

1. See, for example, Conn (1997), Horton (1997), Fynn and Guest (1994), Giulianotti (1999), Lee (1998), Perryman (1997), Dempsey and Reilly (1998), and the more accommodative work by Szymanski and Kuypers (1999). At least two separate editions of the British Broadcasting Corporation's Panorama series have also assessed, with strong criticism, the affect of football's financial boom on its established grassroots spectators and players.

2. In highlighting the abandonment of match attendance by an architect and his wife, the relevant article pointed out that the poorest spectators were not alone in feeling financially and culturally marginalized from football (The Guardian, August, 22, 1999, http://www.guardian.co.uk/Archive/Article/0,4273,3894685,00.html).

3. There is a reasonable range of literature in this area. On North American sports generally, see Alt (1983); on Canadian sports and North American ice hockey, see respectively Gruneau (1983) and Gruneau and Whitson (1994); on basketball, see Andrews (1995).

4. As one football journalist explained, "It is difficult for those who care about their game and, more particularly, care about their team, to comprehend life without this obsession" (Allsop, 1997, p. 95).

5. In South America, most clubs remain private member associations, so that their swimming pool, gym, and other recreation facilities are all available to members in return for a modest annual fee.

6. By far the most successful text on UK football during the 1990s was Nick Hornby's Fever Pitch, which became a major bestseller, acquiring numerous awards before being turned into a stage play and film. Hornby's book is a kind of autobiography, in which the author claims that his football obsession has determined his life course. However, the "subcultural capital" of Hornby as genuine football man has been revalued; for example, some critics point disparagingly to his abandoning of Arsenal as a supporter during his time at university. More generally, some traditionalist supporters also refer critically to spectators who came into football during its 1990s boom as "post-Hornby fans."

7. For example, in Italy during the early 1990s, Sampdoria's ultras were "friendly" with Verona, Inter, Atalanta, Cremonese, and Parma fan groups; they were strongly opposed to fans from the lineage linking Genoa, Torino, Bologna, and Pisa (cf. Roversi, 1992, p. 58).

8. For example, there are the pro-Irish nationalist sentiments of some fans of Celtic and Manchester United, or the "Blues Brothers" network of Unionist fan groups (Chelsea, Glasgow Rangers, and Linfield of Northern Ireland).

9. I am indebted to Bea Vidacs for the first application of this concept to football identity and to her provision of the reference to Cohen.

10. For a discussion of how specific football players appear to fit into traditional (Stanley Matthews), modern (George Best), and postmodern (Paul Gascoigne) identity categories, see Giulianotti and Gerrard (2001b).

11. See, for example, Tester (1994), Featherstone (1995), and Weinstein and Weinstein (1993).

12. This is increasingly apparent at major tournaments such as the World Cup, when the carnival atmosphere before and during matches is often a strikingly sanitized, simulated version of supporter passion. The most extreme illustrations occur when a dead atmosphere among thousands of fans suddenly changes into highly animated collective behavior when the television cameras come into view.

13. Nor should one assume that an attempt to protect the interests of traditional supporters is an act of xenophobia toward those who want to join the football spectator community. There is no credible a priori argument that states that other spectator categories, including flâneurs, are incapable of harboring deeply intolerant attitudes towards some other communities. In addition, as Walzer (in Carleheden & Gabriëls, 1997, p. 129) himself argued, one may quite easily identify those genuinely intolerant communities and seek to remove such traditions, but all the while encourage the community members to adapt to the new conditions, to redefine their values.

Acknowledgments

My thanks to the two anonymous referees for their constructive and helpful suggestions regarding improvements on an earlier version of this article. I am indebted to Adrian Walsh for encouraging me to consider a Walzerian approach to sport sociology and to Mike Gerrard for putting up with my initial ideas on spectator categories in an earlier coauthored paper.

References

Allsop, D. (1997). *Kicking in the wind: The real life drama of a small-town football club.* London: Headline.

Alt, J. (1983). Sport and cultural reification: From ritual to mass consumption. *Theory, Culture and Society,* 1(3), 93–107.

Andrews, D. L. (1995, September 7–9). *The [trans]national basketball association: American commodity-sign culture and global-local conjuncturalism.* Paper presented at the First Annual Conference for Popular Culture, Manchester, UK.

Armstrong, G., & Giulianotti, R. (Eds.). (2001). *Fear and loathing in world football.* Oxford, UK: Berg.

Augé, M. (1995). *Non-places: An introduction to the anthropology of supermodernity.* London: Verso.

Bale, J. (1994). *Landscapes of modern sport.* Leicester, UK: Leicester University Press.

Baudrillard, J. (1990). *Seduction.* London: Macmillan.

Benjamin, W. (1973). *Charles Baudelaire: A lyric poet in the era of high capitalism.* London: NLB.

Benjamin, W. (1999). *The Arcades Project.* Cambridge, MA: Belknap.

Bourdieu, M. (1984). *Distinction.* London: Routledge and Kegan Paul.

Carleheden, M., & Gabriëls, R. (1997). An interview with Michael Walzer. *Theory, Culture and Society,* 14(1), 113–130.

Castells, M. (1996). *The network society.* Oxford, UK: Blackwell.

Cohen, R. (1978). Ethnicity: Problem and focus in anthropology. *Annual Review of Anthropology,* 7, 379–403.

Conn, D. (1997). *The football business.* Edinburgh, Scotland: Mainstream.

Critcher, C. (1979). Football since the war. In J. Clarke, C. Critcher, & R. Johnson (Eds.), *Working class culture: Studies in history and theory* (pp. 161–184). London: Hutchinson.

Dempsey, P., & Reilly, K. (1998). *Big money, beautiful game: Saving soccer from itself.* Edinburgh, Scotland: Mainstream.

Featherstone, M. (1995). *Undoing culture.* London: Sage.

Fynn, A., & Guest, L. (1994). *Out of time: Why football isn't working.* London: Simon & Schuster.

Giulianotti, R. (1999). *Football: A sociology of the global game.* Cambridge, UK: Polity.

Giulianotti, R., & Gerrard, M. (2001a). Cruel Britannia? Glasgow Rangers, Scotland and "hot" football rivalries. In G. Armstrong & R. Giulianotti (Eds.), *Fear and loathing in world football* (pp. 23–42). Oxford, UK: Berg.

Giulianotti, R., & Gerrard, M. (2001b). Evil genie or pure genius? The (im)moral football and public career of Paul "Gazza" Gascoigne. In D. L. Andrews & S. Jackson (Eds.), *Sport stars: The politics of sport celebrity* (pp. 124–137). London: Routledge.

Gruneau, R. (1983). *Class, sport and social development.* Champaign, IL: Human Kinetics.

Gruneau, R., & Whitson, D. (1994). *Hockey night in Canada.* Toronto, Canada: Garamond.

Hargreaves, J. (1986). *Sport, power and culture.* Cambridge, UK: Polity.

Hess, R., & Stewart, B. (Eds.). (1998). *More than a game: An unauthorised history of Australian Rules football.* Melbourne, Australia: Melbourne University Press.

Hochschild, A. R. (1983). *The managed heart: Commercialization of human feeling.* Berkeley: University of California Press.

Hopcraft, A. (1968). *The football man.* London: Simon & Schuster.

Horton, E. (1997). *Moving the goalposts.* Edinburgh, Scotland: Mainstream.

Lash, S. (1994). Expert-systems or situated interpretation? In U. Beck, A. Giddens, & S. Lash, *Reflexive modernization* (pp. 198–215). Cambridge, UK: Polity.

Lash, S., & Urry, J. (1987). *The end of organized capitalism.* Cambridge, UK: Polity.

Lash, S., & Urry, J. (1994). *Economies of signs and space.* London: Sage .

Lee, S. (1998). Grey shirts to grey suits: The political economy of English football in the 1990s. In A. Brown (Ed.), *Fanatics!* (pp. 32–49). London: Routledge.

McLuhan, M. (1964). *Understanding media*. London: Routledge.

Perryman, M. (1997). *Football United: New Labour, the task force and the future of the game*. London: Fabian Society.

Robertson, R. (1992). *Globalization: Social theory and global culture*. London: Sage.

Robson, G. (2000). *'No one likes us, we don't care': The myth and reality of Millwall fandom*. Oxford, UK: Berg.

Roversi, A. (1992). *Calcio, tifo e violenza* [Football, the fan, and violence]. Bologna, Italy: Il Mulino.

Scholte, J. A. (2000). *Globalization: A critical introduction*. Basingstoke, UK: Macmillan.

Szymanski, S., & Kuypers, T. (1999). *Winners and losers: The business strategy of football*. London: Viking Press.

Taylor, I. (1971a). "Football mad": A speculative sociology of football hooliganism. In E. Dunning (Ed.), *The sociology of sport: A selection of readings* (pp. 352–377). London: Frank Cass.

Taylor, I. (1971b). Soccer consciousness and soccer hooliganism. In S. Cohen (Ed.), *Images of deviance* (pp. 134–163). Harmondsworth, UK: Pelican.

Tester, K. (1994). *The flâneur*. London: Routledge.

Thompson, J. B. (1997). *The media and modernity: A social theory of the media*. Cambridge, UK: Polity.

Thornton, S. (1995). *Club cultures: Music, media and subcultural capital*. Cambridge, UK: Polity.

Turner, B. S. (1999). The possibility of primitiveness: Towards a sociology of body marks in cool societies. *Body & Society*, 5(2–3), 39–50.

Walsh, A., & Giulianotti, R. (2001). This sporting mammon: A normative analysis of the commodification of sport. *Journal of the Philosophy of Sport*, 28, 53–77.

Weinstein, D., & Weinstein, M. A. (1993). *Postmodern(ized) Simmel*. London: Routledge.

Williams, R. (1961). *The long revolution*. Harmondsworth, UK: Pelican.

Chapter 25

SOMETHING ABOUT BASEBALL

Gentrification, "Race Sponsorship," and Competing Class Cultures in Neighborhood Boys' Baseball

Sherri Grasmuck

In this ethnographic study, Sherri Grasmuck illustrates how youth sports, aided by gentrification, facilitated the formation of social capital that led to the racial integration of a previously segregated neighborhood in Philadelphia. Her analysis allows us to see how sports can play a key role in affecting race and class dynamics in given political contexts.

In the late 1960s White residents of a Philadelphia neighborhood called Fairmount, north of center city, regularly and often with the support of police, ran off Blacks who walked through the neighborhood.[1] A red-faced, Irish-Ukrainian Fairmounter, looking back at his teenage years, described the neighborhood this way:

> They called our neighborhood "White island" because we were surrounded. . . . When I was growing up there would have been fighting no matter what. We fought everyday. We fought our way to school. We fought our way home from school. We fought everyday.

Thirty years later, on a summer evening in 2001, three police cars surrounded and detained a group of four boys in Fairmount, two Black and two White, under suspicion of attempted car theft. As the police aggressively questioned the 14-year-old boys, a group of White Fairmounter adults surrounded the police cars to defend the interracial group of boys against this "police harassment." Among these adults was the same Fairmounter who had, as a teenager in the 1960s, as described above, fought Blacks transgressing the neighborhood. Yet on that summer night in 2001, after this incident, he loudly explained to a group of listeners why the police had really stopped the boys that night: "You want to know what they did wrong? I'll tell you what. They were guilty of 'walking while Black.' Or they were White and hanging with Blacks. That's what they did wrong."

What had happened in this neighborhood and to these adults to produce such surprising changes? One clue comes from the fact that these were not just any boys. They were baseball players, players who had played in the neighborhood baseball league for almost a decade. Another clue is that both of the Black boys were middle-class, and one of them now lived in the neighborhood. Many other clues to understanding this moment are uncovered by a look at the changes that swept Fairmount, along with its adjacent neighborhood, Spring Garden, in the last decades of the 20th century and at how neighborhood baseball changed over the same period.

Scholars who have studied race and sport have often debated whether sports activities promote social integration or merely reflect broader social inequalities within their games, benches, and locker rooms (Coakley, 2001; Gatz, Messner, & Ball-Rokeach, 2002). Depending on the context, sport can facilitate racial harmony or can contribute to racial division. On the negative side, sport events can become venues for racial hostilities, when teams representing different racial groups compete and give fans and players opportunities to vent game frustrations through racial channels. Other sports practices, such as "stacking"—the segregating of Blacks into certain team positions—or the underrepresentation in professional sports of minorities in leadership or "thinking positions," inflame racial resentments (Edwards, 1970, 1973; Eitzen, 1999; Lapchick and Benedict, 1993; Sage, 2001). On the positive side, sport enthusiasts point to the way sports can bring people of different backgrounds together. For example, three fourths of high school athletes told Louis Harris pollsters in 1993 that they had made friends across racial lines through sport (Eitzen, 1999, p. 18). Thus sports become a means of integration, not just for the participants but also for those who identify with the competing teams (Coakley, 2001). Eitzen (1999, p. 18) has identified some contexts in which sports can help build racial understandings, such as when teams permit players of different races to contribute equally to team success, and when the team with mixed races is successful.

Much of what we do know from the field of the sociology of sport, regarding the ameliorative or destructive impact of sport, comes from research on the top-level of sports, the college and professional levels. With this elite focus comes a heavy emphasis on how organized sports, controlled by a dominant class (Goodman, 1979), or corporate sports, controlled by a power elite, directs spectator attention away from social injustices (Hoch, 1972). This emphasis on "sports as opiate" (Coakley, 2001) leaves little maneuverability to human agents who might find pleasure and community amidst the constraints of sports rules and ideologies or even resist the status quo within sport arenas.

Critical sports sociologists, who have weighed extensive evidence on both sides of this debate, point to a more paradoxical verdict: Under certain conditions the consequences of sport can be destructive, by reinforcing dominant power relations and racial and gender inequalities, and under some conditions constructive, by undermining or challenging them (Gatz et al., 2002, p. 5). The answer might well depend on the type of sport and level of sport, whether it is informal, organized, or corporate sports. The challenge is to understand the particular circumstances when sports experiences are positive and healthy and when they are negative and destructive and to explain how and why (Coakley, 2001; Edwards, 2001).

This paper addresses this challenge by exploring two sets of tensions related to a process of racial integration and new class encounters in a neighborhood baseball league in the two gentrifying Philadelphia neighborhoods described above. There are plenty of stories in America of racial conflict and violence after neighborhood change. Here we explore the opposite—the features of neighborhood baseball that might have made a transition toward racial integration a relatively smooth one. Moreover, the encounter of folks of different socioeconomic backgrounds permits not just a look at how sport structured and processed neighborhood tensions but also how the competing class cultures of diverse parents created conflicting expectations about rights in and responsibilities toward public space and voluntary organizations.

Methods

The findings for this paper are based on a larger study of neighborhood gentrification,

baseball, and masculinity in a gentrifying area of Philadelphia.[2] I warmed the bleachers at the baseball field continuously for thirteen years watching the games and practices of my son and daughter between 1987 and 2002. I began an ethnographic study of the ball club in 1997, its changes over time and its relationship to the neighborhood. Working with a graduate student, over the next three years, we observed 121 games of the 7–9 and 10–12 teams and conducted 41 interviews with parents, coaches, and staff of FSA.[3]

I made the decision to present the real names of these two neighborhoods, following norms of journalism rather than sociology, as I believed the actual historical identities of these spaces mattered to the storytelling. One of my broader goals for this project was to prioritize sociological storytelling rather than to use the community to build abstract theory as an equally valid way of telling the truth (Sparkes, 2002; Grasmuck, 2005). However, I did not extend this "real naming" to individuals

Figure 1

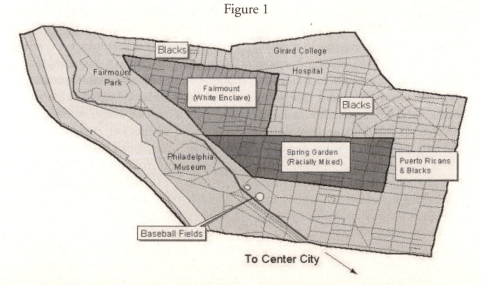

Fairmount/Spring Garden and Surrounding Areas. *Source*: Social Science Data Library, Temple University. This map was created using ArcView with the assistance of Brian Lawton.

in the community. Although some neighborhood folks preferred that I use their real names, some did not. For consistency's sake, all of the names of persons presented here are pseudonyms, even in the case of those who played recognized historical roles in establishing FSA as an organization.

Neighborhood Racial Transition

By the year 2000, most children who played baseball in the Fairmount and Spring Garden neighborhoods of Philadelphia played it on the Von Colln Fields of Fairmount Park, 10 blocks from city hall. Fairmount and Spring Garden physically meet here on their western borders, just opposite the impressive Philadelphia Museum of Art. The ball field is just one block down from the museum at the southwestern corner of the Spring Garden neighborhood (Figure 1). However, before this ball field evolved into a site of social unity for the two neighborhoods, residents of the two neighborhoods lived in different social worlds.

In the early 1950s, both Spring Garden and Fairmount were predominantly White, working-class neighborhoods with a strong representation of Irish, English, Ukrainian, Polish, and Italian ethnic groups. Fairmount remained subdivided into a number of small pockets, where different blocks were often dominated by different first- and second-generation White immigrants (Cybriwsky, 1978, p. 61). As a White enclave bordering poorer Black neighborhoods to the north, Fairmount had a strong race identity. As a 60-year-old barber who had grown up in Fairmount remembered this period:

You had the Italians living on Aspen Street and 23rd Street. The Irish were throughout the neighborhood. The Ukrainians were

down this way and a lot of Greeks were at 27th and 28th. It was pretty mixed with those groups. . . . Blacks would try to come down here, through here and all. This was a tough neighborhood, so it would be like hand-to-hand combat. There *were* some Black families, around 23rd and Oliver, and I went to school with some Blacks and Puerto Ricans, but it was mostly White. This area just seemed to hold on. I called this like "Custer's Last Stand." We got the city here [signaling south], got the park over here [signaling west], Girard College on the north and then the prison [signaling east]. So kind of like boundaries. . . . But things have changed now. The old-timers were more racial than we are.

While Fairmount remained an almost exclusively White area during the 1950s, Spring Garden underwent considerable racial change. First, because of its relative proximity to the first Spanish-speaking church in the city, Spring Garden became the first area of settlement for Puerto Rican migrants arriving from New Jersey agricultural areas in the 1950s (Ericksen et al., 1985), who constituted 31% of the population in Spring Garden by the end of the decade (see Table 1). Second, during the same period the proportion of African Americans in the area just to the east of Spring Garden doubled, growing from 15% to 34% (Whalen, 2001, p. 186).[4] Overall then, while Fairmount remained almost exclusively White in the 1950s, almost half of Spring Garden residents identified as either Latino or Black by the decade's end (Grasmuck, 2005, p. 20).

This racial transition in the Spring Garden area was far from smooth. White residents of Spring Garden, especially the poorer ones, resisted their new neighbors

TABLE 1   *Racial Changes in the Neighborhoods of Fairmount, Spring Garden, and Philadelphia, 1950–2000*

	FAIRMOUNT			SPRING GARDEN				PHILADELPHIA[a]		
Year	Population	% White	% Black	% Latino[b]	Population	% White	% Black	% Latino[b]	% White	% Black	% Latino[b]
1950	10,764	99.3	0.5	—	16,737	84.5	15.5	—	81.7	18.2	0.1
1960	8,769	97.2	2.5	0.1	9,289	81.8	17.8	30.8	79.0	20.4	0.5
1970	7,620	93.0	6.1	2.1	7,436	82.0	14.9	27.7	68.6	30.1	2.3
1980	6,532	94.1	4.7	1.8	5,694	69.1	10.7	22.4	59.2	35.9	3.7
1990	5,882	91.0	6.7	2.7	5,483	74.2	12.8	14.0	53.5	39.6	5.3
2000	5,962	84.1	8.2	2.9	5,386	73.9	16.0	10.4	45.1	43.1	8.5

Source: Years 1950–1990, compiled from an aggregate file of the U.S. Census created by William Yancey with the assistance of Joshua Freely, Social Science Data Library, Temple University; 2000 data from the U.S. Census 2000 Web site, Summary File 3.

[a] Philadelphia is defined here as excluding the two census tracts represented by Fairmount (136) and Spring Garden (134).

[b] Census questions relevant to the categories of race and Latinos changed twice between 1950 and 2000. Throughout the period, "race" and "Hispanic origin" have been operationalized as separate variables in the Census. For the first time in 1960, in addition to the race question, respondents were asked, in a separate ethnicity question, if they were "Puerto Rican" as the only possible Hispanic response. Beginning in 1980, respondents were asked, on a 100% basis, if they were "Latino." Before 1980, the Latino origin question was only asked on a sample basis. Therefore, one cannot always find comparable tabulations on Latinos on the census-tract level in the 1960–1970 period and the 1980–2000 period. Starting in 2000, moreover, people could check off more than one race, making new mixed-race categories possible, and lowering the proportions answering "White" or "Black." These changes explain why in this table the categories White, Black, and Latino sometimes surpass 100% in the same year (1960 and 1970) and sometimes drop below 100% (in 2000), when mixed-race categories are added to the census but not reported here.

with racial riots and violence. During the summer of 1953, one of the worst riots of the city occurred near the corner of Mt. Vernon and 16th Street, with fighting that involved anywhere from 300 to 1,000 people and lasted more than 2 hours. Shawn, a Spring Garden resident, remembered his youth in the neighborhood this way:

> Twenty years ago this was a bad neighborhood. . . . You wouldn't walk past here. The Puerto Ricans would just jump you. Blacks couldn't walk down through the neighborhood. We had fights at the Art Museum all the time. . . . I had a hard time because I lived above Fairmount (in Spring Garden) and we hung out below Fairmount. But I had to go home at night. Puerto Ricans would actually wait up at night. But we had one Puerto Rican kid who lived on Fairmount Avenue, and he used to walk me home at night. . . . But mostly we used to get in fights just be-

cause they were Black and we were White. . . . It was Fairmount. Blacks weren't supposed to walk through Fairmount.

For many Fairmount residents, this racial transition in the area to their south reinforced their long held sense of being a White oasis. The Fairmount area was indeed racially distinct from its surrounding areas (Figure 1). Fairmounters' fears of racial integration were not realized; throughout the period of Spring Garden's racial transformation, Fairmount remained almost 100% White. Cybriwski (1978), who studied Fairmount in the 1970s, identified three factors central to Fairmount's racial stability. First, Fairmounters were much more likely to own their homes, which made the rate of vacancies during this period considerably slower in Fairmount than in Spring Garden.[5] This lower turnover meant fewer opportunities for newcomers in Fairmount than Spring Garden. Second, when vacancies did occur in Fairmount, they were often managed informally through relatives or word of mouth. A village-like cohesiveness made it relatively easy to discriminate against Blacks or Puerto Ricans entering the housing market. Jessie, who lived in the heart of Fairmount all her life, described how it worked:

> Jessie: Thirty years ago this was a very prejudiced neighborhood. I mean everybody in it was prejudiced and that's just . . . the way you were brought up. . . . They kept everything closed mouthed. . . . They called this neighborhood the "Oreo," that's what they used to say, "We're an Oreo cookie." . . . And to hold strong, you stuck together like glue. [You didn't] put a sign on your house if you were selling it. It was word of mouth. . . . I've even been guilty of that. Ten years ago, a woman was renting her house on this block, and I said to her, "Watch what you rent to because while you are out in Bryn Mawr, I'm across the street from the garbage you put in the house."
> S.G.: And what you had in mind then was someone Black?
> Jessie: Right. And she knew what I was saying, and she said, "I wouldn't do that to you." [laughter] I think she was afraid I'd come for her. [laughter]

Third, beyond the closed housing market, Fairmount's youth had a well-established reputation for violently defending its space against transgressors.[6] Well after Puerto Ricans and Blacks had established a strong presence in surrounding areas, Fairmounter corner youths continued their violent confrontations with Blacks who passed through the neighborhood. And, although lower-class families were often harshly criticized by other Fairmount residents as "white trash," they were also often the ones "taking care of business" by enforcing racial boundaries, just as the poorest Whites in Spring Garden were associated with street fighting with Puerto Ricans in the 1950s (Cybriwsky, 1978; Whalen, 2001). These internal divisions, however, had always paled in comparison with the boundaries drawn between this White enclave and the surrounding areas. Then, as the neighborhood to the south changed again, this time with the arrival of new higher income Whites, a new "other" emerged. This both alleviated the racial fears of Fairmounters and posed a threat of a different nature to the old neighborhood.

Gentrification

If the high concentration of rental property in Spring Garden helped facilitate the entrance of Puerto Ricans in the 1950s, it also helped push them out. In the 1970s, Spring Garden began to gentrify. With its close proximity to downtown Philadelphia and its large stock of historic townhouses and rental properties, Spring Garden started to attract many young professional newcomers. The rapidly rising rents and housing values of the 1970s hit hard the poorer sectors of Spring Garden, the struggling Puerto Rican community. Despite resistance, the poorer sectors of the Latino population were pushed out and moved toward the growing community of Latinos in northeast Philadelphia. While Latinos constituted 30% of the Spring Garden area in 1970, they represented only 14% by 1990 and 10% by 2000 (Grasmuck, 2005, p. 20).

TABLE 2   *Economic and Housing Changes in Fairmount and Spring Garden Neighborhoods Compared with Citywide Changes, 1960–2000*

| | FAIRMOUNT | | | | SPRING GARDEN | | | | PHILADELPHIA | | | |
Year	Owner occupied (%)	Poor (%)	Median income ($)	Average housing value	Owner occupied (%)	Poor (%)	Median income ($)	Average housing value	Owner occupied (%)	Poor (%)	Median income ($)	Average housing value
1960	51.3	16.3	5,015	6,700	14.5	44.1	2,508	7,400	59.9	17.6	6,039	9,842
1970	48.5	9.7	9,009	7,100	10.4	21.1	9,083	9,200	56.2	12.2	9,834	12,683
1980	50.9	10.7	17,249	37,700	16.6	24.0	15,005	73,900	55.4	17.6	17,336	30,760
1990	48.6	9.8	34,503	94,400	31.3	16.8	34,691	168,200	62.0	20.7	24,603	48,400
2000	58.5	11.0	46,250	100,600	40.0	19.9	41,536	191,300	64.4	22.9	30,746	61,000

Note: Poverty was not officially computed in 1960; the 1960 numbers in this table are based on a calculation using the 1970 poverty level, the rate of inflation, and changes in the consumer price index between 1960 and 1970. Philadelphia is defined as excluding the two census tracts represented by Fairmount (136) and Spring Garden (134); "Owner occupied" is based on all housing units; "Median income" is based on the household; "Average housing value" refers only to owner occupied residences. *Source:* Years 1950–1990, compiled from an aggregate file of the U.S. Census created by William Yancey with the assistance of Joshua Freely, Social Science Data Library, Temple University; 2000 data from the U.S. Census 2000 Web site, Summary File 3.

From a working-class area with significant pockets of poverty, numerous basement bars, corner taverns, small industries, and three neighborhood Catholic schools in the 1960s, grew a visibly more affluent one. As the price of real estate in Spring Garden rose, gentrification also extended into Fairmount. Both neighborhoods were transformed by the arrival of more affluent professional residents but in different degrees. With gentrification proceeding at a more rapid pace in Spring Garden than in Fairmount, the proportion of college-educated residents in Spring Garden was already notably higher by the early 1970s (16.4% compared with 7.4%) and stayed significantly higher throughout the 1980s (Grasmuck, 2005, p 25). This disparity established new grounds for suspicion between the two areas, disparities now based more on class than on race. But as gentrification continued northward into the Fairmount area throughout the 1980s, these same educational disparities became more salient *within* the two neighborhoods. Just

as the arrival of new professionals in the more southern neighborhood, Spring Garden, had pushed out many Puerto Ricans in the 1960s and 1970s, the continued movement of professionals northward into Fairmount in the 1980s also squeezed out many White Fairmounters.

Despite early tensions and suspicions between old-timers and newcomers, the arrival of new White professionals marked a consolidation of Spring Garden as a predominantly White neighborhood again. This gradual transition eased racial fears to the extent that some of the racial riots in the early 1970s in Fairmount against the entrance of new Black families[7] subsided over the next decade. But this was a gradual process, and although more middle-class professionals entered Spring Garden and Fairmount in the 1990s without incident, some of the first Black professionals who had arrived in the 1970s remembered a hostile welcoming. One Black professor, Helena, whose family moved into Fairmount in 1973, described how they bypassed the

TABLE 3   *Changes in Educational Background of Fairmount and Spring Garden Residents Compared with the City of Philadelphia, 1970–2000*

Year	Fairmount college graduates (%)	Spring Garden college graduates (%)	Philadelphia[a] college graduates (%)
1970	7.4	16.4	6.8
1980	19.4	27.8	12.8
1990	45.2	56.7	15.2
2000	54.3	57.4	17.9

Source: Years 1970–1990, compiled from an aggregate file of the U.S. Census created by William Yancey with the assistance of Joshua Freely, Social Science Data Library, Temple University; 2000 data from the U.S. Census 2000 Web site, Summary File 3.

[a]Philadelphia is defined here as excluding the two census tracts represented by Fairmount (136) and Spring Garden (134).

closed real estate market with help from an interracial couple and defended themselves in the early years of their arrival.

It was rough when we first moved here. We used to live in "Pig Alley," in a house two doors down from here. But we were renting. We entered from the back. The first couple of weeks, the local guys threw something into the window. Earl [her husband] had to go out there and straighten them out . . . the teenagers, the White gang that hung out down at the corner. There was a lot of drugs. . . . He knew who the kid was. Earl went up there and nearly killed him. He ran and got him and really shook him up. . . . And another day, Earl was sitting on the front porch and his wallet was sitting there next to him, and somebody ran by and took the wallet. He chased him down too. He got his wallet back and scared them. After that we haven't had any problems.

As she recounted these events, 30 years later, in the living room of her home that borders the Fairmount–Spring Garden divide, she contrasted these experiences and her early feelings with her current, extremely positive feelings about the neighborhood. She noted the importance of baseball to her integration. Beyond the fact that Helena and her husband were highly educated professionals, another critical piece of information is that her son and daughter were excellent athletes who had played in the neighborhood baseball league. The theme of baseball in this story of a Black professional family's gradual feeling of acceptance in the neighborhood parallels the baseball connection established in the vignette at the beginning of this article about the White Fairmount man who, as a youth, had fought Blacks in the area and yet who, as an adult, defended their right of passage in the 1990s. Both cases of transformation, however understood, are deeply embedded in youth baseball, the center-piece of recreation in Fairmount.

Over this 30-year period of neighborhood change, the local youth baseball organization changed even more dramatically. Although historically an all-White organization, by the mid 1990s approximately one third of the boys playing in the younger division were children of color. And peace prevailed. Given this neighborhood's past, how did this happen? The answer to this question must begin with a brief history of neighborhood baseball and its evolution from informal play to structured, competitive games.

Baseball as the Soul of the Neighborhood

Neighborhood play in Fairmount in the 1950s centered on baseball. Kids played informal games for years at 24th Street and Fairmount Avenue, a prominent block between the two neighborhoods. Sometime in the early 1960s, a neighborhood man wanted to organize games among the boys. He got together some friends and began a baseball club, originally called simply, the Braves, out of the Catholic War Veterans Post and recruited boys from the families connected to the post. Because there was no longer a field in the neighborhood, the neighborhood guys would have them all meet at a specified corner in Fairmount and drive the boys about 3 miles north to "the Dairy," a section of Fairmount Park off Kelly Drive, in an old station wagon they called the "Fairmount Bomber." They organized teams according to "corners," where different clusters of boys hung out.

Around the same time, when Tom O'Connors,[8] another Fairmounter who had

grown up playing ball with these teams, turned 21, he started his own traveling team sponsored by a different veterans' post in the neighborhood, the Parkway VFW, and recruited about 15 of the best players from the original Braves. By the next year, O'Connors had 50 players and had to organize several teams. These traveling teams continued to practice at "the Dairy" and began to play competitive games in South Philadelphia. O'Connors looked to his friends to help him out with the coaching and thereby established a pattern that was to continue for decades in the organization whereby coaches were recruited strictly by word of mouth from neighborhood friendship networks, some of whom were parents and some of whom were not. Both the in-house teams and the traveling teams worked as a loose coalition until 1967, when personality conflicts and internal divisions provoked the men more associated with the travel teams to break away and form a separate organization newly named the Fairmount Sports Association (FSA). Both the Fairmount Braves and FSA coexisted for a brief period, until the original Braves folded, and FSA emerged as the exclusive neighborhood baseball club, still organizationally based at the Catholic War Veterans Post.

The driving of kids back and forth from the neighborhood to the Dairy in Fairmount Park continued until the late 1960s, when the coaches decided they needed to play closer to the neighborhood and selected a nearby city-owned block, formally part of Fairmount Park, the largest urban park in the United States. Their eventual success in securing permission to use this parkland is all the more surprising when one considers that this block is strategically located among major historic landmarks of

Philadelphia. It borders a broad, tree-lined boulevard called the Ben Franklin Parkway, which dramatically connects the vast Philadelphia Museum of Art, situated on a granite hill on one end, with the impressive late 19th-century structure, city hall, at the other end. One of the obstacles to the use of this contested space was that, while it was city-owned, it was not controlled by the recreation office of the city but was officially part of Fairmount Park. The Fairmount Park Commission saw it as an open green space visible from the Franklin Parkway (some even described it as the "Champs-Elysées of Philadelphia") and wanted its park image to remain.

Gaining the right to use this public space was a gradual process requiring street smarts, persistence, and a "quiet confrontation" with local police officers. This case stands in sharp contrast to Goodman's (1979) description of the way dominant economic and cultural groups imposed organized sports on working-class youth in the Lower East Side of Manhattan to eliminate immigrant street culture in the early 20th century. Here we have working-class residents fighting dominant cultural groups for rights to public parkland to serve their own definitions of legitimate use of public space, in this case organized baseball. By the early 1970s they had succeeded: FSA received formal permission to use the land and spent 2 years leveling the field. Neighborhood men built two batting backstops on the property and began devoting themselves to the arduous task of maintaining the rough fields. And they continued to maintain the fields as a condition for the leasing of the grounds for the price of $1 a year from the city for the next 30 years. This block, soon to become known in the neighborhood as "the field," and remain so for

the next 40 years, also immediately borders the Rodin Museum, also on the Parkway. Any visitor contemplating the outdoor, gateway statute of Rodin's "Thinker" in the springtime only need glance left to see the ballgames that came to be a regular feature, after the late 1960s, of this vast, open, public space.

The original terms for the use of the public space included a substantial commitment to maintain the physical appearance of the land as parkland. The neighborhood men took up the challenge and transformed the block into a beautiful lush green surface of well-manicured grass and turf. Inevitably, this kind of transformation, built on neighborhood labor, instilled a sense of ownership and territoriality into the space. The claiming of this space for community use left with it collective "memory traces" that established baseball and this voluntary association as central to the "character" of this community (Molotch, Freudenburg, & Paulsen, 2000) and defined baseball as a "beauty asset" that Fairmounters would defend for the next 3 decades.

Letting Outsiders In

In these early years of FSA baseball, all the kids came from the neighborhood and almost exclusively from the three Catholic schools in Fairmount that existed then. Although there was some limited involvement of local Latino families who were part of the same Catholic schools, these children were overwhelmingly White.[9] The organization did not draw upon the large population of Black children from bordering neighborhoods. For one thing, the origins of the organization as an informal operation out of a veterans post meant that it was next to impossible to know when and where to sign up to play in the spring if you were outside of the social networks of these neighborhood men. Up until the mid 1980s, registration for the spring season occurred over two weekends in February at the Catholic War Veterans Post, where all the baseball equipment was stored for the year and where neighborhood men regularly congregated to drink beer together and socialize. The inaccessibility of the registration also fed into a culture of racial exclusion that had dominated in the neighborhood. As one Fairmounter coach described it,

Listen. We have our own Halloween. We call it "Whiteween." Parents are notified in their mailboxes when our Halloween is, so they don't have to be attacked on regular Halloween, or be run over by wolf packs. We have our own Halloween separate for that reason. . . . Twenty years ago that's how it would be here (with baseball). We would notify who we wanted to about registration. It would be delivery to your house, instead of putting it in the newspaper and publicizing everything. That's how it would have been handled 20 years ago. Registration wouldn't be open. It would be closed.

The tightness of the neighborhood, the reputation for racial exclusion, and the inaccessibility of the sign-ups meant few people needed to be turned away. They simply did not turn up.

Fairmount baseball first started to change in the early 1970s when several things happened that would permanently transform its insular nature. First, the rapid gentrification of the area meant a rather dramatic loss of population, especially in the relative numbers of children in the area. This meant a relative scarcity of children eligible for baseball. Between 1950 and 1990, the pop-

ulation of Fairmount dropped by almost half, from 10,764 to 5,882. Spring Garden's population declined even more sharply over the same period. By 1990 it had dropped to approximately one third of its 1950 size (Table 1). As the local population declined, and the social backgrounds of Fairmount and Spring Garden residents changed, the traditional base of the Catholic schools in the area declined dramatically. The lack of children in the area meant the viability of strictly "local" baseball was at risk. This was recognized by the original leadership of FSA in the early 1970s, who made a series of strategic decisions to insure an ample supply of children for the organization and its ability to launch a full spectrum of teams for each division. The organization would have to be "opened" up, first to the children of the new professionals in the area, who were already entering, and second to children from other Center City areas.

Second, beyond the scarcity of children, the friendship networks of local children, newcomers, and Fairmounters expanded to include children from outside the neighborhood. As the neighborhood gentrified, the presence of a growing group of children who attended non-Catholic private schools, Quaker, and secular, public, and nonparish Catholic schools outside the neighborhood also grew. Because a growing proportion of these children attended schools outside the neighborhood, the networks of information about the neighborhood and its recreational opportunities expanded. Many of these children had strong networks to middle-class minority children. These children and their parents played a part in sponsoring middle-class children of color into FSA. Quite a number of Black parents I interviewed mentioned that they learned about FSA's programs through these private school networks. Thus, ironically, although the entry of these largely White professionals into Spring Garden had played a part in pushing out Latino residents from the area, their sponsorship of middle-class children of color into neighborhood baseball also played a part in breaking down the racial isolation of Fairmount. But only a part. In addition, the fact that the one surviving Catholic school in the area, St. Francis, could no longer rely predominantly on neighborhood children to sustain itself, and drew increasingly from neighborhoods of color in the surrounding areas, also played a role. As this school increasingly integrated over time, some White Fairmounter children also sponsored the entrance of their school friends of color into the ranks of FSA. Both of these sources provided a kind of "race sponsorship" into the local space.

Third, several factors combined to give FSA greater visibility and political accountability in the city in the mid 1980s. Before this time, there were no physical markers of the organization at the ball field. Children desperate for restroom facilities were often shepherded to a tolerant neighbor's house a few blocks away. Several years after my family had moved to Spring Garden in 1984, I remember driving by the field and seeing kids playing baseball in uniforms. I tried to find out how to sign up my daughter to play T-ball. No one I asked seemed to know until it occurred to me to ask the mother of two girls on the block who went to the neighborhood Catholic school. She explained that I should go to a smoke-filled backroom, "kind of a bar," up at one of the veterans' posts in Fairmount, on one of two Saturday nights, a few months before the season starts. They would collect the registration fee, and then a coach would call about a month later to tell me what team my daughter was on and where to go to practice. "How would I find all this out if I didn't know you?" I asked. "You wouldn't," she replied.

The ball field remained essentially a large, leveled lot until 1985, when the president of FSA and the local ward leader persuaded John Street, the local city council representative, to secure Mayor Wilson Goode's approval for the construction of a clubhouse with bathroom facilities, a concession area, and a meeting room for the organization. Five years later, in the middle of the season of 1990, the new building with its concession stand and restrooms opened with an agreement from the City that FSA, in exchange for the maintenance of the field, the grounds, and the building by its volunteers, would rent the space and facilities for $1 a year, ratified in 5-year contracts.

From that point on, anyone driving by and seeing large groups of children playing organized games could inquire at the concession stand on one side of the new building and receive information about sign-up procedures. It is of no small significance that the city council representative, and the mayor who ultimately supported this neighborhood initiative, were African-American politicians who represented large minority constituencies beyond the neighborhood. The completion of this building, and the involvement of city officials, was a turning point for the organization, as it marked a visible transition of organizational headquarters from an insulated informal club within a Catholic veterans' organization, controlled by a small group of neighborhood men, to a highly visible building constructed with city funds with a new accountability to public officials.

Finally, although White gentrification in Spring Garden had contributed to pushing out many residents of color, largely Puerto Rican, in the 1970s and 1980s, throughout the 1990s growing numbers of Black professional residents began to appear in the area. The entrance of the children of these Black newcomers from Spring Garden into FSA, combined with the other, largely middle-class minority children from outside the area who had already entered FSA, meant that by the mid 1990s, approximately one third of the youngest children playing organized baseball in Fairmount were children of color. Anyone in the 1960s closely monitoring how Blacks were excluded and sometimes violently expelled from this area, would have found such an outcome surprising indeed. One Fairmounter mother who had grown up playing baseball in the neighborhood said the rapid racial change in FSA took her by surprise:

Well I know my reaction to opening day and the day after it was like, "Did they send flyers out all over the city?" I was just like, "Where did they all come from, I mean, where did they all find out about us?" And it's like word of mouth. And I mean there's nothing you can really do. When you have a league and it's opened up for enrollment, that's it.

This racial transformation of neighborhood baseball occurred not only relatively rapidly, compared to the two surrounding neighborhoods, but relatively harmoniously. How was that? Beyond the demographic changes and the new accountability to Black politicians, the answer relates to two factors, "race sponsorship" and the nature of baseball itself.

Race Sponsorship

The importance of what I call race sponsorship in the smooth integration of FSA cannot be underestimated. Race sponsorship, as I define it, occurs when an individual or family enters a formerly exclusive space aligned with or sponsored by an individual with legitimate membership status. This is similar to the moment Pee Wee Reese of the Brooklyn Dodgers called a timeout to embrace Jackie Robinson in 1947, as a dramatic silent confrontation to screaming bigots in the stands of Cincinnati.[10] In FSA, race sponsors helped create pockets of safe space for new minority members in this early stage of integration. Sometimes this was a "remote sponsorship," where a leader of the organization would extend a welcome to a minority stranger in the face of members who demonstrated a more hostile reception. The motives for this kind of sponsorship are almost irrelevant and might be little more than a strategic move on the part of the sponsor to fill the ranks of the organization. The important function of such a leader or sponsor is to resist the "race bulldogs"—the more overt racists in the organization, those who dedicate themselves to "boundary work," and would exclude Blacks, for example, under almost any circumstance if not kept in check by fellow insiders.

I saw this kind of sponsorship on numerous occasions by strategic leaders of FSA in the 1990s. Several examples can illustrate this. On two weekends in February of every year, organizational leaders of FSA, some insider coaches and their friends from the neighborhood, often congregate in the small, windowless meeting room of the clubhouse to await the arrival of parents signing up their children for the next season of baseball.

A good deal of socializing occurs over the course of these two weekends. It is also a good strategic place to be if you're a coach who is looking to pick up new talented kids who might not be known to the other coaches. Once this registration is over, the league selects its coaches, holds a draft, and has no formal obligations to accept any late-comers into the league. Accepting those who come late and charging them a late fee is a discretionary decision. This makes the postregistration period an opportune time for excluding anyone who might be considered undesirable.

During one of these weekends, in the mid 1990s when the number of Black children was just beginning to noticeably increase, I went to this "office" to pay the $80 inscription fee and register my son. There were two chairs seated in front of the sign-up desk for those registering. I was seated at one, filling out forms, while a heavy-set Black mother, filling out a registration form for her son, sat next to me. After she left, a Fairmounter named Carl, who regularly hangs out at the clubhouse and qualifies for what I have called a "race bulldog," softly mumbled to a small group of men standing around something about, "Watch out, that chair is still warm." I glanced up to see the expression of Brian, one of the leaders of the organization seated opposite me. As he looked up he frowned disapprovingly in Carl's direction. The reprimand was subtle and involved no overt loss of face for Carl but served to silence him and the snickers of another listener.

Commentary from two other FSA coaches also confirms the importance of sponsorship by strategic FSA leaders as well as coaches. William, a Black school principal I interviewed whose two sons had played for 5 years in the league, also stressed the role of certain FSA strategic leaders in welcoming new people of color "without a lot of ruffled feathers,"

> I've heard other people who have complained but when I ask questions about it, I think sometimes they may be overly reacting, you know, overly sensitive to what has been, what someone has said or done to them. . . . If there is a problem, I think that there are ways to deal with that problem. I think Brian is very approachable. I think the commissioners are approachable. But Brian, specifically, is very approachable about problems, and I think he's very open to looking for solutions.

It would be rather surprising if a social space like Fairmount, with the kind of racial exclusion and racism that had plagued the neighborhood in the past, would have produced a group of adult men where racist feelings or subtle racist behaviors were entirely absent. The integration of the baseball space certainly did not mean this. But the extent to which the leadership of FSA reached out on a regular basis to a stream of new Black families, and sponsored their entry with a welcoming stance, was remarkable. Their willingness to do this, while holding their "race bulldogs" mostly in check, set the stage for the race integration that followed.

Coupled with the sponsorship of early Black children into FSA by strategic leaders, the relatively low level of interest of their parents in getting very involved in the organization of FSA meant they posed little threat to insiders. The first Black parents who entered the organization lived largely outside the neighborhood, in Center City

or surrounding areas, and were primarily interested in a safe space for their children
that would not require a large time commitment. As one Black lawyer expressed it:

> I don't feel like they necessarily need me to
> do anything, and that's fine. I'm just happy
> that we have the league. If they can handle
> it, fine. But nobody really asked me to par-
> ticipate in any leadership way anyway. . . .
> But I don't have the time. There's a lot
> about FSA that I would like to see changed,
> but I don't have the time to really make it
> happen, so there's no point to complain
> about something you can't do a thing
> about.

Beyond the organizational leadership, at
the city level, the consolidation of Black
politicians in strategic positions of power,
including as neighborhood representatives
to the city council, added an additional incentive to facilitate the smooth reception of
new Black families into FSA. One White
Fairmount mother contrasted the current
openness of the organization to the past she
remembered in this way:

> I think it can happen now because of the
> way the laws are set up. It kind of ties your
> hand. Where 20 years ago I think them
> laws were like stuck in a box somewhere.
> And everybody just closed their eyes to it.
> Ignorance. Whatever you want to call it.

And 20 years before, a White leadership
also dominated the city, and baseball was
strictly a neighborhood affair. A Black father, William, who gave several FSA leaders
the bulk of the credit for welcoming in
families of color, nonetheless noted the importance of this background political cli-

mate and two strategic African-American
politicians:

> Well I think the leadership set the tone. I
> think the other thing, from a practical
> standpoint, the leadership, Fairmount's
> Sport Association, has received a lot of sup-
> port from John Street and he was the coun-
> cilman then and now from, what's his
> name, Darrell Clark. You know they get
> state money. They get city money. And I
> think they understand that part of that, in
> order to do that, you have to show that
> there is some, you know some positive, af-
> firmative kind of plan for the . . . for what
> they do, and it's worked out fine.

Remote race sponsorship by a few strategic leaders, however, could not bring about
the kind of race integration seen at FSA if it
were not also occurring in multiple ways at
a more grassroots level as well. In addition
to sponsorship by leaders, and greater accountability to Black leaders, more intimate
forms of race sponsorship were also significant to the integration process. Numerous
Black professional parents I interviewed
mentioned that they originally found out
about FSA through their child's White
friends at the private school they attended
outside the neighborhood. These friendships structured the context of entry, such
that an exclusion of one child could easily
translate into conflicts with another, whose
exclusion could not be justified along racial
lines and whose parents might have had
more social resources to resist.

Helena, the Black professor, and her family, whom I described above as one of the
early Black families in Fairmount who had
been tormented by hostile teenagers, provides another example of race sponsorship.

This family's very entrance into the neighborhood had been sponsored originally by a Black real estate agent who rented them their first apartment in Fairmount.

> Helena: "Michelle [a Black real estate agent] used to live above us and owned the building. They were an interracial marriage, and they would catch it upstairs, and we would catch it downstairs. They [the neighbors] would really just throw things at them. So when Earl, my husband, went out there and took care of them, it slowed up a lot because they just thought he was crazy."
>
> S.G.: "So when you guys lived up there, were those two apartments the only Black people in the neighborhood? On that block?"
>
> Helena: "Almost in the neighborhood. There were very few African Americans in the neighborhood. Michelle was probably the pioneer. And then, she rented to us. Later she sold us this house."

But it was sponsorship into baseball that provided their eventual social acceptance in the neighborhood. One year, a very competitive coach who lived on their block "discovered them" before the draft and recruited them into FSA. They entered under his direct personal sponsorship, although they had already formed an opinion about the organization from another professional Black mother whose daughter had played the year before with no problems.

> But if it weren't for that [baseball] we would probably never have really gotten involved with the neighborhood. It forced us to become "Fairmounters." That's basically what happened. Real Fairmounters! Accepted by Fairmounters! You know, it's hard to be a Fairmounter. You almost have to be in the sports. One thing that puts you in their league is the sports team. . . . I just think that Fairmount is a unique little area. It really is, when you think about it. There's a 2- to 3-mile radius, and it never ceases to amaze me. Even this little block, my neighbors. They are interesting people. There's the different cultures, the different economic brackets. One person lives over here and makes $500,000 and another person doesn't work.

Interracial couples or mixed-race families constitute obvious instances of "intimate race sponsorship." Those prone to exclude a Black child, for example, may come to see the child in a different light when his behaviors are regularly being interpreted by his White father with little social distance from the racially suspicious. As one Black mother, married to a White man, Fritz, who was active in the league for years, explained her son's positive experience in FSA: "Want to know why Sonny had such a good experience down there [the field]? One and only one reason: Fritz. They could all relate to Fritz. So I tried to keep a distance and just watch from far off."

Similarly when two middle-class children of different races demonstrate a casual comfort, as well as an implied history, despite the fact that they may have different cultural styles, their friendship proves a model for those with no such experience. The modeling might be for other racially exclusive children, or it might be for their own, wary parents. Shawn, a Fairmount parent in the league who had described his own adolescence as one constant battle with Black kids, expressed amazement at how his son, Jimmy, had Black friends from the ball field who ran in and out of his house "like nothing."

As a different kind of example, a Black parent who suspects a White coach is treating his child unfairly might be less likely to read in racial motives if the coach regularly selects a Black parent as his assistant, and this Black parent can testify by example of a non-exclusionary style of the suspected coach. In this case, the Black parent is sponsoring the acceptance. Intimate race sponsorship is vital, because the reception and the interpretation of the behaviors of those defined as "the other" always happen in a context, and the extent to which the context links the potentially excluded to internal bases of support, via distant or intimate race sponsorship, the more likely the entry will be smooth and judgments about behaviors tolerant, or at least not overtly hostile.

Although the integration process at FSA occurred relatively harmoniously, it also happened unevenly. I noticed over the years, and numerous parents I interviewed also brought up, that the children of color were often not randomly distributed among the White coaches; certain White coaches were more likely to have more Black kids on their teams than others. This pattern of "selective recruitment" resulted from a variety of factors. Some coaches worked hard to recruit known neighborhood kids who were largely White. Others either had no such preferences, or once they had a Black child on their team they tried to draft him again because he was known to them. Black parents who had had positive experiences with a coach sometimes volunteered to assist with the coaching so as to secure a place on this coach's team for their child. In any case, these coaches carved out a safe social space for these new children and their parents,

which served as an important filter for their overall interpretations of the organization. Sal was one such coach, whom a Puerto Rican father had included in his list of a handful of White coaches he viewed as most likely to have more mixed teams. In my interview with Sal, he described how he perceived his role in the racial encounter of the organization:

The direction of this interview was interesting to me because it's stuff I think about all the time—when you asked me about race. I watch these interactions all the time. I'm supposed to . . . and I'm not one of these crusaders. I'm not gonna come out and say [pause]. I mean I have to coexist here. But I don't agree all the time with what's going on. . . . Last year I had a lot of Black kids on my team again. Years ago, I used to work as an exterminator, and I worked in some Black homes where the kids would come up to me and touch my arms, like they had never seen a White person in their lives. I always remembered that. My experience here has been such that, having these kids on my team, I don't try to be anything special. I'm jus', I'm just a White guy who's not half bad. That's what I'm trying to be. White kids get a lot of preconceptions from their parents and so do Black children—what to expect. There's a guy, Phil, a Black janitor where I work, who lives way up North Philly and told me he wanted his kids to play baseball and experience other types of children. So he came down and I got him on my team. The kid got the sportsmanship award, for being there all the time. . . . They said he had a great time and is coming back.

When asked how he could explain the overall smooth integration in the league:

Why is it so smooth? Because of the diversity of the White people. You have people with better educational backgrounds; it's not all the [pause]. I don't know how to explain this. I think about this a lot, but I can't verbalize it. I think there were more non–Fairmount Whites who could lessen the impact of the change. Does that make sense?

Jessie, a White Fairmounter, whose small neighborhood business brings her into frequent contact with newcomers, also mentioned the impact of more liberal professional attitudes on neighborhood change:

No, I think it [race integration] has been relatively smooth, considering this neighborhood and its background. . . . I guess you gotta give credit where credit's due. If the yuppies didn't move in, I don't think there wouldn't be any change. I think they moved in with different attitudes, and you kind of got a little eye opening here and there and you start to think. Well, you know, they're right. . . . And I think time itself.

Recognizing the segmented nature of the racial integration that did occur in FSA is crucial to understanding the uneven process by which the transformation occurred. Its unevenness also meant that not all families of color who played baseball at FSA came away with good feelings. Some were isolated on teams whose coaches were less sympathetic, or were concentrated on teams whose coaches were in disfavor with the leadership or umpires, and came away with judgments that race issues were still alive and well at FSA. But many more families of color stayed and found enough welcoming

space at FSA to transform the organization into a multicultural one.

Class and Competing Community Values

The professionals gentrifying Fairmount and Spring Garden fit the description of the "cultural new class," (Ley 1994) or the liberal sector of the middle-class that concentrated in the social and cultural fields of the economy typically unconnected to the corporate sector, i.e. doctors, lawyers, professors. The newcomer coaches and parents I interviewed also came almost exclusively from the sector of the middle-class consisting of social and cultural professionals. Almost all of the twenty newcomer coaches and parents interviewees held professional jobs in governmental, educational, or legal services unconnected to the corporate sector. Almost half of them were educators—teachers, principals, and professors. When describing their motivations for moving to this area of the city, newcomers often spoke of their preference for the cultural lifestyle of the city, and, specifically, the diversity of the city as a plus. Many had working-class parents who had helped them achieve upward mobility through educational advancement, and they remained positive toward, and emotionally comfortable with, the social style of many of the Fairmounters.

Part of the intensity that Fairmounters felt about the outcomes of games and championships stemmed from their definition of baseball as the only sport, perhaps the only social activity, that mattered. A Fairmounter coach complained that newcomers' over-involvement in multiple leisure activities and other sports translated into "jack of all trades and master of none," namely, their general lack of baseball talent. Part of what was at stake for Fairmounters as newcomers entered their sports association was not just organizational control but the preservation of baseball itself, the game as it was meant to be played and had been played in the neighborhood: adeptly, thoughtfully, strategically, and with discipline. Playing baseball well was a source of pride for many in Fairmount. Seeing local boys compete in city-wide competitions, representing the neighborhood at Philadelphia's Veterans stadium, and following the championships of local teams were important neighborhood rituals. But essential to maintaining a respectable neighborhood baseball identity was the dedication of a cadre of coaches who both knew enough about the game and its intricacies and had enough time to train the next generation of players. But as time passed, there weren't enough old-timers to do this job and newcomers and outsiders were brought in.

The gap in the amount of time dedicated to maintaining the FSA by an inner core of mostly old-timer volunteers, whose participation ranges from 10 to 53 hours every week of the season (or an average of 270 hours each season per "activist"), and the outer circle of regular parents, who contribute only four hours once during a season, is a source of significant resentment by insiders in the organization. The different degrees of involvement in the FSA became a central focus of tensions between old-timers and the newcomers in FSA, tensions, as we have seen, already established in the neighborhood. But time devoted to the organization was just one symbolic issue that divided them. Just as Fairmounters complained that newcomers had weak ties to the neighborhood with little local mixing, instrumental friendships, and minimal community sup-

port, they saw newcomers approach the baseball organization in a similar manner—for the instrumental needs of their individual children and not as a neighborhood treasure that needed nurturing. Many newcomers were oblivious to this resentment. Others countered with their own complaints about Fairmounters' coolness to outsiders, about unfair access to insider information about teams and opportunities, about the adult-centered, competitive way that Fairmounters ran an organization for children.

The Fairmount tradition established in the 1960s of neighborhood men volunteering to coach baseball, whether or not they had a son in the league, continued in a modified way for decades. In the 1990s, many teams in the FSA were still associated with a Fairmounter coach who "kept his team" year after year. That is, a particular man coaches the Rangers, or the Angels, in the 7–9 age division year after year. Teams came to be identified as "The Padres—John's team," or "The Grays—Bob's team." Most newcomer coaches, on the other hand, were father-coaches and often coached, unlike Fairmounters, their sons in other sports, like soccer. Their reference group was more their own son, and other players and parents on the team, rather than spectators outside this small group. They were less likely to stay with the same team or the same age division over time and more likely to move up age divisions as their sons did.[11] They almost never coached or maintained contact with the organization beyond the playing careers of their children. This way, they established less identification with a particular team and less of an investment with the organization beyond their team.

If Fairmounters saw newcomers as individualistic and not community minded enough, newcomers would counter that, at least, it was a child-centered individualism. The sharpest newcomer critique related to their view that the FSA prioritized adult socializing over children's interests. While Fairmounters might devote lots of time to the organization, they argued, a good amount of that time was devoted to hanging out in the clubhouse and drinking beer, which set a bad example for the kids. The clubhouse has a keg refrigerator so that cold beer is always on tap. Insiders have only to grab a plastic cup, pull down a lever, and fill up.

The complaint that the FSA was adult-centered went beyond discomfort with beer drinking in the clubhouse. Actually many newcomers thought that drinking beer in the staff office and using the clubhouse year round as a hangout place was perfectly acceptable, even appropriate compensation for the hours they spent holding the organization together. When newcomers said that the organization wasn't enough about children they usually had in mind an emphasis on winning games, winning championships, and winning in the city-wide league. Among the parents I interviewed, it was disproportionately newcomers who felt the FSA leaned excessively in the competitive direction and who longed for more emphasis on individual instruction of players. In contrast, Fairmounter parents tended to see the organization as more balanced, with an appropriate emphasis on teaching skills as well as competitively winning games.[12] Typical among newcomer parents were this father's comments,

At FSA they are very much playing games to win, very competitive. This is one of the things I don't like. See. Certain kids are not going to get a base hit because the coach just teaches them to bunt, so he can win the game. They learn to bunt but should be learning to hit and [then they would] have a slightly better chance to get on base than by [just] bunting. I prefer to teach kids how to play baseball and not how to win.

Another newcomer father described FSA as "less instructional and more about winning" and related it to the need of coaches to have bragging rights in the neighborhood. This argument relates back to the issue of "clubhouse teams" versus the newcomer teams. Baseball as a central element of Fairmount neighborhood's identity meant that losing a game, especially for a "clubhouse team" took on a weighted significance. The association of particular teams with insiders focused energy on the importance of winning to prove something to some other group of *adults*. Many newcomers thought that that somebody was them.

The differences in the way that Fairmounters and newcomers related both to the neighborhood as described above, and to the league, reflected a competing set of cultural values related to individual responsibility, group solidarity, and how best to promote children's interests. The different orientations toward the community could be described as hierarchical communalism versus child-centered individualism. While there was a range of opinion about most of these concerns within the two groups, when differences did appear, they often took this form. Fairmounters, on the one hand, regularly brought up resentments about the way newcomers used the organization for the narrow benefit of their own children without appropriate levels of support, or deference, to the needs of the broader group and its leadership, similar to their approach to the neighborhood. Newcomers complained that their interests were ignored, that Fairmounters too often listened only to other Fairmounters and ran the organization to benefit themselves and their adult friends, with children a distant secondary concern.

A United "Inner-City" Identity

Despite the emphasis in this discussion on the divisions and tensions between Fairmounters and more affluent newcomers, there were also many forged understandings and feelings of connection across these groups. Indeed, the cross-class sympathies may even have been stronger than some of the strains between the deep insiders and newcomers. Most importantly, many newcomers cherished being a part of the FSA, despite its warts and their somewhat marginal position. In the words of one newcomer, "We represent some of the outsiders. But I think the mixture of kids here is terrific. I'm not aware of any tensions. I think it's one of the few places where kids of different colors, different ethnicities, and different socioeconomic incomes come together for a common purpose in this city. It's wonderful."

The sympathies that emerged across class and racial lines at the FSA were especially apparent in encounters that the ball club had with the outside world, such as in traveling team championships played in remote neighborhoods of the city and suburbs. Professional parents at the FSA were sometimes surprised to learn that suburban teams viewed Fairmount in an undifferentiated way, as a low-class, inner-city team. The generalized apprehension of suburbanites for anything inside the city translated into nervousness about even neighborhoods as affluent as Spring Garden had become. This

external judgment stimulated community loyalty. This was salient one year when the Fairmount's 12-and-under traveling team faced an all-white, extremely affluent, suburban team. FSA's team was about one-third boys of color and their team was all white. Neighborhood men and women had driven over an hour to see this important Fairmount game, many with no child on the team. After the Council Rock parents had left their BMWs and slick SUVs in the immense parking lot behind their practice field, Fairmounter adults began lining behind FSA's dugout. Seeing the crowd of adult Fairmounters outside our neighborhood, all of us looking particularly ragtag compared to the well-dressed suburban parents we faced, I could see the "insider/newcomer" problem slip away. As the game proceeded, many Fairmounters shouted out non-stop, encouraging comments to each of the Fairmount players. Although some were still strangers to me, they called out my son by name. They called out also the names of our black catcher and third baseman in a raucous, public testimony of solidarity for the community we sometimes achieved.

Although Fairmounters had many complaints about newcomers' individualism, some also recognized the importance of contributions by professionals who were strategically placed in the city. Newcomers were sometimes generous in tapping their networks and resources to provide a different kind of financial support, one that was more lucrative than "booster day," where ball players knocked on neighborhood doors with FSA cups asking for donations. As one FSA staffer acknowledged, "They're [the newcomers] able to get us sponsored money. Where in the past, we used to knock on doors. Now they just email each other, and it's here. That really helps. So it's less work for the twelve people most involved. It's less work because, they can call two friends and a check comes in the mail. It's beautiful." While receiving mailed-in checks might produce more revenue, knocking on doors builds community support for the field and connects the baseball children with locals who might not have children in the league. It was this combination of both orientations, reaching inward to capitalize on community solidarity, and reaching outward for inclusion and external support, which built on the strengths of the two worlds of Fairmounters and newcomer professionals.[13] So while different cultural orientations divided some Fairmounters from some newcomers within the FSA, important cross-class ties of solidarity and understanding coexisted in this local public space of sports, more so than the organizational gatekeepers acknowledged.

Something About Baseball

This article has explored the factors behind a delicate process of racial and class integration in the neighborhood baseball league of these two Philadelphia neighborhoods. Turning to the role of sports itself, we could extend the question and ask, "Were all the features mentioned above sufficient to bring about the transformation of this exclusive, white, baseball league into a relatively harmoniously integrated recreational space? Were all these factors, the passion of the neighborhood men for preserving the integrity of the game when faced with a scarcity of local children, mixed-race alliances and the race sponsorship of new children, the lure of the visible new clubhouse, and the new accountability to black politicians, enough?" We could further ask, "Did it matter that it was baseball? Would

the same thing have happened if it had been football, or soccer, or a neighborhood basketball league? Could the social change that happened in Spring Garden and Fairmount have been embodied in any other sport?" My answer would be no. Something about baseball itself did matter to this transformation.

For one thing, baseball is a highly structured encounter, inherent in which is a great deal of waiting. And it is precisely because of all that waiting, that requirement of patience while tracking the contingencies and possibilities of a play, that baseball offers such social opportunities. Think of the spectators' experience of the game, not just that of the players. Parents sit together on bleachers, often separated from the parents of the other teams who are sitting on different bleachers, each team's parents sitting with their child's teammates' parents. Parents of different backgrounds sit together, but in a very highly structured context. They do not have to figure out how to relate to one another. The differences that might cause problems among them are not right on the surface, or are at least deflected by the bigger concern: the game. You're part of this team, and you're part of that team. You just sit, and wait, and you don't have to do anything. But at the same time, there is a bonding that goes on, because, at least for this season, you share a common fate. And this common fate produces conversation: what the other team did wrong, what the other coach should have done, what our coach should have done, how Rickie didn't fall asleep until midnight worrying about the playoffs, what if the sun goes down before we score? Over a fairly short period of time, a deep sense of "we" develops. Parents don't like it, for example, when parents from another team forgetfully sit on their bleachers (even when they know one another). They want to be able to feel happy with "their group" when the poor little seven-year old on the other team strikes out. They want to feel okay about it, to mumble, "Thank God." So there is that structure to baseball. There is enough time between the moments of intensity to permit human connections. Precisely what looks like a boring moment to baseball's detractors, is often a deeply felt moment of shared wonder to the informed spectator. And those who don't at first "get the religion" are often seduced into believing by the collective reverence around them. Because baseball is a game of waiting for long periods with occasional, intense peaks of emotion, it provides a conducive space for parents and children of diverse backgrounds to sit patiently, controlled by a ritualistic drama, clustered in teams not of their own choosing, while trying to figure each other out.

Baseball is also a game of hope, and a game that spotlights individual failures. Pitchers break down. Batters fail. Fielders drop the ball. There are a lot of collectively shared feelings about the errors and mishaps of individual players, most of whom, almost all of whom, will not be your own son or daughter. A kind of identification evolves, not just with the group, but with particular kids over what happened to them that day, that game. We now care intensely about what happened today to the kid we didn't even know three weeks ago. Mothers will commiserate with each other with a, "You're gonna have a rough night tonight!" when one of the boys has three strikeouts in a game.

So the slow pace of baseball, punctuated as it is by moments of such intensity and drama—that long plateau with its occasional upsurges—matters. It allows parents

of different backgrounds to come together on the bleachers and feel comfortable, without the need to do much, and yet to share the passion, the disappointments, and the triumphs. And just before all this "we" feeling gets out of control (at least usually before), the season comes to an end. And then comes the reshuffling. So that, the next season the parents are on the same bleachers, but with a different group of people. And after four seasons, they have come to know a lot of people in the community, and learned a lot, very specifically, about different individuals and their children. While they may at first have thought of a given child as a "jerk," after months on the bleachers with that child's parents they often learn more about why a given child behaves poorly, and may feel less removed from that child's "problem."

On the bleachers, parents share that baseball "suspension of time." In contrast, parents who sit together watching basketball do not get the same opportunities. In basketball, too much happens against the pressure of the clock. The same is true for soccer. So, it mattered that it was baseball. Because it was baseball, we waited, and hoped together, and experienced moments of communion, pain, and redemption in the process.

Last but not least, Fairmount baseball is played on that lush, green, rectangle of grass and red earth, before the backdrop of the open skyline of Center City, Philadelphia, and its most majestic museums. This space offers all its participants a constant grounding in beauty on a scale grander than the baseball diamond. The deep longing begins around the end of February. "When will practices start?" "Has your coach called yet?" Opening Day becomes an aesthetic re-entrance into a community of friends, neighbors, and former strangers where, just as you feel the first warmth of the spring, you begin tracking the inevitable growth and changes in this year's crop of children. "Oh, my gosh, look at how much Jonathan grew." "I can't believe George is no longer afraid of the ball." "Look at that green! I say to my wife, you want a yard? A yard? This is all the grass I need."

To say that the racial integration of FSA occurred relatively smoothly and without major conflicts is not to say that there were not tensions, grumblings, or conflicts, including stacking, selective recruitment, and questionable calls against outsiders, in which racism played a real or perceived role. These certainly did happen. But given the history of racial conflict in this neighborhood, the fact that the central cleavages to emerge in this organization were not along racial lines, but, rather along lines of class, or along the divide between the old timers and the new professionals, is striking.

One of the sweetest intricacies of baseball is the rule about a dropped third strike. This rule permits a player who strikes out the chance to run to first base if the catcher drops the ball on the third strike. It builds a strong element of hope into baseball. While individual failures are spotlighted in baseball, small possibilities of redemption like this are laced throughout the game. In reviewing the history of baseball in this neighborhood, we have seen that old-timer residents cared enough about baseball to turn their backs on their exclusionary past and make room for outsiders, first their "class competitors" and, second, children of color. Did the newcomers get to be deep insiders? For the most part, no. But their children were allowed in and gathered rich experiences in a beautifully orchestrated game. And all this happened in a city that had distinguished itself as having one of the last professional teams in baseball to integrate in the mid 1950s.[14] A neighborhood that had represented the ugly racial segregation that marked many American cities, which had racially defended itself against outsiders with violence, had a chance to redeem itself in the later decades of the 20th century, and took it. Responding to population loss, and in the context of a new scrutiny by Black politicians in a post–civil rights era, locals watched as children and parents of color were sponsored in. The neighborhood reformed itself, slowly and unevenly, to move beyond its failures, at least on the turf of baseball. It received a second chance and took it—just like a dropped third strike.

Notes

1. This article draws on research that was conducted with the aid of a study leave from Temple University and a research grant from the Department of Sociology, Temple University. I wish to thank John Landreau, Debbie Rogow, Gideon Sjoberg, Nancy Theberge, and Michael Messner for comments and criticism that helped to improve the quality of distinct parts of this paper. I am grateful to Kevin Delaney for his help and collaboration on an early rendition of this project, and to Joshua Freely and Dylan Galaty for their research assistance in the fieldwork for this project, and to Nadine Sullivan for her assistance in finalizing this piece.

2. For a more detailed description of my research methodology and additional ethnographic reflections see Grasmuck 2005: 206–222.

3. Lidz (1991, p. 84) distinguishes a "participant observer" from an "observing participant," in that the former, "enters the group or situation to be studied as a natural member meeting all the usual qualities or requirements of participa-

tion. . . . One is a member who then asks the group for permission to carry out social scientific observation in conjunction with one's other activities of membership." As a "bench Mom" for years, I then requested permission to study the organization.

4. Whalen's data (2001, p. 186) extends the area defined as Spring Garden to include an additional census tract 133, one tract to the east of tract 134.

5. Cybriwski (1978, p. 22) calculates the rates of homeownership in Fairmount as even higher, almost three quarters of Fairmount residents in the 1960s, based on real estate directories.

6. See Taylor (1988, pp. 79–131) for a conceptual discussion of socially defended territories.

7. Ley and Cybriwsky (1974, p. 503) report two cases of large anti-Black actions against Black families settling in the area in the early 1970s.

8. Although I wanted to include the real name of Tom O'Connors in recognition of his important historical role in the creation of the ball club, he preferred that I use a pseudonym in describing his involvement.

9. Although some Puerto Ricans and other Latinos do self-identify as both Latino and White, the use of *White* here refers to non-Latino Whites, unless otherwise specified.

10. This occurred in the early Jackie Robinson days, in 1947, when Pee Wee Reese left his short-stop position to walk to first base and stand with his arm around his lone Black teammate on the Dodgers, Jackie Robinson, as they confronted racist taunts from the Cincinnati fans. Roger Kahn considers this the greatest moment in the history of American sports (MacNeil/Lehrer, 1997). This is not to portray Reese as more heroic than Robinson. It just underscores the need of all heroes and heroines for help from friends.

11. Between 1996 and 1999, 65% of Fairmounter head-coaches agreed to take a team when they had no son playing in the division compared to only 20% of the newcomer head-coaches who had a son on the team they coached over this same period. After 1998, newcomers came to dominate in numbers, hovering around 60 percent of head-coaches over the next several years. This ushered in an increase in "father coaches" since newcomers

typically coached only when they had a son on the team, 80% of those managing the 7–12 age groups between 1996 and 1999 compared to 35% of their Fairmounter counterparts.

12. Seven of the ten newcomer parents described the FSA as stressing competition (playing games to win) over instruction (teaching individual and team skills), whereas only two of the ten Fairmounters described the ball club as relatively competitive. Most Fairmounters saw the FSA as appropriately balancing competition with instruction.

13. Putnam (2000) makes a distinction between "bonded social capital" and "bridging social capital" similar to this inward and outward reaching set of networks of Fairmounters and newcomers and the need for communities to have both.

14. In the mid 1950s, the Phillies had the only all-White baseball club in the National League, with their first Black member, John Kennedy, arriving in 1957 (see Kuklick, 1991, p. 148). Two years later, the Red Sox signed Pumpsie Green, making it the last team in Major League Baseball to integrate, with the Phillies coming in next to last (see Bryant, 2002).

References

Bryant, H. (2002). *Shut out: A history of race and baseball in Boston*. New York: Routledge.

Coakley, J.J. (2001). Sport in society: An inspiration or an opiate? In D.S. Eitzen (Ed.), *Sport in contemporary society: An anthology* (pp. 20–36). New York: Worth.

Cybriwsky, R. (1978). Social aspects of neighborhood change. *Annals of the Association of American Geographers, 68*, 17–33.

Edwards, H. (1970). *The revolt of the Black athlete*. New York: Free Press.

Edwards, H. (1973). *Sociology of sport*. Homewood, IL: Dorsey Press.

Edwards, H. (2001). An end of the golden age of Black participation. In D.S. Eitzen.(Ed.), *Sport in contemporary society: An anthology* (pp. 285–291). New York: Worth.

Eitzen, D.S. (1999). *Fair and foul: Beyond the myths and paradoxes of sport*. Lanham, MD: Rowman & Littlefield.

Ericksen, E.P., Bartelt, D., Feeney, P., Foeman, G., Grasmuck, S., Martella, M., et al. (1985). The state of Puerto Rican Philadelphia. Philadelphia: Institute for Public Policy, Temple University.

Gatz, M., Messner, M.A., & Ball-Rokeach, S.J. (Eds.). (2002). *Paradoxes of youth and sport*. Albany: State University of New York Press.

Goodman, C. (1979). *Choosing sides: Playground and street life on the Lower East Side*. New York: Schocken Books.

Hoch, P. (1972). *Rip off the big game: The exploitation of sports by the power elite*. Garden City, NY: Anchor Books.

Kadaba, L. (1998, March 3). Relentlessly striving for more. *The Philadelphia Inquirer*, p. H3.

Kuklick, B. (1991). *To every thing a season: Shibe Park and urban Philadelphia, 1909–1976*. Princeton, NJ: Princeton University Press.

Lapchick, R. & Benedict, J. (1993). Racial report card: improvement badly. *Crisis*, 100, 38–40.

Lareau, A. (2000). *Home advantage: Social class and parental intervention in elementary education*. Lanham, MD: Rowman & Littlefield Publishers.

Ley, D. (1994). Gentrification and the politics of the new middle class. *Environment and Planning D: Society and Space*. 12, 53–74.

Ley, D., & Cybriwsky, R. (1974). Urban graffiti as territorial markers. *Annals of the Association of American Geographers*, 64, 491–505.

Lidz, V. (1991). The sense of identity in Jewish-Christian families. *Qualitative Sociology*, 14, 77–102.

MacNeil/Lehrer Productions. (1997). *Memories of summer: The golden days of baseball*. Transcript of interview between Roger Kahn and David Gergen, Online News Hour: http://www.pbs.org/newshour/gergen/april97/kahn.

Molotch, H., Freudenburg, W., & Paulsen, K. (2000). History repeats itself, but how? City character, urban tradition, and the accomplishment of place. *American Sociological Review*, 65, 791–823.

Putnam, R. D. (2000). *Bowling alone: The collapse and revival of american community*. New York: Simon and Schuster.

Sage, G. (2001). Racial inequality and sport. In D.S. Eitzen (Ed.), *Sport in contemporary society: An anthology* (pp. 275–284). New York: Worth.

Sparkes, A.C. (2002). Fictional representations: On difference, choice and risk. *Sociology of Sport Journal*, 19, 1–24.

Taylor, R. (1988). *Human territorial functioning: An empirical, evolutionary perspective on individual and small group territorial cognitions, behaviors, and consequences*. Cambridge: Cambridge University Press.

Whalen, C.T. (2001). *From Puerto Rico to Philadelphia: Puerto Rican workers and postwar economics*. Philadelphia: Temple University Press.

Chapter 26

HARDBALL AIN'T THE ONLY GAME IN BROOKLYN ANYMORE

Lee Jenkins and Michael Schmidt

Shawon Dunston's tour of Brooklyn baseball stops at the high rises where he used to throw rocks, the street corners where he used to throw snowballs, and the legendary sandlot where he put that powerful throwing arm on display.

The sandlot was the final stop in a tour that Dunston, whose 17-year major league career included a trip to the 1999 postseason with the Mets, gave his son this summer. Standing on the edge of the Parade Ground in Prospect Park, Shawon Dunston Jr. noticed a bunch of middle-aged men in uniform taking batting practice.

"Why are those guys out there?" Shawon Jr. asked. "They're so old."

In many ways, New York City's rich baseball history is kept alive by guys well past their prime, still wearing uniforms and kicking around local ballparks. This week, two of them will lead the Yankees and the Mets into the playoffs.

Yankees Manager Joe Torre and Mets Manager Willie Randolph, who both played high school baseball in Brooklyn, grew up taking bad hops at the Parade Ground. So did Lee Mazzilli, the Yankees' bench coach, and Omar Minaya, the Mets' general manager. Dirt fields are their common ground.

"It was our Mecca," Minaya said. "It was where we went to be seen."

In many ways, New York City baseball is embodied by Brooklyn. It was there, in the 1940's and 50's, that the Dodgers firmly established the image of the Subway Series in their repeated attempts to beat the Yankees.

Today's Mets and Yankees would not know the Parade Ground from the Polo Grounds. Most of them grew up in California, Texas, Florida, Virginia and Latin America. Mets catcher Paul Lo Duca was born in Brooklyn, but he moved to Arizona when he was 2.

If he had stayed, the odds of ever playing for the Mets would have been stacked against him. In the 1950's, when Brooklyn could lay claim to being recognized as the stickball capital of the world, it produced 26 major league players, according to data obtained from baseballreference.com. This decade, it has produced only six.

Among the last standouts was Dunston, a rifle-armed shortstop who was picked first in the 1982 draft by the Chicago Cubs, the only time a New Yorker has ever been selected No. 1 over all. When Dunston returned to the Parade Ground in August, he was struck by all the football practices, soccer matches and pickup basketball games.

"It used to be just baseball," Dunston said. "From 9 a.m. to 9 p.m., we'd only stop to have a knish for lunch."

"It was all baseball, all the time," Mazzilli said. "The fields were terrible. The conditions were bad, but we didn't know any better. That was what we knew."

There are several reasons for the shortage of home-grown ballplayers from Brooklyn and the rest of New York City—the inclement weather and the proliferation of other sports. On a Sunday afternoon in Brooklyn, cricket is now more common than stickball.

When immigrants from Italy, Ireland and Eastern Europe came to New York in the early 20th century and before, they had few sports to call their own, so they adopted baseball. But the new waves of Pakistani, Indian and Caribbean immigrants have brought along their own games.

"At first they will find whatever grass they can," said Adrian Benepe, the commissioner of the New York City Department of Parks and Recreation. "But when they become engaged and integrated citizens, they lobby for fields."

This spring, the Public School Athletic League will recognize cricket as an official sport. Meanwhile, less than half of the high schools in Brooklyn have their own baseball field. Lafayette High School, which has produced the most major leaguers in the city's history, can no longer fill both a junior varsity and varsity roster.

Lafayette's alumni include a Hall of Fame pitcher (Sandy Koufax), a former All-Star closer (John Franco) and the Mets' principal owner (Fred Wilpon). But the baseball program was shut down in the middle of the 2002 season and did not re-open for nearly two years.

"When I heard that, I almost had a heart attack," said Steve Mandl, the baseball coach at George Washington High School in the Washington Heights section of Manhattan. "It's like Notre Dame stopping football."

Baseball is not gone from Brooklyn, but the baseball geography of the city has clearly been altered. Powerhouses now include George Washington and Monroe High School in the Bronx, which draw on a deep reservoir of players from thriving Latin communities, and Tottenville High School in Staten Island, an area with a deeply ingrained Little League tradition. Brooklyn, which used to be the dominant borough, is suddenly bringing up the rear.

"The intensity is still there in Brooklyn, but the talent pool has increased in North Manhattan, the Bronx and Staten Island," said Robert H. Pertsas, baseball commissioner for the P.S.A.L. "Those areas seem to have the greatest concentration of players."

Still, almost every weekend, the city's best young baseball players ride the subways to Brooklyn. Even if the local high school programs are deteriorating, the club teams for top youth players continue to flourish.

The Mazzillis live in Greenwich, Conn., but his son L. J. came home from a recent game with his club team the Bayside Yankees and said: "Daddy, I played in the Parade Ground, where you played."

Likewise, kids from Washington Heights play for Manny Ramírez's old club team in Brooklyn. Ramírez, the last first-round draft choice from New York, picked 13th in 1991 out of George Washington, came up with the Youth Service League, a group of club teams, at the Parade Ground. Since then, most Youth Service League games have moved to the American Legion field in South Brooklyn's Canarsie. It is a baseball-only facility.

"There's no soccer," said Mel Zitter, director of the Youth Service League. "Kids get on trains and take 90-minute trips each way because they know what we offer is much better than what they can get in their own area. That much hasn't changed."

Zitter acknowledged that New York is losing baseball players, but it can still produce major leaguers. Even though the depth of talent in the city has diminished, the top tier remains capable of winning college scholarships and signing bonuses.

In this year's amateur draft, for instance, the Baltimore Orioles selected Pedro Beato as a supplemental pick between the first and second rounds, and the Yankees chose Dellin Betances in the eighth round. Both played high school ball in Brooklyn.

"With some of the kids from that area, there is probably a little more polish that needs to be applied," said Damon Oppenheimer, the Yankees' vice president of amateur scouting. "But the really talented ones don't seem to have that big a problem."

The only concern is how they handle better competition. Prospects from California and Texas are often used to hitting 90-mile-an-hour fastballs in high school. Prospects from New York must often learn what it feels like to fail.

If the Yankees had not been able to sign Betances, he would have gone to Vanderbilt University and joined another New Yorker, Pedro Alvarez. Last summer, Alvarez rejected a contract from the Boston Red Sox and wound up being the Southeastern Conference's freshman of the year. His transition could not have been simpler. "What I like about recruiting kids in the Northeast is that they tend to improve very, very quickly," said Tim Corbin, the Vanderbilt coach. "Once they have the right facilities and the time to play outside, the talent really comes out."

At the turnstile, baseball is achieving record levels of popularity in New York. But attendance marks at Yankee and Shea stadiums do not equate to huge turnouts at the local sandlots.

Now that the Yankees and the Mets are together at the top, possibly bound for a second Subway Series of their own, coaches are waiting to see if kids will grab their bats and gloves, the way they did when the Yankees used to meet the Brooklyn Dodgers in the 1950's.

"A year ago, I would have told you that baseball in Brooklyn is dead," said Eric (Rock) Eisenberg, the athletic director at Samuel J. Tilden High School, Randolph's alma mater. "Now, with the way the Mets have come back, I'm not so sure.

"Everyone likes success. Everyone is talking baseball."

Dunston reels off the defining characteristics of a New York ballplayer: passion, toughness, persistence. All are hallmarks of successful managers.

He wants to raise his son in an environment where baseball is played all the time, where the competition is fierce and the rewards are great.

He lives in California.

PART VI

SOCIALIZING THE ANATOMY: BODY CULTURE AND SPORT

A number of social-science writers have focused on the various aspects of the body, or body culture, in sport. According to one definition, body culture consists of "everything that people do with their bodies . . . and the elements of culture that shape their doing." This includes, the author writes, "daily practices of health, hygiene, fitness, beauty, dress and decoration, as well as gestures, postures, manners, ways of speaking and eating and so on. It also includes the way these practices are trained into the body, the way the body is publicly displayed, and the lifestyle that is expressed in that display. Body culture reflects the internalization and incorporation of culture. Body culture is embodied culture" (Brownell 1995).

From an interactionist perspective, the body is never simply a physiological organism. Rather, it is a socially constructed object infused with social meanings that adapt it to particular social functions. Think of the contrasts in the bodily demeanor of a Catholic priest, a policeman, a symphony orchestra conductor, and a heavyweight boxer—each *embodies* very different social meanings and functions, developed through long years of training, which are revealed in the pace, the rhythm, and the form of their physical movements. Every "body" internalizes social meanings through socialization that transforms it into an externally defined object (male/female, attractive/ugly, fat/thin, tall/short, etc.) that is distinct from the subjective self.

This has especially important implications in sports, because it is through this socialization that the individual's body makes the transition from being an ordinary object into being an athletic object. In short, the individual learns to view his or her body as an instrument for sports performance: for running (track); for throwing punches (boxing), for catching passes (football), or for hitting a ball (baseball). This experience, in communities where sports are valued and confer social esteem, is likely to transform the individual's identity. It involves an objectification that also gives the individual the motivation and the capacity not only to achieve extraordinary physical discipline and muscular development but also to endure unusual levels of physical exhaustion, characteristics that affirm his or her body's dissimilarity from ordinary human bodies.

The body the individual athlete sees when he or she stands in front of the mirror is an athletic object, an instrument designed for competition against other athletic objects. This perception is sometimes reflected in references to his or her body in the third person—as "it"—particularly when the athlete is talking about training and performance regimens; "it" must be nourished, prepared, and maintained in accordance with objective rules to achieve optimal results.

Another aspect of this objectification is manifested in decorative displays adorning the body (for example, uniforms and other special attire), which transmute and meld it into a larger collective identity—making it a Michigan Wolverine, a New York Yankee, a Green Bay Packer, a Chicago Bull, or a Detroit Red Wing. This is similar to the transmuting and melding of bodies, by means of uniforms and insignia of rank, into soldiers, policemen, firemen, priests, and postmen.

This transmutation of self is directly linked to the athlete's willingness to endure pain and injury—the tendency to give up his or her body in the service of a larger social meaning. The separation of the athlete's body from the subjective self and personal concerns has significant similarities, though it is on a lesser scale, to the bodily sacrifice entailed by what Emile Durkheim termed "altruistic suicide," that is, the type of voluntary self-negation for a higher collective meaning or cause manifested in war or religious martyrdom (Durkheim 1951). Sports often entail committing the body for the sake of a larger, collective, self-transcendent cause: winning.

Among the analytical questions for further research on the body in sport are the following:

• Which male sports are most influenced by the body codes of hegemonic masculinity? Contact or noncontact sports? Working-class, middle-class, or upper-class sports? Amateur or professional sports?
• What is the relationship between the body codes in sports and homophobia?
• What changes have been evidenced in body codes of hegemonic masculinity in sports over the past two decades? To what extent did those changes result from an alternative ideological conception of the body?
• How do women's sports differ in the degree to which they embrace the hegemonic feminine body code? What forms of resistance have emerged to counteract that code? What are the constraints on that resistance?
• To what extent has the globalization of culture changed the conceptions of the proper use or display of the body in sports? Are Asian, African, and Western conceptions of the body converging? What conceptions of the body have remained culturally distinct?

All of the readings in this section view bodies as objects defined and differentiated by social meanings; however, the specific analytical issues engaged by the contributors differ. The first analytical issue addressed is that of resistance to hegemonic body control. Interest in this issue, influenced by the works of Michel Foucault, has been the focus of studies of racial, ethnic, sexual-orientation, and gender groups that resist the social meanings imposed on their bodies by the dominant culture. Sometimes, however, the responses to dominant social meanings, or hegemonic body codes, are an ambivalent mix of resistance and compliance, as illustrated by Molly George in "Making Sense of Muscle: The Body Experiences of Collegiate Women Athletes." George studies a group of college women soccer players and finds that they experience their own physicality, both on and off the playing field, in dynamic and multiple ways, simultaneously resisting and complying with the hegemonic definition of female beauty.

The second analytical issue addressed in this section concerns the cultivation and use of body capital as a means to economic capital and social mobility. There are numerous examples of this capitalization of the body—in the careers of beauty queens, movie actresses, fashion models, and ultimately, athletes. In the article "Managing Bodily Capital," Loïc Wacquant presents an ethnographic essay on the bleak social world of marginal black American professional boxers in Chicago who seek to escape the hardships of ghetto life by pursuing the elusive fame and fortune of big-time fights. Wacquant describes their daily struggles to hone and enhance their bodily capital and to avoid (not always successfully) the dissipating vices of the surrounding environment. Exacerbating these challenges, there looms the inevitable specter of aging, the emerging existential reality of growing older, when the boxer begins to feel that his bodily capital is diminishing.

The third analytic issue concerns the transmission of cultural or political ideologies into bodily disciplines. We are all familiar with the sight of public rituals such as sports fans standing solemnly during the playing of the national anthem, military groups marching in formation, and religious groups practicing meditation, but we do not usually think of these physical acts as embodiments of social doctrines. In "Hindu Nationalism, Cultural Spaces, and Bodily Practices in India," Ian McDonald illustrates the way separate nationalist cultural ideologies in India have been embodied in two distinct physical disciplines. These disciplines, McDonald argues, were designed to elevate India's national esteem and counteract the threats to its cultural identity posed by globalization. However, only one of these Indian physical disciplines is practiced as a martial art. Judo, karate, and tae kwon do are familiar examples of bodily disciplines derived from cultural ideologies that also function as competitive sports.

References

Brownell, S. 1995. *Training the Body for China*. Chicago: University of Chicago Press.
Durkheim, Emile. 1951 [1897]. *Suicide*. New York: The Free Press.
Maguire, J., and K. Young. 2002. *Theory, Sport, and Society*. Boston: JAI Press.

Chapter 27

MAKING SENSE OF MUSCLE

The Body Experiences of Collegiate Women Athletes

Molly George

In this article, Molly George presents an ethnographic study of Division I college women soccer players. She focuses on how the athletes negotiate their own body awareness and physicality with idealized, dominant notions of feminine bodies.

After scoring the winning goal in the Women's World Cup in 1999, U.S. soccer player Brandi Chastain tore off her jersey in spontaneous celebration, revealing her strong, muscular body. Her image was featured in countless magazines and newspapers along with comments both on her risqué action and on her well-defined physique. The world was thus introduced to the powerful image of an elite female athlete. The fact that Chastain received such a tremendous amount of media attention may be attributed in large part to that fact that she represented the new ideal for female beauty.

Numerous scholars have suggested that the past feminine body ideal of ultra-skinny has changed to one which now requires women to not only be slender, but muscular and toned (Bordo 1993; Duncan 1994; Markula 1995). The athletic body type has become the latest standard for female beauty. While there remains a continuum of body ideals, a recent social trend has made musculature for women not only acceptable, but desirable. The fit woman has become ubiquitous in popular culture. Once largely invisible or negatively portrayed in the media, women athletes have recently been embraced as cultural icons (Heywood and Dworkin 2003).

However liberating that sounds. it is not easy to obtain the new toned slenderness ideal embodied by these athletes. This physique requires most women to rid themselves of all fat through exercise and diet and then train to build just the right amount of "sexy, feminine" muscle. Negotiating the precise amount of muscle adds another interesting dimension to this body ideal: having too much muscle is a violation similar to excessive body fat. For female athletes at the collegiate or professional level, the intensity of training for most sports often demands musculature and body mass that surpass the ideal figure. Normative conceptions of beauty impact elite women athletes to a remarkable extent as they work to find a balance between what their bodies allow them to do in sport with expectations of what their physiques should look like. The new fit body ideal has complicated effects on the self-perceptions of young women athletes in particular.

The passage of Title IX has unquestionably impacted gender equality in the institution of sport and created numerous opportunities for women. And although more and more girls and women now energetically participate in sports, hegemonic definitions of femininity and athleticism continue to constrict the participation and representation of women. The celebration of the sporty physique in the media is promising, but should not go unquestioned. As Dworkin (2001:346) observed, "If men are free to pack on thick layers of muscle while women carefully negotiate the upper limits of muscle gains, this symbolizes the gendered nuances of everyday power and privilege and the construction of sexed materiality itself." How does this negotiation affect the way in which elite women athletes view their bodies?

This paper focuses on one group of intercollegiate Division-I women soccer players. Through participant-observation and informal interviewing, I explore how the athletes experience their muscularity and appearance in relation to the body ideal and dominant notions of femininity. My ethnographic fieldwork builds on existing literature in the sociology of sport, as well as research on the body from feminist perspectives.

Method and Setting

I was a member of an intercollegiate soccer team for four years and have played soccer competitively at the club, state, and regional levels for over 15 years. During my third year at the university, I employed "opportunistic" research (Reimer 1977) by turning to my own team in order to study the body experiences of female athletes.[1] This type of research is also referred to as auto-ethnography (Hayano 1979) because as a complete member (Adler and Adler 1987), I maintained equal status and shared common experiences and emotions with others in the setting.[2]

Throughout a two-year period, I conducted participant observation five to six days a week, for two to fifteen hours a day on this particular group. I first announced my interest in studying the team and received informed consent from the coaching staff and each of the players before proceeding with my project. I guaranteed to protect their confidentiality and to use pseudonyms. In addition, I assured all of the participants that they could ask not to be included as members of my research at any time they wished. I observed the team while participating in a variety of different environments such as training sessions, games, weightlifting, formal team gatherings, and countless informal social situations with players, parents, and coaches.

In order to minimize partiality and capture a variety of different players' experiences, I strived to connect with high-, medium-, and low-status players. Fifteen interviews were semistructured and occurred one-on-one, while many occurred in small groups and were less structured. All of the interviews were conducted in person in a variety of different locations, but none were arranged specifically ahead of time. Our conversations took place after practice, in airports and buses while traveling for competition, in the locker room, and in players' homes whenever it was convenient and appropriate. I chose not to audio record our conversations for the purpose of preserving the way in which our conversations often naturally developed while I was participating in the group. The exchanges frequently occurred spontaneously when a player and I would begin talking about our bodies and experiences in soccer. I asked the players, alone or in groups, anywhere from two to ten open-ended questions about their experiences. The interviews ranged from a few minutes to an hour, and I took notes during the conversations.

The setting for my research was a medium-sized private university in the Rocky Mountains. The university had a good reputation academically and was striving to make a name for itself as one of the finer, more competitive liberal arts colleges in the West. The undergraduate enrollment was just under four thousand, with 14 percent of the population made up of minorities, and most of the students came from middle to upper-middle class backgrounds.

The team was comprised of twenty-one female athletes, one male head coach, a male assistant coach, and a female trainer. Similar to the undergraduate population, the overwhelming majority of the players were from middle to upper-middle class families that resided within the state. All of the athletes were White, with the exception of one Latina.

Body Negotiations

The dramatic growth of women's athleticism and involvement in sport *has* allowed women to gain control over their bodies, develop autonomy and self-definition, as well as given many athletes confidence and opportunities in other areas of life. Despite these gains, the institution of sport remains largely defined and controlled by men (Messner 1992). One of the ways in which women continue to be kept from freely enjoying sport and its benefits comes from the societal emphasis placed on attractiveness, which regulates physical strength.

Dworkin (2001) argues that a culturally produced glass ceiling, or upper limit, restricts the amount of musculature that is acceptable for women. So even though it is now popular to look like a "jock," there is a fine line discouraging women from developing their full musculature potential. These social restrictions on muscularity affect elite women athletes in a unique way. For those who venture beyond the toned body ideal, intentionally or not, and obtain powerful bodies, there are often social consequences.

Women who challenge gender norms, through unconventional behavior or appearance, frequently encounter devaluation and stigmatization. This has historically been true for women athletes, who threaten socially constructed definitions of femininity precisely because they possess characteristics usually attributed to men such as strength and competitiveness (Hall 1996). A peculiar tension continues to exist between femininity and athleticism. Numerous sports scholars have explored this presumed conflict that has frequently resulted in women athletes being labeled lesbian through virtue of their participation in sport (Blinde and Taub 1992a, 1992b; Cahn 1994; Griffin 1998; Lenskyj 1986, 1994). The dominant normative system in the United States, as well as in many other cultures, continues to define sport as a primarily male endeavor and equates muscles and strength with masculinity, ultimately discouraging women from fully pursuing physical activity.

Numerous authors have explored the dynamic between dominant notions of femininity and women's physical performance in sport and fitness (Bolin and Granskog 2003; Cox and Thompson 2000; Hall 1996; Hargreaves 1994; Markula 1995; Theberge 2000). This research illuminates how women athletes respond to both the functional aspects of their participation as well as gendered expectations that may influence those experiences. While there is evidence that women athletes' femininity and heterosexuality continue to be called into question, the findings from many of these studies reveal that women frequently experience sport as a vehicle of empowerment and agency. This shows how, despite the contestations that continue to impact women's sports, many participants choose to reject emphasized notions of femininity and welcome the power and autonomy gained through physical activity. Competitive women athletes often need size and power to win and subsequently embrace particular physical attributes and behaviors that have historically denoted masculinity or homosexuality, particularly in nonathletic situations.

Transformations

Many of the players on the team rejected the heavily muscular physique, but a certain amount of musculature was necessary for a player to compete in college. This performance requirement undoubtedly impacted the way in which the athletes felt about their bodies. Rejecting muscle altogether would have impeded the athletes' ability to continue playing soccer at such a high level. After extensive training, almost every woman player inevitably builds significant muscle and although the body types on the team varied, the overwhelming majority of players had physiques that were muscular and trim as a result of their strict training regime.

Over the course of four years that the university transitioned from D-II to D-I athletic competition, the soccer players became bigger and stronger. As the team became more competitive every year, there was a dramatic increase in the level and intensity of athletic conditioning on the soccer team. A specific coach, who was the designated strength coach for all the teams in the athletic department, instructed the players through vigorous Olympic-style weightlifting, which involved the use of the athletes' entire bodies instead of isolating specific muscle groups. This type of training program is designed to add muscle mass while maintaining agility and flexibility. The players lifted year round and increased their lifting amount in the off-season.

Most of the players acknowledged that some type of transformation had occurred in their bodies while playing intercollegiate soccer. Jennifer, a tall junior midfielder, explained how her body developed during and after her freshman year:

In high school, I weighed a good one hundred and five pounds and then went to college, hit the beer and hit the weights and my body changed completely. Now I've got this big ole booty and huge legs.

Bridget, a starting central defender who was known on the team for her well-developed legs, related a similar experience about her body transforming in college:

When I came home for Christmas break, my mom met me when I got off the plane and was like screaming, "What happened to you, Bridget?" She couldn't believe how much bigger I got and was talking about putting me on a diet and all this stuff. I explained to her all the lifting they had us doing at school and then she saw my legs and finally understood it was all muscle.

Each player reacted to her own increased muscularity differently. Some women enjoyed the training and lifting at first, but grew to dislike the way in which their bodies were changing. Ashley, a senior midfielder recruited for her imposing height and strong build, described how her arms began to look different while training for college soccer, "In high school, all my teammates on the basketball team would tease me about how scrawny my arms were. Here, I was really tall and big, but my arms were all weak. But now look at them. They're huge! I hate lifting." While explaining this transformation, Ashley flexed her bicep and looked astonished at its size. She confided to me that she did not like the size of her body and wished that she wasn't "such a giant." In the off-seasons, Ashley avoided the weight room and concentrated on cardiovascular fitness by running long distances several times a week. This type of training trims the body by burning more calories, while not adding muscle mass.[3]

Other players reacted more positively to weight training and to the muscles the activity helped them to build. One player in particular stood out for her enthusiasm for

the gym and her ability to lift more than the majority of women on the team. Mariah was a sophomore forward with extremely low body fat and exceptional arm muscles who only began weight training after joining the university team. She received attention from coaches and teammates for her musculature and became known as the team's "gym rat," a term used to describe someone who spent a lot of time in the weight room. It is important to note, however, that while Mariah was focused on developing big muscles, she was extremely feminine in appearance and conscious of her clothing, makeup, and hair. Mariah expressed pride in her body by frequently displaying her muscles. She often rolled up her sleeves while lifting or playing soccer to reveal her well-defined arms.

Mariah also tended to wear tighter-fitting clothing while working out as well as in social situations. When asked if she liked how lifting was changing her body, Mariah responded, "I love it! Lifting is so fun and I want to get bigger. My goal by the end of the year is to bench press two forty-fives [dumbbells]."

Her passion for weight lifting was positively reinforced by the head coach who complimented Mariah in a team meeting on her "hard work and effort to become a stronger and better player." Mariah represented a new type of athlete in the university's soccer program; one who was more driven to improve her physique for the sport. She stood in sharp contrast to players of the past, when the program was D-II and it was more acceptable for players to be overweight or less fit, as long as their soccer skills were decent.

In order to achieve playing time at the D-I level and maintain the respect of coaches and players, the women had to devote a tremendous amount of energy towards training. Effort in the weight room and on the field transformed both their abilities and physiques.

The Performance Body versus the Appearance Body

As their bodies began to change as a result of training and competing at the elite level, it appeared as though many women experienced and viewed their physiques in conflicting ways. On the one hand, they were developing muscular bodies that allowed them to excel as competitors, and on the other hand, they were still dealing with societal expectations regarding sexualized, as well as racialized and classed, notions of femininity that limited muscle mass. While these are not necessarily opposing body ideals for beauty and sport, a certain amount of consideration occurred as the women reflected on how they experienced their physiques on and off the field. Negotiating a relationship between these two selves can be understood as a task where a woman athlete literally and figuratively embodies two physiques, the performance body and the appearance body. A multiple body perspective is useful for understanding the ways in which women athletes conceive of and use their bodies depending on the context (Cox and Thompson 2000). From this perspective, it is clear that the body becomes a social construct, reflecting ideologies that are embedded in our cultural understandings about sport and gender.

For male athletes, reconciling a performance body with an appearance body is less of a requirement. From young ages, boys experience physical activity as a natural part and privilege of their gender and they are encouraged to explore athletics with few limitations placed on their physical development. And although there has been increased acceptance and appreciation for the athletic body type in women, dominant notions of femininity still exclude women who are exceptionally muscular or powerful. Such women pose a challenge to White, middle-class notions of female frailty and male superiority (Dowling 2000).

In this environment, femininity is often equated with heterosexuality. As Hall (1996) and many others have suggested, an emphasis on a female athlete's appearance is a not so subtle way of critiquing her sexual orientation. Women's resistance to musculature that surpasses the toned body ideal may be interpreted as a technique for avoiding possible deviant labeling. Interestingly, women in sport are often the ones who frequently reinforce assumptions about women athletes and lesbianism. The players on the team were often the most critical of women who gave the slightest indication of being masculine or queer.

For example, a situation occurred where a player on an opposing team was accused of being a lesbian because of her appearance. While sitting on the bench during a game, a player from the other team ran by and Regina, a blonde, thin sophomore, commented in a loud voice, "My god, she's ugly. Is that a man?" Regina's teammates seated nearby on the sidelines laughed at the remark. The player was tall, with visible muscles in her arms and legs, had short hair and a flat chest, traits that commonly denote masculinity or lesbianism (Blinde and Taub 1992a). The teammates used these characteristics to put down their opponent and to distance themselves from her as women athletes.

Such jokes reinforce the notion that being unfeminine, even while competing, is a social violation that should be avoided at all costs. This added to the environment of compulsory heterosexuality on the team and many players actively worked to maintain identities as feminine, "unquestionably straight" women. This was achieved through frequent conversations about men and dating, homophobic jokes, and heterosexual presentations of selves in the locker room, on the field, and away from soccer. For Regina and many other players, one of the most important aspects of their participation was maintaining the perfect balance between their performance and appearance bodies. This was often accomplished through constant self-evaluation of their appearances, and the most feared transgression against femininity and heterosexuality appeared to be size in general, whether it was muscle or fat (Dworkin 2001; Haravon 1995).

Fear of Musculature

There seemed to be a consensus against large muscles, but almost everyone on the team admired toned muscle. This distinction is extremely subjective and the line separating bulk from tone is delicate. Debbie, a junior midfielder with a large upper body and exceptionally muscular legs, explained how she tried to negotiate this perfect amount of muscle:

> It is difficult to strike a balance between being toned and being too buff. I don't want to look like a man, but I don't want to have flabby truck driver arms! Somewhere in between the two is perfect.

This belief was expressed by many women on the team, revealing a popular desire to obtain a body that was in line with the current ideal of beauty, without exceeding the pseudo standard set for muscle mass.

It is important to note that there were also players on the team who seemed unafraid of muscle and intentionally pushed the constructed boundaries set on size. These women were more concerned with their performance during physical competition and devoted time to maximizing their muscle through weightlifting. Anika, a junior goalkeeper with dreadlocks and a tall, powerful physique, often worked out alone and focused a tremendous amount of time on building her arms, back, and core. When I asked her one day in the weight room if she ever worried about getting "too muscular," she laughed at the idea and answered, "Too muscular for who[m]?" It appeared as though for Anika, building muscle was about improving her athletic performance and in this context, being overly powerful for competition was a nonconcern. Another muscular woman on the team was adored for her size, precisely because it helped the team to win games. Sharon, an impressively tall and heavy forward, used her physique to hold the ball under pressure and knock other players down. Because of this, she received the nickname "Big Bird" and a reputation for being one of the most feared players on the team. When I asked Sharon how this made her feel, she explained that the nickname didn't bother her and that she was proud of what her body allowed her to do on the field.

Fear of Fat

The body fat percentages of all the players on the team were considerably lower than the general population of women their age because of the amount of training required for athletic competition at the D-I level. Most of the players burned enough calories daily that extreme attention to diet or weight-loss was unnecessary for health reasons. However, many of the women were still concerned with maintaining a slender physique that was devoid of fat. Similar to the fear of muscle, there were two accounts the players provided to explain their fear of fat, extra body mass impeded their athletic performance and that fat was not an attractive or even an acceptable physical attribute. Preoccupation with fat was expressed in the players' recurring conversations that centered on body fat percentages, fluctuations in weight, diets, and appearances. Often, the women complained to one another about a specific problem area they had personally targeted on their body. Vanessa, the senior walk-on sociology major, complained one day in the locker room to no one in particular. "My butt is huge. I know most of it is muscle, but I wish I could trim it down. I can see little dimples of fat. I hate it. I do a million sit-ups, I run constantly, so how come I still have this flab?"

Some players took their concern with fat more seriously and devoted extra time to cardiovascular training and attention to their diet. Occasionally, some players would go to the fitness center after practice to work out on the stairmaster, stationary bike, or elliptical machine. These types of exercises burn calories and fat and seem to be done specifically for the purpose of appearance, not athletic performance, because they do little to improve fitness directly for soccer. Among these fit, toned athletes, the words "chub" and "flab" were common terms as they spoke with dissatisfaction about their bodies.

With a few cases, extreme preoccupation with body fat led players to develop eating disorders. One player in particular was suspected of having unhealthy issues with food and was subsequently confronted by the team's trainer and some of her teammates.

When confronted about her likely problem, the player defended herself by claiming that her extra fitness and strict diet were merely attempts to get into better shape for soccer. She continued to drop weight rapidly as her disorder got progressively worse. The player ultimately ended up quitting the team because she wasn't able to adequately train or deal with the pressure she was constantly under to seek help. The overall team reaction to this player was sympathy, but not shock.

Having a personal eating disorder, or knowing a friend who had one, is often a part of many young women's lives (Chernin 1981; Hesse-Biber 1996). Because female athletes are exposed to the same societal pressures to conform to the beauty ideal, anorexia and bulimia developed as a way to manage weight and muscle mass (Blinde 1989; Dowling 2000; Heywood 1996; Ryan 1995; Spitzack 1990). The female body remained a constant site for self-scrutiny and evaluation as the players constantly asked themselves, "Am I too muscular? Do I have too much body fat?" The women then turned to various sources when seeking answers to these questions.

Generalized and Specific Audiences

Understanding how the women athletes came to evaluate their appearances by orienting toward both a general audience as well as specific reference groups is central to understanding the motivation behind the constant self-surveillance of the players and the complex relationship women more generally have with their bodies. From very young ages, girls in contemporary Western culture are taught to present an aesthetically pleasing body by learning to gaze evaluatively at themselves (Berger 1972; Duncan

1994; Hesse-Biber 1996; Spitzack 1990). The gaze is used to illustrate how women become both spectator and spectacle when they are socialized to view themselves through the masculine eyes of others (Berger 1972). Although this has historically been conceptualized as a primarily male gaze, recent scholars emphasize how the concept need not necessarily be gendered or patriarchal (Duncan 1994; Dworkin 2003; Spitzack 1990). In this paper, I use the notion of the gaze to refer to dominant prescriptions for gender that are employed by men and women.

Pressure to comply with current definitions of beauty and femininity are manifested through many forms of the media and interaction, but there is not one single, identifiable disciplinarian. The women on the soccer team never pinpointed a specific source that was pressuring them to have a toned, thin body that wasn't overly muscular; rather, they frequently located this drive as internal criteria for themselves. This supports Duncan's claim that "the invisibility and ambiguity of the source of that gaze encourage women to believe that the body standards they apply to their own bodies are personal and private standards" (1994:50).

In addition to internalizing the gaze and communicating with a more ambiguous, general audience, the women identified a number of key reference groups that impacted their self-perceptions.[4] There were four integral groups consistently mentioned by the women athletes as having a significant effect on how they felt about their bodies. Recognizing the tremendous role male coaches, male peers, parents, and teammates played in the women's experiences is consistent with existing research in social psychology that shows how attitudes, self-evaluations, and behavior are shaped by the groups to which the individual belongs (Singer 1981). Reference group theory explains the complicated processes involved when an individual uses the values or standards of particular collectivities as a comparative frame of reference in order to evaluate him or herself (Hyman 1942; Merton 1957; Shibutani 1955; Turner 1956).

In order to understand the diverse ways in which the women felt about their muscular bodies, it is crucial to explore how the players oriented toward multiple, and sometimes conflicting, reference groups.

Male Coaches

The opinions of the male coaches affected the self-esteem of many of the players. This was especially true regarding how the players felt about their athletic abilities because the head coach decided each athlete's position and playing time on the team. If the coach did not regard a player as being skillful or competent, that player sat on the bench. However, the coach's personal opinions about the athletes on the team often extended beyond soccer. In private meetings, in informal settings, and in conversations over the phone, the head coach frequently expressed interest in things seemingly irrelevant to soccer. The head coach would inquire about the player's romantic partners and social lives in addition to their diets and weight. The women on the team interpreted these inquiries in myriad ways. Rennae, the sophomore defender, felt that the coach's questions were an attempt to get to know her as a person away from soccer:

Like once or twice a month he'll ask me about how my boy situation is going and I think that he does that because he knows how important dating and our social lives are to us [the players].

Janet, the senior with strong arms and thin legs, felt that the coach inquired about such issues for another purpose:

> I think he is trying to discourage us from being distracted from things away from the field. He is trying to figure out whether we are preoccupied or if we have our heads on straight and are focused on playing.

Other players felt quite differently about the intentions of the coach and felt that his comments and questions were invasive; although the inquiries were couched in terms of concern for the women as athletes, they were sometimes interpreted by the players as judgments on their lives, actions, or bodies.

These players interpreted the body fat percentage tests as a measure of how toned or attractive their bodies were. Consequently, some female athletes assumed the coaches' reading of the test was based on a similar concern. If the players performed badly on the test, this may be seen as a failure to live up to standards of beauty, reinforced by the coaches' disappointment.

An example of how the male coaches' attitudes were not reserved to athletic performance was apparent in the traditional "best-dressed contest" that occurred during each road trip. After consulting about each player's outfit and appearance, the two male coaches and female trainer would announce which woman athlete had the best outfit. The winner received a free meal or five dollars in addition to a lot of attention. All of the athletes were required to dress up for traveling and the head coach specified this criterion as "wearing the type of clothing you would wear on a first date to make a good impression on a young man." The coach assumed every player on the team was heterosexual and that the women based at-

tractiveness on male approval. This behavior added to the pressure many athletes already felt to present a feminine, heterosexual appearance. One player in particular objected to the head coach's dress code. While discussing the rules of the best-dressed contest privately with me, Anika, the junior goalkeeper with dreadlocks, said:

> It's ridiculous. I understand looking presentable for traveling, but who is he [the head coach] to determine what that is? I am shocked that we're being rated that way and it just makes me laugh that he is the ultimate judge. Who cares!

Other players seemed to be more concerned with meeting the appearance standard outlined by the coach. Sara, a petite junior business major, complained that "I never win, even when I try so hard. I just want to look good and get the five bucks. It never happens. Maybe I'll wear my prom dress next time we go on a trip. I'm not kidding." It seemed important to Sara that she be evaluated as pretty and well dressed by the coaching staff and her teammates.

The comments of the coaches were not merely personal judgments on players' athletic abilities or nutrition regimes, but explicit critiques of appearance and attractiveness. As figures of authority and control, the male coaches' opinions may be construed as representing the views of others in society.

The Guys

For most players, the opinions of their male peers mattered a great deal. Again, none of the athletes identified as nonheterosexual, there was little to no discussion among the women of any player that was "suspected" of being gay, and if there were lesbians on the team, none were out of the closet. This added to the atmosphere of enforced heterosexuality in the group. Men and dating were the center of conversations while the players were in the locker room, while warming up for practice, in the training room, while traveling, and in countless informal social settings. The women discussed which guys at school they thought were cute, which guys should be avoided, and often about what young men thought about the players on the team. One recurring sentiment expressed by the women athletes, both subtly and overtly, was the constant concern if their bodies remained attractive to men. The players' fear of musculature and fear of fat may be interpreted as a resistance to female physical power because it often intimidated the men around them (Dowling 2000; Lowe 1998). Nelson (1994:45) elaborated by explaining "girls learn that female strength is unattractive to men and that being attractive to men is paramount."

Parents

As many studies have shown, the earliest socialization regarding identity is based on familial interaction (Spitzack 1990) with mothers and fathers often playing the largest role in shaping their children's self-image.[5] In many Western middle-class families, relations are intimate, intensive, and relatively enduring. Often, parent-child relationships continue to shape the way in which daughters and sons view themselves throughout their lifetimes. The individual family dynamics of each of the players varied, but most parents were highly involved in their daughters' lives. In order to play intercollegiate soccer, training competitively from childhood was almost always necessary. Soccer remains a relatively elite sport

in the United States, requiring families to devote large amounts of time, energy, and money to ensure that their children remain competitive to play at high levels (Berlage 1982). The majority of the players' parents were financially and emotionally supportive. The gazing power held by mothers and fathers was very powerful and complicated as a result of these typically close relationships (Spitzack 1990). Parental evaluation of athletic performance and physical appearance was important for the majority of the players.

It was frequently the fathers who placed pressure upon the athletes. Many players explained that their fathers were generally supportive of soccer, but still emphasized the importance of looking feminine. Ashley, the tall senior center midfielder, revealed that her father's jokes made her feel confused, "He calls me his little beast. He says it kiddingly, but it makes me feel so big and ugly. It's like he wants me to be the best player on the team and at the same time be the prettiest. I don't get it. What does he want?"

Most of the parents had well-meaning intentions as they encouraged their daughters to excel in sport and in other arenas of life, but some of their comments seemed to add to the pressure many of the women felt to look and be a certain way. Mothers and fathers were impacted by the same societal definitions of femininity and attractiveness and their evaluations in many cases served to intensify the panoptic gaze the players felt.

Teammates

The final group that affected the players' body perceptions was the women on the team. Many of the relationships between players were intense and complicated. For young women in sport, their best friends and worst enemies are often their own teammates. As a team, success was dependent upon the athletes working together as a cohesive unit toward a mutual goal, but group solidarity was compounded by a few factors.

First, like any D-I program, competition for starting positions and playing time was fierce. Second, the interaction between the players was affected on some level by competition for male attention and status within the domain of physical attractiveness (Spitzack 1990). This second factor was especially significant when analyzing how other women contributed to appearance pressure on the team. Lack of support between female athletes has been noted by other sport scholars, such as Lowe (1998), who found that women bodybuilders attributed jealousy and competitiveness to the relative absence of unity and cohesiveness among other women participants.

Players on the team admitted being acutely aware of other players' bodies and appearances. The atmosphere in the locker room was brought up as a site for evaluation, intentional or not, because it was especially tight and personal. Players rarely took showers in this space, but they were frequently in various states of undress. Indirectly looking at other people's bodies was a common and unspoken practice, but there were also times when the women explicitly made body comparisons. Jennifer, the junior transfer, described this atmosphere of heightened body awareness in the locker room:

It's really funny when we go on trips and have to take community showers with everyone [on the team]. It's not like it's weird to be naked in front of each other because we're so close and just run around

nudie laughing at each other. You can tell that everyone is secretly checking one another out—seeing who has big boobs or a good stomach or whatever. I think it would be really uncomfortable to be naked in front of women I don't know because it's like they would be sizing me up or something. But here, we all notice things about each other's bodies, but it's not like we care about the little imperfections or anything.

As I mentioned earlier, the players consistently talked about their bodies in a variety of situations such as before practice, while traveling, and in social situations when the women were just hanging out with one another. The typical interaction about appearance consisted of one player complaining about a specific "problem area" with her body and the other players' responses were usually ones of concern or disagreement about that individual's negative self-evaluation. For example, on a plane trip for an away game, I overheard a conversation between two players. Debbie stated, "I guess I'm most self-conscious about my calves. They're so muscular! I think they look gross." Janet then replied, "Oh my god, no! You have great legs. Your calves are buff, but they look great. Other girls would kill to have those. I have 'cankles'—my calves just run right into my ankles. They are so skinny and undefined. I'd rather have yours."

Another example of this type of interchange about bodies occurred at practice while the team was gathered in a circle stretching for warm-up, Megan, the tallest and most muscularly developed freshmen, poked at her knees and asked the player next to her sarcastically, "Can you get liposuction on your knees? Look at all this fat!" The other player laughed and tried to reassure Megan that the fat she was concerned about was really just muscle and that it didn't look bad. Megan shook her head disbelievingly.

These quotes illustrate how supportive the women athletes were of one another as they attempted to offset individuals' unhappiness with their bodies, but such positive complimentary responses are often expected in interaction among women. It was rare that the women voiced a negative critique about a teammate's body to her face when directly asked for their opinions.[6] Although female friendships are sometimes characterized by jealousy, the women on the team seemed to present a group identity of being cohesive and reassuring of one another. Sara, the petite junior forward, described the feeling she got from the team regarding issues of appearance:

> It's a combination between competitive and supportive, but it's mostly good. I mean, as teammates and friends, we all want each other to do their best—on the field, in school, or whatever. I think other girls that I don't know, like the ones we see when we go out, seem way more judgmental and superficial. And I feel like they're [the non-teammates] judging me on my clothes or body, but here [on the team] everyone knows me and I feel comfortable.

Other players, however, felt that the environment on the team was more contentious and that players were subtly disparaging of one another. Anika, the goalkeeper with the dreadlocks, explained:

> I feel more pressure from these girls [on the team] to look a certain way or wear the best clothes. Most of my other friends are guys and I never feel that competition that goes on with women. I don't like to stress about

it or feel like people are checking me out and rating me.

The Impact of Key Reference Groups and Acts of Resistance

How the women selected among these various reference groups is complicated and variable; the athletes alternately accepted and resisted the opinions of those close to them. This is due in part to the conflicting messages coming from each reference group, as the comments served to both reinforce and challenge dominant assumptions about the female body. The male coaches, male peers, parents, and players themselves drew upon cultural gender stereotypes when considering the appearances of the women athletes, such as labeling certain characteristics as masculine or feminine.

In this way, it becomes clear that gender is more than an individual attribute or social role, but rather, that it is a situated accomplishment forged by social actors (Fenstermaker Berk 1985; Fenstermaker and West 2002; West and Zimmerman 1987). Conceptualizing gender as something that is "done" by people reveals that gender is fundamentally an emergent property of interaction. This is particularly helpful when attempting to understand how key reference groups influenced the ways in which the women athletes ascribed meaning to their self-presentations. Through these social exchanges, the women were continually renegotiating and redefining their own body experiences.

The metaphor of the panopticon is used in the context of my study to reinforce the notion that conceptions of what constitutes a "gender appropriate physique" are socially produced and enforced, yet often experienced as a private struggle to comply with one's personal standards. While Foucault's work is particularly attuned to social control, I do not mean to imply that women are subjugated to these social constructions of beauty from above. Rather, dominant notions surrounding femininity and muscular bodies emerge through social interaction and are ultimately negotiated by the women themselves. So while specific groups may have impacted the women's self-perceptions and attitudes about ideal bodies, there remained alternative forms of behavior and appearances that the women could choose from; their decisions to seek out these alternatives demonstrated individual agency and resistance.

Although my findings indicate that the women were acutely aware of the how their appearances and behaviors might be negatively construed, they remained dedicated to improving their bodies and skills for performance. Most of the women remained somewhat ambivalent about their self-presentations, but predominantly chose to participate fully and enthusiastically in training and competition, regardless of the effect on their bodies. This evidence echoes the findings of other studies of women's subjective experience of sport (Bolin and Granskog 2003; Cox and Thompson 2000; Dworkin 2001; Hall 1996; Hargreaves 1994; Markula 1995; Theberge 2000), which found that women felt empowered through their athletic activity. Through subtle acts of resistance, it is clear that the women soccer players pushed back against ideals that threatened to constrict their participation in sport.

One example can be found in Mariah's dedication to weightlifting despite the fact that her muscular body sometimes elicited negative reactions from her boyfriend, fa-

ther, and teammates. She embraced the power and independence that her physique gave her, instead of scaling back her body to conform to others' opinions of what her body should look like. Another illustration of individual agency can be found with Anika, the junior goalkeeper with dreadlocks, who often distinguished herself from the group by expressing her individuality. On away trips she creatively interpreted the head coach's dress code by wearing sneakers with her skirts, she frequently chose not to participate in gossip or "body talk" that was common among the other players, and she was vocal in her opposition to body fat composition testing. Anika's actions indicate a refusal to embrace the ideology that women athletes must strive to maintain heterosexual attractiveness or conform to stereotypical images of femininity (Hall 1996).

Conclusion

To varying degrees, the women athletes scrutinize their bodies and the bodies of their teammates, checking for signs of excessive fat or muscularity. Such transgressions were interpreted by the women as violations of their own aesthetic standards. However, their resistance to size in general, whether it is fat or muscle, may be interpreted as apprehension to disrupting the gender order for fear of being labeled deviant. As the women soccer players reflected on their own physicality on and off the playing field, it became clear that many were simultaneously resisting and complying with hegemonic definitions of female beauty.

Indeed, it is clear that the female athlete remains "contested ideological terrain" (Messner 1988), where societal expectations surrounding gender play out. The emergence of a new fit body ideal suggested that conceptions of femininity and attractiveness are changing, but are still fraught with tension and complexity.

My findings indicate that women athletes continue to be constrained by gendered expectations of what constitutes appropriate feminine behavior and appearance, suggesting implications that extend far beyond the institution of sport. Exploring the intricate and nuanced ways women athletes "do gender" on a micro level cannot be understood without recognizing the larger macro level allocation of resources and opportunities based on gender (Stewart 2003). In a post–Title IX generation where women have made tremendous social gains both inside and outside the arena of sport, critical questions about gender equity must continue to be posed, along with research that is committed to pursuing those answers.

Notes

1. Originally, this project began as a class assignment, in which the professor had received "blanket approval" from the department's protection of human subjects committee (IRB) for all research conducted in the class. When I decided to expand my research into a senior thesis project, I sought, and received, specific approval to study the team from the committee.

2. My existing role on the team brought unique advantages, as well as constraints, to the research process. By combining my own experience in soccer with my access to other women involved in the sport, I had an intimate familiarity with the scene and was able to interact with others in a natural manner. While I didn't have to worry about gaining entrée or carving out a membership role for the purpose of the investigation, I was faced with a different set of challenges. As a complete member researcher with existing ties to the group, I had to create space for my new research role to emerge, strive to look at the set-

ting with a fresh perspective, and often had to broaden or adjust my existing relationships with other members of the group (Adler and Adler 1987).

3. In her study of women who work out in gyms, Dworkin (2001) found that a large category of women worked out specifically to lose weight or to gain minimal tone. These "nonlifters" expressed fear of developing excessive bodybuilder musculature. They avoided the "masculinizing," anaerobic activity of weightlifting and preferred more aerobic workouts on cardiovascular machines. They expressed notions that these were more feminine ways to exercise and build a gender appropriate physique.

4. One of the major tenets of symbolic interactionist theory is the *looking glass–self* (Cooley 1902), which asserts that we come to see ourselves as we think others see us. This influential concept emphasizes the power of social influence on self-conceptions and further articulates the influence of key reference groups on how the women viewed themselves. However, these reflected appraisals are not passively internalized by the women. The self is formulated through a process of social influence whereby the individual actively selects from the feedback from others, choosing to alternatively ignore or accept their opinions (Blumer 1969; Cooley 1902).

5. This is consistent with symbolic interactionist theory (see Blumer 1969; Cooley 1902).

6. Hochschild (1983) has suggested that feeling rules dictate how women discuss one another's appearances when together. Also, the types of body conversations which occurred between the players can be understood using Goffman's ideas on supportive interchanges (1971) and face work (1955). He describes how social relationships are preserved through interpersonal rituals where people demonstrate their involvement with one another and trade courtesies in order to protect one another's face or self-image.

References

Adler, Patricia A. and Peter Adler. 1994. "Observational Techniques." Pp. 79–104 in *Handbook of Qualitative Research*, edited by Norman

K. Denzin and Yvonna S. Lincoln. Thousand Oaks, CA: Sage.

———. 1987. *Membership Roles in Field Research*. Newbury Park, CA: Sage.

Berger, John. 1972. *Ways of Seeing*. London: Penguin Books.

Berlage, Gai. 1982. "Are Children's Competitive Team Sports Teaching Corporate Values?" *Arena Review* 6:15–21.

Blinde, Elaine M. 1989. "Unequal Exchange and Exploitation in College Sport." *Arena Review* 13:110–21.

Blinde, Elaine M. and Diane E. Taub. 1992a. "Homophobia and Women's Sport: The Disempowerment of Athletes." *Sociological Focus* 25:151–65.

———. 1992b. "Women Athletes as Falsely Accused Deviants: Managing the Lesbian Stigma." *Sociological Quarterly* 33:521–33.

Blumer, Herbert. 1969. *Symbolic Interactionism: Perspective and Method*. Englewood Cliffs, NJ: Prentice-Hall.

Bolin, Anne and Jane Granskog, 2003. *Athletic Intruders: Ethnographic Research on Women, Culture, and Exercise*. Albany: State University of New York Press.

Bordo, Susan R. 1993. *Unbearable Weight: Feminism, Western Culture, and the Body*. Berkeley: University of California Press.

Cahn, Susan K. 1994. *Coming on Strong: Gender and Sexuality in Twentieth-Century Women's Sport*, New York: Free Press.

Chernin, Kim. 1981. *The Obsession: Reflections on the Tyranny of Slenderness*. New York: Harper & Row.

Cooley, Charles H. 1902. *Human Nature and Social Organization*. New York: Scribner's.

Cox, Barbara and Shona Thompson. 2000. "Multiple Bodies: Sportswomen, Soccer, and Sexuality." *International Review for the Sociology of Sport* 35:5–20.

Dowling, Collette. 2000. *The Frailty Myth: Women Approaching Physical Strength and Equality*. New York: Random House.

Duncan, Margaret Carlisle. 1994. "The Politics of Women's Body Images and Practices: Foucault, The Panopticon, and *Shape* Magazine." *Journal of Sport and Social Issues* 18:40–65.

Dworkin, Shari L. 2003. "A Woman's Place is in the . . . Cardiovascular Room?? Gender Relations, the Body, and the Gym." Pp. 131–58 in *Athletic Intruders: Ethnographic Research on Women, Culture, and Exercise*, edited by Anne Bolin and Jane Granskog. Albany: State University of New York Press.

———. 2001. "Holding Back: Negotiating a Glass Ceiling on Women's Muscular Strength." *Sociological Perspectives* 44:332–50.

Fenstermaker Berk, Sarah. 1985. *The Gender Factory: The Apportionment of Work in American Households*. New York: Plenum.

Fenstermaker, Sarah and Candace West. (eds.) 2002. *Doing Gender, Doing Difference: Inequality, Power, and Institutional Change*. New York: Routledge.

Goffman, Erving. 1971. *Relations in Public: Microstudies of the Public Order*. New York: Basic Books.

———. 1955. "On Face-work: An Analysis of Ritual Elements in Social Interaction." *Psychiatry* 18:213–31.

Griffin, Pat. 1998. *Strong Women, Deep Closets: Lesbians and Homophobia in Sport*. Champaign, IL: Human Kinetics.

Hall, Margaret Ann. 1996. *Feminism and Sporting Bodies: Essays on Theory and Practice*. Champaign, IL: Human Kinetics.

Haravon, Lea. 1995. "Fat Bodies and Foucault, or Inside Every Fat Woman Is a Subjugated Knowledge Trying to Get Out." Paper presented at the annual meeting of the North American Society for the Sociology of Sport, Sacramento, CA.

Hargreaves, Jennifer. 1994. *Sporting Females: Critical Issues in the History and Sociology of Women's Sports*. London: Routledge.

Hayano, David M. 1979. "Auto-ethnography: Paradigms, Problems, and Prospects." *Human Organization* 38:99–104.

Hesse-Biber, Sharlene. 1996. *Am I Thin Enough Yet?: The Cult of Thinness and the Commercialization of Identity*. New York: Oxford University Press.

Heywood, Leslie. 1996. *Dedication to Hunger: The Anorexic Aesthetic in Modern Culture*. Berkeley: University of California Press.

Heywood, Leslie and Shari Dworkin. 2003. *Built to Win: The Female Athlete as Cultural Icon.* Minneapolis: University of Minnesota Press.

Hochschild, Arlie Russell. 1983. *The Managed Heart: Commercialization of Human Feeling.* Berkeley: University of California Press.

Hyman, Herbert H. 1942. "The Psychology of Status." *Archives of Psychology* 269:93–126.

Lenskyj, Helen. 1994. "Sexuality and Femininity in Sport Contexts: Issues and Alternatives." *Journal of Sport and Social Issues* 18:356–67.

———. 1986. *Out of Bounds: Women, Sport and Sexuality.* Toronto, ON: Women's Press.

Lowe, Maria R. 1998. *Women of Steel: Female Body Builders and the Struggle for Self-Definition.* New York: New York University Press.

Markula, Pirkko. 1995. "Firm but Shapely, Fit but Sexy, Strong but Thin: The Postmodern Aerobicizing Female Bodies." *Sociology of Sport Journal* 12:424–50.

Merton, Robert K. 1957. *Social Theory and Social Structure.* Glencoe, IL: Free Press.

Messner, Michael A. 1992. *Power at Play: Sports and the Problem of Masculinity.* Boston, MA: Beacon Press.

———. 1988. "Sports and Male Domination: The Female Athlete as Contested Ideological Terrain." *Sociology of Sport Journal* 5:197–211.

Nelson, Mariah Burton. 1994. *The Stronger Women Get, the More Men Love Football: Sexism and the American Culture of Sports.* New York: Avon Press.

Reimer, Jeffery W. 1977. "Varieties of Opportunistic Research." *Urban Life* 5:467–77.

Ryan, Joan. 1995. *Little Girls in Pretty Boxes.* New York: Warner Books Edition.

Shibutani, Tamotsu. 1955. "Reference Groups as Perspectives." *American Journal of Sociology* 60:562–69.

Singer, Eleanor. 1981. "Reference Groups and Social Evaluations." Pp. 66–93 in *Social Psychology*, edited by Morris Rosenberg and Ralph H. Turner. New York: Basic Books.

Spitzack, Caroline. 1990. *Confessing Excess: Women and the Politics of Body Reduction.* Albany: State University of New York Press.

Stewart, Alex. 1998. *The Ethnographer's Method.* Thousand Oaks, CA: Sage.

Stewart, Mary White. 2003. "Gender." Pp. 761–81 in *Handbook of Symbolic Interactionism*, edited by Larry T. Reynolds and Nancy J. Herman-Kinney. Walnut Creek, CA: Alta Mira Press.

Theberge, Nancy. 2000. *Higher Goals: Women's Ice Hockey and the Politics of Gender.* Albany: State University of New York Press.

Turner, Ralph H. 1956. "Role-Taking, Role Standpoint and Reference Group Behavior." *American Journal of Sociology* 61:316–28.

West, Candace and Don H. Zimmerman. 1987. "Doing Gender." *Gender & Society* 1:125–51.

Chapter 28

MANAGING BODILY CAPITAL

Loïc Wacquant

In this excerpt from *Body and Soul: Notebooks of an Apprentice Boxer*, Loïc Wacquant focuses on the social world of black boxers in a gym in Chicago and examines their daily struggles both to enhance their bodily capital and to avoid the dissipating vices of the surrounding inner-city environment. Wacquant's attention to the boxers' "'concrete science' of their own bodies" enriches our understanding of body culture and sport.

There are few practices for which the French expression *"payer de sa personne"* (which literally means "paying with one's person") takes on a more powerful meaning than for boxing. More than in any other sport, the successful pursuit of a career, especially in the professional ranks, presupposes a rigorous management of the body, a meticulous maintenance of each one of its parts (most notably the hands but also the face),[1] an attention of every moment, in and out of the ring, to its proper functioning and protection. In other words, it requires an extraordinarily efficient relation to the specific capital constituted of one's physical resources, at the edge of rational management. This is because the pugilist's body is at once the *tool* of his work—an offensive weapon and defensive shield—and the target of his opponent. Nonetheless, this relation is neither the product of a deliberately maximizing attitude guided by individual decisions made in full knowledge of the facts nor the mechanical effect of external constraints acting onto the body without mediation (in the manner of *"dressage"* according to Foucault),[2] but rather the expression of a *pugilistic practical sense*, a sense of corporeal thrift acquired gradually through long-term contact with other athletes and with coaches, workout after workout and fight after fight, which remains as such inaccessible to conscious and deliberate mastery, in spite of the conjugated efforts of the boxers, trainers, and managers most inclined to the rationalization of their trade.[3] For the knowledge that boxers acquire of the functioning of their bodies, the practical apprehension they have of the limits that must not be exceeded, of the strengths and weaknesses of their anatomy (a low center of gravity or great hand speed, an overly slender neck or brittle hands), the conduct and tactics they adopt in the ring, their conditioning program, and the rules of life they follow pertain not to systematic observation and reflective calculation of the optimal path to follow but, rather, from a sort of "concrete science"[4] of their own bodies, of their somatic potentialities and shortcomings, drawn from daily training and "the often grisly experience of hitting and being hit repeatedly."[5]

There exist many techniques for preserving and making one's *bodily capital* fructify. From the manner of wrapping their hands (and the type of protective bandages used) to the way they breathe during a workout, to all kinds of defensive tricks, to the use of creams, unguents, and elixirs expressly concocted, to special exercises and culinary regimens, the Woodlawn boxers resort to a wide gamut of devices designed to husband and replenish their reserves of energy and protect their strategic organs. Some imitate former champion Jack Dempsey, famed for dipping his hands in brine in order to toughen the skin on his knuckles. Others coat their chest and arms before training with Albolene, an oil that "warms up the body and relaxes the muscles" (according to its directions for use) or spray a vitamin E solution on the ridge of their fists after working out.[6] One slips a dry sponge under his handwraps, so as to cushion the impact of the repeated shocks against the heavy bag, while another, whose bones are fragile relative to his punching power, gets regularly checked out by a hand therapist. Professionals who have the means to hire the services of a paid trainer, such as Ed "Smithie" Smith or former world champion Alphonzo Ratliff, end each workout with a long rubdown under his expert hands. And I could reproduce here nearly word for word the description that Weinberg and Arond offer of the gyms in Chicago in the early 1950s, so closely does it apply to what I observed at the Woodlawn Boys Club.

The boxer comes to consider his body, especially his hands, as his stock-in-trade. Boxers have varied formulas for preventing their hands from excess swelling, from excessive pain, or from being broken. This does not mean a hypochondriacal interest, because they emphasize virility and learn to slough off and to disdain punishment. But fighters continually seek nostrums and exercises for improving their bodies. One practiced Yogi [*sic*], another became a physical cultist, a third went on periodic fasts; others seek out lotions, vitamins, and other means of improving their endurance, alertness, and punching power.[7]

This is one of the main paradoxes of boxing: one must *make use of one's body without using it up*, but the management adapted to that objective does not obey a methodical and considered plan, if only because of the precarious living conditions of those who practice it. The pugilist thus navigates "by eye" between two equally dangerous reefs— all the more dangerous because they are invisible, mobile over time, and to a great extent subjective: on the one hand, an excess of preparation that squanders resources in vain and needlessly shortens a career; on the other, a lack of discipline and training that increases the risk of serious injury and compromises the chances of success in the ring by leaving part of one's fighting capacities unexploited.

The couple formed by Butch and Curtis offer an ideal-typical realization of this opposition. On the one side, Butch is pugilistic frugality incarnate: he trains and boxes with sobriety and economy; he knows how to deny himself for very long periods of time any deviation from the dietary, sexual, emotional, or professional rules of the craft. Everything in his punctilious conditioning expresses an acute sense of equilibrium and the long term. But Butch's asceticism, which, in its rigor, borders on abstinence with respect to anything that could injure his preparation, sometimes turns into anxiety and then pushes him to train too hard, to consume his forces to the point of consummating them. Curtis, on the other side, embodies a deficit in rationality that manifests itself in sometimes irregular training and in fluctuating moral and physical hygiene. Outside of the gym first, where he does not always prove able to deprive himself of the little pleasures of life (carbonated drinks, sweets, fatty foods), and where his sexual temperance knows highs and lows. In the gym next, where he will sometimes go through long stretches without training (especially after a bout), in contrast to Butch who "clocks in" at the club with the regularity of a metronome. Unlike his older gym-mate, Curtis makes tumultuous, unbridled, almost "crazy" use of his body—that is to say, deviant according to the canons of rational boxing—as when he walks up to his opponent, nay his sparring partner, with his guard down so as to offer his uncovered face as a provocation, daring the other to risk an attack. In so doing, he uses up his body for nothing, gratuitously exposing himself to injury and to DeeDee's ill-contained ire.

These differences in disposition between the two boxers are redoubled by their respective constitution and character: Butch is easygoing, placid, and always even-tempered; Curtis's moods are constantly changing and unpredictable, his emotions brusque and edgy, worn on his sleeves, and his energy level as erratic as a fever chart. Whereas Butch's training schedule is rarely perturbed by health troubles, Curtis gets sick frequently (DeeDee likes to say that "Curtis, he gets a cold every other day"), to the point that his manager insists on sending him to spend the middle of winter on his farm in South Carolina so he will not have to sacrifice precious weeks of preparation to a tenacious flu. This contrast of personalities is closely correlated with and reinforced by the gap in social condition between the two club-mates: Butch is a proletarian, a member of the blue-collar aristocracy, endowed with a solid job and income; Curtis is a subproletarian, shorn of all social and economic security, subjected to the cycles of employment in unskilled and unstable labor.[8] And the two diverge even in their economic expectations as regards their trade: Butch recognizes that his chances of making money are minimal; Curtis daydreams of a lightning-quick rise that would miraculously catapult him to the very top of the social ladder.

Curtis: "In One Night, I Can Make a Million Dollars"

At 130 pounds and five feet seven inches, Curtis Strong campaigns in the super lightweight category. He is twenty-seven years old and has been boxing as a professional for three years. He came to the manly art late, after having made a name for himself as a "tough cookie" in his neighborhood. "Since I was short, I always had a whole buncha guys givin' me grief, so I really had to learn how to fight. When I was a kid, I fought *before* school, *during* school and *after* school. Had to defend myself." On the strength of an amateur record of 37 wins for 6 losses, Curtis turned pro in 1986, after taking the title in his division at the Chicago Golden Gloves, the city's most prestigious amateur tournament. Since then, he has confirmed all the hopes pinned on him by the club by winning eight consecutive fights before conquering the Illinois championship in a tough battle, outscoring a Mexican fighter feared for his experience and his punch. (Headlining the card that night was the legendary Roberto "Manos de Piedra" Duran who, at the ripe age of thirty-seven, took his fourth world title in his 97th pro victory.)

Curtis's manager, Jeb Garney, a rich white dog breeder who owns several farms and stables in Illinois and South Carolina and who sits on the board of directors of the Woodlawn Boys Club, harbors great ambitions for him: "Curtis doesn't know how good he is. If you watch films of the truly great boxers, like Johnny Bratton, Sugar Ray Robinson, Sandy Saddler, or Henry Armstrong, you see that he's got some of the punches and some of the moves of the great ones. He's got it in him. He's young and inexperienced, he sure got a lot to learn, but I feel like he can become a great fighter." However, Curtis is passably lacking in personal discipline and does not always impose on himself the hygiene of life that his career demands. To allow him to train under good conditions and to be able to watch over him better, the Boys Club came up with a quarter-time job as janitor for him. After his daily workout, Curtis waits for closing time to clean the gym, mop the locker room, vacuum the carpet in the entry hall, empty the

trashcans, and set the tables in the day-care center back in place.

A catlike and impulsive boxer, gifted with great arm speed and an acute sense of counterpunching, his exceptionally aggressive behavior in the ring, at the edge of losing self-control and breaking the rules, has rightfully earned him the reputation of being a "badass" between the ropes. This nasty athletic persona is in perfect accord with his style, which is to submit his opponent to relentless pressure by marching straight at him and punching from all angles without respite. Yet it is from his Christian faith that Curtis draws his inspiration in the squared circle: he always wears a crucifix on a chain, which he keeps in his boot during fights and never fails to kiss ceremoniously before and after every bout. He never climbs into the ring without first having prayed amid his five brothers and his minister cousin. When I ask him if he "celebrated" after his surprise victory over the state champion at the International Amphitheater, Woodlawn's star boxer answers soberly: "I don't celebrate, I thank God. I dedicated my fight to God. I don't do anything other than what he tell me to do. I'm only executin' his plans for me, in the ring, outside the ring, an' then I thank him, tha's all." Curtis's ambition is that of many young boxers on their way up, who think "the sky's the limit": to win a world title, or, better yet, to unify the three major titles in his weight class and pocket purses numbering in the millions of dollars along the way.

Curtis issues from a subproletarian family at the border of complete destitution (nine children, an absent father, a mother who works sporadically as a barmaid and survives mainly on measly welfare payments), whose reputation is well established in the street.

DeeDee tells that "all his brothers are street fighters. They all know how t'fight. But none of 'em come to d'gym, he's the only one. He got a older brother who's shorter than him but even meaner, *really* mean. (With regret in his voice.) It's a damn shame he don't come to d'gym. He's tough, real tough, he's a natural. But he ain't got too much upstairs, he don't get too tired for usin' his mind. Kinda like Curtis."

Long an avid skirt chaser and the father of a two-year-old boy and a one-year-old girl, Curtis resigned himself to marrying their mother when she threatened to leave him after four years of a rocky life together. When a gym-mate reminds him that "DeeDee say that there's only one thing worse than junk food (for a boxer), that's women," Curtis acquiesces: "Yeah, tha's why I got married. All them fights I lost, that was when I was messin' around with chicks. Afterwards, my wife she told me, if we don't get married, she's gonna leave me, it's over with. It make me think, 'cuz I love her an' stuff, you know, so I said to myself, I don't wanna lose her, no I don't, and then, all this messin' around messes up my boxin'. So I married her."

Owing to the feebleness and irregularity of his income (his job at the Boys Club earns him less than $100 a week after taxes and includes no benefits or medical coverage), it is often hard to make ends meet at the end of the month and the food stamps that the family receives are a vital complement— Curtis sometimes sells me some to generate cash when his finances have run completely dry. His wife, who, like him, dropped out of high school, is taking an evening typing class in the somewhat unrealistic hope of one day becoming secretary to the clerk of the municipal court. In the meantime, she has been working as a waitress in a takeout restaurant owned by a Thai family in an ill-reputed section of the black neighborhood of South Shore, south of Woodlawn.

"See, what's really great, Louie, is that we both got our own career, it's not like one of us has to carry the other on his back. My wife, she has her career, she work hard at it, an' I got my career here, I can concentrate on my career, win for my career. . . . All I gotta do is fight hard an' God will help me win the big fight tha's gonna earn me a lotta money, win the world title and a great pile of dough. I'm gonna become a big man an' stuff." He laughs and throws a series of mock punches to my belly. I laugh with him, but the scene is rather pathetic, he holding his broom and dustpan, painting a picture that is as attractive as it is improbable and rejoicing over "careers" that are so far nonexistent, while I, a young graduate of elite universities, come slumming to this boxing gym to get away from the horror and boredom of academic routine and its privileges. [Field note, 11 October 1988]

Butch: "I Can't Quit Now"

At six feet two inches and 175 pounds of muscle, twenty-nine-year-old Wayne Hankins boxed for seven years among the amateurs before "turning pro" in 1985. Better known at the gym by the nickname "Butch," he is one of the rare members of the club who can boast having a stable and coveted job: he is a firefighter for the City of Chicago, a very well-paid public job (about $3,000 a month) dutifully protected by the powerful civil service union (which affords him unemployment and health coverage as well as paid vacations). On fight nights, "The Fighting Fireman"—Butch's nom de guerre—struts onto the squared circle draped in a magnificent, flaming red robe emblazoned with the municipal firefighters' union seal and logo. And, at each of his appearances, a faithful legion of colleagues from work come to cheer him on noisily from the stands. Married and the father of a large family ("At home I've got four kids, my father, a dog, a cat, seven birds, and a giant aquarium"), Butch supplements his work as a fireman with that, much less prestigious and certainly less remunerative, of bagger at one of the outlets of the Jewel supermarket chain in order to improve the daily standard of living of his household. On weekends, he also occasionally cuts hair and trims moustaches on the barber chair he has installed in his basement garage.

Butch is reputed and admired for his implacable self-discipline, both during training and outside the gym, and for his fierce will to succeed, but also for his equanimity, his sangfroid and total self-control, which are perfectly adapted to his strategy as a "boxer-puncher." Between the ropes, he is the archetype of the economical fighter: every blow is accounted for, every slip planned, every move adjusted to the millimeter so as to minimize his expenditure of energy and to maximize that of his opponent. Does the objective rationalization of life imposed on him by his job as a firefighter (which suffers neither delays nor approximations in matters of schedules and readiness) underpin this pugilistic style, or, conversely, did a general predisposition toward economy and frugal efficiency propel him into both this stable manual profession and into the ring? It is hard to decide in any case, there is a striking affinity between the regularity and predictability of the daily practices required by his occupational at-

tachment—which extends that of his father, a former construction worker—and the manner in which Butch engages his body in the gym and in the ring.

In 1983, Butch also won the Chicago Golden Gloves and nourished the hope of taking the national amateur middleweight title, which would have earned him a spot on the U.S. Olympic team. But, after being seriously weakened by a training injury (lips cut and tongue shredded by an uppercut thrown by his partner after the bell, which required fifteen stitches in his mouth), he was beaten by a hair in the finals, having heroically gotten through four preliminary bouts. With a quaver of admiration in his voice, DeeDee recalls how Butch refused to quit, even though he practically could not eat and was growing visibly thinner as the date of the national tournament drew near. "I told him: 'You can't fight in that shape, it's no use, we're done, you gotta give up the fight.' He replied, 'No way, DeeDee, I've worked too hard, I've suffered too much to get here, I can't quit now.' And he went."

After that bitter disappointment, Butch stopped boxing for three years. He preferred the security of the firefighter's job he was offered at the time to the very uncertain prospects of a career as a prize-fighter. It was at this time that he got married and founded a family. But the demon of the ring soon won out and Butch found his way back to the gym with an exponentially greater will to win. His passion for boxing does not prevent him from remaining lucid and realistic: he wonders about his sporting future and does not envision quitting his job to bet everything in the ring, his success between the ropes will determine how far he goes. For the moment, he has set himself the objective of becoming "the best in

Chicago" and he counts his earnings expectancy in the tens of thousands of dollars at best. His entire family supports him in this pugilistic "second career" which has taken off in a whiz (five straight wins, four of them by kayo, for one draw); his wife and father, who were definitely reticent when he started out, come to all his fights and shower him with encouragement every minute, at home as well as at the boxing cards, where they number among his most demonstrative supporters.

One of the obsessions of the practioners of the manly art is keeping themselves, if not at their optimal weight, at least in the vicinity of their official weight.[9] The old sliding-weight metal scale that sits throne-like in the back room is there to remind everyone of this requirement. Pugilistic folklore abounds with stories of boxers forced to perform fantastic—and often medically dangerous—athletic feats at the last minute in order to lose superfluous pounds before the fateful weigh-in.[10] The members of the Woodlawn Boys Club resort to draconian diets or interminable jogging sessions to rid themselves of impermissible pounds before a fight; others train wearing several layers of clothing or plastic wrappings, or with their chests squeezed by a latex girdle that is supposed to help them slim down. One summer on the eve of a bout, Cliff lost more than eight pounds by running the entire afternoon under a blazing sun dressed in sweaters, a thick wool cap, and two pairs of pants. One fine June evening, I found the locker room closed and so steamed up one would think it was a Turkish bath. Tony was there, shadowboxing and jogging in place next to the shower running full blast and scalding hot, bundled into a heavy track-

suit, his head and torso enveloped in a clear plastic hooded jacket: "Gotta lose nine pounds, Louie, *pfff-pfff,* tha's why I'm in here, *pfff-pfff.* The weigh-in's tomorrow mornin', *pfff-pfff,* I'monna make it, only two more to go."

DeeDee exercises a punctilious surveillance of every moment over the physical state of his charges so as to make sure that they are not straying too far from their "fight weight," either downward, which would signal dangerous overtraining (or the possibility of a malignant ailment),[11] or upward, which is by far the more frequent case. And to lead them back to the straight and narrow path of frugality, he resorts now to humor, now to affection, now to raw authority or sarcasm, as one can see in this field note dated 25 August 1990.

Ashante put on the gloves with Mark, then with Reese, three rounds each. He has a little bit more "gas" this time but he still seems heavy and is dragging himself around the ring. DeeDee is worried: "Ashante ain't doin' well at all. He cain't get rid of those extra pounds and he don't have no speed no more. Reese hit'im with everything he threw today, he was just standin' right in fronta him." It's true that Ashante lacks vivacity and side-to-side movement, he who usually has no trouble making the young amateurs who "move around" with him miss. When he arrived earlier, DeeDee was quick to ask him the supremely humiliating question: "What's *that belly there?*" (when Ashante is in jeans and T-shirt, it's easy to see that he's overweight). Ashante responded with an embarrassed smile, pretending not to understand that DeeDee was talking to him: "What belly, where?" "There, right in front of you, *right under your eyes.*" Ashante didn't squawk and scrammed looking really pissed.

A good trainer needs not make his boxers step on the scale to know whether they are over the limit: he can "read" their weight from their physical appearance, the way they carry themselves, even the mere bounce of their step. One day in August of 1990, Lorenzo shows up at the gym again after several days of unexpected absence and a stormy spat with Eddie, his trainer. Eddie looks him up and down, and snaps in a negative and falsely inquisitive tone: "How much you weighin', a hundred-'n'-fifty?" Lorenzo does not let himself get rattled: he inspects himself from head to toe in the mirror and mentally weighs himself: "I'm a lil' over my weight (of 139 pounds), 'round one forty-five, I think." "You look like you're at least one-fifty when you walkin'." "No, I'm sure I'm 'round forty-five." End of the argument—but not the end of the problem.

One of the major functions of the pair formed by the trainer and the manager is to modulate and adjust the trajectory of their charge over time so as to optimize the "return on pugilistic investment" of the trio, that is, the ratio between the corporeal capital stacked and the dividends procured by fights in the form of money, ring experience, notoriety, and usable contacts with influential agents in the field such as promoters. This management is effected in three relatively independent orders that one must strive to make coincide: the temporality of the boxer's individual career, the trajectory of potential opponents, and the "economic time" of promoters. The ideal is to bring one's boxer to his peak (be it local) at the moment when the opportunity comes to fight, for a meaningful purse, a renowned boxer who is himself at the cusp of a phase of decline, and who thus still bears an accumulated symbolic capital (ranking, titles, and fame) that is well above his current pugilistic capacities.[12] But the higher one climbs in the hierarchy of the boxing field, the more control over time slips away from the fighters to fall into the hands of specialized economic agents, notably promoters and executives in charge of sports programming for the networks that broadcast the big-media bouts. As Thomas Hauser aptly notes, "time [is] the enemy" of boxers, and not only because they get old and wear themselves out.[13]

This management of duration begins among the amateurs, some of whom—left to their own devices or poorly advised—burn themselves out in pursuit of an ephemeral regional or national glory with uncertain economic repercussions so that, when they join the ranks of the "pros," they have already seriously amputated their bodily capital and can hardly hope for a long and fruitful career. According to DeeDee, that was the case of Kenneth "The Candy Man" Gould, a recent U.S. Olympic medalist in Seoul, whom he believes expended himself too much in the amateurs by competing in over three hundred matches: "He already had too many fights. He ain't got enough pep left in him. I dunno, we'll see. I told him to turn pro, it's gotta be years ago." Why did he not do it? Saddled with a manager who was inexperienced or poorly connected within networks of influence, Gould was adamant about fighting in the Seoul Olympics in Korea (where the Frenchman Laurent Boudouani beat him in the semifinals). The future of twenty-two-year-old Kelcie Banks, another young hopeful from Chicago (a Woodlawn Boys Club alumnus and amateur world champion), also defeated in the preliminaries for the last Olympics, appears even more compromised: he has over six hundred amateur fights to his record, as many as three a week in worthless little tournaments: "Tha's a lot of punches and a lotta wear and tear on a young body . . . too much wear and tear," DeeDee grumbles when we evoke his case. A few months later, his prophecy seems to be coming true: "Kelcie ain't doin' nuthin', he's not gonna do nuthin': he's washed up, done. Think about it, nobody wanta sign some guy who's already washed up. He went to that training camp in Texas (where new professional recruits are picked up by the big national promoters), it didn't work out. Nobody signed him. If he'da won in the Olympics, he wouldave gotten a thirty- or forty-thousand-dollar bonus up front. But he got beat and he didn't get a damn thing out of it. He's too beat up now, nobody's gonna put money on a guy who's already washed up" (notes from 7 February and 3 June 1989).

Of a boxer at the end of his career, it is said that "he's done his time" and "his time has passed," that he is "washed up" or "shot" or, worse yet, that he has fallen to the rank of "dead meat": his bodily capital is too devalued for him to hope to beat younger fighters, who are more vigorous and less damaged. At best, he can aspire to be hired by promoters and matchmakers as a foil or "opponent" for up-and-coming boxers, the over-exploitation of his bodily capital allowing the latter to beef up their records at the cost of a lesser expenditure of theirs, as these field notes indicate:

The imperative to hoard corporeal energy also applies in the short term of a workout. Proof is the insistence with which DeeDee forbids us from working on the bag before climbing into the ring to spar: "Slow down, take it easy, Louie, save your strength for sparring. . . . I told you to leave that bag alone, damn it!" [Field notes, 17 December 1988]

This same need to let the body rest justifies the periodic rest phases, especially on the morrow of a rough fight. DeeDee generally grants his boxers a long week off duty after a match—two if the bout was particularly tough physically. After I reluctantly had to interrupt my training for two weeks during the Christmas holidays, the old coach consoles me: "You need to get outa d'gym from time to time, it gives you a breather, it's good for you. Then when you get back to it, you got more juice. But you can't stop too long either. Oherwise you get outa shape, you lose your speed, your timing is off." [Field notes, 5 January 1989]

The regulation of violence in the ring is an integral part of the general setup aimed at preserving the pugilist's body. In the following excerpt from my notebook dated 28 August 1989, DeeDee reminds Eddie of this management rule after a sparring incident.

In the second round, Rodney got his bell rung by Ashante, who explains: "I saw right away that I hurt him, I was ready to hold him up, DeeDee, in case he fall down. I knew we shoulda stopped." But the two club-mates kept on going at it, even though Rodney was barely able to stay on his feet. DeeDee calls over to Eddie, with a stern look in his eye and a sharp tone of reproach in his voice: "When your guy's hurt like that sparrin', you take him outa d'ring. You don't let him take a beating or try to pull through by hisself. *You make him come outa d'ring.* Tha's *your job* to take him out at that point, you understand?" Eddie, sheepish, in a low voice: "Okay, DeeDee, okay. I didn't know. Next time I know, I'll take him out right away."

The practical mastery of time is a central dimension of a successful apprenticeship of the craft of prizefighting. "It takes time," "Take your time," "Keep on workin', it comes with time," "Don't rush yourself" are expressions that come up constantly on the gym floor, whatever the stature of the boxer, and that contribute to making every boxer learn to spread out his physical and emotional investment over the specific duration of the field. It is also this corporeal investment over time, the slow process of incorporation of pugilistic technique and of somatization of its basic principles, that marks the boundary between recreational practitioners and regular boxers and prohibits an immediate passage from one category to the other. Assistant trainer Eddie reminds a visitor who is awkwardly trying to hit the speed bag of that distance with this deliberately exaggerated sarcasm: "Oo-ooh, no! You better stop right there: it takes *years of work* to learn how to hit that bag." A former boxer who has kept himself in good physical shape needs at least three months of intensive conditioning to get back in shape to fight. It takes a minimum of two to three years for an amateur to achieve a reasonable mastery of the basic panoply of the pugilist, and three more years before turning into an accomplished professional. Boxing "teaches patience and discipline and stick-to-itiveness," it is "anti-immediate-gratification."[14]

To persist with patience, to bide your time without recess or respite, to measure out your effort, to spread your expectations over time and smooth over your emotions accordingly: so many critical qualities in a boxing apprenticeship. If the fighter does not possess them, his coach can compensate by imposing them upon him from the outside, for instance by depriving him of sparring for a preset period if he is too impatient or by moving up his bouts so as to quicken the pace of his routine. Aside from the advice of peers and the directives of the coach, it is the body that, of itself, regulates in the final analysis the speed and the slope of progression. A sudden or repeated excess of training provokes injuries that, even when they are minor, quickly prove sufficiently bothersome to force one to slow down the tempo: tenacious little sores on the knuckles or too many broken blood vessels between the fingers limit work on the sandbag; a tender knee prevents you from jumping rope; a rib bruised in a brutal sparring session forbids you from doing situps. More than serious injuries, the accumulation of little injuries and physical annoyances serves as a natural regulator of the workload, as attested by this passage from my journal dated 6 October 1988.

Yesterday, Wednesday, I woke up with my right wrist swollen and very painful: I overdid it on the heavy bag Tuesday, banging it like a brute, and now I'm paying for it! It is still weakened today and I can't turn it or pick up anything heavy with that hand. So I won't be able to work the bag, to my great regret. I'm going to the gym anyway. . . . DeeDee, who gave me plenty of warning, but in vain, advises me to make do with a little shadowboxing so as to take it easy on my wrist. Training is atrociously burdensome: my right hand hurts like hell and I can't jump rope. I do a set on the speed bag with one hand. And shooting pains in my left arm very quickly start giving me trouble as well; it is numb, as if dead, to the point where I feel like quitting after only two rounds in front of the mirror.

The physical exhaustion that results from excessive exercising diminishes your vivacity and tonicity in the ring, increasing the chances of injury and of a protracted interruption, and thereby lack of training. A forced stoppage can in turn push you to resume working out too quickly, leading to yet another excess, and so on. To box over the long run, one must learn, through gradual rationing, to adjust one's effort so as to enter into a virtuous cycle in which training in the gym and clashes in the ring feed and reinforce each other and wherein their respective temporalities come into synergy.

Four Figures in the Management of Bodily Capital

The following two excerpts from my notebooks illustrate the various ways in which boxers encounter the problem of managing their body, preserving its integrity and energy, as much in the gym and in the ring as in daily life.

Boxers themselves are quick to ascribe the sudden downfall of one of their own to a shortfall in the corporeal discipline and hygiene that every pugilist must impose on himself outside the ring. Any infraction of the worldly asceticism that defines the Spartan regimen of the ideal boxer is promptly interpreted as the direct cause of his failings in the ring.

Alphonzo's Physical and Pugilistic Decline

(19 November 1988) Curtis is miming punches, ripping through the air with his fists and a sonorous "*Wham! Wham!*" Butch is watching him attentively. It takes me a few minutes to understand that they're talking about last Thursday's fight, in which Alphonzo Ratliff lost his national title and, according to them, took a tremendous beating (he bit the dust twice in the fourth round before getting kayoed in the fifth).

Curtis: "The man was landin' every punch, every punch landed to the body or the head, not in his gloves. Alphonzo, he was just holdin' his arms like this [he puts his guard up, his head tucked into his forearms] and he wasn't doin' nothin'." Curtis and Butch make no secret of their disapproval of the fact that Alphonzo was bragging so much before the fight. "He be hollerin', 'I'monna knock him cold, he's not gonna last five rounds with me,' you don't say stuff like that before the fight, man! And then he's the one who gets knocked out cold." The match was broadcast on a Chicago cable channel, which makes it all the more damaging to Alphonzo's reputation. Curtis and Butch agree that Alphonzo has come to the end of the road. "He's goin' downhill, for sure. He be better off hangin' em up. He's finished, man, he's finished. He ain't never gonna fight for the title, man."

I ask why Alphonzo got beaten so decisively: was his opponent that much better than him, or didn't Phonzo prepare himself properly for the fight? Butch: "See, the man is thirty-three years old now, Louie. When you get to that age, you gotta stay in shape. Don't mess with alcohol, don't mess with drugs, and don't mess with them women." Sitting on his stool, he mimes copulation with an unmistakable thrust of his hips. "Takes a toll on you. If you don't stay away from that, at thirty-three, man, you're finished, washed up. Check me out, I don't mess around with any of that stuff an' I stay in shape. But Alphonzo, he messes around with all three, especially d'women." Another suggestive movement of the hips. "He's too old for that kinda stuff now, man. He did his time. He should give it up, hang it up for good."

The Scandal of the Smoking Boxer

(28 July 1989) Ashante is chatting with Luke, who's just finished his workout, over the deafening noise Smithie is making nearby banging away on the speed bag. He's telling the story of a guy named Ray, who was "the best heavyweight in the city. Man, that guy was the real deal, he had a helluva punch. But then, he didn't take care of himself, he wasn't serious about it. He do whatever he wanta do and he didn't train hard—everybody knew it. But the day I saw him, with my own eyes, smokin' a cigarette just after his fight, man, I knew he'd never be good again."

Luke remains silent for about ten seconds, without reacting. Then, suddenly, as if he realized the enormity of the thing with a lag, he stares at Ashante with an air of incredulity. And in the tone of a priest who's just heard a curse word uttered in his sacristy, he exclaims, rolling scandalized eyes: "*He was smoking'* after a fight?!! He was smoking' *in the dressing room* after the fight?" [As if this were an inconceivable monstrosity.] "No, not in the dressing room, in the audience. I saw him sittin' in the audience after the fight, puffing away with one of his buddies. *Right away, I knew it was over for him,* man."

The specific wisdom of the coach consists in knowing how to stimulate and calibrate the efforts of his charges, both in relation to their bodies and to the multiple enmeshed temporalities of the institution, and to ensure the harmonious functioning of the complex collective machinery that

transmits knowledge and spurs the investments of the boxers (in the twofold sense of economics and psychoanalysis). By orchestrating the multiple actions that, through their mutual imbrication, define the gym as a mobile configuration of interdependent agents, DeeDee contributes to the production and solidification of pugilistic belief. Contrary to what Weinberg and Arond suggest,[15] this moral function does not come into play only during times of crisis, when disillusionment suddenly threatens, but ongoingly in the everyday routine of the gym. Critical situations, such as the morrow of defeats, which often provoke a practical questioning of the pugilistic *illusio* and in which the trainer overtly fills the roles of confidant, supporter, and proselytizer, obscure the anodyne work of maintenance and the continuous production of belief that takes place on a daily basis, invisibly and unconsciously, through the mediation of the very organization of the gym and its activities.

At the end of this initiatic march—temporarily interrupted by the work required by sociological objectivation—boxing reveals itself to be a sort of "savage science," an eminently social and quasi-scientific practice, even as it might seem to involve only those individuals who risk their bodies in the ring in a singular confrontation that appears rough and unbridled. And the pugilist emerges as the product of a collective organization which, while not thought out and willed as such by anyone, is nonetheless objectively coordinated through the reciprocal adjustment of the embodied expectations and demands of the occupants of the various positions within the space of the gym. These elements of an anthropology of boxing as "biologico-sociological phenomenon"[16] set into relief the central place of practical reason in this limiting case of practice that is pugilism and invite us to move beyond the traditional distinctions between body and mind, instinct and idea, the individual and the institution,[17] by showing how the two terms of these perennial antinomies are constituted together and mutually support one another, specify and reinforce themselves but also weaken each other in the same movement.

Notes

1. These are the two parts of the pugilist's body exposed to the most severe damage: fractures of the hands (metacarpal, thumb, joints), of the nose and jaw, cutaneous cuts, detached retinas, chronic cerebral lesions that can lead to *dementia pugilistica,* repeated hematomas of the ear followed by detachment of the scapha. G. R. McLathchie, "Injuries in Combat Sports," in *Sports Fitness and Sports Injuries,* ed. Tim Reilly (London: Faber and Faber, 1981), 168–174.

2. Michel Foucault, *Discipline and Punish: The Birth of the Prison* (New York: Vintage Books, 1979; orig. 1975), 170–194.

3. Recall that "practical sense . . . orients 'choices' which, though they are not deliberate, are no less systematic, and which, without being ordered and organized in relation to an end, are nonetheless charged with a retrospective finality"; Pierre Bourdieu, *The Logic of Practice* (Stanford, CA: Stanford University Press, 1990), 66. My translation.

4. I borrow this expression from Claude Lévi-Strauss, *The Savage Mind* (Chicago: University of Chicago Press, 1966), especially chap. 1, "The Science of the Concrete."

5. Jeffrey T. Sammons, 1988. *Beyond the Ring: The Role of Boxing in American Society.* Champaign, IL: University of Illinois Press.

6. William Plummer reports similar practices in a gym in New York's East Harlem. William Plummer, 1990. *Buttercups and Strong Boys.* New York: Penguin, 62.

7. S. Kirson Weinberg and Henry Arond, 1952. "The Occupational Culture of the Boxer," *American Journal of Sociology,* 57, 5 (Mar): 460–469.

8. We find here a classic opposition, established by Bourdieu in the case of the Algerian working class, between two types of social position and between the two systems of expectations and dispositions that correspond to them. Peirre Bourdieu, *Algeria 1960,* trans. Richard Nice (Cambridge: Cambridge University Press, 1979).

9. It is always possible to fight in the next weight class up if you happen to put on weight. But that constitutes a considerable handicap, for purely physical reasons of weight (and height) differences between divisions, with which tactical differences are associated. It is a rare pugilist who can go up a division and "bring his punch with him," as the saying goes.

10. On the local and regional levels, amateur as well as professional, differences in weight are rarely decisive, and it is unusual for a manager to decide to pull his fighter out of a bout at the last minute on grounds that his opponent is slightly over the official weight, as he is allowed to do by the contract agreed to in advance, However, the higher one goes in the hierarchy of the Sweet science, the finer weight management becomes, particularly in the intermediate classes, from lightweight to middleweight. A difference of a single pound can suffice to decide the outcome of a close clash, as for example with the first meeting between Thomas "The Motor City Hitman" Hearns and Sugar Ray Leonard in 1981: the specialists readily explain Hearn's defeat by technical knockout in the fourteenth round by the fact that he had for no reason conceded a full pound to his opponent by stepping onto the scale below the maximum authorized for his weight class.

11. This was the tragic case of Big Earl, a truculent heavyweight who enjoyed "moving around" with lighter amateurs to make them work on their offensive technique (I loved to pummel his massive belly in the clinches). DeeDee had worried out loud several times about Big Earl's sudden weight loss, which seemed to him to be disproportionate to the effort expended in the gym, both in its amplitude and its rapidity. Indeed, Big Earl would die in the hospital several weeks later of a virulent strain of leukemia caused by the handling of toxic products at his job as a technician in

a copy shop. The old coach had unfortunately seen correctly when he figured that Big Earl was gravely ill.

12. The fight for the WBC super-welterweight world title held in February of 1989 between René Jacquot and Donald "The Cobra" Curry is a good example of successful management on the part of the French boxer and his entourage. Uplifted by the event, Jacquot caught Curry at the moment when the latter still enjoyed enormous prestige but was in fact already greatly diminished (he had just suffered two stinging defeats, then won his world championship belt back). And what was supposed to be a mere "warmup fight" with a view toward the "second coming of The Cobra," the "live execution" of an obscure and scruffy opponent, turned into an upset, giving the Frenchman the unhoped-for chance to "enter into the legend" of prizefighting. Astolfo Cagnacci, *René Jacquot, l'artisan du ring* (Paris: Denoël, 1989), 13.

13. Thomas Hauser. 1986. *The Black Lights: Inside the World of Professional Boxing.* New York: McGraw Hill, 166.

14. Plummer, *Buttercups and Strong Boys,* 123.

15. Weinberg and Arond, "Occupational Culture of the Boxer," 462.

16. According to the formulation of Mauss, "Techniques du corps," 384, trans. 121. Marcel Mauss. 1934. "Les techniques du corps." *Journal de Psychologie*, XXXII, ne, 3–4, 15 mars–15 avril 1936.

17. For those who would doubt the possibility of generalizing this interpretation of pugilistic practice, one can recommend reading the studies by Jean Lave on the learning of calculus, *Cognition in Practice: Mind, Mathematics, and Culture in Everyday Life* (New York and Cambridge: Cambridge University Press, 1988); Jack Katz on the moral and sensual logic of criminal careers, *Seductions of Crime* (New York: Basic Books, 1989); David Sudnow on improvisation among jazz pianists, *Ways of the Hand: The Organization of Improvised Conduct* (Cambridge, MA: Harvard University Press, 1978); Joan Cassell on the craft of surgery, *Expected Miracles: Surgeons at Work* (Philadelphia: Temple University Press, 1991); and Joseph Alter on the social, moral, and symbolic organization of traditional Indian wrestling (*Bharatiya kushti*) in Benares, India, *The Wrestler's Body: Identity and Ideology in Northern India* (Berkeley: University of California Press, 1992), to take but five deliberately diverse and dispersed universes among others. And recall, with Max Weber, that "in the great majority of cases actual action goes on in a state of inarticulate half-consciousness or actual unconsciousness [*Unbewußtheit*] of its subjective meaning. The actor is more likely to 'be aware' of it in a vague sense than he is to 'know' what he is doing or be explicitly self-conscious about it. In most cases his action is governed by impulse or habit. Only occasionally and, in the uniform action of large numbers, often only in the case of a few individuals, is the subjective meaning of the action, whether rational or irrational, brought clearly into consciousness. The ideal type of meaningful action where the meaning is fully conscious and explicit is a marginal case. Max Weber, *Economy and Society* (Berkeley: University of California Press, 1978), 1:21–22.

Chapter 29

HINDU NATIONALISM, CULTURAL SPACES, AND BODILY PRACTICES IN INDIA

Ian McDonald

In this article, Ian McDonald examines the ways that particular forms of physical training in parts of India articulate with long-term political projects in the context of globalization. Specifically, he discusses the way in which two separate nationalist cultural ideologies have been embodied, through ritual practices, into physical disciplines.

Since the late 1980s, the call to embrace globalization has been the mantra sounded by many of India's economic and political elites. The first tentative attempts by multinational companies to prize open India's vast but hitherto protected consumer markets have brought in their wake a far more tumultuous process of social and cultural globalization. One of the most significant ways in which these processes have been manifest is in debates over national identity. Thus, it is significant that the period in which India embraced the logic and ideology of globalization is also the period in which extreme forms of Hindu nationalism have emerged center stage in the Indian polity. Yet, as Chatterjee (1993) has argued,

it is within civil society, in what he calls the "inner" domain of culture that "nationalism launches its most powerful, creative and historically significant project: to fashion a 'modern' culture that is nevertheless not Western" (p. 6). Here, discourses of Indianness and globalization increasingly frame diverse popular cultural spaces, be it cinema with the narratives of nationalist heroism in Bollywood (Bhatia, 2002) or sport with the claims to global respectability in cricket (McDonald, 1999a).

Although the sporting spaces of contemporary India are dominated by team games that emerged out of the British *Raj*, they have to a greater or lesser extent undergone their own processes of decolonization and what Appadurai (1996, pp. 97–105) has referred to in cricket as "vernacularization." It is in the period since gaining independence in 1947 that cricket emerges as "not so much India's national sport as its national obsession" (Guha, 1994/1995, p. 257) and so becomes heavily imbued with nationalist sentiment. Thus, in opening his account of the cultural significance of the game, Ashis Nandy declares that "cricket is an Indian game accidentally invented by the English" (Nandy, 1989, p. 9). However, as a consequence of its mass following, transcending religious and caste affiliations in its appeal if not so much in its power structures, cricket is an extremely awkward and ambivalent cultural form for Hindu nationalists to exploit (e.g., see Marqusee, 1996). Field hockey is often cited as India's premier sport, based on the fact that India dominated international hockey for decades (not losing a match in the Olympics from 1928 to 1960). However, the introduction of artificial pitches in the 1970s, which has placed a premium on pace and aggression as opposed to skill and trickery, has seen India descend the international rankings, thus divesting it of national prominence and nationalist significance. Soccer is an increasingly popular and growing sport in India (Dimeo & Mills, 2001), but its popularity is as a regional sport, and unlike cricket, the national side is far from one of the world's better teams. So for different reasons, the dominant colonial but decolonized sports of India have hitherto not lent themselves to easy accommodation to a Hindu nationalist agenda. Less understood and analyzed, but arguably more significant, is the impact of globalization and the attendant rise in Hindu nationalism on the micropolitics of bodily practices that are situated in everyday

and mundane public spaces, in the shadows of those theaters of populist spectacle, the cinemas and stadiums.

This article will examine two forms of bodily practice in India, each offering a distinct and contrasting engagement with the challenges posed by globalization and Hindu nationalism. The first bodily practice is *shakha* training. It is a form of physical training undertaken by members of an extreme Hindu nationalist organization called the Rashtriya Swayamsevak Sangh (RSS). In the *shakhas,* a combination of Western-style military drill and indigenous games and exercises are used to inculcate a sense of kin attachment to the Hindu *rashtra,* an exclusionist notion of a future Indian nation-state—a case of "keeping an eye on the body," as work on the body forms the starting point in the creation of the new nation. The second bodily practice is *kalarippayattu,* an indigenous martial art from the state of Kerala in South India. Self-realization is sought through prolonged immersion in this arduous practice, culminating in an optimal state of body-mind consciousness such that the "body becomes all eyes." Thus, there are two forms of bodily practice, both seeking a form of body-mind unity and both embedded in their respective globalizing cultural socioscapes yet offering a contrasting set of cultural meanings and political possibilities.

Globalization and the Rise of Hindu Nationalism

During the early stages of theorizing the cultural significance and ramifications of globalization, many theorists warned against a privileging of homogeneous processes, whether it was called Americanization, McDonaldization, or whatever, against which various local forces either resisted, subverted, or were subsumed (Featherstone, 1990; Robertson, 1992). As Appadurai (1990) commented:

> The central feature of global culture today is the politics of the mutual effort of sameness and difference to cannibalize one another and thus to proclaim their successful hijacking of the twin Enlightenment ideas of the triumphantly universal and the resiliently particular. (p. 308)

Many analyses of the rise of Hindu nationalism in the 1990s situate it firmly in the context of globalization (Jaffrelot, 1996; Kurien, 1994; Rajagopal, 2001; Vanaik, 1997). Hansen (1996, 1999) outlines how the contemporary politics of Hindu nationalism in India can be seen as the postcolonial expression of an attempt to overcome its subordinate position vis-à-vis the West and a desire to be accepted alongside the "great" nations of the world. Drawing on the universalism-particularism dialectic, Hansen surmises that similar to other forms of radical cultural nationalism (e.g., found in Serbia and the Caucasus), the Hindu nationalist imagination has

> sought to compensate for the loss of economic importance of their nation in the world, or the loss of coherence and efficiency of the ruling political project, by the worship of strength, masculinity, cultural purity and radical difference from the west. (Hansen, 1996, p. 613)

Hindu nationalist ideology, known as Hindutva, asserts that to be Indian is to be Hindu and that India's huge Muslim population and other religious minorities are at best conditionally Indian. In fact, advocates of Hindutva argued that the secularist Indian state has in reality discriminated against the majority Hindu population in its protection of India's religious communities (Vanaik, 1997). If India is to become a great nation once again, it has to realize its essential Hindu heritage and culture. In the words of Golwaker, one of the most important ideologues of Hindutva, non-Hindus must

> adopt the Hindu culture and language, must learn to respect and hold in reverence Hindu religion, must entertain no ideas but those of the glorification of the Hindu race and culture, i.e., they must not only give up their attitude of intolerance and ungratefulness towards this land and its age-old tradition but must cultivate the positive attitude of love and devotion instead—in a word they must cease to be foreigners, or may stay in the country wholly subordinate to the Hindu nation, claiming, deserving no privileges, far be any preferential treatment—not even citizen's rights. (cited in Bardhan, 1992, p. 6)

Despite this regionalist obstacle to Hindutva's geographical spread, it has emerged to become the key political force in Indian politics. In the 1998 general elections, the main Hindu nationalist party, the Bharatiya Janata Party (BJP), emerged as the largest single party in Parliament, mirroring the increasing influence of Hindutva throughout India and paving the way for them to establish a coalition government (Hansen & Jaffrelot, 1998). The BJP is but one part of the Sangh Parivar, a combine of organizations operating in different spheres of society to transform India into a Hindu *rashtra*. The ideological and strategic leadership of the Sangh Parivar is supplied by the Rashtriya Swayamsevak Sangh (RSS).

RSS *Shakha* Training: Keeping an Eye on the Body

The role of the RSS is to educate and train a cadre of committed Hindu patriots who will provide leadership in the various spheres of society. It is a long-term strategy "building up hegemony through molecular permeation" (Sarkar, 1993, p. 164) to advance Hindutva's agenda, akin to Gramsci's notion of a fascist "passive revolution" (Forgacs, 1999, p. 247). It is not the ephemeral electoral success in parliament that the RSS believe is key to transforming India but long-term cultural work, particularly as it mediates the quotidian practices (re)shaping the Hindu habitus. Nowhere is this cultural intervention and habitus formation more explicit than in the training camps run by the RSS, a notorious, uniformed, all-male voluntary organization.

For the RSS, the battle for the soul of Indian nationalism starts with the bodies of India's Hindu men and boys and is waged in the daily arenas of the *shakhas*. There are several million *swayamsevaks* (estimates range from 2.5 million to 6 million followers) and about 20,000 *shakhas* throughout India (Bhatt, 2001, p. 113). Each *shakha* will typically be attended by between 10 and 80 volunteers. Significantly, the RSS deliberately targets and attracts boys at the impressionable age of 12 to 15 years (Basu, Datta, Sarkar, Sarkar, & Sen, 1993). *Shakhas* are held every morning and evening in open public spaces such as parks, urban clearings, and school grounds throughout India. The fact they are held in open spaces is extremely important: *Shakhas* are not secret training camps for the creation of formidable *ubermensch*, they are a familiar part of the urban landscape that routinely involves respected members of the community. The regular presence of *shakhas* in mundane public spaces reflects a civic legitimization strategy that is instructive of their fascistic modus operandi.

The *shakha* sessions begin with the participants standing in rows to salute the saffron-colored flag (not the national flag). Known as the *bhagva dhwaj,* the flag is considered the sacred symbol of the nation. The main part of the *shakha* is taken up with an assortment of military drill, exercises, games, and indigenous sports such as *kho-kho* and *kabaddi.* The physical activities are designed to imbue the participants with the desired values such as courage, teamwork, leadership, sacrifice, brotherhood, and utmost loyalty to the Hindu nation (Anderson & Damle, 1987). Significantly, many of the games are framed in a narrative of aggressive nationalism. A *shakha* that I attended while doing field research on the RSS in Mumbai in 1998 contained a game that preached the regional imperialistic ambitions of Hindutva. The boys were holding each other by the arms, forming a circle around a small stone. A slogan about the neighboring Pakistani city of Lahore was repeatedly and each time more aggressively shouted by the *shakha* leader, *Lahore Kiska Hai* ("Whose is Lahore?"). Each time the leader's shout is answered with matching levels of aggression: *Lahore Hamara Hai* ("Lahore is ours"). At the appropriate moment, the *shakha* leader blew a whistle, the signal for the players to let go of each other and be the first to grab the stone, the symbol of Lahore (McDonald, 1999b, p. 352).

In a review of the television documentaries on the RSS by Lali Vachani, Deshpande (2002) reports how one game begins with the boys shouting "Kashmir belongs to us!"

Usually the last quarter of the *shakha* is given over to ideological lessons on Hindu mythology or a discussion on a contemporary issue. A popular myth retold in the *shakha* is taken from the Hindu epic *the Ramayana,* which tells the story of how Rama rescued his wife Sita from her evil abductor, Ravana, demonstrating the virtues of strength, masculinity, and warfare. The *shakha* finishes with a patriotic song and salute to the sacred flag.

An organicist philosophy underpins this physical culture regime. Organicism is a cultural nationalist philosophy that was first developed in 18th century German Romantic thought (Bhatt, 2001). It was Friedrich Jahn who translated such philosophies into concrete organizations, with the formation of open-air gymnasiums in 1811 for the promotion of activities that would elicit the deep and latent nationalist spirit within all Germans (Ueberhorst, 1979). The authoritarian tendencies inherent in organicist approaches were made explicit in its appropriation by interwar fascist movements in Italy and Germany. The Nazi sports theorist Alfred Baeumler declared that "The honour of the body is one part of the collective honour of the nation" (cited in Hoberman, 1984, p. 163). Significantly, European fascist ideology of the 1920s and 1930s provided much inspiration for the founders of Hindutva. In 1938, Golwaker, who was the leader of the RSS from 1940 to 1973, opined,

> To keep up the purity of the nation and its culture, Germany shocked the world by her purging the country of the Semitic races— the Jews. National Pride at its highest has been manifested here. Germany has shown how well nigh impossible it is for races and cultures, having differences going to the root, to be assimilated into one united whole, a good lesson for us in Hindustan to learn and profit by. (cited in Jaffrelot, 1996, p. 55)

Although Golwaker later denied the fascistic nature of the RSS project (Golwaker, 1996, p. 519), contemporary apologists for the RSS, such as Elst, have attempted to rationalize such statements by placing them in their historical context: "At first sight, Guruji's [Golwaker] seemingly laudatory reference to Nazi Germany is highly embarrassing. Upon closer examination, it isn't that bad" (Elst, 2001, p. 136). Archival evidence uncovered by Casolari (2000) demonstrated that there was systematic contact between leaders of the Hindu nationalists and members of the Italian fascist state, including Mussolini, which directly influenced the structure and philosophy of the RSS *shakhas.* In common with fascist ideologists of the interwar years, the RSS recognizes the power of embodied nationalism and the need, therefore, to maintain a close governmental and organizational "eye on the body." It is no accident that understanding and emotional attachment is inculcated through the body to procure the required dominating instincts over the "enemies within."

Kalarippayattu: When the Body Becomes All Eyes

Kalarippayattu is a traditional form of martial art unique to the Southern Indian state of Kerala. Although there are considerable varieties of styles, the common elements in this martial system include a series of physical, breathing, and meditative exercises designed to prepare the practitioner's body and mind for a number of combat forms. These combat forms include empty-hand techniques, fighting with long sticks, fighting with short sticks, and combat with sword and shield. The activities take place in a *kalari,* which is the technical term for a roofed pit dug out of the ground where *pay-attu* (exercise) is practiced. Whereas traditional *kalaris* were literally pits dug into the ground, modern *kalaris* are purpose-built constructions. For example, the *kalari* I visited in Thiruvananthapuram (the capital city of Kerala) is an impressive two-story building that contains a pit *kalari,* a separate massage area, bathing facilities, a medicinal preparation kitchen, living quarters, an office, a waiting room, and a separate viewing area for interested observers. Significantly, many of the observers happened to be Western tourists attempting to capture a slice of authentic Keralite heritage with their smuggled-in cameras.

Kalarippayattu sessions usually begin early in the morning at about 6:30 a.m. The following is a description of a typical session that I observed in the Thiruvananthapuram *kalari* from the designated spectator balcony overlooking the *kalari* pit. After the cacophony of noise and engine smells of the already busy streets outside, the serene and contemplative mood of the *kalari* is immediately apparent. The air is rich with many scents as wicks flicker and gingili oil is burned in small brass oil lamps, strategically placed around the *kalari.* The *kalari* pit is rectangular in shape, measuring approximately 12 meters in length and six meters wide, with high brick wall surrounds and a reddish-brown earthed floor. The pit is actually a poor noun that fails to convey the strict architectural guidelines

that have to be adhered to in order to ensure an appropriate and auspicious *kalari.* It would be better to describe the *kalari* as a form of "exercise-temple." Thus, having changed from their everyday clothes into the traditional loin-cloth (except for the few female students, who wear loose clothing), students descend a few steps to enter the *kalari* with their right-foot first, the tradition upon entering Hindu temples, before touching the floor, the forehead, and chest with the right hand. The students then cross the *kalari* and perform a brief *puja* (worship) by touching the base of a seven-tiered platform known as the *puttara,* the guardian deity of the *kalari,* positioned in a designated corner. A number of other deities are placed around the perimeter to which students, with differing degrees of intensity, pay their respects (see Zarrilli, 1998, pp. 61–83, for explanation and analysis of the different deities). If the students talk at all, it is in hushed tones as they massage oil into their bodies and go through a series of warming up exercises until their bodies begin to glisten with sweat in preparation for the next stage.

Typically, there will be between 15 to 20 students at a session. Similar to the Thiruvananthapuram *kalari,* most are based on Hindu deities, although there is a significant minority of Muslim and Christian *kalaris* in Kerala, reflecting a state population where two fifths are non-Hindus (Chiriyankandath, 1998, p. 204). Students do not need to attend a *kalari* that matches their religious identity, but in reality, this seems to be the pattern. Most of the students are men in their late teens, although it is not uncommon to see boys as young as 12 years and men in their 40s. After 30 minutes of warming-up exercises, in which the students work at their own pace, the instruction phase begins. In steps the *Gurukkal* (master) with his right foot first, touches the floor and then the *puttura* and other deities. The students respectfully acknowledge his entrance by stopping their exercises and touching his feet. All of the students then line up at the correct end of the *kalari* to be led through a series of increasingly strenuous exercise sequences and basic combat techniques. The *Gurrukal* spends a short time with a couple of the newer students, but after 30 minutes or so, all of the less skilled and inexperienced students are instructed to leave, which they do after paying their respect once again to the deities around the perimeter.

With only the more experienced students left, the *Gurrukal* offers instruction in various forms of long-stick combat, spear versus shield and sword, and finally short-stick combat. Even during combat, the silence and calm demeanor of the students are striking. There are no aggressive grunting or intimidatory tactics—just students in intense concentration, bordering on the meditative, engaged in combat using powerfully elegant balletic maneuvers. The *Gurukkal* and the most senior student give an impressive demonstration in short-stick and long-stick combat. Such is the breathtaking rapidity of attacks and counterattacks that I inquire whether such movements are in some sense choreographed. It is explained to me that the key to understanding the almost superhuman pace and skill of the combatants is found in the eyes. With their heads perfectly still and their eyes wide open and fixed on the eyes of the opponent, years of training have positioned the combatants in a heightened state of awareness and self-realization, where the "body becomes all eyes" (Zarrilli, 1998, p. 19). When the body becomes all eyes, body-

mind unity is expressed through a physical capability that transcends the contrasting demands of intuition and control. The final 15 minutes of the session are taken up by two advanced students performing an incredible feat of technique and athleticism, where they manage to leap and then twist in midair in order to kick a football suspended from the ceiling at a height of 2.5 meters. By 8:30 a.m., the *kalari* is emptied, as the two advanced students finish by paying their respect to the deities.

Historically, kalarippayattu emerged in the 11th century in a society dominated by warfare between rival kingdoms in South India. It was used as a form of military training by all castes, but especially by the higher *ksatriyas* and *Brahmins,* and also by Muslims and Christians in the service of particular principalities. Most villages had their own *kalari* where the youth from families whose duty it was to provide military service went for training (Zarrilli, 1998, pp. 25–39). Gradually, in keeping the evolutionary, hierarchical, and ordered caste system, it was one particular *jati* (groups associated with traditional occupations) called the *Nairs* that came to occupy this role. Although it was primarily a male activity, it was not unknown for *Nair* women to receive training. But an ethos of fearlessness, duty, and sacrifice developed among the *Nairs* in the service of their king, and they were soon renowned for their martial spirit and practices, as Zarrilli (1998) notes,

So important was kalarippayattu in medieval Kerala that both its heroic demeanour and its practical techniques were constantly on display whether in "actual" combat, such as interstate warfare or duel, or in forms of cultural performance from mock combats or displays of martial skills at public festivals to dance-dramas where the heroic was virtually displayed as heroes vanquished the forces of evil. (p. 48)

The arrival of Vasco de Gama and the Portuguese at the end of the 15th century heralded the arrival of colonialism in Kerala, and with it the introduction of firearms that was to erode the necessity for martial training and therefore for kalarippayattu. It was not until the 1920s that a revival occurred in sport and physical culture as a reaction against British colonial rule (Dimeo, 2002; Gupta, 1998). In particular, the colonial discourse of the effeminate Indian lacking in Victorian masculine virtues "over time became a pejorative self-image" (Alter, 2000, p. 52) and was targeted by the reawakening of interest in physical culture:

Broadly speaking, the discipline and physical training which characterized this physical fitness movement may be seen as a form of cultural politics wherein the primary concern was to decolonize the subject male body and remasculinize its effete character. (Alter, 2000, p. 53)

Alter's (2000) focus is on the role played by wrestling and in particular on the discourses of nationalism, physical culture, and wrestling in the story of "Gama the Great," the legendary Indian Muslim who was the unbeaten world champion of wrestling from 1910 to 1950. A resurgence of interest in kalarippayattu in the 1920s was part of this reaction against colonial discourses of Hindu effeminacy. Its successful reemergence was worked out and altered in combination with and reaction to precolo-

nial legacies and colonial influences. A revised format simultaneously challenged stereotypes of effeteness while contributing to the forging of a distinctly Kerala (rather than a national) heritage through an emphasis on performance and display. Kalarippayattu was celebrated in public discourse as an encapsulation of Kerala's valorous martial spirit and an idealization of Malayali manhood, and thus symbolized a common Malayali identity and past. Such narratives continued into postcolonial India and were crucial in legitimizing and giving cultural coherence to the Malayali-speaking state of Kerala, which was formally recognized in 1956. Thus, kalarippayattu became inextricably linked to Kerala and its heroic mythico-historical heritage.

There are just more than 100 active *kalaris* throughout Kerala, and the Kerala Kalarippayat Association (KKA) has approximately 600 members, all masters of the martial art (Zarrilli, 1998, pp. 58–59). One of the responsibilities of the KKA is to conduct annual interdistrict and state championships, where competitors are judged on the basis of style and form in preliminary exercises and weapons practice. However, the significance of kalarippayattu does not lie in its competitive structures as a sport. Rather, it is the social and cultural meanings generated as an ancient martial art rooted in Kerala's cultural, mytho-historical heritage; as a traditional psycho-physiological discipline aimed at self-realization; as a technique for effective self-defense and combat; and as a form of training for other dance forms (such as Kathakali) and sports.

One of the most significant impacts of globalization on kalarippayattu has come in the pressure to accommodate to new images of martial arts based on karate and street fighting. Long-standing arts traditions such as kalarippayattu are under pressure to reformulate their ethos and practice to meet the fantasies of contemporary youth, providing an example of how transnational movements of the martial arts as mediated by Hollywood and Hong King film industries are creating "new cultures of masculinity and violence in national and international politics" (Appadurai, 1990, p. 305). As a practitioner schooled in the "traditional" method of training, Zarrilli (1998) is keen to position the new approaches as lacking in authenticity:

> The re-packaging, mediation and transnationalization of kalarippayattu to fit the cosmopolitan self-defense paradigm has transformed it from a complex, embedded, local (martial, therapeutic and fighting) art where its powers are ritually, ethically, spiritually and socially circumscribed into a spectacular and melodramatic one where its powers are either decontextualised or recontextualised. (p. 235)

However, it is not clear how far this process has occurred, and Zarrilli (1998) may be hasty in referring to the transformation of kalarippayattu. Certainly, subjected to an image-centered mediascape that focuses on a discourse of aggressive self-confident masculinity, there are a handful of kalaris that are prepared to adapt kalarippayattu so as to privilege the spectacular and the melodramatic elements. Although further research is required to speak with more confidence, the transformation of the like Zarrilli describes is likely to be a more uneven and contested process. And there are other ways in which the impact of globalization is reshaping kalarippayattu. For exam-

ple, the increasing value of tourism to Kerala's economy is placing increasing demands on kalarippayattu as a form of display representing "Keralite history and culture." At the Thiruvananthapuram *kalari,* the *Gurukkal* expressed his concern over the pressure to emphasize the dance elements in kalarippayattu as a way of training students for stage demonstrations.

It might be expected that given Hindutva's stress on martial history, masculinity, heroism, sacrifice, and street fighting, it would be drawn to appropriating kalarippayattu in the service of the Hindu *rashtra.* It might be thought that under the conditions of global modernity, some means of marrying kalarippayattu to the masculinization of the Hindu man would be found. In fact, there is little evidence of the communalizing of kalarippayattu, although again, this may be due more to lack of research into the issue rather than it not being an issue. However, the fact that the BJP have failed to make significant inroads in Keralite politics suggest that the politics of Hindu nationalism will have a minimal impact on the evolution of kalarippayattu.

In other words, it is the deep association of kalarippayattu with Keralite history and Malayali manhood and identity, coupled with the state's particular political and social trajectory since independence, that has afforded it some immunity from both the influence of Hindutva and the reconstitution of cultural space and its associated physical practices as a manifestation of Hindu *rashtra.* Globalization poses challenges to this indigenous discipline, but it is less in the shape of Hindu nationalism and more through the impact of different consumerist imperatives associated with tourism and the commodification of Asian martial arts.

Concluding Thoughts

These corporeal cultural practices are subjected to a myriad of different influences shaping their production, presentation, and consumption. Yet, the micropolitics of bodily practices is a crucial battleground for the Hindu nationalist movement if it is to maintain the level of patriotic fervor elicited by the bomb tests and secure its hegemonic position in India and its status as a global power. The RSS recognizes this, which is why it places physical training at the center of its strategy for influence. Meanwhile, the relative impermeability of kalarippayattu to Hindutva is testimony to India's diversity and regional politics. When it comes to cultural meanings, all bodily disciplines possess a greater or lesser degree of ambiguity, especially with regard to the possibilities they offer for self-realization and/or to domination. Although there are different and contradictory pressures on the cultural spaces occupied by *shakha* training and kalarippayattu, each in their own way highlights the constitutive role of physical culture in the cultural and political life of a globalizing Indian society.

References

Alter, J. (2000). Subaltern bodies and nationalist physiques: Gama the great and the heroics of Indian wrestling. *Body and Society,* 6(2), 45–72.

Anderson, W. K., & Damle, S. D. (1987). *The brotherhood in saffron: The Rashtriya Swayamsevak Sangh and Hindu revivalism.* New Delhi, India: Vistaar.

Appadurai, A. (1990). Disjuncture and difference in the global cultural economy. In M. Featherstone (Ed.), *Global culture: Nationalism, globalization and modernity* (pp. 295–310). London: Sage.

Appadurai, A. (1996). *Modernity at large: Cultural dimensions of globalization.* Minneapolis: University of Minnesota Press.

Bardhan, A. B. (1992). *Sangh Parivar's Hindutva versus the real Hindu ethos.* New Delhi, India: Community Party of India.

Basu, T., Datta, P., Sarkar, S., Sarkar, T., & Sen, S. (1993). *Khaki shorts and saffron flags: A critique of the Hindu right.* New Delhi, India: Orient Longman.

Bhatia, S. (2002). Even Bollywood. *Index on Censorship.* 31(4), 172–176.

Bhatt, C. (2001). *Hindu nationalism: Origins, ideologies and modern myths.* Oxford, UK: Berg.

Casolari, M. (2000, January 22). Hindutva's foreign tie-up in the 1930s. *Economic and Political Weekly* (Mumbai), pp. 218–228.

Chatterjee, P. (1993). *The nation and its fragments: Colonial and postcolonial histories.* Princeton, NJ: Princeton University Press.

Chiriyankandath, J. (1998). Bounded nationalism: Kerala and the social and regional limits of Hindutva. In T. B. Hansen & C. Jaffrelot (Eds.), *The BJP and the compulsion of politics in India* (pp. 202–227). Delhi, India: Oxford University Press.

Deshpande, S. (2002). Breeding little fascists. *Frontline Online.* Retrieved from http://www.frontlineonnet.com/fl1992/stories/20021108002209000.htm.

Dimeo, P. (2002). Colonial bodies, colonial sport: "Martial" Punjabis, "Effeminate" Bengalis and the development of Indian football. *International Journal of the History of Sport,* 19(1), 72–90.

Dimeo, P., & Mills, J. (2001). *Soccer in South Asia: Empire, nation, diaspora.* London: Frank Cass.

Elst, K. (2001). *The saffron swastika: The notion of "Hindu fascism": Volume I.* New Delhi, India: Voice of India.

Featherstone, M. (Ed.). (1990). *Global culture: Nationalism, globalization and modernity.* London: Sage.

Forgacs, D. (Ed.). (1999). *The Antonio Gramsci reader: Selected writings 1916–35.* London: Lawrence and Wishart.

Golwaker, M. S. (1996). *Bunch of thoughts* (3rd ed.). Bangalore, India: Sahitya Sindhu Prakashana.

Guha, R. (1994/1995). The empire plays back. *Wissenschaftskolleg—Institute for Advanced Study Berlin—Jahrbuch 1994/5,* pp. 253–263.

Gupta, C. (1998, March 28). Articulating Hindu masculinity and femininity: "Shuddhi" and "Sangathan" movements in United Provinces in the 1920s. *Economic and Political Weekly* (Mumbai), pp. 727–735.

Hansen, T. B. (1996, March 9). Globalization and nationalist imagination: Hindutva's promise of equality through difference. *Economic and Political Weekly* (Mumbai), pp. 603–616.

Hansen, T. B. (1999). *The saffron wave: Democracy and Hindu nationalism in modern India.* New Delhi, India: Oxford University Press.

Hansen, T. B., & Jaffrelot, C. (Eds.). (1998). *The BJP and the compulsion of politics in India.* Delhi, India: Oxford University Press.

Hoberman, J. (1984). *Sport and political ideology.* Austin: University of Texas Press.

Ilaiah, K. (1996). *Why I am not a Hindu: A Sudra critique of Hindutva philosophy, culture and political economy.* Calcutta, India: Samya.

Jaffrelot, C. (1996). *The Hindu nationalist movement and Indian politics: 1925 to the 1990s.* London: Hurst & Co.

Kurien, C. T. (1994). *Global capitalism and the Indian economy.* New Delhi, India: Orient Longman.

Marqusee, M. (1996). *War minus the shooting: A journey through South Asia during cricket's World Cup.* London: Heinemann.

McDonald, I. (1999a). Between Saleem and Shiva: The politics of cricket nationalism in "globalising" India. In J. Sugden & A. Bairner (Eds.), *Sport in divided societies* (pp. 213–234). Aachen, Germany: Meyer & Meyer.

McDonald, I. (1999b). "Physiological patriots"? The politics of physical culture and Hindu nationalism in India. *International Review for the Sociology of Sport,* 34(4), 343–358.

Nandy, A. (1989). *The Tao of cricket: On games of destiny and the destiny of games.* Calcutta, India: Viking.

Rajagopal, A. (2001). *Politics after television: Hindu nationalism and the reshaping of the public in India.* Cambridge, UK: Cambridge University Press.

Robertson, R. (1992). *Globalization: Social theory and global culture.* London: Sage.

Sarkar, S. (1993, January 30). The fascism of the Sangh Parivar. *Economic and Political Weekly* (Mumbai), pp. 163–167.

Ueberhorst, H. (1979). Jahn's historical significance. *Canadian Journal of History of Sport and PE,* 10(1), 7–14.

Vanaik, A. (1997). *Communalism contested: Religion, modernity and secularization.* New Delhi, India: Vistaar.

Zarrilli, P. (1998). *When the body becomes all eyes: Paradigms, discourses, and practices of power in kalarippayattu, a South Indian martial art.* New Delhi, India: Oxford University Press.

Chapter 30

ATHLETES EMBRACE SIZE, REJECTING STEREOTYPES

Jeré Longman

The University of Oklahoma tells women's basketball fans a lot about Courtney Paris, the Sooners' 6-foot-4 center. They know that she ranks third in the country in scoring, second in rebounding and that her dream job is to be a novelist. That her best friend is her identical twin and teammate, Ashley Paris, and that her father, Bubba Paris, won three Super Bowls as a lineman for the San Francisco 49ers.

But one piece of information about Paris is not made public by the university: her weight.

The weights of male athletes are widely publicized by college teams, but 35 years after passage of the gender-equity legislation known as Title IX, and 25 seasons after the National Collegiate Athletic Association began sponsoring women's basketball, the weights of amateur female athletes are almost never published, in basketball or any other sport.

Even as women are embracing their size and power, projecting the notion that a wide body can be a fit body, the idea of weighing female athletes is under vigorous debate. Some colleges weigh their basketball players regularly to guard against rapid weight loss or gain. Some weigh them infrequently, others not at all.

"It's a sensitivity about eating disorders," said Jody Conradt, the Hall of Fame coach who has led the Texas Longhorns for three decades. "We're dealing with a population that is vulnerable because it's a Type A personality, driven, the people that want to be perfectionists."

Female athletes still face the same enormous societal pressures that other women face to remain thin and to possess a body type that many find unrealistic, especially for sports. Some experts believe athletes feel even greater pressure, given the assumption—also debatable—that they can improve performance by lowering their weight and percentage of body fat. Thus, many become vulnerable to what is called the female athlete triad: eating disorders, interrupted menstruation and osteoporosis.

The N.C.A.A. recommends that women not be weighed on a regular basis, said Dr. Ron A. Thompson, a psychologist and eating-disorder therapist in Bloomington, Ind., who consults with the collegiate association. He said he opposed making weights public and the practice of weighing female athletes. Lining athletes up for weigh-ins is a form of "public degradation," Thompson said.

"Weighing doesn't accomplish anything, and it can cause undue anxiety and even trigger unhealthy weight-loss practices," Thompson wrote in an e-mail message.

The touchy issue of weight received prominent attention recently when the professional tennis star Serena Williams faced questions about supposedly being out of shape before the Australian Open. After she won the tournament, she faced criticism for appearing to weigh more than a listed 135 pounds.

Williams has led an "in-your-face redefinition of what a strong woman should look like," said Donna Lopiano, executive director of the Women's Sports Foundation. Basketball and tennis courts provide an oasis of freedom for female athletes, she said, although she added that "90 percent of their lives is not lived in that oasis" and that women's sports have "been burdened by a stereotypical view of women."

Thompson said he tried to assist female athletes, not by focusing on their weight, but on their eating and how it is related to their emotions. Many teams have nutritionists and psychologists available. The trend in college is moving away from weighing

athletes, Lopiano said. But colleges are left to make their own decisions.

The female basketball players at top-ranked Duke are weighed once a week, Coach Gail Goestenkors said; they are not given a target weight, but are monitored to guard against quick weight gain, she said. Ohio State's players are also weighed regularly, Coach Jim Foster said, adding, "It's a medical issue; putting your head in the sand is not an attractive alternative."

At Tennessee, players are neither weighed nor measured for body-fat percentage, said Jenny Moshak, the university's assistant athletic director for sports medicine. Instead, players are monitored for performance in such areas as speed, flexibility, vertical jump and weight lifting.

"Far more detrimental things occur when you try to micromanage body shape and size," Moshak said.

At Texas, players are weighed and tested for lean mass two or three times a year, but always privately by sports-science experts. Coaches of women's teams are not permitted to weigh players, set target weights or initiate a conversation about weight.

Some Oklahoma players are weighed up to twice a week during preseason, the strength coach Tim Overman said. During the season, they are weighed and tested for percentage of body fat about once a month, Overman said, adding that too much attention paid to weight loss during the season can lead to calorie deficiency and fatigue.

Courtney Paris's father weighed more than 330 pounds when he was in the N.F.L. He was cut by the 49ers in 1991 when he failed to make their weight limitation of 325 pounds. Overman said he wanted Courtney Paris to lose about 15 pounds, from 240 to 225, so that she could lessen the stress on her body while extending her stamina and the length of her career.

Paris, a 19-year-old sophomore, said she did not generally care if people asked about her weight, saying, "It's not like I can hide who I am." She said she was proud and glad to be in game shape, but "being in shape and being conditioned well are things I really have to work on."

Yet, it is not universally believed that lowering the weight and percentage of body fat of fit athletes will enhance their performance, said Thompson. Some studies indicate improvement, while others do not, he said.

If Paris lost weight, "she might not be as strong or she might be distracted by trying to maintain the weight loss and might not perform as well," said Thompson, an Oklahoma graduate who said he did not know Paris.

Perhaps never have so many influential centers played on so many commanding teams in one season. Alison Bales, a 6-7 center for Duke, leads the nation in shot blocking, while 6-9 Allyssa DeHaan of Michigan State is second. Sylvia Fowles of Louisiana State, is 6-6 and anchors the country's top defense; 6-5 Jessica Davenport of Ohio State can play in the post and beyond the 3-point line; and 6-4 Candace Parker of Tennessee can play any position and has transformed the dunk from a novelty shot to a statement of authority.

"There are more centers of different types across the country than I've ever seen," said Sherri Coale, Oklahoma's coach. "You have graceful, powerful, fundamental, thick, long—all shapes and sizes. To me, that's the greatest evolution in that position."

And there is no more dominant center than Paris, who averages 23 points and 16 rebounds a game. Last season as a freshman she became the first collegiate player, man or woman, to collect at least 700 points, 500 rebounds and 100 blocked shots in a season.

"She's a female Shaquille O'Neal," said Kim Mulkey, who coached Baylor to the 2005 national championship. Kurt Budke, the Oklahoma State coach, said, "She's the best player in the country."

Because Paris has soft hands and a ravenous anticipation for rebounding, nearly 25 percent of her points have resulted from offensive rebounds—often from her own misses.

"She's got much better hands than Terrell Owens," said Foster, the Ohio State coach. "She's not going to lead the league in passes dropped."

Paris represents the evolution of a position that has grown more essential as players have become more skilled in the post and comfortable with their size.

Female players today have professional role models in the Women's National Basketball Association, undergo sport-specific weight training, practice regularly against male scout teams and wear baggy uniforms that allow them to be less self-conscious than athletes like volleyball players, gymnasts and swimmers who participate in more revealing outfits.

"We're women who are not apologizing for being bigger and being different or for being athletic," Paris said. "It's more acceptable in society. For my generation, it's really not a big deal."

Her twin sister, Ashley, a center-forward at Oklahoma, said that their mother, who is 6-1, told of slouching as a girl, and of buying shoes that were too small, in an effort not to stand out.

The difference today, at least in basketball, is that big women are more secure in being and playing big, said Goestenkors, the Duke coach. She said that Bales, the Blue Devils' center, proudly wore three-inch heels, which made her 6-10, while the team was in Cancún, Mexico, in December. Bales said a photograph of her in heels on Duke's Web site had elicited several grateful messages from tall girls or their parents.

"Before, tall girls were all soft and finesse and didn't want contact," Goestenkors said. "Now it's strong, physical, bring on the contact. Courtney epitomizes that."

Growing up in Piedmont, Calif., Courtney Paris developed her skills against four older brothers, who ranged from 6-4 to 6-8.

"Courtney and Ashley had an opportunity to see their father, who was big and winning championships, and have seen their brothers go off and play ball," Bubba Paris said in a telephone interview. "In their mind, being big is good; it benefits you."

That was evident Sunday when Oklahoma overcame an early deficit against Oklahoma State by inserting Ashley Paris in the high post to pass to her sister in the low post. Courtney scored 41 points, 2 below her career high, and grabbed 19 rebounds in a 78–63 victory.

"I think people have fallen away from the stereotype that big means slow and tall means clumsy," Ashley said.

Adam Himmelsbach contributed reporting from College Park, Md.

PART VII

GIVING UP YOUR BODY: VIOLENCE AND INJURIES IN SPORTS

Violence in sports occupies a peculiar and contradictory status. Although some sports prohibit violence and regard it as deviant, others accept—or even normalize—it "as part of the game." Based on the popularity of such sports as boxing, football, hockey, and rugby, it seems clear that violent sports appeal to millions of sports fans. This fact apparently explains their stoical response to injuries caused by sports violence. Nevertheless, certain acts of egregious sports violence persist uneasily in public memory, leaving in their wake a legacy of questions about the need for reforms. The following are examples of sports violence that form part of that disturbing legacy in the United States:

- Benny "the Kid" Paret, a lightweight Cuban boxer, dies after enduring a brutal beating in a boxing match with Emile Griffin.
- Muhammad Ali, shortly after ending his brilliant boxing career, announces that he is suffering from Parkinson's disease, a debilitating neurological disorder, which is linked to the physical punishment he endured in the ring.
- Daryl Stingley, a New England Patriots pro-football player, is permanently paralyzed from the neck down after being viciously tackled by an Oakland Raiders player, Jack Tatum, in a *pre-season* game.

The evidence of the effects of sports violence is clear and indisputable. As one open-source Internet article summed up recent findings: "Research on NFL retirees has shown that those players who sustained three or more concussions during their careers were significantly more likely to fall into clinical levels of depression later in life for no apparent reason other than the concussions" (Mayeda 2008). Despite this evidence, the NFL and the media usually avoid dealing with the problem of violence. When a player is injured in a game, the telecast usually shifts quickly to a commercial. By the time the telecast resumes, the injured player has been whisked from sight and order has been restored; the game proceeds as if nothing has happened. Most significant, the media excludes discourse about the long-term effects of injuries, as the health problems of former players, no matter how serious, are seldom discussed. The problem of violence in boxing is even worse than in football. A neurology journal reported that "due to the constant head strikes in competition and practice, 17 percent of all professional boxers end up punch drunk (with chronic traumatic brain injury) in their elder years" (Lewis 2006). Moreover, as an article in *The Nation* observed, sports media outlets typically ignore the fact that a handful of boxers consistently die each year during or immediately after a match (Newfield 2001). No organization or government agency represents the interests of retired boxers—or other athletes—suffering serious health problems from sports injuries.

It is important to distinguish normative and deviant sports violence from the gray area of tactical sports violence. Tactical sports violence is violence that results not so much from inherent features of the game (such as tackling in football or colliding with a catcher at home plate in baseball) as from deliberate violent tactics used by players or coaches to gain a competitive advantage. Examples would include a baseball pitcher deliberately hitting a batter who was thought to be "too hot"; a basketball player committing a flagrant foul to intimidate a high-scoring opponent; a football offensive linemen "chop blocking" a defensive player with the objective of slamming into his unprotected knees; or a hockey team highsticking or deploying "goons" to take out opposition players. These are all familiar acts of sports violence. Though this kind of violence typically prompts a referee or umpire to impose a minor game penalty, it is unlikely to provoke a severe penalty—such as a season suspension, a heavy fine, or something else that would truly discourage the behavior or even make those tactics obsolete. Instead, the tactics are accepted as unpleasant but inevitable parts of the game. When violent behaviors do provoke severe penalties, such as fighting in the NBA or hitting an opponent with a bat in baseball, these penalties send a clear and certain message: Such behaviors are not tolerated. They exist within the zone of deviance, but most tactical sports violence does not. That is to say, most tactical violence in sports is accepted by both the sports organizations directly involved in that sport and the general public.

Another problem linked to sports violence can be seen in team responses to player injuries. Teams sometimes pressure injured athletes to play, which may entail injecting them with pain-numbing drugs with little concern for the long-term effects on their health. Two former professional basketball stars (Andrew Toney of the Philadelphia Sixers and Bill Walton of the Portland Trailblazers), in different situations, alleged that their playing careers were cut short because their teams pressured them to play with serious injuries. This problem raises complex issues of professional ethics and role conflicts for team physicians. How can they deal with situations in which the health needs of a player and the financial interests of the team conflict? This issue needs to be researched and brought out into the open for discussion.

Social scientists have developed varied theoretical explanations of violence, but none of these explanations has been sufficiently tested in reference to sports violence to gain widespread acceptance as the dominant paradigm. Among the theoretical perspectives that have been used to explain sports violence are the following: the hegemonic masculinity perspective, which views sports violence as a manifestation of dominant cultural norms encouraging athletes to celebrate violence as an expression of masculinity; the psychoanalytic perspective on aggression, which attributes egregious sports violence to insufficiently suppressed or socialized instinctual drives; and the symbolic interactionist perspective, which sees violence as the result of the athlete being socialized into violent sports subcultures.

The study of sports violence raises many analytical questions for research, such as:

- How does the appeal of violent sports differ from the appeal of nonviolent sports?
- What are some of the characteristics of the fan bases of violent and nonviolent sports? Are certain social classes more attracted to violent sports than other social classes? Are there gender differences in attraction to violent sports?
- What criteria are used to distinguish legitimate and illegitimate sports violence? To what extent are these criteria shared among those involved in contact sports?
- How does the appeal of violent sports vary among different societies? Where are violent sports most popular? Where are they least popular? Is there a link between the appeal of violent sports and other types of violence in the society?

All of the readings in this section address analytical issues focused on sports—or sports-related—violence. The first essay, "Male Athletes, Injuries, and Violence" by Michael A. Messner, addresses the analytical issue of why male athletes in high-status sports have a greater proclivity to violence than male athletes in low-status sports. Messner uses the interactionist perspective to explain how socialization in high-status sports predisposes male athletes to both on-field and off-field violence. The second reading shifts to the issue of differential levels of violence among sports. Taking a comparative approach, John Schneider and D. Stanley Eitzen, in "The Structure of Sport and Participant Violence," analyze the levels of illegitimate violence in four major American sports: football, baseball, basketball, and hockey. Using a typology, they distinguish the key organizational features that increase or decrease the likelihood of illegitimate violence in each of the sports.

The third reading uses a comparative approach to explain the discrepancy in levels of violence among sports. In this selection, "On-Field Player Violence," Randall Collins suggests that a number of variables are critical to the understanding of player violence, including the degree to which violence is structured within the game, the amount of protection that players wear, and struggles for emotional dominance at key turning points in the contest. Interestingly, these outbreaks can have major effects on the outcomes of games.

References

Lewis, R. 2006. "Why Haven't We Banned Boxing?" *Neurology* 6, no. 23: 5–6.

Mayeda, D. 2008. "Sporting Violence: The Injuries." Bleacher Report, http://bleacherreport.com/articles/37370-sporting-violence-the-injuries.

Newfield, J. 2001. "The Shame of Boxing." *The Nation*, November 12, 13–22.

Chapter 31

MALE ATHLETES, INJURIES, AND VIOLENCE

Michael A. Messner

In this article, Michael A. Messner explains how the ideology of hegemonic masculinity, internalized by male athletes through sports socialization, creates the will to play even when injured and to endure the pain that ensues. Messner elaborates on how sports normalizes violence and induces pressure on athletes to suppress empathy for others and for themselves.

Men's Violence Against Other Men

In February 2000, a professional basketball player with the San Antonio Spurs, Sean Elliott, announced his impending return to play following a life-threatening illness that resulted in a kidney transplant. Elliott's return was met with considerable media discussion and debate about whether it was appropriate for him to return to play at all, given the grave risks he might face should he receive a blow to his kidney. Lakers star Kobe Bryant, when asked how he would respond to playing against Elliott, said, "As soon as he steps on the court, that means he's healthy. I'll have no problem putting an elbow in his gut."[1] This statement spoke to the routine nature of bodily contact and aggression in basketball. Players and coaches know that in order to be competitive enough to win, they will need to "put their bodies on" opposing players in ways that could cause bodily harm. In football and ice hockey, the overt aggression against other players is even more intense. One former National Football League player told me that before a playoff game, his coach implored his defensive players to hurt the opposing star running back if they had an opportunity to do it. This is apparently not that unusual. A 1998 *Sports Illustrated* cover story on "the NFL's dirtiest players" admiringly described San Francisco 49ers guard Kevin Gogan's tendencies, sometimes even after a play has been whistled dead, to "punch, kick, trip, cut-block, sit on or attempt to neuter the man lined up across from him." Gogan's coach, Steve Mariuchi, expressed his approval: "Coaches want tough guys, players who love to hit and fly around and do things that are mean and nasty. Not everyone can be like that, but if you can have one or two players who are a little overaggressive, that's great."[2]

Bodily aggression toward opponents on the field or court, whether of the "routine" kind that takes place within the rules or of the "dirty" illegal kind that aims to injure an opponent, is often assumed to end when the players cross the boundaries back in the real world. The story of the "gentle giant" football player who growls, curses, and tears opponents limb-from-limb on the field but is a kind and caring teddy bear off the field is part of our national lore. But is aggression on the field against other men related to aggression off the field? Former Dallas Cowboy football star John Niland now says that he and many of his former teammates were involved in drugs, alcohol, and spouse abuse:

> I'm not going to name names, but my wife at the time knew of other wives who were abused. . . . We're paid to be violent. We're paid to beat up on the guy across from you. When you're in the game and your emotions are so high and the aura of the whole environment is so unbelievable. When the game's over, technically, it's to be turned off. But you can't. . . . Quite frankly, if you got every player who did drugs or alcohol or played stoned or who was a spousal abuser, you couldn't field an NFL team. It's still going on.[3]

And consider a comment by NBA coach Pat Riley, of the Miami Heat. Bemoaning an unusually long break between his team's playoff games, Riley said, "Several days between games allows a player to become a person. During the playoffs, you don't want players to be people."[4] If it is acknowledged

that the supposedly civilizing influences of a player's life outside sports can (negatively!) humanize him, then doesn't it follow that it might also work the other way—that dehumanizing attitudes and experiences within sports might spill over into life outside sports? Indeed, sport studies scholars have found evidence that points to this conclusion. Jeffrey Segrave and his colleagues found that Canadian minor league (fifteen- and sixteen-year-old) ice hockey players were more likely than nonathletes to engage in physically violent acts of delinquency.[5] And sociologist Howard Nixon found that male athletes in team contact sports, especially if they reported having intentionally hurt other athletes on the field, were more likely to hurt others outside sports.[6] To understand this connection, it is necessary to look more closely at the ways that boys and men develop their identities and relationships within the culture of sport.

Boys' Embodiments of Toughness

In an earlier book, *Power at Play,* I explored the meanings of athletic participation through life-history interviews with male former athletes. One man, a former NFL defensive back who had been known and rewarded for his fierce and violent "hits," had injured many opposing players in his career, some seriously. I asked him to describe how he felt the first times he had hurt someone on a football field, and he said that hitting and hurting people had bothered him at first:

> When I first started playing, if I would hit a guy hard and he wouldn't get up, it would bother me. [But] when I was a sophomore in high school, first game, I knocked out two quarterbacks, and people loved it. The coach loved it. Everybody loved it. You

never stop feeling sorry for [your injured opponent]. If somebody doesn't get up, you want him to get up. You hope the wind's just knocked out of him or something. The more you play, though, the more you realize that it is just a part of the game—somebody's gonna get hurt. It could be you, it could be him—most of the time it's better if it's him. So, you know, you just go out and play your game.[7]

This statement describes a contextual normalization of violence: "you realize it is just a part of the game." It also illustrates an emotional process, a group-based suppression of empathy for the pain and injury that one might cause one's opponent. Most children are taught that it is unacceptable to hurt other people. In order to get athletes (or soldiers) to be willing and able to inflict harm on others, the opponent must be objectified as the enemy, and the situation must be defined as "either him or me": "somebody's gonna get hurt. It could be you, it could be him—most of the time it's better if it's him." The most obvious force behind this suppression of empathy is the rewards one gets for the successful utilization of violence: "The coach loved it. Everybody loved it." And it's not just this sort of immediate positive reinforcement. The man quoted above, for instance, received a college scholarship, all-American honors, and eventually all-pro status in the NFL.

But rewards do not tell the whole story behind athletes' suppression of empathy for their opponents. In fact, when I probed athletes' early experiences and motivations in sports, I found stories not of victories, trophies, and public adulation. Instead, these men were more likely to drop into stories of early connection with others, especially fathers, older brothers, uncles, and

eventually same-aged male peers. Some found sports to be the primary, sometimes the *only*, site in which they experienced connection with their otherwise emotionally or physically absent fathers. Many also said that they felt alone, unsure of themselves, cut off from others and that it was through sports participation, especially for those who had some early successes and received attention for these successes, that they found acceptance.

Why sports? An important part of the answer is that most boys' early experiences teach them to appear to be invulnerable. This means, don't show any fear or weakness. And little boys begin to learn this at a very young age. Learning to embody and display toughness, even if it is a veneer that covers up a quivering insecurity inside, can be a survival skill that helps boys stay safe in a hostile environment. In his eloquent description of street life for African American boys in poor communities, Geoffrey Canada describes how learning to fight, or at least displaying an attitude that you are ready and willing to fight, was necessary. Losing a fight, and "taking it like a man," was far better (and ultimately *safer*) than being labeled a coward.[8] Learning early to mask one's vulnerability behind displays of toughness may help boys survive on the street, but it can also contribute to boys (and, later, men) having difficulties in developing and maintaining emotional connection with others. Though in an emotional straitjacket, boys and men retain a human need to connect with others. And for those who have some early athletic successes, sports can become an especially salient context in which to receive a certain kind of closeness with others.[9]

A key, then, to understanding male athletes' commitment to athletic careers lies in understanding their underlying need for connection with other people and the ways that society thwarts emotional connection for boys. And there is often an additional layer of emotional salience to sports participation for boys and men from poor and ethnic minority backgrounds. African American men, in particular, when asked about their early motivations in sports, were far more likely to drop into a discussion of "respect" than other men were. Early sports successes, for them, offered the discovery of a group context in which they could earn the respect of family members, friends, schoolmates, and communities. White middle-class men in my study did not talk about the importance of respect in the same way. This is because African American boys and young men are far more likely to face a daily experience of being *suspected* (of a potential crime of violence, of shoplifting in a store, of cheating on an exam, etc.) than of being *respected*. Schools are a major source of African American boys' experience of disrespect. Sociologist Ann Arnett Ferguson observes that elementary school teachers and administrators often treat African American boys as "troublemakers" who are already "beyond redemption."[10] By contrast, most white middle-class boys and men begin each day and enter each situation with a certain baseline, taken-for-granted level of respect that includes an assumption of our competence and trustworthiness, which is then ours to lose. To receive the benefits of this baseline of respect, we simply have to show up. This respect is not earned; rather, it is an unacknowledged but very real benefit that Peggy MacIntosh has called "the invisible Knapsack of White Privilege."[11]

In short, boys' relational capacities and opportunities for expressions of emotional vulnerability tend to be thwarted and suppressed. Some boys find in their early athletic experiences that sports offer them a context in which they can connect emotionally and gain the respect of others. Ironically, though, as one moves farther away from the playful experiences of childhood into the competitive, routinized institutional context of athletic careers, one learns that in order to continue to receive approval and respect, one must be a winner. And to be a winner, you must be ready and willing to suppress your empathy for other athletes. In the context of sports careers, you do not experience your body as a means of connecting intimately with others; rather, your body becomes a weapon, which you train to defeat an objectified, dehumanized opponent.[12] It's a dog-eat-dog world out there; you gotta have that killer instinct.

Booze, Bonding, and Fighting

The lessons learned on the field are important, but athletes also spend large amounts of time not playing sports—in classrooms, at parties, and at other social events with friends. And the kinds of relational patterns that boys and men learn on athletic teams sometimes spill over into these nonsport contexts. Timothy Curry found that college male athletes described life at the campus bar as one of "drinking, picking up women, and getting into fights":

. . . the athletes would try to "own" every bar they frequented. Often, this meant staging bar fights to demonstrate their power. Several of the athletes were good fighters, and they were typically the ones to start the fight. Often, these fighters would pick out a particular victim based on the fact that he looked "queer." The victim need not do anything provocative—sometimes victims were chosen because "they didn't want to fight." After the first punch was thrown, others in the group would enter in, either throwing punches of their own or attempting to break up the fight. The team always backed up its most aggressive members, so that the victim seldom had much of a chance.[13]

Since the athletes were of such high status, Curry explains, they rarely got into any trouble from this fighting. Instead, most often the victim was thrown out of the bar by the bouncer, and the players would be given free drinks from the bartender and would celebrate their "victory" as "a way of building team cohesion and expressing masculine courage."[14] Alcohol consumption is obviously a key part of this process.[15] The athletes would compete among themselves to see who could consume the most free (or nearly free) drinks at the bar. The heavy drinking, an athlete told Curry, is "to prove you're not a pussy."[16]

Curry's description of the sports bar scene mirrors the interactional dynamics of male peer groups that I described earlier concerning violence against women. In the sports bar, we see a premeditated incident of violence, staged to build in-group cohesion (albeit this time in a public place, with a male victim). The victim is a vulnerable-looking man, who is degraded by the group as looking "queer." As a result, the line between "the men," who are inside the group, and others outside the group, be they "queers" or women who are marked for later sexual conquest, is created and reinforced both by the collective act of violence and by the public approval it receives.

This sort of homophobic bullying of nonathlete boys is also a common occurrence on high school and college campuses.

A window was opened on this dynamic in 1999, when Eric Harris and Dylan Klebold, armed to the teeth, entered Columbine High School, in Littleton, Colorado, and proceeded to kill thirteen and wound twenty-one of their schoolmates and teachers. "All jocks stand up," the killers yelled when they began their slaughter. "Anybody with a white hat or a shirt with a sports emblem on it is dead."[17] Much of the aftermath of this tragedy consisted of media and experts discussing the origins of the anger and violence expressed by the two boys, dubbed "the trenchcoat mafia," and how in the future to predict and prevent such individuals from violently "going off." Very little discussion centered on the ways that such outsider boys are so commonly targeted as the "nerds" and symbolic "pussies" that serve as the foil for high-status athletes' construction of their own in-group status. Indeed, Columbine High School was like many other high schools in this regard. There was a "tough little group" of about seven guys, mostly football players and wrestlers, who were known for leading painfully degrading hazing rights among younger male athletes, for harassing and physically abusing girls, for destroying property, and basically getting away with it all. They also abused the outsider boys in the "trenchcoat mafia," one of whom was shoved into a locker by three football players who taunted him, "Fag, what are you looking at?"

Homophobic taunting and bullying does not always result in such serious physical violence.[18] But it is a common part of the central dynamic of male peer groups. The role homophobia plays within male peer groups is akin to Elmer's glue being used to bond two pieces of wood. Once the white glue is dried, it becomes clear, nearly invisible, and it acts simultaneously (and paradoxically) as a bond that holds the two pieces of wood together and as an invisible barrier, or shield, that keeps the two pieces of wood from actually touching each other. Homophobia works the same way. While it bonds boys together as part of the in-group (we are men, they are faggots), it also places clear limits on the extent to which boys and men can make themselves vulnerable to one another (don't get too close, emotionally or physically, or you will make yourself vulnerable). And this, again, is where alcohol often comes in. While it is part of the system of competitive status-enhancement to drink a lot of alcohol, young men also find that one of the short-term benefits of drinking with the guys is that it loosens the constraints on verbal and emotional expression.[19] The key desires underlying boys' and men's affiliations with each other—acceptance, emotional connection, respect—seem more accessible after a few drinks. The constraints normally placed around expressions of physical closeness among men are often relaxed after a few drinks; the arms draped around a teammate's shoulders and the "I love you, man" expression can be conveniently forgotten in the fog of tomorrow's hangover.

In sum, boys in central, aggressive team sports learn early to use their bodies as weapons against an objectified opponent. The empathy that one might be expected to feel for the victim of one's punches, hits, or tackles is suppressed by the experience of being rewarded (with status and prestige, and also with connection and respect) for the successful utilization of one's body against other men. Empathy for one's opponent is also suppressed through the shared contextual ethic that injury is an expected part of the game. These on-the-field values

and practices are mutually constitutive of the off-the-field peer group dynamics, whereby the boundaries of the in-group are constructed through homophobia and violence directed (verbally and sometimes physically) against boys and men who are outside the group.

Male Athletes' Violence Against Themselves

In June 2000, future Hall of Fame quarterback Steve Young ended several months of speculation by announcing his retirement after fifteen years of professional football. Actually, he had played his last down of football ten months earlier, when a "knock out" hit by an opposing player caused Young's fourth concussion in three years. "I'll miss many things," said Young. "What I won't miss are the hits that made my body tingle."[20] Young's announcement was not surprising. In fact, many had wondered why it took him so long to retire, given the mounting evidence concerning the dangerous cumulative effects of head injuries.[21] But Young's desire to continue playing must be seen in the context of an entire career in which he was rewarded for taking tremendous risks on the football field, playing hurt and with reckless abandon. Steve Young is not unusual in this respect. In November 2000, Denver Broncos quarterback Brian Griese suffered a shoulder separation in the first half of the game. Told by team doctors that he had a third-degree separation, the most severe type, he took a painkilling injection and returned to the game to lead his team to victory.

Football players live with the knowledge that small and moderate injuries are an expected outcome of the game and that a serious, career-ending or even life-threatening injury is always a possibility. Indeed, during the 1999 NFL season, 364 injuries were serious enough for a player to miss at least one game. Knee injuries (122) and ankle injuries (52) were the most common. Eleven were concussions.[22] In U.S. high schools, by far the greatest number of fatal, disabling, and serious sports injuries are suffered by football players (though the injury rates per hundred thousand participants are actually higher in ice hockey and gymnastics).[23] Among children, falls and sports-related injuries are now the leading causes of hospital stays and emergency room visits.[24] A survey of hospital emergency rooms and medical clinics in 1997 found a staggering number of sports injuries among U.S. children fourteen years old and under, led by bicycling (901,716 injuries), basketball (574,434), football (448,244), baseball (252,665), and soccer (227,157).[25] In Canada, injuries—a substantial proportion of which are head, neck, and cervical spinal injuries—among children ice hockey players are also escalating.[26]

The Body as Machine

Several years ago, I was watching a football game on television with a friend at his house. A big fan, he knew that his team had to win this game to secure home field advantage for the playoffs. Suddenly, the announcer observed that a key player on my friend's team was hurt. The camera focused on the player, slowly walking off the field and looking at his hand with a puzzled look on his face. His index finger, it turned out, was dislocated and sticking out sideways at a ninety-degree angle. "Oh, good," my friend sighed in relief. "It's only his finger—he can still play." Indeed, a few plays later, the player was back on the field, his hand taped up (and presumably popped back into place by the trainer, and perhaps injected with painkillers). What struck me about this moment was how normal it seemed within the context of football. Announcers, coaches, other players, and fans like my friend all fully expected this man to "suck it up" and get back out there and play. We all have incredibly high expectations of football players' (and indeed, of other professional, college, and even high school athletes') willingness and ability to cope with pain, to play hurt, often risking their long-term health. Injuries and pain levels that in other contexts would result in emergency-room visits, home bed rest, and time off work or school are considered a normal part of the workday for many athletes.

I was struck by the depth to which athletes internalize these cultural standards to endure pain when I interviewed former athletes for *Power at Play.* One man, a former major league baseball player, described an incredible litany of injuries and rehabilitations that spanned not only the everyday aches and bruises that one would expect a catcher to endure but also year after year of ankle, knee, shoulder, neck, and spinal injuries that required several surgeries. In particular, he played out the second half of one season with daily injections of painkillers and cortisone in a shoulder that he knew would require surgery. Players routinely decide to "play hurt," to "give their bodies up for the team" in this way, even with the full knowledge that they are doing so at the risk of long-term disability. But when this man's eleven-year pro baseball career finally came to an end, he described it as a "shock. . . . I had felt that the way I had conditioned myself and taken care of myself that I would play until I was thirty-seven, thirty-eight."[27] Nobody could listen to this man's story and not agree that he had worked very hard and been very dedicated to his craft. But to describe the way he had lived his life as taking care of himself seemed to me to express a particularly alienated relationship to his own body. He, like many other athletes, had a wide range of knowledge about his body. However, this self-knowledge was in some ways shallow; it was not an expansive sense of his body as a living organism, as a self that connects in healthy ways with others and with one's environment.[28] Rather, it was a self-knowledge firmly bounded within an instrumental view of one's body as a machine, or a tool, to be built, disciplined, used (and, if necessary, used up) to get a job done.

This kind of self-knowledge—what psychologist William Pollack calls the "hardening of boys"—starts early in life, especially for athletes.[29] Boys learn that to show pain and vulnerability risks their being seen as "soft," and they know from the media, from coaches, and from their peers that this is a very bad thing. Instead, they learn that they can hope to gain access to high status, privilege, respect, and connection with others if they conform to what sociologist Don Sabo calls "the pain principle," a cultural ideal that demands a suppression of self-empathy and a willingness to take pain and take risks.[30]

Why are so many boys and men willing to take such risks? Again, we must look to the young male's embeddedness in social groups, and again, homophobia and misogyny are key enforcement mechanisms for conformity. The boy who whines about his pain and appears not to be willing to play hurt risks being positioned by the group as the symbolic "sissy" or "faggot" who won't "suck it up and take it like a man for the good of the team." One man I interviewed, for instance, told me that in high school,

when he decided not to play in a big game because of an injury, his coach accused him of faking it. And as he sat in the whirlpool nursing his injury, a teammate came in and yelled at him, "You fucking pussy!"[31] Canadian sport studies scholar Philip White and his colleagues cite a similar example of an ice hockey player who, returning to play after a serious knee injury, was told by teammates "not to ice the swelling and not to 'be a pussy.'"[32]

The fear of being seen by the team as less than a man is not the only reason an athlete will play hurt, though. As pro football player Tim Green wrote in his illuminating book:

Doctors don't coerce players into going out on the field. They don't have to. Players have been conveniently conditioned their entire lives to take the pain and put bodies at risk. Players beg doctors for needles that numb and drugs that reduce swelling and pain. . . . Taking the needle is something NFL players are proud to have done. It is a badge of honor, not unlike the military's Purple Heart. It means you were in the middle of the action and you took a hit. Taking the needle in the NFL also lets everyone know that you'd do anything to play the game. It demonstrates a complete disregard for one's well-being that is admired in the NFL between players.[33]

Green's statement—that demonstrating a complete disregard for one's well-being is so admired in the NFL among players—speaks volumes not just about the normalization of pain and injury in pro football but also about ways that bodily risk and endurance of pain serve as masculine performances that bring acceptance and respect among one's peers. Indeed, writing more generally about men's (often dangerous) health behaviors, Will Courtenay has argued that "health behaviors are used in daily interactions in the social structuring of gender and power. . . . The social practices that undermine men's health are often the signifiers of masculinity and the instruments that men use in the negotiation of social power and status."[34] In short, in the context of the athletic team, risking one's health by playing hurt is more than a way to avoid misogynist or homophobic ridicule; it is also a way of "performing" a highly honored form of masculinity.

There are concrete rewards—status, prestige, public adulation, scholarships, and even money—for men who are willing to pay the price. But we must also remember that underlying men's performances for each other is a powerful need to belong, to connect, to be respected. In refusing to play hurt, especially in the context of a team sport, a player risks losing the tenuous but powerful connection he has with the male group. Given both the negative enforcement mechanisms and the positive rewards a player might expect from choosing to play hurt, it should surprise us more when a player decides *not* to risk his long-term health, by refusing the needle, sitting down, and saying "no más."[35]

Notes

1. "They Said It: Kobe Bryant."
2. Silver, "Dirty Dogs."
3. Glauber, "We're Paid to Be Violent."
4. "Quotebook," *Los Angeles Times.*
5. Segrave, Moreau, and Hastad, "An Investigation into the Relationship between Ice Hockey Participation and Delinquency."
6. Nixon, "Gender, Sport, and Aggressive Behavior outside Sport."
7. Messner, *Power at Play,* 65–66.
8. Canada, *Fist Stick Knife Gun.*

9. I develop this line of argument in much more depth in *Power at Play,* where I argue that the specific kind of connection that boys and men experience in sports is a distant and thus "emotionally safe" form of connection. This has (mostly negative) ramifications for the development of friendships, for intimate relations with women, and for athletes' retirement and disengagement from sports. Psychologist William Pollack reaches a similar conclusion, arguing that boys often find sports to be one place where they emotionally connect. Pollack concedes that "the positive benefits to boys dim when sports cease to be played"; still, he tends to overstate the benefits of sports and ignores the range of social-scientific studies of sport that point to negative outcomes. Pollack, *Real Boys,* 273.

10. Ferguson illustrates how dynamics of gender and race in public schools serve as self-fulfilling prophecies, tracking African American boys into failure in the classroom, into the school's "punishment room," and ultimately (and inevitably, according to some of the teachers) into the criminal justice system. Ferguson, *Bad Boys.*

11. MacIntosh, "White Privilege."

12. Philosopher Brian Pronger has argued that an oppressive territorialization of the male body, which closes off intimate and erotic connection with other bodies and channels desire into violent directions, is the key outcome of modern sport, which he sees as a major expression of fascism. Pronger, "Outta My Endzone"; Pronger, "Homosexuality and Sport."

13. Curry, "Booze and Bar Fights," 168, 169–170.

14. Ibid., 170.

15. Several studies have shown that college male athletes and fraternity members tend to have higher rates of alcohol consumption than other college students, including more drinks per week and higher rates of binge drinking. Boswell and Spade, "Fraternities and Collegiate Gang Rape"; Leichliter et al., "Alcohol Use and Related Consequences among Students with Varying Levels of Involvement in College Athletics." A study of teen athletes found that male and female teen athletes are no more likely to drink than nonathletes, but "highly involved athletes" are more likely to

binge drink than nonathletes. Miller et al., *The Women's Sports Foundation Report*.

16. Curry, "Booze and Bar Fights," 169.

17. Adams and Russakoff, "At Columbine High, a Darker Picture Emerges."

18. Indeed, Messerschmidt points out that although many boys are challenged by bullying, not all respond with violence. Boys' responses to bullying vary, and this variance can be explained by boys' being differently situated in family, school, and peer contexts. Messerschmidt, *Nine Lives*.

19. As Rocco L. Capraro puts it, " . . . college men's drinking appears to be profoundly paradoxical. . . . [They drink] not only to enact male privilege but also to help them negotiate the emotional hazards of being a man in contemporary American college." Capraro, "Why College Men Drink," 307.

20. Young, "Young at Heart," 61.

21. The extent of brain damage to boxers has been well documented for many years. Stories of champions and top contenders suffering from *dementia pugilistica* (a medical term that describes a malady that used to be called punch-drunk) and other forms of boxing-induced brain damage, such as Floyd Patterson, Muhammad Ali, Jerry Quarry, Sugar Ray Robinson, and Wilfredo Benitez are only the most recent high-profile examples of the logical outcome of boxing. These and other cases led to the American Medical Association in 1986 calling for a ban on boxing. More recent research has increased awareness of the danger and extent of head injuries in other sports, especially football and soccer. Crosset cites recent studies that note a connection between men's head injuries and their violence against women: " . . . batterers are more likely to have sustained moderate or severe head injuries than nonbatterers. . . . A history of significant head injury increased the chances of marital violence sixfold. . . . Like alcohol consumption, head injury is not the direct cause of violence against women but clearly one that may play a role in some athlete violence against women." Crosset, "Athletic Affiliation and Violence against Women," 160.

22. These statistics, of course, do not include the much larger number of routine, smaller injuries that do not result in a player sitting out a game. Gutierrez and Mitchell, "Pain Game."

23. Young and White, "Researching Sports Injury."

24. Dwyer Brust, Roberts, and Leonard, "Gladiators on Ice."

25. As reported in Gold and Weber, "Youth Sports Grind Is Tough on Body, Spirit."

26. Dwyer Brust, Roberts, and Leonard, "Gladiators on Ice," 27.

27. Messner, *Power at Play*, 122–23.

28. Brian Pronger has written about sport as a disciplinary practice particular to modernity, through which men learn to close off their bodies to connection with others. Instead, the body is experienced as a means of overcoming others. Pronger, "Outta My Endzone."

29. Pollack, *Real Boys*.

30. Sabo, "Pigskin, Patriarchy and Pain." The pain principle in sport can also be seen as paradigmatic of (and indeed, a pedagogy for) a more general cultural view of men's instrumental orientations to their own bodies. A few scholars have recently pointed to gender-related health patterns among men that help to explain the fact that, on average, men die seven years earlier than women do and have higher death rates from suicide, heart disease, accidents, and other major killers. Research points to the conclusion that these health risks among men are closely correlated with boys' and men's conformity to narrow conceptions of masculinity that include risk taking, violence, and instrumental orientations to the body. For excellent general overviews, see Sabo and Gordon, eds., *Men's Health and Illness*; and Courtenay, "Constructions of Masculinity and Their Influence on Men's Well-Being." Taking this observation to a different level, scholars have pointed out how different groups of men—broken down by social class, race-ethnicity, sexual orientation, age, and so forth—have very different levels of vulnerability to certain diseases and dangers. See, for instance, Staples, "Health among African American Males."

31. Messner, *Power at Play*, 72.

32. White, Young, and McTeer, "Sport, Masculinity, and the Injured Body," 171.

33. Green, *The Dark Side of the Game*, 215, 125.

34. Courtenay, "Constructions of Masculinity and Their Influence on Men's Well-Being," 1385.

35. The "no más" reference is to the famous 1980 welterweight championship fight between Roberto Duran and Sugar Ray Leonard. Feeling that he was losing the fight, Duran refused to return to the ring for a new round, saying "No más." He was roundly criticized for quitting instead of continuing the fight until he was knocked out. I critically examined this idea that boxers must fight until the very end in Messner, "Why Rocky III?"

References

Adams, Lorraine, and Dale Russakoff. "At Columbine High, a Darker Picture Emerges: Were Athletes Given Preferential Treatment and Allowed to Misbehave with Impunity?" *Washington Post National Weekly Edition,* June 21, 1999, 29.

Boswell, A. Ayres, and Joan Z. Spade. "Fraternities and Collegiate Gang Rape: Why Some Fraternities Are More Dangerous Places for Women." *Gender & Society* 10 (1996): 133–47.

Canada, Geoffrey. *Fist Stick Knife Gun.* Boston: Beacon Press, 1995.

Capraro, Rocco L. "Why College Men Drink Alcohol, Adventure, and the Paradox of Masculinity." *Journal of American College Health* 48 (2000): 307–15.

Courtenay, Will H. "Constructions of Masculinity and Their Influence on Men's Well-Being: A Theory of Gender and Health." *Social Science and Medicine* 50 (2000): 1385–401.

Crosset, Todd. "Athletic Affiliation and Violence against Women: Toward a Structural Prevention Project." In *Masculinities, Gender Relations, and Sport,* ed. Jim McKay, Michael A. Messner, and Donald F. Sabo, 147–61. Thousand Oaks, Calif.: Sage Publications, 2000.

Curry, Timothy. "Booze and Bar Fights: A Journey to the Dark Side of College Athletics." In *Masculinities, Gender Relations, and Sport,* ed. Jim McKay, Michael A. Messner, and Donald F. Sabo, 162–75. Thousand Oaks, Calif.: Sage Publications, 2000.

Dwyer Brust, Janny, MPH, William O. Roberts, MD, and Barbara J. Leonard, Ph.D. "Gladiators on Ice: An Overview of Ice Hockey Injuries in Youth." *Medical Journal of Allina* 5 (1996): 26–30.

Ferguson, Ann Arnett. *Bad Boys: Public Schools in the Making of Black Masculinity.* Ann Arbor: University of Michigan Press, 2000.

Glauber, Bob. "We're Paid to Be Violent: Cost Was High for Ex-Dallas Star John Niland." *Newsday,* Sunday, January 12, 1997, B8, B25.

Gold, Scott, and Tracy Weber. "Youth Sports Grind Is Tough on Body, Spirit." *Los Angeles Times,* February 28, 2000, A1.

Green, Tim. *The Dark Side of the Game: My Life in the NFL.* New York: Warner Books, 1996.

Gutierrez, Paul, and Houston Mitchell. "Pain Game." *Los Angeles Times,* January 25, 2000, D1.

Leichliter, J.S., P.W. Meilman, C.P. Presley, and J.R. Cashin. "Alcohol Use and Related Consequences among Students with Varying Levels of Involvement in College Athletics." *Journal of American College Health* 46 (1998): 257–62.

MacIntosh, Peggy. "White Privilege: Unpacking the Invisible Knapsack." In *Gender through the Prism of Difference,* ed. Maxine Baca Zinn, Pierrette Hondagneu-Sotelo, and Michael A. Messner, 247–50. 2d ed. Boston: Allyn and Bacon, 2000.

Messerschmidt, James W. *Nine Lives: Adolescent Masculinities, the Body, and Violence.* Boulder, Colo.: Westview Press. 2000.

Messner, Michael A. *Power at Play: Sports and the Problem of Masculinity.* Boston: Beacon Press, 1992.

———. "Why Rocky III?" In Michael A. Messner and Donald F. Sabo, *Sex, Violence and Power in Sports: Rethinking Masculinity,* 74–81. Freedom, Calif.: Crossing Press, 1994.

Miller, Kathleen E., Donald F. Sabo, Merrill J. Melnick, Michael P. Farrell, and Grace M. Barnes. *The Women's Sports Foundation Report: Health Risks and the Teen Athlete.* East Meadow, N.Y.: Women's Sports Foundation, 2000.

Nixon, Howard L., II. "Gender, Sport, and Aggressive Behavior outside Sport." *Journal of Sport and Social Issues* 21 (1997): 379–91.

Pollack, William. *Real Boys: Rescuing Our Sons from the Myths of Boyhood.* New York: Henry Holt, 1998.

Pronger, Brian. "Outta My Endzone: Sport and the Territorial Anus." *Journal of Sport and Social Issues* 23 (1999): 373–89.

———. "Homosexuality and Sport: Who's Winning?" In *Masculinities, Gender Relations, and Sport,* ed. Jim McKay, Michael A. Messner, and Donald F. Sabo, 222–44. Thousand Oaks, Calif.: Sage Publications, 2000.

"Quotebook." *Los Angeles Times*, May 11, 2000, D-2.

Sabo, Donald. "Pigskin, Patriarchy and Pain." In Michael A. Messner and Donald F. Sabo, *Sex, Violence and Power in Sport: Rethinking Masculinity,* 82–88. Freedom, Calif.: Crossing Press, 1994.

Sabo, Donald, and David F. Gordon, eds. *Men's Health and Illness: Gender, Power, and the Body.* Thousand Oaks, Calif.: Sage Publications, 1995.

Segrave, Jeffrey, Claude Moreau, and Dougas N. Hastad. "An Investigation into the Relationship between Ice Hockey Participation and Delinquency." *Sociology of Sport Journal* 2 (1985): 281–98.

Silver, Michael. "Dirty Dogs." *Sports Illustrated,* October 26, 1998.

"Six Football Players Arrested for Hazing." *High Desert Star,* November 13, 2000. http://www.hidesertstar.com/display/inn_news/news1.txt.

Staples, Robert. "Health among African American Males." In *Men's Health and Illness: Gender, Power, and the Body,* ed. Donald Sabo and David F. Gordon, 121–39. Thousand Oaks, Calif.: Sage Publications.

"They Said It: Kobe Bryant." *Sports Illustrated,* February 21, 2000, 26.

White, Philip G., Kevin Young, and William G. McTeer, "Sport, Masculinity, and the Injured Body." In *Men's Health and Illness: Gender, Power, and the Body,* ed. Donald F. Sabo and David F. Gordon, 158–82. Thousand Oaks, Calif.: Sage Publications, 1995.

Young, Kevin, and Philip White. "Researching Sports Injury: Reconstructing Dangerous Masculinities." In *Masculinities, Gender Relations, and Sport*, ed. Jim McKay, Michael A. Messner, and Donald F. Sabo, 108–26. Thousand Oaks, Calif.: Sage Publications, 2000.

Young, Steve. "Young at Heart." *Sports Illustrated,* June 19, 2000, 55–61.

Chapter 32

THE STRUCTURE OF SPORT AND PARTICIPANT VIOLENCE

John Schneider and D. Stanley Eitzen

The authors of this article, John Schneider and D. Stanley Eitzen, explain the different levels of illegitimate violence in four major sports (football, basketball, baseball, and hockey) by focusing on their distinctive organizational features. They explore how the amount of scoring, the amount of legitimate body contact, the degree to which there are opportunities for retaliation, and the number of intermediate rewards (for example, getting a first down in football or getting a hit in baseball) affect the likelihood of illegitimate violence in given sports.

Player violence in sport is of two types. There is normative violence where it is a part of the game to aggress against the opponent. Examples of normative violence are bodychecking in hockey, blocking and tackling in football, and legitimately sliding hard into a fielder in baseball. Although approved by coaches, peers, and spectators as part of the sport, normative violence can result in injury (Underwood, 1979). Illegitimate violence also occurs in the major American sports. This type of behavior involves the intentional use of force to harm the opponent outside the rules of a sport. Examples of this type of violence are "late hits" in football, "high sticking" in hockey, and fighting. The distinction between legitimate and illegitimate violence is often blurred, however. Some coaches and players may incorporate illegitimate means to intimidate, incapacitate, and exploit opponents with the tacit or even explicit approval of fans and participants.

The purpose of this article is twofold: first, to examine both types of violence, illustrating the prevalence of normative violence in the four major American team sports; and second, our goal is to explain why the incidence of illegitimate violence varies by type of sport. In doing so, we will focus on the structure of sport as the explanatory variable. This emphasis differs from the current theories on player violence.

I. Explanations for Illegitimate Violence

The explanations of player violence vary greatly. There are six theories used to explain violence in sport. . . . Any one of these theoretical approaches may be considered useful in explaining a small portion of violence behavior among participants in a number of sports. But do these theories, alone or in combination, address the issue of participant violence across all sports? If not, are there new ideas that might add to the understanding of this phenomenon across the sports spectrum? The following section reviews each of these theories.

The Violence in Sport Mirrors the Violence Found in Society. The argument is commonly made that sport, like other institutions, is a microcosm of society; that sport simply reflects the prevailing ideologies, values, and behaviors extant in the larger society (Smith, 1979; Eitzen, 1981; Eitzen and Sage, 1982; Edwards and Rackages, 1977; and Smith, 1974). Thus, the investigation of violence in sport must begin with the assumption that sport does not occur in a vacuum but is shaped by the history, culture, and distribution of power in society. We must understand that American society has been and continues to manifest and glorify violence. Several points require emphasis:

- Violence has occurred throughout American history. . . .
- The U.S. ranks higher than other western industrial societies in the proportion of violent crimes (Graham and Gurr, 1979:303).
- The amount of violence in the media is staggering. . . . By the time the aver-age child is 14 he or she has witnessed 11,000 television murders.
- There are cultural norms that support violence. . . .
- The incidence of spouse abuse and child abuse is high. . . .
- Capitalist society creates conditions where workers are exploited, alienated, and treated as commodities (Sugden, 1981), increasing the likelihood of violence.
- Military strength, even in times of peace, is a very high priority, as evidenced by the Reagan Administration's commitment to spend in excess of $1 trillion for defense over a five-year period.

Violence as the Result of Economic Incentives. Another explanation for player violence rests on the assumption that commercialization and economic incentives influence how athletes perform. Gregory Stone (1955) has made the case that sport is comprised of "play" and "dis-play." The element of play refers to the participants' personal concern with the dynamics of the activity; the element of display refers to action that symbolically represents the dynamics of the activity for the expressed purpose of making it more amusing to the spectators. When sport becomes commercialized, the element of dis-play becomes increasingly important so that spectator interests can be maintained at the levels necessary to stage profitable events (Coakley, 1981). Edwards and Rackages (1977) have added to this commercial aspect with their assertion that recent economic developments have been a major contributing factor to the intensification of competitiveness. The demise of the World Football League and the American Basketball Association, for example, left the National Football League and the National Basketball Association as monopolies with considerably fewer player opportunities. This constriction of opportunity could possibly be a major factor in the increase of on-the-field sports violence (Edwards and Rackages, 1977). The play, dis-play model formulated by Stone (1955) does not suggest that skill and finesse are unimportant when a sport becomes entertainment. But skill and finesse in sport have become overshadowed by what Furst (1971) has described as heroic action. When this value transformation takes place, athletes may tend to emphasize actions of daring and courage, which may often take some form of violence. This phenomenon is illustrated by Jerry Kramer's description of his pre-game feelings about the opponents he used to face as an offensive lineman for the Green Bay Packers:

> I've started day-dreaming about Merlin Olsen. I see myself breaking his leg, or knocking him unconscious and then I see myself knocking out a couple of other guys and then I see us scoring a touchdown and always . . . I see myself as the hero. (1968)

Commercialization can change the entire context in which a sporting event takes place. Attention is now focused on the outcome of the event, not on the meaning of the sport experience. Moreover, a "victory at all costs" attitude seems to be a result of commercial productivity.

The Influence of Crowd Behavior on Player Violence. The literature on participant violence in sport is also filled with references pertaining to the influence of spectators upon athletes' performances (Thirer, 1981; Coakley, 1981; Hatfield, 1973; Smith, 1973, Pilz, 1979). The assumption, based on collective behavior theory (Blumer, 1959), is that as spectators become more rowdy and vocal, the participants will become more violent. Fans' encouragement for violence, overall crowd noise, spectator aggression towards players, and game-related tension on the field are all factors that increase the possibility for player aggression.

Genetic Causation for Player Aggression. A fourth existing theory which might explain why players aggress argues that athletes have a genetic predisposition to do so. The Drive-Discharge Hypothesis maintains that aggression is an innate drive in all human beings. This aggressive drive is "somewhat responsive to the environment which acts to generate aggressive pressure on every individual and in society itself" (Brown and Davies, 1978). The assumption is that tension is cumulative within individuals and must be released before it erupts in violence. This tension can grow collectively in society as well. Thus, the Drive-Discharge theory predicts an inverse relationship between the presence of war and aggressive or war-like sports. Sipes (1973) has stated that the probability of war can be reduced, according to this model, by increasing the incidence of alternative behavior similar to warfare (such as combative sports). . . .

Sipes (1973) has suggested, alternatively, that individual aggressive behavior is primarily learned. Utilizing the "Culture Pattern Model" of human aggression, Sipes predicted different levels of aggressive behavior for different cultures. More important, Sipes has argued that the intensity and configuration of aggression is affected predominantly by cultural characteristics. Contrary to the Drive-Discharge Hypothesis, the Culture Pattern Model posits that "behavior patterns and value systems relative to war and warlike sports tend to overlap and support each other's presence" (Sipes, 1973:65). Therefore, periods of intense war activity should be accompanied by less intense sports activity.

Sipes' evidence supports the Culture Pattern Model of human aggression. "Rather than being functional alternatives, war and combative sports activities in a society appear to be components of a broader culture pattern" (Sipes, 1973:80). Therefore, aggression appears to be a learned, rather than instinctive behavior.

Learning Theory and Player Aggression. Yet another existing theory about why athletes aggress is forwarded by the social learning theorists. Social Learning Theory suggests that individuals are influenced by exposure to aggressive models, especially if their subsequent behavior is reinforced (Bandura and Walters, 1963a and 1963b). The concept of aggression is defined as "any sequence of behavior, the goal response to which is the injury of the person toward whom it is directed" (Dollard et al., 1939). A number of sports sociologists and psychologists have discussed the social learning theory in their work on sports violence (Silva, 1978; Cataldi, 1978; Thirer, 1981; Smith, 1974; Goldstein, 1982). Berkowitz (1964) has demonstrated that adults respond with increased aggression after observing a violent model. The research findings supporting these beliefs deal severe blows to the belief that violence in sport is innate. The idea that athletes have a genetic tendency to aggress lacks any solid empirical support (Coakley, 1978).

There are, however, some serious drawbacks to the learning model. Michael Smith (1974) has outlined what he considers to be a number of severe limitations to the learning theory. Among these limitations are: (1) most of the research is based on the responses of young children, and it remains an open question whether some of the findings can be generalized to older children and adults; (2) much of the imitation of aggression via the media seems to apply to "novel" behaviors; (3) it is unclear how long-lasting the effects are of exposure to aggressive models; and (4) Sears (1965) has concluded that the responses imitated in the Bandura experiments are simple and easily recognized, and that more complex behavior may not be learned by modeling (Smith, 1974).

Psychological Stress and Player Violence. Jay Coakley (1978, 1981) has attempted to draw an analogy between a prison setting and player training camps. In this view the repressive aspects of training camp settings reflect many of the same characteristics as a prison setting, which may, in turn, promote player violence. Using the original work of criminologist Gresham Sykes (1971), Coakley has illustrated how training camp settings parallel prison settings. For example, both training camps and prisons promote: (1) the deprivation of liberty: a threat to moral worth; (2) the deprivation of autonomy: a threat to adulthood; (3) the deprivation of security: a threat to physical well-being; (4) the deprivation of heterosexual relationships: a threat to masculinity; and (5) the deprivation of material goods: a threat to person adequacy (Coakley, 1978).

As players respond collectively to these five threats, a social system develops where violent behavior comes to be defined as the normative means for establishing status among peers, maintaining self-esteem, and protecting one's physical well-being. Coakley admits that there are obvious differences between prisons and training camps. A central similarity, though, is that the subjective meanings of the deprivations experienced in prison are akin to the meanings of the deprivations experienced by athletes (1978). Resorting to violent action is perhaps the primary method used by athletes to cope with widespread deprivations.

Each one of these theoretical perspectives provides some general understanding of why illegitimate violence occurs among players. But according to them, the amount of illegitimate violence should be constant across sports. But it is not. The theories are not very helpful because they do not treat violence as a variable. They omit the sport-specific factors that account for the variance. The remainder of this article examines the structure of sport as an independent variable.

II. The Structure of Sport and Player Violence

We have thus far outlined the six major theoretical perspectives that are currently being utilized to understand why participant violence occurs. Aside from some generalities, the insights of sociology are missing from these theories. Sociological research has been negligent in attempting to identify why sports violence exists. During the past ten years, sociologists have investigated illegitimate violence among sports participants, but *only* in contact sports such as football and hockey (Smith, 1974, 1978, 1979; Coakley, 1978, 1981; Vaz, 1974). Since violence also occurs in baseball and basketball, we should examine each of the four major North American sports. This

will permit us to view illegitimate violence as a variable, affected by the characteristics inherent in the structure of each sport.

There are four structural characteristics common to these four sports that will help us understand this phenomenon. We would hypothesize that participant violence in sport is related to: (1) the amount of scoring in each sport; (2) the amount of body contact allowed within the rules of each sport; (3) the amount of retaliatory power players have in each sport; and (4) whether the structure of the sport has high or low rewards throughout the game. These four characteristics of the structure of sport work *in combination* to help explain why illegitimate violence by participants exists. These variables work together simultaneously, not individually. A discussion of how each of these structural characteristics are manifested in each sport will clarify the argument.

Scoring: The Lower the Scoring, the Greater the Potential for Illegitimate Violence. The amount of scoring in a contest could be linked to violent participant behavior. The basic assumption is that if a high score is obtained in a contest, violent behavior will be lessened because an outlet for frustration and aggression has been obtained. Conversely, if scoring in a contest is low, frustration levels among participants will elevate because the outlet for frustration is not available. Moreover, in low scoring sports tension is heightened by the fear of making a crucial error leading to failure. Freischlag and Schmidke (1978) have stated that whether the game is high or low in scoring will have a direct effect on the amount of pent-up tension among participants.

This hypothesis would seem to be valid. Although we do not have the data to support this argument, bench-clearing brawl behavior seems to occur more frequently in hockey and baseball, which have very low scores, than in football and basketball, where scoring for the most part is higher.

Scoring frequency may explain participant violence rather than total scoring, but we think not. For example, on many occasions the frequency of scoring in hockey or baseball is much higher than the frequency of scoring in football, yet baseball and hockey contests are constantly reporting fights. Even in situations where the scoring frequency is identical between baseball or hockey (3–2) and football (21–14), baseball or hockey still appears to have more situations involving player violence. It would be useful if we had data on incidents of violence by sport as well as the frequency relative to the score in each contest. Assuming that our contention is correct that the amount of scoring is more strongly correlated with illegitimate violence, this is explained by the symbolic importance players attach to the number of points given for a score. If so, then high scoring would tend to decrease the pent-up frustration on the part of players. That football and basketball reward a score with more points than do hockey or baseball would seem to be a valuable insight into why these sports may have a lower frequency of illegitimate violence than baseball and hockey.

Body Contact: The Greater the Normative Body Contact, the Lower the Amount of Illegitimate Violence. The amount of legal body contact between players in different sports varies greatly. We hypothesize that there is an inverse relationship between the amount of legitimate body contact allowed and the amount of illegitimate violence found in each sport. As the amount of legitimate body contact increases, the amount of illegitimate violence decreases. Conversely, if legitimate body contact is virtually nonexistent within the structure of the game, we would expect to see high amounts of illegitimate violence among players.

In football, contact between players is simply part of the game. The ability to "move bodies" and "stick" an opponent are ingredients that are mandatory if a team is to be successful. Hard, physical contact, therefore, is expected on every play.

Hockey, like football, demands that body contact be part of the game. The ability to "check" an opponent is an essential part of the game if a team expects to be competitive at all. Yet hockey, unlike football, is not characterized by continuous body contact. Most bodychecking occurs when an opponent has or is near the puck. Penalties are often called if a player simply levels an opponent for no reason. Normative violent contact in hockey seems to center around the man with the puck, whereas in football, possession of the ball by a player is not necessary for contact to be initiated. In summary, hockey allows high levels of contact between participants, but less than in football.

Although some basketball players obtain "enforcer" reputations among their peers, the amount of legitimate body contact allowed in professional basketball is lower than in hockey or football. When picks are set and players "jockey" for position under the boards, there is physical contact. But the violent nature of the contact between players as evidenced in football and hockey is not evident in basketball.

Normative body contact between players is the least in baseball. With the exception of collisions at home plate and an occasional hard "take-out" slide into base, baseball players have little legitimate physical contact with other players.

The hypothesis of an inverse relationship between legitimate body contact in a sport and the amount of illegitimate violence holds true except for hockey. Perhaps the reason for this lack of fit with the hypothesized relationship is that in hockey the amount of legitimized body contact is but one of the four variables which work together in explaining participant violence.

Player Retaliation: The More That a Sport Allows Legitimate Player Retaliation, the Lower the Amount of Illegitimate Violence. This inverse relationship between player retaliation and illegitimate violence is based on the premise that if players are allowed to retaliate immediately against an opponent, frustration cannot build up and brawling behavior will be less likely to occur. Conversely, if players are unable to retaliate immediately against an opponent, frustration will accumulate throughout the course of a game and illegitimate violence, taking shape in the form of brawling behavior, will increase.

The amount of retaliation between players in football is very high. Suppose, for example, that a defensive end "beats his man" and throws the quarterback for a substantial loss. The offensive tackle who was victimized does not need to wait until late in the game to retaliate and make the defensive end "pay" for his sack. Because the match-up system exists between players in football, the offensive tackle knows that he can block extra hard on the very next play to retaliate against the very same defensive end. His frustration level does not have the chance to build up over the course of the game because he has the opportunity to retaliate almost immediately.

Basketball players also have a very high opportunity for retaliation against their opponents but with much less physical contact than in football. Because scoring a goal in basketball occurs very frequently, the ball changes hands quite often. If a forward is faked out by his opponent who then scores an easy lay-in, he has the chance to do the same almost immediately. Because of the matchup system in basketball, where quite often one is guarded by the man he guards, a player has the ability to retaliate by going down floor the next time and scoring on his opponent. This is particularly true of professional basketball, where the 24-second shot clock is used. In addition, basketball has an immediacy of retaliation since players who are recipients of dirty play (flagrant elbows, verbal aggression) can go down floor on the very next possession and do the same.

Hockey presents an interesting situation in terms of the amount of retaliatory power a player has. Hockey is less likely than football and basketball to have woven into its structure the match-up phenomenon. Typically, defensemen play zones and do not follow other players in a man-to-man fashion all over the ice. Hockey is a very "fluid" game, where offensive possessions may change every few seconds. Consequently, the potential for one player to retaliate against a specific other is low. So, for example, if a right-wing scores a goal by beating a defenseman, the defenseman does not have the retaliatory power to go back down the ice and score immediately on the same man or check him hard into the boards. He must wait until the same man has the puck, and then he may legally retaliate in a physical way. Since legal retaliation is relatively low in hockey, retaliation often takes illegitimate forms—high-sticking, tripping, or outright fighting.

Legitimate retaliatory power in baseball is virtually nonexistent. Perhaps even more than in hockey, match-up situations between players do not exist, and body contact is not even allowed. For a player to retaliate in baseball, a hard slide must be administered or a base hit must be achieved. Brush-back pitches and beanballs are techniques employed in order for one team to retaliate against another. The following quote by Pat Zachry, then a pitcher for the Mets, exemplifies retaliation through a brush-back pitch. After giving up back-to-back home runs, Zachry admitted throwing at Ron Cey to even the score. Zachry states: "I don't think it hurt him as bad as it hurt his feelings. . . . After two home runs, a guy should expect something inside" (Wulf, 1980). Legitimate retaliatory power among players in baseball, though, is very low to nonexistent.

The hypothesized relationship concerning the amount of legitimate retaliatory power and the amount of illegitimate violence that occurs in each sport would seem to hold true. In football and basketball, two sports that have high or very high amounts of retaliatory power among players, forms of illegitimate violence, i.e., brawling behavior, is relatively low. Conversely, in hockey and baseball, two sports that have low or nonexistent amounts of retaliatory power among players, illegitimate forms of behavior are often evidenced.

Reward Structure: The Greater the Opportunity for Rewards During a Contest, the Lower the Incidence of Illegitimate Violence. We hypothesize that there is an inverse relationship between the amount of rewards amassed throughout the game and the incidence of illegitimate violence. In other words, the greater the number of rewards achieved throughout the game, the less the tendency for players to aggress illegitimately.

Football is one sport where a team is rewarded throughout the course of an event. Rewards are not necessarily measured in terms of whether points are put on the scoreboard. Rather, events that take place during the course of a game may aid in decreasing the level of frustration experienced on the part of the players. For example, the offensive team in football may not obtain the ultimate goal—a touchdown—but other rewards exist that serve to reduce tension and frustration. Among these rewards are: (1) first downs; (2) completed pass plays; (3) successful trick plays; (4) field goals; (5) long runs; and (6) "coffin-corner" placements on punts. The defensive team also has rewards which are present throughout the course of a game which decrease frustration levels. Among these rewards are (1) quarterback sacks and drops for losses; (2) tipped passes; (3) interceptions; (4) holding the offense on four downs to little or no yardage; (5) goal line stands; (6) blocked field goals or punts; and (7) recovering fumbles. Both the offense and defense, then, have the potential for rewards throughout the course of the game. And, we assume, the greater the rewards, the less frustration which should reduce the likelihood of illegitimate aggressive outbursts.

The structure of basketball also presents teams with the opportunity to amass rewards throughout the course of a game. In addition to lots of scoring opportunities by all players, regardless of position, special rewards may be obtained offensively by: (1) hitting a three-point shot; (2) scoring on a spectacular slam-dunk; (3) making free throws and baskets; (4) running plays in your offense to perfection; (5) making a beautiful pass for an assist; or (6) starting the fast break with an outlet pass off a rebound. Defensive rewards can consists of: (1) blocking a shot; (2) stealing a pass; (3) harassing your opponent into a turnover; (4) boxing-out for a rebound; and (5) drawing a charging foul. As in football, basketball has the potential for rewards throughout the course of a game. This high reward system may lessen tension and decrease the potential for illegitimate violence among participants.

The structure of baseball also presents teams with the opportunity to accumulate rewards throughout the course of a game. The same logic applies to baseball that applies to football and basketball; namely, opportunity for rewards throughout the course of a game may lessen tension and lead to fewer aggressive illegitimate incidents. Potential rewards for the offense in baseball include: (1) singles, doubles, triples, or especially home runs; (2) perfectly executed bunts and sacrifice flies; (3) stolen bases; (4) walks; (5) perfectly executed hit-and-run plays; (6) successful hard slides to break up double-plays; and (7) runs-batted-in. The rewards for the defense include: (1) strike-outs; (2) put-outs; (3) double or triple plays; (4) throwing an opponent out trying to steal; or (5) throwing a runner out trying to take an extra base. In each case, rewards throughout the game may tend to lessen the potential for aggressive illegitimate action. Although we have already argued that bench-clearing brawls often occur in baseball, we still feel that rewards throughout the game dissipate tension on the part of players. The reasons why baseball still abounds with bench-clearing fights will be addressed later. Recall that participant violence in sport may be understood by analyzing the four variables' interactive effects, not their individual effects.

Of the four major sports in America, hockey has the least potential for rewards throughout the course of a game. A few goals (and assists) occur and there are good defensive plays, steals, and checking during the course of a game, but in general the rewards for players are less frequent than in the other sports. Perhaps this is a partial explanation for the extreme violence that occurs in hockey.

III. Why Sports Are Violent: The Interaction of Structural Variables

We have already discussed the four variables which each of the four major sports have in common. These common characteristics of sport can lend some valuable insight into determining why the four major sports vary in the incidence and magnitude of illegitimate violence by participants.

Although football is a contact sport, it may also be considered to be nonviolent in the sense that bench-clearing brawls rarely occur. The middle range amount of scoring, the very high level of player retaliation, the very high level of body contact, and the high number of rewards allowed throughout the game help decrease the pent-up frustration experienced by the athlete. Perhaps football allows too much "legitimate" body contact for an athlete's own safety, but because the other three factors work together to allow the venting of frustration and tension in legal ways, football remains relatively free of illegitimate brawling behavior.

Professional basketball is basically a nonviolent game because the very high amounts of scoring, structural opportunities for player retaliation, and amounts of rewards throughout the game help to diffuse the pent-up frustrations experienced by athletes. In addition, basketball also legitimizes a middle range amount of body contact, which serves to reduce tension.

Baseball, a sport that has long been considered nonviolent, has a good deal of illegitimate violence. Bench-clearing brawls occur with alarming frequency. Yet when the structure of the sport is analyzed, the violent nature is no longer surprising. First of all, the amount of scoring is low. This means that the athletes see little reward for their work, at least in terms of what the scoreboard shows, and tension is heightened by the crucial effects of each play because it may determine the outcome of the game. Second, legitimate body contact between players is rare, which allows even more frustration to build up. And third, the amount of legitimized player retaliation is very low. Apparently, the very high rewards throughout the game are not gratifying enough for players. Some other outlet for frustration needs to be given. The real need for an additional outlet can be evidenced by the fact that when a batter charges the mound to fight, both benches clear almost *immediately*. Seemingly, this brush-back pitch was all that was necessary to send athletes' frustration levels over the edge. Baseball exhibits far more brawling behavior than either basketball or football and the structure of the sport promotes this violence.

Hockey exhibits the most illegitimate violence of the four major sports. The high incidence of violence in hockey is explained in part by the National Hockey League's unwillingness to take a firm stance against it. It could be argued that the league actually encourages violence because that increases spectator interest and revenues. But the structure of the sport is also responsible. Like baseball, hockey has low amounts of scoring. This could add to the high tension and frustration level of players. But more important, hockey is the only one of the four major sports which does not have a high number of rewards throughout the course of the game. Football, basketball, and baseball all have rewards in between scores built into their structure, but hockey has few. When this is added to the high amount of legalized contact and the relatively few opportunities for legitimate player retaliation, then the reasons for the high incidence of illegitimate violence in hockey become more clear.

IV. Summary

Table 1 presents a summary of the four structural variables examined here and a crude rank ordering of each by sport. Our thesis is that the lower the composite ranks of these variables, the more likely that illegitimate violence will occur. Clearly, our hypotheses are speculative. The rank orderings in Table 1 are not interval data and are subject to empirical verification. The structural variables delineated here are likely not to equal weight, and there are probably others that should be included in a definitive analysis. Despite these shortcomings, however, this article presents an important step in understanding why sports vary in the degree of illegitimate violence that occurs because it focuses on the structure of each sport.

This article has attempted to make the case that participant violence in the four major sports exists as a result of the structure of each sport. We believe that the existing theories currently used to understand participant violence explain only a small portion of why violence exists. These theories have attempted to explain violence: (1) as a "microcosm" of society; (2) as

TABLE 1   *The Rank Order of Structural Variables by Sport*

Sport	Amount of Scoring	Amount of Legal Contact	Amount of Appropriate Player Retaliation	Number of Rewards	Rank Total
Football	3*	4	4	3	14
Basketball	4	2	3	3	12
Baseball	2	1	1	3	7
Hockey	1	3	2	1	7

* *These numerals represent ordinal rather than interval measurements.*

TABLE 2   *Factors Leading to Participant Violence in Sport*

Social Factors	Biological and Psychological	Sport Situational	Structure of Sport
Societal values	Genetic	Spectator behavior	Amount of scoring
Economic incentives	Psychological	Importance of game	Amount of legitimate body contact
Economic conditions		Propinquity of opponent	Amount of retaliation power
Cleavages in society (ethnic, religious)		Media intensity	High versus low reward
Violence in society		Stage of contest	
History			
Contemporary		Behavior of coaches, officials	
Punishment			
School		Drugs	
Media			
War and militarization			

caused by commercialization and economic incentives; (3) as caused by violent crowd behavior; (4) as a genetic predisposition to aggress; (5) as a learned behavior; and (6) as caused by psychological deprivation and repression. These theories are limited because they do not address the important issue of why sports vary in illegitimate violence. Second, the sociological explanations for illegitimate violence have addressed only the

types of violence found in contact sports such as football and hockey. Table 2 provides these existing theories of violence with the structural elements of sport considered in this paper added. We contend that the structure of each sport is the one important variable through which all other variables must be channeled in understanding why illegitimate forms of participant violence in sports occur.

The value of this article is that the causes for illegitimate participant violence have been analyzed sociologically by determining what structural characteristics exist in contact as well as non-contact sports that promote illegitimate violence. The addition of the structural elements adds to our understanding of why violence varies by sport. Our hope is that this discussion will encourage research on the structure of the various sports as the independent variable and that it will also encourage research that finds better measures of the dependent variable—illegitimate violence.

References

Bandura, A. K., and R. H. Walters. 1963a. "Aggression," *Child Psychology,* Chicago, National Society for the Study of Education, Part 1; 364–415.

———. 1963b. *Social Learning and Personality Development.* New York: Holt, Rinehart and Winston.

Berkowitz, L. 1964. "The Effects of Observing Violence," *Scientific American* 210 (February):35–42.

Blumer, Herbert. 1959. "Collective Behavior," in *Principles of Sociology,* revised edition, Alfred McClung Lee, Editor. New York: Barnes & Noble.

Brown, J. Marshall, and Nancy Davies. 1978. "Attitude Towards Violence Among College Athletes," *Journal of Sport Behavior* (May):61–70.

Cataldi, Peter, Jr. 1978. "Sport and Aggression: A Safety Valve or a Pressure Cooker?" in *Sport Psychology,* William F. Straub, Editor. Ithaca, N.Y.: Movement Publications: 59–62.

Coakley, Jay J. 1978. *Sport and Society: Issues and Controversies.* St. Louis: C. V. Mosby Company.

———. 1981. "The Sociological Perspective: Alternate Causations of Violence in Sport," *Arena Review* 5 (February):55–57.

Dollard, J. and others. 1939. *Frustration and Aggression.* New Haven: Yale University Press.

Edwards, Henry, and Van Rackages. 1977. "The Dynamics of Violence in American Sport: Some Promising Structural and Social Considerations," *Journal of Sport and Social Issues* 1 (Summer/Fall):3–32.

Eitzen, D. Stanley. 1981. "The Structure of Sport and Society," in *The Social World,* Ian Robertson, Editor. New York: Worth: 59–62.

Eitzen, D. Stanley, and George H. Sage. 1982. *Sociology of American Sport,* second edition. Dubuque: William C. Brown Company, Publishers.

Freischlag, J., and Charles Schmidke. 1978. "Violence in Sports: Its Causes and Some Solutions," in *Sport Psychology,* William F. Straub, Editor. Ithaca, N.Y.: Movement Publications: 161–165.

Furst, Terry R. 1971. "Social Change and the Commercialization of Professional Sports," *International Review of Sport Sociology* 6:153–170.

Gelles, Richard J. and Murray A. Straus. 1979. "Determinants of Violence in the Family," in *Contemporary Theories About the Family,* Volume I, Wesley R. Burr, Editor. New York: Free Press: 549–581.

Goldstein, Jeffrey H. 1982. "Sports Violence," *National Forum* 62 (Winter):9–12.

Graham, Hugh Davis and Ted Robert Gurr, editors. 1979. *Violence in America,* revised edition. Beverly Hills, Calif.: Sage.

Hatfield, Frederick C. 1973. "Some Factors Precipitating Player Violence: A Preliminary Report," *Sport Sociology Bulletin* 2 (Spring):3–6.

Kramer, Jerry. 1968. *Instant Replay,* Dick Schapp, Editor. Cleveland: The World Publishing Company.

Pilz, Gunter A. 1979. "Attitudes Toward Different Forms of Aggressive Behavior in Competitive Sports: Two Empirical Studies," *Journal of Sport Behavior* 2 (February):3–27.

Rubenstein, Richard E. 1970. *Rebels in Eden.* Boston: Little, Brown.

Sears, R. R. and others. 1953. "Some Child-Rearing Antecedents of Aggression and Dependency in Young Children," *Genetic Psychology Monographs* 47 (February):132–234.

Silva, John, III. 1978. "Understanding Aggressive Behavior and Its Effects Upon Athletic Performance," in *Sport Psychology*, William F. Straub, Editor. Ithaca, N.Y.: Movement Publications: 177–186.

Sipes, R. G. 1973. "War Sports and Aggression," *American Anthropologist* 75 (February):64–86.

Skolnick, Jerome H. 1969. *The Politics of Protest.* New York: Ballantine.

Smith, Michael D. 1973. "Hostile Outbursts in Sport," *Sport Sociology Bulletin* 2 (Spring):3–6.

———. 1974. "Significant Others' Influence on the Assaultive Behavior of Young Hockey Players," *International Review of Sport Sociology* 3–4:45–59.

———. 1978. "Hockey Violence: Interring Some Myths," in *Sport Psychology*, William F. Straub, Editor. Ithaca, N.Y.: Movement Publications:187–192.

———. 1979. "Hockey Violence: A Test of the Violent Subculture Hypothesis," *Social Problems* 27 (December):235–248.

Steinmentz, Suzanne K. and Murray A. Straus. 1973. "The Family as a Cradle of Violence," *Society* 10 (September/October):50–56.

Stone, Gregory. 1955. "American Sports—Play and Dis-play," *Chicago Review* 9:83–100.

Storr, A. 1968. *Human Aggression.* New York: Atheneum.

Sugden, John P. 1981. "The Sociological Perspective: The Political Economy of Violence in American Sport," *Arena Review* 5 (February):57–62.

Sykes, Gresham. 1971. *The Society of Captives*, second edition. Princeton, N.J.: Princeton University Press.

Thirer, Joel. 1978. "The Effect of Observing Filmed Violence on the Aggressive Attitudes of Female Athletes and Non-Athletes," *Journal of Sport Behavior* 1 (February):28–37.

———. 1981. "The Psychological Perspective: Analysis of Violence in Sport," *Arena Review* 5 (February).

Underwood, John. 1979 *The Death of An American Game: The Crisis in Football.* Boston: Little, Brown.

Vaz, Edmund W. 1974. "What Price Victory? An Analysis of Minor Hockey League Attitudes Toward Winning," *International Review of Sport Sociology* 2:33–57.

Wulf, Steven. 1980. "They're Up in Arms Over Beanballs," *Sports Illustrated* (July 14):26–31.

Chapter 33

ON-FIELD PLAYER VIOLENCE

Randall Collins

In this selection written for this book, Randall Collins, author of a book on a micro-socio-logical theory of violence, has distilled his larger argument to focus on the context and tim-ing of extracurricular violence in sports. Using a comparative approach (across sports) and micro-observations, Collins suggests that a number of variables are critical to the under-standing of player violence, including the degree to which violence is sanctioned within the game, the amount of protection that players wear, and struggles for emotional dominance at key turning points in the contest. Interestingly, these outbreaks can have major effects on the outcomes of the games.

Sports violence is often explained by conjec-tures about factors extraneous to the game. Causes frequently invoked both in the media and by social scientists include fans' desire for violence, race and class pressures and resent-ments, or the culture of masculinity and pa-triarchalism. These popular explanations are far off the mark. Once we look at it with sys-tematic comparisons of when violence hap-pens and does not happen, it becomes clear that these are neither necessary nor sufficient conditions for violence to occur.

The method of comparison is always the best way to establish causal patterns. Let us make the comparisons: in which sports does violence happen more frequently, less fre-quently, or not at all? This will show us that the structure of the game itself is what causes the propensity to violence. But even

in the more violence-prone sports, players do not fight with each other all the time, or even very much of the time. What causes players to fight with each other during a game is best answered by asking *when* in a game do fights break out. We shall see that just what produces maximal drama in the game is also what produces player violence.

Both sports and violence are emotional processes. By this I mean that both are forms of social interaction, confrontations in which one person or group tries to gain emotional dominance over the other. As I have argued more generally in my book *Violence: A Micro-Sociological Theory* [Collins 2008], vi-olence does not come off successfully unless one side establishes emotional dominance; the subtle and fast-moving details of emo-tional interaction are more important than whatever weapons are used or physical moves are made. Similarly with sports of all kinds: quite apart from any violence which may occur in a sport, the sport itself is a struggle for emotional dominance. The performance of skilled techniques or the use of superior bodily speed, strength or athleticism all take second place to the emotional tone in which these are carried out. At crucial moments in a sporting contest, one side forces the other into an emotional breakdown; and this is what victory and defeat is usually about.

Given this underlying similarity in the emotional dynamics of violence and of sports, we should be able to predict under what conditions violence will break out among players. Violence of course can also occur among fans, both during the game and outside the arena, and between fans and players. These forms of violence have a rather different dynamic, and are not treated here. For a fuller treatment, see Collins [2008].

My method, wherever possible, is direct observation of the details of action. The emphasis is not on the background characteristics of players or fans, but on the actual flow of events in the emotions of lived time. I draw on my own observations of games, largely from television, and from interviewing experienced fans of particular kinds of sports. My generalizations draw also on a news clipping file of incidents of sports violence over the years 1997–2004, and on photographs of those incidents. Sports in recent years is the best recorded of all forms of action, and thus it is possible to see the time sequence of conflict better here than in most other kinds of violence.

Sports as Dramatically Contrived Conflicts

Sports are deliberately contrived for producing exciting and entertaining contests.

What happens during a game is spontaneous and unpredictable in details. But the kinds of things that can happen are structured by procedures selected in advance. A game is the most highly staged of all conflicts; the conflict form itself has been chosen because of the drama it produces. Rules have been formulated and reformulated to channel the action in particular pathways; these conscious choices are usually made to promote more dramatic action in the game. The height of the pitcher's mound is lowered and the strike zone reduced to bring more hitting in baseball games; football games introduce forward passes; basketball games add 3-point shots and narrow the zone in which defenders can stand to block the basket. Sports are real life, and this makes them engrossing; but real life at its most deliberately and artificially organized and controlled. It is larger than life, conflict in its purified forms, better focused and therefore more dramatically satisfying than in ordinary events.

At the center of sports is its emotional appeal. Spectators follow the action above all for the experience of dramatic moments: the surge to go ahead in the scoring; the defensive rally to fend off an attack; the drama of catching up after having fallen behind; the last minute triumph. One's favorite does not always prevail, of course; on average, half the games will be lost. But even a losing effort can be dramatically satisfying, enough to keep spectators coming back for more, if there are enough dramatic moments along the way. The basic elements of drama are simple and repetitive, but they can be varied in many ways. Particular sports have their own patterns in the timing of dramatic moments; baseball with its long rallies of a sequence of players getting on base, building tension which may or may not go over the brink into scoring runs; soccer with its long continuous pressure and sudden release in a rare goal; the intermediate targets in American football with its 4 downs to go 10 yards and another chance to keep moving the ball towards the goal line; the series of nerve-wracking time-outs near the end of a close basketball game as teams struggle for a crucial shot, block or steal.

A literary narrative depends on plot tension; archetypally a protagonist has a problem, launches out on a search to solve it, encounters obstacles, acquires help, goes through set-backs and deceptions, and finally meets the chief obstacle head-on [classically delineated in Propp 1928/1968; cf. Elias and Dunning 1986]. In adventures, romances and comedies, the hero finally wins; in more complex dramas, there may be a tragic failure, losing the external goal but gaining a moral victory by having fought well, making a heroic sacrifice, or by gaining inner insight. Sports rarely have the most complex of these dramatic resolutions, but they are propelled by the basic shape of dramatic narrative.

To fully enjoy the game, one needs to go through these moments of suspense in real time; to merely watch taped replays or to read about the outcome in the news is to miss most of the emotional experience. Without the tension build-up, there is little of the surging joy of triumph, and the letdown of failure is the price people willingly pay for the chance of those moments. Moreover, the emotional experience is a collective one; it is the reverberated sounds and mutually entrained gestures of the crowd that makes it fun to be in the stands watching one's team's rally——even if it doesn't ultimately come off—and which makes the moments of triumph an experience for lifetime memories. That is why spectators will

pack a stadium for an eagerly-anticipated game, even though their seats may be poor, and on the whole they would have a better view on TV. What the fan experiences is not the sights of the game itself so much as the dramatic sequence of emotions, amplified by the presence of a like-minded crowd.

There are additional sources of excitement besides the short-run tensions of the game action. Anticipation and tension can build up from a series of games or matches, and from the standing of teams in a league playing for the season championship or position in a tournament. In some sports (chiefly American ones), secondary goals are elaborated by record-keeping, so that individual players can win batting or scoring championships and get their names in the record books in various ways, apart from whether the team wins or loses. A game may also feature some extraordinary moments of skill display—a shortstop making a spectacular fielding play, a basketball player's flying dunk—but these are unpredictable, not framed by a build-up of prior tension; they are enjoyable for the crowd but off to the side of the drama of conflict. There are also the dramatic aspects of individual player's histories: newcomers and aging veterans; injuries and recoveries; players moving from team to team and recasting old rivalries; quarrels with teammates, coaches and officials. Knowledgeable fans participate in an ongoing serial melodrama, a real-life soap opera; this material makes both for a continuous flow of news copy, and conversational capital for sociable ties among fans. This is why long familiarity with the stories of the players makes the experience of a sports event much thicker in meanings than it does for an outsider, who will likely find the same events uninteresting. For this reason, fans often find sports in other countries boring.

Spectators attend for the collective effervescence, the flow of dramatic emotions building up tension into group energy and solidarity. Players enact these emotional surges in a more complex way. In team sports, they share collective emotions with their teammates, and successful performance depends on emotional resonances that keep the team coordinated as well as energetic; these two features together are colloquially referred to as 'momentum' or 'chemistry' [Adler 1984]. Players also are involved in an emotional interaction with their opponents, whether in individual contests or team sports. Play consists in a contest of skill and effort, but most importantly in moment-by-moment challenges as to who will become emotionally dominant. It is a struggle over emotional energy (EE) in the technical sense of interaction ritual theory; the player or team who gains EE wins at the point where the opponent loses EE. These are the emotional turning points of a game.

These three kinds of emotional dynamics—collective effervescence in build-ups of dramatic tension in the audience; the degree of emotional resonance within a team; EE contests between opponents—make up the background for outbursts of sports violence.

Game Dynamics and Player Violence

When does violence happen? Below I will try to pin down the moments during the game when it is most likely. Consider here a broader comparison: what are the features of sports that make violence more frequent, and (not necessarily correlated) more severe.

Some violence is part of the game itself. Boxers hit each other; American football players block and tackle with as much force as possible; ice hockey players body check.

Injuries frequently happen within the rules of the game. We reserve the term sports violence for violence which happens outside the rules; typically it brings play to a stop. There are overlaps, and some violence on the field of play is quasi-recognized by the rules; there are penalties for fouls, unnecessary roughness, and illicit hits. These make up a continuum from legitimate player force, to fouls, to game-interrupting fights; emotional escalation goes up the continuum.

Sports may be divided into 3 main types: staged combats, in which there is both offense and defense; parallel contests, in which competitors strive to outdo each other towards a goal; and skill exhibitions, where competitors win by impressing a panel of judges. Sports violence is most frequent in staged combats, or rather in a subset of them. Considering why this is so will show us that the structure of the encounter is much more important than dispositional and background explanations which are often invoked to account for sports violence.

Masculinity is often put forward as an explanation of violence, whether in the form of a cultural code of aggression and dominance, or in the physiology of testosterone and bulked-up muscles. But among the most muscular and masculine-looking of athletes are track-and-field performers in shot put, discus and hammer throw; yet fights are almost unheard of at such competitions. This is also the case with weightlifters, the sport with the greatest emphasis upon sheer muscles. These are parallel competitions, with no direct confrontation of offense and defense; the form of the encounter, however tense and competitive, does not promote the dramatic form of violent confrontation. Still further from such confrontations are contests of skill exhibition, such as gymnasts; male gymnasts are very muscular but the structure of their encounters are non-confrontational. This is a reason why men who engage in similar exhibitions (whether they are organized as competitive sports, such as ice dancing, or are considered musical entertainment, such as ballet) tend to be regarded as not very masculine, even though they display a very high level of strength and body coordination.

Sports with both offense and defense are especially dramatic, in that they tend to build up tensions through a series of episodes, and allow for both sudden and creeping reversals of dominance. Players both attempt to execute their offense and to block their opponents. There is the tension and drama of fending off threats and thwarting the juggernaut; and the emotional triumph of finally breaking through a strong defense; there can be bitter emotions over having one's skill disrupted and team flow broken down. The clash of offenses and defenses through a series of such episodes is most likely to produce emotional turning points.

Sports which take the form of staged combats have the most frequent violence, but this in itself is not enough. The sports which are closest to real fights are boxing and wrestling. But these rarely lead to extracurricular fighting. An extreme instance occurred in a heavyweight championship in 1997, when Mike Tyson, frustrated at losing the fight, bit off a piece of Evander Holyfield's ear. Holyfield was so furious that he stomped around the ring and refused to continue fighting. Fighting is so completely incorporated into the sport itself that there is no way to make a dramatic statement by escalating fighting. In other sports, player fights are ways of showing that the mock-fight which constitutes the game has now escalated into a real fight; the dramatic form of boxing, which pretends to be a real fight, precludes this, or at any rate leaves little dramatic resources for framing one's dispute and one's anger as above and beyond the normal.

Wrestling is even more extreme in avoiding extracurricular violence. [i.e. real sport wrestling as practiced in school or amateur federation matches. In contrast, professional wrestling, which has little to do with the rules and techniques of sport wrestling, is heavily staged to give an impression of all-out violence, and includes regular occurrences of wrestlers fighting their opponents outside the ring, persisting in blatantly illegal weapons and techniques of attack. This is staged and rehearsed; in my opinion, a serious amateur wrestler would be able to tie up a professional exhibition wrestler very easily by applying standard take-down and immobilization moves.] Skilled wrestlers operate at close range, where more violent moves of kicking and punching are virtually impossible to mount with any force; the standard wrestling moves involve taking down the opponent to the ground and then leveraging the other into a defenseless position on his back. Even relatively unskilled wrestlers generally know how to tie up the opponent and to stall; such a match tends to turn into a muscular endurance contest. The dramatic form here is rather simple, and instead of building up to peak moments of tension, tends to wind down into a gradual establishment of dominance, or near-stalemate. Highly skilled wrestlers can make sudden attacks and escapes; but the momentary result of each such move is generally to make the opponent more harmless. Thus wrestling, as the form of sport fighting which involves the most direct and prolonged muscle-on-muscle confrontation, is caged by its very form into keeping fighting confined to the main lines of the event.

A third sport very close to real violence is fencing; but such matches seem never to lead to extraneous fighting. Fighting is so strongly incorporated into the sport itself that it does not overlap it. [On fencing and martial arts schools generally: Collins 2008; Draeger 1974.]

Player violence is most frequent in offensive/defensive combats organized as teams rather than individuals, even though the fights themselves are generally between individuals. This fits the general pattern that violence depends upon group support. There are two main features which predict violence: the extent to which violent moves, efforts or threats are incorporated into the game action itself; and the extent to which players are protected from being hurt.

Systematic data on player violence is comparatively rare. [Shields 1999; and data sources cited in Collins 2008] In the absence of other direct observational counts of fights during games, I offer the following from my own checking of news reports and televised games, and from questioning experienced fans: Hockey fights occur at a rate of about one per game (in professional hockey). Football players' fights occur once or twice per weekend (comprising about 15 games) in the professional season, but more concentrated in tense games near the end of the season. Baseball fights occur about once a week: i.e. out of 90 professional games. Basketball fights are rare, below 1% of the games. Soccer player fights appear to be very rare.

How is this ordering to be explained?

In some games, direct bodily impedance of opponents is the main form of action. In American football, violence is the normal play itself, the bodily collisions of tackling, blocking, and running through tacklers. Hockey involves body checking, and slam-ming speeding skaters into the boards; basketball includes a certain amount of pushing and grappling for position, as well as the possibility of charging or blocking in the movement of players on the way to the basket or in scrambling for the ball. Baseball has legitimate forms of running into or blocking a player, notably in close plays at home plate between the catcher applying a tag and an oncoming runner. It seems obvious that normal playing violence would carry over into angry fights which stop the play of the game, or that the tensions and frustrations of normal playing violence break out in extracurricular violence. Nevertheless, although body contact sports of this kind are the main locus of player violence, this is not enough to explain either the frequency with which different kinds of sports have violence, or the particular moments when violence breaks out.

Games with impedance of the opponent's scoring efforts structurally promote fights. Games without impedance thus almost never have fights. But impedance may arise obliquely in the same locations where it is formally absent. Golf is a parallel contest in which the players, small numbers of whom are playing together on the same hole, are not physically separated but are very peaceful. Fights do sometimes happen on golf courses; the only ones I have personally witnessed, heard or read about, have occurred not between golfers who are competing with each other, but in non-tournament situations where golfers become angry at those in front of them for slow play; they will sometimes try to hit the slow players with a ball, or physically confront them. This is an instance of impedance, which occurs in the context of a game but separate from the actual competition itself. This shows that golfers are generally peaceful, not because they are more polite and upper-middle class than other athletes, but because the dramatic structure of tensions in the game is not organized to produce confrontations with one's competitors.

Similarly, tennis players, although in a sport traditionally connected with the polite upper classes, are not above angry outbursts (and among female as well as male players). Tennis is a form of offensive-defensive combat, with players directly impeding each other's scoring efforts. But the players are physically separated by a net, and the form of the action is to keep the ball away from the opponent rather than forcefully hitting at him or her. The tension of sudden efforts and reversals of movement and the dramatic failures in losing a point can lead to emotional outbursts; but these are directed at referees rather than opponents [Baltzell 1995]. Anger is not enough to produce a fight.

Rules have been manipulated so as to take into account violence which gets out of hand. In football, there are penalties for unnecessary roughness; clipping or hitting a player from behind or in vulnerable parts like the knees; hitting especially vulnerable or non-violent players such as the quarterback; impeding a pass receiver or pass defender who has not yet caught the ball; etc. These penalties in varying degrees affect the possibility of winning the game; however since both teams tend to commit penalties (and penalties for violent play are treated in the same way as penalties for other violations such as off-sides), there is a tendency for penalties to balance out among both teams, and there is no overwhelming incentive for players to avoid violence penalties. Similarly, in hockey there are a variety of penalties including those for forms of violence which are beyond the rules: high-sticking, hooking the opponent with one's stick, as well as especially violent body checks. More serious fighting is itself penalized as a normal, expectable violation that occurs frequently in the course of a game. The penalties (sitting for a certain number of minutes in the penalty box) affect the chances of winning, but are incorporated into both offensive and defensive strategies ('power plays' when the other side is short-handed for penalties, but also tactics for killing a power play). In basketball, rough play is penalized by penalty shots; given the high rate of scoring, these do not usually give enough points in any one occasion to make a big difference in winning the game, although they might in the aggregate or at crucial moments. Penalties are so frequent on both sides that they are normalized and incorporated into the flow and tactics of the game; the game includes a range of play which is strictly speaking illegal but expectable, another arena of risk and competition that good players and teams must be proficient at. A penumbra of controlled violence surrounds the main play of the game. Penalties allow for a form of protected violence, kept within bounds which are implicitly understood by everyone involved; penalties are ways of making violence possible, overcoming confrontational tension/fear by socially organizing the violence in a limited form.

The influence of penalty regimes can be seen by comparing games which have quite severe penalties. Soccer is normally a low-scoring game, because of the presence of a goalie (as compared to games with an open goal and prohibitions on goal-tending) and off-sides rules which favor the defense. Rather draconian rules against tackling by body contact set up unimpeded penalty kicks on goal which often decide a game;

moreover since players who are sent off the field for penalties cannot be replaced, the offending team is very disadvantaged by playing short-handed. Severe penalties of this sort deter borderline violence within the game; and this sets an atmosphere in which extracurricular fights are rare.

Nevertheless, institutionalization of frequent mild penalties does not itself predict very well the level of player violence. Hockey, football, and basketball all have penalty structures which normalize violence beyond the rules; but hockey has very frequent fights, football moderately frequent, and basketball very infrequent fights among players. In addition, baseball, which does not have much in the way of a normalizing penalty structure for rough play (but instead a comparatively severe rule on fighting—expulsion from the game, sometimes with fines and suspension from future games—in this last respect similar to soccer) also has rather frequent fights of a distinctive kind. Another condition for fighting must be invoked.

This is the extent to which players are protected from being hurt if a fight breaks out.

Hockey players wear heavy padding, including helmets and gloves; although they carry sticks which can operate as weapons, these are virtually never used in a fight itself, although hooking or high-sticking might be a provocation to a fight. Typically in a hockey fight players drop their sticks and pummel each other with (or without) gloves on and with helmets in place. The equipment operates both to protect them against attacks, and to limit the damage they can do to each other during a fight. The most serious injuries in hockey violence come not from fights when the game action has stopped, but from vicious hits in the course of the game itself: e.g. when a player blind-sided an opponent skating up the ice away from the puck, in retaliation for an earlier confrontation. Moreover, the fighters are usually soon surrounded by other players, who scuffle and push but generally limit the space in which fighters can maneuver, constricting what good blows can be gotten off. Fighters on skates do not have good footing and are not in a position to carry out an effective boxing match.

Football players are heavily padded, and wear helmets with face-guards. Football players fairly often get into fist fights, but these do little damage, since the fist is a poor weapon against such protection; thus fights are less damaging than what can be normally done during play, where most injuries occur. The most dangerous weapon carried by a football player is his helmet, which are used as effective striking weapons for spearing an opponent with a full-body lunge. But this can only be done while a play is going on. There is also a certain amount of punching, even biting and gouging in pile-ups, out of sight of the referees and the audience. But although some players have reputations as dirty players for behind-the-scenes violence, this appears to be a self-contained arena, that does not spill over into other kinds of more publicly visible, and therefore more dramatic violence. It is minor violence compared to the ordinary violence of the game.

Basketball is played without protective equipment. When rare fights among players break out, they usually take the form of posturing and gesturing, and solid punches are rarely thrown. Thus one of the two most protected games (hockey) has the most fights, the least protected (basketball) has the fewest among combat sports. Other unprotected games, like soccer, also have low violence, although we have seen multiple reasons for keeping player violence low.

Football, by my estimate, has somewhat fewer fights than hockey, although still at the medium-high end of the range. Both sports are approximately equally protected from physical injury by equipment, and both regularize violent violations under penalty rules (although one could argue that hockey fights are more regularized). But football players have more opportunity to fight, legitimately, in the course of play itself; rough checking is only part of the game of hockey, but blocking, tackling or breaking tackles happens for almost all players on every play in football. The vast majority of football injuries happen during play, not during fights; if a player is angry enough to want to injure an opponent, the most effective way to do so is to continue with the game. Football has the most room for legitimately demonstrative violence during the course of the game; although there are perhaps the greatest abundance of game situations from which violence could overflow, it is more dramatically satisfying to carry out the strongest violence within the rules.

The pattern is: the more protected the participants, the more frequent the fight. Hockey players, like football players, in an extracurricular scuffle, are in the position of children scuffling with each other near adults who can break it up; they are bigger and stronger, but the damage they can do is limited by both their padding and their social surroundings. It is the same pattern that appears in the contrast between German student duellists in the *Mensur*, literally measuring each other's mettle for a fight while padded from waist to neck, in protective goggles and using shallow unpointed swords; and on the other hand French duellists with much less body protection but keeping their distance in sword and pistol fights; the German students hack away energetically and at length to produce a few honorable scars; the French make their duels a display of bluster but statistically manage to avoid most injuries. Hockey and football players closely resemble the bundled-up German students playing a prolonged game of mild punishment; most other players of confrontational games resemble French duellists. [For analysis of dueling, see Collins 2008.]

Comparison with baseball shows that protection can be social rather than physical. Baseball is not a body contact sport (with a few exceptions), so one might expect a low level of fights on that score. And its players are generally unprotected by equipment; they wear gloves on defense, but these are usually discarded during a fight. Batters wear helmets, although these do not protect the face, and sometimes elbow and shin guards, but these have little relevance to fights. Only the catcher, with chestguard, shin guards, and face mask, is heavily protected (against his own pitcher, chiefly).

Almost all baseball fights begin after a pitcher hits a batter with a pitch; in the following inning (usually), the opposing pitcher retaliates by hitting a batter on the opposing team, which batter then angrily shouts at, insults or attacks the pitcher with his fists. The rest of both teams then run onto the field, including the reserve players. Usually there is little violence; other members of both teams grab each other, and may wrestle the most excited fighters to the ground, where pummeling with fists is little effective.

There is more of a mêlée in a baseball fight than in other sports fights; basketball fights have few mêlées but more of an individual face-off; football and hockey fights are generally restricted to those already on the field and usually just to those closest to the action. This difference in team participation results from the fact that baseball pitcher-retaliation fights are an explicit code (although forbidden by the formal rules, very similar to dueling in relation to formal law); all members of the team are expected to make at least a token show of solidarity. Bench players will indicate that they ran onto the field because everybody else did, and they felt expected to do so too; while on the field, much of the action consisted in a mixture of grabbing opposing players—as a hostile gesture, but also in a defensive move to keep them from grabbing and knocking down one's own players—and grabbing one's own players to restrain them from getting further into the fight, ostensibly to avoid penalties for fighting.

Leaving aside the ostensible motivations and justifications, the micro-sociological process of a baseball fight is that a few angry principals carry out a ritual retaliation and honor defense; other players who are closely connected to them join in with some degree of anger, but also to restrain them; other players bodily mass together, as if in one huge ritual of body contact, mixing solidarity and hostility. Players are rarely hurt during such mêlées; and the most dangerous weapon—the batter's bat—is virtually never used in such a fight, but is always discarded just before the fight begins. (Baseball bats are sometimes used as weapons in street fights and in hold-ups (e.g. Felson 1994: 32; Morrison and O'Donnell 1994). In general, baseball lies in an anomalous position among other games in degree of danger; getting struck by a pitch can sometimes cause death or crippling injury, and there are some other rough plays in baserunning

(especially when a catcher blocks a runner at home plate; also when a runner breaks up a double play at second base by upending the fielder), but the level of bodily hitting is much more intermittent than in football or hockey. Rough baserunning plays rarely lead to fights, in comparison to hit by pitch, nor are they retaliated for by hitting by pitch. Partly this is because close baserunning plays happen only occasionally and at unpredictable times, whereas the pitcher can at any time deliberately throw at a batter, just as a duel can be scheduled at will. Highly motivated violence needs to be dramatic violence; and dramatic staging takes tension build-up to an appropriate, well-anticipated moment.

Here again the exception or historical variant helps confirm the rule. Baserunning was much more violent in the period before 1920, when attention shifted to the home run and hence to the hitter-pitcher confrontation. Prior to a rule change in 1897, stolen bases included extra bases taken on a teammate's hit. In the next 2 years, the new stolen base record was established at 77 for the season. In the 7-year period between 1909 and 1915, heated competition built up among half a dozen players who came near to breaking the record, several of whom successively raised the record to 81 (Eddie Collins), 83 (Ty Cobb), 88 (Clyde Milan), and finally 96 (Cobb again). [Thorn et al. 2001: 543, 547; Stump 1994] It was during this time that Cobb acquired the reputation for sharpening his spikes to bloody defensive players with his violent high slides. The reputation was in part bluster, an image and strategy of intimidation; Cobb also perfected techniques of guile and timing by carefully observing the moves of opposing pitchers. Rival base-stealers developed similar strategies and techniques. After this period of competition, the record remained stable until 1962; base-stealing was no longer an object of rapt attention; the yearly totals of Cobb and the other contenders dropped off considerably, and fights centering on baserunning virtually disappeared.

A thought-experiment will illustrate the theory to this point. Soccer is a game with very low extracurricular fighting, for a head-to-head mutual impedance sport of offense vs. defense. But soccer could be changed into a high-fight game, similar to hockey or American football, by making 2 modifications: players wearing more padding (such as light-weight synthetic body armor) so they are less vulnerable to being hurt; and changing the penalty structure so that rough play does not count so much in the dramatic action of winning or losing the game. This could be done by adopting football or hockey type penalty rules, in which rough players are sent off for only short periods of requiring the team to play short-handed, or allowing substitutions if players are ejected from the game. This mental exercise should show that it is these kinds of structural features which determine on-field player violence, rather than something intrinsic to the ethos of particular games.

Winning by Practical Skills for Producing Emotional Energy Dominance

Sports as staged combats are unusually prolonged face-to-face struggles, compared to the usual brevity of real-life fights. Techniques of winning a game are applied on each play; they are a matter of establishing dominance over the person right in front of you—momentarily physically, and in a

longer time-frame emotionally. Football linemen charge ahead while defenders push back; winning this contest happens in surges of momentum as one team imposes its will on the other. The struggle is over emotional energy (EE) dominance, just as it is in the climax of military battles, where the winning side becomes energized into a frenzied attack while the other side gets caught in confusion and paralyzing passivity; just as it is in armed robberies where the robber tries to get the jump on a victim. The difference in sport, apart from the restrictions on violence, is that the struggle for dominance is usually stretched out and visibly displayed for the sake of spectators. Where holdup artists seize the jump suddenly and soldiers go into an outburst of forward panic after a period of tension, athletes often go through prolonged efforts yielding temporary and partial dominance at best, occasionally building up to spectacular and decisive momentum-swings.

EE is collective in several senses. It spreads through the team, who become high or low on EE as a unit. More precisely, some segments of the team may have more collectively shared emotion than other players; teams vary in emotional cohesiveness, both high and low; and it varies over time. The inner history of each game played is the sequence of emotional coordination and its level. Collective emotion can be both good and bad: collective confidence and initiative, or collective depression or frustration; at the low end this turns into quarreling among teammates.

Teams that are being beaten not only lose emotional dominance, but lose their cohesion. [Interview question:] "How could you tell when a defense was cracking?" [Eric Dickerson, record-holder for most rushing yards in a season:] "What you'd have is, you'd have a team bickering. That's when you knew you'd got them. You'd have them, 'Why don't you guys make a tackle up front!' Then, 'Why don't you make a tackle in the back!'" [*Los Angeles Times*, Dec. 27, 2003]

There is simultaneously a reciprocal interaction with opponents so that one side gains EE at the expense of the other side losing it. It is often noted at such moments that the defense is getting tired out, allegedly from being on the field a long time; but this cannot be simply physical tiredness, since the opposing offense is on field the same amount of time. The physical tiredness is a manifestation of losing EE; the bodies of the yielding defenders are losing their emotional charge. Another way to say it is that they are being emotionally beaten in a fight, perhaps all the more so because the fight is restricted rather than all-out violence. Sports tactics aim to destroy the opponent emotionally rather than physically.

Players' techniques for blocking and fighting through blocks, for knocking the other player down, for causing him to miss a catch or a running man, are what wins the game as well as the little segments within it. These are techniques of a violent contest in two senses: both to physically control the opposing player so that the play can be executed or stymied; and to establish EE dominance, charging oneself up further and taking away the other's EE.

Such conflicts can spill over rather naturally from violence-within-the-rules into extracurricular violence or player fighting in the sense we are using the term here. In football, the most effective violence happens within normal play, and hence fights are largely expressions of the emotional dominance which has already been established. In other sports, notably baseball,

fights can be dramatic high points and turning points of the game.

In baseball, the chief head-to-head battle is between pitcher and batter. Part of this struggle is a guessing game: the batter tries to anticipate what kind of pitch will be thrown, its speed and location, while the pitcher varies his pitch selection to try to make the batter guess wrong. There is also an aspect of sheer physical control of the batter: a pitcher with overpowering speed can freeze a batter's swing, or make him look awkward in trying to catch up with it. What makes pitch speed overpowering is not purely a matter of how high over 90 mph it is thrown; it is often a matter of the rhythms built up through a series of pitches; especially in strike-outs, a pitcher makes batter fall into his dominant rhythm.

It is notable in this regard that batters and pitchers rarely look at each other's eyes, or even faces. They seem to be attempting to maximize the trickiness of the guessing game by assuming the demeanor of poker players. Another aspect of the situation is that players take direct looks as hostile gestures; eye contact triggers a fight as much as verbal insult. The Texas Rangers, leading the AL West by 4 games over the Anaheim Angels in July 2004, got into a fight during pre-game warm-ups at the Angels' stadium. The Ranger's catcher, Gerald Laird, had quarreled in the previous game with the Angels' batter, Adam Kennedy, accusing the latter of deliberately trying to be hit by a pitch with the bases loaded to force in a run. Kennedy came up to Laird at the batting cage, intending to make amends; instead the two got into a tussle, which brought all the other players into pushing, shoving and grabbing each other for 4 minutes. "He kind of saw that I was making eye contact with him, and I expected a different response and a more cordial conversation than I got," Kennedy said. "It was a little misunderstanding that probably got a little out of control." The Angels went on to win the game, 2 to 0. Laird did not play in the game; Kennedy went 1 for 3. [*San Diego Union*, July 28, 2004] The fight—starting with the struggle over who controls eye contact—set the tone for the game.

Sports commentators conventionally use terms like "the pitcher is in his rhythm" when he is making an effective series of pitches for a strikeout, and also getting one batter after another for a series of outs. This raises an issue: if the pitcher establishes a rhythm, why doesn't the batter know what pitch is coming, and adjust to it? Nevertheless, he plays the passive role. There are parallels in other areas [discussed in Collins 2004: 122–124]. In swimming and other races, habitually winning competitors establish a pace that the others must adjust to. If we think of the race through the technical details of interaction ritual theory, the dominant person is the one who makes him/herself the focus of attention—the winner focuses on the goal, the loser focuses on the winner. Chambliss [1989] emphasizes especially the cognitive interpretations made by winners and losers. There is also an emotional aspect, which he refers to as 'the mundanity of excellence'—the winner is calmer and more detached, focusing on performing the micro-detailed techniques which s/he has confidence will bring victory; the loser has more anxiety, feeling that there is a mysterious power that superior athletes have that s/he does not share. The winner's technique includes, perhaps above all, methods for setting the rhythm and making the other competitors adapt to it.

There is further evidence in another area of micro-sociology: the fine-grained rhythms of conversational speech. In high-solidarity interaction, conversationalists fall into the same temporal rhythm. In some interactions, there is a struggle over who sets the conversational rhythm; tape-recorded data shows instances both of the struggle at these moments and of the emergence of one speaker as dominant over the other, who gives in and lets the other set the rhythm. This is analogous to the pitcher who achieves rhythmic dominance over a batter.

There are also more complicated, reflexive ways of pitching, disrupting the batter's swing by change-ups which are slower than they appear; as well as curves thrown in various directions as they cross the plate. Pitching is partly deception, partly sheer physical dominance through speed, and partly a form of explicit intimidation. Pitchers throw inside, both to catch the inner corner of the plate (especially if a batter has a weakness there), and to back the player up, making it more difficult for him to hit the next pitch on the outside. The brush-back pitch, thrown directly at the batter so he has to jump or fall away to avoid being hit, is a standard technique for all these purposes. On top of this, it also can have an intimidating effect, changing EE dominance between that batter and that pitcher. Some pitchers, such as Roger Clemens, or historically Bob Gibson, are known for their intimidating manner; these are pitchers who have set strike-out and ERA records, although other record-setting pitchers did not have the same confrontational style. Intimidation is one technique among others.

Batters are in a Goffmanian face contest with the pitcher; to let oneself appear intimidated is to give an advantage to the pitcher, and controlling one's external expression may be an attempt at controlling one's interior emotions as well. A batter who has been brushed back, knocked down, or hit by a pitch may become angry precisely because he feels a bit of fear which he cannot control; it is better to mask this by anger, to keep up a dramatic front by making a gesture (usually ineffective) of intimidating the pitcher in return.

Some batters take the other tack and make it part of their technique to stand close to the plate, even to risk getting hit often as a way of getting on base and of disrupting the pitcher's pattern. Thus the same players lead the league yearly in being hit by pitch. A hypothesis in keeping with my observations is that such batters do not become angry when they are hit by a pitch, nor become involved as principals in brawls. Just as there are pitchers who rely on deception and those who emphasize overt domination, there are batters who rely more on cool-headed technique and others who rely on energy surges. (Recent examples of the former would include Barry Bonds, Ichiro Suzuki, and Tony Gwynn; of the latter, Manny Ramirez.) It is the latter who we would expect to start more fights. Similarly, we would expect pitchers who try to overpower batters are more likely to get into fights than pitchers who rely on deception and fine placement. Thus a fight would be most likely where a power pitcher faces a batter who relies on sheer muscular dominance or sheer emotional intensity.

Aggressive pitching is largely a form of bluster rather than actual violence, although occasionally batters do get hurt; it is the threat of violence more than its actual occurrence; its success comes when it gives EE dominance, with physical dominance coming in its train in the form of batter's poor performance. Baseball fights almost always start when the batter escalates in reply to the pitcher's bluster. But in fact the pitcher is usually just as angry as the batter, sometimes more so (as I have shown by the analysis of facial expressions and gestures), showing that fear of getting hurt is not essential to the anger.

Escalation does not happen all the time. As usual, we run astray by sampling on the dependent variable. Although it is true that most baseball fights start because of pitcher's conflicts with batters, if we count incidents of bean-balls, we find they are much more frequent than fights. In an 8-day period, for example, there were 64 incidents of hit by pitch in 105 games, but only 2 fights (42 games had at least one HBP, and 22 games had multiple incidents); i.e. 40% of games had an incident, but only 3% of these resulted in a fight. [calculated from *San Diego Union-Tribune* and *Los Angeles Times*, Aug. 25-Sept. 3, 2004] It takes additional dramatic elements to turn an incident into a fight.

In hockey, most of the action consists in passing and disrupting passing, and in fighting for the loose puck. Such fights are especially vehement in the corners behind the goal; defensemen consider these their special turf, and incursions by the offense have to be especially aggressive, both to have a chance of winning the practical fight over the puck, and to meet the high level of emotional confrontation.

"I know a lot of times a guy will go into the corner. That's where you find out if the guy is going to come back at you or challenge you or anything. You see what he can take." [Interviewer question:] "So the corners are important?" "Sure, you go in and really rap him hard with the elbow and let him have it in the head maybe and the next time you won't have any problems with the guy. Maybe he'll come in the corner but not as hard as he did the first time, he's taking a chance of getting another elbow in the mouth. Maybe you get a penalty, but you take him out of the play, that's a good penalty . . . I'll give 'em an elbow and, you know, hit guys dirty. Now I wouldn't hit a guy in the head with a stick, but you get 'em solid with a good check. This is your job, and you watch, he won't come back into the corner too quick.

"The guy you've got to worry about is the guy who turns around and really hits you back, bang, right in the nose, and the guy who keeps going into the corner to dig it out. The next time you're thinking, he's got you going. You've got to respect him because you know he'll take it and give it back. He doesn't back away." [Faulkner 1976: 98–99]

The borderline between normal play and fouls is itself part of players' consciousness of the game. Players distinguish between good fouls and stupid fouls; good fouls not only serve a purpose in the game, but are precisely the fouls which are delivered most aggressively and send the message of domination. 'Cheap shots' are looked down upon because they are not violent enough.

"To intimidate a guy you've got to rap him, cheap penalties are no good really, a hooking penalty is a cheap penalty, tripping, holding is a cheap penalty. A good penalty is charging provided you hit the guy and he *knows* he's been hit. If you trip the guy, it won't hurt him, it doesn't even bother him, he won't care. Tripping is really stupid, the only time you'll trip a guy is if he gets behind you or if you miss the puck and hit his feet. These are stupid because you haven't really done *your* job. This means the guy's beaten you and you have to slow him down so you can hook him or hold him. If you can intimidate him he won't get in this position in the first place." [Faulkner 1976: 99]

The course of a game, as well as longer stretches of players' careers, depends on the cumulative effect of these contests for emotional dominance. "It's a known fact that there are certain guys on certain teams that if you nail 'em once or twice, if you show 'em you're going to take charge, well, they can't take the hitting and so they've got to respect you. They'll be looking, so you can kill their game." [Faulkner 1976: 99]

This is not simply a matter of masculine identity; in hockey, testing the opponent's aggressiveness is a key part of the game. Lack of aggressiveness makes one perform badly, and be taken advantage of by opponents in normal play.

"I know we've got a couple of guys on our team, well you know he's scared. He's just scared. You can tell him not to worry that if anything happens don't worry about it, the guys will back you up. But this guy is just scared, you'll make a pass to him and he'll let the pass go off his stick, he'll make a stupid play, he'll move away from the trouble. Last week we got the puck out to him across the blue line and their defensemen came in to take him out of the play and our guy just let the puck go off his stick. So this guy on the other team got it and went in to make a shot on net. Now damn, that's really bad. My defense partner and myself were on the bench and he said, Look at that goddamned chicken. And you just look at that type of thing and it makes you mad. This guy better change his attitude or everybody will tell him." [Faulkner 1976: 101]

Faulkner notes that the experience of being called upon by others to protect them seems to increase a player's sense of confidence in his own skills. Ritualistic fights give EE to the entire sports performance. Fighting is not just encapsulated as separate activity, or expression of masculinity apart from the process of winning the game.

"If the other team knows that when one of your players is in trouble the whole team will back him up, then we *all* have confidence. This is why some teams are feared, like with S., everyone is there. Someone will put a stick in to stop a punch, if a guy is trying to throw a sucker punch from behind. As a team they're tougher because they back each other up all the way. You never let your teammates get beat because it can swing a whole game around. A guy works your teammate over pretty bad, that gives the rest of them a lift and if we don't go out and challenge him and straighten him out we're *dead.*" [Faulkner 1976: 105]

Violence in hockey acts as a high intensity interaction ritual, riveting collective attention and producing emotional entrainment. It is a common cliché to complain that fights in hockey are more important than the game; this is not strictly true (since goal scoring and saves are the apex of the game), but fights are often the moments which are most successful in stirring up collective energy. This can be the result of entrainment both among teammates and between them and fans.

"The first thing that comes into my head is the cheering every time somebody gets hit into the boards and a fight breaks out everyone stands up and cheers that kind of thing, and when they see blood. A lot of fans came to see that and they got bored if there wasn't some kind of violence going on. In my personal conversations with them and how they react to the game, it was enough for me to see that they wanted to see that violence thing, and it does promote it. I mean, when the crowd is behind you and cheer when you knock people into the boards I'm not going to lie, it gets you fired up and wants to make you do more banging of guys into the boards, and lots of times, if it takes that to get the team fired up, then that's what you're going to do. It always helps to get the fans behind you they definitely have a role in promoting violence in the sport." [Pappas et al. 2004: 302]

Violent techniques are just part of the techniques of a hockey team; some players specialize as scorers, and these (along with goalies) seem to be rarely involved in fights, or even in rough play. Wayne Gretzky, the all-time scoring leader in professional hockey, had a reputation among opponents as a 'sneaky' player, deft and surprising in his moves to the goal rather than confrontational. Other players are known as the 'heavies', and these in turn fall into subtypes. Some are regarded as 'policemen', who intimidate opponents, respond to their aggression, and readily join in fights to back up embattled teammates. Some of them regard their role as protecting the fast-skating and slick stick-handling scorers. A 'good policeman' is oriented to the game, and avoids penalties in crucial situations. Others, who fight too recklessly, earn the reputation as 'goons'; they are disliked by opponents for hits beyond the normal level of intimidation, but also by teammates for involving them in more group fights than necessary. This division of labor shows again that hockey violence comes not simply from a generalized commitment to masculinity, or even to producing violence for the fans; but rather particular techniques concentrated at particular places in the game. [cf. Pappas et al. 2004; Weinstein et al. 1995; Smith 1979] Every team needs one or two 'policemen', but it is not necessary for every player to be one. Even more than scorers, goalies are treated as high-skill specialists who are not expected to fight. If they are hit in front of the goal by encroaching opponents, their defensemen gather around protectively, and may fight on their behalf. In rare instances, when a full-scale mêlée occurs between teams, the two goalies will square off at center ice, against each other, trading token punches. Thus even in an all-out fight, the specialized organization of the teams in terms of violence is maintained.

The Timing of Player Violence: Loser-frustration Fights and Turning Point Fights

Now we are concerned, not with normally violent or intimidating game action but the points at which it turns into specifically bracketed fights. When do fights in this sense happen during a game?

One type of player fight arises from frustration. Frustrated fighting occurs late in a game. This happens most noticeably in football, around just the time when one team recognizes it has lost the possibility of winning the game. The fight is a way of staving off admitting being dominated; it is a last gasp of resistance, at the last moment when the players are still struggling hard. Such frustration fights are usually ineffective as violence (as football fights normally are), and never seem to turn the momentum around. Fights in hockey are especially likely after a team has clearly lost the game. The losing players start these fights, as if to show they still have a presence on the ice, even though they can no longer win the game.

A second type of player violence changes the emotional situation so dramatically that it determines the outcome of the game. Turning point fights occur after the tension of the contest has been going on for some time, and thus usually in the last third or quarter of the game.

August 10, 2001: a big bench-clearing brawl in baseball game. This one is unusual because the initiator is really angry, a batter who throws his batting helmet at the pitcher; wrestles him to the ground, and punches him while he is on the ground; as both benches rush the field, other players trade punches too, and the instigator keeps pursuing the pitcher, tackles him again near homeplate as he is trying to get away, again punching him on the ground. The manager of the team on the receiving side of the helmet-throwing calls it "the most vicious thing I've ever seen." The brawl stops play for 12 minutes, and the instigator plus one coach on each side are thrown out of game. The fight is unusual in the amount of punches thrown, although there is also the usual milling around, pushing each other at arms length, and angry shouting. [*Los Angeles Times*, Aug. 11, 2001]

The immediate lead-up to the fight: Mike Sweeney, Kansas City Royals' first baseman and clean-up hitter, complains that the Detroit Tiger's pitcher, Jeff Weaver, is leaving the white resin bag on top of the mound so that it distracts the hitter's vision. At his second complaint to the umpire, the pitcher says something: quoted by Sweeney afterwards in an interview: "He said, 'You (expletive expletive), (expletive)-you.' [i.e. something like 'You fucking asshole, fuck you.'] For me, I wish it never happened, but in the same breath, he called me out." Weaver is 6 ft. 5, a big macho guy. Sweeney is the clean-up hitter, a fairly big muscular guy, too (6 ft. 1, over 200 pounds). Sweeney had a reputation as mild-mannered, according to press reports—so it's not personality. Instead there is the build up of tension in several kinds of interaction ritual chains.

First: the long-term frustrations and expectations. Both teams, earlier highly regarded, are having very bad seasons, at the point in mid-August where it's clear they are just fighting to stay out of the cellar. KC is in last place in the American League Central division, 19 1/2 games back; Detroit is just ahead of them in 4th place, 15 1/2 games back. But Detroit is sliding, KC has been gaining ground on them and sees a chance of catching up in this head-to-head series, of which this is the first game. Moreover, KC is playing at home, with a crowd of 22,000 behind them.

Second: the tension build-up in the game. It started badly for KC: Detroit jumped ahead in top of first inning, the first 4 batters all hitting singles and 2 runs scoring. KC comes back with 1 run in bottom of the first, which Sweeney drove in with a sacrifice fly; but thereafter the Detroit pitcher settles down and allows no hits and no walks in the next 4 2/3 innings. KC pitching settles down too, allowing no more runs. So when Sweeney comes to bat in the bottom of the 6th, the game is tense: they've been 1 run back for 5 innings (over an hour). Finally after 2 outs the Royals get a base runner on with a double, putting a man in scoring position. Sweeney feels all the pressure on him to tie the game. He also has the expectation—the EE—to do so: over the course of the season, he is leading the team in RBI's (82), and in batting average (.311); and in this game, he drove in the team's only run with a sacrifice in his first at bat. But he still doesn't have a hit for the game. Weaver, on the other hand, is Detroit's best pitcher (at this point, 10 W 10 L); he's been cruising since the first inning, until giving up a double with two outs. It's crunch time for him too. He apparently tries to upset the batter by playing with the

resin bag; and deliberately taunts him when Sweeney complains.

Then the fight, unusually prolonged anger on the part of the batter, and prolonged chasing and punching the pitcher (although punching someone while both are on ground, in wrestling position, isn't very dangerous). Notice that the pitcher, although he provoked the fight by taunting, and is the bigger man with a more macho reputation, is passive; tries to get away; is wrestled to the ground several times; doesn't hit back.

Third: the switch in EE dominance. After the fight, Sweeney is ejected from the game; the pitcher stays in. But Sweeney has won the fight, making the pitcher back down, manhandling him and emotionally dominating him during the fight. The angrier person, charged up with EE, wins the fight. Then the pitcher's performance breaks down: Weaver walks the next batter (having walked no one in the game up to that point); then he gives up a single which scores a run and ties the game (losing his potential victory); then he throws a wild pitch to next batter, which advances the runners to 2nd and 3rd; then he hits the batter with a pitch, loading the bases.

Then the entire team's EE gives way. Weaver is taken out for a reliever, who gets the next batter to hit a routine fly ball; but the Detroit center fielder bobbles it for an error, allowing 3 runs to score. The reliever walks the next batter; the following batter hits a double to drive in 2 more runs. This momentum swing results in 6 runs scoring, all after the fight (when Detroit only needed to get 1 out, but failed to do so for 6 straight batters, only 2 of whom got hits). During all this, from the fight onwards, the home crowd has been roaring (and had been building up spirit since the double just before Sweeney came up). After the crowd settles down, Detroit comes back for 1 run in top of the 7th, but the rest of the game is routine and KC wins, 7 to 3. In the following 2 days, KC continues on a roll and defeats Detroit twice to sweep the series.

Winning the turning point fight is crucial for winning the game; both are about establishing emotional dominance. Conversely, fights may break out when the game is on the line, but if the fight is a stalemate, the momentum is not broken.

An example from football: Of 4 NFL first-round playoff games televised on Jan. 5, 2003, only one had fights during game. This was the hardest fought game (2 others were blowouts; the third had one momentum swing as the trailing team came from behind to win).

San Francisco 49ers vs. New York Giants. First quarter swings back and forth, each scoring 2 touchdowns, 14–14. Second quarter and most of third quarter dominance swings to Giants, who open up 38–14 lead—scoring on 4 consecutive drives while SF could neither stop them on defense nor move on offense. Giants control momentum for a total of 14 minutes playing time, but it seems much longer in real time since it also includes the half-time break. Then momentum swings again: SF mounts 2 drives, scoring touchdowns and 2-point conversions, while the Giants can't move the ball; the score is cut to 38–30. Then SF drives again, but can only kick a field goal as the defense stiffens, leaving the score 38–33 with under 8 minutes to go. SF has now dominated for 11 minutes until stopped. During these 3 drives, the Giants defense looks very tired, panting, out of breath, while SF performs a no-huddle fast-paced offense. Of course both opposing offense and defense participate in same number of plays and make just as much physical effort; the apparent tiredness is an emotional let-down, a loss of EE.

Having finally broken the 49ers' momentum, the Giants move the ball for 5 minutes but cannot score. SF gets the ball back with 3 minutes to go, and mounts a drive. During this last drive, only 1 NY player—defensive safety Shaun Williams—hustles to make plays, and temporarily saves a touchdown. Then SF scores on a pass, to go ahead 39–38; star receiver Terrell Owens, a very tall, dominant receiver, known for showing off celebrating his touchdowns, taunts the Giants safety, who punches him furiously. Both players are called for fouls; this is especially irrational for the Giants, since they will get the ball back on the kickoff, and a 15 yard penalty on their opponent would move them close to field goal range. But the penalties offset, so there is no effect.

SF tries for a 2-point conversion, which if successful would give them a 3 point lead, so that a field goal would do no more than tie them. But the Giants intercept the pass, and try to run the ball back out (which is against the rules, since the defense can't advance on an extra point try). Owens comes over and hits the Giant ball carrier (a defensive back) out of bounds—another flagrant foul; but the Giants retaliate, in fact, twice: another of the Giant defensive backs hits Owens; plus the same Giant safety who got the previous foul (Shaun Williams) punches a big SF lineman (100 pounds bigger than himself) who had intervened in the first fight. The same set of players can't stop fighting with each other. So again it's offsetting fouls—again SF gives the other side a penalty break, but the other side can't take advantage of it because of retaliation. Giants then move the ball down the field rapidly; another brief fight breaks out; then

Giants try for a field goal, which they miss as time runs out. 49ers win.

What we see is an extremely hard-fought game; momentum swings very strongly first to Giants; then to SF; the most effective defensive player in trying to break the momentum swing starts a fight in response to boasting by the SF performance leader after he finally scores to take the lead; then the SF star angrily attacks after their insurance play has been foiled, and the NY defensive leader counterattacks. The individuals with the highest EE and most personal dominance initiate the fighting and keep it going with retaliation. The fighters are those who have put in the most effort to shift the momentum swings of the game. But no one wins these fights. The fights do not change the momentum, but only confirm it. The team in EE decline also fades out in their last-ditch effort to win.

Tension can build up over a series of games, compounded out of team rivalries, the pressures of elimination tournaments, and accumulating incidents of in-game intimidation. The fights that result can become the dramatic centerpiece of the action. This is most notable in professional baseball and basketball playoff series, where teams and their fans store up emotional memories of previous confrontations, and winning or losing a fight tends to determine the following sequence of action on the field, for a whole series of games.

An example is the 2003 American League championship series between the New York Yankees and the Boston Red Sox [*Los Angeles Times*, Oct. 10–13, 2003]. The Red Sox, which had not won a world series in 85 years, was heavily hyped as having their best chance in years. The Red Sox started the series by winning the first game at Yankee Stadium, and took an early lead in the second

game but then fell behind, missed a scoring opportunity to tie the game in the top of the 7th inning, and eventually lost as the Yankees scored two more runs in the bottom of the 7th. In the following inning both Red Sox and Yankee pitchers threw knock-down pitches at opposing star batters; since the game was largely out of hand by that point (Yankees leading 6 to 2, which remained the final score), these were merely expressions of hostility for what was to come.

The Red Sox had blown an opportunity to win two games on the opponents' home field, but they were returning home with their best pitcher, Pedro Martinez, scheduled to pitch against the Yankee's ace, Roger Clemens. These were both regarded as hall-of-fame pitchers, having excellent seasons and riding recent winning streaks, and they had a previous history of bitter rivalry in previous crucial games. Earlier in the season, Clemens had hit a Boston batter, and Martinez promised to retaliate, which he did 3 days later by putting Yankee stars Alfonso Soriano and Derek Jeter out of the game with first-inning pitches hitting their hands. These past events were vividly recounted in the press, and no doubt among players and fans, in the build-up to the 3rd game, touted as the biggest pitching match-up of the year.

The game started well for the Red Sox; 3 of their first 4 batters got hits to go ahead 2–0. But Martinez gave up runs in the second and third innings, leaving the game tied 2–2 going into the top of the 4th. The Yankees then rallied to get their first 3 men on base, the third hitting a double which put the Red Sox behind 3–2, with no outs. Martinez then hit the next batter with a high pitch, Karim Garcia, who yelled angrily at the pitcher before taking first base.

Martinez replied by pointing to the Yankee dugout and then to his own head, and yelled several times "I hit you right here!" Garcia angrily bowled over the Red Sox second baseman on the next play, a double-play grounder, while another Yankee run scored to make it 4–2.

In the bottom of the inning, Clemens took the mound for the Yankees; he had been warned by the umpires that any retaliation would result in being thrown out of the game; teammates said the veins were popping out of his neck from the tension as he attempted to keep his emotions under control. The next batter was the Red Sox slugger, Manny Ramirez, who had driven in the first run of the game in the first. Clemens threw a pitch high, but not inside; although the pitch was not near his head, Ramirez reacted as if it were, and stepped toward the mound, waving the bat in his hand—the dangerous weapon that batters almost never use in a fight. (The bat-waving was bluster; it was never used.) Both teams ran onto the field in a mêlée that lasted for 15 minutes. But the players held each other back and little damage was done, except when the Yankee bench coach, 72-year-old Don Zimmer, took a swing at Pedro Martinez, who tossed him to the ground; Zimmer was taken off on a stretcher but later proved to have no injuries beyond minor cuts and bruises. Martinez was not pitching at the time, since the Red Sox were batting, but merely standing near the dugout; but the Yankee coach took him as responsible for the fight—an accurate enough perception.

Immediately after play resumed, Manny Ramirez struck out flailing at the first pitch Clemens threw, even though it was far outside the strike zone. Ramirez was emotionally out of control in the entire fight

sequence, and failed to get a hit the rest of the game. After the game he acted ashamed, dressing rapidly and walking out of the clubhouse without a word to anyone. Martinez too seemed embarrassed by having knocked down the old coach, and refused to comment on the bean-ball war he had started. The Red Sox went flat after the fight, and ended up losing the game 4–3.

The Yankees, however, were charged up, and took the offensive in 2 more fights at the end of the game. In the top of the 9th inning, the Yankees got a man on but the Red Sox turned a double play to end the inning; a member of the local stadium grounds crew stationed in the Yankee bullpen cheered and waved a flag. Since the relief pitchers no doubt regarded their bullpen as their own turf, one of them turned angrily to him and said "If you want to cheer for them, why don't you go over in their bullpen?" The groundskeeper allegedly took a swing at the pitcher, was knocked down and kicked by at least 2 players. The Yankee right fielder who was just coming out to take up his position, saw the fight and jumped over the fence into the bullpen; this was Karim Garcia, the same man whose beaning had started the whole fight sequence earlier in the game. Garcia sprained his hand in the fight and had to leave the game.

There were no more fights in the remaining games. The Red Sox and Yankees alternated close victories the rest of the way. Clemens and Martinez faced each other again in the decisive 7th game; neither pitched particularly well. Clemens was knocked out of the game in the 4th inning; he did not wave in response to the crowd's ovation (although he was believed to be retiring after the game), keeping his head down as he shuffled off the field and down the tunnel to the locker room. Martinez blew a 3-run lead in the 8th inning to tie the game. The Red Sox lost in the 11th inning and failed again to make the World Series.

Fights also punctuate a swing in dominance among closely contending teams. In late June 2004, the Los Angeles Dodgers went into San Francisco for a series with the Giants; the Dodgers lost all four games and fell from first place to second, 2 1/2 games behind the Giants. In the third game, the Giants were leading 3 to 2 in the fifth inning, when the Giants' Michael Tucker, attempting to beat out a bunt, ran into Dodger pitcher Jeff Weaver who tagged him out at first base; the two continued running down the line, Tucker shoving the pitcher (a much bigger man), who shoved back, shouted and pointed at Tucker's face. Both dugouts emptied onto the field, but umpires restored order after the teams milled around shoving each other, and no one was ejected. There was no further scoring and the Giants went on to win. In the next game, the Giants were far ahead, 9 to 1 in the 9th inning when the Dodgers brought in their star closer, Eric Gagne, just to give him some exercise (Gagne was then riding a record-setting string of perfect saves). Gagne threw his famous 97 mph fastball high and inside, but not really close to Tucker, who dropped to the ground, and then got up and motioned and shouted at Gagne. The pitcher responded by dropping his glove and walking towards Tucker, shouting "Let's go." "He was charging, so I dropped my glove," Gagne said. "You can't throw in anymore? It's pretty sad. He knows it wasn't even close. He knows he just got carried away because he tried to hurt our players [the day before]. I guess he thought it was payback." The teams again charged

the field, holding each other back; eventually Tucker and Gagne were ejected; the Giants went on to win 9–3. [*Los Angeles Times*, May 24–25, 2004]

Tucker had done no hitting in either game, going 0 for 4 and then 0 for 5 the next day; but in each instance he stood up against the Dodgers' best pitchers (starter and closer) by instigating a fight. This appears to be a combination of personal frustration (by an unsuccessful player on the winning team), generalized frustration by the losing team (notably by the pitchers used to their accustomed success), and the ebullience of the team that was consistently dominating the other. One might call this a rubbing-it-in fight—the counterpart on the side of the victors of a frustration fight by the losing team.

Turning points can also occur in the kinds of non-contact sports that involve no fights but emotional tests of dominance. In the Wimbledon tennis championship in 2004, Maria Sharapova battled the prior champion Serena Williams in an exchange of 21 volleys at break point in her first service game of the second set (having won the first set already). Finally Sharapova hit a forehand deep in the corner, and Williams slipped and fell. Sharapova gave Williams a hard stare and pumped her fist, while Williams lay on the ground, an expression of agony on her face. Sharapova went on to ace the next serve and to take the rest of the match easily. [*San Diego Union Tribune*, July 4, 2004] The loser is beaten both physically and emotionally, at the turning point, while the winner goes on from that point demonstrably and self-consciously full of confidence. Battles for dominance are not gender specific, but are shaped by the dramatic sequence of the game. We see this also in photos of women pitchers in softball games making the same gestures that men pitchers do after recording a crucial strike-out: jaw thrust forward, fist punching the air. [Collins 2008]

Basketball fights often happen in a climax of frustration when a team blows a lead and loses momentum. This may take the form of especially rough play rather than a frame-breaking fight. In the final game of the 2004 NBA Eastern Conference championship, the Indiana Pacers had led by 14 points in the first half, but the Detroit Pistons slowly caught up, and tied the score with just under 4 minutes to play. The Pacers's best defender, Ron Artest, then knocked down the Piston's best scorer, Richard Hamilton—a much smaller man—with a forearm shiver to the jaw. Hamilton picked himself up, made the two penalty shots, and his team never trailed again, going on to win the series (and eventually the NBA championship). The team that won the fight physically did not win it dramatically, and was emotionally knocked out of the game. [*Los Angeles Times*, June 2, 2004]

Further light is cast on the dynamics of player fights by asking when they do *not* occur. After all, only a minority of games have frustrated game-losing violence, or turning-point violence, although most games have a point at which a team becomes aware it has lost. I have argued (in Collins 2008) for the structural limit of one fight per venue or dramatic sequence. The same pattern of filling the emotional attention space predicts when fights will not happen. After the build-up to a dramatic climax, further fights become emotionally superfluous. Based on this principle, I predicted successfully that after the dramatic American League championship series be-

tween the Yankees and the Red Sox in 2004, coming to an emotional climax in the 6th game collision between Yankees star Alex Rodriguez and Red Sox pitcher Bronson Arroyo, there would be no further fights, either in the remaining 7th game, nor in the following World Series.

Conclusion: And the Beat Goes On

These examples come from the period when this chapter was written; by the time you, the reader, reads this, you will no doubt find them a bit out of date. They are yesterday's news, old gossip now gone stale because it has been eclipsed by the latest confrontation, the latest fight, the latest meltdown or dramatic turn-around in current sporting events. But that is the nature of sports as a social institution: contrived to produce a dramatic story over and over again, with new details and new protagonists. Underneath the surface of the particular details, the patterns are the same. Sports are contrived to create drama; and the high points of drama are also what creates player violence.

It is sometimes said that violence is getting out of control. If the implication is that violence is getting worse now than it has ever been, that is surely wrong. We have no systematic data about incidents of sports violence (and the professional leagues are not very interested in keeping such records); but whatever period of sports we dip into the historical record, we find violence [e.g. Dunning 1999]. Violence is built into the social structure of the game: not necessarily directly in the rules, but in the underlying emotional dramatics that make sports appealing. Intense moments in these emotional confrontations on the playing field are what create violence. What makes the game exciting is what causes the moments when players fight.

References

Adler, Peter. 1984. *Momentum*. Beverly Hills: Sage.

Baltzell, E. Digby. 1995. *Sporting Gentlemen*. New York: Free Press.

Chambliss, Daniel F. 1989. "The Mundanity of Excellence." *Sociological Theory* 7: 70–86.

Collins, Randall. 2004. *Interaction Ritual Chains*. Princeton: Princeton Univ. Press.

Collins, Randall. 2008. *Violence: A Micro-Sociological Theory*. Princeton: Princeton University Press.

Draeger, Donn F. 1974. *The Martial Arts and Ways of Japan*. (3 vols.) New York & Tokyo: Weatherhill.

Dunning, Eric. 1999. *Sport Matters*. London: Routledge.

Elias, Norbert, and Eric Dunning. 1986. *Quest for Excitement; Sport and Leisure in the Civilizing Process*. Oxford: Blackwell.

Faulkner, Robert F. 1976. "Making Violence by Doing Work: Selves, Situations, and the World of Professional Hockey." In Daniel M. Landers (Ed.), *Social Problems in Athletics: Essays in the Sociology of Sport*. Urbana, IL: University of Illinois.

Felson, Marcus. 1994. *Crime and Everyday Life*. Thousand Oaks, CA: Pine Forge Press.

Morrison, Shona and Ian O'Donnell. 1994. *Armed Robbery: A Study in London*. University of Oxford Centre for Criminological Research, Occasional Paper No. 15.

Pappas, Nick T.; Patrick C. Mckenry; Beth Skilken Catlett. 2004. "Athlete Aggression on the Rink and off the Ice: Athlete Violence and Aggression in Hockey and Interpersonal Relationships." *Men and Masculinities* 6: 3, 291–312.

Propp, Vladimir. 1928/1968. *Morphology of the Folk Tale*. Austin: University of Texas Press.

Shields, Jr., Edgar W. 1999. "Intimidation and Violence by Males in High School Athletics." *Adolescence*, 34: 135, 503–521.

Smith, Michael D. 1979. "Towards an Explanation of Hockey Violence: A Reference Other Approach." *Canadian Journal of Sociology*, 4: 105–124.

Stump, Al. 1994. *Cobb: A Biography*. New York, NY: Workman Publishing.

Thorn, John, Pete Palmer, and Michael Gershman. 2001. *Total Baseball: The Official Encyclopedia of Major League Baseball*. Kingston, NY: Total Sports Publishing.

Weinstein, Marc D; Michael D. Smith; David L. Wiesenthal. 1995. "Masculinity and Hockey Violence." *Sex Roles*, 33: 11–12, 831–847.

Chapter 34

BACKTALK

Violence, Redemption and the Cost of Sports

Robert Lipsyte

The trial balloon with Marv Albert's toupee on top has long since returned to ground. The broadcaster politely declined even discussing an offered radio job until after his sentencing this week and then presumably more time for jail or psychological counseling. But the brief flurry 10 days ago accomplished the mission of preparing us for his return. Most people polled seemed to think that after a decent interval (after the bite marks fade?), Albert should resume what has been a notable career. Sports, after all, is about second chances, coming back from all the bad bounces of life, from knee injuries to rape convictions.

In removing Albert from their air, television executives alluded to the difference between broadcasters and their subjects. They implied that a player could be more quickly forgiven for a transgression than an "interpreter" of events, although they said they would consider rehiring Albert. With the likes of Lawrence Phillips on the Rams, Christian Peter on the Giants and enough active athletes who have left significant marks on others to fill the rosters of domestic violence week, there was all the more reason to return Marv to the booth. Who better to report on all the bad boys than a redeemed bad boy?

Besides, the crime for which he pleaded guilty, assaulting a woman, has never been a deal-breaker in Sports World.

Evidence of this boys-will-be-boys defense has been collected in "Public Heroes, Private Felons" (Northeastern University Press), Jeff Benedict's controversial study of athletes and their crimes against women. There are few major revelations—the usual suspects, Mike Tyson, Warren Moon and too many Cincinnati Bengals make appearances—but the depth of Benedict's research and the pattern of his details lead us to an unsettling revelation of its own. This kind of behavior is no aberration; to some coaches it seems to be almost an acceptable cost of doing business with troubled young men who have superior skills.

Often in packs, like wolves on a deer, college and pro athletes bring down a woman as they would sack a quarter-back, play with her, physically hurt her and then toss her away. Should she complain, the college or pro team pays for a lawyer whose standard ploy is to contrast the popularity and value of the defendant with the contemptible star-chasing sexuality of the victim.

It works. According to Benedict, more than 400 professional and college athletes have been publicly reported for violent crimes against women in the past 10 years, and few have been successfully prosecuted, much less jailed. This has "dulled public consciousness of their increasing levels of deviance," he writes. And as we are numbed, the athletes, aided by a "diminishing sense of shame over their socially degenerate behavior," continue the assaults.

Obviously, there is more than a little avenging angel to Benedict, a law student in Boston. He is former research director of the Center for the Study of Sports and Society, which has distanced itself from the book's statistical methods and its prosecutorial tone.

Richard Lapchick, the center's director, believes that Benedict's book is counterproductive to his group's national violence-prevention program, which uses athletes as speakers and mentors. He points out that Coach Tom Osborne, a center honoree, would never have invited the antiviolence program to Nebraska if its approach to Phillips and Peter, former Nebraska players, were accusatory.

Osborne's protectiveness of his team, perennially among the nation's best and most felonious, is condemned by Benedict. One troubling case history involved Kathy Redmond, a Nebraska student who claimed to have been raped twice by Peter. She cannot discuss the case as part of a gag order agreed to in a civil settlement that resulted from her allegations. Her more general opinions and suggestions are elsewhere on this page.

Benedict's book should be no surprise. Even as basically positive a book as Peter Golenbock's enormously entertaining oral history of Dallas football, "Cowboys Have Always Been My Heroes" (Warner Books), makes clear that the sense of entitlement bestowed on athletes is over-whelming. The forgiving attitude toward John Niland running naked through the streets, Lance Rentzel exposing himself to a child, Hollywood Henderson snorting cocaine, etc. (as long as they are producing for the team, of course) sets the scene for Michael Irvin's destructive behavior and the reason people were quick to believe the false accusations of sexual assault made against him last season.

Golenbock and Benedict agree that racism has been a factor in what seems to be a proportionately higher incidence of reports on black athletes. However, more to the point, both agree, is the cynicism of college and pro teams in signing on poor, semi-literate, unsocialized gladiators without bothering to prepare them for the alien experience of a middle-class college or sudden millionaire status in a city that wants to love them to death.

In such a milieu, a poised, established, well-educated, middle-class white man from a nuclear family landing in tabloid hell seemed like a surprise. But the Albert story has an element of sensation that made Sports World squirm, a dangling thread that no one has wanted to tug too hard. In the trial testimony, Albert's group sex activities included other men. In Golenbock's book, group sex looks like a team-bonding romp. In Benedict's book, it is a vicious gang rape. But a number of other observers, including gay athletes and feminist academics, have wondered how much of it is really covert homosexual activity.

The sports industry—unlike other cultural arts—has treated any hint of homosexuality with denial, even if it is casual, experimental and has no visible connection to gay life. This has been damaging to athletes confused about their sexuality; they don't dare even ask for counseling. The Albert case briefly offered the possibility of a window, but that has been shut. Keeping it closed may be part of the price he will pay to come back.

ABOUT THE EDITORS

Robert E. Washington

After serving two years as a Peace Corps Volunteer in Afghanistan, Robert Washington attended graduate school at the University of Chicago where he received his PhD in sociology. He is currently a professor of sociology and Africana studies at Bryn Mawr College. His research interests and teaching focus on race relations, deviance, the sociology of culture, African development, and the sociology of sports. He played football during his youth but eventually realized that his talents were more suited to analyzing social phenomena than to making open field tackles. He is now an avid fan and sociological observer of sports.

David Karen

David Karen received his BA in Sociology at Queens College–City University of New York and his MA and PhD from Harvard University. He is currently a professor of sociology at Bryn Mawr College and an elected school board member in Eastern Pennsylvania. In addition to focusing on sociology of sport, Karen's research and teaching interests range broadly: from politics and social movements to inequality and education. Karen's participation in organized sports started inauspiciously when the first points he ever scored in an official scholastic basketball game were for the other team! Nevertheless, he continues to play and follow sports rather fanatically.

INDEX